QM Library

23 1361264 4

KU-113-552

WITHDRAWN
FROM STOCK
QMUL LIBRARY

EC PUBLIC PROCUREMENT:
CASE LAW AND REGULATION

EC PUBLIC PROCUREMENT: CASE LAW AND REGULATION

Christopher Bovis

Professor of Law and Jean Monnet Chair in European and Business Law, Lancashire Law School

OXFORD

UNIVERSITY PRESS

This book has been printed digitally and produced in a standard specification
in order to ensure its continuing availability

OXFORD
UNIVERSITY PRESS

Great Clarendon Street, Oxford OX2 6DP

Oxford University Press is a department of the University of Oxford.
It furthers the University's objective of excellence in research, scholarship,
and education by publishing worldwide in

Oxford New York

Auckland Cape Town Dar es Salaam Hong Kong Karachi
Kuala Lumpur Madrid Melbourne Mexico City Nairobi
New Delhi Shanghai Taipei Toronto
With offices in
Argentina Austria Brazil Chile Czech Republic France Greece
Guatemala Hungary Italy Japan South Korea Poland Portugal
Singapore Switzerland Thailand Turkey Ukraine Vietnam

Oxford is a registered trade mark of Oxford University Press
in the UK and in certain other countries

Published in the United States
by Oxford University Press Inc., New York

© Christopher Bovis, 2006

The moral rights of the author have been asserted

Crown copyright material is reproduced under Class Licence
Number C01P0000148 with the permission of OPSI
and the Queen's Printer for Scotland

Database right Oxford University Press (maker)

Reprinted 2009

All rights reserved. No part of this publication may be reproduced,
stored in a retrieval system, or transmitted, in any form or by any means,
without the prior permission in writing of Oxford University Press,
or as expressly permitted by law, or under terms agreed with the appropriate
reprographics rights organization. Enquiries concerning reproduction
outside the scope of the above should be sent to the Rights Department,
Oxford University Press, at the address above

You must not circulate this book in any other binding or cover
And you must impose this same condition on any acquirer

ISBN 978-0-19-927792-6

Printed and bound in Great Britain by CPI Antony Rowe,
Chippenham and Eastbourne

For Jakov

ACKNOWLEDGEMENTS

It would have been very difficult to complete this project without the involvement of a number of people to whom I record here my great indebtedness. First of all, my thanks go to the publishers for their professionalism and the assistance they provided.

It is also with deep appreciation that I express my gratitude to Professor Alan Rosas, Professor Walter van Gerven, Professor Brian Bercusson, Professor Robert Merkin, Professor Alan Dashwood, Professor John Bell, Professor Hugh Beale, Professor John Usher, Professor Takis Tridimas, Professor Anthony Arnull, Professor Harry Arthurs, Dr Christine Cnossen, Dr Andreas Bartosch, Mr Terrence Bramall, Mr Richard Watson, Mr David Blunt, and Mr Brian Clark.

Finally, I am eternally indebted to H. J. Lamar, President and CEO of LE Group Inc., for his invaluable support, guidance, and inspiration through difficult times.

Christopher Bovis
September 2005

CONTENTS—SUMMARY

IV. ENFORCEMENT AND COMPLIANCE AT NATIONAL LEVEL

CONTENTS

II. PUBLIC PROCUREMENT REGULATION

III. PUBLIC PROCUREMENT AND
THE EUROPEAN COURT OF JUSTICE

7. Public Contracts and Contracting Authorities

IV. ENFORCEMENT AND COMPLIANCE AT NATIONAL LEVEL

10. Public Procurement and Public–Private Partnerships

11. Enforcement and Compliance

APPENDICES

TABLE OF CASES BEFORE THE EUROPEAN COURT OF JUSTICE

TABLE OF CASES

TABLE OF DECISIONS

TABLE OF NATIONAL CASES

Belgium

France

Sweden

United Kingdom

United States

TABLE OF EUROPEAN LEGISLATION

Conventions

Regulations

Directives

TABLE OF NATIONAL LEGISLATION

Netherlands

Portugal

Spain

Sweden

United Kingdom

INTRODUCTION

The regulation of public procurement in the European Union has multiple **I.01** dimensions as a discipline of European law and policy, directly relevant to the fundamental principles of the common market, and as a policy instrument in the hands of member states. The purpose of the regulation of public procurement is to insert a regime of competitiveness in the relevant markets and eliminate all non-tariff barriers to intra-community trade that emanate from preferential purchasing practices which favour national undertakings. Apart from reasons relating to accountability for public expenditure, avoidance of corruption and political manipulation, the regulation of public procurement represents best practice in the delivery of public services by the state and its organs.

Public procurement is a powerful exercise. It carries the aptitude of acquisition; **I.02** it epitomizes economic freedom; it depicts the nexus of trade relations amongst economic operators; it represents the necessary process to deliver public services; and it demonstrates strategic policy options. Public procurement as a discipline expands from a simple topic of the common market to a multi-faceted tool of European regulation and governance, covering policy choices and revealing an interesting interface between centralized and national governance systems. This is where the legal effects of public procurement regulations will be felt most.

This book aims to provide the reader with a comprehensive analysis of the law and **I.03** jurisprudence which have shaped the landscape of the regulation of public procurement in the European Union and its member states. It covers the *acquis communautaire* prior to the recent enlargement of the European Union. Part I considers public procurement as a discipline within the European economic and legal integration. In Chapter 1, public procurement is positioned within the context of the common market. The objective of this chapter is to provide the necessary links between the regulation of public procurement and the remit of European Community law. This chapter reveals the concept of public markets and the economic policy dimension in the regulation of public procurement. It also points out the policy rationale of the relevant legal structure and the overall framework of Community and national competence. Chapter 1 examines the anti-trust dimension in public procurement regulation and justifies the influence of neo-classical economic theory upon the integration of public markets. This finding will also reflect on the public policy dimension of public procurement and the interplay of

1

public purchasing with state aid. As a result, the industrial policy dimension in public procurement emerges, and the remit of public procurement regulation demonstrates its flexibility and complementary relation with other policies in the European integration process. Chapter 2 examines the judicial nature of the regulation of public procurement. Its main objective is to identify the key characteristics of public procurement litigation before the European Court of Justice and before national legal *fora*. It investigates judicial control of public procurement at centralized level by examining the role of the European Commission in public procurement litigation, and by exposing the nature of proceedings before the European Court of Justice, the consequences of its judgments, and the availability of interim measures before the Court. Chapter 2 also addresses judicial control at domestic level. In particular, it examines public procurement litigation within national legal structures by observing the profile of national *fora* and, specifically, issues of enforcement and compliance, such as the award of damages under Community law before national courts, and the possibility of set aside and annulment of decisions of contracting authorities. Such analysis reveals the importance of the decentralized application of public procurement rules, and the relative significance of the Compliance Directives for the award of damages to aggrieved undertakings that have suffered harm as a result of a violation of public procurement rules on the part of contracting authorities. The role of the European Commission under the Compliance Directives is exposed and such exposure reveals the close links between centralized and decentralized judicial control of public procurement. Finally, Chapter 2 addresses issues of compliance with, and enforcement of, the public procurement rules under the WTO Government Procurement Agreement. Chapter 3 provides a detailed analysis covering the historical evolution of public procurement regulation. It exposes the legal and socio-economic background of the attempts to reform the public sector purchasing patterns of the member states. It investigates the evolution of the public supplies regime, the public works regime, the utilities regime, the public services regime, and the thrust of the Compliance Directives. It also delineates the extra-territorial application of the public procurement regime through the GATT Agreement on Government Procurement and the WTO Government Procurement Agreement. Chapter 3 also depicts the concepts and principles of public procurement regulation which have emerged through its evolution. The concepts of public procurement regulation refer to the mechanism for the applicability and engagement of the relevant rules and provide for different notions and definitions which are necessary for the harmonization of national legal and political systems with a view to integrating their respective public markets. The principles of public procurement regulation include the principle of mandatory advertisement and publication of public contracts, the principle of non-discrimination, and the principle of objectivity. Chapter 3 provides for the interplay of these principles and the way they have influenced the evolution of public procurement regulation.

In Part II, the newly-enacted public procurement regime is examined after the   **I.04**
culmination of reforms and the maturity of the public procurement regulation
resulting from the application of the rules and the jurisprudential inferences of the
European Court of Justice. Chapter 4 provides a thorough analysis of the reasons
behind the introduction of the new public procurement regime. It offers a critical
assessment of public procurement regulation by exposing the inherent shortcomings in the public procurement rules, the problems with regard to the dimension-
ality of public procurement, the effects of the principle of transparency, the abuse
of award procedures which may restrict competition, the obstacles posed by public monopolies to the integration of public markets, the harmonization issues of
standardization and specification, and, finally, the reluctance of the private sector
in initiating litigation. Chapter 4 presents a thematic overview of the new public
procurement regime by revealing the new concepts in public procurement regulation relevant to the public sector and also relevant to the procurement of utilities. It also exposes the new dynamics with regard to the new public procurement
regime and the WTO, and provides insights to future developments in public
procurement regulation, in particular, public procurement and public–private
partnerships and the future revision of the Compliance Directives. Chapter 5 covers the applicability of the public sector rules, the coverage and scope of the new
Public Sector Directive, the requirements for advertisement and publicity of public contracts, the process of qualitative selection of tenderers and candidates, and
the use of award procedures and award criteria. Chapter 6 reflects on the applicability of the utilities rules, the coverage and scope of the Utilities Directive, the
activities which are covered and the activities which are excluded from
the Utilities Directive, publicity and advertisement requirements, qualification
and qualitative selection systems, award procedures, framework agreements, and
award criteria.

Part III covers public procurement regulation from the perspective of the   **I.05**
European Court of Justice. The European Court of Justice has been instrumental
in interpreting the public procurement legal framework. The Court has provided
intellectual assistance to the efforts of European institutions in order to
strengthen the three principles (non-discrimination, objectivity and transparency) underlying the regulation of public procurement, to eliminate discrimination and non-tariff barriers in the fields of technical standards (product
specification and standardization), and the selection procedures (quantitative and
qualitative suitability criteria). The jurisprudence of the Court also reflects on a
strategic goal of the European judiciary: to vest the regime wherever possible with
direct effect. Arming the public procurement rules with direct effect will enhance
access to justice at national level, improve compliance, increase the quality of the
regulatory regime and finally streamline the public procurement process across
the common market by introducing an element of uniformity. By conferring
direct effect upon the Public Procurement Directives and inviting national courts

to play a prominent role in future public procurement litigation, the Court has hinted at its preference for a decentralized enforcement of the public procurement regime. However, the most important lesson which law and policymakers have learnt from the Court's jurisprudence reflects on a 'rule of reason' approach which propels public procurement regulation as an instrument of policymaking at national and European levels. Chapter 7 examines case-law relating to the notion of public contracts and the concept of contracting authorities. The Court has dealt with the notion of public contracts in cases regarding public service concessions, vertical procurement and subcontracting, procurement and state aid, procurement and services of general interest, needs in general interest, and contracts financing public services. Chapter 7 provides also for a codified approach of the concept of contracting authorities under the Court's jurisprudence, their relation with private sector undertakings, the conditions for pursuing services of general interest as part of public procurement contracts, especially the criteria for defining bodies governed by public law, and the tests used by the Court to define the existence of state control over an entity which is construed as the contracting authority. Chapter 8 reflects on selection and qualification of tenderers and candidates. It examines jurisprudence on technical standards, selection and qualification requirements, consortia participation in tendering procedures, reliance of tenderers on other sources, substitution of consortia members, and reasons for exclusion and disqualification of tenderers. Chapter 9 examines award procedures and award criteria in public procurement. The objective of this chapter is to focus on the reasoning of the Court in its attempt to provide a dynamic analysis of the procedures applicable to the award of public contracts. It demonstrates the nature and characteristics of the award procedures, as viewed by the Court and their utilization by contracting authorities. It elaborates upon the restrictive interpretation of the negotiated procedures and attempts to define the framework for their utilization, the grounds for their legitimate use, and the justification and causality requirements for negotiated procedures without prior publicity, particularly the use of negotiated procedures for technical reasons or reasons of extreme urgency, or as a result of repetition of similar works within three years. Chapter 9 also investigates the Court's case law in relation to award criteria and presents a comprehensive analysis of the two criteria laid down in the Public Procurement Directives. It provides for the conditions under which contracting authorities award public contracts. The Court has many opportunities to pronounce on the features of the award criteria, namely the lowest price or the most economically advantageous offer. The chapter explores the Court's views in relation to the following topics: the meaning of abnormally low offers, the compatibility of mathematical matrices, the evaluation of the lowest offer, the factors included in the most economically advantageous offer, and policy considerations such as employment and protection of the environment as part of the award criteria.

Part IV covers the evolution of the phenomenon of public–private partnerships, **I.06** and provides a comprehensive analysis of the structure of remedies and access to justice at national level and the jurisprudence of the Court relating to compliance issues of public procurement regulation. Chapter 10 evaluates the relationship between public procurement and public–private partnerships. It appraises recent legal, policy and judicial developments that have emerged as a result of the involvement of the private sector in the delivery of public services and, in particular, their financing. The concept of public–private partnerships is gaining momentum across the common market and policy makers are keen to see the relevant model as a credible and effective delivery mechanism. Chapter 10 demonstrates that the procurement of public–private partnerships must adhere to the enshrined principles of transparency, objectivity and non-discrimination that underlie the public procurement regime, and provides a detailed analysis of legal developments in the fields of concession contracts at Community level. Finally, Chapter 11 deals with legal remedies available to individuals at national level and access to justice in public procurement disputes. The objective of this chapter is to assess the progress made by member states to decentralize enforcement of public procurement rules by creating the appropriate legal frameworks that encourage aggrieved contractors to seek justice. Chapter 11 compares the way member states facilitate the creation of such frameworks, and assesses their effectiveness by investigating the reception of the public procurement legal framework by member states, the legal structure of member states in relation to public procurement grievances, and remedies available to aggrieved tenderers.

PART I

PUBLIC PROCUREMENT AND EUROPEAN INTEGRATION

1

PUBLIC PROCUREMENT IN THE COMMON MARKET CONTEXT

A. Public Procurement and European Integration

The establishment of the common market, as the core objective envisaged by the **1.01** Treaty of Rome (the Treaty creating the European Economic Communities) and reinforced by the Treaty of Maastricht (the Treaty creating the European Union) is to be achieved through the progressive approximation of the economic policies of member states.[1] The concept of the common market embraces the legal and economic dynamics of the European integration process, with clear political ambitions from its accomplishment, and presents the characteristics of a genuine integral market. Such a market is a place where unobstructed mobility of factors of production[2] is guaranteed and where a regime of effective and undistorted competition regulates its operation. These characteristics reflect on the four fundamental freedoms of a customs union (free movement of goods, persons, capital and services)[3] and, to the

---

[1] *See* Arts. 2 and 3 of the Treaty of Rome (EC).
[2] *See* Arts. 48 and 67 EC respectively.
[3] The Court of Justice has recognized a fifth freedom, the free movement of payments, which is closely related to the freedom of movement of capital, *see* Joined Cases 286/82 and 26/83, *Luisi and Carbone v. Ministero del Tesoro* [1984] ECR 377, Case 308/86, *Ministere Public v. Lambert* [1988] ECR 478. The Treaty of Rome provides also for the accomplishment of this freedom in Arts. 67(2).

extent that the customs union tends to become an economic and a monetary one,[4] on the adoption of a common economic policy and the introduction of a single currency. The adherence by member states to the above-mentioned fundamental principles of European economic integration will result in the removal of any restrictions or obstacles to inter-state trade. The level of success of economic integration in Europe would determine the level of success of political integration among member states, which is the ultimate objective stipulated in the Treaties.

1.02 The law of the European Union has conceived the creation of a supranational legal system alongside existing domestic legal systems, where the supremacy of the former over national laws has been declared by the European Court of Justice.[5] The economic integration of the European Union requires the assistance of a legal order that can facilitate its functioning and observe its evolutionary progress. The new legal order is a conglomerate of mutual rights and duties between the European Union and its subjects, both member states and private persons, and provides for the procedures which are necessary for adjudicating infringements of the law of the European Union. The new legal order does confer rights and obligations not only to member states but also to individuals (physical or legal persons).

1.03 Two strategic plans have facilitated the economic integration of the member states. These plans were enacted by European institutions and have been subsequently transposed into national laws and policies by member states. The first plan included a series of actions and measures aiming at the abolition of all tariff and non-tariff barriers to intra-community trade. The second plan has focused on the establishment of an effective, workable and undistorted regime of competition within the common market, in order to prevent potential abuse of market dominance and market segmentation, factors which could have serious economic implications in its functioning. The first plan, the abolition of all tariff and non-tariff barriers to intra-community trade, reveals a static effect which aimed at eliminating all administrative and legal obstacles to free trade, and had as its focal point member states and their national administrations. The second plan, the establishment of an effective, workable and undistorted regime of competition within the common market, has been implemented at industry level and has a rather on-going and dynamic effect.

---

and 106. The free movement of payments, a complementary principle of the free mobility of capital as a production factor, plays an extremely important role in the process of integration of public markets, and in particular in financing public projects either through indirect or direct investment.

[4] *See* Art. 102a EC.

[5] *See* Case 26/62, *NV Algemene Transport-en Expeditie Onderneming Van Gend en Loos v. Nederlandse Administratie der Belastigen* [1963] ECR 1.

All tariff barriers appear to have been abolished by the end of the first transitional **1.04** period,[6] so customs duties, quotas, and other forms of quantitative restrictions could no longer hinder the free flow of trade amongst member states. Non-tariff barriers, however, have proved more difficult to eliminate, as they involve long-established market practices and patterns that could not change overnight. Non-tariff protection represents a disguised form of discrimination and can occur through a wide spectrum of administrative or legislative frameworks relating to public monopolies, fiscal factors such as indirect taxation, state aid practices and subsidies, technical standards, and, last but not least, public procurement. Non-tariff barriers are by no means confined to the European integration process. The existence of non-tariff barriers is a common phenomenon in world markets and their elimination is the main objective of regulatory instruments of international trade. It has been maintained that non-tariff barriers could seriously distort the operation of the common market and its fundamental freedoms and derail the process of European integration.

The European Commission's *White Paper for the Completion of the Internal* **1.05** *Market*[7] identified existing non-tariff protection and provided the framework for specific legislative measures[8] in order to address the issue at national level. The enactment of a set of Directives was deemed necessary for the completion of the internal market by the end of 1992, and the timetable was set out in the Single European Act, which in fact amended the Treaty of Rome by introducing *inter alia* the concept of the internal market. The internal market, in quantifiable terms, could be considered as something less than the common market but, perhaps the first and most important part of the latter, as it 'would provide the economic context for the regeneration of the European industry in both goods and services and it would give a permanent boost to the prosperity of the people of Europe and indeed the world as a whole'.[9]

The internal market, as an economic concept, could be described as an area **1.06** without internal frontiers where the free circulation of goods and the unhindered provision of services, in conjunction with the unobstructed mobility of factors of production, are ensured. The concept of the internal market is a reinforcement of the principle of the customs union as the foundation stone of the common

---

[6] The first transitional period covers the time period from the establishment of the European Communities until 31 December 1969, *see* Art. 8(7) EC.

[7] *See* European Commission, *White Paper for the Completion of the Internal Market*, COM (85) 310 final.

[8] The completion of the internal market required the adoption at Community level and the implementation at national level of some 300 Directives on the subjects specified in the Commission's White Paper, *see also* European Commission, *Third Report of the Commission to the European Parliament on the Implementation of the White Paper*, COM (88) 134 final.

[9] *See* Lord Cockfield's quotation in the Cecchini Report, *1992: The European Challenge: The Benefits of a Single Market* (Aldershot: Wildwood House, 1988).

market. The internal market embraces, obviously, less than the common market to the extent that the economic and monetary integration elements are missing. The Single European Act, as a legal instrument amending the Treaty of Rome, reveals strong public law characteristics, since the regulatory features of its provisions promote the importance of certain areas that had been previously overlooked. As a result, there has been both centralized and decentralized regulatory control by European institutions and member states over environmental policy, industrial policy, regional policy and the regulation of public procurement. The above areas represented the priority objectives in the process of completing the internal market. Public procurement was specifically pointed out as a significant non-tariff barrier and a detailed plan was devised to address the issue. The European Commission based its action on two notable studies.[10] Those studies provided empirical proof of the distorted market conditions in the public sector and highlighted the benefits of the regulation of public procurement.

1.07 The regulation of public procurement in the European Union has been significantly influenced by the internal market project. The *White Paper for the Completion of the Internal Market*[11] and the Single European Act represent the conceptual foundations of the regulation of public markets of the member states. The identification of public procurement as a significant non-tariff barrier has offered ample evidence on the economic importance of its regulation.[12] Savings and price convergence appeared as the main arguments for liberalizing the trade patterns of the demand (the public and utilities sectors) and supply (the industry) sides of the public procurement equation.[13] The regulation of public procurement exposes an economic and a legal approach to the integration of public markets in the European Union. On the one hand, the economic approach to the regulation of public procurement aims at creating an integral public market across the European Union. Through the principles of transparency, non-discrimination and objectivity in the award of public contracts, it is envisaged that the public procurement regulatory system will bring about competitiveness in the relevant product and geographical markets, will increase import penetration of products and services destined for the public sector, will enhance the tradability of public contracts across the common market, will result in significant price convergence,

---

[10] *See* European Commission, *The Cost of Non-Europe, Basic Findings, Vol. 5, Part A; The Cost of Non-Europe in Public Sector Procurement* (Luxembourg: Official Publications of the European Communities, 1988), also the Cecchini Report, op. cit. (n. 9).

[11] *See* European Commission, op. cit. (n. 7).

[12] *See* European Commission, op. cit. (n. 10), also the Cecchini Report, op. cit. (n. 9).

[13] The European Commission has claimed that the regulation of public procurement could bring substantial savings of ECU 20 billion or 0.5 per cent of GDP to the (European) public sector. *See* European Commission, op. cit. (n. 10).

and finally will be the catalyst for the needed rationalization and industrial restructuring of the European industrial base.[14]

The legal approach to the regulation of public procurement, on the other hand, reflects on a medium which facilitates the functions of the common market. In parallel with the economic arguments, legal arguments have emerged supporting the regulation of public procurement as a necessary ingredient of the fundamental principles of the Treaties, such as the free movement of goods and services, the right of establishment, and the prohibition of discrimination of nationality grounds.[15] The legal significance of the regulation of public procurement in the common market has been well documented through the Court's jurisprudence. The liberalization of public procurement indicates the wish of European institutions to eliminate preferential and discriminatory purchasing patterns by the public sector and create seamless intra-community trade patterns between the public and private sectors. Procurement by member states and their contracting authorities is often susceptible to a rationale and a policy that tend to favour indigenous undertakings and *national champions*[16] at the expense of more efficient competitors (domestic or Community-wide). As the relevant markets (product and geographical) have been sheltered from competition, distorted patterns emerge in the trade of goods, works, and services destined for the public sector. These trade patterns represent a serious impediment in the functioning of the common market and inhibit the fulfilment of the principles enshrined in the Treaties.[17]

1.08

Legislation, policy guidelines, and jurisprudence have all played their role in determining the need for integrated public markets in the European Union, where sufficient levels of competition influence the most optimal patterns in resource allocation for supplying the public sector as well as the public utilities with goods, works, and services. Public procurement has now been elevated as a milestone of the vision of the European Union in becoming the most competitive economy in the world by 2010.[18]

1.09

---

[14] *See* European Commission, *Statistical Performance for Keeping Watch over Public Procurement*, 1992. Also European Commission, op. cit. (n. 10).

[15] *See* Bovis, 'Recent Case Law Relating to Public Procurement: A Beacon for the Integration of Public Markets', *Common Market Law Review*, 39 (2002), 1–49.

[16] The term implies a firm with more than a third of its turnover made in its own country and which has enjoyed formal or informal government protection. The term has been defined by Abravanel and Ernst, 'Alliance and Acquisition Strategies for European National Champions', *McKinsey Quarterly*, 2 (1992), 45–62.

[17] *See* Nicolaides (ed.), *Industrial Policy in the European Community: A Necessary Response to Economic Integration* (Martinus Nijhoff, 1993).

[18] *See* Communication from the European Commission to the Council, the European Parliament, the Economic and Social Committee, and the Committee of the Regions, *Working Together to Maintain Momentum* (2001 Review of the Internal Market Strategy, Brussels, 11 April 2001), COM (2001) 198 final. Also, European Commission, Commission Communication, *Public Procurement in the European Union* (Brussels, March 11, 1998), COM (98) 143.

B. The Concept of Public Markets

1.10 The main reason for regulating public sector and utilities procurement is to bring their respective markets in parallel to the operation of private markets. European policy makers have recognized the distinctive character of *public markets* and focused on establishing conditions similar to those that control the operation of private markets. The public markets reflect an economic equation where the demand side is represented by the public sector at large and the utilities, whereas the supply side covers the industry.

1.11 The state and its organs would enter the market place in pursuit of public interest.[19] However, the activities of the state and its organs do not display the commercial characteristics of private entrepreneurship, as the aim of the public sector is not the maximization of profits but the observance of public interest.[20] This fundamental difference emerges as the ground for the creation of *public markets* where public interest substitutes profit maximization.[21] However, further variances distinguish private from public markets. These focus on structural elements of the market place, competitiveness, demand conditions, supply conditions, the production process, and, finally, pricing and risk. They also provide for an indication as to the different methods and approaches employed in their regulation.[22]

1.12 Private markets are generally structured as a result of competitive pressures originating in the interaction between buyers and supplier, and their configuration can vary from monopoly or oligopoly conditions to models representing perfect competition. Demand arises from heterogeneous buyers with a variety of specific needs, is based on expectations, and is multiple for each product. Supply, on the other hand, is offered through various product ranges, where products are standardized using known technology, but constantly improved through research and development processes. The production process is based on mass-production patterns and the product range represents a large choice including substitutes, whereas the critical production factor is cost level. The development cycle appears

---

[19] *See* Valadou, 'La Notion de Pouvoir Adjudicateur en Matière de Marchés de Travaux', *Semaine Juridique*, Ed. E, No. 3 (1991); Bovis, 'La Notion et les Attributions d'Organisme de Droit Public comme Pouvoirs Adjudicateurs dans le Régime des Marchés Publics', *Contrats Publics*, Septembre 2003.

[20] Flamme et Flamme, *Enfin l'Europe des Marchés Publics* (Actualité Juridique—Droit Administratif, 1989).

[21] On the issue of public interest and its relation with profit, *see* Cases C-223/99, *Agora Srl v. Ente Autonomo Fiera Internazionale di Milano* and C-260/99 *Excelsior Snc di Pedrotti Runa & C v. Ente Autonomo Fiera Internazionale di Milano* [2001] ECR 3605; C-360/96, *Gemeente Arnhem Gemeente Rheden v. BFI Holding BV* [1998] ECR 6821; C-44/96, *Mannesmann Anlangenbau Austria AG et al. v. Strohal Rotationsdurck GesmbH* [1998] ECR 73.

[22] *See* Bovis, *The Liberalisation of Public Procurement in the European Union and its Effects on the Common Market* (Aldershot: Ashgate-Dartmouth, 1998), Chapter 1.

to be short- to medium-term and, finally, the technology of products destined for the private markets is evolutionary. Purchases are made when an acceptable balance between price and quality is achieved. Purchase orders are multitude and at limited intervals. Pricing policy in private markets is determined by competitive forces and the purchasing decision is focused on the price-quality relation, where the risk factor is highly present.

On the other hand, public markets tend to be structured and to function in a **1.13** different way. The market structure often reveals monopsony characteristics.[23] In terms of its origins, demand in public markets is institutionalized and operates mainly under budgetary considerations rather than price mechanisms. It is also based on fulfilment of tasks (pursuit of public interest) and it is single for many products. Supply also has limited origins, in terms of the establishment of close ties between the public sector and industries supplying it, and there is often a limited product range. Products are rarely innovative and technologically advanced, and pricing is determined through tendering and negotiations. The purchasing decision is primarily based upon the life-time cycle, reliability, price, and political considerations. Purchasing patterns follow tendering and negotiations, and often purchases are dictated by policy rather than price/quality considerations.

The intellectual support of public procurement regulation in the European **1.14** Union draws inferences from economic theories. Although the regulation of public procurement aims primarily at the purchasing patterns of the demand side, it is envisaged that the integration of public markets through enhanced competition could bring about beneficial effects for the supply side. These effects focus on the optimal allocation of resources within European industries, the rationalization of production and supply, the promotion of mergers and acquisitions, and the creation of globally competitive industries. Public procurement has cyclical dynamics. It purports to change both behavioural and structural perceptions and applies its effects to both the demand and supply sides.

The integration of the public markets of the European Union is achieved solely by **1.15** reference to the regulation of the purchasing behaviour of the demand side (the contracting authorities). The behaviour of the supply side is not the subject of public procurement legislation, although its regulation would arguably be of equal importance to the integration of public markets in the European Union. The supply side in the public procurement equation is subject to the competition law and policy of the European Union, although there is not any integral mechanism in the public procurement legislation which is capable of introducing the anti-trust rules to the supply side. *Stricto sensu*, anti-competitive behaviour of

---

[23] Monopsony is the reverse of monopoly power. The state and its organs often appear as the sole outlet for an industry's output.

undertakings or collusive tendering do not appear as reasons for disqualification from the selection and award procedures of public contracts.

1.16 European institutions have assumed that encouraging the public and the utilities sectors in the European Union to adopt a purchasing behaviour which is homogenous and is based on the principles of openness, transparency, and non-discrimination will achieve efficiency gains and public sector savings and stimulate industrial restructuring in the supply side.

1.17 The European Commission has claimed that the regulation of public procurement throughout the European Union and the resulting elimination of non-tariff barriers arising from discriminatory and preferential purchasing patterns of member states could bring about substantial savings estimated around 0.5 per cent of the GDP of the European Union. Combating discrimination on grounds of nationality in the award of public procurement contracts and eliminating domestic preferential purchasing schemes could result in efficiency gains at European and national levels through the emergence of three major effects which would primarily influence the supply side. These include a *trade effect*, a *competition effect*, and a *restructuring effect*.

1.18 The trade effect represents the actual and potential savings that the public sector will be able to achieve through lower cost purchasing. The trade effect is a result of the principle of transparency in public markets (compulsory advertisement of public contracts above certain thresholds). However, the principle of transparency and the associated trade effect in public markets do not in themselves guarantee the establishment of competitive conditions in the relevant markets, as market access—a structural element in the process of integration of public markets in Europe—could be subsequently hindered by the discriminatory behaviour of contracting authorities in the selection stages and the award stages of public procurement. The trade effect has a static dimension, since it emerges as a consequence of enhanced market access in the relevant sector or industry.

1.19 The competition effect relates to the changes of industrial performance as a result of changes in the price behaviour of national firms which had previously been protected from competition by means of preferential and discriminatory procurement practices. The competition effect derives also from the principle of transparency and appears to possess rather static characteristics. Transparency in public procurement breaks down information and awareness barriers in public markets, and, as mentioned above, it brings a trade effect in the relevant sectors or industries by means of price competitiveness. The competition effect comes as a natural sequence to price competitiveness and inserts an element of long-term competitiveness in the relevant industries in aspects other than price (e.g. research and development, innovation, customer care). The competition effect will materialize in the form of *price convergence* of goods, works, and services destined for the public sector. Price convergence could take place both nationally and Community-wide, in as much as competition in the relevant markets would equalize the prices of similar products.

Finally, the restructuring effect reveals the restructuring dimension and the re-organizational dynamics in the supply side, as a result of increased competition in the relevant markets. The restructuring effect is a dynamic one and refers to the long-term industrial and sectoral adjustment within industries that supply the public sector. The restructuring effect will encapsulate the reaction of the relevant sector or industry to the competitive regime imposed upon the demand and supply sides, as a result of openness and transparency and the sequential trade and competition effects. The response of the relevant sector or industry and the restructuring effect itself would depend on the efficiency of the industry to merge, diversify, convert or abort the relevant competitive markets and would also reflect upon contemporary national industrial policies.[24]   **1.20**

As a result of the policy momentum gathered in the mid-eighties, the regulation of public procurement in the European Union became a priority. The inefficiency of the relevant primary and secondary Community provisions to combat discriminatory practices and preferential public purchases of contracting authorities throughout the common market was disclosed, as statistical results revealed considerably low cross-border import penetration in public contracts. Furthermore, a disturbing picture emerged as to the extent of differentiation of market access in public procurement opportunities in the member states of the European Union. Market access reflects the effectiveness of import penetration strategies (marketing, predatory pricing, venture alliances) of an undertaking and very much depends upon the regime of competition reigning in the relevant market place.   **1.21**

If scale economies were important in defining the most desirable purchasing pattern for the public sector and if competition were to increase amongst industries which supply the latter, an efficient European industrial structure would support less firms operating at full capacity.[25] Strategic mergers and cross-border investments would reshape the industries and reorganize the operation of firms. Within this reorganization process, the structural adjustment would constantly change in order to adapt to the new market environment introduced by the legal regime on public procurement. In the process of developing new industrial strategies, two factors appear essential: the need for integration of industrial activities[26] and the need to meet local demands.   **1.22**

---

[24] *See* European Commission, *The Opening-up of Public Procurement to Foreign Direct Investment in the European Community*, CC 93/79 (1995).

[25] *See* Dunning, 'Explaining Changing Patterns of International Production: in Defence of the Eclectic Theory', *Oxford Bulletin of Economics and Statistics*, 41/4 (1979), 269–295.

[26] *See* Dunning, *The Globalisation of Business, The Challenge of the 1990s* (London and New York: Routledge, 1993).

1.23   During the past, many of the advantages offered to national champions and locally-operating firms in public procurement markets had discouraged the tradability of public contracts[27] amongst European industries.[28] Persistently low import penetration in protected public procurement sectors dictated a corporate strategy to the relevant industries. Before the opening-up of the public procurement in Europe, the typical strategic choice was low on integration and high on responsiveness, including the replication of all major corporate functions (production, research and development, marketing) in each member state. The ongoing realization of the common market and the regulation of public procurement in the European Union have been forcing undertakings to revise their strategies and to build-up *network organizations,* which combine local responsiveness with a high degree of centralization and co-ordination of major supporting activities. The new strategy has the characteristics of a multi-focal strategy.

1.24   The adoption of multi-focal strategies or global integration strategies involves a major shift in location patterns of key functions within firms.[29] The old decentralized multinational organizations that duplicated major functions in each country in which they operated need to transform into an integrated system whose key elements show a different degree of regional concentration.[30] As a consequence of the new organizational structure, different types of international transactions are expected to occur.[31] Specialization and concentration of activities in certain regions will lead to more trade between certain member states. In addition, as a result of the corporate network system, trade will increasingly develop into intra-firm trade and intra-industry trade with greater exchange of intermediary products.[32] The organizational rationalization following the development of network organizations may result in a problem of ownership and location of the corporate headquarters. Some member states may fear losing strategic control in the restructuring process,[33] and therefore may resist the rationalization process that the industry has been undergoing, by imposing various restrictions in terms of ownership or control structures of locally operating firms.

---

[27] The term 'tradability of public contracts' denotes the effectiveness of the supply side to engage in transactions with public authorities in member states other than the state of its residence or nationality.

[28] *See* McLachlan, 'Discriminatory Public Procurement, Economic Integration and the Role of Bureaucracy', *Journal of Common Market Studies,* 23/4 (1985), 357–372.

[29] Porter, *The Competitive Advantage of Nations* (London: MacMillan, 1990).

[30] Prahalad and Doz, *The Multinational Mission, Balancing Local Demands and Global Vision* (The Free Press, 1987).

[31] Dunning, 'Multinational Enterprises in the 1970s', in Klaus J. Hopt (ed.), *European Merger Control* (Berlin: Walter de Gruyter, 1982).

[32] Vandermerwe, 'A Framework for Constructing Euro-networks', *European Management Journal,* 11/1 (1989), 55–61.

[33] Tirole, *The Theory of Industrial Organization* (Cambridge: The MIT Press, (1988).), Cambridge.

C. The Economic Policy Dimension in Public Procurement Regulation

Viewing public procurement from the prism of an economic exercise, its **1.25** regulation displays strong neo-classical influences. Such influences embrace the merit of efficiency in the relevant market and the presence of competition, mainly price competition, which would create optimal conditions for welfare gains. The connection between public procurement regulation and the neo-classical approach to economic integration in the common market is reflected upon the criterion for awarding public contracts based on the lowest offer.[34] This feature of the public procurement legal framework focuses on price competition being inserted into the relevant markets, and, assisted by the transparency requirement to advertise public contracts above certain thresholds,[35] it would result in production and distribution efficiencies and drive the market towards an optimal allocation of resources.

The lowest offer as an award criterion of public contracts is a quantitative method of achieving market equilibrium between the demand and supply sides. The sup- **1.26** ply side competes in costs terms to deliver standardized (at least in theory) works, services, and goods to the public sector. Price competition is bound to result in innovation in the relevant industries where, through investment and technological improvements, firms could reduce production and/or distribution costs. The lowest offer criterion could be seen as the necessary stimulus in the relevant market participants in order to improve their competitive advantages.

The lowest offer award criterion reflects on, and presupposes, low barriers to entry in a market and provides for a type of predictable accessibility for product or geo- **1.27** graphical markets. This is a desirable characteristic in a system such as public procurement regulation, which is charged with integrating national markets and creating a common market for public contracts which is homogenous and transparent. In addition, the low barriers to enter a market, together with the competitive and transparent price benchmarking for awarding public contracts through the lowest offer criterion, would inevitably attract new undertakings in public

---

[34] *See* Art. 26(1)(a) of Directive 93/36; Art. 30(1)(a) of Directive 93/37; Art. 34(1)(b) of Directive 93/38; Art. 36(1)(b) of Directive 92/50.

[35] The thresholds laid down by the Directives are as follows:

€5 million for all work and construction projects (Art. 3(1) of Directive 93/37; Art. 14(c) of Directive 93/38).

€200,000 for supplies contracts within the European Union (Art. 5(1)(a) of Directive 93/36) and €136,000 for supplies contracts from third countries (Art. 5(1)(c) of Directive 93/36) which participate in the WTO Government Procurement Agreement.

€600,000 for supplies of telecommunication equipment under the Utilities Directive (Art. 14(b) of Directive 93/38) and €400,000 for all other supplies contracts awarded by public utilities (Art. 14(a) of Directive 93/38).

€200,000 for services contracts (Art. 7(1) of Directive 92/50).

procurement markets. This can be seen as an increase of the supply-side pool, a fact which would provide the comfort and the confidence to the demand side (the public sector) in relation to the competitive structure of an industry. Nevertheless, the increased number of participants in public tenders could have adverse effects. Assuming that the financial and technical capacity of firms is not an issue,[36] the demand side (the public sector) will have to bear the cost of tendering and, in particular, the costs relating to the evaluation of offers. The more participants enter the market for the award of public contracts, the bigger the costs attributed to the tendering process would have to be borne by the public sector.

1.28 However, competitiveness in an industry is not reflected solely by reference to low production costs.[37] Efficiencies which might result through production or distribution innovations are bound to have a short term effect on the market for two reasons: if the market is bound to clear with reference to the lowest price, there would be a point where the quality of deliverables is compromised (assuming a product or service remains standardized). Secondly, the viability of industries which tend to compete primarily on cost basis is questionable. Corporate mortality will increase and the market could revert to oligopolistic structures.

1.29 The welfare gains emanating from a neo-classical approach of public procurement regulation encapsulate the actual and potential savings the public sector (and consumers of public services at large) would enjoy through a system that forces the supply side to compete on costs (and price). These gains, however, must be counterbalanced with the costs of tendering (administrative and evaluative costs borne by the public sector), the costs of competition (costs related to the preparation and submission of tender offers borne by the private sector) and litigation costs (costs relevant to prospective litigation borne by both aggrieved tenderers and the public sector). If the cumulative costs exceed any savings attributed to lowest offer criterion, the welfare gains are negative.

1.30 A neo-classical perspective of public procurement regulation reveals the zest of policy makers to establish conditions which calibrate market clearance on price grounds. Price competitiveness in public procurement raises a number of issues with anti-trust law and policy. If the maximization of savings is the only (or the

---

[36] The demand side often omits risk assessment tests during the evaluation process. The Directives remain vague as to the methods for assessing financial risk, leaving a great deal of discretion in the hands of contracting authorities. Evidence of financial and economic standing may be provided by means of references including: i) appropriate statements from bankers; ii) the presentation of the firm's balance sheets or extracts from the balance sheets where these are published under company law provisions; and iii) a statement of the firm's annual turnover and the turnover on construction works for the three previous financial years. *See* Case C-27/86, *Constructions et Entreprises Industrielles SA (CEI) v. Association Intercommunale pour les Autoroutes des Ardennes*; Case C-28/86, *Ing. A. Bellini & Co. SpA v. Regie de Bâtiments*; Case C-29/86, *Ing. A. Bellini & Co. SpA v. Belgian State* [1987] ECR 3347.

[37] *See* Lawton (ed.), *Industrial Policy and Competitiveness in Europe* (Macmillan, 1998).

primary) achievable objective for the demand side in the public procurement process, the transparent/competitive pattern cannot provide any safeguards in relation to under-priced (and anti-competitive) offers.

The price-competitive tendering reflects on the dimension of public procurement **1.31**
regulation as an economic exercise. On the one hand, when the supply side responds to the perpetually competitive purchasing patterns by lowering prices, the public sector could face a dilemma: *what would be the lowest offer it can accept?* The public sector faces a considerable challenge in evaluating and assessing low offers other than 'abnormally low' ones.[38] It is difficult to identify dumping or predatory pricing disguised behind a low offer for a public contract. On the other hand, even if there is an indication of anti-competitive price fixing, the European public procurement rules do not provide for any kind of procedure to address the problem. The anti-trust rules take over and the suspension of the award procedures (or even the suspension of the contract itself) would be subject to a thorough and exhaustive investigation by the competent anti-trust authorities.

Evidence of the neo-classical approach in public procurement regulation can be **1.32**
found in guidelines[39] issued by the European Commission. The Commission adopted a strict interpretation of the rules and focused member states on an economic approach in the application of the Public Procurement Directives. The Commission has championed the neo-classical approach for two reasons: first, to bring an acceptable level of compliance of member states with the public procurement regime and, secondly, to follow the assumptions made through the internal market process that procurement represents a significant non-tariff barrier and its regulation can result in substantial savings for the public sector.

It is interesting to follow the Commission's approach[40] in litigation before the **1.33**
European Court of Justice, where, as an applicant in compliance procedures, or as an intervening party in reference procedures, it consistently regarded public

---

[38] The European rules provide for an automatic disqualification of an 'obviously abnormally low offer'. The term has not been interpreted in detail by the judiciary at European and domestic levels and serves rather as a 'lower bottom limit'. The contracting authorities are under duty to seek from the tenderer an explanation for the price submitted, or to inform him that his tender appears to be abnormally low and to allow a reasonable time within which to submit further details, before making any decision as to the award of the contract. *See* Case 76/81, *SA Transporoute et Travaux v. Minister of Public Works* [1982] ECR 457; Case 103/88, *Fratelli Costanzo SpA v. Comune di Milano* [1989] ECR 1839; Case 296/89, *Impresa Dona Alfonso di Dona Alfonso & Figli snc v. Consorzio per lo Sviluppo Industriale del Comune di Monfalcone* [1991] ECR 2967; Case C-285/99 & 286/99, *Impresa Lombardini SpA v ANAS* [2001] ECR 9233.

[39] *See* Commission Communication, *Social and Regional Aspects of Public Procurement*, 22 September 1989, COM (89) 400, [1989] OJ C311.

[40] *See* the Commission's arguments in the *Beentjes* case (Case 31/87, *Gebroeders Beentjes BV v. State of Netherlands* [1988] ECR 4635), *Nord-Pas-de-Calais* (Case C-225/98, *Commission v. French Republic* [2000] ECR 7445), and *Concordia* (Case C-513/99, *Concordia Bus Finland v. Helsingin Kaupunki et HKL-Bussiliikenne* [2002] ECR 7213).

procurement regulation as an economic exercise. The backbone of such approach has been the price approach to the award of public contracts, predominately through the lowest offer award criterion, but also through the most economically advantageous offer criterion, where factors other than price can play a role in the award process. Even in the latter category, where some degree of flexibility is envisaged by the legal regime, the Commission has been sceptical of any attempts to apply so-called 'qualitative' factors in the award process. Along these lines, the European Court of Justice pursued a neo-classical approach of public procurement regulation through its rulings relating to i) compliance procedures against Member States for not observing the publicity and mandatory advertisement requirements, ii) procedures concerning standardization and technical specifications[41] and iii) procedures relating to the notion of abnormally low offers.[42]

D. Anti-trust and the Public Policy Dimension in Public Procurement Regulation

1.34 The regulatory weaponry for private markets evolves around anti-trust law and policy, where the influence of the neo-classical economic approach has been evident.[43] Public markets are *fora* where the structural and behavioural remedial tools of competition law also apply. However, they focus on the supply side (the industry) which *ipso facto* is subject to the relevant rules relating to cartels and abusive dominance.

1.35 There is a conceptual difference relating to the application of anti-trust in public markets. The demand side (the public sector, the state and its organs) can hardly be embraced by its remit, except in the case of state aids and illegal subsidies. In private markets, anti-trust law and policy seek to punish cartels and the abusive dominance of undertakings. The focus of the remedial instruments of anti-trust is the supply side, which is conceived as the commanding part in the supply/demand equation due to the fact that it instigates, and often controls, demand for a product. In private markets, the demand side of the equation (the consumers at large) is susceptible to exploitation, and the market equilibria are prone to distortion as a result of collusive behaviour of undertakings or abusive monopoly position. On the other hand, the structure of public markets reveals

---

[41] *See* Case C-45/87, *Commission v. Ireland* [1988] ECR 4929; Also Case C-359/93, *Commission v. The Netherlands* [1995] ECR 151.

[42] *See* Case 76/81, *SA Transporoute et Travaux v. Minister of Public Works* [1982] ECR 457; Case 103/88, *Fratelli Costanzo SpA v. Comune di Milano* [1989] ECR 1839; Case 296/89, *Impresa Dona Alfonso di Dona Alfonso & Figli snc v. Consorzio per lo Sviluppo Industriale del Comune di Monfalcone* [1991] ECR 2967; Case C-285/99 & 286/99, *Impresa Lombardini SpA v ANAS* [2001] ECR 9233.

[43] *See* Posner, *Antitrust Law* (2nd edn., University of Chicago Press, 2000).

a different picture. In the supply/demand equation, the dominant part appears to be the demand side (the state and its organs as purchasers), which initializes demand through purchasing, where the supply side (the industry) fights for access to the relevant markets.

In public markets, market segmentation occurs as a result of concerted practices attributed to the demand side. Since such concerted practices of Member States and their contracting authorities (e.g. excluding foreign competition, application of buy-national policies, and application of national standards policies) focus on the origin of a product or a service or the nationality of a contractor, market segmentation in public markets tends to possess geographical characteristics and results in the division of the European public market into different national public markets.

The regulation of public markets requires more than the control of the supply side **1.36** through anti-trust. The primary objective is *market access* and the abolition of barriers and obstacles to trade. Therefore, the regulation aims at the demand side, which effectively controls access and can segment the relevant market. Whereas price competition is the main characteristic of anti-trust,[44] public procurement regulation pursues, firstly, market access. This perspective reflects on the *sui generis* nature of public markets and has provided ground for developing a regulatory system which is strongly influenced by neo-classical economics, whilst at the same time integrating the relevant market. Such system has also strong public law characteristics, to the extent that it has been branded as public competition law (*droit public de la concurrence*).[45]

The vehicle of harmonization has been entrusted to carry the progress of public **1.37** procurement regulation. Directives, as legal instruments, have been utilized to provide the framework of the *acquis communautaire*, but at the same time afford the necessary discretion to the member states as to the forms and methods of their implementation. This is where the first deviation of anti-trust from the traditional economic approach of public procurement occurs. Anti-trust law and policy is enacted through the principle of uniformity across the common market, utilizing directly-applicable regulations. By allowing for discretion to the Member States, an element of public policy is inserted in the equation, which often has decentralized

---

[44] *See* Monti, 'Article 81 EC and Public Policy', *Common Market Law Review*, 39 (2002), 1057–1099, where it is argued that public policy considerations balance the legality test of *ab initio* illegal restrictive agreements by virtue of Art. 81(1)(2) EC with a set of requirements contained in Art. 81(3) EC and also developed by the EC Commission in its jurisdictional capacity to provide individual exemptions.

[45] *See* Bazex, 'Le Droit Public de la Concurrence', *RFDA*, 4/4 (1998), 780–800; Arcelin, *L'Enterprise en Droit Interne et Communautaire de la Concurrence*, (Paris: Litec, 2003); Guézou, 'Droit de la Concurrence et Droit des Marchés Publics: Vers une Notion Transversale de Mise en Libre Concurrence', *Contrats Publics*, Mars 2003.

features. Traditionally, discretion afforded by Directives takes into account national particularities and sensitivities as well as the readiness of domestic administrations to implement *acquis* within a certain deadline. In addition, individuals, who are also subjects of the rights and duties envisaged by the Directives, do not have access to justice, unless provisions of Directives produce direct effect.

1.38 However, the public policy dimension of public procurement regulation is not exhausted in the nature of the legal instruments of the regime. The genuine connection of an ordo-liberal perspective[46] with public procurement regulation is reflected in the award criterion relating to the most economically advantageous offer. The public sector can award contracts by reference to 'qualitative' criteria, in conjunction with price, and thus can legitimately deviate from the strict price competition environment set by the lowest offer criterion.[47] There are three themes emanating from such approach: one reflects on public procurement as a complementary tool of the European integration process; the second regards public procurement as an instrument of contract compliance; lastly, the ordo-liberal perspective can reveal a rule of reason in public procurement, where the integration of public markets in the European Union serves as a conveyer belt of common policies, such as environmental policy, consumer policy, social policy, and industrial policy, and takes into account a flexible and wider view of national and community priorities, and a type of 'European public policy'.

1.39 Policy makers at both European and national levels have not overlooked the effects of public procurement on the formulation of the industrial policy of the European Union. The objective of the public procurement regulation has to a large extent acquired an industrial policy background, which mainly focuses on the achievement of savings for the public sector and the much desired restructuring and adjustment of the European industrial base. However, public spending in the form of procurement is indissolubly linked with adjacent policies and agendas in all member states. The most important policy associated with public purchasing is social policy. Such an argument finds justification in two reasons: the first relates to the optimal utilization of human resources in industries supplying the public sector; the second reason acquires a strategic dimension, in the sense that public purchasing serves aims and objectives stipulated in the European Treaties, such as social cohesion, combating of long-term unemployment, and, finally, the

---

[46] *See* Jacquemin and de Jong, *European Industrial Organization* (Macmillan, 1997); Möschel, 'Competition Law from an Ordo Point of View', in Peacock and Willgerodt (eds.), *German Neo-Liberals and the Social Market Economy* (London: MacMillan, 1989).

[47] *See* European Commission, *Interpretative Communication on the Community Law Applicable to Public Procurement and the Possibilities for Integrating Social Considerations into Public Procurement*, COM (2001) 566, 15 October 2001. Also, European Commission, *Interpretative Communication on the Community Law Applicable to Public Procurement and the Possibilities for Integrating Environmental Considerations into Public Procurement*, COM (2001) 274, 4 July 2001.

achievement of acceptable standards of living. The underlying objectives of the European regime on public procurement relating to enhanced competition and unobstructed market access in the public sector at first sight appear incompatible with the social dimension of European integration, particularly in an era where recession and economic stagnation have revealed the combating of unemployment as a main theme of European governance.

As mentioned above, the award of public contracts can be based on two criteria: **1.40** i) the lowest price, or ii) the most economically advantageous offer. Contracting authorities have absolute discretion in adopting the award criterion under which they wish to award their public contracts. The lowest price award criterion is mostly used when the procurement process is relatively straightforward. On the other hand, the most economically advantageous offer award criterion is suited for more complex procurement schemes.

The most economically advantageous offer as an award criterion represents a **1.41** flexible framework for contracting authorities wishing to insert a qualitative parameter in the award process of a public contract. Needless to say, price, as a quantitative parameter plays an important role in the evaluation stage of tenders, as the meaning of 'economically advantageous' could well embrace financial considerations in the long run. So, if the qualitative criteria of a particular bid compensate for its more expensive price, potential savings in the long run could not be precluded. It is not clear whether the choice of the two above mentioned award criteria has been intentional with a view to providing contracting authorities with a margin of discretion to take into account social policy objectives when awarding their public contracts, or if it merely reflects an element of flexibility which is considered necessary in modern purchasing transactions. If the most economically advantageous offer represents elements relating to quality of public purchasing other than price, an argument arises here supporting the fact that the enhancement of the socio-economic fabric is a 'qualitative' element which can fall into the framework of the above criterion. This argument would take away the assumption that the award of public contracts is a pure *economic exercise*. On the other hand, if one is to insist that public procurement should reflect only *economic choices*, the social policy considerations that may arise from the award of public contracts would certainly have an economic dimension attached to them, often in public service activities which are parallel to public procurement. To what extent contracting authorities should contemplate such elements remains unclear.

The regulation of public procurement and the integration of the public markets **1.42** of the member states do not operate in a vacuum. Irrespective of the often publicized nature of public procurement as the most significant non-tariff barrier for the functioning of the common market, and the clinical presentation of the arguments in favour of an integrated public market across the

European Union,[48] public purchasing is indissolubly linked with national policies and priorities.[49] In the history of European economic integration, public procurement has been an important part of the member states' industrial policies. It has been utilized as a policy tool[50] in order to support indigenous suppliers and contractors and protect national industries and the related workforce.

1.43   The public procurement legal framework can also accommodate *contract compliance* through its award criteria and, in particular, the most economically advantageous offer. The most economically advantageous offer as an award criterion has provided the Court for the opportunity to balance the economic considerations of public procurement with policy choices. Although in numerous instances the Court has maintained the importance of the economic approach[51] to the regulation of public sector contracts, it has also recognized the relative discretion of contracting authorities to utilize non-economic considerations as part of the award criteria.

1.44   The term 'contract compliance'[52] could be best defined as the range of secondary policies relevant to public procurement, which aim at combating discrimination on grounds of sex, race, religion or disability.[53] When utilized in public contracts, contract compliance is a system whereby, unless the supply side (the industry) complies with certain conditions relating to social policy measures, contracting authorities can lawfully exclude tenderers from selection, qualification, and award procedures. The potential of public purchasing as a tool capable of promoting social policies has been met with considerable scepticism. Policies relevant to

---

[48] *See* European Commission, *Special Sectoral Report no. 1, Public Procurement* (Brussels, November 1997).   [49] *See* European Commission, op. cit. (n. 39).

[50] The legislation on public procurement in the early days clearly allowed for 'preference schemes' in less favoured regions of the common market which were experiencing industrial decline. *See* Arts. 29(4) and 29(a) of the EC Public Works Directive 71/305; also Art.26 of EC Public Supplies Directive 77/62. Such schemes required the application of award criteria based on considerations other than the lowest price or the most economically advantageous offer, subject to their compatibility with Community Law in as much as they did not run contrary to the principle of free movement of goods and to competition law considerations with respect to state aids. Since the completion of the internal market (1992) they have been abolished, as they have been deemed capable in contravening directly or indirectly the basic principle of non-discrimination on grounds of nationality stipulated in the Treaty of Rome.

[51] *See* Case C-380/98, *The Queen and HM Treasury, ex parte University of Cambridge*, judgment of 3 October 2000, at paragraph 17; Case C-44/96, *Mannesmann Anlangenbau Austria AG et al. v. Strohal Rotationsdurck GesmbH* [1998] ECR 73, paragraph 33; Case C-360/96, *Gemeente Arnhem Gemeente Rheden v. BFI Holding BV*, judgment of 10 November 1998, at paragraphs 42 and 43; C-237/99, *Commission v. France*, judgment of 1 February 2001, at paragraphs 41 and 42.

[52] *See* Bovis, 'The Compatibility of Compulsory Tendering with Transfer of Undertakings: The Case of Contract Compliance and the Acquired Rights Directive', in Collins, Davies and Rideout (eds.), *Legal Regulation of the Employment Relations* (Kluwer, 2000), Chapter 21.

[53] *See* Inner London Education Authority, *Contract Compliance: A Brief History* (London: ILEA Contract Compliance Equal Opportunities Unit, 1990).

affirmative action or positive discrimination have caused a great deal of controversy, as they practically accomplish very little in rectifying labour market equilibria. In addition to the practicality and effectiveness of such policies, serious reservations have been expressed with regard to their constitutionality,[54] since they could limit, actually and potentially, the principles of economic freedom and freedom of transactions.[55]

Contract compliance legislation and policy is familiar to most European member **1.45** states, although the enactment of Public Procurement Directives has changed the situation dramatically.[56] The position of European institutions on contract compliance has been addressed in three instances before the European Court of Justice.[57] The Court maintained that contract compliance with reference to domestic or local employment cannot be used as a selection criterion in tendering procedures for the award of public contracts. The selection of tenderers is a process which is based on an exhaustive list of technical and financial require-ments expressly stipulated in the relevant Directives and the insertion of contract compliance as a selection and qualification requirement would be considered *ultra vires*. The Court ruled that social policy considerations can only be part of award criteria in public procurement, and especially in cases where the most economically advantageous offer is selected, provided that they do not run contrary to the basic principles of the Treaty and that they have been mentioned in the tender notice.

The Court's approach has also opened an interesting debate on the integral **1.46** dimensions of contract compliance and the differentiation between the *positive* and *negative* approaches. The concept of positive approach within contract com-pliance encompasses all measures and policies imposed by contracting authorities on tenderers as suitability criteria for their selection in public procurement con-tracts. Such positive action measures and policies intend to complement the actual objectives of public procurement which are confined in economic and

---

[54] In particular in the US, *see* Case 93–1841, *Adarand Constructors* v. *Pena*, 515 US 200 (1995). The United States Supreme Court questioned the constitutionality in the application of contract compliance as a potential violation of the equal protection component of the Fifth Amendment's Due Process Clause and ordered the Court of Appeal to reconsider the employment of socio-economic policy objectives in the award of federal public procurement contracts.

[55] For an overview of the social policy in North American systems, *see* Cnossen and Bovis, 'The Framework of Social Policy in Federal States: An Analysis of the Law and Policy on Industrial Relations in USA and Canada', *International Journal of Comparative Labour Law and Industrial Relations*, 12 (1996).

[56] For example, in the United Kingdom, every initiative relating to contract compliance has been outlawed by virtue of the Local Government Act 1988. Contract compliance from a public law per-spective has been examined by Daintith, 'Regulation by Contract: The New Prerogative', *Current Legal Problems*, 32 (1979), 41.

[57] *See* Case 31/87, *Gebroeders Beentjes BV* v. *The Netherlands* [1988] ECR 4635. Also Case C-360/89, *Commission* v. *Italy* [1992] ECR 3401.

financial parameters and are based on a transparent and predictable legal background. Although the complementarity of contract compliance with the actual aims and objectives of the public procurement regime was acknowledged, the Court (and the European Commission) were reluctant in accepting such an over-flexible interpretation of the Directives and, based on the literal interpretation of the relevant provisions, disallowed positive actions of a social policy dimension as part of the selection criteria for tendering procedures in public procurement.

1.47 However, contract compliance can incorporate not only unemployment considerations, but also promote equality of opportunities and eliminate sex or race discrimination in the relevant market.[58] Indeed, the Directives on public procurement stipulate that the contracting authority may require tenderers to observe national provisions of employment legislation when they submit their offers. The ability to observe and conform to national employment laws in a member state may constitute a ground of disqualification and exclusion of the defaulting firm from public procurement contracts.[59] In fact, under such interpretation, contract compliance may be a factor of selection criteria specified in the Directives, as it contains a *negative approach* to legislation and measures relating to social policy.

1.48 There are arguments in favour and against incorporating social policy considerations in public procurement.[60] The most important argument in favour focuses on the ability of public procurement to promote parts of the member states' social policy, with particular reference to long-term unemployment, equal distribution of

---

[58] There are a number of legal instruments relevant to social policy at Community level that may apply to public procurement. They include, in particular, Directives on safety and health at work (for example, Council Directive 89/391 on the Introduction of Measures to Encourage Improvements in the Safety and Health of Workers at Work, and Directive 92/57 on the Implementation of Minimum Safety and Health Requirements at Temporary or Mobile Construction Sites), working conditions and the application of employment law (for example, Directive 96/71/EC of the European Parliament and of the Council Concerning the Posting of Workers in the Framework of the Provision of Services, OJ L18/1 of 21 January 1997, and Directive 2001/23 on the Safeguarding of Employees' Rights in the Event of Transfers of Undertakings, Businesses or Parts of Undertakings or Businesses, OJ L82/16 of 22 March 2001, codifying Directive 77/187/EEC), Directive 2000/43/EC of 29 June 2000 implementing the principle of equal treatment between persons irrespective of racial or ethnic origin ([2000] OJ L180/22) and Directive 2000/78/EC of 27 November 2000 establishing a general framework for equal treatment in employment and occupation ([2000] OJ L303/16).

[59] It should be mentioned that adherence to health and safety laws has been considered by a British court as part of the technical requirements specified in the Works Directive for the process of selection of tenderers; *see General Building and Maintenance v. Greenwich Borough Council* [1993] IRLR 535. Along these lines, *see* European Commission, op. cit. (n. 47).

[60] *See* Krüger, Nielsen, and Bruun, *European Public Contracts in a Labour Law Perspective* (Copenhagen: DJØF Publishing, 1997).

income, social exclusion, and the protection of minorities. Under such a positively oriented approach, public purchasing could be regarded as an instrument of policy in the hands of national administrations with a view to rectifying social equilibria. Contract compliance in public procurement could also cancel the stipulated aims and objectives of the liberalization of the public sector. The regulation of public markets focuses on economic considerations and competition. Adherence to social policy factors could derail the whole process, as the public sector will pay more for its procurement by extra or hidden cost for the implementation of contract compliance in purchasing policies.[61]

The nomination of regional or national firms in the award process of public **1.49** contracts, as well as the promotion of socio-economic considerations relevant to policies of member states under such premises could, legitimately, elevate preferential procurement as an instrument of industrial policy. This might shift the debate from the potential violation of internal market provisions, such as state aids and the free movement principles, towards the overall compatibility of the regime with national or common market-wide industrial policies, thus positioning preferential public procurement in the remit of anti-trust.

Secondly, there is a fundamental change in perceptions about the role and **1.50** responsibilities expected from governments in delivering public services. The public sector not only initiates and facilitates the delivery of public services but also can actively be involved in the actual delivery process. Such changes, in practical terms viewed through the evolution of public–private partnerships,[62] are translated into a new contractual interface between public and private sectors,[63] which in turn encapsulates an era of *contractualized governance*.

---

[61] *See* Bovis, 'Social Policy Considerations and the European Public Procurement Regime', *International Journal of Comparative Labour Law and Industrial Relations*, 3 (1998).

[62] An example of such approach is the views of the UK Government in relation to the involvement of the private sector in delivering public services. The so-called *Private Finance Initiative* (PFI) has been utilized as a procurement and contractual system in order to create a framework between the public and private sectors working together in delivering public services. *See*, in particular, Department of Environment, *Working Together—Private Finance and Public Money* (DoE, 1993). HM Treasury and Private Finance Panel, *Private Opportunity, Public Benefit—Progressing the Private Finance Initiative* (HM Treasury, 1995).

[63] Of interest is the recent case *ARGE* (paragraphs 26 *et seq.* of the Court's judgment), where even the receipt of aid or subsidies incompatible with the Treaty by an entity may be a reason for disqualification from the selection process, as an obligation to repay an illegal aid would threaten the financial stability of the tenderer in question. *See* Case C-94/99, *ARGE Gewässerschutzt v. Bundesministerium für Land- und Forstwirtschaft*, judgment of 7 December 2000, where the Court concluded that if the legislature wanted to preclude subsidized entities from participating in tendering procedures for public contracts, it should have said so explicitly in the relevant Directives.

E. The Industrial Policy Dimension in Public Procurement

1.51 The implementation of industrial policies through public purchasing focuses on either the sustainability of strategic national industries, or the development of infant industries. In both cases, preferential purchasing patterns can provide the economic and financial framework for the development of such industries, at the expense of competition and free trade. Although the utilization of public procurement as a means of industrial policy in member states may breach directly or indirectly primary Treaty provisions on free movement of goods and the right of establishment and the freedom to provide services, it is far from clear whether the European Commission and the European Court of Justice could accept public procurement as legitimate state aids.

1.52 The industrial policy dimension of public procurement is also reflected in the form of strategic purchasing by public utilities. Public utilities in the European Union, which in their majority are monopolies, are accountable for a substantial magnitude of procurement, in terms of volume and in terms of price. Responsible for this are the expensive infrastructure and high technology products that are necessary to procure in order to deliver their services to the public. Given the fact that most of the suppliers to public utilities depend almost entirely on their procurement, and that, even when some degree of privatization has been achieved, the actual control of the utilities is still vested in the state, the first constraint in liberalizing public procurement in the European Union is apparent. Utilities, in the form of public monopolies or semi-private enterprises, appear prone to perpetuate long-standing over-dependency purchasing patterns with certain domestic suppliers. Reflecting the above observations, it is worth bearing in mind that until 1991 utilities were not covered by European legislation on procurement. The delay in their regulation can be attributed to the resistance from member states in privatizing their monopolies and the uncertainty of the legal regime that will follow their privatization.

1.53 Nevertheless, the public procurement legal framework is positively in favour of strategic subcontracting.[64] Subcontracting plays a major role in the opening up of public markets as it is the most effective way of small and medium sized enterprises' participation in public procurement. All Directives on public procurement, influenced by the Commission's Communications on subcontracting and small and medium enterprises, encourage the use of subcontracting in the award

---

[64] *See* European Commission, *SME Task Force: SMEs and Public Procurement* (Brussels, 1988); European Commission, *Pan European Forum on Sub-contracting in the Community* (Brussels, 1993). Also, Mardas, 'Sub-contracting, Small and Medium Sized Enterprises (SMEs) and Public Procurement in the European Community', *Public Procurement Law Review*, 3 (1994), CS 19.

of public contracts. For example, in public supplies contracts, the contracting entity in the invitation to tender may ask the tenderers about their intention to subcontract to third parties as part of the contract. In public works contracts, contracting authorities awarding the principal contract to a concessionaire may require the subcontracting to third parties of at least thirty per cent of the total work provided for by the principal contract. A public works concession is defined by the Works Directive[65] as a written contract between a contractor and a contracting authority concerning either the execution or both the execution and design of a work, and for which remunerative considerations consist, at least partly, in the right of the *concessionaire* to exploit exclusively the finished construction works for a period of time. The regulation of concession contracts was introduced to the *aquis communautaire* by virtue of Directive 89/440 which amended Directive 71/305. In fact, it incorporated the Voluntary Code of Practice, which was adopted by the representatives of member states meeting within the Council in 1971.[66] The Code was a non-binding instrument and contained rules on the advertising of contracts and the principle that contracting authorities awarding the principal contract to a concessionaire were to require him to subcontract to third parties at least thirty per cent of the total work provided for by the principal contract.

The industrial policy dimension of public procurement evolves around public **1.54** monopolies in the member states which predominately operate in the utilities sectors (energy, transport, water, and telecommunications) and have been assigned with the exclusive exploitation of the relevant services in their respective member states. The legal status of these entities varies from legal monopolies, where they are constitutionally guaranteed, to delegated monopolies, where the state confers certain rights on them. During the last decade they have been the target of a sweeping process of transformation, from underperforming public corporations to competitive enterprises. Public monopolies very often possess a monopsony position. As they are state-controlled enterprises, they tend to perform under different management patterns than private firms. Their decision-making responds not only to market forces but mainly to political pressure. Understandably, their purchasing behaviour follows, to a large extent, parameters reflecting current trends of domestic industrial policies. Public monopolies in the utilities sector have sustained national industries in member states through exclusive or preferential procurement. The sustainability of 'national champions', or in other terms, strategically-perceived enterprises, could only be achieved through discriminatory purchasing patterns. The privatization of public monopolies, which absorb, to a large extent, the output of such industries will most probably discontinue

---

[65] *See* Art. 1(d) of Directive 93/37.   [66] *See* [1971] OJ C82/13.

such patterns. It will also result in industrial policy imbalances as it would be difficult for the 'national champions' to secure new markets to replace the traditional long dependency on public monopolies. Finally, it would take time and effort to diversify their activities or to convert to alternative industrial sectors.

1.55 The protected and preferential purchasing frameworks between monopolies and 'national champions', and the output dependency patterns and secured markets of the latter, have attracted considerable foreign direct investment, to the extent that European Union institutions face the dilemma of threatening to discontinue the investment flow when liberalizing public procurement in the common market. However, it could be argued that the industrial restructuring following the opening-up of the procurement practices of public monopolies would possibly attract similar levels of foreign direct investment, which would be directed towards supporting the new structure. The liberalization of public procurement in the European Union has as one of its main aims the restructuring of industries suffering from overcapacity and sub-optimal performance. However, the industries supplying public monopolies and utilities are themselves, quite often, public corporations. In such cases, procurement dependency patterns between state outfits, when disrupted, can result in massive unemployment attributed to the supply side's inadequacy to secure new customers. The monopsony position when abolished could often bring about the collapse of the relevant sector.

1.56 Industrial policies through public procurement can also be implemented with reference to defence industries, particularly for procurement of military equipment. The Procurement Directives cover equipment of dual-use purchased by the armed forces, but explicitly exclude from their ambit the procurement of military equipment. It should also be mentioned here that every member state in the European Union pursues its own military procurement policy by virtue of Article 223 of the Treaty of Rome. In the light of the Maastricht Treaty on European Union, the creation of a framework within which a common European Defence Policy should be established, defence contracts and procurement of military equipment by member states should be harmonized to the extent that a centralized mechanism regulating them should take over independent national military procurement practices.

1.57 Attempts have been made to liberalize, to a limited extent, the procurement of military equipment at European level under the auspices of European Defence Equipment Market (EDEM). This initiative is a programme of gradual liberalization of defence industries in the relevant countries and has arisen through the operation of the Independent European Programme Group, which has been a forum of industrial co-operation in defence industry matters amongst European NATO members. The programme has envisaged, apart from collaborative research and development in defence technology, the introduction of a competitive regime in defence procurement and a modest degree of transparency, subject to the draconian primary Treaty provisions of Article 223. Award of defence procurement contracts under the EDEM should follow a similar rationale with civilian procurement, particularly in the introduction of award criteria based on economic and financial considerations and a minimum degree of publicity for contracts in excess of €1 million.

The establishment of a Common European Defence Policy could possibly bring **1.58** about the integration of defence industries in the European Union and this will inevitably require a change in governments' policies and practices. Competitiveness, public savings considerations, value for money, transparency, and non-discrimination should be the principles of the centralized mechanism regulating defence procurement in Europe. The establishment of a centralized defence agency with specific tasks of *contractorization, facilities management,* and *market testing* represent examples of new procurement policies which would give an opportunity to the defence industry to adopt its practices in the light of the challenges, risks, policy priorities, and directions of the modern era. In particular, risk management and contracting arrangements measuring reliability of deliveries and cost compliance, without penalizing the supply side, are themes which could revolutionize defence procurement and play a significant role in linking such strategic industries with national and European-wide industrial policies.

Public procurement as a discipline expands from a simple internal market topic to **1.59** a multi-faceted tool of European regulation and governance, covering policy choices and revealing an interesting interface between centralized and national governance systems.

F. Public Procurement and State Aid

The frequently exposed nature of public procurement as the most significant **1.60** non-tariff barrier for the functioning of the common market[67] and the presentation of the arguments in favour of an integrated public market across the European Union[68] have contributed to the debate that public purchasing is indissolubly linked with national policies and priorities.[69] In the history of European economic integration, public procurement has been an important part of the member states' industrial policies. It has been utilized as a policy tool[70] in order to

---

[67] *See* European Commission, op. cit. (n. 7). Also, European Commission, op. cit. (n. 10). Also, the Cecchini Report, op. cit. (n. 9). [68] *See* European Commission, op. cit. (n. 48).
[69] *See* European Commission, op. cit. (n. 39).
[70] *See* Arts. 29(4) and 29(a) of the EC Public Works Directive 71/305; also Art. 26 of EC Public Supplies Directive 77/62.

support indigenous suppliers and contractors and preserve national industries and the related workforce. The legislation on public procurement in the early days clearly allowed for 'preference schemes' in less favoured regions of the common market which were experiencing industrial decline. Such schemes required the application of award criteria based on considerations other than the lowest price or the most economically advantageous offer, subject to their compatibility with Community law in as much as they did not run contrary to the principle of free movement of goods and to competition law considerations with respect to state aids. Since the completion of the internal market in 1992 they have been abolished, as they have been deemed capable in contravening directly the basic principle of non-discrimination on grounds of nationality.

1.61 There has been a great deal of controversy over the issue of the compatibility of preferential procurement with EU law. The justification of preference schemes as a ground to promote regional development policies has revealed the interaction of public procurement with state aids.[71] Preferential procurement reflects protectionism, and, as such, is regarded as non-tariff barrier. However, protectionist public procurement, when strategically exercised, has resulted in the evolution of vital industries for the state in question.[72] Preferential public procurement can be seen through a multi-dimensional prism. First, it appears in the form of an exercise which aims at preserving some domestic sectors or industries at the expense of the principles of the European integration process. Impact assessment studies undertaken by the European Commission showed that the operation of preference schemes had a minimal effect on the economies of the regions where they had been applied, both in terms of the volume of procurement contracts, as well as in terms of real economic growth attributed to the operation of such schemes.[73] Thus, in such format, preferential public procurement perpetuates the sub-optimal allocation of resources and represents a welfare loss for the economy of the relevant state. On the other hand, preferential purchasing in the format of strategic investment to the sustainability of selected industries might represent a viable instrument of industrial policy, to the extent that the infant industry, when specialized and internationalized, would be in a position to counterbalance any welfare losses during its protected period. In the above format, preferential public procurement, as an integral part of industrial policy could possibly result in welfare gains.[74]

1.62 Preference schemes have been indissolubly linked with regional development policies, but their interpretation by the European Court of Justice has always been

---

[71] *See* Fernadez-Martin and Stehmann, 'Product Market Integration versus Regional Cohesion in the Community', *European Law Review*, 16 (1991).   [72] *See* Bovis, op. cit. (n. 22).
[73] European Commission, op. cit. (n. 39).
[74] *See* European Commission, op. cit. (n. 14).

restrictive.[75] Although the utilization of public procurement as a tool of regional development policy may breach directly or indirectly primary Treaty provisions on free movement of goods, the right of establishment, and the freedom to provide services, it is far from clear whether the European Commission or the Court could accept the legitimate use of public procurement as a means of state aids. Prior notification to the European Commission of the measures or policies intended to be used as state aid apparently does not legitimize such measures and absolve them from adherence to the judicially well-established framework of the four freedoms. The parallel applicability of rules relating to state aids and the free movement of goods, in the sense that national measures conceived as state aids must not violate the principle of free movement of goods, renders the thrust of regional policies through state aids practically ineffective. It appears that the Court has experimented with the question of the compatibility between state aids and free movement of goods in a number of cases where, initially, it was held that the two regimes are mutually exclusive, to the extent that the principle of free movement of goods could not apply to measures relating to state aids.[76] The acid test for such mutual exclusivity was the prior notification of such measures to the European Commission. However, the Court departed from such a position when it applied free movement of goods provisions to a number of cases concerning state aids which had not been notified to the Commission.[77] Surprisingly, the Court also brought notified state aids measures under the remit of the provision of free movement of goods and reconsidered the whole framework of the mutual exclusivity of states aids and free movement of goods.[78]

State aids jurisprudence has revealed the catalytic position of public procurement **1.63** in the process of determining whether subsidies or state financing of public services represent state aids. The significance of the subject is epitomized in the attempts of the European Council[79] to provide for a policy framework of greater

---

[75] *See* Case 84/86, *Commission v. Hellenic Republic*, not reported; Case C-21/88, *Dupont de Nemours Italiana SpA v. Unita Sanitaria Locale No. 2 di Carrara* [1990] ECR 889; Case C-351/88, *Laboratori Bruneau Srl v. Unità Sanitaria Locale RM/24 di Monterotondo* [1991] ECR I-3641; Case C-360/89, *Commission v. Italy* [1992] ECR I-3401; Case C-362/90, *Commission v. Italy* [1992] ECR I-2353.

[76] *See* Case C-74/76, *Ianelli & Volpi SpA v. Ditta Paola Meroni*, [1977] 2 CMLR 688.

[77] *See* Case C-18/84, *Commission v. France* [1985] ECR 1339; Case 103/84, *Commission v. Italy* [1986] ECR 1759; also Case C-244/81, *Commission v. Ireland* [1982] ECR 4005.

[78] *See* Bovis, 'Public Procurement as an Instrument of Industrial Policy in the European Union', in Lawton (ed.), *Industrial Policy and Competitiveness in Europe* (MacMillan Publishers, 1998), Chapter 7; Fernadez-Martin and Stehmann, op. cit. (n. 71).

[79] *See Conclusions of the European Council of 14 and 15 December 2001*, paragraph 26; *Conclusions of the Internal Market, Consumer Affairs and Tourism Council Meeting of 26 November 2001 on Services of General Interest*; *Commission Report to the Laeken European Council on Services of General Interest of 17 October 2001*, COM (2001) 598; *Communication from the Commission on the Application of the State Aid Rules to Public Service Broadcasting*, [2001] OJ C32, 5; *see also* the two general Commission Communications on services of general interest of 1996 and 2000, in [1996] OJ C281, 3 and [2001] OJ C17, 4.

predictability and increased legal certainty in the application of the state aid rules to the funding of services of general interest. Along the above lines, public procurement rules have served as a yardstick to determine the nature of an undertaking in its contractual interface when delivering public services. The funding of services of general interest by the state may materialize through different formats, such as the payment of remuneration for services under a public contract, the payment of annual subsidies, preferential fiscal treatment, or lower social contributions. The most common format is the existence of a contractual relation between the state and the undertaking charged to deliver public services. The above relation should, under normal circumstances, pass through the remit of public procurement framework, not only as an indication of market competitiveness but mainly as a demonstration of the nature of the deliverable services as services of 'general interest having non industrial or commercial character'.

1.64 There are three approaches under which the European judiciary and the Commission have examined the financing of public services: *the state aids approach, the compensation approach* and *the quid pro quo approach*. The above approaches reflect not only conceptual and procedural differences in the application of state aid control measures within the common market, but also raise imperative and multifaceted questions relevant to the state funding of services of general interest.

1.65 The state aids approach[80] examines state funding granted to an undertaking for the performance of obligations of general interest. It thus regards the relevant funding as state aid within the meaning of Article 87(1) EC[81] which may however be justified under Article 86(2) EC,[82] provided that the conditions of that derogation are fulfilled and, in particular, if the funding complies with the principle of proportionality. The state aids approach provides for the most clear and legally certain procedural and conceptual framework to regulate state aids, since it positions the European Commission in the centre of that framework.

1.66 The compensation approach[83] reflects upon a 'compensation' being intended to cover an appropriate remuneration for the services provided or the costs of

---

[80] *See* Case C-387/92, *Banco Exterior de España v Ayuntamiento de Valencia* [1994] ECR I-877; Case T-106/95, *Fédération Française des Sociétés d'Assurances and others v Commission* [1997] ECR II-229; Case C-174/97 P, *Fédération Française des Sociétés d'Assurances v Commission* [1998] ECR I-1303; Case T-46/97, *SIC v Commission* [2000] ECR II-2125.

[81] Art. 87(1) EC defines state aid as 'any aid granted by a Member State or through State resources in any form whatsoever which distorts or threatens to distort competition by favoring certain undertakings or the production of certain goods . . . , in so far as it affects trade between Member States'.

[82] Art. 86(2) EC stipulates that 'Undertakings entrusted with the operation of services of general economic interest . . . shall be subject to the rules contained in this Treaty, in particular to the rules on competition, insofar as the application of such rules does not obstruct the performance, in law or in fact, of the particular tasks assigned to them. The development of trade must not be affected to such an extent as would be contrary to the interests of the Community'.

[83] *See* Case 240/83, *Procureur de la République v. Association de Défense des Brûleurs d'Huiles Usagées* [1985] ECR 531; Case C-53/00, *Ferring v. ACOSS* [2001] ECR I-9067; Case C-280/00,

providing those services. Under that approach, state funding of services of general interest amounts to state aid within the meaning of Article 87(1) EC only if, and to the extent that, the economic advantage which it provides exceeds such an appropriate remuneration or such additional costs. European jurisprudence considers that state aids exist only if, and to the extent that, the remuneration paid, when the state and its organs procure goods or services, exceeds the market price.

The *quid pro quo* approach distinguishes between two categories of state funding;   **1.67**
in cases where there is a direct and manifest link between the state financing and clearly-defined public service obligations, any sums paid by the state would not constitute state aid within the meaning of the Treaty. On the other hand, where there is no such link or the public service obligations were not clearly defined, the sums paid by the public authorities would constitute state aids.

The choice between the state aids approach and the compensation approach does   **1.68**
not only reflect upon a theoretical debate; it mainly reveals significant practical ramifications in the application of state aid control within the common market. Whilst it is generally accepted that the pertinent issue of substance is whether the state funding exceeds what is necessary to provide for an appropriate remuneration or to offset the extra costs caused by the general interest obligations, the two approaches have very different procedural implications. Under the compensation approach, state funding which does not constitute state aid escapes the clutches of EU state aid rules and need not be notified to the Commission. More importantly, national courts have jurisdiction to pronounce on the nature of the funding as state aid without the need to wait for an assessment by the Commission of its compatibility with *acquis*. Under the state aid approach, the same measure would constitute state aid which must be notified in advance to the Commission. Moreover, the derogation in Article 86(2) EC is subject to the same procedural regime as the derogations in Article 87(2) and (3) EC, which means that new aid cannot be implemented until the Commission has declared it compatible with Article 86(2) EC. Measures which infringe that stand-still obligation constitute illegal aid. Another procedural implication of the compensation approach is that national courts must offer to individuals the certain prospect that all the appropriate conclusions will be drawn from the infringement of the last sentence of Article 88(3) EC, as regards the validity of the measures giving effect to the aid, the recovery of financial support granted in disregard of that provision, and possible interim measures.

The *quid pro quo* approach[84] positions at the centre of the analysis of state funding   **1.69**
of services of general interest a distinction between two different categories:

Altmark Trans GmbH and Regierungspräsidium Magdeburg v Nahverkehrsgesellschaft Altmark GmbH, judgment of 24 July 2003.

[84] *See* Opinion of Advocate General Jacobs in Case C-126/01, *Ministre de l'Economie, des Finances et de l'Industrie v GEMO SA*, 30 April 2002.

i) the nature of the link between the financing granted and the general interest duties imposed; and ii) the degree of clarity in defining those duties. The first category would comprise cases where the financing measures are clearly intended as a *quid pro quo* for clearly defined general interest obligations, or in other words where the link between, on the one hand, the state financing granted and, on the other hand, clearly defined general interest obligations imposed is direct and manifest. The clearest examples of such a direct and manifest link between state financing and clearly defined obligations are public service contracts awarded in accordance with public procurement rules. The contract in question should define the obligations of the undertakings entrusted with the services of general interest and the remuneration which they will receive in return. Cases falling into that category should be analysed according to the compensation approach. The second category consists of cases where it is not clear from the outset that the state funding is intended as a *quid pro quo* for clearly defined general interest obligations. In those cases, the link between state funding and the general interest obligations imposed is either not direct or not manifest, or the general interest obligations are not clearly defined.

1.70 The *quid pro quo* approach appears at first instance consistent with the general case law on the interpretation of Article 87(1) EC. Also, it gives appropriate weight to the importance of services of general interest, within the remit of Article 16 EC and of Article 36 of the EU Charter of Fundamental Rights. On the other hand, the *quid pro quo* approach presents a major shortcoming: it introduces elements[85] of the nature of public financing into the process of determining the legality of state aids. According to state aids jurisprudence, only the effects of the measure are to be taken into consideration[86] and, as a result of the application of the *quid pro quo* approach, legal certainty could be undermined.

---

[85] For example, the form in which the aid is granted (*see* Cases C-323/82, *Intermills v. Commission* [1984] ECR 3809, paragraph 31; Case C-142/87, *Belgium v. Commission*, cited in note 18, paragraph 13; and Case 40/85, *Belgium v. Commission* [1986] ECR I-2321, paragraph 120), the legal status of the measure in national law (*see* Commission Decision 93/349/EEC of 9 March 1993 Concerning Aid Provided by the United Kingdom Government to British Aerospace for its Purchase of Rover Group Holdings Over and Above those Authorised in Commission Decision 89/58/EEC Authorizing a Maximum Aid to this Operation Subject to Certain Conditions [1993] OJ L143, 7, point IX), the fact that the measure is part of an aid scheme (*see* Case T-16/96, *Cityflyer Express v. Commission* [1998] ECR II- 757), the reasons for the measure, and the objectives of the measure (*see* Case C-173/73, *Italy v. Commission* [1974] ECR 709; *Deufil v. Commission* [1987] ECR 901; Case C-56/93, *Belgium v. Commission* [1996] ECR I-723; Case C-241/94, *France v. Commission* [1996] ECR I-4551; Case C-5/01, *Belgium v. Commission* [2002] ECR I-3452), and the intentions of the public authorities and the recipient undertaking (Commission Decision 92/11/EEC of 31 July 1991 Concerning Aid Provided by the Derbyshire County Council to Toyota Motor Corporation, an Undertaking Producing Motor Vehicles [1992] OJ L6, 36, point V).

[86] *See* Case C-173/73, *Italy v. Commission* [1974] ECR 709, paragraph 27; *Deufil v. Commission* [1987] ECR 901; Case C-56/93, *Belgium v. Commission* [1996] ECR I-723, paragraph 79; Case C-241/94, *France v. Commission* [1996] ECR I-4551, paragraph 20; and Case C-5/01, *Belgium v. Commission* [2002] ECR I-3452, paragraphs 45 and 46.

The application of the state aid approach creates a *lex and policy lacuna* in the **1.71**
treatment of funding of services of general economic interest and normal services.
In fact, it presupposes that the services of general economic interest emerge in a
different market, where the state and its emanations act in a public function. Such
markets are not susceptible to the private operator principle[87] which has been
relied upon by the Commission and the European Courts[88] to determine the borderline between market behaviour and state intervention.

European jurisprudence distinguishes the economic nature of state intervention **1.72**
and the exercise of public powers. The application of the private operator principle is confined to the economic nature of state intervention[89] and is justified by the
principle of equal treatment between the public and private sectors.[90] Such treatment requires that intervention by the state should not be subject to stricter rules
than those applicable to private undertakings. The non-economic character of
state intervention[91] renders immaterial the test of private operator, for the reason
that profitability, and thus the *raison d'être* of the private investment, is not
present. It follows that services of general economic interest cannot be part of
the same demand/supply equation, as other normal services the state and its

---

[87] *See* the Communication of the Commission to the Member States Concerning Public
Authorities' Holdings in Company Capital, *Bulletin EC*, 9–1984, point 3.5.1. The Commission
considers that such an investment is not aid where the public authorities authorized it under the
same conditions as a private investor operating under normal market economy conditions. *See also*
Commission Communication to the Member States on the Application of Articles 92 and 93 of the
EEC Treaty and of Article 5 of Commission Directive 80/723/EEC to Public Undertakings in the
Manufacturing Sector [1993] OJ C307, 3, point 11.

[88] *See* in particular Case 234/84, *Belgium v. Commission* [1986] ECR 2263, paragraph 14;
Case C-142/87, *Belgium v. Commission* ('*Tubemeuse*') [1990] ECR I-959, paragraph 26; and Case
C-305/89, *Italy v. Commission* ('*Alfa Romeo*') [1991] ECR I-1603, paragraph 19.

[89] For example, where the public authorities contribute capital to an undertaking (Case 234/84,
Belgium v. Commission [1986] ECR 2263; Case C-142/87, *Belgium v. Commission* [1990] ECR
I-959; Case C-305/89, *Italy v. Commission* [1991] ECR I-1603), grant a loan to certain undertak-
ings (Case C-301/87, *France v. Commission* [1990] ECR I-307; Case T-16/96, *Cityflyer Express v.
Commission* [1998] ECR II-757), provide a state guarantee (Joined Cases T-204/97 and T-270/97
EPAC v. Commission [2000] ECR II-2267), sell goods or services on the market (Joined Cases
67/85, 68/85 and 70/85 *Van der Kooy and Others v. Commission* [1988] ECR 219; Case C-56/93,
Belgium v. Commission [1996] ECR I-723; Case C-39/94, *SFEI and Others* [1996] ECR I-3547), or
grant facilities for the payment of social security contributions (Case C-256/97, *DM Transport*
[1999] ECR I-3913), or the repayment of wages (Case C-342/96, *Spain v. Commission* [1999] ECR
I-2459).

[90] *See* Case C-303/88, *Italy v. Commission* [1991] ECR I-1433, paragraph 20; Case C-261/89,
Italy v. Commission [1991] ECR I-4437, paragraph 15; and Case T-358/94, *Air France v.
Commission* [1996] ECR II-2109, paragraph 70.

[91] For example, where the public authorities pay a subsidy directly to an undertaking (Case
310/85, *Deufil v. Commission* [1987] ECR 901), grant an exemption from tax (Case C-387/92,
Banco Exterior [1994] ECR I-877; Case C-6/97, *Italy v. Commission* [1999] ECR I-2981; Case
C-156/98, *Germany v. Commission* [2000] ECR I-6857), or agree to a reduction in social security
contributions (Case C-75/97, *Belgium v. Commission* [1999] ECR I-3671; Case T-67/94, *Ladbroke
Racing v. Commission* [1998] ECR II-1).

organs procure.[92] Along the above lines, a convergence emerges between public procurement jurisprudence and the state aid approach in the light of the reasoning behind the *BFI*[93] and *Agora*[94] cases. Services of general economic interest are *sui generis*, having as main characteristics the lack of industrial and commercial character, where the absence of profitability and competitiveness are indicative of the relevant market place. As a rule, the procurement of such services should be subject to the rigour and discipline of public procurement rules and, in analogous *ratione*, classified as state aid in the absence of the competitive award procedures. In consequence, the application of the public procurement regime reinforces the character of services of general interest as non-commercial or industrial and the existence of public markets.[95]

1.73 The compensation approach relies heavily upon the real advantage theory to determine the existence of any advantages conferred to undertakings through state financing. Thus, the advantages given by the public authorities and threaten to distort competition are examined together with the obligations on the recipient of the aid. Public advantages thus constitute aid only if their amount exceeds the value of the commitments the recipient enters into. The compensation approach treats the costs offsetting the provision of services of general interest as the base line over which state aids should be considered. That base line is determined by the market price, which corresponds to the given public/private contractual interface, and is demonstrable through the application of public procurement award procedures.

1.74 The real advantage theory runs contrary to the apparent advantage theory which underlines Treaty provisions[96] and the approach that relies on the economic effects and the nature of the measures in determining the existence of state aids. The borderline of the market price, which will form the conceptual base above which state aids would appear, is not always easy to determine, even with the presence of public procurement procedures. The state and its organs as contracting authorities (state emanations and bodies governed by public law) have wide discretion to award public contracts under the public procurement rules.[97] Often,

---

[92] *See* the analysis in the Joined Cases C-278/92 to C-280/92, *Spain v. Commission* [1994] ECR I-4103.

[93] *See* Case C-360/96, *Gemeente Arnhem Gemeente Rheden v. BFI Holding BV*, op. cit.

[94] *See* Cases C-223/99, *Agora Srl v. Ente Autonomo Fiera Internazionale di Milano* and C-260/99, *Excelsior Snc di Pedrotti Runa & C v. Ente Autonomo Fiera Internazionale di Milano*, op. cit.

[95] *See* Bazex, op. cit. (n. 45); Arcelin, op. cit. (n. 45); Guézou, op. cit. (n. 45).

[96] According to Advocate General Léger in his Opinion on the *Altmark* case, the apparent advantage theory occurs in several provisions of the Treaty, in particular in Art. 92(2) and (3), and in Art. 77 of the EC Treaty (now Art. 73 EC). Art. 92(3) of the Treaty provides that aid may be regarded as compatible with the common market if it pursues certain objectives such as the strengthening of economic and social cohesion, the promotion of research, and the protection of the environment.

[97] According to Art. 26 of Directive 93/36, Art. 30 of Directive 93/37, Art. 34 of Directive 93/38 and Art. 36 of Directive 92/50, two criteria provide the conditions under which contracting authorities

price plays a secondary role in the award criteria. In cases when the public contract is awarded to the lowest price, the element of *market price* under the compensation approach could be determined. However, when the public contract is to be awarded by reference to the most economically advantageous offer,[98] the market price might be totally different to the price the contracting authority wishes to pay for the procurement of the relevant services. The mere existence of public procurement procedures cannot, therefore, reveal the necessary element of the compensation approach: the market price which will determine the 'excessive' state intervention and introduce state aids regulation.

An indication of the application of the compensation approach is reflected in the **1.75** *Stohal*[99] case, where an undertaking could provide commercial services and services of general interest without any relevance to the applicability of the public procurement rules. The rationale of the case runs parallel with the real advantage theory, up to the point of recognizing the different nature and characteristics of the markets under which normal (commercial) services and services of general interest are provided. The distinction begins where, for the sake of legal certainty and legitimate expectation, the activities of undertakings of dual capacity are equally covered by the public procurement regime and the undertaking in question is considered as *contracting authority* irrespective of any proportion or percentage between the delivery of commercial services and services of general interest. This finding might have a significant implication for the compensation approach in state aids jurisprudence: irrespective of any costs offsetting the costs related to the provision of general interest, the entire state financing could be viewed under the state aid approach.

award public contracts: *the lowest price* or the *most economically advantageous offer*. The first criterion indicates that, subject to the qualitative criteria and financial and economic standing, contracting authorities do not rely on any other factor than the price quoted to complete the contract. The Directives provide for an automatic disqualification of an 'obviously abnormally low offer'. The term has not been interpreted in detail by the Court and serves rather as an indication of a 'lower bottom limit' of contracting authorities accepting offers from the private sector tenderers. *See* Case 76/81, *SA Transporoute et Travaux v. Minister of Public Works* [1982] ECR 457; Case 103/88, *Fratelli Costanzo SpA v. Comune di Milano* [1989] ECR 1839; Case 296/89, *Impresa Dona Alfonso di Dona Alfonso & Figli snc v. Consorzio per lo Sviluppo Industriale del Comune di Monfalcone*, judgment of 18 June 1991. In Case C-94/99, *ARGE Gewässerschutz*, the Court ruled that directly or indirectly subsidised tenders by the state or other contracting authorities, or even by the contracting authority itself, can be legitimately part of the evaluation process; it did not elaborate on the possibility of rejection of an offer which is appreciably lower than those of unsubsidised tenderers by reference to the of abnormally low disqualification ground. *See* paragraphs 26 *et seq.* of the Court's judgment. Although the case has relevance in the fields of selection and qualification procedures and award criteria, the Court made no references to previous case law regarding state aids in public procurement, presumably because the *Dupont de Nemours* precedence is still highly relevant.

[98] The meaning of the most economically advantageous offer includes a series of factors chosen by the contracting authority, including price, delivery or completion date, running costs, cost-effectiveness, profitability, technical merit, product or work quality, aesthetic and functional characteristics, after-sales service and technical assistance, commitments with regard to spare parts and components and maintenance costs, and security of supplies. The above list is not exhaustive.

[99] Case C-44/96, *Mannesmann Anlangenbau Austria AG et. al. v. Strohal Rotationsdurck GesmbH* [1998] ECR 73. *See also* the analysis of the case by Bovis, in [1999] 36 CMLR 205–225.

1.76   Finally, the *quid pro quo* approach relies on the existence of a direct and manifest link between state financing and services of general interest, existence indicative through the presence of a public contract concluded in accordance with the provisions of the Public Procurement Directives. Apart from the obvious criticism the *quid pro quo* approach has received, its interface with public procurement appears as the most problematic facet in its application. The procurement of public services does not always reveal a public contract between a contracting authority and an undertaking.

G. The Remit of Public Procurement Regulation

1.77   Whereas the regulatory weaponry for private markets is dominated by anti-trust law and policy, public markets are *fora* where the structural and behavioural remedial tools of competition law emerge as rather inappropriate instruments of a regulatory framework. The applicability of competition law to public markets is limited, mainly due to the fact that anti-trust often clashes with monopolistic structures which exist in public markets. State participation in market activities is regularly assisted through exclusive exploitation of a product or a service within a geographical market. The market activities of a public entity are protected from competition by virtue of laws on trading and production or by virtue of delegated monopolies. Another reason for the limited applicability of anti-trust law and policy in public markets is the fact that conceptual differences appear between the two categories of markets—private and public—in the eyes of anti-trust, which could be attributed to their different nature. In private markets, anti-trust law and policy seek to punish cartels and abusive dominance of undertakings. The focus of the remedial instruments is the supply side, which is conceived as the commanding part in the supply/demand equation due to the fact that it instigates and controls demand for a product. In private markets, the demand side of the equation (the consumers in general) is susceptible to exploitation and the market equilibria are prone to distortion as a result of collusive behaviour of undertakings or abusive monopoly position. On the other hand, the structure of public markets reveals a different picture. In the supply/demand equation, the dominant part appears to be the demand side (the state and its organs as purchasers), which initializes demand through purchasing, whereas the supply side (the industry) fights for access to the relevant markets. Although this is normally the case, one should not exclude the possibility of market oligopolization and the potential manipulation of the demand side.[100] These advanced market structures can occur more often in the future, as a result of well-established trends of industrial concentration.

---

[100] *See* Konstadacopoulos, 'The Linked Oligopoly Concept in the Single European Market', *Public Procurement Law Review*, 4 (1995), 213.

Another argument which has relevance to the different regulatory approach of **1.78** public and private markets reflects on the methods of possible market segmentation and abuse. It is maintained that the segmentation of private markets appears different from the partitioning of public ones. In private markets, market segmentation occurs as a result of cartels and collusive behaviour which would lead to abuse of dominance, with a view to driving competitors out of the relevant market, increasing market shares, and ultimately increasing profits. Private markets can be segmented both geographically and by reference to product or service, whereas public ones can only be geographically segmented. This assumption leads to the argument that the partition of the public markets would probably be the result of concerted practices attributed to the demand side. As such, concerted practices focus on the origin of a product or a service or the nationality of a contractor, and then the only way to effectively partition the relevant market would be by reference to its geographical remit. In contrast, as far as private markets are concerned, the segmentation of the relevant market (either product or geographical) can only be attributed to the supply side. The argument goes further to reveal the fact that the balance of powers between the supply and the demand side is reversed in public markets. In the latter, it is the demand side that has the dominant role in the equation by dictating terms and conditions in purchases, initiation of transactions, as well as by influencing production trends.[101]

In public markets, concerted practices of the demand side (e.g. excluding foreign **1.79** competition, application of buy-national policies, and application of national standards policies) represent geographical market segmentation, as they result in the division of the European public markets into different national public markets. It could also be maintained that public markets are subject to protection—rather than restriction—from competition, to the extent that the latter are quasi-monopolistic and monopsonistic in their structure. Indeed, the state and its organs, as contractors, possess a monopoly position in the sense that no one competes against them in their market activities.[102] Even in cases of privatization, the monopoly position is shifted from the public to private hands. The situation is different in cases of an open privatized regime pursuing an operation of public interest. In that case, it would be more appropriate to refer to oligopolistic competition in the relevant market. Also, in privatized regimes interchangeability of supply is very limited, to an extent that monopoly position characteristics survive the transfer of ownership from public to private hands. The state and its organs also possess a monopsony position, as firms engaged in transactions with them have no alternatives to pursue business. Access barriers to geographical public markets are erected by states as a result of exercising their discretion to conclude

---

[101] *See* Bovis, 'The Regulation of Public Procurement as an Element in the Evolution of European Economic Law', *European Law Journal*, Spring (1998).

[102] *See* Swann, *The Retreat of the State* (Harvester-Wheatsheaf, 1988), Chapters 1–2.

contracts with national undertakings. This type of activity constitutes the partition of public markets in the European Union, whereas undertakings operating in private markets must enter into a restrictive agreement between themselves in order to split up the relevant markets. Due to their different integral nature, private and public markets require different control. The control in both cases has a strong public law character, but while anti-trust regulates private markets, it appears rather inappropriate for public ones. Anti-trust law and policy is a set of rules of a negative nature; undertakings must *restrain* their activities to an acceptable range pre-determined in due course by the competent authorities. On the other hand, public markets require a set of rules that have positive character. It should be recalled that the integration of public markets is based on the abolition of barriers and obstacles to national markets; it then follows that the type of competition envisaged for their regulation is mainly *market access competition*. This primarily indicates that price competition is expected to emerge in European public markets, only after their integration.

1.80 It appears, however, that in both private and public markets, two elements have relevance when attempting their regulation. The first element is the *price differentiation* of similar products; the second element is *access* to the relevant markets. As the European integration is an economic process which aims at dismantling barriers to trade and approximating national economies, the need to create acceptable levels of competition in both public and private markets becomes more demanding. In fact, a regime of genuine competition in public markets would benefit the public interest as it will lower the price of goods and services for the public, as well as achieve substantial savings for the public purse.

1.81 The evolution of public procurement regulation in the European Union points towards a strategy for eliminating discriminatory public procurement amongst member states which have posed significant obstacles to the fundamental principles of free movement of goods, the right of establishment, and the freedom to provide services. That strategy has been based on two principal assumptions: the first assumption acknowledged the fact that, in order to eliminate preferential and discriminatory purchasing practices in European public markets, a great deal of *transparency* and *openness* was needed; the second assumption rested on the premise that the only way to regulate public procurement in the member states in an effective manner was through the process of *harmonization* of existing laws and administrative practices which had been in operation, and not through a *uniform* regulatory pattern which would replace all existing laws and administrative practices throughout the Community. The latter assumption indirectly recognized the need for a decentralized system of regulation for public procurement in the Community, well ahead of the pronouncement of the principle of *subsidiarity*, which was introduced in the European law jargon some years later by virtue of the Maastricht Treaty on European Union.

Since harmonization was adopted as the most appropriate method of regulation **1.82** of public procurement in the common market, and the decentralized character of the regime was reinforced through legislation, the onus then was shifted to the national administrations of the member states, which had to implement the Community principles into domestic law and give a certain degree of clarity and legitimate expectation to interested parties. Occasionally, the European Commission is criticized for not reserving for itself or other Community institutions central powers, other than those already available, and in its disposal as the guardian of the Treaty, in relation to the enforcement of and compliance with public procurement rules. The critics often refer to the applicability of competition law and policy of the European Union and the regime which legally implements it through specific Regulations. However, although in principle competition law of the European Union may apply to the award of public contracts,[103] the *effectiveness* and *efficiency* of a regulatory regime in the public markets through basic anti-trust remedies remains a challenge for the law and policy maker. A rigid regime in its application through a uniform way across the common market would not take into account national particularities in public procurement, and a highest common denominator would probably eliminate any elements of *flexibility* in the system. Public procurement, as the *nexus* of transactions in the supply chain of the public sector, does not differ in principle from the management of purchasing practices in the private sector, which remains unregulated.

The legal instruments opted for by European institutions to achieve the objective **1.83** of flexibility are Directives. Public markets and their regulation are dominated by different legal regimes and legal approaches that diverge to a considerable extent from each other. Directives, as flexible legal instruments, leaving a great deal of discretion in the hands of member states with respect to the forms and the methods of their implementation, can harmonize public markets taking into account existing divergences in domestic legal systems. The appropriateness of Directives, to achieve the desired degree of competition in public markets and establish a regime where optimal resource allocation benefits the public interest, is unquestionable. The nature and character of Directives, as *framework* legal instruments, aim at harmonizing existing legal systems, bringing them in conformity with Community envisaged objectives. Directives attempt to approximate

---

[103] *See* Case 47/73, *Cooperative Vereniging 'Suiker Unie' UA v. Commission* [1975] ECR 1663, in which the European Court of Justice recognised the adverse effects of concerted practices in tendering procedures on competition in the common market. This case appears to have opened the way for the application of competition law on public procurement in the Community. The applicability of competition law provisions of the Treaty (Arts. 85, 86) in controlling collusive tendering and anti-competitive behaviour of suppliers, was also the subject of Commission Decision 92/204, [1992] OJ L92/1. It could be argued that competition law and policy applies equally to private as well as public markets, but the explicit provisions of the Directives on consortia participation in tendering procedures might limit the scope of Arts. 85, 86 in public procurement.

different national laws and achieve a similar legal regime throughout the common market based on the lowest common denominator amongst the systems of the member states. Divergences will inevitably remain, as the European Union lacks the powers to abolish existing domestic legal regimes and impose *ab initio* a different one.[104] Nevertheless, it should be pointed out that Regulations aim at unification of the regimes governing the member states' legal orders and have been extensively used in the anti-trust field. It could be further argued that Regulations reveal all the characteristics of instruments of public law, in particular to the extent that they are directly applicable and produce vertical and horizontal direct effectiveness. Apart from the creation of a uniform system common to the internal legal orders of the member states, other notable advantages by having recourse to Regulations instead of Directives would have been the fact that individuals could directly rely on their provisions not only against the state but also against other individuals before domestic courts.

1.84   Directives, on the other hand, appear to have strong characteristics of instruments of public law, in as much as they constitute the legal framework within which the state must enact rules that regulate the relevant sector. Directives, unlike Regulations, lay down duties and obligations addressed only to member states. Regulations, in addition, introduce rights of individuals to be respected by member states and also other individuals. Directives resemble circulars at domestic administrative level, to the extent that the latter provide the framework for action by central government to the competent decentralized authority. The difference is that Directives are binding legal instruments and may be relied upon before national courts by individuals under certain circumstances restrictively interpreted by the European Court of Justice (the case of direct effect), whereas administrative circulars produce no binding effects. Directives, as Community legal instruments were thought to be the most appropriate method to regulate public markets in the European Union. As mentioned above, fundamental differences in existing national legal systems dictated the continuation of domestic public market regimes, but the main concern was their enforcement at national level. In fact, it was the range of procedural and substantive sensibilities and peculiarities found in the judicial infrastructure of the member states, especially the system through which judicial review of public procurement is channelled, that prevented legal unification at Community level by means of Regulations.

1.85   Treaty provisions on non-discrimination, on the prohibition to barriers to intra-community trade, on the freedom to provide services, on the right of establishment,

---

[104] For the constitutional aspects of the application of a Regulation in domestic legal orders, see the reservations of the French Government after the adoption of the SEA and in particular Art. 100A EC, which constitutes the legal basis of all Public Procurement Directives after 1986, in Kapteyn and Verloren van Themaat, *Introduction to the Law of the European Communities* (2nd edn., Kluwer-Deventer, 1989), 470–479.

on public undertakings and undertakings to which member states grant special or exclusive rights, and on state monopolies providing services of general economic interest, although capable of embracing the legal relations arising from public procurement in the common market and regulating intra-community trade of public contracts according to the principles stipulated in the Treaties, seemed insufficient on their own in eliminating protection afforded to domestic under-takings through preferential public procurement. The diversity of legal systems within the member states of the European Union, and the differences in existing domestic public procurement rules, would have rendered the regulation of public markets ineffective, if recourse solely to primary Community legislation was sought. The negative character of the primary Community provisions which may apply to public procurement, to the extent that they provide for a legal framework which prohibits any obstructions, distortions and hindrances to intra-community trade and the relevant fundamental principles, could be seen as the main reason for the need by European institutions to intervene and introduce a set of rules which, although based upon the above primary Community rules, have a positive character in the sense that they allow a margin of discretion in their implementation. Due to the decentralized nature of any regulatory form of public procurement in the common market, the normative character of the primary Community rules was diluted in favour of a process of harmonization of existing laws and practices in the member states.

2

THE JUDICIAL NATURE OF PUBLIC PROCUREMENT

A. Introductory Remarks

The implementation of Public Procurement Directives by member states through **2.01** the enactment of national legislation or the employment of administrative practices has been subject to judicial control at Community level and at national level. The judicial control of the implementation of the public procurement regime at Community level has a centralized orientation and reveals its horizontal effects, as it is directed to the demand side of the public procurement equation (contracting authorities) and focuses primarily on compliance procedures under Article 169 EC before the European Court of Justice, where the European Commission asks the Court to condemn a member state's failure to comply with European Community law. On a number of occasions the Commission has enacted proceedings relating to interim measures which are ordered by the European Court of Justice under Article 185 EC. The horizontal effect of the centralized judicial control of public procurement aims at the correct application and appropriate implementation of the relevant Directives within domestic legal orders.

2.02 At the same time, the public procurement regime is subject to a decentralized judicial control at national level, where disputes between the demand and supply sides of the public procurement equation arise. The decentralized judicial control has a vertical nature, to the extent that it reveals disputes arising from the operation of public procurement legislation at domestic level, after their incorporation within the national legal systems. However, it should be mentioned that the decentralized judicial control often ends with a reference by the national court to the European Court of Justice under Article 177 EC, for a preliminary ruling in relation to the interpretation of the provision of the Public Procurement Directives or in relation to the compatibility of national laws implementing the Public Procurement Directives with Community law.

2.03 The centralized judicial control of the public procurement regime aims at the compliance of member states, whereas the decentralized judicial control focuses on the enforcement of the public procurement regime at national level. The centralized and decentralized judicial control of public procurement law has also revealed the formulation of two distinctive patterns which address the impact of public procurement legislation on the demand and supply sides of public procurement. The first pattern is linked with compliance proceedings against defaulting member states that failed to implement correctly Public Procurement Directives, and often occurs during the early stages of implementation of public procurement legislation into domestic legal orders. It reveals the impact of the new regime on existing national systems, although it is not surprising that, well after the completion of the internal market, compliance proceedings are still being brought before the European Court of Justice. The second pattern relates to the utilisation of the Court's rulings as a guide for the direct effectiveness of the provisions of the Public Procurement Directives or the interpretation of provisions of the relevant Directives. This pattern can be identified in case law related to Article 177 EC proceedings and occurs in cases where clarification and interpretation of provisions of the relevant Directives is needed; it can be associated with the post implementation era, where the Directives have been transplanted into the domestic legal orders.

B. Judicial Control at Centralized Level

2.04 Since the forms and methods of incorporation of secondary Community legislation into national provisions rely mainly on the discretion of member states,[1] the EC Treaty envisaged primarily a centralized judicial control at Community in order to

---

[1] *See* Art. 189 EC.

ensure that member states fulfil their obligations. This type of judicial control involves proceedings under Articles 169, 170, and 171 of the EC Treaty, which include actions against a member state for failure to fulfil Treaty obligations. Under Article 169 EC, it is the European Commission that brings a member state before the European Court of Justice. Other member states may avail themselves of the provisions laid down in Article 170 EC to ask the Court to condemn a member state's infringement of the Treaty. Interestingly, both proceedings lack an effective enforcement mechanism and the Court's judgment has only a declaratory character. Even under Article 171 EC, where the Court may continue to condemn a member state's failure to comply with a previous judgment, enforcement proceedings are not present. The completion of the internal market in 1992 has witnessed fifteen compliance cases under Article 169 EC,[2] the majority of which were attributable to the failure on the part of the relevant states to implement or comply with provisions of Public Procurement Directives. Interestingly, during the same period, the European Court of Justice, after an application by the European Commission, considered the award of interim measures under Article 185 EC in three cases, one against Ireland and the other two against Italy, in which the award of the contract in question was suspended.

It has been suggested[3] that Community institutions may take sanctions against a **2.05** member state that has failed to fulfil its obligations under the Treaty and to comply with a Court's judgment. There is a parallel under the European Coal and Steel Community Treaty[4] but, in fact, such action has never been used. It should be mentioned here that, in the area of public procurement, non-compliance with the European Directives may lead to withdrawal of Community funds allocated to the defaulting member state. This appears an effective form of sanction, initiated by the European Commission, after a decision of the European Court of Justice pronouncing on the non-compliance issue.[5] Centralized judicial control also covers proceedings under Article 177 EC, where national courts make references to the Court of Justice asking for a preliminary ruling on the interpretation of Community law and the compatibility of national laws with the former, but this type of judicial cooperation lies in the borderline between Community and national jurisdictions.

By virtue of Article 169 EC, the European Commission may initiate proceedings, **2.06** on its own initiative[6] or in response to a complaint, against a defaulting member

---

[2] Nine out of fifteen Art. 169 cases have been brought against Italy; two against Greece and one against Ireland, Spain, Portugal, and Denmark respectively.

[3] *See* Kapteyn and VerLoren van Themaat, *Introduction to the Law of the European Communities* (2nd.edn., Deventer: Kluwer, 1989), 35.   [4] *See* Art. 88 ECST, paragraphs 3 and 4.

[5] *See* European Commission, *Public Procurement and Community Financing* [1989] OJ C22.

[6] Individuals cannot force the Commission to bring a state before the Court under Art. 169 EC procedure, Case C-48/65, *Alfons Luttucke GmbH v. Commission* [1966] ECR 19.

state for failure to fulfil its obligations under the Treaty. Existence of specific legal interest is not required[7] as a condition of the admissibility of the action, since it is in the general interest of the Commission to observe, supervise, and ensure the correct application of Community law. Even in cases where the national litigation (*Farmaindustria v. Consejeria de Salud de la Junta de Andalucia*)[8] was withdrawn, the Commission proceeded in launching an action against Spain for failure to comply with the provisions of the Public Supplies Directive 77/62, on the basis of the incompatibility with the principles and provisions of public procurement law of a framework agreement entered into by Spanish public authorities and the national association of pharmaceutical companies (*Farmaindustria*), in which the prices and other terms and conditions governing the direct purchase of pharmaceutical products destined for social security institutions and the indirect purchase of such products for institutions non-related to social security were set in advance.

2.07 The enactment of the Compliance Directives[9] has introduced a special procedure of centralized nature, the so-called *correction procedure*. Under the Compliance Directives, there is the opportunity for the European Commission to intervene in cases where it feels there has been a breach of the procurement rules, under the provisions laid out in Article 3 of the Public Sector Compliance Directive and Article 8 of the Utilities Compliance Directive. However, as far as the Public Sector Compliance Directive is concerned, the relevant provision applies only where there appears to have been a breach of the rules relating to contracts covered by the Public Works Directive (93/37/EC) and the Public Supplies Directive (93/36/EC). There seems to be nothing in the Public Services Directive to make a particular provision applicable to public services contracts, although the rest of the Compliance Directive applies to award procedures under the Services Directive, as well as to those covered by Public Works and Supplies Directives. This was, apparently, due to an oversight in the drafting stages and was not intentional. The oversight in relation to public sector services is not, however, important, since the provision adds nothing to the powers which the Commission has already had under Article 169 EC. Basically, the corrective procedure may be invoked whenever the Commission considers that there has been a *clear and manifest* breach of the public procurement law. When the procedure is invoked, the Commission must notify both the relevant state and the contracting authority of the reasons which have led it to this conclusion, and request that the infringement be corrected (Article 3(2)). The member state concerned must reply within

---

[7] *See* Casecase C-167/73, *Commission v. France*, [1974] ECR 359.

[8] *See* Case C-179/89, *Farmaindustria v. Consejeria de Salud de la Junta de Andalucia* [1989] OJ C160/10.

[9] *See* the Public Works and Public Supplies Compliance Directive 89/665 [1989] OJ L395, and the Utilities Compliance Directive 92/13 [1992] OJ L76/7.

21 days of receipt of notification, and must either confirm that the infringement has been corrected or give an explanation as to why no correction has been made (unless the award procedure has already been suspended, in which case it is simply required to notify the Commission of this). Failure by a member state to give a reply which is to the satisfaction of the Commission does not attract any specific sanctions under Article 3, nor does the Commission enjoy any special powers where this 'corrective mechanism' is invoked. It was originally proposed that the Commission should be able to suspend the relevant award procedure on its own initiative, but the proposal was dropped because of opposition from the member states. Thus, if a satisfactory reply is not received, the Commission may initiate proceedings under Article 169 EC in the usual way. It is the Commission's practice to treat a notification of a breach given under the Article 3 procedure as a 'letter of infringement' for the purpose of the Article 169 EC procedure. If the member state does not give a satisfactory reply within the 21 day period stated in Article 3, a reasoned opinion will be issued on expiry of that period. It is submitted that 21 days is a 'reasonable' period for a state to prepare a response, and that the Commission's practice in this respect is consistent with the requirements of Article 169 EC. The effect of the corrective procedure under the Compliance Directives appears to demonstrate in an official manner that a member state is in breach of the law, if it does provide a satisfactory reply or does not provide a reply at all. The corrective procedure does not in practice facilitate the powers of the Commission to effectively enforce public procurement law.

(1) Proceedings before the European Court of Justice

2.08 The European Commission has an important role to play in ensuring that the public procurement rules are complied with and enforced, and positively encourages complaints from aggrieved undertakings. In practice, the Commission follows all genuine complaints with the member state concerned, in an attempt to negotiate an amicable satisfactory solution. A complaint to the Commission is, thus, always a potentially useful avenue of redress for an aggrieved contractor. In those cases where no satisfactory solution can be reached, the Commission may, as a last resort, consider bringing compliance proceedings before the European Court of Justice, under the provisions of Article 169 EC. Proceedings are brought against member states as such, and not against the particular contracting authorities which are responsible for the breach. Thus, states are not only held responsible for breaches of Community law committed by the central or local government but also for breaches by other public authorities and bodies over which they exercise a certain degree of control. Based on the Court's case law, it appears likely that the state will be held responsible under Article 169 EC for the award procedures of bodies which are defined as 'contracting authorities' for the purposes of the

Public Procurement Directives, since these are all bodies which have sufficient connection with central authority for that authority to be held accountable for all their activities.

2.09 However, it may be that the state will not be held accountable for all those bodies which are caught as 'contracting authorities' under the Utilities Directive.[10] In particular, in many member states, entities operating in the telecommunications, energy, water, and transport sectors, which have been privatized, may have insufficient connection with the state. A leading case which has defined the ambit of the state from a functional perspective is *Foster v. British Gas*,[11] in which the European Court of Justice ruled that a Directive capable of having direct effect could be invoked against a body which is subject to the *control* of the state and has been delegated special powers. The House of Lords then held that this applied to the *British Gas Corporation* (a publicly controlled entity), the predecessor of *British Gas* (a privatized utility). However, it is not clear that the privatized utilities could be covered by the *Foster* principle,[12] thus state accountability under the compliance proceedings of Article 169 EC could not embrace privatized enterprises.[13] Nevertheless, it may be pointed out that in those cases where the state is not generally held responsible for the activities of a contracting authority, the state may be held accountable where it exercises some specific control (e.g. auditing, or regulation) over the contractual activities of the entity concerned.

(2) The consequences of a judgment by the Court of Justice

2.10 Compliance procedures before the European Court of Justice lack an enforcement character to the extent that the Court only pronounces on the failure of the defaulting member state to comply with Community law, although, as a result of the Masstricht Treaty, there is the possibility of periodic fines of dissuasive character imposed on a member state which is in default of a Court's judgment. The nature of the Court's judgment is to give the State in question the opportunity to take all the necessary measures to avoid future violations, rather than penalize it for the particular breach. Unfortunately, the compliance procedure under Article 169 EC represents a rather soft approach to monitoring the correct application of, and adherence to, Community law when it comes to member states' infringement of the spirit and the letter of the Treaties. A mere declaration of a member state's inability to comply with its obligations apparently does not create the right level of confidence in the centralized judicial control system, nor does it reflect the

---

[10] *See* Directive 93/38 EC.
[11] *See* Case C-188/89, *Foster v British Gas* [1990] ECR1-3313
[12] *See* Trepte, *Public Procurement in the EC* (Bicester: CCH, 1993), 197–198
[13] This was the view of Advocate General Lenz in Case C-247/89, *Commission v. Portugal* [1991] ECR I-3659.

degree of commitment by European institutions in the European integration process. Failure by a member state to take into account the outcome of compliance procedures may bring an action under Article 171 EC, where the member state concerned comes under an obligation to take all the necessary measures to comply with the judgment. Again, here the Court's decision has declaratory character and no specific enforcement measures are attached to it.

In public procurement cases, the European Commission has instigated compliance procedures in order to have the Court declare the failure of a member state to align general legal measures or specific administrative practices with primary and secondary Community law relevant to public procurement. It follows that, after the Court's judgment, and under Article 171, there is a concrete obligation imposed upon the member state in question to repeal any legislation and to abandon any unlawful practices that might contravene the Court's judgment. If this is not done, the member state concerned may be brought before the Court in a further Article 169 EC action, based this time on a breach of Article 171 EC. **2.11**

An issue which is less clear, however, and which deserves careful consideration, is whether there is an obligation imposed on a member state to set aside any contract which has actually been concluded and which has not yet been finally performed. This assumption would imply that the relevant award procedure would be reopened and conducted in a lawful manner, if the case relates to an individual award procedure rather than the challenge of general implementing measures. The main argument in favour of setting aside a public contract is the confidence in the legal system in observing and enforcing public procurement law. On the other hand, the main argument against is the unfairness which this may cause to the successful tenderer or to the public interest as a result of the delay. It should be mentioned here that, under the Compliance Directives, the question of whether national courts or review bodies should be allowed to set aside a contract which has already been awarded or concluded is expressly left to the discretion of member states. **2.12**

It is suggested, however, that where the Court pronounces the failure of a member state to implement public procurement law in an appropriate manner under Article 169 EC, the duty of the member state under Article 171 EC to comply with the judgment reflects an obligation to set aside a contract which is affected by the judgment. This argument is substantiated by virtue of the *Lottomatica* case, where the Court exercised its powers under Articles 185 and 186 EC to *suspend* a concluded contract. The same line of argumentation is found in the opinion of Advocate General Lenz in *Commission v Italy*.[14] This case concerned an alleged breach of the procurement rules relating to a contract for the construction of a **2.13**

---

[14] *See* Case C-199/85, *Commission v Italy* [1987] ECR 1039.

waste recycling plant. The crucial question which was raised was whether the state in question had complied with the reasoned opinion issued by the Commission. Apparently it had not, thus the Advocate General suggested that compliance with the reasoned opinion presupposed the setting aside of the contract. Although the substantial case before the Court was compliance procedures under Article 169 EC, the requirements of an action for failure to act under Article 171 EC do not preclude the conclusion that the content of the obligation to comply with a reasoned opinion is the same as that under Article 171 EC. In both cases, the knowledge of the successful tenderer of any illegality or its complicity in a particular breach was not considered to be a relevant factor in determining whether the contract should be set aside.

(3) Interim measures

2.14 The postponement of a particular procurement procedure leading to the award of a public contract, or the postponement of the performance of the contract after an award is made, can be sought by obtaining an order through interim measures, until the substantial or the procedural disputes have been finally settled. Interim measures refer to the case where aggrieved tenderers challenge the legality of the selection or the award stages of public procurement and wish to delay the process in order to avoid damages. Interim measures are very important legal remedies in public procurement cases. Where contracting authorities refuse to delay the award procedure and no interim relief is available, by the time the substantive or the procedural matter has been finally determined by national courts or by the European Court, it is likely that the contract will have been finalized. If this is the case, then in practice it would not be possible to reopen the award procedure, and an action for damages would generally be the only remedy available to those who have been prejudiced by the breach.[15] Perhaps even more important than the outcome in a particular case, the availability of interim relief is also likely to act as an important deterrent to a breach of the rules, possibly more than any award of damages or any financial penalty. Although the availability of interim measures may be more important in the context of national review procedures than in the context of procedures before the European Court of Justice, since the prospect of an action under Article 169 EC would seem much more remote a possibility than a national review action, the overall thrust of interim measures at centralized level appears as an effective *modus* of judicial control in public procurement.

---

[15] This is certainly likely to happen in the context of proceedings before the European Court of Justice, where the average length of proceedings for cases decided in 1991 was 24.2 months. *See* 'Proceedings of the Court of Justice and of the Court of First Instance of the European Communities', No. 23191, 30 January 1992.

On an application by the European Commission the Court may grant interim **2.15** measures under a general power which is found in Article 186 EC. The detailed rules governing the application are set out in Articles 83 to 88 of the *Rules of Procedure of the European Court of Justice*. Applications are made to the President of the Court, who may hear the matter himself or refer it to the Court. However, it is not possible for the Commission to apply for interim relief until Article 169 EC proceedings have actually been instituted before the Court. This is arguably implicit in Article 186 EC, and is stated in Article 83(2) of the *Rules of Procedure*, which permits an application only if made by a party to a case before the European Court. It was explained earlier that the Commission must follow certain formal requirements before compliance proceedings under Article 169 EC can be instituted, which are concerned notably with providing an opportunity for the state concerned to dispute the allegations made and to redress any breach. There might be some delay between observation of the breach, and commencement of proceedings and the opportunity to obtain interim relief.

It was once thought that this delay might cause considerable problems, to the **2.16** extent that contracting authorities might rush to conclude a contract before interim relief could be sought to suspend the award procedure, and in this way make it difficult for the Court to affect the outcome of the procedure. It was partly in response to this fear that a proposal was originally made in the Compliance Directive to allow the Commission to suspend the procedure of its own motion when a breach appeared to be *clear* and *manifest*; but the suggestion was eventually dropped. That fear was based on the assumption that the Court might not consider itself to have the power to prevent the performance of a contract once it had actually been concluded. It now seems, however, that this fear was groundless, since the Court does indeed have a power to suspend the implementation and the performance of a concluded contract. This was accepted by the Court in the *Lottomatica* case.[16] This case concerned the award by the Italian government of a concession contract for the establishment and operation of a computerized lottery system. Participation in the competition was limited to firms (or groups of firms) which had the majority of their shares in Italian public ownership, which condition the Commission contended contravened Articles 52 and 59 EC. It was also alleged that there had been a breach of Article 30 EC, and of some of the provisions of the Supplies Directive. Article 169 EC proceedings were instituted, and interim relief sought under Article 186 EC. At the relevant time the award decision by the contracting authorities had already been made, and it seems that the contract might actually have been entered into. The application for interim relief thus requested not simply the suspension of the award procedure, but also

---

[16] *See* Case C-272/91 R, *Commission v Italy (Lottomatica)*, and the orders of 31 January 1992 and 12 June 1992 [1994] ECR I-1409.

suspension of: i) the legal effects of the Ministerial Decree awarding the contract, and also ii) the legal effects of *any contract actually concluded*. This relief was granted by the President in the order of 31 January (a later application to have the order discharged was rejected on 12 June 1992). Thus, the Court was prepared to order the parties to suspend the execution of an actual contract. It is suggested that this decision also seems to indicate that a public contract would be required to be set aside if the action is successful at the final hearing concerning the substantive requirements of the alleged breach (the hearing under Article 169 EC). If this appears to be the case, the inevitable delay between the opening of negotiations over an alleged breach (initiation of compliance procedures) and any application to suspend the award procedure (interim measures) would not be of much practical importance if the power to set aside an illegally awarded public contract, either at the interim relief stage or at the substantive stage, is vested in the Court of Justice.

2.17 However, interim relief is not given automatically in every case. There are a number of conditions which must be met. First, the applicant must establish a *prima facie* case, which means that the application should not be 'manifestly without foundation'. It must then be shown that the need for measures is 'urgent'. A second condition will be satisfied when it can be shown that interim measures are needed to prevent 'serious and irreparable' damage to the applicant. There is some doubt over whether, in the case of actions brought by the Commission, it is necessary in order to meet this requirement to show some specific and concrete damage to Community interests, or whether it is sufficient that there is a *prima facie* breach of Community law, the effects of which are irreversible. In public procurement cases it will often be difficult to show any concrete effect on the competitive market structure brought about by a breach of the law which relates merely to an isolated award procedure. However, specific and concrete damage to Community interests can be demonstrated by serious and irreparable injury to tenderers interested in the particular contract. Although third party interests cannot, in principle, be taken into account in applications for interim measures, this is permissible where the European Commission is the applicant, as it represents all affected interests in the Community.[17] This approach, however, raises the question of whether the damage to interested parties is indeed irreparable, given the availability of remedies for the award of damages before national courts. In the three cases concerning interim measures before it, the Court did not make clear the basis for its decision in this respect—whether it relied on damage to individual contractors, or simply took the view that it is appropriate to award interim measures in order to prevent any irreversible breach of Community law.[18]

---

[17] *See* Case 61/77 R, *Commission v Ireland* [1977] ECR 1411.
[18] *See* Case 45/87 R, *Commission v Ireland* [1987] ECR 1369; and Case 194/88 R, *Commission v Italy* [1988] ECR 5647.

Another important consideration for the award of interim measures is the 'balance **2.18** of interests' of the relevant parties. This condition requires the Court to examine the merits of the case against any injury which would be caused by an award of interim measures and in particular the possible harm to the public interest which would be caused by the delay to the procurement of goods, works, or services in question. Balancing the interests of the relevant parties in a public procurement case appears to be a difficult exercise, as the hierarchical classification of the interests in question would determine the outcome of the interim relief proceedings.

On the one hand, the economic interests of a tenderer or a number of tenderers **2.19** which might be prejudiced by the unlawful behaviour of a contracting authority could be protected by recourse to decentralized judicial control, in the sense that aggrieved contractors may generally obtain damages in actions before national courts or some sort of interim relief, as the case may be. On this side of the balance, the adverse effects arising from the violation of Community law should be also added. On the other hand, every public procurement project serves the public interest, and the possible suspension of its award or the set aside of the particular contract could cause unnecessary delays which may inevitably have an effect upon public interest aspects such as public health, public safety, and the protection of the environment.

Balancing, on the one hand, individual economic interest damaged by breaches of **2.20** Community law, against the general public interest potentially harmed by delays in the provision of public service has revealed the priorities of European institutions, particularly the European Court of Justice, in the process of the integration of the Community. The reluctance of some member states to recognize the relative importance of individual interests harmed through violations of European law was reflected in the early case of law of the European Court of Justice. In the *Dundalk* pipeline case[19] which concerned the award of a contract for the construction of a water pipeline, although interim relief was initially granted in order to assess the situation, at a later stage the Court refused the suspension of the contract on the basis of a possible threat to public health and safety caused by the shortage of water and the potential delay of the project. Along the same lines, in an earlier case,[20] the Court was also reluctant to delay the award of a construction project on the grounds of public interest. The case concerned an Ethiopian government contract for the construction of a hydro-electric dam, which was subject to the supervision of the Commission under the terms of the Lomé Convention. One of the aggrieved tenderers sought interim measures against the Commission in an attempt to secure the suspension of the procedure. Interim relief was refused

---

[19] *See* Case C-45/87, *Commission v. Ireland* [1988] ECR 4929.
[20] *See* Case 118/83 R, *CMC Co-operativa Muratori e Cementisti v. Commission* [1983] ECR 2583.

by the Court on the basis that delays in the award procedures would inevitably reflect upon the conclusion of the contract and the public interest would be prejudiced as a result. In both cases where interim measures were refused, the Court emphasized the potential damage to the public interest which would be caused by delays in public procurement and counterbalanced any adverse effects of Community law violations on individual economic interests and the principles stipulated in the Treaties.

2.21   However, the balancing exercise between individual economic interests and public interest at large revealed a completely different dimension in two cases, where a refusal of interim relief on the grounds of public interest is likely to be the exception rather than the rule. The first case is *Commission v. Italy (La Spezia)*,[21] which concerned a contract for the renovation of a waste disposal plant. The Court awarded interim measures despite acceptance of the fact that damage to both public health and the environment might result from the delay. The differentiating factor which distinguishes this case from *Dundalk* was that the urgency of the renovations was due to the fault of the contracting authorities themselves in not acting earlier on the matter, although it might be that the Court would normally refuse interim measures in cases where this is not a fault by contracting authorities and there is an immediate and serious threat to public health. However, in this case the Court prioritized the individual economic interests and the violation of Community procurement law over the possible prejudice to the public interest as a result of delays in the procurement process. The Court is not only the guardian of the public interest of the subjects of European law, but also, and more importantly, it is the guarantor of the success in the European integration process. *La Spezia* certainly showed the commitment of European institutions to the principles and rule of the public sector integration and could be seen to pave the way for interim relief where the prejudice to public interest is less serious, even when there is no fault on the part of the contracting authority. As was noted above, relief has now also been given in the *Commission v. Italy (Lottomatica)*[22] case In this case Italy argued that the measures requested should be refused on the balance of interests because of, firstly, the loss of revenue which the government would suffer, and, secondly, the fact that delay to the computerized lottery system would delay the government's fight against illegal gambling schemes. However, these arguments were quickly dismissed by the Court on the basis that the interests of the Community should prevail over those of member states. *Lottomatica* seems to have redefined the concept of public interest in applications for interim measures relating to public procurement projects to an extent that the concept should be narrowly construed.

---

[21] *See* Case 194/88 R, *Commission v. Italy* [1988] ECR 4547.

[22] *See* Case C-272/91 R, *Commission v Italy (Lottomatica)*, and the orders of 31 January 1992 and 12 June 1992 [1994] ECR I-1409.

The spirit of *Dundalk* returned in interim measures litigation in the *Wallonia* case, **2.22** interestingly after the completion of the internal market. The Commission initiated interim measures against Belgium[23] under Article 185 EC in order to suspend the award of a contract relating to the purchase of buses for public transport in Wallonia. The Commission had already opened proceedings under Article 169 EC against Belgium for infringement of the Utilities Directive 90/531, particularly the selection of tender offers and their evaluation. The Commission argued that interim measures with suspension of the award procedures were justified by conditions of manifested urgency dictated by the possibility of serious and irreparable damage and to an aggrieved tender. The Court in balancing the interest of the parties in question ruled that the performance and completion of the contract should take precedence over potential economic damage, on the grounds of public interest. The contract concerned the purchase and operation of new buses by a transport authority, and delays in its execution could seriously harm the lives of individuals and commuters who rely on the modernisation of the transport fleet. The President of the Court refused the interim measures requested.

C. Judicial Control at Domestic Level

National courts can claim jurisdiction for a member state's failure to fulfil Treaty **2.23** obligations, when primary and secondary Community legislation is directly applicable and directly effective. Direct applicability of Community law means that there is no need for implementing measures to be taken by member states,[24] whereas direct effectiveness implies the reliance of individuals upon Community law before national courts.[25] Individuals may avail themselves of legal remedies before national courts relying on provisions of Community law armed with direct effectiveness. With respect to Public Procurement Directives, actions may be launched by individuals against the state, central government, local government, and other contracting authorities, provided that the particular provisions of the Directives upon which individuals rely produce *vertical direct effect*. The verticality of direct effectiveness implies the responsibility of the state vis-à-vis individuals, arising from obligations stipulated in the particular Directive in question, and assimilates the direct effect of the Directives with the direct applicability of Regulations. Direct effectiveness in its vertical dimension provides for access to

---

[23] *See* Case C 87/94 R, *Commission v. Belgium*, order of 22 April 1994 [1994] ECR I-1395.

[24] *See* Winter, 'Direct Applicability and Direct Effect: Two Distinct and Different Concepts in Community Law', *Common Market Law Review*, 9 [1972], 425.

[25] *See* the Court's judgment in Case C-26/62, *NV Algemene Transport-en Expeditie Onderneming Van Gend en Loos v. Nederlandse Administratie der Belastigen* [1963] ECR 1. Also Cases 57/65, *Alfons Luttucke GmbH v. Haupzollampt Saarlouis* [1966] ECR 205, and C-28/67, *Firma Molkerei Zentrale Westfalen/Lippe GmbH v. Haupzollampt Paderborn* [1968] ECR 143.

justice for individuals against the state in situations where judicial review is otherwise unattainable, due to the fact that Directives are addressed to member states only, thus requiring legislative incorporation into domestic legal systems in order to confer rights and duties upon individuals. On the other hand, *horizontal direct effectiveness* may allow individuals to rely on Community law in actions against other individuals.[26] Interestingly, the Court rejected the argument that Directives may produce horizontal direct effect[27] on the grounds that their binding nature exists only in relation to the member states to which they are addressed.

2.24 The legal nature of Directives precludes them from being directly applicable, as member states are required to introduce implementing measures, and the direct effectiveness of their provisions depends on three cumulative conditions, as defined by the European Court of Justice:[28] i) the sufficient clearness and precision of their provisions, ii) their unconditionality, and finally, iii) the lack of discretion on the part of member states when implementing them. The concept of direct effectiveness is closely linked with the normative character of Community law. However, access to justice before national *fora* based upon reliance of directly effective Community law requires judicial precedent set by the European Court of Justice. Judicial control at domestic level relies heavily on the utilisation of the Court's rulings as a guide for the direct effectiveness or the interpretation of provisions of the relevant Directives through Article 177 EC proceedings. In cases, where there is no clear precedent, clarification and interpretation of provisions of the relevant Directives is needed; thus the national court embarks upon a reference procedure asking the assistance of the European Court of Justice.

2.25 Public procurement litigation which has been the subject of domestic judicial control is based on the doctrine of vertical direct effectiveness of the provisions of public procurement Directives and focuses particularly at the *post* implementation era,[29] where the Directives have been transplanted into the domestic legal orders. Individuals claim the existence of direct effectiveness requesting the court to apply the provision of the Directive in question directly, irrespective of any implementing measure adopted by the state. In most cases, national courts feel

---

[26] The concept of horizontal direct effect has been defined by the Court of Justice in Case C-13/61, *Kledingverkoopbedrijf de Geus en Uitdenbogerd v. Robert Bosch GmbH* [1962] ECR 45.

[27] *See* Case C-152/84, *Marshal v. Southampton and South West Hampshire Area Health Authority* [1986] ECR 723.

[28] *See* Cases C-6/64, *Costa v. ENEL* [1964] ECR 585; 27/67, *Firma Fink-Frucht GmbH v. Haupzollamt Munchen Landsbergerstrasse* [1968] ECR 223; C-13/68, *SpA Salgoil v. Italian Ministry for Foreign Trade* [1968] ECR 453; C-41/74 *Van Duyn v. Home Office* [1974] ECR 1337.

[29] Most Directives provide for a period between their enactment and their coming into force in order to give member states the time necessary to adjust their national systems to Community standards and also gear their legislative machinery with a view to introducing laws implementing the Directives. *See* Lauwaars, *Lawfulness and Legal Force of Community Decisions* (Leiden: AW Sijthoff, 1973), 28–37.

safer to ask the Court of Justice for a reference regarding the direct effect of the relevant provision, even if the case is obviously clear or a previous materially-identical reference to the Court has been made.[30] The majority of cases initiated before national courts and later referred to the European Court of Justice relate to the meaning and definition of the term 'contracting authorities' and the application of selection and award criteria defined in the Public Procurement Directives. Until the completion of the internal market, there have been nine cases before national courts relying on Public Procurement Directives' provisions, which have been referred to the Court of Justice for a preliminary ruling under Article 177 EC. In five other cases before national courts,[31] the latter dealt with them without having recourse to Article 177 proceedings. The post-internal market era has witnessed litigation which was mainly concerned with the interpretation and clarification of provisions of the Public Procurement Directives.

The decentralized judicial control of the public procurement regime has revealed **2.26**
the perpetuation by some member states of preferential and discriminatory procurement as a major persisting obstacle to the integration of public markets in the European Union. Failure to comply with the provisions of the relevant Directives, as well as incorrect application of them by contracting authorities, constitutes the most important non-tariff barrier in the European integration process. While technical standards and specifications have been harmonized to a considerable degree to eliminate any potential ground for discrimination based on nationality, the movement of goods and services related to public markets appears more distorted than the movement of good and services destined for private markets.

(1) The award of damages under Community law

In the absence of specific remedies available to individuals before national courts **2.27**
in order to rectify infringements of Community law, two questions arise with respect to the award of damages suffered by individuals as a result of the state's violation of Community law. The first question is whether an infringement of a directly effective primary or secondary Community provision may be used by individuals before national courts as grounds for an action for damages against the state. The second question approaches the problem from a different perspective; if the infringed provision does not produce direct effect, is, then, the state liable to

---

[30] *See* Case C-283/81, *Srl CILFIT v. Ministry of Health* [1982] ECR 3415: the theories of *acte éclaire* and *acte claire*.

[31] *See* Case No. 10475, *SA SHV Belgium v. La Maison Ideale et Societé Nationale du Logement*; judgment of 24 June 1986 of the Belgian *Conseil d'Etat*; Case 194/84, *Steinhauser v. Ville de Biarritz*, before the *Tribunal Administratif du Pau*; judgment of 24 December 1987 before the District Court of Maastricht, and finally, an arbitration award of the *Raad van Arbitrage* of 31 March 1987.

compensate individuals who have suffered as a result of its infringement or of its wrongful implementation of Community law?

2.28 In public procurement cases, Article 30 EC establishing the free movement of goods, and Article 52 concerning the right of establishment, produce direct effect.[32] Also, the European Court of Justice has recognized that specific (substantive) provisions of the relevant Directives produce direct effect. There are also cases in which national courts have awarded compensation to individuals who suffered damages due to a mere breach of Community law.[33] More intriguing are those cases before national courts where infringement of Community law has already been pronounced directly by the European Court of Justice through a proceeding under Article 169 EC. In those cases, national courts are confronted with national legislation, the incompatibility of which with Community law has been unequivocally and authoritatively declared by the Court. Is the existence of incompatible national legislation a ground for an action for damages before national courts?

2.29 The whole matter goes further to question whether the European Court of Justice may require the courts of the member states to make declarations of invalidity in respect of national legislation found to infringe Community law or to make declaration of awards of damages to the victims. By virtue of Article 171 EC Treaty, the Court said in the *Waterkeyn* case[34] that national courts are bound to draw the 'necessary inferences' from judgments under Article 169 EC. What is meant by this expression is not clear. In the *Waterkeyn* case, the Court did not expressly require national courts to declare invalid a national law or an administrative rule that violates directly effective primary or secondary Community legislation. On the other hand, there is a strong suggestion, in the same case, that such measures should be considered as invalid.

2.30 The assertion of a national rule that violates Community law as valid, probably justified by public interest, would leave individuals with the possibility of being compensated only through judicial review based on the system of non-fault liability, where a wrongful act is not required. This appears contrary to the principles of good faith and legitimate expectation and beyond the spirit of the Treaty.[35] On the other hand, if national courts recognize the unlawful nature of an infringement of

---

[32] This occurred at the end of the transitional period (31 December 1969); *see also* Cases 2/74, *Reyners v. Belgian State* [1974] ECR 631 and 33/74, *Van Bisbergen v. Bestuur van de Bedrijfsvereniging voor de Metaalinijverheid* [1974] ECR 1299.

[33] *See* Case C-213/89, *The Queen v. Minister of Agriculture, Fisheries and Food* [1990] ECR I-2433; also Case C-14/68, *Wilhem v. Bundeskartellampt* [1969] ECR 1, at 27; Case 78/70, *Deutsche Grammophon GmbH v. Metro-SB Grossmarkte GmbH* [1971] ECR 1, at 31; Case 44/84, *Hurd v. Jones* [1986] ECR 29.

[34] *See* Cases 314–316/81and 314–316/82, *Procureur de la République et al. v. Waterkeyn* [1982] ECR 4337.

[35] All the above-mentioned principles—legal certainty, legitimate expectation, Community loyalty, and Community solidarity—are inherent in the fundamental provision of Article 5 EC.

Community law as such, they should, normally, open the door for compensation on the basis of fault.

With respect to the second question, that of the possibility of relying upon a **2.31** provision of Community law that does not have direct effect as ground for an action for damages against the State before national courts, the Court in one of its most important recent judgments[36] answered it in the affirmative. The cases referred to it concerned the non-implementation by Italy of a Directive on the protection of employees in the event of the insolvency of their employer, and reached the Court through a reference under Article 177 EC. The questions the Court faced, at the request of national courts, were: i) whether provisions of the Directive in question were capable of producing direct effect, thus being relied upon by individuals, and ii) the above being answered in the negative, whether individuals had a right to receive compensation from the member state for the negative effects of its failure to implement the Directive. The Court found that the provisions of the Directive were not sufficiently clear, precise, and unconditional to produce direct effect, thus answering the first question in the negative. In considering whether an individual has a right to be compensated by a state that has failed to implement a Directive, the Court held that, in principle, an individual is entitled to compensation in such circumstances.[37] In order to found state liability, it relied on Article 5 of the EC Treaty, the principle of Community loyalty and solidarity, which provides that member states are under an obligation to take all the necessary measures to ensure that Community law is properly applied. It has been held by the Court[38] that Article 5 EC (especially its negative obligation) is capable of producing direct effect, but only in conjunction with other substantive Treaty provisions or in circumstances in which this obligation is further developed in implementing legislation or through case law. Based on the above considerations, as well as on the doctrine of the useful effect (*effet utile*) of Community rules and the rights being acknowledged therein, and which would be weakened if individuals were not provided with the possibility of compensation in the case of their rights being affected by a violation of Community law by a member state, the Court proceeded further and examined the specific conditions that should be met in order for an individual suffering damages to be entitled to compensation by the defaulting state.

Three conditions should be fulfilled: firstly, the result required by the Directive **2.32** must involve the granting of rights to individuals; secondly, these rights must be

---

[36] Joined Cases C-6/90 and C-9/90, *Francovich and Bonifaci v. Italian Republic* [1995] ICR 722.
[37] *See also* Case C-213/89, *The Queen v. Minister of Agriculture, Fisheries and Food* [1990] ECR I-2433.
[38] *See* Case C-14/68 *Wilhem v. Bundeskartellampt* [1969] ECR 1, at 27; Case 78/70 *Deutsche Grammophon GmbH v. Metro-SB Grossmarkte GmbH* [1971] ECR 1, at 31; Case C-44/84, *Hurd v. Jones* [1986] ECR 29.

identifiable on the basis of the provisions of the Directive, and thirdly, there must be a clear causal link between the breach of its obligations by the member state and the damage suffered by the individual concerned. The above conditions being met, then an individual may benefit from a right to compensation at national level based on Community law which is not directly effective. The amount of compensation payable should be determined by national courts in accordance with relevant domestic legislation. The *Francovich* judgment was a landmark decision with respect to state liability under Community law. Individuals may rely upon Community law which does not produce direct effect before their national courts. The European Court of Justice laid down the required conditions for the admissibility of an action for damages before national courts submitted by an individual claiming damages against a member state which has failed to implement a Directive, hereby injuring a right conferred therein. How strict the national courts will be when confronted with such actions remains to be seen in due course. Obviously, harmonization of domestic provisions on award of compensation will be required.

2.33   What appears to be the most important element is the importance that is given to the interest of individuals. According to the judgment of the Court in the *Francovich* case,[39] the individual must be granted rights conferred by the Directive itself. This means that member states and their competent national authorities must not have any discretion in determining the content and extent of such rights. Here, it should be recalled that lack of discretion in the hands of a member state is perhaps the most fundamental condition for the direct effect of provisions of Directives. Thus, the relevant provisions of the Directive should be close to producing direct effect, being deprived of it due to their conditionality or to their insufficient clarity and precision.

2.34   The whole issue came to test in 1993, when the Divisional Court of the Queen's Bench Division of the Supreme Court of England and Wales made a reference to the European Court of Justice on the interpretation of Directive 90/531 concerning procurement procedures in the utilities. The national case[40] concerned the definition of the relevant provision of the Directive relating to the application of procurement rules to entities operating in the telecommunications sector. Also, a request was made for clarification of the possibility of award of damages to individuals in case of wrongful implementation of the relevant provision by member states. In the preliminary ruling, the European Court of Justice elucidated the member states' obligation to award damages to individuals who suffered from

---

[39] *See* Joined Cases C-6/90 and C-9/90, *Francovich and Bonifaci v. Italian Republic* [1995] ICR 722.

[40] *See* Case C-392/93, *The Queen and HM Treasury, ex parte British Telecommunications Plc* [1993] OJ C287/6.

wrongful implementation of Directives. The Court held that the conditions laid down in the *Brasserie du Pêcheur* and *Factortame* cases[41] concerning state liability applied where a member state had incorrectly implemented a Directive; however, in this case, the breach of Community law was not sufficiently serious, as the relevant provision of the Utilities Directive (Article 8(1)) was imprecisely worded and reasonably capable of bearing the interpretation given to it by the UK government in good faith: no guidance had been available from previous case law as to the interpretation of the relevant provision, and the Commission had not raised the matter when the national relevant legislation was adopted. The Court, therefore, held that no liability could be attributed to the state in question.

Since many provisions of the Public Procurement Directives are deemed to produce direct effect, the question of whether an infringement of them can be considered as sufficient ground for an action for damages at national level, is combined with the duty of national courts to afford an effective protection mechanism in the form of remedies for the protection of rights conferred on individuals by directly effective Community law.   **2.35**

D. National Legal Structures and Public Procurement Litigation

(1) The profile of national fora

Access to justice for individuals before domestic *fora* in public procurement cases is of paramount importance as it constitutes the mechanism for judicial control at national level. Existing national legal systems channel public procurement disputes through either public law review proceedings or through civil law review proceedings, as a result of their conceptual predisposition of public market transactions. In principle, and to a certain degree in practice, arbitration through the operation of non-judicial *fora* and alternative dispute resolution systems appears in many jurisdictions. Although a detailed investigation of domestic procedural and substantive legal regimes of member states is provided in Chapter 11 of this work, the following analysis intends to expose the main difference between national legal systems when dealing with public procurement disputes. The level and degree of access to justice for interested parties is exposed by reference to the remedies and actions available to them for review procedures, interim measures, and, finally, actions for the award of damages.   **2.36**

---

[41] *See* Cases C-46 and 48/93, *Brasserie du Pêcheur SA v. Germany* and *Regina v. Secretary of State for Transport, ex parte Factortame Ltd* [1996] 1 CMLR 889.

2.37 French law regards public procurement contracts as subject to the exclusive jurisdiction of administrative courts.[42] Administrative courts are competent to deal with actions concerning the award of public procurement in most cases, even where the awarded contract itself is governed by private law. Indeed, the action is not directed against the contract, but against the decision adopted by the awarding authority (which is normally a public administration), and which is 'severable' from the contract itself.

2.38 There are two types of action available: an action for annulment and an action for damages. Both can be lodged at the same time, provided the time limits required have been met. Interim measures may be ordered in cases of urgency. An action for annulment may be brought before the competent administrative court within two months from the issue of the administrative act in question. French courts apply the *théorie de l'acte detachable* and separate the act awarding the contract or the act calling for tender or the act that approves the award, or preparatory acts before the award of the contract in question, from the contract itself. Thus, they focus on the administrative part of the public procurement contract. The most common ground on which to base an action for annulment is *excès de pouvoir*, a concept which hardly coincides with misuse of powers found in English law. *Excès de pouvoir* means the grave disregard of the limits by the authority in question, which would have acted in a manner beyond the competence and the powers attributed to it. In addition to the above-mentioned ground, the plaintiff may plead the direct effect of a provision of a Directive. Although the *Conseil d'Etat* has recognized the supremacy of Community law over national law, sometimes it is reluctant to pronounce on the direct effectiveness of Directives, thus following a restrictive interpretation of Article 189 EC. On the merits, the claimant may attack the external legality of the administrative act, as well as its internal legality. The former provides for the following grounds: i) incompetence of the awarding authority, ii) irregularities as to its composition and function, and iii) any violation of a rule relating to the award of the contract in question (this should be a substantial one capable of nullifying the act). As to the internal legality, four grounds may be invoked against the authority: i) material inaccuracy of the act, ii) non-respect of the principle of equality among the candidates, iii) *detournement de pouvoir* (misuse of powers attributed to the authority), and iv) manifestly wrong exercise of its discretion. Under those grounds, the plaintiff may achieve the annulment of the detachable act (awarding act, or the act calling for tender etc.), but not the annulment of the contract itself. An action for damages should also be addressed to the administrative courts. To award compensation, they look for

---

[42] For a detailed analysis of the French legal order with respect to public procurement regulation, *see* the report by C. Brechon-Moulenes in *Application in the Member States of the Directives on Public Procurement: the 14th FIDE Congress* (Madrid: Centro de Publicaciones del Ministerio de Justicia, 1990).

a *faute de service* (a wrongful act of the administration). With respect to public procurement, such a *faute* includes: i) the illegal selection of a candidate, and ii) the illegal award of a contract. Plaintiffs must prove the existence of actual damages, in particular damages resulting from the preparation for the bid, expected profits had the contract been awarded to them, and, finally, damages for the bad reputation attaching to their undertakings in cases where the authority illegally rejected their offer and revealed the reasons for that rejection. It must be said that the causal link between the damage and the *faute* must be proved by the plaintiffs.

Before the contract is concluded, an action may be lodged before the president of the **2.39** administrative court ('pre-contractual action'). The president must decide within 20 days and may suspend the award procedure, make injunctions to the administration, and annul all measures taken by the awarding authority,[43] in particular decisions covering technical specifications. Where the awarding authority is operating in the utilities sectors and is an entity governed by private law, or in certain cases governed only partially by public law, the president of the competent court (which is the administrative court, the commercial, or the civil court, depending on the nature of the awarding authority) may only make an injunction to the awarding entity and impose a periodic penalty payment in order to comply with its obligations.[44]

After the contract is concluded, an action for annulment of the decision of the **2.40** administrative authority to conclude such a contract may be lodged before the administrative court. However, the contract does not disappear when the decision to conclude it is set aside. Only the parties to the contract may lodge an action before the administrative court (or the civil or commercial court in cases where the contract is governed by private law) in order to have the contract declared void. An injunction or a periodic penalty payment may be imposed by the court having set aside the decision to award the contract, in order to force the administrative authority to lodge such an action. Finally, an interested party which has suffered an economic loss because of the violation of the public procurement rules, may lodge an action in order to ask for damages.

Litigation on the award of public contracts is relatively frequent in France. The **2.41** nature of disputes includes cases concerning alleged incomplete or unlawful amendment of tender material, communication with undertakings before or during the tender procedure, confusion between selection and award criteria, and whether reservations in tender proposals actually constitute alternative proposals. The existing remedies do not provide aggrieved contractors with the possibility of

---

[43] *See* Art. L22 of the Code of Administrative Courts and Administrative Courts of Appeal.

[44] *See* Art. L23 of the Code of Administrative Courts and Administrative Courts of Appeal., or Art. 11-1 of Act 91-3 of 3 January 1991, as subsequently amended, and Arts. 1441-1 to 1441-3 of the new Civil Procedure Code.

being awarded a contract which should have been awarded to them, had the contracting authorities been complied with public procurement rules.

2.42 The pre-contractual action was conceived in order to give a more effective remedy. It has been negatively affected by the case law of the *Conseil d'Etat*. The *Conseil d'Etat* held that, where the contract has been concluded after the action was lodged, but before the judge rendered its decision, the action is inadmissible. This is considered to constitute an incentive for the awarding authority to try to sign the contract as quickly as possible, especially when it is informed that there is a risk that its choice might be challenged before the administrative court. Moreover, French law provides that, before lodging a pre-contractual action, the applicant must request the awarding authority to comply with its obligations and, if the authority does not reply, then the action may be lodged only ten days after this demand. This delays the action and increases the risk that it may be considered inadmissible. Consequently, in many cases, possible actions are not lodged because their chances of success are considered to be too low.

2.43 In Belgium, the incorporation of the provisions of Public Procurement Directives through *Arrêtés Royaux* has created a nexus of rights and duties which are enforceable before the *Conseil d'Etat*, in case of an action for annulment, and before tribunals and ordinary courts in case of an action for damages.[45] The Belgian remedial system in the field of public procurement reveals a split of competencies between the administrative courts and the civil courts. Actions for annulment of decisions of the administrative authorities may be lodged before the *Conseil d'Etat*.[46] Decisions taken by the awarding authority before the conclusion of the contract, and in particular the decision awarding the contract, are considered to be decisions of an administrative authority. However, the question of whether an entity normally governed by private law is to be considered as an administrative authority because of its obligation to comply with the public procurement rules has not been settled.[47] As in French law, the annulment of the decision does not affect the contract that may be cancelled by the competent court (in Belgium the civil court) only on request of the parties to the contract.

2.44 An action for annulment does not suspend the application of the challenged act. An action may be lodged before the *Conseil d'Etat* in order to have suspended the application of the act.[48] Such an action may be lodged at the latest with the action for annulment. In spite of this power of the *Conseil d'Etat*, civil courts may also grant interim measures, at least in certain circumstances.

---

[45] *See* the report by Yvon Hannequart and Andre Delvaux in *14th FIDE Congress*, op. cit. (n. 42).
[46] *See* Art. 14 of the Coordinated Laws on the Conseil d'Etat.
[47] *See* Act of 24 December 1993, which is notably applicable to certain entities governed by private law, which operate in the so-called 'excluded sectors'.
[48] *See* Act of 19 July 1991, codified in Art. 17 of the Coordinated Laws on the Conseil d'Etat.

Actions for damages must be lodged before civil courts that are the only ones **2.45** competent to deal with matters concerning 'subjective rights'. In cases where the award criterion is the lowest price, a bidder that should have been awarded the contract if the law had not been infringed is automatically entitled to compensation equal to ten per cent of the amount of its bid.[49] In other cases, the candidate or bidder may claim a compensation for the loss of the chance to win the contract.

Actions for annulment before the Belgian *Conseil d'Etat* are time-consuming **2.46** exercises (often in excess of two years), and the judgment is usually not rendered before the contract has been signed and at least partially implemented. The authority of the judge is limited because of the discretionary power that is recognized to the awarding authority in most of the cases. However, the rate of success of actions is far from negligible. The most common ground for annulment seems to be the lack of a statement of reasons in the challenged decision. Actions for a suspension of the decisions of the awarding authorities have been a matter of controversy between the Flemish-speaking and the French-speaking chambers of the *Conseil d'Etat* since the entry into force of the Act of 1991. This dispute turns on the question of whether or not the loss of a contract, and any resulting financial impact on the company concerned, constitutes an irreparable damage, which justifies a suspension of the award procedure.

The Belgian administrative law accepts the theory of detachable acts. Under this **2.47** doctrine, the courts are allowed to separate the defaulting part of an act, seeking to save the remaining legitimate part(s). (To some extent, this doctrine is also recognized in common law jurisdictions, known as the doctrine of severance). Under the *théorie de l'acte detachable*, the decision of the administration awarding a public procurement contract constitutes an act separable from the contract itself. In fact, only those administrative acts that award contracts fall under the jurisdiction of the *Conseil d'Etat*, which may annul them on the grounds of excess or misuse of powers (*excès ou détournement de pouvoir*), or order their suspension in the form of interim measure, as the case may be. On the other hand, the contract itself falls under the jurisdiction of private law in a case where disputes and grievances concerning damages may arise between the parties. It should be mentioned that, in both cases (before the *Conseil d'Etat* and tribunals or ordinary courts), third parties may also avail themselves of the appropriate remedies provided they can show and prove the existence of a legal/legitimate interest. This means that third parties (mainly unsuccessful tenderers) must prove not only a personal link with the dispute in question, but also the legal consequences arising from this personal link. In respect of public law jurisdiction, the *Conseil d'Etat* may annul the decision awarding a public procurement contract, either because of substantial irregularities that derogate from the framework of powers attributed

---

[49] *See* Art. 15 of the Act of 24 December 1993.

to the contracting authority, or because of non-substantial irregularities due to arbitrary exercise of its margin of appreciation. A successful request for annulment of the act awarding the contract will normally open the door for an action for damages under private law, as the *Conseil d'Etat* will pronounce on the illegality of that act. Before the tribunals and ordinary courts the plaintiff should prove, apart from the existence of a legal interest, the wrongful act of the contracting authority (*faute de service*), the actual damage caused by that act, and the existence of a causal link between the wrongful act and the damage suffered.

2.48   Both public and private law regulate the settlement of public procurement disputes in Luxembourg. The control of the award of public contracts (the act awarding them) relies on the jurisdiction of the *Conseil d'Etat*, which may annul on grounds of want of authority, infringement of essential procedural requirement, *ultra vires* and misuse of powers, the act or decision awarding a contract, or any unilateral administrative act carried out under the award procedure. In principle, the *Conseil d'Etat* may suspend the execution of the contract or order any other appropriate interim measure. Damages resulting from a breach of the rules governing public procurement are under the jurisdiction of ordinary courts. Private law regulates state liability in public procurement as a quasi-tort,[50] and action for damages before ordinary courts normally requires the prior annulment of the act awarding the contract by the *Conseil d'Etat*.

2.49   Under Greek law, all administrative disputes (disputes where one party is the state, legal or regional authorities, and bodies governed by public law) fall under the jurisdiction of administrative tribunals and of the *Conseil d'Etat*. The latter has also unlimited jurisdiction to examine the legality of the act awarding the contracts. Thus, applying the *théorie de l'acte detachable*, the *Conseil d'Etat* may annul the awarding (administrative) act of a contract, as it considers it an act separable from the contract itself. In such a case, an aggrieved participant in the tender may sue for damages before the administrative courts. He may also sue directly before ordinary (civil) courts,[51] seeking compensation and contesting the legality of the award at the same time but, in that case, he will not be able to ask for the suspension of the latter. It should be noted that the power to annul the act awarding the contract is exclusively vested in the hands of the *Conseil d'Etat*.[52]

2.50   In Spain, review procedures for public procurement contracts are channelled through administrative and judicial routes. Under the former, the Bureau of

---

[50]   *See* Art. 1382 of the Civil Code.

[51]   In both cases the action will be based on Art. 105 of the Introductory Law to the Civil Code, which lays down state liability (non-fault liability) for illegal actions performed by its organs in pursuit of the exercise of official authority.

[52]   For a general introduction to the Hellenic administrative law *see* the report by P. Stathopoulos in *14th FIDE Congress*, op. cit. (n. 42).

Supervision of Projects is vested with the power to examine technical aspects in the award of the contract in question, and to adjudicate of possible disputes arising therein; in addition, the Intervention of the State, another administrative organ, deals with aspects concerning the financial control of the award, the formal legality of the contract and the decision awarding it. Furthermore, under the adjudication stage within the administrative review procedures, the *Mesa de Contratació*, (also an administrative organ) is empowered, upon request from one of the parties concerned, to pronounce on the validity of the offers, on the conditions for participation in the tender competition, and on the qualitative criteria for the selection of the tenderer to whom the contract has been awarded. It also has the power to make provisional award of contracts based on the criterion of the best (lowest) price, and it may modify the conditions of the award in case of infringement of the law, or in case of an abnormally low or disproportional price with regard to the project. The lengthy administrative review proceedings constitute a requirement of admissibility in order to pursue judicial review at a later stage.[53] Judicial review denotes the involvement of administrative tribunals, in the case that the dispute has not been settled through the administrative stage or in case of a claim for damages. Under the former, the tribunals have competence to declare the act awarding a public contract void, mainly on grounds of want of authority, failure to comply with procedural or substantive requirements, *ultra vires*, and misuse of powers. What is interesting is that such a declaration results in rendering the contract itself void. An action for damages must fulfil very strict requirements, as Spanish courts are very stringent in awarding compensation for damages which can be attributed to the state. Interim measures are available on request of the applicant in accordance with a separate procedure before the same forum.

2.51 In the Spanish legal system, actions before the courts may be lodged only after an administrative complaint to a superior authority, if there is one. The competent courts are the administrative courts. They may set aside the decisions taken by the awarding authority, and, in particular, decisions awarding contracts. Contrary to French and Belgian laws, the contract normally becomes void by the fact that the decision to conclude it has been set aside. However, the administrative authority may decide, on the grounds of public interest, to continue with implementation of the contract.

2.52 Administrative complaints and actions for annulment do not have the effect of suspending the execution of the administrative decision at stake. However, interim measures may be granted both at the stage of the administrative review procedure and by the administrative court. In particular, the decisions of the awarding authority may be suspended. In cases where no other remedy is available that can correct the effects of the violation of public procurement rules, the court

---

[53] The latter must be lodged within two months of dismissal of the former.

may also grant compensation for damages. Specific remedies rules have been provided for by the act on utilities procurement.[54] An administrative complaint must first be lodged before the administrative authority that is in charge of controlling the awarding entity (which may be an entity established under private law). Certain trends appear from the case law published in the Supreme Court report and in law journals. Litigation is not rare in this field, but cases concerning award procedures are much less frequent than cases concerning disputes on the performance of public contracts.

2.53 Traditionally, the courts have been quite reluctant to grant interim measures. This is a serious problem, since the Spanish administrative court procedures can result in long delays. Actions often take between two years and five years to reach a conclusion. Nevertheless, the application of the new Act on Administrative Courts, which is intended to make the adoption of interim measures easier, could lead Spanish courts to grant such measures more frequently in the future. The annulment of the decisions of the awarding authority is not in itself satisfactory for the complainant, especially when it takes place several years later. Actions for damages have been infrequently successful so far. In cases where damages are granted, they are usually equal to six per cent of the amount of the bid. Such awards are not regarded as a sufficient incentive for bidders who are victims of a violation of the public procurement rules to go to court.

2.54 In Portugal, administrative courts have jurisdiction on matters concerning the validity, interpretation, and annulment of the act which awards a public procurement contract. Portuguese law follows to a large extent the notion of *administrative act* which emanates form the French *droit administratif*. The relative importance of the awarding act is reflected also in the fact that it constitutes the most crucial stage in the public procurement process. The plaintiff may submit before administrative courts an application for annulment of the act awarding the contract, which is subject to an appeal before the same courts. It is also possible to lodge an action for damages before administrative courts, after the administrative law review process has been exhausted and the act awarding the relevant public contract has been found unlawful. Damages are in most cases nominal, to the extent that the courts award compensation only with respect to the exact amount the plaintiff has suffered as a result of the unlawful behaviour of the contracting authority. The substantive disputes arising out of a public contract between the successful tenderer and the contracting authority are the subject of the civil law jurisdiction. Interim relief in relation to the award of public contracts is in theory available to affected parties, although the administrative courts are often reluctant to award measures which have a suspensive effect upon the awarding act. The reason for such reluctance is probably attributed to the relatively slow process of

---

[54] *See* Act 48/1998 on Utilities Procurement of December 1998.

judicial review of the administrative act which awards a public contract, and the need to avoid the prejudice of the public interest.

In the Italian legal system, apart from administrative redress available to aggrieved **2.55**
contractors, where the hierarchical superior authority is entitled to review the act awarding a public contract, reviewing both its legality and its substance, there are legal remedies available to them before administrative and ordinary courts. The Italian system is interesting, as in cases where an injury caused by an administrative act relates to a right of the contractor or a third party, ordinary courts have jurisdiction; where, on the other hand, the dispute concerns the legality of the administrative act awarding the contract, then ordinary courts take over. Administrative courts have not only the power to suspend the award of the contract, by means of interim measure, but also to set aside it or any other administrative act performed in the course of the awarding procedure. Action for damages brought by the contractor or a third party against the contracting authority before ordinary courts is admissible only when a 'subjective right' is in breach. State responsibility embraces contractual and pre-contractual liability, but it is only for the successful tenderer who has been awarded the contract to seek remuneration. Unsuccessful tenderers are not entitled to pursue an action for damages as they have only a 'lawful interest' and not a 'subjective right'. Actions for damages before ordinary courts are allowed to proceed on condition of a previous delivery of judgment concerning the annulment of the act awarding the contract by an administrative court.

In the public procurement field, a distinction must be made between two phases, i.e. **2.56**
the procedure for selecting the contractor and the execution of the contract once it has been awarded. Under Italian law, private citizens do not have unrestricted rights to bring cases against the government, but can only claim an interest in the government acting appropriately and in compliance with the law (what are known as 'legitimate interests'). From a judicial standpoint, this has always been a key distinction, and there are two different courts with jurisdiction in such cases, depending on whether citizens' individual rights or legitimate interests are concerned. In particular, administrative tribunals, which handle appeals against illegal acts of government and thereby safeguard the legitimate interests of citizens, are organized on a regional basis. These administrative courts may not award compensation for damages (which traditionally is granted by ordinary courts and only for the infringement of plaintiffs' individual rights), but may only annul illegal acts.

Consequently, any matters that arise during the tendering phase are the jurisdiction **2.57**
of administrative courts, since enterprises may only challenge government action on the basis of the defence of their legitimate interest. However, during the execution of the contract phase, the government is deemed to act as a normal private party, and is therefore liable, like any contracting party, if it fails to meet its contractual obligations.

2.58 As a result, in such cases claims are brought before the ordinary courts. With regard to public works contracts, an accelerated procedure has been introduced in Italy that has reduced the appeals process from sixty days to thirty days, from the time at which the appeal against the illegal act is lodged. The administrative court can then make an immediate ruling to suspend the act being appealed. Furthermore, under the influence of the Compliance Directives 89/665 and 92/13, an important innovation has recently been introduced by Legislative Decree 80/1998, which has given the administrative courts exclusive jurisdiction over all procedures for awarding contracts for public works, supplies, and services related to the management of public services. Administrative courts can also award compensation for damages in these fields. In practice, appeals most often contest procedures for awarding contracts, or calls for tenders and specifications, that the parties concerned consider to be directly harmful to their legal positions. However, this field is continually changing, as is shown by a recent ruling of the Supreme Court of Appeal that allows damages to be awarded when parties' legitimate interests are harmed by an illegal act of government, thus overturning one of the most longstanding tenets of Italian law. There is also a growing use of extrajudicial methods in the public procurement sector. These methods of resolving conflicts that arise during the execution of the contract generally consist of arbitration and, in special cases, of 'amicable agreements'. They undoubtedly make it possible to resolve conflicts more rapidly than through the ordinary courts, even though their cost is often considerable.

2.59 Under Danish law, there is no distinction between administrative and civil disputes in public procurement contracts. There are no administrative courts. The decision awarding a public procurement contract may be reviewed by a higher administrative authority. This sort of review is not a judicial one, but rather seeks the adjudication and conciliation of the dispute. The offended party or third parties (unsuccessful tenderers) may resort to ordinary courts seeking compensation for damages caused by a wrongful act of the authority awarding contracts. There is no statutory rule-governed state liability. but well-established judicial precedent regulates the issue. The plaintiff has the burden of proof as regards the wrongful act of the administration, the actual damage suffered, and the causal link between the wrongful act and the damage. Compensation covers any economic loss caused by the fault of the contracting authorities, but the plaintiff's contribution (negligence) to that loss may reduce or exempt the state from an obligation to compensate.

2.60 A specific system for public procurement review has existed in Denmark[55] since 1995. The Public Procurement Review Board was established to implement the

---

[55] See *Lovbekendtgørelse nr. 1166 af 20 December 1995 om Klagenævnet for Udbud.* Detailed rules on the activities of the Board are contained in a Decree issued by the Minister of Trade and Industry—*Bekendtgørelse nr. 26 af 23 Januar 1996 om Klagenævnet for Udbud.*

public procurement regime. The system allows complaints in the first instance to be brought before the normal courts or the Public Procurement Review Board, which has been established as an independent entity by the Ministry of Industry and Trade. The decisions of the Board can be appealed to the normal courts. The Public Procurement Review Board is assisted by the Competition Board, which is part of the Ministry of Industry and Trade and is responsible for administering the Law and acting as the Secretariat to the Public Procurement Review Board.

The Public Procurement Review Board can decide on any alleged infringement of **2.61** the Public Procurement Directives, including those concerning the utilities sector,[56] as well as the relevant Treaty provisions concerning, for example, the free movement of goods. This means that the Board can review tenders below the thresholds defined in the Directives. The Public Procurement Review Board is composed of judges and independent experts and is headed by a judge. The status and procedures of the Board are similar to those of national courts with the possibility for both parties to submit written observations in support of their claims. Any person with an interest in a particular contract can lodge a complaint with the Public Procurement Review Board. This includes situations where the complaint is that a contract has been made without any tender procedure at all. The Competition Board and certain business organisations can also register complaints.

The Public Procurement Review Board can take all the types of decisions **2.62** foreseen in the Directives, including suspension of tender procedures and annulment of unlawful decisions of the contracting entity. Normal courts determine the effects of such decisions on the relation between parties in cases when a contract exists according to general Danish rules on contractual relationships. The Public Procurement Review Board cannot take decisions about damages, which is the responsibility of the courts. Since 1996, the Competition Board has dealt with approximately 100 cases annually. It can act on the basis of any complaint from any person and on its own initiative lodge complaints with the Public Procurement Review Board. The Board has no power of decision, but usually the contracting entity will comply with the Board's recommendations.

To ensure the application of Public Procurement Directives both at *Bund* and at **2.63** *Länder* levels, Germany has enacted administrative instructions[57] that are legally binding by means of, and through, pertinent budgetary laws. Under the principle of legality of administration,[58] the state and local authorities are entitled to act on

---

[56] An important modification in this respect is that complaints regarding contracts involving the utility entities dealing with exploration of oil and gas fall outside the competence of PPB but can be lodged at a specific Commercial Court (*Soe- og Handelsretten*).
[57] *Verdingungsordnung für Leistungen- ausgenommen Bauleistungen* for public works and *Verdingungsordnung für Bauleistungen* for public supplies contracts.
[58] Art. 20, para.3 of the German Basic Law.

their own initiative in cases where a violation of provisions of Public Procurement Directives occurs. Nationals and non-nationals (from other EC member states or non-EC member states) enjoy the same treatment, as a consequence of the principle of equal treatment laid down in the German Basic Law. Disputes concerning the award of public contracts fall under the jurisdiction of administrative control. The power of supervision over acts and decisions of the contracting authorities is based on similar principles at the *Bund* and *Länder* levels.[59] The organs finally responsible for the administration, the state and the *Länder*, exert their supervision over inferior authorities controlling the legality of acts awarding public contracts. In particular, they have powers to suspend the act awarding a public contract, to order new tendering procedures, to rescind the act that invites tenders for a public contract, and even to invite tenders on their own initiative in cases where the contracting authority does not comply with the instructions given within a certain time. What is interesting is the fact that, once the contract has been awarded, administrative control is no longer applicable. The award is considered to be the acceptance of the contractor's or the supplier's offer and, according to principles of German law, the contractor must not be burdened with the uncertainty of a potential cancellation of the contract due to the violation of rules by the contracting authority. Thus, aggrieved contractors may only apply before ordinary courts against public authorities seeking damages. Their claim requires a fault on the part of the contracting authority in concluding the contract or in its preparation—*culpa in contrahendo*.[60] The claim is based on the relationship of confidence, which resembles that of contract, arising between the contracting authority and the contractor by virtue of the invitation to tender. The amount of damages depends on the actual damage which the contractor can prove. The damage may be limited to the cost of taking part in the tendering process. This might be the case when the supervisory administrative authority cancels an illegitimate invitation for tender. On the other hand, if the contractor can prove that the contracting authority has illegally discriminated against him in awarding the contract to another, then he is entitled to damages to the amount of his lost profits, on condition that he can substantiate that he would have been awarded the contract had the contracting authority not discriminated. If the contracting authority holds a monopoly or a dominant position, the applicant who has been denied the award of the contract may base his claims for damages against the former also on the provisions of the Statute against Distortions of Trade or on the Statute against Unfair Competition. He may suspend the award process by requesting an injunction from the court.

---

[59] The constitutionally established right of organization, Art. 65, sentence 2 of the German Basic Law.   [60] *See* Paragraph 242 of the Civil Codebook.

By virtue of the 4th Chapter of the Act against Restraints of Competition,[61] review **2.64** procedures that guarantee effective remedies for complaints against violations of the procurement rules have been established. The Act grants bidders the right to complain against infringements of the procurement rules during an award procedure, thus enforcing compliance with the procurement rules. Since 1 January 1999, 'Procurement Chambers' (*Vergabekammer*) have been in charge of deciding about complaints lodged in connection with an award procedure. This (independent) administrative review body is an integral part of the German Federal Cartel Office (*Bundeskartellamt*). It is also possible that other parties, in particular other bidders, may formally participate in the proceeding. The parties involved have standing to appeal against the Procurement Chamber's decision. A procedure for judicial review of the Chambers' decisions was introduced by the Act. New bodies, the 'Procurement Senates' (*Vergabesenate*) were established at the level of the Higher Court of Appeals (*Oberlandesgericht*). These senates form part of the ordinary courts in Germany.

As Germany is a federal state, review bodies have to be established both at the **2.65** federal level (i.e. at the Federal Cartel Office) and the state level. The sixteen German states have chosen very different solutions for the establishment of Procurement Chambers. The Higher Court of Appeals in each state is in charge of appeals. The remedies against an infringement of the procurement rules have proven to be very efficient since the award procedure is suspended during the proceeding at the Procurement Chamber and, if the complainant is successful, also during the proceeding in the Higher Court of Appeals. Both the Procurement Chambers and the Higher Court of Appeals are bound by very strict time limits in order to guarantee a speedy resolution of procurement disputes. The Procurement Chambers have to decide within five weeks after a complaint has been lodged. On the basis of the information available, it appears that such time limits have not been observed in only a very few cases. The Higher Court of Appeals has also to make a decision within a reasonable period but this period is not precisely defined in law.

In the Netherlands, the judicial review of the award of public contracts is subject **2.66** to the control of civil courts and also to arbitration. Supplies and services contracts are under the jurisdiction of ordinary courts, whereas public works contract are channelled through a special institution (*Raad van Arbitrage*).[62] The appropriate forum for judicial control of public procurement is determined by virtue of the laws implementing the relevant Directives. In practice, the legal forum which handles the majority of public procurement disputes is the *Raad van Arbitrage*,

---

[61] *See Gesetz gegen Wettbewerbsbeschränkungen* of 26 August 1998, *Bundesgesetzblatt* (Federal Gazette), I (1998), 2512.

[62] *See* the report by P. Glazener, E. H. Pijnacker Hordijk and E. M. A van der Riet in *14ᵗʰ FIDE Congress*, op. cit. (n. 42).

as the laws implementing the Directives contain arbitral clauses under which the jurisdiction of civil courts is secondary. Both the civil courts and the *Raad van Arbitrage* are competent in awarding damages to aggrieved tenderers, on condition that the applicant can prove that he would have won the contract.

2.67 By virtue of a Resolution on public procurement,[63] the Dutch legal system entrusted public procurement compliance at domestic level to the Dutch Court of Justice and the Council of Arbitration (the latter for remedies concerning works). Interim measures such as suspension of the tendering procedure are handled by the Dutch Court of Justice through urgent procedures or injunctive relief (*spoedprocedure, kortgeding*). When arbitration is required, especially in construction projects, the Dutch system offers a form of accelerated arbitration (*spoed arbitrage*). Damage awards vary between six and seventeen per cent of the total contract value. The claiming party has to prove that it suffered genuine damage and to provide evidence that it had a good chance to win the contract had the contracting authority followed the provisions of the Public Procurement Directives.

2.68 In the United Kingdom, an aggrieved contractor could initiate judicial review proceedings against a contracting authority under public law or seek redress through private actions, in a case where there has been a breach of a statutory duty. In addition to the remedies which have been created under the Statutory Instruments implementing the Directives specifically for enforcing the procurement rules,[64] an aggrieved contractor may also make use of the more general remedies which may be used in order to ensure that public bodies act lawfully.[65]

---

[63] *See Besluit overheidsaanschaffingen* of 4 June 1993 on public procurement of goods, works and services, and *Besluit aanbestedingen Nutssector* of 6 April 1993 on public procurement in the utilities sectors.

[64] Remedies which are required to be available under the Compliance Directive in the United Kingdom include: i) provision for the court to 'set aside' a decision or action which is in breach of the Regulations. The effect of an order of set aside will be that the decision or action has no legal effect and cannot be acted upon. For example, if the government makes an award decision in breach of the Regulations, and that award decision is set aside, the government may not go ahead and conclude a contract with the selected firm, but must take the award decision again in a lawful manner. ii) provision that the court may order the contracting authority to amend any document. Thus if a contract document contains unlawful specifications, for example, the court may order the authority to amend them. This is a useful power: it allows a firm effectively to ensure documents are amended without the need to strike down the whole call for tenders. iii) provision that a remedy in damages must be available to disappointed contractors who suffer loss.

[65] Among the main remedies available in an action for judicial review are *certiorari, prohibition* and *mandamus*. The first will annul, with retrospective effect, an order or decision of a person or a body of persons having legal authority to determine questions affecting the rights of subjects; the second has a prospective effect, prohibiting an administrative authority from acting either at all or in the way it proposes; the last is an order requiring a public body to do something on condition that the applicant has first called on it unsuccessfully to do its duty.

The right of damages under judicial review is not an independent remedy. What is peculiar in comparison with continental legal systems is that the High Court or the Court of Appeal must be satisfied that there is a claim for damages before it fulfils all the conditions in order to be successful under private law; that means the breach of a statutory duty. The award of damages is in the discretion of the court and when the applicant (aggrieved contractor) claims damages alternatively (in a case where the application for annulment of the act awarding the contract is dismissed), the court may order the continuation of proceedings as if they had begun by writ. Action for damages in tort represents the private way of judicial redress of public procurement cases in the United Kingdom. Such actions can be based on breach of statutory duty or negligence. The plaintiff is entitled to compensation for the loss he suffered, on condition that he can prove that the tort has caused his loss.

In Ireland, the appropriate forum for the review of public procurement cases is the **2.69** High Court, which has general jurisdiction over administrative, civil, or criminal cases. The Irish legal system does not provide for an administrative law forum; however, a number of *ad hoc* administrative tribunals have been established and are under the supervision of the High Court. Judicial remedies available to aggrieved contractors in public procurement cases before the High Court include the general public law remedies in the form of *certiorari, prohibition* and *man-damus*. Through these remedies the Court has the power to quash unlawful administrative decisions (practically the same results with setting aside a decision under the Compliance Directive), to prevent an unlawful decision being made, and to order a decision to be taken in a lawful manner. The general remedies of *declaration*, where the Court simply declares the legal position in the case before it, and *injunction* are also available. The challenge of an unlawful administrative act through the above public law remedies requires prior application for judicial review. However, declarations and injunctions are also available in plenary proceedings. Damages may be sought by the applicant on grounds of deliberate breach of public law rules by virtue of the tort of misfeasance in public office.[66]

The Swedish legal system has established review procedures for both dimensional **2.70** (those with values above the thresholds stipulated by the Directives) and sub-dimensional (those with values below the thresholds stipulated by the Directives) public procurement contracts. Prior to the conclusion of a public procurement contract, administrative courts are responsible to deal with public procurement cases. The County Administrative Court is a judicial body dealing with issues of public law and has jurisdiction to hear disputes on public procurement. The County Court may decide to suspend a tender proceeding until the complaint has been reviewed by the court and a final decision taken. The County Court will

---

[66] *See* the report by Mary Robinson in *14th FIDE Congress*, op. cit. (n. 42).

abstain from suspending the proceedings if the negative consequences of such a decision are judged to be greater than the advantages, i.e. the damage to the procuring entity is greater than the advantage to the complainant. The County Court may decide to cancel the tender proceedings and order re-tendering. It may also order the correction by the contracting entity of deficiencies found in the tender proceedings. In the case of a complaint procedure brought against a public utility, the decision may also include a fine.

2.71 A decision of the County Court may be challenged in higher administrative courts and, in such cases, the tender proceeding will be suspended until the court takes its final decision. Before contract signing, there are no time limits for filing a complaint, nor is there any maximum period of time for the County Court or higher courts to finalize the complaint review. After the contract is signed, the only remedy remaining available to aggrieved contractors is to request damages in an ordinary (civil) court. Such a request must be filed within one year of signing the contract. To be successful in court, the supplier must prove not only that the contracting entity acted unlawfully but also that the supplier in question would have been awarded the contract if the tender proceedings had been carried out lawfully. If the supplier succeeds in proving his case, he is entitled to compensation for loss incurred.

(2) Set aside and annulment of decisions

2.72 The possibility for setting aside the act awarding the contract is provided in most member states. In some jurisdictions, administrative courts have power to set aside unlawful administrative acts and deal with claims concerning the act awarding the contract. With respect to the contract itself, they follow the theory of detachable acts, whereby the validity of administrative acts leading to the conclusion of a public contract may be viewed in isolation from the contract itself and challenged on grounds of their unlawfulness, without the validity of the contract necessarily being affected. However, in other jurisdictions, the validity of the contract may be automatically affected if the award decision is set aside.

2.73 The theory of detachable act, which operates in French-influenced continental jurisdictions, presents considerable weaknesses when applied to public procurement cases. Under that theory, the public procurement process is subject to both public and private law jurisdiction. The above jurisdictional separation lies in the fact that the decision of a contracting authority under which a particular public contract is awarded is considered an administrative act which is subject to the jurisdiction of public law and, as such, is separated from the contract itself, which falls under civil law jurisdiction. However, it is undisputed that the administrative act awarding the contract constitutes an integral part of the whole procurement process and forms the legal justification for the conclusion of the contract between the contracting authority and the successful tenderer. By the separation, both jurisdictional and actual, of the act of awarding the contract and the contract itself, there is the possibility that the whole procurement process could be thrown to legal uncertainty in the event that the legality of the awarding act is contested. If the contract itself has not yet been concluded, its suspension represents the most logical solution and, in principle, falls under the same jurisdiction as the action to annul the awarding decision. If the act is annulled, then the contract remains without a legal basis. In cases where the contract itself has not yet been concluded this does not represent a major problem. The administrative act will be re-issued by the contracting authority without defaults this time. However, a question remains as to whether the contracting authority has liability to compensate the previously successful contractor in the award stage of the procurement process, when the re-issued act awards the contract to a different tenderer. If, for example, the act awarding the contract is declared illegal and the contracting authority is ordered to re-open the tendering procedures for its award, the contracting authority should compensate the existing contractor for losses of profits should the contract be finally awarded to another tenderer. The issue remains unclear, although the European Court of Justice, in proceedings concerning interim measures before it, did not consider the successful contractor's knowledge of the illegality of the awarding act and this was not considered to be a relevant factor in determining whether the contract should be set aside.[67]

Problems arise when the parties have concluded the agreement (by signing the **2.74** relevant contract) or even when the contract is in its performance stage. An action to annul the administrative act which awarded the contract would probably shake the entire legal foundation of the latter. Two elements deserve attention here: firstly, if the administrative act is annulled, the legal basis of the concluded contract or the contract under performance disappears. This means that the contract, as a private law covenant, cannot be executed; therefore it should be suspended. Even in the event of the re-issued act awarding the contract to the same contractor, this new administrative act cannot *stricto sensu* be the legal foundation of the contract already awarded by the first one. The second element refers to the prejudice or the harm of the public interest as a result of the amount of legal uncertainty which covers the period during which the case concerning the legality of the awarding act is pending, as well as the period during which the performance of the contract is suspended.

On the other hand, the *doctrine of severance* utilized in common law jurisdictions **2.75** may have more balanced results. In contrast with the theory of detachable acts, the doctrine of severance allows the courts, in principle, to separate the defaulting

---

[67] *See* Case C-199/85, *Commission v. Italy* [1987] ECR 1039. Also, Case C-272/91 R, *Commission v Italy (Lottomatica)*, and the orders of 31 January 1992 and 12 June 1992 [1994] ECR I-1409.

parts of a contract, thus saving the legitimate ones. If the contract is viable only with the latter then it could be legally executed, otherwise it should be declared null and void. The viability, in legal terms, of a public procurement contract after severance of any unlawful or illegal parts of the procurement process may insert an element of *qualitative evaluation* of the stages under which public contracts are awarded. Such evaluation, perhaps, would classify in hierarchical order the relative importance of violation of procurement law. For example, a breach over the time limits for the receipt of tenders under open procedures could not in itself be a sufficient reason to nullify the award of a public contract. However, violations of rules relating to the qualification of tenderers or the selection and award criteria cannot be severed by other legitimate parts of a public contract, as they considerably affect its substantive validity. The doctrine of severance cannot be applied in legal systems where public law and private law jurisdiction co-exist. In such a case, the doctrine could scarcely give an answer.

E. The Compliance Directives

2.76 The public procurement sector is by nature decentralized and requires a decentralized control. In some member states there are already remedies for breach of public procurement laws, and it is the responsibility of all the member states to provide legal remedies to the parties concerned, capable of enforcing the provisions of the Public Procurement Directives. The aim of the European institutions should be to provide for the possibility of having uniform remedies in all member states, of harmonizing procedures or at least of coordinating national laws and administrative provisions relating to the application of procedures for reviewing public procurement contracts.[68] Uniformity of application, as far as legal remedies are concerned, is a desirable situation but it is an ideal which is difficult to achieve, since there are different ways, already established, for solving public procurement disputes. It is almost impossible to have one law applicable in all member states due to separate legal traditions and procedures. Any attempt to abolish existing national systems would be extremely difficult, useless and a waste of time. Similarly, harmonisation of national procedures concerning the availability of legal remedies for breach of public procurement contracts is neither possible nor necessary. In order to achieve harmonisation, that is, approximation of national legal orders, one should start from a common point; in other words, the national legal orders to be harmonized should be homogeneous.

2.77 In the case of public procurement, the existing national remedies are addressed to civil or administrative courts, or administrative bodies, or arbitrators.

---

[68] This is the aim of Art. 100 EC and, to a certain point, of Art. 100A EC.

Furthermore, the national law applicable in each member state varies from civil to public administrative law. Finally, the cost of initiating proceedings differs from member state to member state, depending on the cost of living or the judicial cost in each country. Under those conditions, it is hardly possible to achieve harmonization. What remains is to coordinate these national legal remedies with a view to ensuring a procedure and a sanction for the application of the underlying Public Procurement Directives.

In an attempt to give an answer to these questions, the Council enacted a **2.78** Directive on the harmonization of laws, regulations and administrative provisions relating to the application of review procedures to the award of public works and public supply contracts (Directive 89/665 EC).[69] In addition, Directive 92/13[70] extends the remedies and review procedures covered by Directive 89/665 to the water, energy, transport and telecommunication sectors. According to the Compliance Directives, member states should be left to implement procedures consistent with their own judicial practices to achieve effective and rapid review rules. This approach is consistent with the provisions in Article 189 EC, that a Directive shall be binding as to the result to be achieved, leaving the form and the methods to the discretion of the member states. In some member states, highly developed systems of monitoring public procurement procedures already exist. Both Directives aim at coordinating existing procedures and procedures to be introduced with a view to a uniform application of the underlying Directives concerning public supplies, public works, and utilities. It seems that neither Directive produces direct effect.

According to Article 1 of Directive 89/665 and Article 1 of Directive 93/13, **2.79** member states must ensure effective and rapid review of decisions taken by contracting authorities which infringe public procurement provisions. Undertakings seeking relief from damages in the context of a procedure for the award of a contract should not be treated differently under national rules implementing European public procurement laws and under other national rules. This means that the measures to be taken concerning the review procedures should be similar to national review proceedings, without any discriminatory character.

Any person having or having had an interest in obtaining a particular public **2.80** supply or public works contract, and who has been, or risks being, harmed by an alleged infringement of public procurement provision, must be entitled to seek review before national courts. This is laid down in the third paragraph of Article 1 of Directive 89/665 and Article 3 of Directive 92/13 and, in both cases, is followed by a stand-still provision concerning the prior notification by the person seeking review to the contracting authority of the alleged infringement, and of his

---

[69] *See* [1989] OJ L395.   [70] *See* [1992] OJ L76/7.

intention to seek review. However, with respect to admissibility aspects, there is no qualitative or quantitative definition of the interest of a person in obtaining a public contract. As to the element of potential harm by an infringement of public procurement provisions, it should be cumulative with the first element, that of interest. The prior notification should intend to exhaust any possibility of amicable settlement before the parties have recourse to national courts.

2.81 However, by virtue of Article 2 of Directive 89/665 and Article 2 of Directive 92/13, the measures concerning the review procedures shall include interim measures, by way of interlocutory procedures, with the aim of correcting the alleged infringement or preventing further damages. Provision shall be made for measures to suspend, or to ensure the suspension of, the procedure for the award of a public contract or the implementation of any decision taken by the contracting authority. In most of the member states, suspension of a contract would be achieved through an injunction. National courts have the power to grant an injunction to restrain unlawful acts. It should be borne in mind that suspension of the whole procedure or of the implementation of any decision will create some problems.

2.82 Firstly, review procedures should not have an automatic suspensive character. Indeed, Article 2(3) in both Directives reads so. Secondly, in practical terms, a disappointed tenderer would ask the court to order the procuring authority to reconsider its bid and not to enter into a contract in the meantime. Many times, this will cause disproportionate hardship. Therefore, the national courts or administrative bodies should take into account the probable consequences to all interests likely to be harmed as well as the public interest. In fact, Article 2(4) in both instruments introduces the principle of proportionality. The provision stipulates that where any grant of a review measure causes negative consequences, such consequences must not exceed the benefits. For the sake of history, it is worth mentioning that Article 3 of the draft Directive 89/665[71] gave the Commission the right to suspend a contract award procedure for a period of up to three months. Since this would have led to legal uncertainty, as at the same time national courts have suspensive powers, it has been deleted from the final text.

2.83 In addition to interim measures correcting the alleged infringement or suspending the award procedure, Article 2(1)(b) provides for measures to set aside unlawfully taken decisions by the contracting authority, including the removal of discriminatory technical, economic or financial specifications in the invitation to tender, the contract document or any other document relating to the award procedure. The present texts of the Directives are not sufficiently clear in respect of the execution of the contract itself. It could be argued that contracts might be set aside, even after

---

[71] *See* COM (88) 733 final.

having been awarded. The effect of annulling contracts would be to render uncertain for several years the basis for proceeding with important public works and could cause damages extending well beyond the authority under challenge. The Commission has made clear its intention that contracts once awarded should not be at the risk of being overturned. However, the fact of setting aside a decision leaving the contract unaffected causes serious doubts as to the validity of the contract. In some continental legal orders, the theory of detachable acts has been developed and permits the validity of administrative acts leading to the making of a contract to be considered distinct from the contract itself and for them to be open to challenge on grounds of their illegality, without affecting the validity of the contract. In these legal orders, the attack of the unlawful decision is a pre-requisite to an action for damages. In other jurisdictions, the setting aside of the decision without touching the contract will create problems, as the legal basis of the contract has been removed.

It is the discretion of the national court to decide whether it should set aside the   **2.84** decision to enter into a contract or simply to declare illegalities in the award procedure and therefore grant damages. Directive 92/13 recognizes explicitly the theory of detachable acts and provides in Article 2(d) that, prior to an award of damages, the contested decision must first be set aside or declared illegal. The power to order the removal of discriminatory specifications in the contract documents is a different matter. Such an order should not be made in a way which would hinder the procurement process and it should ensure that the procedure is in accordance with the Community principle of non-discrimination.

(1) The award of damages under the Compliance Directives

Article 2(1)(c) in both Directives provides for award of damages to persons   **2.85** harmed by an infringement of public procurement law. The purpose behind this provision is to mobilize the interested contractors in order to supervise the application of public procurement Directives.

As already mentioned above, European law does not require the provision of a   **2.86** remedy for the award of damages when there is a breach of a directly effective rule. The reasons for that absence vary: in some cases the national court has held that the authority in breach of Community law did not owe any obligation directly to the plaintiff, or that the claimant's losses were the results of foreseeable economic risk; in others, the award of damages has been seen as an unacceptable fetter on the freedom of authorities to enact legislative measures or administrative rules in good faith, pursuant to their general duty to safeguard public interest, such as human health. Damages may be available as a consequence of provisions of national law which make a national authority liable to compensate for breach of its obligations. Procuring authorities are subject to a duty to observe European rules and are liable for damages in breach of those rules. In the context of the Compliance Directives, a question arises as to whether an aspiring contractor seeking damages should prove that he would have been accepted as a tender or he would have won the contract, if not for the infringement.

2.87 Under the restrictive procedures, a limited number of contractors or suppliers are invited to tender pursuant to Article 22 of the Public Works Directive, or Article 19 of the Public Supplies Directive. Where a contractor or a supplier has applied as a candidate, but he has not been invited to tender and the contracting authority has infringed the Directive, the assessment of loss would be difficult, since tender costs have not been incurred and the contractor or supplier might not, in any case, have been awarded the contract.

2.88 In the case that he has submitted a tender, it may be easier to show that he has suffered a quantifiable loss in respect of which he should be indemnified, at least so far as the expenses of tendering are concerned. Any additional loss would be more difficult to prove. Under the Utilities Compliance Directive, the undertaking claiming damages must prove the infringement of public procurement law and the effect of this infringement on his chance of being awarded the contract. He does not have to prove that, in the absence of the infringement, he would have been awarded it.[72]

2.89 Where the complaint is that the procuring authority has failed to accept the most economically advantageous tender, as required by the Public Procurement Directives, there is probably no alternative; the procuring authority will be required to advise unsuccessful tenders of the reason for their failure. Then, it is for the unsuccessful tenders to assess whether these reasons are so defective as to justify legal proceedings for compensation. It should be recalled that the criteria laid down in the Public Procurement Directives are wide-ranging, leaving a great deal of discretion to the contracting authority. The burden of proof will be on the unsuccessful tenderer to persuade the court that his tender was more economically advantageous than that of the winning tender. On the other hand, where the potential tenderer complains of unlawful exclusion from the tendering process, he should be entitled, on proof, to recovery of costs actually incurred, which will usually not be substantial. Under the draft Compliance Directive on the utilities sectors, the amount of damages refunded should be deemed to be one per cent of the value of the contract, in a case where a contractor is preparing a bid or participating in an award procedure, unless he proves that his costs were greater. This provision has been deleted from the final text of Directive 92/13. It should be noted that the draft Directive 89/665 mentioned three grounds of action for damages: the cost of unnecessary studies, forgone profits, and lost opportunities. The final

---

[72] *See* Recital 11 of Directive 92/13.

text of the Directive, interestingly, remains silent and refers only to award of damages generally (Article 2(1)(c)). There have been fears that the inclusion of forgone profits and lost opportunities could have lead to speculative and wasteful litigation.

There are two observations relating to damages litigation in public procurement. **2.90** First, as is generally admitted, undertakings will be hesitant to bring a contracting authority before a court, since they want to maintain good relations in the future. Litigation between a supplier and a contracting authority often results in an irrevocable breakdown of their relationship. Secondly, if damages are too great and too readily awarded, contracting authorities would find themselves proceeding so extremely carefully as to seriously impede any public work or supplies contract. It remains to be seen how, in practice, national courts will deal with the matter. Since there are a number of different jurisdictions throughout the Community, it also follows that there would be great differences in the amounts awarded as compensation by national courts. This could prevent some undertakings from taking any proceedings in member states that provide for low sanctions. In this case, the member state is obliged to introduce more effective procedures, similar, though not necessarily identical, to those of the rest of the member states of the Community. The Commission could launch an action under Article 169 EC and request the Court to declare that a member state has not conformed to the Compliance Directive.

The Compliance Directives provide that member states should establish judicial **2.91** or administrative bodies responsible for their enforcement. Member states, therefore, have a choice as to the forum and procedures provided for hearing disputes or otherwise achieving the required result. In addition, they require that all decisions taken by bodies responsible for review procedures shall be effectively enforced.

As explained above, since contracting authorities are involved in a public contract, **2.92** in many continental jurisdictions public law will be applied and the dispute is to be addressed before administrative courts. In other cases, civil law applies in public procurement litigation, whereas in the Netherlands, for example, there is a remarkably swift arbitration system for construction contracts. Consequently, the question of enforcement of the decisions is relevant to the choice of the forum. Normally, national courts have the power, the prerogative, and the means to enforce their decisions. An administrative body, without judicial powers to order discovery or injunctions, could not ensure effective enforcement of its decisions. In the case of arbitration, the winning party, in order to have the arbitration award enforced, has to go before national courts and exhaust the relevant proceedings. Moreover, there are some doubts as to the consistency of tribunals' decisions. National courts are skilled at construing contracts and statutory provisions, knowledgeable about the principles of damages, and staffed by judges. On the other hand, an administrative body or a tribunal, normally staffed by lawyers and laymen experienced in public procurement, is a swift, flexible, and rapid institution with simple proceedings to resolve disputes, since it will deal exclusively with this matter.

2.93 Where the Compliance Directive in the utilities sectors[73] is really novel is in Chapter 2. Member states are required to give the contracting entities the possibility of having their purchasing procedures and practices *attested* by persons authorized by law to exercise this function. Indeed, this attestation mechanism may investigate in advance possible irregularities identified in the award of a public contract and allow the contracting authorities to correct them. The latter may include the attestation statement in the notice inviting tenders published in the *Official Journal*. The system appears flexible and cost-efficient and may prevent wasteful litigation. Quite promisingly, the attestation procedure under Directive 92/13 will be the essential requirement for the development of European standards of attestation.[74]

(2) The role of the European Commission under the Compliance Directives

2.94 As mentioned above, under the draft Directive 89/665, the Commission had extensive powers, namely to intervene in an administrative or judicial procedure and to suspend unilaterally the procedure for award of a public procurement contract. Those powers were indeed far beyond the provision of Article 100A of the EC Treaty and could only be justified under Article 235 EC. The Commission's intervention was a novel provision since it has no power to be a party or to intervene in a trial before national courts. The *vires* of this provision was questioned, since the draft Directive was unclear at that particular point; it did not specify whether the Commission would have had a certain right to intervene or whether its intervention was subject to invitation or the permission of the court. In the latter case, it would have been considered as an *amicus curiae*, advising the court upon the correct interpretation of European Community law. On the other hand, it could be argued that the Commission's intervention would have been desirable, since it can only be heard in a case of interim measures before the Court of Justice or under the proceedings of Article 169 EC. Interim measures may be taken by the Court only if the case in question is pending before it, and an Article 169 EC action is a heavy, cumbersome and time-consuming procedure, as far as public procurement cases are concerned.

2.95 The Commission's suspension power could lead to legal uncertainty and undermine the independence of the courts. Control by both court and the Commission simultaneously is not desirable. In the final text of Directive 89/665,

---

[73] *See* Directive 92/13 [1992] OJ L76/7.   [74] *See* Art. 7 of Directive 92/13.

all these powers have been deleted and the Commission has been left with the right to invoke the procedure of Article 3 by way of notification of an infringement of Community law provisions to a member state requiring its correction. The same regime is provided for in Directive 92/13 (Article 8). Interestingly, the Commission's action is limited. It can only notify a clear and manifest infringement of Community law provisions in the field of public procurement, before a contract has been concluded. The former requirement introduces a kind of qualitative test. Clear and manifest infringement probably means an outspoken breach of a relevant provision. Unclear and ambiguous situations will fall outside the scope of the notification procedure. The latter requirement serves the principle of legal certainty, since, after the contract has been concluded, it is extremely costly and undesirable to start investigating it, probably with a view to suspending it.

After twenty-one days, in the case of Directive 89/665, and thirty days, in the case **2.96** of Directive 92/13, from the Commission's notification to a member state, the latter is obliged to communicate to the former: i) its confirmation that an infringement has been corrected, or ii) a justification as to why no correction has been made, or iii) a notice that a suspension of the award procedure has been ordered. When the suspension is lifted, the member state is obliged to inform the Commission. It is apparent that the Commission's role has been limited on the insistence of member states and, from a power to intervene or to suspend award procedures, the Commission's powers consists of the mere possibility of notification.

There have been two cases[75] so far where the Commission utilized the procedure **2.97** provided in Article 3 of Directive 89/665. The Court had the opportunity to declare that the special procedure of Article 3 is a preliminary measure which can neither derogate from nor replace the powers of the Commission to initiate proceedings under Article 169 EC. In both cases, the communication of the Commission's position under Article 3 of Directive 89/665 served as the reasoned opinion for the subsequent compliance proceedings under Article 169 EC.

The Commission's role is really innovative under Directive 92/13, where **2.98** provision has been made for a conciliation procedure, apart from the attempt to achieve an amicable settlement laid down in Article 1(3), as an endeavour to avoid any litigation between the parties. The conciliation procedure shall be distinguished from the judicial/administrative procedures at national level. Interestingly, there is no provision concerning the relationship between the two proceedings, and if the same person were to initiate conciliation and judicial review proceedings under the Directive simultaneously, the relation between

---

[75] *See* Case C-359/93, *Commission v. The Netherlands* [1995] ECR I-157; Case C-79/94, *Commission v. Greece* [1995] ECR I-1071.

them is unclear. Article 11(2)(a) of the Directive stipulates that conciliation proceedings shall be without prejudice to proceedings under Articles 169 or 170 EC and the rights of the parties or any other person under national laws (Article 11(2)(b). Any person having an interest and feeling that a breach of relevant public procurement law rules occurs may notify the Commission or the competent authorities of a member state. The possibility of the interested person choosing either the Commission or a member state's authorities creates some uncertainty, since it is admitted that the whole public procurement problem is decentralized. The Commission or the national authorities may refer the case to the Advisory Committee for Public Contracts[76] or the Advisory Committee on Telecommunications.[77] These Committees will set up working groups with a view to reaching an agreement between the parties.

2.99 The degree of compliance with Public Procurement Directives is in close relation to the degree of enforcement of their provisions at national level. Enforcement concerns legal remedies available to individuals before national courts, in particular actions for damages. Judicial review concerning the administrative part of a public procurement contract, in almost all member states,[78] is subject to public law. The award of damages to an aggrieved contractor reflects the approach of each national legal system vis-à-vis state liability.

F. Compliance with and Enforcement of the Rules under the WTO Government Procurement Agreement

2.100 The extra-territoriality of the legal regime regulating the public procurement of the member states of the Community has been achieved by virtue of the special inter-governmental agreements concluded between the European Community and member/signatories to the GATT Agreement. It was initially the GATT Agreement on Government Procurement (AGP), which was concluded during the Tokyo Round of negotiations that provided third-country contractors with access to European public markets. The AGP was amended by virtue of the WTO Government Procurement Agreement (GPA) during the Uruguay Round. In principle, access to the public sector markets of the member states has been guaranteed, as far as the framework of provisions in relation to procedural and substantive stages of public procurement is concerned. However, even the most comprehensive set of rules would be ineffective, if its enforcement appeared not

---

[76] This Committee has been set up by EC Council Decision 71/306 ([1971] OJ L185) as amended by EC Council Decision 77/63 ([1977] OJ L152).

[77] *See* Art. 31 of Directive 90/531.

[78] The notable exception is Denmark, where there is no distinction between administrative and civil disputes in a public contract.

sufficient. Access to justice for third-country providers under the GATT/WTO agreements is thus equally important with the principles of access to the public markets of the member states of the Community.

Both the WTO Government Procurement Agreement and its predecessor (the GATT AGP) are considered inter-governmental instruments which are addressed to states and do not intend to confer rights and duties upon individuals as such. Irrespective of the clearness and precision, the unconditionality of their provision, and the lack of discretion reserved to states for their implementation, international agreements are not deemed to produce direct effect,[79] thus depriving individuals from taking advantage of directly effective provisions in litigation before national courts. The Decision of the European Council which incorporates the WTO GPA into Community law specifically stipulates that the provisions under the GPA do not have direct effect. However, there is apparently a contradiction between the difficulties arising from applying the theory of direct effectiveness to the GPA provisions and the spirit and wording of the agreement. Express provision of remedies for aggrieved providers is made under Article XX of the GPA, where the remedies provided should be as favourable as those conferred upon Community contractors. Also, Article III of the GPA stipulates that signatories to the agreement should not be treated in a less favourable manner than national providers or providers from other parties. In practice, how these provisions concerning access to justice at national level for third-party providers will operate remains to be seen.[80]

2.101

As with its predecessor, the WTO Government Procurement Agreement has created an inter-governmental mechanism for settling disputes arising from its application. The mechanism is referred to as the *Understanding on Rules and Procedures Governing the Settlement of Disputes* (DSU) and is attached to the Annex II of the Agreement. The mechanism provides for a dispute settlement procedure between parties to the Agreement, that is states and not individuals. The DSU apparently elevates the pre-contractual or the contractual dispute between a third-party provider and a contracting authority to a grievance of an inter-governmental dimension. To invoke the Dispute Settlement Understanding, a state must first exhaust all possible ways of settling the dispute in an amicable manner by means of direct consultation and negotiations with the state allegedly in breach. If settlement cannot be reached, the state then may request the WTO Dispute Settlement Body for a Panel to be established in order to hear the case. The Panel is appointed in consultation with the parties and comprised of persons

2.102

---

[79] *See* Joined Cases C-21 to 24/72, *International Fruit Co NV v. Produktschap voor Groenten en Fruit* [1972] ECR 1236. Also Case C-280/93, *Germany v. Council* [1994] ECR-I 4973.

[80] *See* Footer, 'Remedies under the New GATT Agreement on Government Procurement', *Public Procurement Law Review*, 4 (1995), 80–86.

with experience in the area of government procurement. The Panel has as its task the provision of a report to the parties concerned, which then is adopted by the Dispute Settlement Body. The latter would then request the state in breach to repeal all the measures which contravene the principles of the WTO Government Procurement Agreement. Failing to do so, the Dispute Settlement Body may authorize *unilateral suspension* of the application of the GPA or any other agreement under the WTO in the territory of the state affected by the violation.

3

THE EVOLUTION OF PUBLIC PROCUREMENT REGULATION

A. The Public Supplies Regime

Attempts to regulate public procurement in the European Community were **3.01** recorded even before the end of the first transitional period.[1] For the purposes of giving guidance to Community institutions and member states in the implementation of Articles 52, 53 EC (right of establishment) and 59, 60 EC (freedom to provide services), in 1962 the Council of Ministers adopted two *General Programmes*[2] for the elimination of existing restrictions on inter-state trade. Among the restrictions to be abolished were rules and practices of member states

---

[1] The transitional period covered the period from the establishment of the European Communities until 31 December 1969, *see* Art. 8(7) EC.   [2] *See* [1962] JO 36/62.

which '. . . *exclude, limit or impose conditions upon the capacity to submit offers or to participate as main contractors or subcontractors in contract awards by the state or legal persons governed by public law*'. Those rules and practices resulted in blunt discrimination based on nationality grounds and practically fragmented the entire common market in relation to public procurement. Both Programmes envisaged a gradual and balanced removal of restrictions in the form of quotas and the coordination of national procedures for the award of public contracts to nationals of other member states through agencies or branches or directly to persons or undertakings established in other member states.

3.02 With respect to the abolition of all quotas and measures having an effect equivalent to quantitative restrictions upon trade amongst member states, the Commission in 1966 introduced Directive 66/683[3] which required the elimination of measures prohibiting the use of imported products or prescribing that of domestic products, thus favouring them. However, public supplies contracts were exempted pending the adoption of a specific Directive. Four years later, in 1970, the Commission enacted Directive 70/32[4] on the basis of Article 33(7) EC, hence introducing the prohibition of measures having an effect equivalent to quantitative restrictions in the public procurement arena. That Directive applied to all products of whatever description which were admitted to free circulation within the Community by virtue of Articles 9 and 10 EC. These were products originating in a member state, and third country products admitted to free circulation within the Community through a member state. It indicated two types of barriers that states, territorial authorities and other public corporate bodies could impose upon procurement of public supplies:[5] i) those preventing or inhibiting the supply of imported products, and ii) those favouring the supply of domestic products or granting preferential treatment (other than state aids which must be assessed under the framework of Article 92 EC and taxation) to domestic suppliers. In addition, the Directive (Article 3(3)) listed a number of forms of discrimination against foreign goods. Among those were technical specifications which, though applicable to both domestic and imported products, had restrictive effects on trade. The aims behind the introduction of Directive 70/32 were similar to the aims and objectives of Directive 66/683. However, the very first Community instrument to regulate public supplies contracts (Directive 70/32) came into force when the transitional period had virtually expired (at the end of 1969), thus rendering Article 30 EC directly effective. One might question the logic behind the decision of European institutions to introduce secondary legislation (the Directive) which had as its main thrust the free movement of goods within the Community, when the primary Treaty provision which guarantees the principle of free movement of goods (Article 30) had become directly effective.

---

[3] *See* [1966] JO L220/3748.   [4] *See* [1970] JO L13/1.
[5] *See* Arts. 3(1) and 3(2) of EC Directive 70/32, as well as the preamble of the Directive.

A possible answer could be that the direct effect of Article 30 EC would have **3.03** facilitated the incorporation of the Directive into national legal orders. On the other hand, this delay on the part of the Community in adopting an instrument which aimed at regulating public supplies revealed a highly complicated and sensitive regime that was related, not only to the free movement of goods, but expanded further covering aspects in the fields of competition and common commercial policy. Directive 70/32 attempted to integrate markets relating to the supply of goods destined for the public sector from within and from outside the Community. It indirectly made clear to national administration and law and policy makers that public supplies markets could not be confined within the geographical territory of the Community, let alone the national border of member states, but encompassed a broader field of sourcing of goods, a fact that cultivated the ground for the introduction of common commercial policy consideration in public procurement.[6] Indeed, ten years later, the European Commission was concluding on behalf of the member states the Agreement on Government Procurement during the GATT Tokyo Round, thus expanding the territorial application of the EC internal regime to members/signatories to the Agreement.[7]

In 1977, the Council adopted Directive 77/62[8] pursuant to Articles 30 and 100 **3.04** EC, concerning the coordination of procedures for the award of public supply contracts. This instrument, which came into force in 1978, was designed to ensure a more effective supervision of compliance with the negative obligations of Article 30 EC and Directive 70/32, by means of the imposition of a number of positive obligations on purchasing bodies (Article 1(b): contracting authorities specified in Annex I).

The imposition of a positive obligation on a member state by a Directive reveals **3.05** that a margin of appreciation as to the forms and methods of the result to be achieved is allotted to it. Of course, there is no doubt that Directives are binding only with respect to the result to be achieved,[9] thus requiring member states to opt for the appropriate methods and forms to implement their provisions into domestic law, but the fact that a Directive imposes a positive obligation may affect the direct effectiveness of its provisions, in case of wrongful or non-implementation. Positive obligations, in contrast to negative ones, allot to member states a greater margin of discretion. Member states should not only abstain from action that hinders a Community aim, but, in addition, they must take all the appropriate

---

[6] *See* Bovis, 'The Extra-territorial Effect of EC Public Procurement Directives—The Situation under the GATT Uruguay Round', *Legal Issues of European Integration*, II (1993), 83–93. Also, Bovis, 'Public Procurement under the Framework of the EC Common Commercial Policy', *Public Procurement Law Review*, 4 (1993), 211–220.

[7] For a detailed analysis of the GATT AGP and its successor WTO GPA, *see* below in this Chapter.　　　　　　　　　　　　　　　　　　　[8] *See* [1977] OJ L13/1.

[9] *See* Art. 189 EC.

measures to enhance the function and operation of that aim. A positive obligation seems to contain two requirements: that of abstention and that of introduction of further measures to secure the results of the former. With respect to direct effectiveness of provisions of Directives imposing positive obligations on member states, the Court, initially, was reluctant[10] to accept that the margin of discretion deriving from a positive obligation was capable of rendering the provision in question directly effective. Interestingly, in two cases[11] it ruled that even positive obligations contained in a Directive may produce direct effect.

3.06   The fact that Directive 77/62 imposed a number of positive obligations on member states raised a number of questions as to the direct effectiveness of its provisions. The principal aim of the Directive was to enhance public market efficiency by ensuring that conditions of competition were not distorted and that contracts were allocated to suppliers and contractors under the most favourable conditions for the contracting authorities. That aim could be achieved through transparency and improved market information. The Directive introduced three fundamental principles: i) Community-wide advertising of contracts; ii) prohibition of technical specifications capable of discriminating against potential bidders; and iii) application of objective criteria of participation in tendering and award procedures. However, the scope of the Directive was rather limited. It explicitly excluded from its coverage public supplies contracts by public utilities (authorities in the transport, energy, water, and telecommunications sectors). Apparently, the main legal reason for that exclusion was that these entities had different legal status and operated under different regimes in member states. Some of them were completely covered by public law, others governed by private law, while some were in the process of privatization, although the essential control remained in the hands of the state. On the other hand, it could be argued that this is not a valid argument, since the instruments employed for the regulation of this sort of entities were Directives, which implement Community envisaged standards into national law, taking into account existing national sensibilities. It appears that the regulation of the public utilities in respect to their purchasing requirements had been rather premature for the time.

3.07   Directive 77/62 contained a kind of *de minimis* rule; it was applicable only to public supply contracts with a value of more than 200,000 EUA.[12] Its legal basis (Articles 30 and 100 EC) rendered it inapplicable to products originating in and supplied by third countries. The Directive was also inapplicable to public supplies contracts awarded: i) pursuant to an international agreement between a member

---

[10]   *See* Case 57/65, *Alfons Luttucke v. Hauptzollampt Saarlouis* [1966] ECR 205.
[11]   *See* Case C-28/67, *Firma Molkerei-Zentrale Westfalen/Lippe GmbH v. Haupzollampt Pederborn* [1968] ECR 143; Case C-13/68, *SpA Salgoil v. Italian Ministry of Foreign Trade* [1968] ECR 453.
[12]   *See* Art. 5(1)(a) of Directive 77/62. EUA refers to the European Unit of Account, the predecessor of the ECU. The threshold of the Directive was exclusive of VAT.

state and one or more non-member countries; ii) pursuant to an international agreement relating to the stationing of troops between undertakings in a Member State or a non-Member country; and iii) pursuant to a particular procedure of an international agreement.[13]

In 1980, Directive 77/62 was amended by Directive 80/767[14] in order to take **3.08** account of the 1979 GATT Agreement on Government Procurement.[15] The Agreement committed the Community and its member states to providing suppliers from third countries with better access, through the application of lower thresholds, to central government purchasing and to some defence procurement, than suppliers from the Community enjoyed under Directive 77/62. Clearly, Directive 80/767 instituted an element of multilaterality in access to international public markets based on the principle of *reciprocity*.[16] That Agreement became part of Community law as it was approved by Council Decision 80/271.[17]

In 1984, the Commission's *Communication to the Council on Public Supply* **3.09** *Contracts*[18] revealed an unsatisfactory situation with respect to the implementation of the Supplies Directives in the legal orders of member states. The list of factors responsible for the lack of success includes *inter alia*:

— failure to advertise contracts in the *Official Journal*, as a result of intentional or unintentional splitting up of contracts;[19]
— ignorance of the relevant rules on the part of contracting authorities or deliberate omission of these rules;
— excessive use of the exceptions permitting non-competitive tendering (negotiated procedures) instead of open or restricted procedures;
— discriminatory requirements posed by contracting authorities by means of compliance with national technical standards, to the exclusion of European standards or equivalent standards of other countries; and
— unlawful disqualification of suppliers or contractors or discriminatory use of the award criteria.

The Commission's *White Paper on the Completion of the Internal Market*[20] reiterated **3.10** that there was a serious and urgent need for improvement and clarification of the relevant Public Procurement Directives. In accordance with the Commission's

---

[13] This may be the case of supplies under ECSC and Euratom Treaties.
[14] *See* [1980] OJ L215/1.   [15] *See* [1980] OJ L71/1.
[16] *See* Birkinshaw and Bovis, *The EC Public Supplies Directive; Public Procurement: Legislation and Commentary* (Butterworths European Law Service, 1992).
[17] *See* [1980] OJ L215/1.   [18] *See* COM (84) 717 final.
[19] It was anticipated that EC Directive 83/189, [1983] OJ L165/1, enacted in order to assist suppliers to fulfil the requirements of norms and standards referred to EC Directive 77/62 and to eliminate discrimination arising through their use would end the intentional or unintentional splitting up of public contracts in order to avoid the mandatory advertisement requirements.
[20] *See* COM (85) 310 final.

action programme, the Council in 1988 adopted Directive 88/295[21] amending all previous Supplies Directives. The main improvements were:

— with open tendering procedures as the norm, negotiated ones were allowed in exceptional circumstances;[22]
— the definition of the types of supplies contracts was widened[23] and the method of calculation of the thresholds was clarified;[24]
— the exempted sectors were more strictly defined;[25]
— purchasing authorities had to publish in advance information on their annual procurement programmes and their timetable, as well as a notice giving details of the outcome of each decision of award;[26]
— the rules on technical standards were brought in line with the new policy on standards, which is based on the mutual recognition of national require-ments, where the objectives of national legislation are essentially equivalent, and on the process of legislative harmonization of technical standards through non-governmental standardization organisations (CEPT, CEN, CENELEC).[27]

3.11 In an attempt to consolidate all previous legislation relating to public supplies and align it in conformity with the relevant Directives on Public Works[28] and Public Services,[29] and the Utilities Sector,[30] Directive 93/36[31] has been adopted since June 1993. The consolidated Directives aim at introducing a similar procedural regime in their relevant sectors and at enhancing clarity of some of the previously existing provisions.[32]

B. The Public Works Regime

3.12 The two General Programmes adopted by the Council for the purpose of guiding the Community institutions in the implementation of the provisions of Articles 52, 53, 59 and 62 of the EC Treaty, took account of the special features of public works contracts. A gradual and balanced removal of restrictions based on quotas and the coordination of national procedures for awarding public works contracts to nationals of other member states were the main aims envisaged therein.

---

[21] *See* [1988] OJ L127/1.   [22] *See* Art. 7(2) of Directive 88/295.
[23] *See* Art. 1(a) of Directive 88/295.   [24] *See* Art. 6(1)(c) of Directive 88/295.
[25] *See* Art. 3(2)(a)(b)(c) of Directive 88/295.   [26] *See* Art. 9 of Directive 88/295.
[27] *See* Art. 7 of Directive 88/295. *See also* the *White Paper on Completing the Internal Market,* paras. 61–79; also Council Resolution of 7 May 1985 on a new approach in the field of technical harmonization and standards [1985] OJ C136.   [28] *See* Directive 93/37 [1993] OJ L199.
[29] *See* Directive 92/50 of 18 June 1992 [1992] OJ L209.
[30] *See* Directive 93/38 [1993] OJ L199.   [31] *See* Directive 93/36 [1993] OJ L199.
[32] *See* Birkinshaw and Bovis, op. cit. (n. 16).

The issue of public sector activities related to construction contracts after the   **3.13**
transitional period was addressed by Directive 71/304,[33] which required member
states to abolish restrictions on participation of non-nationals in public procurement contracts. However, it came into force after the completion of the transitional period, when Articles 59 and 60 EC concerning the freedom to provide
services, became directly effective, thus leaving few aspects to be implemented by
member states. It now serves mainly to list professional trade activities which
constitute public works.

The aims envisaged in Article 52 *et seq.* on the right of establishment and Article   **3.14**
59 *et seq.* on the freedom to provide services, were further enhanced by the adoption of Directive 71/305,[34] which was the primary vehicle for the opening up of
the public works contracts. Based on the prohibition of discriminatory technical
specifications, the adequate and prompt advertising of contracts, the establishment of objective selection, and award criteria and a procedure of joint supervision both by member states' authorities and the EC Commission to ensure the
observation of these principles,[35] the Directive sought the coordination of
national procedures in the award of public works contracts. The Directive's major
objective was the establishment and enhancement of a transparency regime in the
public works sector, where conditions of undistorted competition would ensure
that contracts are allocated to contractors under the most favourable terms for the
contracting authorities. However, like the Supplies Directive 77/62, Directive
71/305 had a limited aim. It did not introduce new tendering procedures nor
were existing national procedures and practices replaced by a set of Community
rules. Member states remained free to maintain or adopt substantive and procedural rules on condition that they comply with all the relevant provisions of
Community law and, in particular, the prohibitions following from the principles
stipulated in the Treaty regarding the right of establishment and the freedom to
provide services.[36]

The concept of public works contracts under the first Works Directive was very   **3.15**
extensive[37] and covers those contracts concluded in writing between a contractor
and a contracting authority for pecuniary interest concerning either the execution
or both the execution and design of works related to building or civil engineering
activities listed in class 50 of the NACE Classification,[38] or the execution by whatever means of a work corresponding to the requirements specified by the contracting authority. The above formula was wide enough to embrace modern forms

---

[33] *See* [1971] OJ L185/1.   [34] *See* [1971] OJ L185/5.
[35] *See* the Preamble of Directive 71/305.
[36] *See* Cases 27, 28 and 29/86, *CEI and Bellini* [1987] ECR 3347.
[37] Art. 1(a) of Directive 71/305 as amended by Directive 89/440.
[38] General Industrial Classification of Economic Activities within the European Communities,
see Annex II to Directive 71/305.

of works contracts such as project developing contracts, management contracts and concession contracts.[39] With reference to the latter type of contracts, a public works concession is defined by the Works Directive[40] as a written contract between a contractor and a contracting authority concerning either the execution or both the execution and design of a work and for which remunerative considerations consist, at least partly, in the right of the *concessionaire* to exploit exclusively the finished construction works for a period of time. The initial Works Directive 71/305 did not apply to concession contracts, except in the case that the concessionaire was a public authority covered by the Directive. In such situations, only the works subcontracted to third parties would be fully subject to its provisions. In any other case, the only provisions of the Directive applicable to works concessions were that the *concessionaire* should not discriminate on grounds of nationality when it itself awarded contracts to third parties.[41] The regulation of concession contracts was introduced to the *acquis communautaire* almost two decades later by virtue of Directive 89/440 which amended Directive 71/305. In fact, it incorporated the Voluntary Code of Practice, which was adopted by the representatives of member states meeting within the Council in 1971.[42] The Code was a non-binding instrument and contained rules on the advertising of contracts and the principle that contracting authorities awarding the principal contract to a concessionaire were to require him to subcontract to third parties at least thirty per cent of the total work provided for by the principal contract. Obviously, these requirements could not easily be incorporated in a binding instrument such as Directive 89/440, thus a more relaxed regime occurred. As a result, the coordination rules of the Directive applied to concession contracts only in respect of their advertising. The Directive's rules on tendering procedures, suitability criteria, selection and qualification, technical specifications, and award procedures and criteria were inapplicable. Interestingly, Article 3(3) of Directive 71/305 on the prohibition of discrimination on grounds of nationality by a *concessionaire* awarding subcontracts has disappeared from the text of the amending Directive 89/440. The reason could be that, by the end of the transitional period, Articles 7, 48, 52, 59 and 119 EC were directly effective and, in addition, their horizontal direct effect had been pronounced by the European Court of Justice.[43]

3.16 The amended Works Directive adopted a special, mitigated regime for the award of concession contracts.[44] The provisions of the Directive only applied to

---

[39] Concession contracts are public works projects under which the consideration for the works consists of a franchise (concession) to operate the completed works, or of a franchise plus payment. For more details *see* the Guide to the Community Rules on Opening Government Procurement [1987] OJ L358/1, at 28. [40] *See* Art. 1(d) of Directive 93/37.

[41] *See* Art. 3(3) of Directive 71/305. [42] *See* [1971] OJ C82/13.

[43] *See* Case C-36/74, *Walrave and Koch v. Association Union Cycliste International et al.* [1974] ECR 1423; Case C-43/75, *Drefenne v. SABENA* [1976] ECR 473.

[44] *See* Art. 3 of Directive 93/37.

concession contracts with a value of at least 5 million ECU. No rules were given as to the way in which the contract value must be calculated. For the award of concession contracts, contracting authorities must apply similar rules on advertising to the advertising rules concerning open and restricted procedures for the award of every works contract. Also, the provisions on technical standards and on criteria for qualitative selection of candidates and tenderers applied to the award of concession contracts. The Directive does not prescribe the use of specific award procedures for concession contracts. The Directive presupposes that concession contracts should be awarded in two rounds, such as in the case of restricted procedures or negotiated procedures for ordinary works contracts. Nothing, however, prevents contracting authorities from applying a one-round open procedure. The Directive contained no rules on the minimum number of candidates which have to be invited to negotiate or to submit a tender. It would seem that a contracting authority may limit itself to selecting only one single candidate, provided the intention to award a concession contract has been adequately published. A contracting authority may under no circumstances refrain from publicizing a notice in the *Official Journal* indicating its intention to proceed with the award of a concession works contract.[45]

The definition of contractors comprised any legal or natural person involved in construction activities and, for the purposes of the Directive, the contracting authority might impose a requirement as to the form and legal status of the contractor that won the award.[46] The above requirement covers the case of *consortia participation* in public procurement contracts. To facilitate market access and provide as many opportunities as possible for interested tenderers, the Directive specifically prohibits contracting authorities from disqualifying groups or consortia of tenderers without corporate structure. This means that contracting authorities must apply all the relevant selection and qualification procedures equally in evaluating an offer made by a consortium and award the contract to the consortium, if the offer meets the award criteria. However, after the award of the contract and, for reasons dictated by legal certainty and legitimate expectation, as well as for reasons associated with the supervision of the contract and its management, contracting authorities may require the incorporation of the consortium into a more concrete entity. As far as contracting authorities are concerned, their definition was very wide and covers bodies governed by public law which is defined as being any body *'established for the specific purpose of meeting needs in the general interest and not having an industrial or commercial character, which has legal personality and is financed for the most part by the State or is subject to management* **3.17**

---

[45] *See* Bovis, *EC Public Procurement Law* (Longman, European Law Series, 1997), 67–68.
[46] *See* Art. 21 of Directive 71/305 as amended. The same requirement is found also in the Supplies Directive (Art. 18 of Directive 77/62).

supervision by the latter.[47] There is a list of such bodies in Annex I of Directive 71/305, which is not an exhaustive one like that in the Supplies Directive, and member states were under an obligation to notify the Commission of any changes in that list.

3.18 Works contracts in the utilities and defence sectors and those contracts awarded in pursuance of certain international agreements were explicitly excluded by virtue of Articles 4 and 5 of the Directive. These provisions are identical in effect to the corresponding ones of the Supplies Directive.[48] This revealed the fact that public contracts under the framework of the Works Directive covered mainly construction projects in the education, health, sports, and leisure facilities sectors, in as much as the state or regional or local authorities undertake such projects. In cases where entities involved in this sort of activity (e.g. a hospital or a university) enjoyed considerable independence from the state or local government as to the undertaking of works contracts, Directive 71/305 was inapplicable, since they were not included in its Annex I as bodies governed by public law for the purposes of the Directive in question. This seems to have limited the scope of the Directive only to cases where the state or local government had direct control over the above mentioned entities. Given the fact that works contracts in the utilities sectors were also excluded from the framework of the Directive, its applicability covered a rather modest portion of the construction sector. In order to moderate this apparently undesirable result, the amending Directive 89/440[49] provides for an obligation upon member states to ensure compliance with its provisions when they subsidize directly, by more than fifty per cent, a works contract awarded by an entity involved in activities relating to certain civil engineering works, and to the building of hospitals, sports, recreation and leisure facilities, school and university buildings, and buildings used for administrative purposes. These conditions seem not to impose a heavy duty on member states, as only direct subsidies trigger the applicability of the Directive. Indirect ways of subsidizing the entities in question, such as tax exemptions, guaranteed loans, or provision of land free of charge, render it inapplicable. It should be noted that, under both the original Supplies and Works Directives, preference schemes in the award of contracts were allowed. Such schemes required the application of award criteria based on considerations other than the lowest price or the most economically advantageous tender, which are common in both regimes.[50] However, preferences could only be compatible with Community law in as much they did not run contrary to the principle of free movement of goods (Article 30 EC *et seq.*) and to competition law considerations

---

[47] This definition resembles the Court's ruling on state controlled enterprises in Case C-152/84, *Marshall v. Southampton and South West Hampshire Area Health Authority* [1986] ECR 723.

[48] *See* Art. 3 of Directive 77/62 as amended by Directive 88/295.

[49] *See* Art. 2 of Directive 71/305 as amended by Directive 89/440.

[50] *See* Arts. 29(4) and 29(a) of Directive 71/305; also Art. 26 of Directive 77/62.

in respect of state aids.[51] Preference schemes have been abolished since the completion of the internal market at the end of 1992.

Works contracts which are subsidized directly by more than fifty per cent by the state **3.19** can still fall within the scope of the Directive.[52] Works which are not subsidized directly, or for less than fifty per cent, fall outside this anti-circumvention provision. Not all subsidized works fall within the scope of the Directive: only civil engineering works, such as the construction of roads, bridges, and railways, as well as building work for hospitals, facilities intended for sports, recreation and leisure, university buildings, and buildings used for administrative purposes, are referred to as subsidized works contracts.[53] This list is exhaustive. The Works Directive does not apply to works contracts which are declared secret or the execution of which must be accompanied by special security measures[54] in accordance with the laws, regulations, or administrative provisions in force in the member state concerned; nor does the Directive apply to works contracts when the protection of the basic interests of the member states' security so requires. Finally, the Works Directive does not apply to public works contracts awarded in pursuance of certain international agreements;[55] nor does the Directive apply to public works contracts awarded pursuant to the particular procedure of an international organisation.[56] Several international organisations, such as NATO, have their own rules on the award of public works contracts.

In 1993, the Council enacted a Directive with a view to consolidating all existing **3.20** legislation in the field of public works. The consolidated Directive 93/37[57] has embraced all relevant Community legislation relating to public works with some minor amendments and clarifications of existing provisions of Directive 89/440.

C. The Utilities Regime

As previously mentioned, both supplies and works contracts in the transport, **3.21** water, energy, and telecommunications sectors were excluded from the relevant Supplies and Works Directives.[58] The exclusion of the above-mentioned sectors from the framework of Supplies Directives (77/62 and 88/295) had been attributed to the fact that the authorities entrusted with the operation of public utilities had been subject to different legal regimes in the member states, varying from completely state controlled enterprises to private controlled ones. With respect to Works Directives, the above justification appears valid, although the apparent

---

[51] *See* the Commission's Communication on the *Regional and Social Aspects of Public Procurement*, where it gives an overview of the preference schemes still existing in member states, COM (89) 400 final.   [52] *See* Art. 2(1) of Directive 93/37.
  [53] *See* Art. 2(2) of Directive 93/37.   [54] *See* Art. 4(b) of Directive 93/37.
  [55] *See* Art. 5(a) of Directive 93/37.   [56] *See* Art. 5(c) of Directive 93/37.
  [57] *See* Directive 93/37 [1993] OJ L199.
  [58] *See* Art. 2 of Directive 77/62 as amended; Art. 3 of Directive 89/440.

connection between construction projects and the excluded sectors leads to the conclusion that Directives 71/305 and 89/440 have very limited application.

3.22   As far as supplies contracts were concerned, a convincing reason behind the exclusion of these sectors is that the projects covered therein could not fall within the thresholds of Directives 77/62 and 88/295. Energy, telecommunications, transport, and, to a lesser extent, the water industry, are technical sectors requiring state-of-the-art technology (especially telecommunications and energy). The prices in the contracts are very high, in comparison with (simple) supplies ones, so the only way these sectors could be brought within Directive 77/62 would have been either to increase the thresholds (200,000 ECU) of the supplies contracts to such a level as to catch a substantial amount of contracts of the excluded sectors, or, on the other hand, to lower the envisaged thresholds of contracts in telecommunications, energy, transport and water industry sectors[59] to the level of the (simple) supplies ones (200,000 ECU). Either option would have resulted in a very undesirable situation; if the first option was chosen, the bulk of supplies contracts would have escaped from the framework of Directive 77/62. On the other hand, reducing the thresholds of the excluded sectors to 200,000 ECU would have eliminated the *de minimis* rule for those sectors. A *de minimis* rule is a *conditio sine qua non* where quantitative criteria for regulation of a sector are chosen, thus the administrative burdens on contracting authorities would have made the award of public contracts a rather slow and costly exercise.

3.23   With respect to works contracts, the exclusion of the telecommunications, transport, energy, and water industry sectors from Directives 71/305 and 89/440 could be justified, due to the different legal positions of the entities in question in the member states. If a private controlled entity operating in the above sectors were to be involved in a construction project, Works Directives would be inapplicable, as the former was not included among the contracting authorities specified in Annex I (bodies governed by public law). To cover both private and public controlled entities operating in the relevant utilities sectors, the Works Directives should have expanded the definition of contracting authorities; but this would have resulted in an internal disturbance in the operation of the Directives, which are envisaged as regulating construction project awards exclusively by the state or local government, or bodies governed by public law. Thus, the only viable and reasonable solution was to introduce a separate instrument, applying the same principles as those found in Directive 77/62, in order to regulate the transport, telecommunications, energy, and water sectors.

3.24   A more sceptical explanation for the late regulation of utilities procurement could be attributed to the fact that, due to their purchasing volume and relative

---

[59] *See* Art. 12 of Directive 90/531; 400,000 ECU for water, energy, and transport supplies, and 600,000 ECU for telecommunications supplies.

magnitude, public utilities procurement constituted an important domestic industrial policy instrument. Member states appeared reluctant in subjecting the procurement of their utilities to the rigorous transparent and competitive regime of public works and supplies purchasing, as they have relied upon preferential and closed utilities procurement in order to sustain certain strategic industries.[60]

The Commission was requested by the Council to follow the progress of the **3.25** CEPT proceedings[61] on harmonization in the field of telecommunications, and to submit to the latter a timetable for measures ensuring effective competition in the field of supply contracts awarded for telecommunications services. The Commission, in its Recommendations on Telecommunications,[62] also expressed its desire to ensure that the objective of an open market, in particular for suppliers within the Community, was being achieved without undesirable consequences for the pattern of Community trade with non-member countries. In its *Communication to the Council of 1984 on Public Supply Contracts*[63] and its *White Paper on the Completion of the Internal Market*,[64] the Commission reiterated the need to liberalize the so far excluded sectors, particularly telecommunications.

The European Parliament's Committee on Economic and Monetary Affairs and **3.26** Industrial Policy presented a report in the European Parliament[65] stressing the need for extension of the scope of the Supplies Directives to cover excluded sectors. In its Resolution,[66] the Parliament approved all the Commission's and Council's actions so far, and called them to submit a proposal for a Directive to govern the excluded sectors. The Council, in its Recommendation 84/550,[67] shared the Commission's considerations as to the opening of access to public telecommunications contracts, providing that governments of member states should offer opportunities for Community undertakings to tender on a non-discriminatory basis for the supply of specified telecommunications equipment, and should also report to the Commission on implementing measures and practical effects. The Commission in 1988 issued Directive 88/301[68] on competition in the markets in telecommunications terminal equipment.

Finally, in 1990, the Council adopted Directive 90/531[69] on the procurement **3.27** procedures of entities operating in the water, energy, transport, and telecommunications sectors. The regime imposed is rather similar to the Supplies Directives with

---

[60] *See* European Commission, *Statistical Performance Indicators for Keeping Watch over Public Procurement*, 1992. Also, *see* Chapter 6 below.

[61] CEPT is the European Conference of Postal and Telecommunications Administrations, established in Montreux in 1959, and aiming at closer relations between member administration to improve their administrative and technical services, [1977] OJ C11/3.

[62] *See* COM (80) 422 final.   [63] *See* COM.(84) 717 final.

[64] *See* COM.(85) 310 final.   [65] *See* the von Wogau report, DOC.A2-38/85.

[66] *See* [1985] OJ C175/241.   [67] *See* [1984] OJ L289/51.

[68] *See* [1988] OJ L131/73.   [69] *See* [1990] OJ L297.

some important differences as to the flexibility given to the contracting authorities over the choice of methods to be used to make the award process competitive.[70] The Utilities Directive has been amended by Directive 93/38,[71] which mainly incorporates the newly enacted Public Services Directive 92/50[72] into the utilities regime.

3.28 The legislative background of the Utilities Directive and the ordeal of the regulation of public utilities procurement justify the high complexity of the regime. The fact that public utilities often have an unclear legal status or their legal nature varies within the member states' legal systems has obviously rendered it difficult to introduce a single legal instrument to regulate their purchasing, although such a prolonged delay should be attributed to other factors. It may be recalled that public utilities absorb the vast majority of high technology equipment designated to the public sector. Protectionism in strategic industrial sectors has been pursued through preferential purchasing with a view to either sustaining the relevant industries or to assisting the development of infant industries in member states. The regulation of utilities purchasing not only had to overcome the significant legislative barriers accountable to their nature but also the abandoning of individual industrial policies of member states through strategic procurement. In addition to these constraints, the fear of an uncontrolled flow of direct investment which would target vulnerable European-based high technology industries and the subsequent possible increase in take-overs and acquisitions, mainly from Japanese and American investors, poured cold water on the attempts of European institutions to integrate the utilities procurement within the common market.

3.29 The Utilities Directive has been the most radical approach to the public sector integration in Europe and its enactment coincided with the envisaged international liberalization of public procurement during the Uruguay GATT negotiations. One could question such a strategy by European institutions, particularly bearing in mind the vulnerability of Europe's high-tech industry in comparison with that in the USA and Japan. However, the GATT regime has introduced a new era in the accessibility of international public markets, to the extent that highly protectionist countries like the USA and Japan must, under the new regime, abolish their buy-national laws and policies, and open, on a reciprocal basis, their public markets to international competition.

3.30 The ambit of the Utilities Directive and the field of its application appear more complicated than those in the Supplies and Works Directives, although the internal legal structure among the three Directives is very similar. Articles 1 and 2

---

[70] The Directive provided different implementing periods for Spain, Greece and Portugal. Spain has to implement its provisions by January 1, 1996 whereas Greece and Portugal by January 1, 1998 respectively. The delay in the uniform implementation of the Utilities Directive could be attributed to the preparations needed for the integration of the public utilities sectors in the respective countries.
[71] *See* [1993] OJ L199.   [72] *See* [1992] OJ L209.

of the Utilities Directive form the broad framework of the Directive's application, by providing various definitions and the scope of some preliminary exemptions. The Utilities Directive devotes a substantial amount of provisions in an attempt to exempt from its application certain contracts or activities that have been deemed ineligible for Community-wide regulation.

Apart from the normal exemptions under the grounds of defence and security, and confidentiality, the major exemptions are provided for under Articles 1 and 2. Radio and television broadcasting have not been classified as telecommunications activities and have been specifically excluded from the ambit of the Directive by virtue of Article 2. Also, bus transport services to the public are excluded on condition that their providers operate under a regime of competitive conditions, which means that other potential contractors or suppliers of similar services are allowed to enter the relevant geographical and product markets and compete against the existing utilities provider Article 2(4). A similar rule applies to telecommunications services which operate within a competitive market.[73] **3.31**

Under the same Article 2, special exemptions are also provided to private entities supplying gas, heat, drinking water, and electricity. Although the wording and spirit of the Directive covers private entities operating under exclusive and special rights in the utilities sectors, nevertheless, under certain conditions, these entities can be exempted from the application of the rules of the Directive. In the case of the production of drinking water and electricity, if a private entity is able to show that it does so for its own purposes, which are not related to the provision of drinking water or electricity to the public, it is exempt. Similarly, if a private entity is able to show that it supplies to the public network drinking water or electricity which is destined for its own consumption, and that the total so supplied to the network is not more than thirty per cent of the total produced by that network in any one year over a three year period, it is also exempt.[74] **3.32**

In the case of gas and heat supplies, if the production by a private entity is related to an activity other than the supply to a network for public consumption, then these entities are also exempt. On the same lines, if the supply of gas and heat by a private entity to a public network relates to economic exploitation only, and does not exceed twenty per cent of the firm's turnover in any one year, taking an average of the preceding three years and the current year, then such an entity is also exempt.[75] These exemptions predominantly cover entities which have research and development as their main objective in the relevant utilities sector, or which do not play a major role in supplying public networks with water or energy.[76] **3.33**

---

[73] *See* Art. 2(4) and Art. 8 of the Utilities Directive as amended by Directive 93/38.
[74] *See* Art. 2(5)(a) of the Utilities Directive as amended by Directive 93/38.
[75] *See* Art. 2(5)(b) of the Utilities Directive as amended by Directive 93/38.
[76] *See* O'Loan, 'Implementation of Directive 90/531 and Directive 92/50 in the United Kingdom', *Public Procurement Law Review*, (1993), 29. Also, A. Cox, *Public Procurement in the*

3.34   There are also exemptions for entities exploring for gas, oil, coal, and other solid fuels under Article 3. Entities operating in these sectors will not be regarded as having an exclusive right provided that certain conditions are fulfilled. These conditions are cumulative and stipulate that, when an exploitation right is granted to the entity in question, the latter is exempt from the Utilities Directives provided that other bodies are able to compete for the same exclusive rights under free competition; that the financial and technical criteria to be used in awarding rights are clearly spelt out before the award is made; that the objective criteria are specified as to the way in which exploitation is to be carried out; that these criteria are published before requests for tenders are made and applied in a non-discriminatory way; that all operating obligations, royalty, and capital and revenue participation agreements are being published in advance; and, finally, that contracting authorities are not required to provide information on their intentions about procurement except at the request of national authorities.[77] Furthermore, member states have to ensure that these exempted bodies apply, at least, the principles of non-discrimination and competition. They are obliged to provide a report to the Commission on request about such contracts. However, this requirement is less stringent than the mandatory reporting rules in the Supply and Works Directives. It should be mentioned that the Utilities Directive does not apply to concession contracts granted to entities operating in utilities sectors, awarded prior to the coming into force of the Directive. All exemption provisions within the Utilities Directive are subject to assessment in the light of the four year overall review of the process.[78]

3.35   Other exemptions cover entities in the relevant sectors which can demonstrate that their service and network associated contracts are not related to the specific supplies and works functions specified in the Directive, or if they are related, they take place in a non-member state and they are not using a European public network or a physical area.[79] The member states are under an obligation to inform the European Commission, on request, of the cases when these exemptions have been allowed. There are also provisions which allow for resale and hire contracts to third parties to be exempt when the awarding body does not possess an exclusive or special right to hire or sell the subject of the contract, and there is competition already in the market from other suppliers or producers to provide the commodity or service to third parties.[80] Similar relaxed reporting and monitoring requirements are found in Article 8 which applies to telecommunications exemptions.[81]

European Community: The Single Market Rules and the Enforcement Regime after 1992 (Earlsgate Press, 1993).

   [77]   *See* Art. 3(1) of the Utilities Directive as amended by Directive 93/38.
   [78]   *See* Art. 3(2) to (4) of the Utilities Directive as amended by Directive 93/38.
   [79]   *See* Art. 6(1) of the Utilities Directive as amended by Directive 93/38.
   [80]   *See* Art. 7(2) of the Utilities Directive as amended by Directive 93/38.
   [81]   *See* Art. 8(2) of the Utilities Directive as amended by Directive 93/38.

In 1993, the Divisional Court of the Queen's Bench Division of the Supreme   **3.36**
Court of England and Wales made a reference to the European Court of Justice
on the interpretation of Directive 90/531 concerning procurement in public
utilities. The national case[82] concerned with the definition of the relevant
provision of the Directive relating to the application of procurement rules to
entities operating in the telecommunications sector. Article 8(1) of the Utilities
Directive provides for an exemption from the regime, and for the inapplicability of the Directive, when contracting authorities in the telecommunications
sector operate under substantially the same competitive conditions within the
same geographical market. The national court asked for an interpretation of
Article 8(1) of the Utilities Directive and, in particular, the competence of
member states to determine the sufficiently genuine competitive regime and the
criteria for such evaluation, in a geographical area between telecommunications
operators in order to exclude them from the application of the Directive. In the
preliminary ruling, the European Court of Justice exposed the so far contro-
versial interpretation of Article 8(1) and the exemption schemes within the
Utilities Directive, as well as determining the member states' obligation to
award damages to individuals who suffered from wrongful implementation of
Directives. The Court followed the Conclusions of the Advocate General and
held that a member state could not decide, when implementing the Directive,
which telecommunications services were excluded from the scope of the Directive,
as that power was reserved for the telecommunications entities themselves.
Answering the second question, the Court maintained that, in order for the
criterion in Article 8(1) to be satisfied, other contracting entities had, in all
the circumstances of the case, to be able to compete as a matter of fact as well
as of law.

3.37

Another set of significant exemptions is provided for water authorities under
Article 9. Under this provision water authorities specified in Annex 1 are specifically exempt from the rules when they purchase water. They are, however, covered by the Directive when they purchase other supply and construction
products.[83] Similarly, there are specific exemptions for the electricity, gas and
heat, oil and gas, and coal and other solid fuels entities outlined in Annex II, III,
IV and V, but only when they award contracts for the supply of energy or for fuels
for the production of energy. For all other relevant contracts these bodies are
included in the rules. These exemptions were provided because of the need to allow
contracting authorities to buy from local sources of supply, which may not always
be the cheapest, but which are important on the basis of regional development
policies or environmental grounds, and because these purchases are central to the

---

[82] *See* Case C-392/93, *The Queen and HM Treasury, ex parte British Telecommunications Plc*
[1993] OJ C287/6.
[83] *See* Art. 9(1)(a) of the Utilities Directive as amended by Directive 93/38.

entities' operations and not part of normal supply and works procurement process.[84]

3.38 Finally, specific exemptions under the Utilities Directive are provided for those carriers of passengers and providers of transport services by air and by sea. In the preamble of the Directive it is stated that, under a series of measures adopted in 1987 with a view to introducing more competition between firms providing public air services, it was decided to exempt such carriers from the scope of the legislation. Similarly, because shipping has been subject to severe competitive pressures, it was decided to exempt certain types of contracts from the Directive.[85]

3.39 The Utilities Directive intends to open up procurement practices in the four previously excluded sectors mainly to EC-wide competition. With respect to goods (and services) originating in third countries, things are more complicated. A product outside the Community, in order to be subject to a public contract regulated by one of the EC Public Procurement Directives, must lawfully be put in free circulation in at least one member state.[86] Except where there has been an international agreement which grants comparable and effective access for Community undertakings to public markets of a third country (reciprocity principle), Article 29 renders it possible for European contracting authorities in the utilities sector to reject offers from outside the Community, and requires Community preference where Community offers are equivalent to offers from third countries (where the price difference does not exceed three per cent). With reference to an international agreement granting access to public markets, the Utilities Directive opens the door for the application of the GATT Agreement on Government Procurement in the utilities sector.

D. The Public Services Regime

3.40 Whilst the liberalization of trade, as envisaged in international agreements such as the GATT or in supranational organisations such as the European Union, embraces primarily the free movement of goods, provisions regulating the provision of services are often described as inadequate. Modern economies have witnessed a shift in trade patterns from product manufacturing industries to

---

[84] It has been considered that these exemptions might be the appropriate framework to introduce a common energy policy.

[85] In the future sea-ferry operators would be excluded, but their position has been kept under review. Inland water ferry services and river ferry services operated by public authorities were to be brought within the rules.

[86] For the concept of origin of goods and their lawful free circulation in the Common Market, *see* Regulation 802/68 [1968] OJ (1), English Special Edition, 165.

markets where the provision of services is the predominant sector of the industry. The lack of regulation of services at a global level has given rise to economic controversies. Trade wars have been taking place and the international legal community currently attempts to adopt measures towards regulation of trade in services within the context of the GATT Uruguay Round of multilateral trade negotiations.

In line with the above considerations, European institutions enacted Directive **3.41** 92/50[87] on the award procedures relating to public services contracts in an attempt to pave the way for liberalization of services in public markets. The Directive follows the same principles as the rest of the Community's legislation on public procurement, which is compulsory Community-wide advertising of public contracts, prohibition of technical specification capable of discriminating against potential bidders, and uniform application of objective criteria of participation in tendering and award procedures. The Services Directive has introduced a special type of award procedure, namely *design contests*, with reference to planning projects. According to Article 1(g), *design contests* are those national procedures which enable the contracting authority to acquire in the fields of area planning, town planning, architecture, and civil engineering, a plan or a design selected by a jury, after being put out to competition with or without the award of prizes. The award of *design contests*, according to the Services Directive, must follow specific rules. The admission of participants to the contest shall not be limited either by reference to the territory or part of a member state, or on the grounds that, under the law of the member state in which the contest is organized, participants would have been required to be either natural or legal persons. Furthermore, where design contests are restricted to a limited number of participants, the contracting authorities must lay down clear and non-discriminatory selection criteria which ensure sufficient and genuine competition among the participants. The jury shall be composed exclusively of natural persons who are independent.

Under the Services Directive, public services contracts are contracts which have **3.42** as their object the provision of services classified in the *Common Product Classification (CPC) Nomenclature of the United Nations*, as a nomenclature for classification of services at Community level is lacking. The United Nations Common Product Classification covers almost every conceivable service an undertaking may provide, although the services description is rather plain.

The Services Directive is the first legal instrument which attempts to open the increasingly important public services sector to intra-community competition. It should be mentioned that the Directives on Public Supplies, Public Works, and Utilities contain provisions where the provision of services is regarded as ancillary

---

[87] *See* [1992] OJ L209.

to the main contract under their regime, provided that the value of the services is less than the value of the supplies or works. Such services are covered by the relevant Directive.

3.43 Specific services contracts are excluded from the scope of the Services Directive. It should be mentioned that not all of these specific exclusions are listed in the amended Utilities Directive 93/38, because they would not, in any event, fall within the ambit of a defined activity. Apart from those contracts which are covered by the relevant provisions of the Works, Supplies and Utilities Directives, and therefore not considered as services, the other contracts excluded from the Services Directive and amended Utilities Directive 93/38 are:

   (i) contracts for the acquisition or rental, by whatever financial means, of land, existing buildings, or other immovable property or concerning rights thereon. However, financial service contracts concluded at the same time as, before or after the contract of acquisition or rental, in whatever form, will be subject to the Directive;

   (ii) contracts for the acquisition, development, production, or joint production of programme material by broadcasters and contracts for broadcasting time;[88]

   (iii) contracts for voice telephony, telex, radiotelephony, paging and satellite services;[89]

   (iv) contracts for arbitration and conciliation services;

   (v) contracts for financial services in connection with the issue, sale, purchase or transfer of securities or other financial instruments, and central bank services;[90]

   (vi) employment contracts;

   (vii) research and development service contracts other than those where the benefits accrue exclusively to the contracting authority for its use in the conduct of its own affairs, on condition that the service provided is mostly remunerated by the contracting authority.

---

[88] This includes the purchase of, on the one hand, services producing audio-visual works such as films, videos and sound recording, including advertising and, on the other hand broadcasting time (transmission by air, satellite or cable). In principle, these services would be covered but are given derogations in so far as they are connected with broadcasting activities, *see* Armin-Trepte, *Public Procurement in the EC* (CCH Europe, 1993), 101.

[89] These have been excluded because they are not part of the Community liberalization package for the telecommunications services market.

[90] This refers to contracts which constitute transactions concerning shares, for example. In the public sector, it will also include within the derogation contracts awarded to financial intermediaries to arrange such transactions because these are specifically excluded from the scope of investment services (Category 6 of Annex IA). However, this exclusion does not appear in the Utilities Directive so that contracts for the services of intermediaries who will make the arrangements for such transactions would be subject to the provisions of the Utilities Directive; *see* de Graaf, 'The Political Agreement on a Common Position Concerning the Utilities Services Directive', *Public Procurement Law Review*, (1992), 473. Choice of such intermediaries is often difficult in practice since it is quite often made on the basis of the perceived quality of the intermediary or on references from existing clients and past experience. This choice will be made no easier by the application of the procurement rules which do not necessarily best fit such services; see Armin-Trepte, op. cit. (n. 88), 101.

Research and development services contracts are covered in identical terms in both. **3.44**
The exclusion of such contracts under both the Services and the Utilities Directives
lies in the assumption that research and development projects should not be
financed by public funds.[91] However, where research and development contracts
are covered by the procurement rules, a provision in the Utilities Directive allows a
contracting entity to award a contract without a prior call for competition where it
is purely for the purpose of research, experiment, study, or development, and not
for the purpose of ensuring profit or of recovering research and development costs,
and in so far as the award of such contract does not prejudice the competitive award
of subsequent contracts which have in particular these purposes.[92]

Interestingly, service concessions, although included in the draft Directive,[93] have **3.45**
been excluded from the provisions of Directive 92/50. The exclusion of service
concessions falls short of the aspirations to regulate concession contracts for the
public sector under the Works Directive and breaks the consistency in the two
legal instruments. The reasons for the exclusion of service concessions from the
regulatory regime of public procurement could be attributed to the different legal
requirements in member states to delegate powers to concessionaires. The delegation of services by public authorities to private undertakings in some member
states runs contrary to their constitutional provisions.

The Directive adopts a two-tier approach in classifying services procured by **3.46**
contracting authorities. This classification is based on a 'priority' and a 'non-
priority' list of services, according to the relative value of such services in intra-
community trade. *Priority services* include:

— maintenance and repair services;
— land transport services (except for rail transport services), including armoured
   car services and courier services, except transport of mail;
— air transport services of passengers and freight, except transport of mail;
— transport of mail by land and by air;
— telecommunications services (except voice telephony, telex, radiotelephony,
   paging and satellite services);
— financial services including
   i) insurance services
   ii) banking and investment services (except contracts for financial services in
       connection with the issue, sale, purchase or transfer of securities or other
       financial instruments, and central bank services)
— computer and related services;
— research and development services;

---

[91] *See* de Graaf, op. cit. (n. 90) and Armin-Trepte, op. cit. (n. 88).
[92] *See* Art. 20(2)(b) of Utilities Directive 93/38 as amended.
[93] *See* COM (90) 372 final, SYN 293 and COM (91) 322 final, SYN 293.

— accounting, auditing and book-keeping services;
— market research and public opinion polling services;
— management consultant services (except arbitration and conciliation services) and related services;
— architectural services;
— engineering services and integrated engineering services;
— urban planning and landscape architectural services;
— related scientific and technical consulting services;
— technical testing and analysis services;
— advertising services;
— building-cleaning services on a fee or contract basis;
— publishing and printing services on a fee or contract basis;
— sewage and refuse disposal services;
— sanitation and similar services.

Non-priority services include:

— hotel and restaurant services;
— rail transport services;
— water transport services;
— supporting and auxiliary transport services;
— legal services;
— personnel placement and supply services;
— investigation and security services;
— education and vocational education services;
— health and social services;
— recreational, cultural, and sporting services.

3.47 The division is not permanent and the European Commission has the situation under constant review, by assessing the performance of 'non-priority' services sectors. The two-tier approach, in practical terms, means that the award of priority services contracts is subject to the rigorous regime of the Public Procurement Directives (advertisement, selection of tenderers, award procedures, and award criteria), whereas the award of non-priority services contracts must follow the basic rules of non-discrimination and publicity of the results of the award.

3.48 Article 6 of the Services Directive provides for the inapplicability of the Directive to service contracts which are awarded to an entity which is itself a contracting authority within the meaning of the Directive on the basis of an exclusive right which is granted to the contracting authority by a law, regulation, or administrative provision of the member state in question.[94] Article 13 of the

---

[94] This practice resembles the market testing process often employed in the United Kingdom between a contracting authority and an in-house team; *see* Harden, 'Defining the Range of

Utilities Directive provides for the exclusion of certain contracts between contracting authorities and affiliated undertakings.[95] These are service contracts which are awarded to a service provider which is affiliated to the contracting entity, and service contracts which are awarded to a service provider which is affiliated to a contracting entity participating in a joint venture formed for the purpose of carrying out an activity covered by the Directive.[96] The exclusion from the provisions of the Directive is subject, however, to two conditions:the service provider must be an undertaking affiliated to the contracting authority, and at least eighty per cent of its average turnover arising within the European Community for the preceding three years derives from the provision of the same or similar services to undertakings with which it is affiliated. The Commission is empowered to monitor the application of this Article and to request the notification of the names of the undertakings concerned and the nature and value of the service contracts involved.

E. The Compliance Directives

European Community law remains silent as to the availability of remedies to   **3.49** individuals at national level in cases of infringement of primary or secondary legislation. To address the issue of the protection of individuals under Community law when their rights have been violated, one should first seek clarification of a crucial factor:the direct effectiveness of Community law and, in particular, whether an infringement of a directly effective primary or secondary Community provision may be used by individuals before national courts as sufficient ground for an action for damages against the state. As many provisions of Community legislation concerning public procurement (Directives) are deemed to produce direct effect, the question of whether an infringement of them can be considered as a sufficient ground for an action for damages at national level is combined with the duty of national courts to afford an effective protection mechanism (remedies) of the rights conferred on individuals by directly effective Community law. In an

---

Application of the Public Sector Procurement Directives in the United Kingdom', *Public Procurement Law Review*, 1 (1992), 362.

[95] An affiliated undertaking, for the purposes of Art. 1(3) of the Utilities Directive, is an undertaking the annual accounts of which are consolidated with those of the contracting entity in accordance with the requirements of the Seventh Company Law Directive (Council Directive 83/349 [1983] OJ L193/1).

[96] *See* the explanatory memorandum accompanying the text amending the Utilities Directive (COM (91) 347, SYN 361) which states that this provision relates, in particular, to three types of service provision within groups. These categories, which may or may not be distinct, are: the provision of common services such as accounting, recruitment, and management; the provision of specialized services embodying the know-how of the group; and the provision of a specialized service to a joint venture.

attempt to complement the substantive procurement rules enacted by virtue of the Supplies, Works, and Services Directives, and to provide a system of effective protection of individuals in cases of infringements of their provisions, European institutions enacted the Compliance Directive on the harmonization of laws, regulations and administrative provisions relating to the application of review procedures in the award of public works and public supply contracts (Directive 89/665 EC).[97] To encompass the utilities procurement rules, Directive 92/13[98] extends the remedies and review procedures covered by Directive 89/665 to the water, energy, transport, and telecommunications sectors.

3.50 The scope and thrust of the Compliance Directives focuses on the obligation of member states to ensure effective and rapid review of decisions taken by contracting authorities which infringe public procurement provisions. Undertakings seeking relief from damages in the context of a procedure for the award of a contract should not be treated differently under national rules implementing European public procurement laws and under other national rules. This means that the measures to be taken concerning the review procedures should be similar to national review proceedings, without any discriminatory character. Any person having, or having had, an interest in obtaining a particular public supply or public works contract, and who has been, or risks being, harmed by an alleged infringement of public procurement provision, shall be entitled to seek review before national courts. This particular obligation is followed by a stand-still provision concerning the prior notification by the person seeking review to the contracting authority of the alleged infringement and of his intention to seek review. However, with respect to admissibility aspects, there is no qualitative or quantitative definition of the interest of a person in obtaining a public contract. As to the element of potential harm by an infringement of public procurement provisions, it should be cumulative with the first element, that of interest. The prior notification should intend to exhaust any possibility of amicable settlement before the parties have recourse to national courts. A novelty in the Compliance Directive of the utilities sectors[99] is the introduction of the *attestation procedure*. Member states are required to give the contracting entities the possibility of having their purchasing procedures and practices *attested* by persons authorized by law to exercise this function. Under the attestation mechanism, possible irregularities in the award of a public contract may be identified in advanced and provide for the opportunity to contracting authorities to correct them. The latter may include the attestation statement in the notice inviting tenders published in the *Official Journal*. The system appears flexible and cost-efficient and may prevent wasteful litigation. Quite promisingly, the attestation procedure under Directive 92/13

---

97 *See* [1989] OJ L395. 98 *See* [1992] OJ L76/7.
99 *See* Directive 92/13 [1992] OJ L76/7.

will be the essential requirement for the development of European standards of attestation.[100]

F. The Extra-territorial Application of the Public Procurement Regime

(1) The GATT Agreement on Government Procurement

The procurement legal regime of the European Union has been extended in order **3.51** to cover signatories to the GATT Agreement on Government Procurement.[101] Foreign firms (from third countries) can participate in tendering procedures for the award of public contracts from public entities in the common market and vice-versa; European firms can participate in tendering procedures in foreign public markets. The GATT Agreement on Government Procurement embraces the following countries: the USA, Canada, Japan, EFTA countries, Singapore, Hong Kong, and Israel, and it promises considerable improvement in reciprocal market access.

The first Public Procurement Directives were inapplicable to products originating **3.52** in and supplied by third countries. In practical terms, the meaning of this limitation was that a product outside the Community, in order to be subject to a public contract regulated by one of the Directives, had to be lawfully put in free circulation in at least one member state.[102] The Council, being conscious of the above limitation, adopted a Resolution[103] concerning access to Community public supply contracts for products originating in non-member states. At the same time, negotiations in the international framework were being carried out under the GATT Tokyo Round (1973–1979). Finally, on 12 April 1979, the GATT Agreement on Government Procurement (AGP) was concluded and became part of the Community's legal order by virtue of Article 228(2) EC and Council Decision 80/271.[104]

The primary aims of the AGP were similar to those of Supplies Directive 77/62, **3.53** *viz*, transparency of laws and procedures on government procurement and elimination of protection for domestic suppliers and discrimination between foreigner suppliers.[105] However, the AGP provisions went further than those of Directive 77/62 by introducing more favourable conditions for tenders from

---

[100] *See* Art. 7 of Directive 92/13.
[101] *See* Council Regulation 1461/93 ([1993] OJ L146) and EC Council Decision 93/324 ([1993] OJ L125).
[102] For the concept of origin of goods and their lawful free circulation in the common market, *see* Regulation 802/68, [1968] OJ, English Special Edition (1), 165.   [103] See O.J.1977 C11/1.
[104] See O.J.1980 L 215/1.
[105] See Weiss, *Public Procurement in the EC—Public Supply Contracts* (1988) European Law Review.

outside the Community; the AGP was envisaged as the vehicle for establishing an international framework of rights and obligations with respect to government procurement with a view to achieving liberalization and expansion of world trade. As a consequence, third countries or signatories to the AGP are under obligation to provide the same opportunities for access to Community tenderers in their respective public markets, as those provided for by EC member states to undertakings from these countries. Due to the above modifications, Directive 77/62 was amended. The result of this amendment is that the AGP rules are now incorporated in the Supplies regime,[106] which is the only regime in the Public Procurement sector, the application of which produces extra-territorial effects.

3.54   The situation under the AGP (Tokyo Round) rules, which have been incorporated in Directive 88/295 is the following:foreign undertakings (from third countries) which have subsidiaries within the Common Market will have the same access to public supplies contracts as European undertakings and can invoke and enforce Community law both at Community and (mainly) at national level. Obviously, it is required that undertakings from outside the Community must have an economic presence in it. Subsidiaries should take the form of a corporate personality subject to tax laws of the member state within which they operate. It should also be noted that under all Public Procurement Directives, contracting authorities have the right to impose an obligation on one or more undertakings awarded a contract, that the latter take a specific legal form. Suppliers, signatories to the GATT, but not established in the Community, will still be subject to the GATT Agreement on Government Procurement, although they cannot invoke and enforce Community law. They cannot even enforce GATT rules, unless the competent forum (EC member state or third state-GATT signatory) provides for the appropriate remedies. The AGP lays down a rather inoffensive dispute settlement and enforcement procedure, where consultation and conciliation between the aggrieved contractor and the contracting authority play the dominant role. With respect to enforcement of the AGP rules, the Committee on Government Procurement (composed of representatives from each of the Parties), as the body responsible for consultation on matters relating to the operation of the AGP or the furtherance of its objectives has the right to authorize any measure adopted by a Party aiming at suspending the reciprocity principle, between that Party and a Party that refuses access to public markets for undertakings of the former. State retreat represents a very interesting compliance method of international trade, which, however, may result in unsatisfactory consequences, as it represents a complex interrelation of private and public law rights. Undertakings which are non-signatories to GATT may face trade restrictions by

---

[106] See Directives 80/767 and 88/295, *supra*.

member states according to Article 115 EC, which governs the Community's Common external policy.

Despite its promising aims and purposes,[107] the AGP-EC regime on public supplies **3.55** contracts has had a rather limited application as i) it embraced only its signatories, ii) it covers only the supply of products and services that are incidental to the supply contract and not services contracts per se and iii) it applied only to centrally controlled authorities, thus leaving local or regional authorities outside its scope.

The above-mentioned regime has left large areas of procurement activity unregul- **3.56** ated by the GATT or by EC secondary legislation. Works and utilities contracts and supply of services have been excluded. Both Community and global public procurement markets are very promising business fields. The Council in its 1977 Resolution[108] noted that the opening up of the public procurement market in respect of non-Community countries could only be accomplished through reciprocity in treatment and mutual balance of advantages. The reciprocity doctrine or the 'mirror principle' requires that non-member states provide in their domestic markets similar opportunities to those provided by the European member states to undertakings coming from those countries. This means that the element of reciprocity should occur between all European member states and the third country in question. This is a rather unlikely situation, so the Commission in its statement in 1977 concerning Article 115 EC[109] was prepared to permit a limited and controlled use of it by individual member states, which have established economic and commercial relations with non-member countries in the field of Public Procurement. During the Tokyo Round negotiations, the Council noted also that Community undertakings were participating in contracts awarded in third countries. This reveals that reciprocity was a bilateral phenomenon in economic activities between a member state and a third country. At first sight, this appears contradictory with the centralized policy that European institutions seek to apply in the public procurement sector. In this regard, the Commission stated that, in order to prevent deflection of trade between a member state and a third country, it would authorize the former, under Article 115 EC, to exclude from public contracts certain products, originating in third countries, which are in free circulation in another member state, where similar arrangements (reciprocity effects) have been made for products imported directly. In other words, it was thought that the use of Article 115 EC might eliminate the 'free rider' phenomenon and 'protect' the benefits gained through a bilateral trade flow between a member state and a third country. From an economic point of view, this tactic may prevent deflection and diversification of trade, but on the other hand, it creates what is sometimes

---

[107] *See* the FIDE Congress on *The Application in the Member States of the EC Directives on Public Procurement* (Madrid, 1990).   [108] *See* [1977] OJ C11/1.
[109] *See* [1977] OJ C11/2.

more serious: non-tariff barriers to intra-Community trade. It is difficult, in the framework of an economic union such as the EC, to strike the balance between a common external tariff and individual commercial policies pursued by one or more member states.

3.57 One could question the reason that the AGP did not extend its scope to cover works contracts also. It should be recalled that supplies and works contracts were the only regimes covered by Public Procurement Community legislation during the GATT Tokyo Round (1979). A possible answer could be that supply of products was the maximum that could be agreed, at least at the first stage in the cumbersome and laborious negotiations between the European Communities and GATT signatories. Like the EC Treaty, GATT does not prohibit discrimination by government purchasing agencies in favour of national products. Under the EC regime, discrimination based on economic reasons is justified. National authorities may justify their discriminatory purchasing practices invoking concerns for employment and social equity, under the broader goal of promoting greater economic efficiency and industrial adjustment. Under the GATT regime, Article III 8(a) excludes government procurement from the principle of national treatment regarding its regulation. Thus, free movement of goods was considered, with respect to public procurement, to be the first step under the framework of the Multilateral Agreements between the EC and GATT signatories with a view to liberalizing trade and preventing non-tariff barriers arising from national procurement policies.

3.58 Another possible justification of the limitation of the AGP rules to supplies of goods only could have been that works and construction contracts involve further aspects that must be taken into account in an attempt to liberalize their regime. They involve social and regional policy, short and long term employment considerations, peripheral development of the EC regions, etc. Liberalizing the public works regime between the Community and third countries will not only bring into play free trade area considerations (free movement of goods), but will also go further, trespassing on the field of economic union, where labour, capital, payments and services need also to circulate freely.[110]

3.59 The Utilities Directive 90/531 intends to open up procurement practices in the four previously excluded sectors—water, energy, telecommunications and transport-mainly to EC-wide competition. With regard to goods (and services) originating in third countries, things are more complicated. A product outside the Community, in order to be subject to a public contract regulated by one of the EC Public Procurement Directives, must lawfully be put in free circulation in at least one

---

[110] See Gormley, *Some reflections on Public Procurement in the EC,* (Nov.1990) European Business Law Review.

member state.[111] Except where there has been an international agreement which grants comparable and effective access for Community undertakings to public markets of a third country (reciprocity principle), Article 29 of Directive 90/531 renders it possible for EC contracting authorities in the utilities sector to reject offers from outside the Community and requires Community preference where Community offers are equivalent to offers from third countries (where the price difference does not exceed 3%). With reference to an international agreement granting access to public markets, Directive 90/531 opens the door for the application of the GATT Agreement on Government Procurement in the utilities sector, concluded between the European Community and 11 GATT signatories during the GATT Tokyo Round in 1979. The AGP embraces only supplies contracts, which are currently the only public sector regime open to international competition. The European Union's commitment towards international liberalization of public markets has been demonstrated by its offer to the GATT AGP signatories during the Uruguay Round, to eliminate all discrimination regarding contracts in urban transport, ports, airports, and heavy electrical and telecommunications equipment.[112]

Expansion of the AGP framework to embrace supplies and works contracts in the **3.60** utilities sector and services contracts has being pursued during the GATT Uruguay Round.[113] The new regime introduced substantial changes in the application of the AGP with respect to types of contracts and coverage of contracting authorities as well as remedies. Works and services contracts are now covered and the list of contracting authorities embraces not only central government departments and their agencies, but regional and local authorities, and some utilities in the form of public authorities or public undertakings. Certain exemptions between the signatories do apply but, based on bilateral agreements, the new regime promises a significant expansion of the existing European procurement legislation.[114]

With respect to EFTA countries, the EC reached an agreement on 22 October **3.61** 1991 with the seven states (European Economic Area) to participate in the Single Market from 1 January 1993. This will change the so far existing framework under the preferential agreement regime existing until 1991[115] to a free trade area, as the EFTA states will be required to implement Community law, and, of course,

---

[111] For the concept of origin of goods and their lawful free circulation in the Common Market see Regulation 802/68, [1968] OJ, English Special Edition (1), 165.

[112] *See* Council Regulation 1461/93 on access to public contracts for tenderers from the United States [1993] OJ L146; Council Decision 93/323 on the conclusion of agreement between the EC and USA on government procurement [1993] OJ L125.

[113] Art. XXIV 1 AGP, signed on 15 April 1994 by all the previous signatories except Hong Kong and Singapore.

[114] The applicability of the new GPA by its signatories is subject to its ratification before 1 January 1996.

[115] *See* Weiss, 'The Law of Public Procurement in EFTA and the EC; The Legal Framework and its Implementation', *Yearbook of European Law*, 1987.

EC Public Procurement Directives in their national legal orders. The regime applies also to Hungary and Poland, by virtue of their Association Agreements.[116]

(2) The WTO Government Procurement Agreement

3.62 The Government Procurement Agreement (GPA) is based on a number of general principles, which depict the principles of the old AGP regime. The most important of them is the principle of *national treatment*. Under this principle, the parties to the GPA must give the same treatment afforded to national providers and products to providers and products of other signatory states. Reinforcing the principle of national treatment, the *most favoured nation* (MFN) principle guarantees treatment no less favourable than that afforded to other parties. In addition to the above principles, the principle of *non-discrimination* prohibits discrimination against local firms on grounds of the degree of their foreign affiliation or ownership, or on the grounds of origin of the goods or services where these have been produced in one of the states which is party to the Agreement.

3.63 The GPA stipulates a set of procedures for contracting authorities in the signatory parties which must be followed when awarding contracts within its scope. These procedures aim to ensure transparency and openness, as well as objectivity and legitimacy, in the award of public contracts, and to facilitate cross-border trade between the signatories. The influence of the European Community on the GPA regime is apparent, an indication of the maturity and validity of the regulatory process of the European public markets integration. The procedures are, however, less strict than those applicable for the award of public sector contracts under the Community regime, and depict the integral flexibility envisaged by the regulatory regime for utilities procurement.

3.64 The GPA intends to regulate access specifically to the government procurement markets. General market access between the signatories is, in principle, dealt with under other agreements, notably the GATT (on the import of goods) and the GATS (on access to services markets). The detailed scope and coverage of the GPA with regard to the entities covered, the type of procurement, and monetary thresholds is set out in Appendix I of the Agreement. The Agreement applies in principle to all bodies which are deemed as 'contracting authorities' for the purposes of the European Public Sector Directives. With reference to utilities, the GPA applies to entities which carry out one or more of certain listed 'utility' activities, where these entities are either 'public authorities' or 'public undertakings', in the sense of the Utilities Directive. However, the GPA does not cover entities operating in the utilities sector on the basis of *special and exclusive rights*. The utility activities which are covered include: (i) activities connected with the

---

[116] *See* [1993] OJ L347/36 and [1993] OJ L348/36.

provision of water through fixed networks; (ii) activities concerned with the provision of electricity through fixed networks; (iii) the provision of terminal facilities to carriers by sea or inland waterway; and (iv) the operation of public services in the field of transport by automated systems, tramway, trolley bus, or bus or cable. The provision of public transport services by rail is included in principle, but there is exclusion for entities listed in Annex VI of the European Utilities Directive, designed to exclude non-urban transport services. However, the trust of the applicability of the GPA in relation to utilities activities appears short in comparison with that under the European regime. Activities connected with the distribution of gas or heat, and the exploration or extraction of fuel are notable exceptions from the GPA's ambit.

The thresholds for the applicability of the GPA regime to public contracts of **3.65** signatories are as follows: For supplies and services it is SDR 130,000 for central government; 200,000 for local government; and 400,000 for all contracts in the utilities sectors (including those awarded by central and local government). For works contracts, the threshold is SDR 5 million, for all entities.

Although in principle the GPA regime represents a significant improvement in **3.66** relation to the old AGP regime in terms of coverage and thrust, certain important derogations from its applicability would result in diluting the principal aims and objectives envisaged by the signatories. As far as central or federal government works and supply contracts are concerned, the Agreement is expected to facilitate market access and enhance cross-border trade patterns in public contracts. However, for contracts relating to services and for certain contracts in the utilities sector, as well as for contracts awarded by local, municipal or regional authorities, the effect of the Agreement appears considerably moderate. A number of signatories have been unable, or unwilling, to offer for coverage all of their entities or contracts in the above categories. Political and legal particularities in the systems of the signatories have prevented similar coverage between the parties. In addition, by applying the principle of *reciprocity* in negotiating the GPA, the result would probably have been very similar to the old AGP regime in covering central or federal public contracts. The solution to this apparently fundamental deadlock was to be found in a rather peculiar method. Each signatory should effectively negotiate with each other signatory, to come to a satisfactory agreement on coverage based on reciprocity on a bilateral basis. This approach constitutes a significant departure from the premise of the *principle of most favoured nation* (MFN) and has resulted in some considerable divergence in the applicability of the GPA by virtue of derogations and limitations imposed by signatories on access to their public markets. Thus, for example, coverage in the utilities sector does not apply to Canada, since that country did not commit itself to opening its own markets to the European Community. When the Agreement was first concluded in December 1993, there was also no coverage for utilities with respect to the United

States, but there have since been modifications to the EC-US coverage as a result of a subsequent EC-US bilateral agreements. Also outside the coverage of the Agreement in the utilities sector is, in relation to Japan, urban transport and electricity; in relation to South Korea, urban transport and airports; and in relation to Israel, urban transport. There are also significant derogations for certain categories of services and for specified types of equipment.

3.67 The scope and coverage the GPA, as well as the structure of its applicability present a unique instrument of international law which is based on a series of bilateral agreements rather than a multilateral arrangement. This represents a significant compromise of the most favoured nation principle, which is a fundamental premise of the majority of international trade agreements. Members of the World Trade Organisation joining the GPA, at their discretion, need to reach separate agreements on the scope of coverage with all existing parties to the Agreement. The GPA thus, has acquired a *plurilaterality* status, a fact that weakens its thrust and complicates its applicability.

G. The Concepts and Principles of Public Procurement Regulation

(1) Concepts of public procurement regulation

3.68 The internal structure of the public procurement law intends to embrace all the phases of the purchasing behaviour of the demand side of the equation (the contracting authorities) in an attempt to introduce the envisaged regulatory system. Of paramount importance to the internal structure of the EC Public Procurement Directives, is the comprehensive and clear definition of the term *contracting authorities*, a factor which would determine the applicability of the relevant rules. The term *contracting authorities*, for the purposes of public purchasing regulation, should not pose considerable conceptual difficulties; it should cover authorities which disperse public funds in pursuit of or on behalf of public interest. EC public procurement law characterizes as contracting authorities the state and its organs interpreted in functional terms. The term *state* covers central, regional, municipal, and local government departments. The above contracting authorities are primarily responsible for the core procurement requirements of supplies, works, and services in a society. The Public Procurement Directives include detailed lists of all central and regional government departments that fall under their ambit.[117] However, the state in its function as a procurer of goods, works, and services does not contain a range of purchasing operations which are attributed to its *organs*. By

---

[117] *See* the Annexes attached to the Public Procurement Directives.

the term *organs*, procurement law has envisaged all entities which somehow deliver public interest functions and has described them as *bodies governed by public law*. The latter category is subject to a set of cumulative criteria[118] in order to be classified as contracting authorities for the purposes of the Directives. *Bodies governed by public law* must be established for the specific purpose of meeting needs in the general public interest. Although they must have legal personality, their operations should not have industrial or commercial character. These entities must be financed, for the most part, by either the central government, or regional or local authorities, as well as be under their management and supervision control.

Contracting authorities for the purposes of public procurement law also include **3.69** entities which are considered part of the state and its organs *in functional terms*. The definition of *authorities awarding contracts* under the public works regime was sought through reference procedures by a Dutch court.[119] In particular, the European Court of Justice was requested to clarify whether a *local land consolidation committee* could fall within Article 1(b) of Directive 71/305. Pursuant to that provision, the state, regional. or local authorities, and legal persons governed by public law, are to be regarded as *authorities awarding contracts*. The consolidation committee in question had no legal personality, but its functions and compositions were specifically governed by legislation. The Court interpreted the term *state* in functional terms and considered that the local consolidation committee, which depended on the relevant public authorities for the appointment of its members, was subject to their supervision of its operations and had as its main task the financing and award of public works contracts, as falling within the notion of *state* for the purpose of the above-mentioned provision (Article 1(b)), even though it was not part of the state administration in *formal terms*.[120] The Court held that the aim of the Public Works Directive 71/305, which was to ensure the effective attainment of freedom of establishment and freedom to provide services in respect of public works contracts, would be jeopardized if the provisions of the Directive were to be held to be inapplicable, solely because a public works contract is awarded by a body, which, although it was set up to carry out tasks entrusted to it by legislation, was not formally part of the state's administration.

The enactment of the Utilities Directive brought an end to the exclusion of **3.70** procurement of entities operating in the water, energy, transport, and telecommunications sectors of the member states. A wide range of these entities is covered by the term *bodies governed by public law*, which is used by the Utilities Directives for the contracting entities operating in the relevant sectors.[121] Interestingly,

---

[118] *See* Art. 1(b) of Directive 93/36 and Art. 1(b) of Directive 93/37.
[119] *See* Case C-31/87, *Gebroeders Beentjes BV v. State of Netherlands* [1988] ECR 4635.
[120] *See* Case 249/81, *Commission v. Ireland* [1982] ECR 4005.
[121] *See* Art. 1(1) of Directive 93/38.

another category of contracting authorities under the Utilities Directives includes *public undertakings*.[122] The term indicates any undertaking over which the state may exercise direct or indirect dominant influence by means of ownership, or by means of financial participation, or by means of laws and regulations which govern the public undertaking's operation. Dominant influence can be exercised in the form of majority holding of the undertaking's subscribed capital, in the form of majority controlling of the undertaking's issued shares, or, finally, in the form of the right to appoint the majority of the undertaking's management board. Public undertakings cover utilities operators which have been granted exclusive rights of exploitation of a service. Irrespective of their ownership, they are subject to the Utilities Directive in as much as the *exclusivity* of their operation precludes other entities from entering the relevant market under substantially the same competitive conditions. Privatized utilities could, in principle, be excluded from the procurement rules when a genuinely competitive regime[123] within the relevant oligopsonistic market structure would rule out purchasing patterns based on non-economic considerations.

3.71 Under the Tokyo Round GATT Agreement on Government Procurement, the term *public authorities* confined itself to central governments and their agencies only.[124] The new World Trade Organisation Government Procurement Agreement applies in principle to all bodies which are deemed as 'contracting authorities' for the purposes of the Public Supplies and Public Works Directives. As far as utilities are concerned, the GPA applies to entities which carry out one or more of certain listed 'utility' activities,[125] where these entities are either 'public authorities' or 'public undertakings', in the sense of the Utilities Directive. However, the GPA does not cover entities operating in the utilities sector on the basis of *special and exclusive rights*.

(2) The principle of mandatory advertisement and publication of public contracts

3.72 One of the most important principles of the Public Procurement Directives is the principle of transparency. The principle of transparency serves two main

---

[122] *See* Art. 1(2) of Directive 93/38.

[123] The determination of a genuinely competitive regime is left to the utilities operators themselves. *See* Case C 392/93, *The Queen and HM Treasury, ex parte British Telecommunications Plc* [1993] OJ C287/6. This is perhaps a first step towards self-regulation which could lead to the disengagement of the relevant contracting authorities from the public procurement regime.

[124] Council Decision 87/565 [1987] OJ L345.

[125] The listed utility activities which are covered under the new GPA include: (i) activities connected with the provision of water through fixed networks; (ii) activities concerned with the provision of electricity through fixed networks; (iii) the provision of terminal facilities to carriers by sea or inland waterway; and (iv) the operation of public services in the field of transport by automated systems, tramway, trolley bus, or cable bus.

objectives: the first is to introduce a system of openness in public purchasing of the member states, so a greater degree of accountability should be established and potential direct discrimination on grounds of nationality should be eliminated. The second objective aims at ensuring that transparency in public procurement represents a substantial basis for a system of best practice for both parts of the equation, but in particular relevant to the supply side, to the extent that the latter has a more *proactive* role in determining the needs of the demand side. Transparency in public procurement is achieved through community-wide publicity and advertisement of public procurement contracts over certain thresholds by means of publication of three types of notices in the *Official Journal of the European Union*:

i. Periodic Indicative Notices (PIN). Every contracting authority must notify its intentions for public procurement contracts within the forthcoming financial year.[126] By doing so, it provides for an estimate intention of its purchasing and gives the supply side the necessary time for planning and response to future contract opportunities. The publication of Periodic Indicative Notices, if properly observed, also serves as a useful indicator in determining the relevant market size for the supply side, as well as the relevant procurement magnitude for a type of contracting authorities on an annual basis. The fact that, through PIN notices, contracting authorities produce only an estimated figure for forthcoming contracts they intend to award, does not absolve them from their responsibilities in strictly adhering to their publication. The Commission brought the Italian State before the European Court of Justice[127] for a declaration that it had not observed EC law, for failing to communicate by publication in the *Official Journal*, an indicative notice summarizing all the contracts which the Italian Ministry of Finance planned to award during that year, and then by failing to publish a notice inviting tenders for the concession of the system for the computerization of the lottery.

ii. Invitations to tender. All contracts above the relevant thresholds should be tendered, and the notice containing the invitation to tender must include the award procedures and the award criteria for the contract in question.[128] The invitation to tender is the most important publicity and advertisement requirement for the creating of transparent and open public markets in the European Community. The publication of the invitation to tender refers

---

[126] *See* Art. 9(1) of Directive 93/36; Art. 11(1) to (3) of Directive 93/37; Art. 22(1)(a) to (c) of Directive 93/38; Art. 15(1) of Directive 92/50.

[127] *See* Case C-272/91 R, *Commission v Italy (Lottomatica)*, and the orders of 31 January 1992 and 12 June 1992 [1994] ECR I-1409.

[128] *See* Art. 9(2) of Directive 93/36; Art. 11(2) of Directive 93/37; Art. 21 of Directive 93/38; Art. 15(2) of Directive 92/50.

only to a particular contract or a range of similar contracts of repetitive nature, and provides the supply side with the opportunity to respond and make an offer in order to meet the needs and requirements of the demand side. The invitation to tender is part of the contractual nexus in the public procurement process between the relevant contracting authority and the tenderers/candidates competing for the award of the contract in question. It is through the invitation to tender that the supply side has a clear view as to the award procedures and the award criteria which contracting authorities intend to utilize, thus being able to respond accordingly. The invitation to tender represents the first step towards the award of public contracts, and failure by contracting authorities to adhere to the minimum requirements specified in the Directives, could invalidate the whole process.

iii. Contract Award Notices (CAN). This is a form of notification after the award of the contract of the successful tenderer and the price of its offer, as well as the reasons for its selection by the contracting authority.[129] In principle, Contract Award Notices publicize the reasoning of contracting authorities during the selection and award stages of the process, but quite often price information of the successful tenderers and other candidates is withheld for reasons of commercial confidentiality. The publication of CAN notices can be used as an effective indicator in monitoring the purchasing patterns of contracting authorities, as well as in providing a picture relevant to the tradability of public contracts.

3.73 All types of notices are published by the Publications Office of the European Communities. Within twelve days (or five days in the case of the accelerated form of restricted or negotiated procedures), the Publications Office publishes the notices in the Supplement to the *Official Journal* and via the TED (Tenders Electronic Daily) database. Two notices are published in full in their original language only, and in summary form in the other Community languages. The Publications Office takes responsibility for the necessary translations and summaries. The cost of publishing notices in the Supplement to the *Official Journal* is borne by the Community.

(a) The monetary applicability of the rules

3.74 The European rules of public procurement and all the requirements and procedures laid down therein are triggered only if certain value thresholds are met. The application of the Directives is subject to monetary considerations in relation to the value of the relevant contracts. There is a clear-cut distinction of coverage of the public procurement rules upon contracts representing transactions between

---

[129] *See* Art. 9(3) of Directive 93/36; Art. 11(5) of Directive 93/37; Art. 24 of Directive 93/38; Art. 16(1) of Directive 92/50.

the public sector and the industry of a certain economic substance and volume. Contracts below the required thresholds are not subject to the rigorous regime envisaged by the Directives. However, contracting authorities are under the explicit obligation to avoid discrimination on nationality grounds and apply all the provisions related to the fundamental principles of the Treaties of Rome and Maastricht. The thresholds laid down are as follows:

— ECU 5 million for all work and construction projects.[130]
— ECU 200,000 for supplies contracts within the European Union,[131] and ECU 136,000 for supplies contracts from third countries[132] which participate in the WTO Government Procurement Agreement.
— ECU 600,000 for supplies of telecommunication equipment under the Utilities Directive,[133] and ECU 400,000 for all other supplies contracts awarded by public utilities.[134]
— ECU 200,000 for services contracts.[135]

One could question the reason behind the separation of public procurement **3.75** regulation into dimensional and sub-dimensional nature as a result of the relevant thresholds. Interestingly enough, it was thought that contracts above the thresholds laid down by the Directives could embrace the majority of the public procurement requirements in the member states, thus eliminating the danger of discriminatory public purchasing for those contracts left outside the ambit of the Directives. However, a careful monitoring of procurement systems in the member states has revealed that sub-dimensional procurement appears at least three times the size of dimensional public purchasing,[136] a fact that renders the application of the Directives only partly responsible for the integration of public markets in the European Community.

The way in which the value of a contract is calculated is crucial for the application **3.76** of the relevant Directive. To ensure that identical calculation methods are used throughout the member states of the European Community, and to prevent intentional avoidance of the procurement Directives by artificially low contract valuations, the Directives lay down specific rules.[137] Where the contract is to be concluded in the form of a lease, rental or hire-purchase agreement, the calculation method varies according to the duration of the contract. The estimated value

---

[130] *See* Art. 3(1) of Directive 93/37; Art. 14(c) of Directive 93/38.
[131] *See* Art. 5(1)(a) of Directive 93/36. [132] *See* Art. 5(1)(c) of Directive 93/36.
[133] *See* Art. 14(b) of Directive 93/38. [134] *See* Art. 14(a) of Directive 93/38.
[135] *See* Art. 7(1) of Directive 92/50.
[136] *See* European Commission, *The Use of Negotiated Procedures as a Non-Tariff Barrier in Public Procurement*, Brussels, CC 9364, 1995.
[137] *See* Art. 5(2) to (6) of Directive 93/36; Art. 6(1) to (5) of Directive 93/37; Art. 14(4) to (13) of Directive 93/38; Art. 7(2) to (8) of Directive 92/50.

is to be calculated on the basis of the following requirements:

— where its term is twelve months or less, the total value for the contract's duration;
— where its term exceeds twelve months, the total value for the contract's duration, including the estimated residual value of the products;
— where the contract is concluded for an indefinite period or where its term cannot be defined, the monthly value multiplied by forty-eight;
— where contracts are of a regular nature or are to be renewed over a given period, the following must be taken into account:
— either the actual aggregate value of similar successive contracts awarded over the previous twelve months or accounting period, adjusted where possible for anticipated changes in quantity or value over the subsequent twelve months;
— or the estimated aggregate value of the successive contracts concluded during the twelve months following the initial delivery or accounting periods where this exceeds twelve months. In any event, the choice between these two valuation methods must not be made with the intention of keeping contracts outside the scope of the Directive.

3.77 If a proposed procurement of supplies of the same type may lead to contracts being awarded at the same time in separate lots, the estimated value of all the lots must be taken into account. If it reaches the relevant threshold, all the lots must be awarded in compliance with the Directive. The same rules apply when estimating the value of leasing, rental or hire-purchase contracts. Where provision is explicitly made for options, the basis for calculating the estimated contract value must be the highest possible total permitted for the purchase, lease, rental, or hire options included.

3.78 When calculating the value of a public works contract, account has to be taken of the estimated value of the works and of the estimated value of the supplies needed to carry out the works, even if these supplies are made available to the contractor by the contracting authorities. The estimated value of work which the contracting authority intends to have carried out later by the contractor awarded the current contract, and which consists in a repetition of the work to be carried out under the current contract, must be included in the contract value.

3.79 The Works Directive provides for special rules when a contract is subdivided into several lots. When the aggregate value of the lots is over 5 million ECU, the provisions of the Directive apply to all lots. A work or a contract may not be split up with the intention of avoiding the applicability of the Directive. However, lots of a value, net of VAT, less than 1 million ECU may be exempted from the scope of the Directive, provided that the total estimated value of all the lots exempted does not exceed twenty per cent of the total estimated value of all lots.

(b) Selection and qualification

After the advertisement and publicity requirements the next phase in the public **3.80** procurement process is the selection and qualification of the tenderers. At this stage, contracting authorities vet all the responses received and determine the suitability of the candidates according to objectively defined criteria which aim at eliminating arbitrariness and discrimination. The selection criteria are determined through two major categories of qualification requirements: i) legal, and ii) technical/economic. Contracting authorities must strictly follow the homogeneously-specified selection criteria for enterprises participating in the award procedures of public procurement contracts, in an attempt to abolish potential grounds for discrimination on grounds of nationality and exclude technical specifications which are capable of favouring national undertakings.

On the Procurement Directives relating to the criteria of a tenderer's good **3.81** standing and are directly effective.[138] These criteria comprise grounds for exclusion from participation in the award of public contracts, such as bankruptcy, professional misconduct, failure to fulfil social security obligations, and obligations relating to taxes. They also refer to the technical ability and knowledge of the contractor, where proof of these may be furnished by educational or professional qualifications, previous experience in performing public contracts, and statements on the contractor's expertise. In construction projects, the references which the form of certificates issued or invitation to tender.[139] They include the contractor's educational and professional qualifications or those responsible for carrying out the works; and a list of the works carried out over the past five years, accompanied by certificates of satisfactory execution for the most important works. These certificates shall indicate the value, date, and site of the works and shall specify whether they were carried out according to the rules of the trade and properly completed. Where necessary, the competent authority shall submit these certificates direct to the authority awarding the contracts; a statement of the tools, plant, and technical equipment available to the contractor for carrying out the work; a statement of the firm's average annual manpower and number of managerial staff for the last three years; and a statement of the technicians or technical divisions which the contractor can call upon for carrying out the work, whether or not they belong to the firm.

On the other hand, in supplies contracts, the references which may be requested[140] **3.82** must be mentioned in the invitation to tender and are the following: a list of the principal deliveries effected in the past three years, with the sums, dates, and recipients, public or private, involved in the form of certificates issued or countersigned

---

[138] *See* Case C-76/81, *SA Transporoute et Travaux v. Minister of Public Works* [1982] ECR 457.
[139] *See* Art. 27 of Directive 93/37 and Art. 31 of Directive 93/38.
[140] *See* Art. 22 of Directive 93/36.

by the competent authority; a description of the undertaking's technical facilities, its measures for ensuring quality, and its study and research facilities; an indication of the technicians or technical bodies involved, whether or not belonging directly to the undertaking, especially those responsible for quality control; samples, descriptions or photographs of the products to be supplied, the authenticity of which must be certified if the contracting authority so requests; certificates drawn up by official quality-control institutes or agencies of recognized competence attesting to conformity with certain specifications or standards of goods clearly identified by references to specifications or standards; and, where the goods to be supplied are complex or, exceptionally, are required for a special purpose, a check carried out by the contracting authorities (or on their behalf by a competent official body of the country in which the supplier is established, subject to that body's agreement) on the production capacities of the supplier and, if necessary, on his study and research facilities and quality control measures. The provisions covering the contractors' eligibility and technical capacity constitute an exhaustive list.

3.83 In principle, there are automatic grounds for exclusion,[141] when a contractor, supplier or service provider: i) is bankrupt or is being wound up; ii) is the subject of proceedings for a declaration of bankruptcy or for an order for compulsory winding up; iii) has been convicted for an offence concerning his professional conduct; iv) has been guilty of grave professional misconduct; v) has not fulfilled obligations relating to social security contributions; and vi) has not fulfilled obligations relating to the payment of taxes.

3.84 However, for the purposes of assessing the financial and economic standing of contractors, an exception to the exhaustive list covering the contractors' eligibility and technical capacity is provided for,[142] where, in particular, contracting entities may request references other than those expressly mentioned therein. Evidence of financial and economic standing may be provided[143] by means of references including: i) appropriate statements from bankers; ii) the presentation of the firm's balance sheets or extracts from the balance sheets where these are published under company law provisions; and iii) a statement of the firm's annual turnover and the turnover on construction works for the three previous financial years. The non-exhaustive character of the list of references in relation to the contractors' economic and financial standing was recognized by the European Court of Justice,[144] where the value of the works which may be carried out at one time may

---

[141] *See* Art. 20 of Directive 93/36; Art. 24 of Directive 93/37; Art. 31 of Directive 93/38; Art. 29 of Directive 92/50.   [142] *See* Art. 25 of Directive 71/305.

[143] *See* Art. 22 of Directive 93/36; Art. 26 of Directive 93/37; Art. 31(b) of Directive 93/38; Art. 31 of Directive 92/50.

[144] *See* Case C-27/86, *Constructions et Enterprises Industrielles SA (CEI) v. Association Intercommunale pour les Autoroutes des Ardennes*; Case 28/86, *Ing. A. Bellini & Co. SpA v. Regie de Bâtiments*; Case 29/86, *Ing. A. Bellini & Co. SpA. v. Belgian State* [1987] ECR 3347.

constitute a proof of the contractors' economic and financial standing. The contracting authorities are allowed to fix such a limit, as the provisions of the public procurement Directives do not aim at delimiting the powers of member states, but at determining the references or evidence which may be furnished in order to establish the contractors' financial and economic standing. The Court in another case referred to it by a Dutch court[145] maintained that the examination of a contractor's suitability based on its good standing and qualifications and its financial and economic standing may take place simultaneously with the award procedures of a contract.[146] However, the two procedures (the suitability evaluation and bid evaluation) are totally distinct processes which should not be confused.[147]

(c) Legal requirements for the qualification of contractors

The definition of a contractor wishing to submit a tender for the award of a public **3.85** contract comprises any legal or natural person involved in supplies, construction, or services activities. It also includes private consortia, as well as joint ventures or groupings. Contracting authorities may impose a requirement as to the form and legal status of the contractor that wins the award.[148] This requirement focuses only on the post selection stage, after the award of the contract, and indicates the need for legal certainty. Specific legal form and status required by contracting entities facilitates monitoring of the performance of the contract and allows better access to justice in case of a dispute between the contracting entity and the undertaking in question. The successful contractor should also fulfil certain qualitative requirements concerning his eligibility and technical capacity[149] and his financial and economic standing. An opportunity to elaborate on consortia participation under Public Procurement Directives occurred in 1992 when the Belgian *Raad van Staat* asked the European Court of Justice for a preliminary ruling on the interpretation of the relevant provisions of the Works Directives, which were in dispute in a case before the former.[150] The national litigation concerned with the dispute of a holding company against the Belgian State for failure to include the former in an official list of recognized contractors for future public works contracts, on the grounds that the holding company did not possess any technical expertise in relation to construction projects. The Works Directives require

---

145 *See* Case C-31/87, *Gebroeders Beentjes BV v. State of Netherlands* [1988] ECR 4635.

146 *See Bellini*, Case C-28/86 [1987] ECR 3347, op. cit.

147 *See* Case C-71/92, *Commission v. Spain* [1993] ECR I-5923.

148 *See* Art. 21 of Directive 71/305 as amended by Directive 89/440, and Art. 18 of Directive 77/62 as amended by Directive 88/295. The same regime is followed in the Utilities Directive 90/531, Art. 26, and the Services Directive 92/50, Art. 26.

149 *See* Arts. 20 to 23 of Directive 77/62; Arts. 23 *et seq.* of Directive 71/305; Arts. 29 *et seq.* of Directive 90/531; Arts. 29 *et seq.* of Directive 92/50.

150 *See* Case C-389/92, *Ballast Nedam Groep NV v. Belgische Staat* [1994] 2 CMLR.

specific qualitative technical criteria for selection of tenderers (Articles 23 to 26 of the Works Directive 71/305) and the official list of recognized contractors refers to these criteria (Article 28 of the Works Directive 71/305). The Court proceeded by endorsing the wide interpretation of the definition of works contracts under the original Works Directive 71/304 and under the amending Works Directive 88/295, and declared that, even when an undertaking does not possess the relevant expertise to perform the actual works, contracting authorities by no means should exclude it from tendering procedures. The Court also made reference to the explicit provision of group tendering through consortia and the obligation of contracting authorities to require specific legal personality from the group only after the award of the contract to that group.

(d) Lists of recognized contractors

3.86 Registration in lists of recognized contractors that exist in various member states may be used by contractors as an alternative means of proving their suitability, also before contracting authorities of other member states.[151] Information deduced from registration in an official list may not be questioned by contracting authorities. Nonetheless, the actual level of financial and economic standing, and technical knowledge or ability, required of contractors is determined by the contracting authorities. Consequently, contracting authorities are required to accept that a contractor's financial and economic standing, and technical knowledge and ability, are sufficient for works corresponding to his classification only in so far as that classification is based on equivalent criteria with respect to the capacities required.

3.87 A reference for a preliminary ruling from the *Conseil d'Etat* of the Grand Duchy of Luxembourg was made to the European Court of Justice[152] in an attempt to clarify the relevant provisions. An establishment permit imposed by national legislation[153] on foreign undertakings seeking to participate in the award of public works and public supplies contracts was held incompatible with the relevant provisions of the Public Works Directive 71/305 and Article 59 EC (the freedom to provide services). The Court held that official registration in a list in a member state[154] constitutes a means of proving, before the authority of another member state awarding contracts, that the tenderer satisfies the qualitative criteria referring to the technical capacity and ability specified in the Directives.[155] In another similar case referred by a national court,[156] the European Court maintained that the inclusion of a contractor

---

151 *See* Art. 25 of Directive 93/36; Art. 29 of Directive 93/37; Art. 35 of Directive 92/50.
152 *See* Case C-76/81, *SA Transporoute et Travaux v. Minister of Public Works* [1982] ECR 457.
153 *See Reglement Grand-Ducal du 6 Novembre 1974.*
154 *See* Arts. 24 and 28(3) of the Public Works Directive 71/305.
155 *See* Arts. 23 to 26 of the Public Works Directive 71/305.
156 *See* Case C-27/86, *Constructions et Enterprises Industrielles SA (CEI) v. Association Intercommunale pour les Autoroutes des Ardennes*; Case 28/86, *Ing. A. Bellini & Co. SpA v. Regie de Bâtiments*; Case 29/86, *Ing. A. Bellini & Co. SpA. v. Belgian State* [1987] ECR 3347.

in an official list of recognized contractors in a member state may be used as an alternative means of proving, before the authority of another member state awarding contracts, the qualitative criteria listed in the relevant Directive. However, as harmonization of official lists of recognized contractors concerns only the references attesting to financial and economic standing, and their technical knowledge and ability, the criteria for their classifications are not harmonized. In regard to evidence of contractors' economic and financial standing, and good standing and qualifications, registration in a official list of recognized contractors may replace the references laid down in the provisions relating to technical requirements and ability, as well as financial and economic standing, in so far as such registration is based upon *mutually equivalent* information.[157] Thus, a request from a contractor recognized in another member state to furnish proof that his undertaking has the minimum funds, manpower, and managerial staff required by the domestic law of the contracting authority is compatible with Directive 71/305. The possible rejection of his tender by the awarding authority, if he fails to meet these domestic provisions, would appear legitimate even if the tenderer is recognized in a class equivalent to that required by domestic law governing the conditions of the contract to be awarded.

(3) The principle of non-discrimination in public procurement regulation

(a) Tendering procedures

Participation in tendering procedures is channelled through open, negotiated or restricted procedures. **3.88**

— Open procedures are those where every interested supplier, contractor, or service provider may submit an offer.[158]

— Negotiated procedures[159] are such procedures for the award of public contracts whereby contracting authorities consult contractors of their choice and negotiate the terms of the contract with one or more of them. In most cases they follow restricted procedures and they are heavily utilized under framework agreements in the Utilities sectors.[160] There are two different kinds of negotiated procedures: i) negotiated procedures with prior notification, and ii) negotiated procedures without prior notification.

---

[157] *See* Bovis, 'The Eligibility of Enterprises to Participate in Tenders for the Award of Public Procurement Contracts', *European Business Law Review*, 5 (January 1994), 1–36.

[158] *See* Art. 1(d) of Directive 93/36; Art. 1(e) of Directive 93/37; Art. 1(7)(a) of Directive 93/38; Art. 1(d) of Directive 92/50.

[159] *See* Art. 1(f) of Directive 93/36; Art. 1(g) of Directive 93/37; Art. 1(7)(c) of Directive 93/38; Art. 1(c) of Directive 92/50.

[160] *See* the section on framework agreements under *Specific Types of Contracts under the Public Procurement Directives*, op. cit.

i. Negotiated procedures with prior notification[161] provide for selection of candidates in the first round, all interested contractors may submit their tenders, and the contracting authority selects, from the candidates, those who will be invited to negotiate. In the second round, negotiations with various candidates take place and the successful tender is selected. In principle, the minimum number of candidates to be selected is three, provided that there are a sufficient number of suitable candidates.

ii. Negotiated procedures without prior notification[162] are the least restrictive of the various award procedures laid down in the Directive and may be conducted in one single round. Contracting authorities are allowed to choose whichever contractor they want, begin negotiations directly with this contractor, and award the contract to him. The Directive provides for only a few rules with which this procedure must comply. A prior notice in the *Official Journal* is not required.

— Finally, restricted procedures[163] are those procedures for the award of public contracts whereby only those contractors invited by the contracting authority may submit tenders. The selection of the winning tender usually takes place in two rounds. In the first round, all interested contractors may submit their interest, and the contracting authority selects, from the candidates, those who will be invited to tender. In principle, the minimum number of candidates to be selected is five. In the second round, bids are submitted and the successful tender is selected.

3.89 An accelerated form of restricted or negotiated procedure may be used[164] where, for reasons of urgency, the periods normally required under the normal procedures cannot be met. In such cases, contracting authorities are required to indicate in the tender notice published in the *Official Journal* the grounds for using the accelerated form of the procedure. The use of an accelerated procedure must be limited to the types and quantities of products or services which it can be shown are urgently required. Other products or services must be supplied or provided under open or restricted procedures.

3.90 The Directives stipulate that open procedures, where possible, should constitute the norm. Open procedures increase competition without doubt and can achieve

---

[161] Art. 6(2) of Directive 93/36; Art. 7(2) of Directive 93/37; Art. 20(1) of Directive 93/38; Art. 11(2) of Directive 92/50.

[162] *See* Art. 6(3) of Directive 93/36; Art. 7(3) of Directive 93/37; Art. 20(3) of Directive 93/38; Art. 11(3) of Directive 92/50.

[163] *See* Art. 1(e) of Directive 93/36; Art. 1(f) of Directive 93/37; Art. 1(7)(b) of Directive 93/38; Art. 1(d) of Directive 92/50.

[164] *See* Art. 12 of Directive 93/36; Art. 13 of Directive 93/37; Art. 26(2) of Directive 93/38; Art. 19(4) of Directive 92/50.

better prices for the contracting authorities when purchasing goods in large volumes. Price reduction based on economies of scale can bring about substantial cost savings for the public sector. Open procedures are mostly utilized when the procurement process is relatively straightforward, and are combined with the lowest price award criterion. On the other hand, competition in tendering procedures is limited by using the restricted and negotiated procedures. By definition, the number of candidates that are allowed to tender is limited (five in restricted procedures and three in negotiated procedures); therefore, the Directives have attached a number of conditions for the contracting authorities to justify when they intend to award their contracts through restricted or negotiated procedures. Restricted and negotiated procedures are utilized in relation to the most economically advantageous offer award criterion and are suited for more complex procurement schemes. Although contracting authorities can freely opt for open or restricted procedures, the latter should be justified by reference to the nature of the products or services to be procured, and the balance between contract value and administrative costs associated with tender evaluation. A more rigorous set of conditions applies for the use of negotiated procedures. When negotiated procedures with prior notification are used, they must be justified on grounds of irregular or unacceptable tenders received as a result of a previous call. Negotiated procedures without prior notification are restrictively permitted in absence of tenders, when the procurement involves manufactured products or construction works purely for research and development, when for technical or artistic reasons, or reasons connected with the protection of exclusive rights, a particular supplier or contractor is selected, in cases of extreme urgency brought by unforeseeable events not attributable to the contracting authorities, when additional deliveries and supplies or works would cause disproportionate technical operational and maintenance difficulties.

All negotiations with candidates or tenderers on fundamental aspects of contracts, **3.91** in particular, on prices, are prohibited in open and restricted procedures; discussions with candidates or tenderers may be held, but only for the purpose of clarifying or supplementing the content of their tenders or the requirements of the contracting authorities, and provided that this does not involve discriminatory practices.[165] The need for such a prohibition is clear, since the possibility to negotiate may allow the contracting authority to introduce subjective appraisal criteria. A Declaration on the above subject has been made by the European Council and the Commission of the European Communities.[166] Also the European Court of Justice has condemned post-tender negotiations as in Case 243/89, *Commission v. Denmark.*[167]

---

[165] *See* Art. 24 of Directive 93/36.   [166] *See* [1994] OJ L111/114.
[167] *See* the Court's judgment of 22 June 1993 in [1993] ECR I-3353.

3.92 It should be clear that the selection process must be completely distinguished from the award process. Quite often, contracting authorities appear to fuse the two basic processes of the award of public procurement contracts. This runs contrary to legal precedent of the European Court of Justice and, in particular, case 31/87 *Gebroeders Beentjes v. Netherlands*.[168] The Court stated expressly that suitability evaluation and bid evaluation are distinct processes which shall not be confused. The same line was adopted by the Court in Case C-71/92, *Commission v. Spain*.[169]

(4) The principle of objectivity in public procurement regulation

(a) The award criteria

3.93 In principle, there are two criteria laid down in the Public Procurement Directives for awarding public contracts:

— the lowest price;
— the most economically advantageous offer.

3.94 The lowest price criterion is self-explanatory.[170] The tenderer who submits the cheapest offer must be awarded the contract. Subject to the qualitative criteria and financial and economic standing, contracting authorities do not rely on any other factor than the price quoted to complete the contract. The reasons for utilizing the lowest price criterion are simplicity, speed, and less qualitative consideration during the evaluation of tenders.

3.95 The appreciation of what is the most economically advantageous tender offer[171] is to be made on a series of factors and determinants chosen by the contracting entity for the particular contract in question. These factors include: price, delivery or completion date, running costs, cost-effectiveness, profitability, technical merit, product or work quality, aesthetic and functional characteristics, after-sales service and technical assistance, commitments with regard to spare parts and components and maintenance costs, and security of supplies. The above list is not exhaustive, and the factors listed therein serve as a guideline for contracting authorities in the weighted evaluation process of the contract award. The order of appearance of these factors in the invitation to tender or in the contract documents is of paramount importance for the whole process of evaluation of the tenders and award of the contract. The most economically advantageous factors must

---

[168] *See* [1988] ECR 4635.
[169] *See* the Court's judgment of 30 June 1993 in [1993] ECR I-5923.
[170] *See* Art. 26(1)(a) of Directive 93/36; Art. 30(1)(a) of Directive 93/37; Art. 34(1)(b) of Directive 93/38; Art. 36(1)(b) of Directive 92/50.
[171] *See* Art. 26(1)(b) of Directive 93/36; Art. 30(1)(b) of Directive 93/37; Art. 34(1)(a) of Directive 93/38; Art. 36(1)(a) of Directive 92/50.

be in hierarchical or descending sequence so tenderers and interested parties can clearly ascertain the relative weight of factors other than price for the evaluation process. However, factors which have no strict relevance to the particular contract in question, or factors which are irrelevant in economic terms are classified as subjective. It is clearly stated in the *European Commission's Guide to the Community Rules on Open Government Procurement*[172] that '.....only objective criteria which are strictly relevant to the particular project may be used ...' Along the same lines, the European Court of Justice has established a precedent in Case 31/87, *Gebroeders Beentjes v. Netherlands*,[173] where the award criteria concern only the qualities of the service the provider can offer.

Along the same lines, in 1993, a reference to the European Court of Justice was made **3.96** by the High Court (Queen's Bench Division) on, *inter alia*, the utilization of Public Procurement Directives for the purchasing of pharmaceutical products (narcotic drugs previously being supplied under licence) by the competent health authorities.[174] The national court requested a preliminary ruling on the interpretation of Article 25 of the Supplies Directive 77/62, particularly the meaning of the 'most economically advantageous offer'. The national court asked whether factors concerning continuity and reliability, as well as security of supplies, fall under the framework of the most economically advantageous offer, when the latter is being evaluated. The Court of Justice, following previous case law,[175] reiterated the flexible and wide interpretation of the relevant award criterion, and had no difficulty in declaring that contracting authorities may use the most economically advantageous offer as award criterion by choosing the factors which they want to apply in evaluating tenders, provided these factors are mentioned, in hierarchical order, in the invitation to tender and or the contract documents. Two member states intervened in the case and submitted that a restricted system of supply of potentially dangerous substances could be justified by having recourse to Article 6(1) and (4) of the Supplies Directive, which permits the use of negotiated procedures when, for technical reasons, the supply of goods in question can be guaranteed by only a particular supplier (Article 6(1)), or when, for security reasons, the supply of goods in question is declared secret, or when their delivery must be accompanied by the application of administrative laws or regulations that guarantee the secrecy of the delivery (Article 6(4)).

(b) Framework agreements

The Utilities Directives have introduced a new selection and tendering procedure, **3.97** namely framework agreements, which is influenced to a large extent by the

---

[172] *See* [1987] OJ C385/1, at 36.   [173] *See* [1988] ECR 463.
[174] *See* Case C-324/93, *R. v. The Secretary of State for the Home Department, ex parte Evans Medical Ltd and Macfarlan Smith Ltd* [1995] ECR I-563.
[175] See Case C-31/87, *Gebroeders Beenjes v. The Netherlands* [1988] ECR 4635, op. cit.

benefits of chain supply management and partnership schemes. The Supplies, Works, and Services Directives do not refer to framework agreements. A framework agreement is an agreement between a contracting authority and one or more suppliers, contractors or service providers, the purpose of which is to establish the terms, in particular with regard to prices, and, where appropriate, the quantity envisaged, governing the contracts to be awarded during a given period. A framework agreement does not possess binding character and should not be considered as a contract between the relevant parties.[176] In practical terms it represents a sort of a standing offer which remains valid during its time-span. Within the provisions of the Utilities Directive, when a contracting authority awards a framework agreement under the relevant procedures which are common to other public contracts covered therein, subsequent individual contracts concluded under the framework agreement may be awarded without having recourse to a call for competition. Individual contracts which have been awarded under a framework agreement are subject to the requirement of the publication of a contract-award notice in the *Official Journal*. The Directive specifically stipulates that misuse of framework agreements may distort competition and trigger the application of the relevant rules, particularly with reference to concerted practices which lead to collusive tendering.

(c) In-house contracts and contracts to affiliated undertakings

3.98   Article 6 of the Services Directive provides for the inapplicability of the Directive to service contracts which are awarded to an entity which is itself a contracting authority, within the meaning of the Directive, on the basis of an exclusive right which is granted to the contracting authority by a law, regulation, or administrative provision of the member state in question.[177] Article 13 of the Utilities Directive provides for the exclusion of certain contracts between contracting authorities and affiliated undertakings. An affiliated undertaking is one the annual accounts of which are consolidated with those of the contracting entity, in accordance with the requirements of the Seventh Company Law Directive (Council Directive 83/349 ([1983] OJ L193/1)). These are service contracts which are awarded to a service provider which is affiliated to the contracting entity, and service contracts which are awarded to a service provider which is affiliated to a contracting entity participating in a joint venture formed for the purpose of carrying out an activity covered by the Directive. The explanatory memorandum accompanying the text amending the Utilities Directive[178] states

---

[176] Framework agreements should not be confused with framework contracts, the latter producing binding effects; *see* Armin-Trepte, op. cit. (n. 88), 93.

[177] This practice resembles the market testing process often employed in the United Kingdom between a contracting authority and an in-house team; *see* Harden, op. cit. (n. 94).

[178] *See* COM (91) 347, SYN 361.

that this provision relates, in particular, to three types of service provision within groups. These categories, which may or may not be distinct, are: the provision of common services such as accounting, recruitment and management; the provision of specialized services embodying the know-how of the group; and the provision of a specialized service to a joint venture. The exclusion from the provisions of the Directive is subject, however, to two conditions: the service-provider must be an undertaking affiliated to the contracting authority, and at least eighty per cent of its average turnover, arising within the European Community for the preceding three years, derives from the provision of the same or similar services to undertakings with which it is affiliated. The Commission is empowered to monitor the application of this Article and require the notification of the names of the undertakings concerned and the nature and value of the service contracts involved.

(d) Design contests

Under the Services Directive, provision has been made for a fourth type of award **3.99** procedure, namely *design contests*, with particular reference to planning projects. According to the Services Directive, *design contests* are those national procedures which enable the contracting authority to acquire in the fields of area planning, town planning, architecture, and civil engineering, a plan or a design selected by a jury, after being put out to competition with or without the award of prizes. The award of *design contests*, according to the Services Directive must follow specific rules. The admission of participants to the contest shall not be limited either by reference to the territory or part of a member state, or on the grounds that under the law of the member state in which the contest is organized, participants would have been required to be either natural or legal persons. Furthermore, where design contests are restricted to a limited number of participants, the contracting authorities must lay down clear and non-discriminatory selection criteria which ensure sufficient and genuine competition among the participants. The jury shall be composed exclusively of natural persons who are independent. The award criteria for design contests remain the same with other public contracts (the lowest price or the most economically advantageous offer).

(e) Concession contracts

The Public Works Directive has adopted a special, mitigated regime for the award **3.100** of concession contracts the value of which is 5 million ECU or more. There are no specific rules as to the way the value of the contract must be calculated or rules referring to aggregation. For the award of concession contracts, contracting authorities are obliged to follow the advertising rules concerning open and restricted procedures for the award of ordinary works contracts. Also, the provisions on technical standards and on criteria for qualitative selection of candidates and tenderers do apply. However, the Works Directive does not prescribe the use of specific award procedures for concession contracts. The Directive presupposes the concession contracts are awarded in two rounds, such as in the case of restricted procedures or negotiated procedures for works contracts. Nothing, however, prevents contracting authorities from applying a (one round) open procedure. The Directive contains no rules on the minimum number of candidates which have to be invited to negotiate or to submit a tender. It would seem that a contracting authority may limit itself to selecting only one single candidate, provided the intention to award a concession contract has been adequately published. A contracting authority may under no circumstances refrain from publishing a notice.

(f) Additional award criteria

3.101 *Subcontracting and public procurement.* Subcontracting plays a major role in the opening up of public markets as it is the most effective means of small and medium sized enterprises' participation in public procurement. All Directives on public procurement, influenced by Commission's Communications on subcontracting and small and medium enterprises, encourage the use of subcontracting in the award of public contracts. Particularly, in public supplies contracts, the contracting entity in the invitation to tender may ask the tenderers on their intention to subcontract to third parties part of the contract. This reveals the importance of subcontracting for regional development in public procurement. In public works contracts, contracting authorities awarding the principal contract to a concessionaire may require him to subcontract to third parties at least thirty per cent of the total work provided for by the principal contract.

3.102 *Local labour employment and public procurement.* Contracting authorities are often faced with the dilemma of utilizing public procurement contracts, particularly in construction projects, as a tool for combating long-term unemployment within their region. Although, at first instance, local labour clauses appear to fall foul of the relevant Treaty provisions on non-discrimination (Article 7) and right of establishment (Article 52), the European Court of Justice, in a seemingly important case[179] on public procurement, pronounced that the utilization of local labour clauses could be included in the non-exhaustive list of factors determining award criteria, especially the most economically advantageous offer, if they did not have discriminatory effects. The Court apparently rejected the possible utilization of local labour clauses as a selection criterion, a decision which runs in consistency with previous case law, recognizing the exhaustive character of selection criteria stipulated by the Public Procurement Directives.

---

[179] *See* Case C-31/87, *Gebroeders Beentjes BV v. State of Netherlands* [1988] ECR 4635.

The award of public housing schemes. The award of public housing contracts[180] may **3.103** deviate from the normal regime of the Directive for the purpose of selecting a contractor who meets the requirements specified by the public authority. The design and construction of a public housing scheme, and the size and complexity of the project, as well as the estimated duration of the work involved, require that planning be based from the outset on close collaboration within a team comprising representatives of the contracting authorities, experts, and the contractor to be responsible for carrying out the works. In these cases, the contracting authorities have to apply the advertising rules and the criteria for qualitative selection relating to the restricted procedure. Moreover, the contracting authorities have to include in the contract notice as accurately as possible, a description of the works to be carried out. With respect to quantitative selection, no restrictions apply. Hence, there is no obligation for the contracting authorities to select more than one single contractor to negotiate admission to the building team.

---

[180] *See* Art. 9 of Directive 93/37.

PART II

PUBLIC PROCUREMENT REGULATION

4

THE NEW PUBLIC PROCUREMENT REGIME

A. A Critical Assessment of Public Procurement Regulation

4.01 The process of the liberalization of public procurement in the European Union has two primary objectives: i) to achieve an open and competitive regime of public purchasing which would yield substantial savings to the public sector, and ii) to act as a stimulant for the much needed restructuring and adjustment of the European industrial base. When compared with other advanced integrated economic or political systems, the regulation of public procurement in the European Union has no precedence. It is not only the aspiration for the creation of a genuinely integrated public sector market within the Community, but to a large extent, the impact of such a regime upon the overall process of European integration that deserves further attention. The mechanism of the public purchasing regulation has revealed a considerable range of socio-economic considerations which interact with the envisaged aims and objectives of the regime. The public procurement sector in the European Union is by no means readily receptive to the parameters of any legislative framework. Rather, it is a *forum* of well established socio-economic and legal patterns which, for a long time, have served national interests.

4.02 One should not expect a dramatic and unprecedented transformation of the way public procurement has been conducted in the member states of the European Union, for two main reasons. Firstly, what has been asked by European law and policy on public procurement represents a significant change of the *modus operandi* of contracting authorities, which quite often have regarded the European rules as a burden. The unwillingness of public authorities to change well-established public purchasing patterns and practices not only reflects their reservations over the financial implications of such an exercise, but mostly their concern over domestic policy considerations which are closely associated with public procurement. The second reason for the modest progress in adapting to the new regime can be attributed to a number of factors which may not only slow the progress of public sector integration, but also hinder the delivery of the envisaged results and the accomplishment of the objectives under the relevant framework. The primary concern of European institutions over the progress of public procurement regulation is the simple assumption that the member states and their contracting authorities do indeed comply with the stipulated requirements of the Public Procurement Directives. However, the integration of the public markets in the European Union has encountered problems which focus on four main areas: a) inherent constraints in the legislation, b) the existence of public monopolies and the process of their privatization in the member states, c) harmonization of standards and specifications, and d) the reluctance of the supply side in initiating litigation.

(1) Inherent shortcomings in the public procurement rules

The legislation on public procurement is far from perfect. It has envisaged the **4.03** creation of a framework which will enhance competition in public markets, but the actual mechanism in delivering the objectives has revealed a number of limitations with its impact on the demand and supply sides. The most significant danger in the legislative framework of public procurement in the Community is the potential elements of non-tariff protection which might be arising from its application. Indeed, inherent shortcomings in the legislation could pose considerable obstacles to the integration of the public sector in Europe. The impact of the law and policy of public purchasing upon the demand side in particular has exposed two fundamental limitations which are integral to the legislative framework. The first limitation refers to the quantitative division of public markets in dimensional public contracts (above certain thresholds) and sub-dimensional ones (below the thresholds which trigger the applicability of the Directives). The second limitation is concerned with the potential adverse effects of the principle of transparency upon the public procurement process.

(2) The dimensionality of public procurement

The main objective of the European rules on public procurement, as implemented **4.04** by member states in the form of domestic laws, is the establishment of the principle of transparency in the award of public contracts. The rules stipulate that public contracts of estimated value which exceeds certain thresholds shall be advertised in the *Official Journal of the European Union*.[1] The legislation on public procurement has put much faith on the principle of transparency. Transparency and openness in the public sector in Europe represent prerequisites for its integration. The principle of transparency encompasses the principle of accountability in the public sector, and is materialized through the advertisement and publicity of procurement requirements of contracting authorities. However, the ambit of the law does not encapsulate all public procurement contracts awarded by contracting authorities. It rather introduces a *de minimis rule*, where certain thresholds in relation to the value of the contracts are utilized for the applicability of the Directives. The dimensional public procurement should, in principle, encompass the majority of procurement requirements of member states and their contracting authorities.

---

[1] €5 million for all work and construction projects (Art. 3(1) of Directive 93/37; Art. 14(c) of Directive 93/38). €200,000 for supplies contracts within the European Union (Art. 5(1)(a) of Directive 93/36), and €136,000 for supplies contracts from third countries (Art. 5(1)(c) of Directive 93/36). €600,000 for supplies of telecommunications equipment under the Utilities Directive (Art.14(b) of Directive 93/38), and ECU 400,000 for all other supplies contracts awarded by public utilities (Art. 14(a) of Directive 93/38). €200,000 for services contracts (Art. 7(1) of Directive 92/50).

However, the legislation on public procurement has had little effect on the principle of transparency, as empirical investigation of the patterns of contracting authorities of member states concerning their publication record in relation to their contracts reveals a rather gloomy picture. The volume of public purchasing which is advertised and tendered according to the requirements of the relevant Directives in comparison with the total volume of public procurement of the member states appears disproportionate and beyond expectation, bearing in mind the vital importance that has been given to the principle of transparency for the opening-up of the public markets in the European Union. The percentages of public contracts advertised in the *Official Journal* by member states reveal the relatively low impact of the public procurement legislation on the principle and objectives of transparency in European public markets. Clarification of the above impact of the law upon the transparency patterns which contracting authorities have established should be sought by exploring three scenarios.

4.05 The first scenario is based on the distinction between dimensional and sub-dimensional public procurement in the member states. The European Directives allow the division of public contracts into lots[2] without any justification from contracting authorities. This, in most cases, may result in intentional contravention of the Directives, as sub-dimensional (below certain thresholds) public contracts escape their applicability. As sub-dimensional public procurement escapes from the mandatory publication requirement, contracting authorities tend to divide contracts into separate lots. It should be mentioned that the Directives stipulate the prohibition of intentional division of contracts into lots with a view to avoiding the relevant thresholds, but the provision presents practical difficulties in its observance and enforcement. At the time of writing, there is no case or complaint before national courts or before the European Court of Justice relating to the intentional division of contracts into lots with lower thresholds in order to avoid the application of the Directives. The relevant thresholds which require the mandatory publication requirement clearly result in a segmentation of the public markets in quantitative terms by creating a *dimensional forum* which is subject to the rigorous legal regime. A *de minimis* rule applies to contracts below the thresholds, which exempts them from the provisions of the Directives. The sub-dimensional public procurement is only subject to the principle of non-discrimination at European level, whereas, at domestic level, national tendering rules regulate the award of these contracts.

4.06 The second scenario is based on the excessive utilization of award procedures without prior publication. Indeed, the Directives allow, under certain circumstances, the award of contracts through direct negotiations with a contractor. Although the European Court of Justice condemned the above practice in

---

[2] *See* Arts. 17 and 20 of the Public Supplies (93/36) and Public Works (93/37) Directives respectively.

a number of cases before it, the actual utilization of negotiated procedures without prior publication is widespread. Finally, the third scenario implies the blunt violation of Community law by member states by avoiding the publication of tender notices in the *Official Journal of the European Union*.

Bearing in mind the relative absence of complaints and subsequent litigation **4.07** concerning non-advertisement of public contracts before national courts or the European Court of Justice, the third scenario reflects to a large extent the underlying reason for the lack of transparency in public procurement. In fact, intentional division of contracts into lots with a view to avoiding the Directives, and excessive and unjustified recourse to award procedures without prior publication, amounts to a blunt violation of member states' obligations arising from the relevant Directives and also from primary Treaty provisions.

(3) *The effects of the principle of transparency*

Transparency, as a principle in public purchasing, has an obvious trade effect, that **4.08** of price competitiveness. If more interested suppliers are aware of a contracting authority's determination to procure, an element of competition occurs automatically; this sort of competitive pattern would probably be reflected in the prices received by the contracting authority, when it evaluates the offers. The fact that more suppliers are aware of a forthcoming public contract and the fact that interested suppliers are aware that their rivals are informed about it, indicates two distinctive parameters which are relevant to savings and value for money. The first parameter focuses on value for money for the demand side of the equation of public purchasing, and reveals the possibility for contracting authorities to compare prices (and quality). The second parameter has an effect on the supply side of the equation (the suppliers) which, amongst other things, can no longer rely on the lack of price comparisons when serving the public sector. Openness in public procurement, by definition, results in price competition and the benefits for contracting authorities appear achievable.

However, transparency and openness in public purchasing pose a question over **4.09** long-term savings and value for money considerations. Price competition, as a result of the awareness of forthcoming public contracts, represents a rather static effect in the value for money process. The fact that more and more interested suppliers are aware and do submit tenders, in the long run, appears rather as a burden. If transparency and the resulting price competitiveness are based on a *win-to-win* process, the potential benefits for contracting authorities could easily be counterbalanced by the administrative costs in tender evaluation and replies to unsuccessful tenders. Furthermore, the risk management factor is much higher in a win-to-win purchasing scenario. Price competitiveness also represents some threats for contracting authorities, to the extent that quality of deliverables as well as the delivery process itself could be jeopardised, if contracting authorities deal with different and unknown contractors. It could thus be argued here that price competitiveness, as a trade effect potentially beneficial for the demand side of the public purchasing equation, has a static character. It seems that it does not take into account medium- or long-term purchasing patterns, as well as counter-effects of competition. Two elements deserve further analysis here.

4.10 The first raises questions over the aggregate loss of the economy through transparent competitive purchasing patterns. For example, if a large number of interested suppliers submit their offer to a particular contracting authority, two types of costs should be examined. Firstly, the cost which is attributed to the response and tendering stage of the procurement process. Human and capital resources are directed by the suppliers towards the preparation of documents and the submission of the offers. If one of these suppliers wins the contract, the remaining would have suffered an unrecoverable loss. If that aggregate loss exceeds the benefit/saving accomplished by the contracting authority by following transparent and competitive purchasing patterns, value for money has not been achieved. Secondly, along the same lines, the evaluation and selection process during tendering represents a considerable administrative cost for the contracting authorities. If the principle of transparency complements the principle of equal treatment, contracting authorities should give the same attention to all interested suppliers that have submitted a response. Downsizing the list through evaluation and assessment based on stipulated criteria is by no means an inexpensive exercise. Human and capital resources have to be directed by contracting authorities towards meeting that cost. If the latter exceeds the potential savings achieved through the competitive tendering route, then value for money is not accomplished.

4.11 The second element that deserves attention relates to the definition of price competitiveness in public purchasing, as well as its interrelation with anti-trust law and policy. A question which arises in price competitive tendering patterns is, *What would be the lowest offer contracting authorities can accept?* If the maximization of savings is the only achievable objective in the public procurement process, the transparent/competitive pattern cannot guarantee and evaluate safeguards in relation to under-priced offers. If the supply side responds to the perpetuated competitive purchasing pattern by lowering prices, contracting authorities could face a dilemma: where to stop. It should be mentioned here that the European rules provide for an automatic disqualification of an 'abnormally low offer'.[3] The term has not been interpreted in detail by the judiciary at European and domestic levels and serves rather as a 'lower bottom limit'.[4] Also, when an offer appears low,

---

[3] *See* Art. 29(5) of Directive 71/305 as amended by Directive 89/440.
[4] *See* Case 76/81, *SA Transporoute et Travaux v. Minister of Public Works* [1982] ECR 457; Case No. 104/75, *SA SHV Belgium v. La Maison Ideale et Societé Nationale du Logement*, before the Belgian *Conseil d'Etat*, judgment of 24 June 1986 of the Belgian *Conseil d'Etat*.

Table 1 Transparency Rates by Member State (%)

	1995	1996	1997	1998	1999	2000	2001	2002
Belgium	6.9	7.6	10.9	13.8	15.6	15.6	18.6	15.8
Denmark	16.4	13.4	13.4	13.5	14.3	20.9	15.8	14.5
Germany	5.1	5.6	6.3	6.5	5.2	5.6	5.7	7.5
Greece	34.1	37.7	42.9	45.1	39.9	31.9	35.3	45.7
Spain	8.5	11.0	11.5	11.5	16.8	25.4	23.4	23.6
France	5.5	6.8	8.4	11.0	11.7	14.6	16.8	17.7
Ireland	11.4	16.3	19.3	16.1	16.8	21.4	19.3	18.0
Italy	9.8	9.9	11.3	10.7	13.2	17.5	15.3	20.3
Luxembourg	5.2	7.0	9.2	14.3	12.9	12.3	10.7	13.3
Netherlands	4.8	5.1	5.5	5.2	5.9	10.8	12.5	8.9
Austria	4.5	7.5	7.5	8.3	7.0	13.5	14.6	15.5
Portugal	15.5	17.7	15.1	15.5	14.6	15.0	17.7	19.4
Finland	8.0	9.2	8.2	9.2	9.8	13.2	15.1	13.9
Sweden	10.5	10.6	11.5	11.6	12.5	17.9	23.4	19.3
UK	15.0	15.6	17.9	16.9	15.1	21.5	21.5	21.1
EU 15	8.4	9.2	10.7	11.1	11.2	14.9	15.4	16.2

Source: Internal Market Directorate General

contracting authorities may request clarifications from the tenderer in question. Contracting authorities face a dilemma in evaluating and assessing low offers other than abnormal ones. It is difficult for them to identify dumping or predatory pricing disguised behind a low offer for a public contract. In addition, even if there is an indication of anti-competitive price fixing, the European public procurement rules do not provide for any kind of procedure. The suspension of the award procedures (or even the suspension of the conclusion of the contract itself) would be unlikely without a thorough and exhaustive investigation by the competent anti-trust authorities.

(4) The abuse of award procedures which may restrict competition

The participation of the supply side of the public procurement equation in the tendering process is channelled through open, negotiated, or restricted procedures. Open procedures are those where every interested supplier, contractor, or service provider may submit an offer.[5] Negotiated procedures[6] are such procedures for the award of public contracts whereby contracting authorities consult contractors of their choice and negotiate the terms of the contract with one or

4.12

---

    [5] *See* Art. 1(d) of Directive 93/36; Art. 1(e) of Directive 93/37; Art. 1(7)(a) of Directive 93/38; Art. 1(d) of Directive 92/50.
    [6] *See* Art. 1(f) of Directive 93/36; Art. 1(g) of Directive 93/37; Art. 1(7)(c) of Directive 93/38; Art. 1(c) of Directive 92/50.

more of them. Finally, restricted procedures[7] are those procedures for the award of public contracts whereby only those contractors invited by the contracting authority may submit tenders. The selection of the winning tender takes place in two rounds. In the first round, all interested contractors may submit their tenders and the contracting authority selects, from the candidates, those who will be invited to tender. In principle, the minimum number of candidates to be selected is five. In the second round, bids are submitted and the successful tender is selected.

4.13 The Utilities Directives have introduced a new selection and tendering procedure, namely framework agreements, which is influenced to a large extent by the benefits of chain supply management and partnership schemes. The Supplies, Works, and Services Directives do not refer to framework agreements. A framework agreement is an agreement between a contracting authority and one or more suppliers, contractors, or service providers, the purpose of which is to establish the terms, in particular with regard to prices, and, where appropriate, the quantity envisaged, which govern the contracts to be awarded during a given period.[8] A framework agreement does not possess a binding character and should not be considered as a contract between the relevant parties. In practical terms it represents a sort of a standing offer which remains valid during its time-span. Within the provisions of the Utilities Directive, when a contracting authority awards a framework agreement under the relevant procedures which are common to other public contracts covered therein, subsequent individual contracts concluded under the framework agreement may be awarded without having recourse to a call for competition.[9] Individual contracts which have been awarded under a framework agreement are subject to the requirement of the publication of a contract-award notice in the *Official Journal*. The Directive specifically stipulates that misuse of framework agreements may distort competition and trigger the application of the relevant rules, particularly with reference to concerted practices which lead to collusive tendering.

4.14 Certain types of award procedures (particularly negotiated with or without prior publication in the *Official Journal*) are prone to abuse by contracting authorities in order to avoid the publicity requirement in advertising public contracts and in order to favour certain suppliers or contractors. Negotiated procedures[10] are such procedures for the award of public contracts whereby contracting authorities consult contractors of their choice and negotiate the terms of the contract with one or

---

[7] *See* Art. 1(e) of Directive 93/36; Art. 1(f) of Directive 93/37; Art. 1(7)(b) of Directive 93/38; Art. 1(d) of Directive 92/50. [8] *See* Art. 1(5) of Directive 93/38.

[9] *See* Art. 20(2)(i) of Directive 93/38.

[10] *See* Art. 1(f) of Directive 93/36; Art. 1(g) of Directive 93/37; Art. 1(7)(c) of Directive 93/38; Art. 1(c) of Directive 92/50.

more of them. In most cases, they follow restricted procedures and they are heavily utilised under framework agreements in the utilities sectors. There are two different types of negotiated procedures: i) negotiated procedures with prior notification, and ii) negotiated procedures without prior notification.

i. Negotiated procedures with prior notification[11] provide for selection of candidates in two rounds. In the first round, all interested contractors may submit their tenders and the contracting authority selects, from the candidates, those who will be invited to negotiate. In the second round, negotiations with various candidates take place and the successful tender is selected. In principle, the minimum number of candidates to be selected is three, provided that there are a sufficient number of suitable candidates.

ii. Negotiated procedures without prior notification[12] are the least restrictive of the various award procedures laid down in the Directive, and may be conducted in one single round. Contracting authorities are allowed to choose whichever contractor they want, begin negotiations directly with this contractor, and award the contract to him. The Directive provides for only a few rules with which this procedure must comply. A prior notice in the *Official Journal* is not required.

An accelerated form of negotiated procedures may be used[13] where, for reasons of **4.15** urgency, the periods normally required under the normal procedures cannot be met. In such cases, contracting authorities are required to indicate in the tender notice published in the *Official Journal* the grounds for using the accelerated form of the procedure. The use of an accelerated procedure must be limited to the types and quantities of products or services which it can be shown are urgently required. Other products or services must be supplied or provided under open or restricted procedures.

The Public Procurement Directives stipulate that open procedures, where possible, **4.16** should constitute the norm. Open procedures increase competition without doubt and can achieve better prices for the contracting authorities when the latter purchase goods in large volumes. Price reduction based on economies of scale can bring about substantial cost savings for the public sector. Open procedures are mostly utilised when the procurement process is relatively straightforward and are combined with the lowest price award criterion. On the other hand, competition in tendering procedures is limited by using the restricted and negotiated

---

[11] *See* Art. 6(2) of Directive 93/36; Art. 7(2) of Directive 93/37; Art. 20(1) of Directive 93/38; Art. 11(2) of Directive 92/50.
[12] *See* Art. 6(3) of Directive 93/36; Art. 7(3) of Directive 93/37; Art. 20(3) of Directive 93/38; Art. 11(3) of Directive 92/50.
[13] *See* Art. 12 of Directive 93/36; Art. 13 of Directive 93/37; Art. 26(2) of Directive 93/38; Art. 19(4) of Directive 92/50.

procedures. By definition, the number of candidates that are allowed to tender is limited (five in restricted procedures and three in negotiated procedures); therefore, the Directives have attached a number of conditions for the contracting authorities to justify when they intend to award their contracts through restricted or negotiated procedures. Restricted and negotiated procedures are utilized in relation with the most economically advantageous offer award criterion and suited for more complex procurement schemes. Although contracting authorities can freely opt for open or restricted procedures, the latter should be justified by reference to the nature of the products or services to be procured and the balance between contract value and administrative costs associated with tender evaluation. A more rigorous set of conditions apply for the use of negotiated procedures. When negotiated procedures with prior notification are used, they must be justified on grounds of irregular or unacceptable tenders received as a result of a previous call. Negotiated procedures without prior notification are restrictively permitted in absence of tenders, when the procurement involves manufactured products or construction work purely for research and development, when for technical or artistic reasons or reasons connected with the protection of exclusive rights a particular supplier or contractor is selected, in cases of extreme urgency brought by unforeseeable events not attributable to the contracting authorities, or when additional deliveries and supplies or works would cause disproportionate technical operational and maintenance difficulties.

4.17 Negotiated procedures with prior publication, since they restrict the number of tenderers, may constitute an element of non-tariff protection and may encourage practices which appear to run counter to effective competition. If they are being employed as a non-tariff barrier, negotiated procedures may give rise to discrimination on grounds of nationality, preference, and support of domestic uncompetitive suppliers, all of which would or could be detrimental to the position of foreign firms which will be placed at a competitive disadvantage. However, the use of negotiated procedures may have certain positive effects in public procurement, as it may reduce the economic costs of the contracting entities, particularly in cases where product complexity, which requires negotiations for the quality of procurement, or a large number of tenderers makes tender evaluation relatively expensive. Contracting authorities also have abusive recourse to award procedures without prior notification and claim a number of reasons, varying from extreme urgency to the protection of industrial or commercial property rights and the need to guarantee the flow of supplies or works, to award public contracts through direct negotiations with the contractor(s) of their choice. They also claim (particularly the utilities) that the utilization of framework agreements or list of approved vendors has resulted in cost-efficiency gains of administrative costs relating to the evaluation of tenders.

4.18 The European Court of Justice has always been reluctant in accepting the use of negotiated procedures, particularly without prior advertisement. In a number of notable cases before it relating to improper use of the award procedures, the Court has maintained the exceptional character of negotiated procedures and the extremely onerous obligation of contracting authorities to justify them. It might be construed from the case law of the Court of Justice that the particular procedure stipulated by the rules requires some sort of clearance prior to its utilization. This is not, however, the case, as the only form of official notification by contracting authorities when using negotiated procedures takes place after the award of the contract in question, where a notice containing the reasons for having recourse to negotiation should be communicated to the European Commission. This rather reinforces the exceptional character of the negotiated procedures rather than their prohibitive use. A number of cases before the European Court of Justice have clarified the position of European Institutions vis-à-vis the use of negotiated procedures.

(5) *Public monopolies*

Public monopolies in the European Union, which in the majority are utilities, are **4.19** accountable for a substantial magnitude of procurement, in terms of volume and in terms of price. Responsible for this are the expensive infrastructure and high technology products which are necessary for them to procure, in order to deliver their services to the public. Given the fact that most of the suppliers to public utilities depend almost entirely on their procurement and that, even when some degree of privatization has been achieved, the actual control of the utilities is still vested in the state, the first constraint in liberalizing public procurement in the European Union is apparent. Utilities, in the form of public monopolies or semi-private enterprises, appear prone to perpetuating long-standing over-dependent purchasing patterns with certain domestic suppliers. Reflecting the above observations, the reader should bear in mind that, until 1991, utilities were not covered by European legislation on procurement.[14] The delay in their regulation can be attributed to the resistance from member states in privatizing their monopolies and the uncertainty of the legal regime that will follow their privatization.

Public monopolies[15] operating in the utilities sector (energy, transport, water, and **4.20** telecommunications) have been the target of a sweeping process of transformation from monolithic and sub-optimal public corporations to competitive enterprises. These legal or delegated monopolies have been assigned with the exclusive exploitation of the relevant services in their respective member states (production, distribution of water and any form of energy, and the provision of telecommunications and transport) and very often possess a monopsony position.

---

[14] Utilities were first regulated in their procurement by virtue of EC Directive 90/531 [1990] OJ L297. [15] *See* Arts. 37 and 90 EC.

State-controlled enterprises perform a different management pattern to private ones in their market activities. Profit maximization is not their main objective, and decision-making responds not only to market forces, but mainly to political pressure. Understandably, their purchasing behaviour follows, to a large extent, parameters reflecting current trends of the industrial policy of the government in power. It has become apparent that public monopolies in the utilities sector have sustained industries in member states through exclusive or preferential procurement. Preferential and protectionist purchasing behaviour could not easily withstand the competitive forces under which private firms are exposed. One of the most important elements of corporate performance is sourcing and the associated costs. The private firm which is exposed to competitive forces for its deliverables would certainly be compelled to have recourse to the most cost-efficient sources. This covers not only procurement but also extends to a wide range of legal and corporate activities such as subcontracting, research and development, and maintenance services. Sustainability of 'national champions' or, in other terms, strategically perceived enterprises, could only be achieved through discriminatory purchasing patterns. The privatization of public monopolies which absorb, to a large extent or even entirely, the output of such industries will most probably discontinue such patterns and will result in industrial policy imbalances, as it would be difficult for the 'national champions' to secure new markets to replace the traditional long dependency on public monopolies, and it would take time and effort to diversify their activities or to convert to alternative industrial sectors. Imbalances in social policy (unemployment) will also occur, as a result of the restructuring of the public monopoly and also the industries which are dependent on it.

4.21 The protected and preferential purchasing frameworks between monopolies and 'national champions' and the output dependency patterns and secured markets of the latter have attracted considerable foreign direct investment, to the extent that Community institutions face the dilemma of threatening to discontinue the investment flow when liberalizing public procurement in the common market. However, it could be argued that the industrial restructuring following the opening-up of the procurement practices of public monopolies would possibly attract similar levels of foreign direct investment, which would be directed towards supporting the new structure.

4.22 As mentioned above, the liberalization of public purchasing aims *inter alia* at achieving a restructuring effect in the common market, particularly in industries suffering from overcapacity and sub-optimal performance. However, the industries supplying public monopolies and utilities are themselves quite often public corporations. In such cases, procurement dependency patterns between state outfits, when disrupted, can result in massive unemployment attributed to the supply side's inadequacy to secure new customers. The monopsony position, when abolished, could often bring about the collapse of the relevant sector.

(6) Standardization and specification

National technical standards, industrial product and service specifications, and **4.23** their harmonization were considered priority areas for the internal market programme. The European Commission's *White Paper for the Completion of the Internal Market* stipulated a number of Directives to be adopted and implemented with a view to eliminating discrimination based on the description of national standards. The rules on technical standards and specifications have been brought in line with the new policy, which is based on the mutual recognition of national requirements, where the objectives of national legislation are essentially equivalent, and on the process of legislative harmonization of technical standards through non-governmental standardization organizations (CEPT, CEN, and CENELEC).[16] However, the persistence of contracting authorities in specifying their procurement requirements by reference to national standards poses obstacles in the public sector integration[17]. The European Commission has been for some time aware of the most notable examples of circumvention of the policy on standards and specifications[18]. These include: the exclusive familiarity of national suppliers with technical data existing in a particular member state; over-specification by contracting authorities in order to exclude potential bidders; and, finally, favouritism and discrimination by contracting authorities as a result of the availability of technical standards and specifications to certain suppliers only.

Standardization and specification can act as a non-tariff barrier in public procure- **4.24** ment contracts in two ways: firstly, contracting authorities may use apparently different systems of standards and specifications as an excuse for disqualification of tenderers. It should be maintained here that the description of the intended supplies, works or services to be procured is made by reference to the Common Product Classification, the NACE (General Industrial Classification of Economic Activities within the European Communities), and the Common Procurement Vocabulary (CPV); however, this type of description is of generic nature and does not cover industrial specifications and standardization requirements. Secondly, standardization and specification requirements can be restrictively defined in order to exclude products or services of a particular origin, or narrow the field of competition amongst tenderers. National standards are not only the subject of domestic legislation, which, of course, need to be harmonised and mutually

---

[16] *See* Art. 7 of Directive 88/295. *See* the *White Paper on Completing the Internal Market*, paras.61–79; also, Council Resolution of 7 May 1985 on a New Approach in the Field of Technical Harmonization and Standards [1985] OJ C136.

[17] *See* the Documents of the Advisory Committee for the Opening up of Public Procurement, *Policy Guidelines on the Obligation to Refer to European Standards*, CCO/91/67 final.

[18] *See* the report of the Advisory Committee for the Opening up of Public Procurement, *Standards for Procurement*, CCO/92/02.

recognized across the common market. One of the most significant aspects of standardization and specification appears to be the operation of voluntary standards, which are mainly specified at industry level. The above category is rather difficult to harmonize, as any approximation and mutual recognition relies on the willingness of the industry in question. Voluntary standards and specifications are used quite often in the utilities sector, where the relevant procurement requirements are complex and cannot be specified solely by reference to 'statutory' standards, thus leaving a considerable margin of discretion in the hands of the contracting authorities, who may abuse it during the selection and qualification stages of the procurement process.

(7) Reluctance in initiating litigation

4.25 The litigation before the European Court of Justice and national courts in relation to public procurement contracts has pointed out the areas of contention between defaulting contracting authorities and the Commission or aggrieved contractors. The most common disputes subject to centralised or decentralised judicial control include the following:

— advertisement and preferential purchasing frameworks between monopolies; and
— 'national champions' and standardization;
— award procedures;
— award criteria.

4.26 Interestingly, all the relevant provisions of the Directives covering the above areas are capable of producing direct effect, thus maximizing the opportunities for access to justice for aggrieved contractors. The impact of public procurement legislation on the demand and supply sides identified certain areas which represent obstacles to public market integration. Although the relevant legislation has provided for a great deal of flexibility, in terms of implementing methods and time, national legal systems responded slowly to the envisaged regime. The limited number of cases relating to public procurement, in contrast with its volume and the economic importance for member states, reflects a false picture. One may assume that, because of the relatively disproportionate number of cases before the European Court of Justice or before national courts, the integration of public markets is on a good course and has progressed satisfactorily.

However, examination and analysis of the case law on public procurement as the impact of the relevant legislation on the demand and supply sides reveals the nature of public procurement as a *nexus* of transaction activities between the state and its organs on the one hand, and the private sector on the other. Such a nature appears to have strong *endocentric* characteristics, in terms of the reluctance in initiating litigation, the secrecy and confidentiality of the dispute itself, and, finally, the belief that litigation represents the *ultium refugium* in resolving the dispute. Furthermore, the contractual relation between the supply and the demand side after the litigation of a dispute between them appears to be irretrievably broken. This means that, prior to having recourse to legal proceedings, parties in a public procurement dispute appear to have comprehensively exhausted all the routes in dissolving the issue in an amicable way. Therefore, the relevant litigation and its outcome serve as the epitaph in a rather unclear nexus of legal relations. The supply side appears reluctant to take contracting authorities to court for a number of reasons: psychological, legal, and financial.

The psychology behind enforcement and compliance with public procurement legislation is the key point for understanding the behaviour of the supply side. The supply side is often afraid of the vindictive behaviour of the contracting authorities. A contractor who initiates litigation (or some form of official complaint) against a contracting authority would find himself on a 'black list' and would not continue doing business with the latter. Even in the unlikely event that a contract is awarded to a supplier who had previously created some form of trouble for the contracting authority, the latter could make the performance of the contract intolerable, ensuring minimization of margins of profit and delaying payments. The psychology in public procurement enforcement and compliance works against the supply side, as the latter initiates the majority of litigation against contracting authorities. Even where the European Commission takes the defaulting member state before the European Court of Justice, there is a complaint from an aggrieved contractor who has identified himself. **4.27**

The supply side also appears reluctant in initiating litigation against contracting authorities because of financial reasons. If the court found that the contracting authority breached the law, the damages that could be awarded would be disproportionate to the legal costs. The extent to which compensation is awarded varies among legal orders. Compensation for loss of incurred expenses, for loss of profits, and for loss of opportunity is theoretically available in all member states, in accordance with the Compliance Directives. However, in practice, the only relatively certain heading of damages that an aggrieved contractor may count on is that of out-of-pocket expenses, *viz.* the cost of preparing the bid. Foregone profits and losses of opportunities would be deemed as elements of speculative litigation by the courts, and would probably be rejected. It is worth mentioning that, in Italy, due to the very strict requirement that only successful tenderers that have been awarded the contract may lodge an action for damages against the contracting authority, losses of profits are not easily granted; on the other hand, under the relevant arbitration proceedings for public contracts in the Netherlands, compensation is available for injury to a firm's commercial reputation. Direct compensation from administrative bodies, without judicial interference, is **4.28** theoretically available in Denmark and Spain. These examples demonstrate the diversity of national systems as far as enforcement of public procurement law is concerned.

4.29 Finally, legal obstacles appear to have constrained the supply side in its attempts to enforce its rights under public procurement law. These obstacles act as non-tariff barriers, particularly in cases of cross-country litigation, where the nature of the competent forum, the cost of initiating a suit, legal and expert fees, translation costs, and the chances of a favourable outcome, deter aggrieved contractors from taking defaulting contracting authorities to court. The complexity of domestic legal regimes relating to public procurement disputes, in conjunction with the uncertainties arising from the parallel application of public and private law remedies in some member states, appears to be a major deterrent for initiating litigation against contracting authorities.

4.30 In December 1996, the European Commission published the *Green Paper on Public Procurement: Exploring the Way Forward*. In this document, the Commission has reflected on the law and policy of public procurement, particularly since the completion of the internal market. The Green Paper does not proclaim a huge success by the regime or any unprecedented impact upon the demand and supply sides of the public purchasing equation. Rather, it acknowledges the modest effect of the law and policy on the principles envisaged in the opening up of the public sector markets in the European Community. It invited all interested parties to submit written evidence on the effect of the regime upon them and possible suggestions as to future improvements.

The Green Paper has recognized the case-law on public procurement as the impact of the economic importance of public procurement as a *nexus* of public purchasing in the European Community is considered as fundamental to the success of the common market. The effectiveness of the public procurement regime would bring about cost-efficiency gains for the public sector, which could consequently affect the success of fiscal deficit reduction policies imposed by the Maastricht convergence criteria. Thus, the European Commission has made clear the possible links between public sector savings and convergence criteria of the European Monetary Union. However, to what extent the success of monetary integration in the European Community would be affected by the outcome of the public sector integration process of the common market, deserves thorough and in-depth quantitative and qualitative research for the years to come.

4.31 Although the Commission acknowledged some improvements in the transparency of the public procurement process as a result of the obligatory publicity and advertisement requirements, substantial progress in the implementation of the Directives within domestic systems has not been recorded. The Green Paper raised the thorny question of *qualitative implementation* of the public procurement regime into national legal orders. To what extent the member states have failed to meet the expectations of European institutions, and share their aspirations for an integrated procurement system in the common market, is a matter for the European Court of Justice to decide. The reservations of the successful implementation of the regime expressed by the author, in relation to the limited amount of litigation and the relatively low number of complaints in public procurement, could perhaps trigger the need for a new approach to member state's obligations arising from Directives. The acid test for the *qualitative implementation* of the Public Procurement Directives is *access to justice* at national level. Moreover, the expectations of the new regime in relation to the actual or potential savings for the public sector have not fully materialized. The author has pointed out the relatively limited economic impact of the public procurement law and policy on the demand and supply side respectively, and, in particular, the effects on price convergence and the public sector import penetration.

The 1996 Commission's *Green Paper on Public Procurement*[19] paved the way for the 1998 Commission's Communication, in which European institutions attempted to assess the progress of the regime in the common market. The Public Procurement Directives have been seen as an instrument of economic reform. As a consequence, they are an integral part of the Commission's 2000 Work Programme, which pledges to modernize the relevant legislation for the completion of the internal market and, at the same time, implement the Lisbon European Council's call for economic reform within the internal market.   **4.32**

The *Green Paper on Public Procurement* and the subsequent policy developments adopted by the European Commission called for a modernization of the public procurement regime. The previous legal framework of public sector procurement separated supplies, works, and services, as well as the utilities procurement, into different legal instruments. The jurisprudence of the European Court of Justice has been the main influence of the need to codify the public procurement regime into two mainstream Directives: the Public Sector Directive and the Utilities Directive.   **4.33**

The codification of the Supplies, Works, and Services Directives into a single legal instrument is intended to simplify the public procurement framework and enhance legal certainty. In addition, it is expected to facilitate legal efficiency and compliance in the sense that it could streamline its implementation process by national governments, and provide for a one-stop shop reference point in national legal orders. On the other hand, the utilities procurement remains a separate regime due to complexity of the regulatory regimes applicable by member states to utilities undertakings and their respective markets. It should be noted that the character of the utilities markets reflects a quasi-oligopolistic environment, as the   **4.34**

---

[19] See European Commission, *Green Paper on Public Procurement in the European Union: Exploring the Way Forward*, 1996.

existence of special or exclusive rights granted by the member states for the supply, provision, or operation of networks for providing the service concerned necessitates a special regulatory regime for the procurement requirements of these undertakings. Such a regime must be compatible with the principles of transparency and competitiveness which underpin the public sector procurement, and, more importantly, adhere to the fundamental principles of European Union law.

B. The New Public Procurement Regime

4.35 The European Union has adopted a new set of rules which govern the award of public contracts in the supplies, works, and services sectors, as well as in the public utilities[20] after a considerable amount of debate and consultation.[21] The new Directives reflect on the 1996 European Commission's *Green Paper on Public Procurement*[22] and the following 1998 Commission's Communication.[23] The Directives have been seen as an integral part of the Commission's 2000 Work Programme, which pledges to modernize the relevant legislation for the completion of the internal market and, at the same time, implement the Lisbon European Council's call for economic reform within the internal market. The new public procurement regime will become operational after 31 January 2006, when member states are expected to transpose the Directives into national law.[24] In the meantime, the existing regime is still applicable.[25]

---

[20] *See* Directive 2004/18 on the Coordination of Procedures for the Award of Public Works Contracts, Public Supply Contracts and Public Service Contracts [2004] OJ L134/114, 30 April 2004, and Directive 2004/17 Coordinating the Procurement Procedures of Entities Operating in the Water, Energy, Transport and Postal Services Sectors [2004] OJ L134/1, 30 April 2004.

[21] *See* the Proposal from the European Commission [2001] OJ C29/E, 30 January 2001, 11, and [2002] OJ C203/E, 27 August 2002, 210; the Opinion of the Economic and Social Committee [2001] OJ C193, 10 July 2001, 7; the Opinion of the Committee of the Regions [2001] OJ C144, 16 May 2001, 23; the Opinion of the European Parliament of 17 January 2002 [2002] OJ C271/E, 7 November 2002, 176; Council Common Position of 20 March 2003 [2003] OJ C147/E, 24 June 2003, 1; and the Position of the European Parliament of 2 July 2003. *See also* the Legislative Resolution of the European Parliament of 29 January 2004 and Decision of the Council of 2 February 2004.   [22] *See* European Commission, op. cit. (n. 19).

[23] *See* European Commission, Communication on Public Procurement in the European Union, COM (98) 143.

[24] *See* Art. 80 of Directive 2004/18, regarding implementation, where member states are obliged to bring into force the laws, regulations, and administrative provisions necessary to comply with the Public Sector Directive no later than 31 January 2006, and, by that deadline, to inform the European Commission on the measures they intend to introduce in order to incorporate the Directive's provisions into national laws. The application of the new rules on the postal sector has been postponed until 1 January 2009.

[25] The current public procurement regime includes the Public Supplies Directive 93/36/EC [1993] OJ L199/1, as amended by Directive 97/52/EC [1997] OJ L328/1 and Directive 2001/78/EC [2001] OJ L285/1; the Public Works Directive 93/37/EC [1993] OJ L199/54,

(1) A thematic overview of the new public procurement regime

The new Directives are based upon two premises: *simplification* and *modernization*. **4.36**
Drawing on the wealth of experience from the application and implementation of
previous legal regimes and the Court's jurisprudential inferences to public procurement regulation, the new Directives are set to achieve the challenging objective
to fully integrate public sector purchasing in the common market and abolish any
remaining non-tariff barriers.

Although the same fundamental principles underpin procurement liberalization **4.37**
in government and utilities sectors, the new regime maps a clear-cut *dichotomy*
between the public sector and the utilities. Their separate regulation reveals the
diametrically-opposed nature of the contracting authorities/entities under these
sectors, and reflects on the process of transformation that utilities have been
undergoing over the past decade. Their change in ownership from public to
private has stimulated commercialism and competitiveness, and provided for the
justification of a more relaxed regime and the acceptance that utilities, in some
form or another, represent *sui generis* contracting authorities which do not need a
rigorous and detailed regulation of their procurement.

The dichotomy in regulation which the new public procurement regime has **4.38**
established to separate public sector procurement from utilities procurement
exposes an insight of current market conditions and political priorities across the
European Union, as well as an indication that the main emphasis should be placed
on attempts to open up the public sector.

The merger of the rules governing supplies, works, and services procurement into a **4.39**
single legal instrument represents a successful attempt on the part of the European
Union to codify supranational administrative provisions which aim to harmonize
domestic legal regimes, public or private, which coordinate the award of public contacts. The codification, apart from the obvious benefits of legal certainty and legitimate expectation, has two important implications: legal efficiency, and compliance
discipline. As far as legal efficiency is concerned, the new codified Directive will speed
up and streamline its implementation process by member states, especially the new
arrivals from the 2004 Accession Treaty, and provide for a one-stop shop reference
point in national legal orders, augmented by the Court's vesting of direct effectiveness
upon the Directive's predecessors in numerous occasions. On the other hand,
codification will enhance compliance, as it will remove any remaining uncertainties

---

amended by Directive 97/52/EC [1997] OJ L328/1 and Directive 2001/78/EC [2001] OJ L285/1;
the Utilities Directive 93/38/EC [1993] OJ L199/84, amended by Directive 98/4/EC [1998] OJ
L101/1; the Public Services Directive 92/50/EEC [1992] OJ L209/1, amended by Directive
97/52/EC [1997] OJ L328/1 and Directive 2001/78/EC[2001] OJ L285/1; the Remedies Utilities
Directive 92/13/EEC [1992] OJ L076/14, 23 March 1992; and the Public Remedies Directive
89/665/EEC [1989] OJ L395/33, 30 December 1989.

over the applicability of the previously fragmented regime, and afford contracting authorities a disciplined method of dispersing their procurement functions. The main influence of the codified Public Sector Procurement Directive can be traced in important recent case law developments[26] from the European Court of Justice, in particular case law on the definition of contracting authorities, the use of award procedures and award criteria, and the possibility for contracting authorities to use environmental and social considerations as criteria for the award of public contracts.[27]

4.40 As far as the utilities procurement is concerned, the two main reasons for the introduction of a distinctive legal regime which aims at coordinating procedures for the award of contracts in the utilities sectors evolve around the relations of the state with such entities. Firstly, the numerous ways in which national authorities can influence the purchasing behaviour of these entities, such as participation in their capital and representation in their administrative, managerial, or supervisory bodies. Secondly, the closed nature of the markets in which utilities operate, as a result of special or exclusive rights granted by the member states, necessitates the operation of a procurement regulatory regime which ensures, on the one hand, compliance with the fundamental principles of the EU Treaties and, on the other hand, compatibility with anti-trust and sector-specific regulation in the utilities sectors.

(2) The new concepts in public sector procurement

4.41 The codified Public Sector Directive has introduced a series of new concepts which are the product of jurisprudential inferences and policy refining of the previous legal regimes. They intend to modernize public purchasing and align the procurement of government and its agencies with that of utilities, which operate in a more commercially oriented environment.

(a) Eligibility of bodies governed by public law to tender

4.42 The new Public Sector Directive clearly accepts that entities which are covered by its rules can participate in the award of public contracts, alongside private sector

---

[26] For a comprehensive analysis of the public procurement case law, *see* Bovis, 'Recent Case Law Relating to Public Procurement: A Beacon for the Integration of Public Markets', *Common Market Law Review*, 39 (2002), 1025–1056.

[27] *See* Communication from the European Commission to the Council, the European Parliament, the Economic and Social Committee, and the Committee of the Regions, 'Working together to maintain momentum' *2001 Review of the Internal Market Strategy*, (Brussels, 11 April 2001), COM (2001) 198 final. Also, European Commission, *Commission Communication, Public Procurement in the European Union* (Brussels, 11 March 1998), COM (98) 143. *See* European Commission, *Commission Interpretative Communication on the Community Law Applicable to Public Procurement and the Possibilities for Integrating Social Considerations into Public Procurement*, 15 October 2001, COM (2001) 566. Also, European Commission, *Commission Interpretative Communication on the Community Law Applicable to Public Procurement and the Possibilities for Integrating Environmental Considerations into Public Procurement*, 4 July 2001, COM (2001) 274.

undertakings. Member states should ensure that the participation of a body governed by public law as a tenderer in a procedure for the award of a public contract does not cause any distortion of competition in relation to private tenderers. The eligibility of bodies governed by public law to participate in tendering procedures has been influenced by case law.[28] There is a protection mechanism built in Article 55(e) of the Public Sector Directive, which specifies that, in case of abnormally law tenders, the contracting authority may reject those tenders, if it establishes that the tenderer is the recipient of state aid which may have been granted illegally. The onus to prove the legitimacy of the state aid rests with the tenderer.

It should be mentioned that the existing Directives provide for an automatic **4.43** disqualification of an 'obviously abnormally low offer'. The term has not been interpreted in detail by the Court and serves rather as an indication of a 'bottom limit'.[29] The Court, however, pronounced on the direct effect of the relevant provision requiring contracting authorities to examine the details of the tender before deciding the award of the contract and to seek from the tenderer an explanation for the price submitted.

The debate over the terminology of 'obviously abnormally low' tenders surfaced **4.44** when the Court held[30] that rejection of a contract based on mathematical criteria without giving the tenderer an opportunity to furnish information is inconsistent with spirit of the Public Procurement Directives. The Court, following previous case law,[31] ruled that the contracting authorities must give an opportunity to tenderers to furnish explanations regarding the genuine nature of their tenders, when those tenders appear to be abnormally low. However, the Court did not analyze the meaning of 'obviously'. It seems, in the author's view, that the term 'obviously' indicates the existence of precise and concrete evidence as to the abnormality of the low tender. On the other hand, the wording 'abnormally' implies a quantitative criterion left to the discretion of the contracting authority. Nonetheless, if the tender is just 'abnormally' low, it could be argued that it is within the discretion of the contracting authority to investigate the genuine offer of a tender. *Impresa Lombardini*[32] followed *Transporoute*, and maintained the unlawfulness of mathematical criteria used

---

[28] *See* Case C-94/99, *ARGE Gewässerschutzt v. Bundesministerium für Land- und Forstwirtschaft*, paragraph 30, judgment of 7 December 2000, where the Court ruled that directly or indirectly subsidized tenders by the state or other contracting authorities, or even by the contracting authority itself, can legitimately be part of the evaluation process.

[29] Case 76/81, *SA Transporoute et Travaux v. Minister of Public Works* [1982] ECR 457.

[30] *See* Case 103/88, *Fratelli Costanzo SpA v. Comune di Milano* [1989] ECR 1839; Case 296/89, *Impresa Dona Alfonso di Dona Alfonso & Figli snc v. Consorzio per lo Sviluppo Industriale del Comune di Monfalcone*, judgment of 18 June 1991.

[31] *See* Case 76/81 *Transporoute* [1982] ECR 417, op. cit.

[32] *See* Case C-285/99 and 286/99, *Impresa Lombardini SpA v ANAS*, judgment of 27 November 2001.

as an exclusion of a tender which appears abnormally low. Yet, it held that such criteria may be lawful if used for determining the abnormality of a low tender, provided an *inter partes* procedure between the contracting authority and the tenderer who submitted the alleged abnormal low offer offers the opportunity to clarify the genuine nature of that offer. Contracting authorities must take into account all reasonable explanations furnished and avoid limiting the grounds on which justification of the genuine nature of a tender should be made. In *ARGE*,[33] the rejection of a tender based on the abnormally low pricing attached to it got a different twist in its interpretation. Although the Court ruled that directly or indirectly subsidized tenders by the state or other contracting authorities, or even by the contracting authority itself, can legitimately be part of the evaluation process, it did not elaborate on the possibility of rejection of an offer which is appreciably lower than those of unsubsidized tenderers by reference to the abnormally low disqualification ground.[34]

(b) Joint and centralized procurement

4.45 The Public Sector Directive aims at introducing a regime where procurement can benefit from scale economies and streamlining planning, operation, and delivery. In the light of the diversity of public procurement contracts in member states, contracting authorities have been given the freedom to make provision for contracts for the design and execution of work to be awarded jointly. The decision to award contracts jointly must be determined by qualitative and economic criteria, which may be defined by national law. According to Article 1(10) of the Public Sector Directive, a central purchasing body is a contracting authority which: i) acquires supplies and/or services intended for contracting authorities, or ii) awards public contracts or concludes framework agreements for works, supplies, or services intended for contracting authorities.

(c) Official list of contractors

4.46 The Public Sector Directive provides for a central system of certification of private and public organizations for the purposes of providing evidence of financial and economic standing as well as levels of technical capacity in public procurement selection and qualification procedures. Such systems must be mutually recognized by all member states and registration of entities in official lists of contractors,

---

[33] *See* Case C-94/99, *ARGE Gewässerschutzt v. Bundesministerium für Land- und Forstwirtschaft*, paragraph 30, judgment of 7 December 2000.

[34] In *ARGE* the Court adopted a literal interpretation of the Directives and concluded that, if the legislature wanted to preclude subsidized entities from participating in tendering procedures for public contracts, it should have said so explicitly in the relevant Directives, see paragraphs 26 *et seq.* of the Court's judgment. Although the case has relevance in the fields of selection and qualification procedures, and award criteria, the Court made no references to previous case law regarding state aids in public procurement, presumably because the *Dupont de Nemours* precedence is still highly relevant.

suppliers, or service providers is influenced by the Court's case law,[35] where an economic operator belonging to a group claims the economic, financial, or technical capabilities of other companies in the same group in support of its application for registration. Member states may determine the level of requirements to be met for such registrations and the period of their validity, in particular, requirements for joint and several liability where an operator relies on the financial standing of another company in the same group.

(d) The competitive dialogue

The competitive dialogue is the most publicized change brought about by the new **4.47** public procurement regime. Its inception is attributed to three reasons: i) the inability of open or restricted procedures to facilitate the award of complex public contracts, including concessions and public–private partnerships, ii) the exceptional nature of negotiated procedures without prior advertisement,[36] and iii) the restrictive interpretation[37] of the grounds for using negotiated procedures with prior advertisement.

Article 29 of the Public Sector Directive establishes the competitive dialogue as an **4.48** award procedure, alongside open, restricted and negotiated procedures. The

---

[35] *See* Case C-76/81, *SA Transporoute et Travaux v. Minister of Public Works* [1982] ECR 457; Case C-27/86, *Constructions et Enterprises Industrielles SA (CEI) v. Association Intercommunale pour les Autoroutes des Ardennes*; Case C-28/86, *Ing. A. Bellini & Co. SpA v. Regie de Bâtiments*; Case C-29/86, *Ing. A. Bellini & Co. SpA v. Belgian State* [1987] ECR 3347; Case C-89/92, *Ballast Nedam Groep NV v. Belgische Staat* [1994] 2 CMLR; Case C-5/97, *Ballast Nedam Groep NV v. Belgische Staat*, judgment of 18 December 1997; Case C-176/98, *Holst Italia v Comune di Cagliari*, judgment of 2 December 1999.

[36] Negotiated procedures without prior advertisement are exceptionally allowed '. . *when for technical or artistic reasons or reasons connected with the protection of exclusive rights the services could only be procured by a particular provider . . . and . . . in cases of extreme urgency brought about by events unforeseeable by the contracting authority'*. In Cases C-199/85, *Commission v. Italy* [1987] ECR 1039, and C-3/88, *Commission v. Italy* [1989] ECR 4035, the Court rejected the existence of exclusive rights and regarded the abuse of this provision as contrary to the right of establishment and freedom to provide services which are based on the principle of equal treatment and prohibit not only overt discrimination on grounds of nationality, but also all covert forms of discrimination, which, by the application of other criteria of differentiation, lead to the same result. Interestingly, in Case 199/85, *Commission v Italy*, op. cit, the Court elucidated that exclusive rights might include contractual arrangements such as know-how and intellectual property rights. For urgency reasons brought by unforeseen events to contracting authorities, the Court established two tests: i) the need for a justification test based on the proportionality principle, and ii) the existence of a causal link between the alleged urgency and the unforeseen events (*see* C-199/85, *Commission v Italy*, op. cit; C-3/88, *Commission v Italy*, op. cit., C-24/91, *Commission v Spain* [1994] CMLR 621; C-107/92, *Commission v Italy*, judgment of 2 August 1993; C-57/94, *Commission v Italy*, judgment of 18 May 1995; C-296/92, *Commission v Italy*, judgment of 12 January 1994).

[37] The grounds for using this procedure are confined to situations where: i) the nature of the works or services or risks attached thereto do not permit overall pricing and ii) the nature of the services is such that specifications cannot be established with sufficient precision. *See* Art. 7(2)(c) of the Works Directive and Arts. 11(2)(b) and 11(2)(c) of the Services Directive.

competitive dialogue must be used exceptionally in cases of particularly complex contracts, where the use of the open or restricted procedures will not allow the award of the contract, and the use of negotiated procedures cannot be justified. A public contract is considered to be particularly complex where the contracting authorities are not able to define in an objective manner the technical specifications which are required to pursue the project, or they are not able to specify the legal or financial make-up of a project.

4.49 The procedure is very complex, as it has three main phases and many options within these phases. Firstly, the advertisement phase according to Article 29(2) obliges contracting authorities to publish a contract notice or a descriptive document outlining their needs and basic specifications of the project. After that phase, and before launching a competitive dialogue for the award of a contract, contracting authorities may, using a technical dialogue, seek or accept advice which may be used in the preparation of the specifications, provided that such advice does not have the effect of precluding competition.

4.50 Secondly, a selection phase reduces the candidates to be invited to the competitive dialogue according to the relevant provisions of Articles 44 to 52 of the Public Sector Directive.[38] The minimum number of candidates should be three but it could be lower if there is sufficient evidence of competitiveness in the process or the limited number of initial respondents to the contract notice precludes the invitation of at least three candidates.

4.51 Thirdly, the competitive dialogue is opened by the commencement of the award phase in accordance with Article 29(3). Contracting authorities must open a dialogue with the candidates selected, the aim of which is to identify the means best suited to satisfying their needs. They may discuss all aspects of the contract with the chosen candidates, ensuring equality of treatment among all tenderers. In particular, they must not provide information in a discriminatory manner which may give some tenderers an advantage over others. Contracting authorities may not reveal to the other participants the solutions proposed, or other confidential information, communicated by a candidate participating in the dialogue, without prior agreement granted from that candidate.

4.52 Contracting authorities may provide for the competitive dialogue to take place in successive stages in order to reduce the number of solutions to be discussed with the candidates in accordance with Article 29(4). They may continue the dialogue until they can identify the solution or solutions which are capable of meeting their needs. Having declared that the dialogue is concluded, and having informed the

---

[38] Arts. 44 to 46 of the Public Sector Directive 2004/18 govern the conduct of the procedure for verification of the suitability and choice of participants and award of contracts, criteria for qualitative selection, and suitability to pursue a professional activity.

participants, contracting authorities must ask them to submit their final tenders on the basis of the solution or solutions presented and specified during the dialogue.

After this phase is over (closure of the competitive dialogue), there are four stages **4.53** until the contract award. Firstly, contracting authorities must ask all remaining candidates to submit their final tenders (Article 44(4)). Secondly, these tenders need to be finalized prior to their evaluation (Article 29(6)). Thirdly, the selection of the winning tenderer must take place in accordance with the criteria stipulated in the contract notice (Article 29(7)) and fourthly the winning tenderer must provide further clarification and his commitment to undertake the project (Article 29(7)).

The tenders must contain all the elements required and considered necessary for **4.54** the performance of the project. They may be clarified, specified, and fine-tuned at the request of the contracting authority. However, any additional information must not involve any changes to the basic features of the tender or the call for tender, nor allow for variations which are likely to distort competition or have a discriminatory effect. In the author's view, there is a great deal of uncertainty over the meaning of clarification, additional provision of tender specification, and the extent of fine-tuning, to the degree of compromising the competitiveness and integrity of the procedure.

Contracting authorities must assess the tenders received on the basis of the award **4.55** criteria laid down in the contract notice or the descriptive document, and must choose the most economically advantageous tender in accordance with Article 53. At the request of the contracting authority, the tenderer identified as having submitted the most economically advantageous tender may be asked to clarify aspects of the tender, or confirm commitments contained in the tender, provided this does not have the effect of modifying substantial aspects of the tender or of the call for tender, and does not risk distorting competition or discriminating against other candidates.

Overall, the competitive dialogue has addressed many of the features that are **4.56** important during the award of complex projects and are currently being addressed by negotiated procedures with prior advertisement. In comparison with these procedures, the competitive dialogue allows also for a limited number of participants (three in number), introduces a staged approach to tendering, and permits elimination of participants during its internal phases. However, it allows significant scope for post-tender negotiations, but it restricts the award of a contract to complete offers.

(e) Framework procurement

The existing Utilities Directives have introduced framework agreements as a **4.57** selection and tendering procedure which is influenced to a large extent by the benefits of chain supply management and partnering schemes operating in the private sector. The new Utilities Directive has maintained the framework agreements regime in virtually unaltered format as laid down in Article 17(3). Within the provisions of the new Utilities Directive, when an entity established a framework agreement under the relevant procedures which are common to other public contracts covered therein, subsequent individual contracts concluded under the framework agreement may be awarded without having recourse to a call for competition. Individual contracts which have been awarded under a framework agreement could be subject to the reopening of tendering procedures, provided the contracting entity does not invite new tenderers to participate. The Directive specifically stipulates that misuse of framework agreements may distort competition and trigger the application of the relevant rules, particularly with reference to concerted practices which lead to collusive tendering.

4.58 The new Public Sector Directive has, for the first time, introduced framework procurement to the public sector contracting authorities. According to Article 1(5) of the Public Sector Directive, a framework agreement is an agreement between one or more contracting authorities and one or more economic operators, the purpose of which is to establish the terms and conditions of public contracts to be awarded during a given period, in particular with regard to price and, where appropriate, the quantity of supplies, works, or services envisaged.

4.59 Contracting authorities may establish framework agreements in accordance with the provisions of the Public Sector Directive relating to advertising, time limits, and conditions for the submission of tenders. The parties to the framework agreement must be chosen by applying the award criteria set in accordance with Article 53. Article 53 refers to the award criteria being the most economically advantageous offer or the lowest price. When the award is made to the tender most economically advantageous from the point of view of the contracting authority, various criteria are linked to the subject-matter of the public contract in question, for example, quality, price, technical merit, aesthetic and functional characteristics, environmental characteristics, running costs, cost-effectiveness, after-sales service and technical assistance, delivery date, and delivery period or period of completion. When the award criterion refers to the lowest price only, no other factors should play a part. Contracting authorities may subsequently enter into contracts based on such framework agreements during their term of validity either by applying the terms set forth in the framework agreement or, if terms and condition for the conclusion of contracts have not been fixed in advance, by reopening competition between the parties to the framework agreement. The reopening of competition should comply with certain rules,[39] the aim of which is to guarantee the required

---

[39] According to Art. 32(4) of the Public Sector Directive 2004/18, the conditions for reopening competition within a framework agreement include: (a) for every contract to be awarded, contracting authorities must consult in writing the economic operators capable of performing the

flexibility and to guarantee respect for the general principles, in particular the principle of equal treatment.

Contracts based on a framework agreement must be awarded in accordance with **4.60** the procedures of Article 32, which must be applied only between the contracting authorities and the economic operators originally party to the framework agreement. The duration of a framework agreement may not exceed four years, unless exceptional cases justify its extension. Framework agreements can be established between contracting authorities and a single economic operator, according to Article 32(3), in exceptional circumstances which must be justified by the nature of the framework agreement, or with several economic operators, according to Article 32(4). The latter must be at least three in number, provided that there are a sufficient number of economic operators to satisfy the selection criteria or there are a sufficient number of admissible tenders which meet the award criteria. Contracting authorities are under an obligation not to use framework agreements improperly or in such a way as to prevent, restrict, or distort competition.

(f) Electronic procurement

The rapid expansion of electronic purchasing systems in private sector procurement **4.61** and the continuous development of electronic purchasing techniques have made an impact with the Public Sector Directive. Electronic procurement can contribute in increasing competition and streamlining public purchasing, particularly in cases where repetitive purchasing allows efficiencies to be achieved both in time and in financial terms.

(i) Dynamic purchasing systems

Article 1(6) of the Public Sector Directive provides for the establishment of **4.62** dynamic purchasing systems. A dynamic purchasing system is an electronic process which allows contracting authorities to utilize techniques available to the private sector in order to procure supplies or services of repetitive nature. Any economic operator which submits an indicative tender in accordance with the specification and meets the selection criteria should be allowed to join such a system. This purchasing technique allows contracting authorities, through the establishment of a pre-selected list of tenderers, to have a particularly broad range of tenders as a result of the electronic facilities available, and to ensure, in principle, optimum use of public funds through broad competition.

---

contract; (b) contracting authorities must fix a time limit which is sufficiently long to allow tenders for each specific contract to be submitted, taking into account factors such as the complexity of the subject-matter of the contract and the time needed to send in tenders; (c) tenders must be submitted in writing, and their content must remain confidential until the stipulated time limit for reply has expired; and (d) contracting authorities must award each contract to the tenderer who has submitted the best tender on the basis of the award criteria set out in the specifications of the framework agreement.

4.63 The use of dynamic purchasing systems is described in Article 33 of the Public Sector Directive. In order to set up a dynamic purchasing system, contracting authority, the tenderer identified as having submitted the system and does not risk distorting competition or discriminating against other candidates.

    (a) publish a contract notice making it clear that a dynamic purchasing system is involved;

    (b) indicate in the specification, amongst other matters, the nature of the purchases envisaged under that system, as well as all the necessary information concerning the purchasing system, the electronic equipment used and the technical connection arrangements and specifications;

    (c) offer by electronic means, on publication of the notice and up to the expiry of the system, unrestricted, direct and full access to the specification and to any additional documents and must indicate in the notice the internet address at which such documents may be consulted.

4.64 Contracting authorities must give every economic operator participating in the dynamic purchasing system the possibility of submitting an indicative tender throughout the entire period of such system. Each specific contract must be the subject of an invitation to tender. Before issuing the invitation to tender, contracting authorities must publish a simplified contract notice inviting all interested economic operators to submit an indicative tender within a time limit of at least fifteen days. The duration of a dynamic purchasing system may not exceed four years, except in duly justified exceptional cases. Contracting authorities are under an obligation not to levy any charges attributed to the operation of dynamic purchasing systems to the interested economic operators admitted to such systems.

(ii) Electronic auctions

4.65 According to Article 1.7 of the Public Sector Directive an electronic auction is a repetitive process involving an electronic device for the presentation of new prices which are revised downwards, or new values concerning certain elements of tenders. The presentation of such financial information occurs after an initial full evaluation of the tenders, enabling them to be ranked using automatic evaluation methods.

4.66 Article 54 of the Public Sector Directive has for the use of electronic auctions. In open, restricted, or negotiated procedures, contracting authorities may decide that the public contract must be preceded by an electronic auction when the purpose of which is to establish the same circumstances, an electronic auction may be held on the reopening of competition among the parties to a framework agreement, as provided for in the second indent of the second subparagraph of Article 32(4), and on the opening for competition of contracts to be awarded during a given period, in particular with regard to price and, where appropriate, the quantity of supplies, works or services envisaged.

Contracting authorities who decide to hold an electronic auction must indicate **4.67** their intention in the contract notice. The contract specifications must include, *inter alia*, the following details:

(a) the features, the values for which will be the subject of electronic auction, provided that such features are quantifiable and can be expressed in figures or percentages;

(b) any limits on the values which may be submitted, as they result from the specifications relating to the subject of the contract;

(c) the information which will be made available to tenderers in the course of the electronic auction and, where appropriate, when it will be made available to them;

(d) the relevant information concerning the electronic auction process;

(e) the conditions under which the tenderers will be able to bid and, in particular, the minimum differences which will, where appropriate, be required when bidding;

(f) the relevant information concerning the electronic equipment used and the arrangements and technical specifications for connection.

When the contract is to be awarded on the basis of the most economically advan- **4.68** tageous tender, the invitation must provide the full evaluation framework in accordance with the respective weighting of the award criteria. The invitation must also state the mathematical formula to be used in the electronic auction to determine automatic re-rankings on the basis of the new prices or new values submitted. That formula must incorporate the weighting of all the criteria fixed to determine the most economically advantageous tender. Where variants are authorized, a separate formula must be provided for each variant. After closing an electronic auction, contracting authorities must award the contract in accordance with Article 53 on the basis of the results of the electronic auction. Contracting authorities may not have improper recourse to electronic auctions, nor may they use them in such a way as to prevent, restrict, or distort competition, or to change the subject-matter of the contract, as specified in the contract notice and defined in the specifications.

(g) The award criteria and the introduction of policies in public procurement

(i) Contractual performance and public procurement

Conditions relating to the performance of public contracts are compatible with **4.69** the Public Sector Directive provided that they are not directly or indirectly discriminatory and are indicated in the contract notice or in the contract documents. They may, in particular, be intended to favour on-site vocational training, the employment of people experiencing particular difficulty in achieving integration, the fight against unemployment, or the protection of the environment.

4.70   The new Public Sector Directives and the new Utilities Directives remain silent over the possibility of expressly authorizing social or environmental consideration as part of the award criteria of public contracts. Although the draft Directives, at the insistence of the European Parliament, contained specific provisions relevant to workforce matters as part of the award criteria, such provisions were omitted from the final text. The Commission has adopted a myopic view that considerations related to contractual performance cannot be used as criteria for the award of the contract. The Court had the opportunity to correct the Commission's interpretation and point to the right direction of its judgments,[40] where a condition relating to the employment of long-term unemployed persons or the protection of the environment can legitimately constitute a criterion for the award of the contract. However, the new public procurement regime has failed to adopt previous jurisprudential inferences and clarify the position of contacting authorities over the legitimacy of pursuing socio-economic and environmental policies through public procurement.[41]

4.71   Examples of conditions relevant to contractual performance in public contracts may include requirements to recruit long-term job-seekers or to implement training measures for the unemployed or young persons, to comply in substance with the provisions of the International Labour Organization (ILO) Conventions, assuming that such provisions have not been implemented in national law, and to recruit more handicapped persons than are required under national legislation.

4.72   However, according to Article 19 of the Public Sector Directive, a specific category of public sector contracts are regarded as reserved contracts. This is the only concession the Commission afforded member states in relation to the socio-economic dimension of the award criteria of public contacts. Member states may reserve the right to participate in public contract award procedures to sheltered workshops or provide for such contracts to be performed in the context of sheltered employment programmes where most of the employees concerned are handicapped persons who, by reason of the nature or the seriousness of their disabilities, cannot carry on occupations under normal conditions. The contract notice must make reference to this provision.

4.73   In addition, the laws, regulations and collective agreements, at both national and Community level, which are in force in the areas of employment conditions and safety at work, apply during performance of a public contract, providing that such

---

[40] *See* Case 31/87, *Gebroeders Beentjes v. The Netherlands* [1989] ECR 4365, at paragraph 14; Case C-225/98, *Commission v. French Republic (Nord-Pas-de-Calais)* [2000] ECR 7445, at paragraph 52; Case C-513/99, *Concordia Bus Finlandia v. Helsingin Kaupunki et HKL-Bussiliikenne* [2002] ECR 7213, at paragraph 31.

[41] For a detailed analysis of the ordo-liberal versus the neo-classical approach in public procurement regulation, see Bovis, 'Public Procurement and the Internal Market of the 21st Century: Economic Exercise versus Policy Choice', in *EU Law for the 21st Century: Rethinking the New Legal Order*, Chapter 17, footnote 9, op. cit.

rules, and their application, comply with Community law. In cross-border situations, where workers from one member state provide services in another member state for the purpose of performing a public contract, Directive 96/71/EC concerning the posting of workers in the framework of the provision of services[42] lays down the minimum conditions which must be observed by the host country in respect of such posted workers. If national law contains provisions to this effect, non-compliance with those obligations may be considered to be grave misconduct, or an offence concerning the professional conduct of the economic operator concerned, liable to lead to the exclusion of that economic operator from the procedure for the award of a public contract.

(ii) The most economically advantageous offer

The most economically advantageous offer as an award criterion has provided the Court with the opportunity to balance the economic considerations of public procurement with policy choices. Although, in numerous instances, the Court has maintained the importance of the economic approach[43] to the regulation of public sector contracts, it has also recognized the relative discretion of contracting authorities to utilize non-economic considerations as award criteria. **4.74**

The meaning of the most economically advantageous offer[44] includes a combination of factors chosen by the contracting authority, including price, delivery or completion date, running costs, cost-effectiveness, profitability, technical merit, product or work quality, aesthetic and functional characteristics, after-sales service and technical assistance, commitments with regard to spare parts and components and maintenance costs, and security of supplies. The above list is not exhaustive and the factors listed therein serve as a guideline for contracting authorities in the weighted evaluation process of the contract award. The Court reiterated the flexible and wide interpretation of the relevant award criterion[45] and had no difficulty in declaring that contracting authorities may use the most economically advantageous offer as the award criterion by choosing the factors which they want to apply in evaluating tenders,[46] provided these factors are mentioned, in hierarchical order or descending **4.75**

---

[42] *See* [1997] OJ L18/1, 12 January 1997.

[43] *See Case* C-380/98, *The Queen and HM Treasury, ex parte University of Cambridge* [2000] ECR 8035, at paragraph 17; Case C-44/96, *Mannesmann Anlangenbau Austria AG et al. v. Strohal Rotationsdurck GesmbH* [1998] ECR 73, at paragraph 33; Case C-360/96, *Gemeente Arnhem Gemeente Rheden v. BFI Holding BV* [1998] ECR 6821, at paragraphs 42 and 43; Case C-237/99, *Commission v. France*, judgment of 1 February 2001 (OPAC), at paragraphs 41 and 42.

[44] *See* Art. 26 of Directive 93/36, Art. 30 of Directive 93/37, Art. 34 of Directive 93/38 and Art. 36 of Directive 92/50.

[45] Case 31/87, *Gebroeders Beentjes v. The Netherlands* [1989] ECR 4365.

[46] Case C-324/93, *R. v. The Secretary of State for the Home Department, ex parte Evans Medical Ltd and Macfarlan Smith Ltd*, judgment of 28 March 1995, where the national court asked whether factors concerning continuity and reliability as well as security of supplies fall under the framework of the most economically advantageous offer, when the latter is being evaluated.

sequence, in the invitation to tender or the contract documents,[47] so tenderers and interested parties can clearly ascertain the relative weight of factors other than price for the evaluation process. However, factors, which have no strict relevance in determining the most economically advantageous offer by reference to objective criteria do involve an element of arbitrary choice and therefore should be considered as incompatible with the Directives.[48]

4.76 A question was put before the Court in *Concordia*[49] intended to assess the integral function of the factors that comprise the most economically advantageous offer for contracting authorities. The question was as to whether, under the most economically advantageous offer, each individual award factor has to provide an economic advantage which directly benefits the contracting authority, or it is sufficient that each individual factor has to be measurable in economic terms, without the requirement that it directly provides an economic advantage for the contracting authority in the given contract.

4.77 Although there is wide discretion conferred to contracting authorities in compiling the relevant factors, subject to the requirements of relevance to the contract in question and their publicity, their relative importance, in economic terms, remains somehow unknown. In other words, the discretion conferred to contracting authorities would permit a wide range of factors to feature as part of award criteria in public contracts, without the need to demonstrate a direct economic advantage to a contracting authority which is attributable to each of these factors. On the contrary, if each individual factor has to establish a measurable (in quantifiable terms) economic advantage to the contracting authority, which is directly attributed to its inclusion as part of the award criterion, the discretion of contracting authorities is curtailed, since they would be required to undertake and publicise in the tender or contract documents a clear cost-benefit analysis of the relevant factors that comprise in their view the most economically advantageous offer.

4.78 **Social considerations**   In *Beentjes*,[50] the Court ruled that social policy considerations and, in particular, measures aiming at the combating of long term unemployment, could only be part of the award criteria of public contracts, especially in cases where the most economically advantageous offer is selected. The Court accepted that the latter award criterion contains features that are not exhaustively defined in the Directives; therefore there is discretion conferred on contracting authorities to specify what would the most economically advantageous offer for them. However, contracting authorities cannot refer to such measures as a

---

[47] *See* paragraph 22 of *Beentjes*.   [48] *See* paragraph 37 of *Beentjes*.
[49] *See* Case C-513/99, *Concordia Bus Finlandia v. Helsingin Kaupunki et HKL-Bussiliikenne* [2002] ECR 7213. The case concerns, *inter alia*, the permissibility of environmental considerations as part of the award criteria.
[50] *See* Case 31/87, *Gebroeders Beentjes BV v. The Netherlands* op. cit.

selection criterion and disqualify candidates which could not meet the relevant requirements. The selection of tenderers is a process, which is based on an exhaustive list of technical and financial requirements expressly stipulated in the relevant Directives, and the insertion of contract compliance as a selection and qualification requirement would be considered *ultra vires*. The Court held that a contractual condition relating to the employment of long-term unemployed persons is compatible with the Public Procurement Directives, if it has no direct or indirect discriminatory effect on tenders from other member states. Furthermore, such a contractual condition must be mentioned in the tender notice.[51] Rejection of a contract on the grounds of a contractor's inability to employ long-term unemployed persons has no relation to the checking of the contractors' suitability on the basis of their economic and financial standing and their technical knowledge and ability. The Court maintained that measures relating to employment could be utilized as a feature of the award criteria only when they are part of a contractual obligation of the public contract in question, and on condition that they do not run contrary to the fundamental principles of the Treaty. The significance of that qualification has revealed the Court's potential stance over the issue of contract compliance in public procurement.

In the recent case *Nord-pas-de-Calais*, the Court considered whether a condition **4.79** linked to a local project to combat unemployment could be considered as an award criterion of the relevant contract. The Court held that the most economically advantageous offer does not preclude all possibility for the contracting authorities to use as a criterion a condition linked to the campaign against unemployment, provided that that condition is consistent with all the fundamental principles of Community law, in particular the principle of non-discrimination deriving from the provisions of the Treaty on the right of establishment and the freedom to provide services.[52] Furthermore, even if such a criterion is not in itself incompatible with Directive 93/37, it must be applied in conformity with all the procedural rules laid down in that Directive, in particular the rules on advertising.[53] The Court therefore accepted the employment considerations as an award criterion, part of the most economically advantageous offer, provided it is consistent with the fundamental principles of Community law, in particular, the principle of non-discrimination, and it is advertised in the contract notice.

The Court's rulings in *Beentjes* and *Nord-pas-de-Calais* have opened an interesting **4.80** chapter in public procurement jurisprudence. *Beentjes* started a debate on the integral dimensions of contract compliance, and differentiated between the

---

[51] *See Bellini*, Case 28/86 [1987] ECR 3347.   [52] *See Beentjes*, paragraph 29.
[53] *See*, to that effect, paragraph 31, where the Court stipulated that an award criterion linked to the campaign against unemployment must be expressly mentioned in the contract notice so that contractors may become aware of its existence.

positive and *negative* approaches. A positive approach within contract compliance encompasses all measures and policies imposed by contracting authorities on tenderers as suitability criteria for their selection in public procurement contracts. Such positive action measures and policies are intended to complement the actual objectives of public procurement, which are confined to economic and financial parameters and are based on a transparent and predictable legal background. Although the complementarity of contract compliance with the actual aims and objectives of the public procurement regime was acknowledged, the Court has been reluctant in accepting such a flexible interpretation of the Directives and, based on the literal interpretation of the relevant provisions, disallowed positive actions of a social policy dimension as part of the selection criteria for tendering procedures in public procurement. However, it should be mentioned that contract compliance could incorporate not only unemployment considerations, but also promote equality of opportunities and eliminate sex or race discrimination in the relevant market.[54] Indeed, the Directives on public procurement stipulate that the contracting authority may require tenderers to observe national provisions of employment legislation when they submit their offers. The ability to observe and conform to national employment laws in a member state may constitute a ground of disqualification and exclusion of the defaulting firm from public procurement contracts. In fact, under such interpretation, contract compliance may be a factor of selection criteria specified in the Directives, as it contains a *negative approach* to legislation and measures relating to social policy.[55]

4.81 **Environmental considerations** In *Concordia*,[56] the Court was asked, *inter alia*, whether environmental considerations such as low emissions and noise levels of vehicles could be included amongst the factors of the most economically

---

[54] There are a number of legal instruments relevant to social policy at Community level that may apply to public procurement. They include, in particular, Directives on safety and health at work, (for example, Council Directive 89/391 on the Introduction of Measures to Encourage Improvements in the Safety and Health of Workers at Work, and Directive 92/57 on the Implementation of Minimum Safety and Health Requirements at Temporary or Mobile Construction Sites), working conditions, and the application of employment law (for example, Directive 96/71/EC of the European Parliament and of the Council Concerning the Posting of Workers in the Framework of the Provision of Services [1997] OJ L18/1 of 21 January 1997, and Directive 2001/23 on the Safeguarding of Employees' Rights in the Event of Transfers of Undertakings, Businesses or Parts of Undertakings or Businesses [2001] OJ L82/16 of 22 March 2001, codifying Directive 77/187/EEC), Directive 2000/43/EC of 29 June 2000 Implementing the Principle of Equal Treatment Between Persons Irrespective of Racial or Ethnic Origin [2000] OJ L180/22, and Directive 2000/78/EC of 27 November 2000 Establishing a General Framework for Equal Treatment in Employment and Occupation [2000] OJ L303/16.

[55] It should be mentioned that adherence to health and safety laws has been considered by a British court as part of the technical requirements specified in the Works Directive for the process of selection of tenderers, *see General Building and Maintenance v. Greenwich Borough Council* [1993] IRLR 535. Along these lines, *see* European Commission, op. cit. (n. 27).

[56] *See* Case C-513/99, *Concordia Bus Finlandia v. Helsingin Kaupunki et HKL-Bussiliikenne* [2002] ECR 7213.

advantageous criterion, in order to promote certain types of vehicles that meet or exceed certain emission and noise levels. The Advocate General in his opinion[57] followed the *Beentjes* principle, established that contracting authorities are free to determine the factors under which the most economically advantageous offer is to be assessed, and that environmental considerations could be part of the award criteria, provided they do not discriminate over alternative offers, as long as they have been clearly publicized in the tender or contract documents. However, the inclusion of such factors in the award criteria should not prevent alternative offers that satisfy the contract specifications being taken into consideration by contracting authorities.[58] Criteria relating to the environment, in order to be permissible as additional criteria under the most economically advantageous offer, must satisfy a number of conditions, namely they must be objective, universally applicable, strictly relevant to the contract in question, and clearly contribute an economic advantage to the contracting authority.[59]

Under Article 6 of the EU Treaty, environmental protection requirements are to **4.82** be integrated into the definition and implementation of the Community policies and activities referred to in Article 3 of that Treaty, in particular with a view to promoting sustainable development. The Public Sector Directive clarifies how contracting authorities may contribute to the protection of the environment and the promotion of sustainable development, whilst ensuring the fairness and competition in the award of public contracts. Article 50 of the Public Sector Directive deals with environmental management standards. It provides that contracting authorities may require the production of certificates drawn up by independent bodies attesting the compliance of the economic operator with certain environmental management standards; if so, they must refer to the Community Eco-Management and Audit Scheme (EMAS), or to environmental management standards based on the relevant European or international standards certified by bodies conforming to Community law, or the relevant European or international standards concerning certification. Contracting authorities must recognize equivalent certificates from bodies established in other member states. They must also accept other evidence of equivalent environmental management measures from economic operators.

In appropriate cases, in which the nature of the works and/or services justifies **4.83** applying environmental management measures or schemes during the

---

[57] *See* the Opinion of Advocate General Mischo delivered on 13 December 2001.

[58] Clearly the Advocate General wanted to exclude any possibility of environmental considerations being part of selection criteria, or disguised as technical specifications, capable of discriminating against tenderers who could not meet them. *See* the debate on selection and qualification and technical standards, in Bovis, op. cit. (n. 26).

[59] See the analysis of the Advocate General Mischo in his opinion of *Concordia*, paragraphs 77 to 123.

performance of a public contract, the application of such measures or schemes may be required. Environmental management schemes, whether or not they are registered under Community instruments such as Regulation (EC) No. 761/2001 (EMAS),[60] can demonstrate that the economic operator has the technical capability to perform the contract. Moreover, a description of the measures implemented by the economic operator to ensure the same level of environmental protection should be accepted as an alternative to environmental management registration schemes as a form of evidence.

(h) Small and medium-sized enterprises and subcontracting

4.84 In order to encourage the involvement of small and medium-sized undertakings in the public contracts procurement market, it is advisable to include provisions on subcontracting. According to Article 25 of the Public Sector Directive, the contracting authority, in the contract documents, may ask or may be required by a member state to ask the tenderer to indicate in his tender any share of the contract he may intend to subcontract to third parties and any proposed subcontractors. This indication must be without prejudice to the question of the principal economic operator's liability. The theme of public procurement and subcontracting originates in the original Works Directives, where contracting authorities are allowed to specify to concessionaires a minimum percentage of the works to be subcontracted. Along these lines, Article 60 of the Public Sector Directive provides that the contracting authority may either: (a) require the concessionaire to award contracts representing a minimum of thirty per cent of the total value of the work for which the concession contract is to be awarded to third parties, at the same time providing the option for candidates to increase this percentage, this minimum percentage being specified in the concession contract, or (b) request the candidates for concession contracts to specify in their tenders the percentage, if any, of the total value of the work for which the concession contract is to be awarded which they intend to assign to third parties.

(i) Procurement and culture

4.85 The award of public contracts for certain audiovisual services in the field of broadcasting should allow aspects of cultural or social significance to be taken into account which render application of procurement rules inappropriate. For these reasons, an exception must therefore be made for public service contracts for the purchase, development, production, or co-production of off-the-shelf programmes and other preparatory services, such as those relating to scripts or artistic performances necessary for the production of the programme and

---

[60] *See* Regulation (EC) No. 761/2001 of the European Parliament and of the Council of 19 March 2001 Allowing a Voluntary Participation by Organizations in a Community Eco-Management and Audit Scheme (EMAS) [2001] OJ L114/1, 24 April 2001.

contracts concerning broadcasting times. However, this exclusion should not apply to the supply of technical equipment necessary for the production, co-production, and broadcasting of such programmes. A broadcast should be defined as transmission and distribution using any form of electronic network.

(j) Procurement and probity

The award of public contracts to economic operators who have participated in a **4.86** criminal organization or who have been found guilty of corruption or of fraud to the detriment of the financial interests of the European Communities, or of money laundering, should be avoided. Where appropriate, the contracting authorities should ask candidates or tenderers to supply relevant documents and, where they have doubts concerning the personal situation of a candidate or tenderer, they may seek the cooperation of the competent authorities of the member state concerned. The exclusion of such economic operators should take place as soon as the contracting authority has knowledge of a judgment concerning such offences rendered in accordance with national law that has the force of *res judicata*. If national law contains provisions to this effect, non-compliance with environmental legislation or legislation on unlawful agreements in public contracts, which has been the subject of a final judgment or a decision having equivalent effect, may be considered an offence concerning the professional conduct of the economic operator concerned, or grave misconduct. Non-observance of national provisions implementing Council Directives 2000/78/EC[61] and 76/207/EC[62] concerning equal treatment of workers, which has been the subject of a final judgment or a decision having equivalent effect, may be considered an offence concerning the professional conduct of the economic operator concerned or grave misconduct.

Article 45 of the Public Sector Directive deals with the personal situation of the **4.87** candidate or tenderer. It provides that any candidate or tenderer who has been the subject of a conviction by final judgment of which the contracting authority is aware for one or more of the reasons listed below must be excluded from participation in a public contract:

(a) participation in a criminal organization, as defined in Article 2(1) of Council Joint Action 98/733/JHA;[63] (b) corruption, as defined in Article 3 of the Council Act of 26 May 1997[64] and Article 3(1) of Council Joint Action

---

[61] *See* Council Directive 2000/78/EC of 27 November 2000 Establishing a General Framework for Equal Treatment in Employment and Occupation [2000] OJ L303/16, 2 December 2000.

[62] *See* Council Directive 76/207/EEC of 9 February 1976 on the Implementation of the Principle of Equal Treatment for Men and Women as Regards Access to Employment, Vocational Training and Promotion, and Working Conditions [1976] OJ L39/40, 14 February 1976. Directive amended by Directive 2002/73/EC of the European Parliament and of the Council [2002] OJ L269/15, 5 October 2002.   [63] *See* [1998] OJ L351/1, 29 December 1998.

[64] *See* [1997] OJ C195/1, 25 June 1997.

98/742/JHA,[65] respectively; (c) fraud within the meaning of Article 1 of the Convention relating to the protection of the financial interests of the European Communities;[66] (d) money laundering, as defined in Article 1 of Council Directive 91/308 on prevention of the use of the financial system for the purpose of money laundering.[67]

(3) The new concepts in utilities procurement

(a) Remit and extent of coverage

4.88 As a result of the liberalization process in public utilities across the European Union and the introduction of sector-specific regulation covering the operational interface of such entities, the regulation of their purchasing practices no longer requires the rigidity and disciplined structure of that of public sector authorities. Under the remit of flexibility envisaged by the new regime, utilities procurement has undergone a dramatic restructuring with effects varying from the relaxation of the competitive tendering regime to the total disengagement of the public procurement rules in industries that operate under competitive conditions, especially in the telecommunications and water sectors. The new Utilities Procurement Directive does not regard telecommunications utilities as contracting entities, since the sector has been subjected to competitive forces adequate enough to ensure its commercial character operation.

4.89 The existing Utilities Directive 98/38/EC covers, at present, certain contracts awarded by contracting entities operating in the telecommunications sector. One of the consequences of telecommunications regulation has been the introduction of effective competition, both *de jure* and *de facto*, in this sector. The Commission, being aware of this development has published a list of telecommunications services[68] which may already be excluded from the scope of the existing Utilities Directive by virtue of Article 8 of the existing Utilities Directive.

4.90 There are three milestones in EU telecommunications regulation. Firstly, the actions, which followed the 1987 Green Paper[69] and open the door for partial sector liberalization, and set in motion the process of an integrated telecommunications market. Although the corporate structure of operators was left untouched, and voice telephony and television broadcasting were excluded, some fundamental principles were established and this created the necessary conditions for subsequent regulatory

---

[65] *See* [1998] OJ L358/2, 31 December 1998.
[66] *See* [1995] OJ C316/48, 27 November 1995.
[67] *See* [1991] OJ L166/77, 28 June 1991. Directive as amended by Directive 2001/97/EC of the European Parliament and of the Council of 4 December 2001 [2001] OJ L344/76, 28 December 2001.
[68] *See* [1994] OJ L336/1, 23 December 1994.
[69] *See* European Commission, *Towards a Dynamic Economy—Green Paper on the Development of the Common Market for Telecommunications Services and Equipment*, COM (87) 290.

reforms. In particular, the liberalization of terminal equipment,[70] the community-wide interoperability,[71] the separation of regulatory and operation functions of public telecommunications operators,[72] the application of competition law to public telecommunications operators and private sector providers,[73] and the installation of an Open Network Provision (OPN) to determine the level competitiveness between public monopolies and private telecommunications providers.[74] The period that followed the 1992 Review[75] and the 1994 Green Paper[76] resulted, gradually, in a full liberalization of alternative infrastructures,[77] cable television networks, and mobile networks. Voice telephony regulation and the liberalization of the relevant market were envisaged as the subsequent phase.

Secondly, the fully liberalized period earmarked a period which includes the **4.91** introduction of a competition regime in the telecommunications sectors with the so-called full competition Directive (Directive 96/19EC).[78] This period witnessed significant regulatory adjustments in the field of Open Network Provision, such as interconnectivity and licensing provisions and voice telephony and universal service liberalization.[79] In addition, common frameworks for interconnection of networks and licensing and authorization were provided by Directive 97/33EC[80] (the so-called Interconnection Directive) and by Directive

---

[70] Directive 88/301EEC on liberalizing terminal equipment in telecommunications is the first instrument that followed the 1987 Green Paper. The Directive required the abolition of exclusive rights for import, marketing, connection, bringing into service, or maintenance of telecommunications terminal equipment.

[71] *See* Directive 91/263EEC replacing Directive 86/361EEC on the initial stage of the mutual recognition of type approval for telecommunications terminal equipment. The Directive has been consolidated by Directive 98/13EC on telecommunications terminal equipment and satellite earth station equipment, including mutual recognition of its conformity. The system has been replaced with a mutual recognition framework by virtue of Directive 99/5EC on radio equipment and telecommunications terminal and mutual recognition of their conformity.

[72] *See* Directive 90/388EC (the Services Directive) as subsequently amended. The original Directive did not apply to television or radio broadcasting, telex mobile telephony paging, satellite services, and voice telephony.

[73] *See* the European Commission, *Commission's Guidelines on the Application of EC Competition Rules in the Telecommunications Sector* [1991] OJ C233/2.

[74] *See* Directive 90/387EEC on the OPN Framework, and Directive 92/44EEC on the OPN Leased Lines.

[75] *See* European Commission, *Review of the Situation in the Telecommunications Services Sector*, SEC (92) 1048 final.

[76] *See* European Commission, *Part I—Principles and Timetable, 1994*, COM (94) 440 final, and *Part II—A Common Approach to the Provision of Infrastructures for Telecommunications in the European Union, 1995*, COM (94) 682 final.

[77] Telecommunications infrastructure owned by parties different than local telecommunications operators.

[78] *See* Directive 96/19EC [1996] OJ L74, amending Directive 90/388EEC with regard to the implementation of full competition in telecommunications markets.

[79] The envisaged regulatory adjustments were enacted by virtue of Directive 97/51EC [1997] OJ L295/23 and Directive 98/10EC on the application of OPN to voce telephony and universal service for telecommunications in a competitive environment.

[80] *See* Directive 97/33EC [1997] OJ L199/32.

97/13EC[81] (the so-called Licensing Directive), respectively. The advent of competitiveness in the relevant markets introduced the notion of significant market power (SMP) in telecommunications markets,[82] a development which will provide a regulatory yardstick for future generations of legal and policy instruments.

4.92 Thirdly, the current phase of telecommunications regulation embraces the notion of convergence and the creation of a common regulatory framework for telecommunications, media, and information technologies.[83] The most significant legislative measure has been the adoption of the Competition Directive 2002/76EC,[84] on competition in the markets for electronic communications networks and services. The Directive consolidates all previous instruments, and its main purpose is to reaffirm the obligation of member states to abolish exclusive and special rights in the field of telecommunications. Furthermore, four additional Directives consolidate the telecommunications regime and, in particular, the Framework Directive 2002/21EC[85] on a common regulatory framework for electronic communications networks and services, the Authorization Directive 2002/20/EC,[86] the Universal Service Directive 2002/22/EC[87] on universal service and users' rights relating to electronic communications networks and services, and the Access Directive 2002/19/EC[88] on access to interconnection of electronic communications networks and associated facilities.

4.93 The regulatory process of telecommunications in the European Union is centred on the national regulatory authorities (NRAs), which will provide the necessary interface for implementing Community principles in line with national legal frameworks and market conditions. As a consequence of the above progress in the telecommunications sector and its relevant markets, the Commission considers that it is no longer necessary to regulate purchases by entities operating in this sector.

---

[81] *See* Directive 97/13EC [1997] OJ L117/15.

[82] *See* Art. 4(3) of the Interconnection Directive 97/33EC regarding universal service and operability through the applications of OPN.

[83] *See* European Commission, *Green Paper on the Convergence of Telecommunications, Media and Information Technologies*, COM (97) 623.

[84] *See* Directive 2002/76EC [2002] OJ L249/21, which consolidates the Services Directive 90/388EEC as amended by the Satellite Directive 94/46EC, the Cable Directive 95/51EC, the Mobile Directive 96/2EC, the full Competition Directive 96/19EC, and the Cable Ownership Directive 1999/64 amending the Services Directive in relation to the requirement that telecommunications networks and cable TV networks owned by a single operator are separate legal entities.

[85] *See* Directive 2002/21EC [2002] OJ L108/33, which effectively replaces the OPN Framework Directive 90/387EEC, as amended by Directive 97/51/EC, and repeals Directives 90/387EEC, 92/44, the Interconnection Directive 97/33EC, the Licensing Directive 97/13EC, the Voice Telephony Directive 98/10EC, and the Telecommunications Data Protection Directive 97/66EC.

[86] *See* Directive 2002/20/EC, which effectively repeals all existing licensing and authorization instruments.

[87] *See* Directive 2002/22/EC [2002] OJ L108/51 which replaces the relevant provisions of the Interconnection Directive 97/33/EC and the Voice Telephony Directive 98/61/EC.

[88] *See* Directive 2002/19 [2002] OJ L108/7, which replaces the relevant provisions of the Interconnection Directive 97/33/EC and OPN Leased Lined Directive 92/44/EC.

On the other hand, Directive 93/38/EC excludes from its scope purchases of **4.94** voice telephony, telex, mobile telephone, paging, and satellite services. Those exclusions were introduced to take account of the fact that the services in question could frequently be provided only by one service provider in a given geographical area because of the absence of effective competition and the existence of special or exclusive rights. The introduction of effective competition in the telecommunications sector removes the justification for these exclusions. The Commission has therefore included the procurement of such telecommunications services within the remit of the new Utilities Directive.

Conversely, the postal sector which was previously excluded from procurement **4.95** regulation is now covered, but not until 1 January 2009, in order to allow sufficient time for transitional measures in the postal services sector of member states. Taking into account the further opening up of Community postal services to competition and the fact that such services are provided through a network by contracting authorities, public undertakings, and other undertakings, contracts awarded by contracting entities providing postal services should be subject to the rules of this Directive, creating a framework for sound commercial practice and allowing greater flexibility than is offered by the new Utilities Directive 2004/18/EC. For a definition of the activities in question, it is necessary to take into account the definitions of Directive 97/67/EC on common rules for the development of the internal market of Community postal services and the improvement of quality of service.[89]

The new concepts of Directive 2004/17 embrace the links of the state with utilities **4.96** through special or exclusive rights and the notion of affiliated undertakings as a potential subject of utilities procurement coverage. Finally, the new regime introduces grounds for exemption for entities operating in competitive markets.

(b) Special or exclusive rights in the utilities

The remit and thrust of public procurement legislation has traditionally relied on **4.97** the connection between contracting authorities and the state. However, that connection might be weak to cover entities, which operate in the utilities sector and have been privatised. The *Foster* principle[90] established that state accountability could not embrace privatized enterprises.[91] The enactment of the Utilities Directives[92] brought under the procurement framework entities operating in the

---

[89] *See* [1998] OJ L15/14, 21 January 1998. Directive as last amended by Regulation (EC) No. 1882/2003 [2003] OJ L284/1, 31 October 2003.

[90] *See* Case 188/89, *Foster v British Gas* [1990] ECR-1313, in which the European Court of Justice ruled that a Directive capable of having direct effect could be invoked against a body which is subject to the *control* of the State and has been delegated special powers.

[91] This was the view of Advocate General Lenz in Case 247/89, *Commission v. Portugal*, [1991] ECR I 3659.

[92] EC Directive 90/531, as amended by EC Directive 93/38 [1993] OJ L199/84.

water, energy, transport, and telecommunications sectors. A wide range of these entities are covered by the expression 'bodies governed by public law', which is used by the existing Utilities Directives for the contracting entities operating in the relevant sectors.[93] Interestingly, another category of contracting authorities under the existing Utilities Directives includes *public undertakings*.[94] The term indicates any undertaking over which the state may exercise direct or indirect dominant influence by means of ownership, or by means of financial participation, or by means of laws and regulations, which govern the public undertaking's operation. Dominant influence can be exercised in the form of a majority holding of the undertaking's subscribed capital, in the form of majority controlling of the undertaking's issued shares, or, finally in the form of the right to appoint the majority of the undertaking's management board. Public undertakings may cover utilities operators, which have been granted exclusive rights of exploitation of a service. Irrespective of their ownership, they are subject to the Utilities Directive in as much as the *exclusivity* of their operation precludes other entities from entering the relevant market under substantially the same competitive conditions.

4.98 Entities in the utilities sector enjoying special or exclusive rights conferred to them by member states have been covered by the utilities procurement regime. The intention of the legislature was to eliminate government interference over the purchasing behaviour of the recipients of such rights arising from the pressure exercised by the respective governments as a condition of granting the special or exclusive rights and the inability of the recipient entity to resist such pressure as a result of the non-competitive environment of its operation. Traditionally, special or exclusive rights were demonstrable when the right to expropriate property or the right to place utility networks on, under, or over highways were conferred upon the recipient. Also, a connection with an entity enjoying special or exclusive rights brought any supplier of a utility network within the remit of utilities procurement.

4.99 For the purposes of the new Utilities Directive, and in accordance with Article 2(3), 'special or exclusive rights' means rights granted by a competent authority of a member state by way of any legislative, regulatory, or administrative provision the effect of which is to limit the exercise of activities defined in Articles 3 to 7[95] to one or more entities, and which substantially affects the ability of other entities to carry out such activity.

4.100 The new Utilities Directive provides for a more restrictive definition of the notion of special or exclusive rights than its predecessor. The consequence of the definition is depicted in three ways: first, the availability of a procedure for the

---

[93] *See* Art. 1(1) of Directive 93/38.   [94] *See* Art. 1(2) of Directive 93/38.

[95] The activities covering special or exclusive rights embrace the following utilities sectors: gas, heat and electricity, water, postal services, transport services, exploration for, or extraction of, oil, gas, coal or other solid fuels, as well as ports and airports.

expropriation or use of property and the ability of an entity to place network equipment on, under, or over a public highway for the purpose of constructing networks or port or airport facilities, does not automatically constitute exclusive or special rights within the meaning of the Directive; secondly, a special or exclusive right does not exist merely due to the fact that an entity supplies drinking water, electricity, gas or heat to a network which is itself operated by an entity enjoying special or exclusive rights granted by a competent authority of a member state; and, thirdly, rights granted by a member state through acts of concession, to a limited number of undertakings on the basis of objective, proportionate and non-discriminatory criteria that allow any interested party fulfilling those criteria to enjoy those rights, are not considered special or exclusive rights.

The practical implication of the definition of special or exclusive rights under the new Utilities Directive is the non-applicability of the regime to the entities that do not meet the conditions but are still covered under the existing regime. **4.101**

The influence of the Court's jurisprudence in the restrictive application of special or exclusive rights is evident. The Court's approach in the *British Telecommunications*[96] case does not allow the application of the sector-specific definition of leased (licensed) lines in the telecommunications sector to the respective utilities procurement definition of special or exclusive right. In that case, the Court ruled that special or exclusive rights under the Leased Lines Directive[97] did not exist as a result of the licenses conferred by member states to entities. **4.102**

The situation could be more complicated as entities compete for such special or exclusive rights such as concessions or public–private partnerships on the basis of objective, proportionate, and non-discriminatory criteria which can restrict market access to other undertakings and, by definition, limit the number of interested parties. The analogous application of the *British Telecommunications* judgment is dubious, as the Court remained silent over such a scenario. The Commission however has indicated[98] that, where member states do not enjoy discretion in the conferral of special or exclusive rights, by definition they cannot detrimentally influence the procurement behaviour of the recipient of such rights and, as a consequence, the utilities procurement regime need not apply. **4.103**

(c) Affiliated undertakings

Article 13 of the existing Utilities Directive provides for the exclusion of certain contracts between contracting authorities and affiliated undertakings. The term **4.104**

---

[96] *See* Case C-302/94, *R. v. Secretary of State for Trade and Industry ex parte British Telecommunications Plc* [1996] ECR 6417. [97] *See* EC Directive 92/44 [1992] OJ L165/27.
[98] *See* European Commission, *Explanatory Memorandum of the Proposal for the Directive Coordinating the Procurement Procedures of Entities Operating in the Water, Energy and Transport Sectors*, COM (2000) 276 final.

affiliated undertaking, for the purposes of Article 1(3) of the Utilities Directive, is one the annual accounts of which are consolidated with those of the contracting entity in accordance with the requirements of the Seventh Company Law Directive.[99] These are service contracts which are awarded to a service provider which is affiliated to the contracting entity, and service contracts which are awarded to a service provider which is affiliated to a contracting entity participating in a joint venture formed for the purpose of carrying out an activity covered by the Directive.

4.105 The explanatory memorandum of the Utilities Directive[100] stated that this provision relates to three types of service provision within groups. These categories, which may or may not be distinct, are: the provision of common services such as accounting, recruitment, and management; the provision of specialized services embodying the know-how of the group; and the provision of a specialized service to a joint venture. The exclusion from the provisions of the Directive is subject, however, to two conditions: the service provider must be an undertaking affiliated to the contracting authority, and at least eighty per cent of its average turnover arising within the European Community for the preceding three years derives from the provision of the same or similar services to undertakings with which it is affiliated. The Commission is empowered to monitor the application of this Article and require the notification of the names of the undertakings concerned and the nature and value of the service contracts involved.

4.106 Interestingly, the new utilities regime also excludes from its remit contracts awarded to affiliated undertakings. Article 23 of the new Utilities Directive excludes contracts awarded by a contracting entity to an affiliated undertaking, or by a joint venture, formed exclusively by a number of contracting entities for the purpose of carrying out activities which are covered by the Utilities Directive to an undertaking which is affiliated with one of these contracting entities.

4.107 Under the new utilities procurement regime, the term 'affiliated undertaking' means any undertaking the annual accounts of which are consolidated with those of the contracting entity in accordance with the requirements of the Seventh Council Directive 83/349 on consolidated accounts.[101] In cases of entities which are not subject to that Directive, affiliated undertaking means any undertaking over which the contracting entity may exercise, directly or indirectly, a dominant influence within the meaning of Article 2(1)(b), or any undertaking over which the contracting entity may exercise a dominant influence by virtue of ownership, financial participation, or the rules which govern it.

---

[99] *See* Council Directive 83/349 [1983] OJ L193/1.   [100] *See* COM (91) 347-SYN 361.
[101] *See* [1983] OJ L193/1, 18 July 1983, as last amended by Directive 2001/65/EC [2001] OJ L283/28, 27 October 2001.

(d) Competitive markets in utilities

Privatized utilities could, in principle, be excluded from the procurement rules **4.108**
when a genuinely competitive regime[102] within the relevant market structure
would rule out purchasing patterns based on non-economic considerations.
The new Utilities Directive should not apply to markets where the participants
pursue an activity which is directly exposed to competition in markets to which
access is not limited within the relevant member state. The new Utilities Directive
has therefore introduced a procedure, applicable to all sectors covered by its
provisions, which will enable the effects of current or future opening-up to
competition to be taken into account. Such a procedure should provide legal
certainty for the entities concerned, as well as an appropriate decision-making
process, ensuring, within short time limits, uniform application of standards that
result in the disengagement of the relevant procurement rules.

Direct exposure to competition should be assessed on the basis of objective **4.109**
criteria, taking account of the specific characteristics of the sector concerned. The
implementation and application of appropriate Community legislation liberalizing a utility sector will be considered to provide sufficient grounds for determining if there is free access to the market in question. Such appropriate legislation
should be identified in an annex which will be provided by the Commission. In
particular, the Commission will take into account the possible adoption of measures entailing a genuine opening up to competition of sectors other than those
for which legislation is already mentioned in Annex XI, such as that of railway
transport services. Where free access to a given market does not result from
the implementation of appropriate Community legislation, it should be
demonstrated that such access is uninhibited *de jure* and *de facto*.

Article 30 of the new Utilities Directive provides for the procedure for establishing **4.110**
whether a given activity of a utility entity is directly exposed to competition. The
question of whether an activity is directly exposed to competition shall be decided
on the basis of criteria that are in conformity with the Treaty provisions on competition, such as the characteristics of the goods or services concerned, the existence of alternative goods or services, the prices, and the actual or potential
presence of more than one supplier of the goods or services in question. When a
member state considers that access to the relevant market activity is free, it must
notify the Commission and provide all relevant facts, and, in particular, details of
any law, regulation, administrative provision, or agreements, where appropriate,

---

[102] The determination of a genuinely competitive regime is left to the utilities operators
themselves. *See* Case C 392/93, *The Queen and HM Treasury, ex parte British Telecommunications Plc*
[1993] OJ C287/6. This is perhaps a first step towards self-regulation which could lead to the
disengagement of the relevant contracting authorities from the public procurement regime.

ogether with the position adopted by an independent national authority that is competent in relation to the regulation of the activity concerned. The Commission can issue a Decision which verifies that the relevant activity is provided in a competitive environment. Such verification is also presumed if the Commission has not adopted a Decision concerning the inapplicability of the Utilities Directive within a certain period.[103]

4.111 The disengagement of the utilities procurement regime as a result of the operation of the relevant entities in competitive markets by virtue of Article 30 of the new Utilities Directive does not apply to the WTO Government Procurement Agreement. This represents a legal *lacuna* as the procedural flexibility envisaged in the European procurement regulatory regime does not cover entities covered under the GPA. Rectification of the problem would require amendment to the GPA with the conferral of concessions and reciprocal access rights to the GPA signatories.

C. The New Public Procurement Regime and WTO

4.112 Council Decision 94/800/EC, which covered the Agreements reached in the Uruguay Round multilateral negotiations (1986 to 1994),[104] approved the WTO Agreement on Government Procurement, the aim of which is to establish a multilateral framework of balanced rights and obligations relating to public contracts with a view to achieving the liberalization and expansion of world trade. The scope and coverage of the WTO Government Procurement Agreement, as well as the structure of its applicability, present a unique instrument of international law which is based on a series of bilateral agreements rather than a multilateral arrangement. This represents a significant compromise of the most favoured nation principle, which is a fundamental premise of the majority of international trade agreements. Members of the World Trade Organisation joining the GPA, at their discretion, need to reach separate agreements on the scope of coverage with all existing parties to the Agreement. The GPA thus, has acquired a *plurilaterality* status, a fact that weakens its thrust and complicates its applicability.

4.113 The Government Procurement Agreement (GPA) under the WTO is based on a number of general principles, which depict the principles of the old GATT-AGP regime. The most important principle reflects the significance of *national treatment* in international trade. Under this principle, the parties to the GPA must give

---

[103] According to Art. 68(2), for the adoption of a Decision, the Commission shall be allowed a period of three months commencing on the first working day following the date on which it receives the notification or the request. However, this period may be extended once by a maximum of three months in duly justified cases, in particular if the information contained in the notification or the request or in the documents annexed thereto is incomplete.

[104] *See* [1994] OJ L336/1, 23 December 1994.

the same treatment afforded to national providers and products to providers and products of other signatory states. Reinforcing the principle of national treatment, the *most favoured nation* (MFN) principle guarantees treatment no less favourable than that afforded to other parties. In addition to the above principles, the principle of *non-discrimination* prohibits discrimination against national undertakings on grounds of the degree of their foreign affiliation or ownership, or on the grounds of origin of the goods or services where these have been produced in one of the states which are party to the Government Procurement Agreement.

The GPA stipulates a set of procedures for contracting authorities in the signatory parties which must be followed when awarding contracts within its scope. These procedures aim to ensure transparency and openness as well as objectivity and legitimacy in the award of public contracts and to facilitate cross-border trade between the signatories. The influence of the European Community on the GPA regime is apparent, an indication of the maturity and validity of the regulatory process of the European public markets integration. The procedures are, however, less strict than those applicable for the award of public sector contracts under the Community regime, and depict the integral flexibility envisaged by the regulatory regime for utilities procurement. **4.114**

The GPA intends to regulate access specifically to the government procurement markets. General market access between the signatories is in principle dealt with under other agreements, notably the GATT (on the import of goods) and the GATS (on access to services markets). The detailed scope and coverage of the GPA with regard to the entities covered, the type of procurement, and monetary thresholds is set out in Appendix I of the Agreement. The Agreement applies in principle to all bodies which are deemed as 'contracting authorities' for the purposes of the European Public Sector Directives. With reference to utilities, the GPA applies to entities which carry out one or more of certain listed 'utility' activities, where these entities are either 'public authorities' or 'public undertakings', according to the existing Utilities Directive. However, the GPA does not cover entities operating in the utilities sector on the basis of *special and exclusive rights*. The utility activities which are covered include: (i) activities connected with the provision of water through fixed networks; (ii) activities concerned with the provision of electricity through fixed networks; (iii) the provision of terminal facilities to carriers by sea or inland waterway; and (iv) the operation of public services in the field of transport by automated systems, tramway, trolley bus, or bus or cable. The provision of public transport services by rail is included in principle, but there is exclusion for entities listed in Annex VI of the existing Utilities Directive, designed to exclude non-urban transport services. The trust of the applicability of the GPA in relation to utilities activities appears short in comparison with that under the European regime. Activities connected with the distribution of gas or heat, the exploration or extraction of fuel are notable exceptions from the GPA's ambit. **4.115**

4.116 Although, in principle, the GPA regime represents a significant improvement in relation to the old GATT-AGP regime in terms of coverage and thrust, certain important derogations from its applicability would result in diluting the principal aims and objectives envisaged by the signatories. As far as central or federal government works and supply contracts are concerned, the Agreement is expected to facilitate market access and enhance cross-border trade patterns in public contracts. However, for contracts relating to services and for certain contracts in the utilities sector, as well as for contracts awarded by local, municipal or regional authorities, the effect of the Agreement appears considerably moderate. A number of signatories have been unable, or unwilling, to offer for coverage all of their entities or contracts in the above categories. Political and legal particularities in the systems of the signatories have prevented similar coverage between the parties. In addition, by applying the principle of *reciprocity* in negotiating the GPA, the result would probably have been very similar to the old AGP regime in covering central or federal public contracts. The solution to this fundamental, apparently, deadlock was to be found in a rather peculiar method. Each signatory should effectively negotiate with each other signatory, to come to a satisfactory agreement on coverage based on reciprocity on a bilateral basis. This approach constitutes a significant departure from the premises of the principle of *most favoured nation* (MFN) and has resulted in some considerable divergence in the applicability of the GPA by virtue of derogations and limitations imposed by signatories on access to their public markets.

D. Future Developments in Public Procurement Regulation

(1) Public procurement and public–private partnerships

4.117 At European level, as part of the Initiative for Growth, the Council has approved a series of measures designed to increase investment in the infrastructure of the trans-European transport networks, and also in the areas of research, innovation and development,[105] as well as the delivery of services of general interest.[106] European Community law does not lay down any special rules covering the award or the contractual interface of public–private partnerships. Nevertheless, such arrangements must be examined in the light of the rules and principles resulting from the European Treaties, particularly as regards the principles of freedom of establishment and freedom to provide services (Articles 43 and 49 of the EC Treaty),[107] which encompass, in particular, the principles of transparency, equality of treatment,

---

[105] Conclusions of the Presidency, Brussels European Council, 12 December 2003.

[106] *See* COM (2003) 270 final.

[107] The rules on the internal market, including the rules and principles governing public contracts and concessions, apply to any economic activity, i.e. any activity which consists in

proportionality, and mutual recognition,[108] and the Public Procurement Directives.[109] The Commission has already taken initiatives under public procurement law to deal with the award of public–private partnerships. In 2000, it published an *Interpretive Communication on Concessions and Community Public Procurement Law*,[110] in which it defined, on the basis of the rules and principles derived from the Treaty and applicable secondary legislation, the outlines of the concept of concession in Community law and the obligations incumbent on the public authorities when selecting the economic operators to whom the concessions are granted.

The *Green Paper on Public Private Partnerships* distinguishes two major formats of **4.118** public private partnerships: the contractual formant, also described as the concession model, and the institutional format which is often described as the 'joint-venture model'. Public authorities in the member states often have recourse to public–private partnership arrangements to facilitate mainly infrastructure projects. Budget constraints confronting national governments and the widespread assumption that private sector know-how will benefit the delivery of public services appear as the main policy drivers[111] for selecting a public–private partnership route. Also, the accounting treatment of public–private partnership contracts benefits national governments as the assets involved in a public–private partnership should be classified as non-government assets, and therefore recorded off balance sheet for public accountancy purposes,[112] subject to two conditions: i) that the private partner bears the construction risk, and ii) that the private partner bears at least one of either availability or demand risk. However, it is necessary to assess whether a public–private partnership option offers real added value compared with the conclusion of traditional public contracts.[113]

---

providing services, goods, or carrying out works in a market, even if these services, goods or works are intended to provide a 'public service', as defined by a member state.

[108] *See Interpretive Communication of the Commission on Concessions in Community Law*, [2000] OJ C121, 29 April 2000.

[109] In addition to the public procurement regime, in certain sectors, and particularly the transport sector, the organization of a PPP could be subject to specific sectoral legislation. *See* Regulation 2408/92 of the Council on access of Community air carriers to intra-Community air routes, Council Regulation 3577/92 applying the principle of freedom to provide services to maritime transport within Member States, Council Regulation 1191/69 on action by Member States concerning the obligations inherent in the concept of a public service in transport by rail, road and inland waterway, as amended by Regulation 1893/91, and the amended proposal for a Regulation of the European Parliament and of the Council on action by member states concerning public service requirements and the award of public service contracts in passenger transport by rail, road and inland waterway, COM (2002) 107 final.   [110] op. cit. (n. 108).

[111] *See* Communication from the Commission of 23 April 2003, *Developing the Trans-European Transport Network: Innovative Funding Solutions—Interoperability of Electronic Toll Collection Systems*, COM (2003) 132, and the Report of the high-level group on the trans-European transport network of 27 June 2003.

[112] *See* Eurostat, (Statistical Office of the European Communities), press release STAT/04/18 of 11 February 2004.

[113] *See* Communication from the Commission to the Council and to the Parliament, 'Public Finances in EMU 2003', in *European Economy* No. 3/2003, COM (2003) 283 final.

(2) Revision of the Remedies Directives

4.119   The Remedies Directives 89/665 (review procedures for public supply, and public works, and public services contracts) and 92/13 (review procedures for public contracts in the water, energy, transport, and telecommunications sectors) were enacted in order to ensure effective implementation of the Public Procurement Directives at national level and to guarantee access to justice to aggrieved contractors and interested parties against illegal or wrongful award decisions of contracting authorities.

4.120   It has emerged that the progress of implementation of the public procurement *acquis* is not uniform. The fact that only a small percentage of calls to tender are published (16.2% for the European Union in 2002), and that the figure varies appreciably amongst member states, leaves little room to celebrate. Public procurement is the weakest link of the common market. Initial consultations launched by the Commission with the member states, economic operators, and their representatives have revealed that the operation of national review procedures does not always make it possible to correct implementation failures. It has also become apparent that the effectiveness of national review mechanisms in public procurement differs considerably, a fact that may discourage economic operators from tendering for public contracts.

4.121   The process of revising the Remedies Directives will not be launched until the public procurement legislative package is in force. The Commission is of the view that any amendments should merely adapt and improve certain provisions of the Remedies Directives, without altering the philosophy and principles which underpin their structures. For example, the principle of the member states' *procedural autonomy* will not be questioned. Thus, member states will be able to retain the power to select a court, a tribunal or an independent authority as the competent forum to deal with public procurement law. However, the unsatisfactory situation brought about mainly by the very heterogeneous operation of member states' national review procedures, and recent developments in case law, require clarification of the existing legislative framework in order to establish greater precision and to ensure that any sanctions are effective and proportionate and have a deterrent effect on infringements of Community law on public procurement.

E. Assessment of the New Public Procurement Regime

4.122   The new generation of legal instruments intends to simplify and modernize a regulatory regime which aims at establishing gradually a public market in the European Union. This regime seeks to accomplish unobstructed access to public markets through transparency of public expenditure relating to procurement, improved market information, elimination of technical standards capable of discriminating against potential contractors, and uniform application of objective criteria of participation in tendering and award procedures. The new regime has three principal objectives: simplification, modernization, and flexibility.

The objective of simplification has been met to a large extent. The new Public **4.123** Sector Directive represents a notable example of codification of supranational administrative law. The objective of modernization is partly met, mainly as a result of the enormity of the newly introduced concepts. The ability of bodies governed by public law to tender for public contracts among private undertakings is a significant development. The use of framework procurement could assist in bringing the public sector closer to a seamless supply chain management. The introduction of electronic procurement and the use of information technology in public purchasing could process the logistics of public sector purchasing faster and more efficiently. However, the introduction of the competitive dialogue to facilitate the award complex projects such as public–private partnerships and trans-European networks leaves many practical questions over its nature and conduct unanswered. This represents the biggest problem for the new regime. The exceptional nature of the competitive dialogue and its hierarchy with other award procedures (the wording of the Public Sector Directive puts the procedure at a par with the negotiated procedures with prior advertisement); the discretion of contracting authorities to initiate the procedure (who is to determine the nature of a particularly complex contract, the inability of the contracting authorities to draw precise specifications, and the contract's financial and legal make-up); the internal structure and conduct of the procedure (the confusion surrounding the different stages pre- and post-tender); the response of the private sector (the predictably very high costs in participating); the degree of competition achieved (there is great potential for post-tender negotiations); and, finally, the overall value for money results (in many instances the completive dialogue is less flexible than the negotiated procedures), are pertinent questions that have not been addressed by the new public procurement regime.

The objective of flexibility is the surprise element of the new regulatory package. **4.124** The relaxation of the competitive tendering regime and the disengagement of the public procurement rules in industries that operate under competitive conditions in the utilities sectors indicate the links between procurement regulation and anti-trust. The non-applicability of the regime to telecommunications entities is an important development indicative of the future legal and regulatory blueprints. A rather disappointing feature of the new regime is the lack of clarity over the potential use of socio-economic and environmental considerations as part of the award criteria. Contrary to the Court's jurisprudential inferences, the new Directives do not confer the much needed flexibility in this matter to contracting authorities, thus inviting the Court to continue its *rule of reason* approach into the legitimacy of policies, other than economic ones, through public procurement regulation.

4.125 The regulation of public procurement reflects on two opposite dynamics: one of a community-wide orientation and one of national priorities. The influence of neo-classical economic theory on public procurement regulation has taken the relevant regime through the paces of the liberalization. However, we have witnessed the emergence of a *sui generis* market place where the mere existence and functioning of anti-trust is not sufficient to achieve the envisaged objectives. Public markets require a positive regulatory approach in order to enhance market access. Whereas anti-trust and the neo-classical approach to economic integration depend heavily on price competition, public procurement regulation requires a system which primarily safeguards market access. In the author's argument, such regulatory system could be described as public competition law.

4.126 The above scenario represents a departure from the *stricto sensu* neo-classical perspective of public procurement. A policy orientation has emerged mainly through the jurisprudential approach of the regime and the willingness of the Court to expand on the element of flexibility that is inherent in the Public Procurement Directives. The Court has allowed for a flexible policy-oriented application of public procurement, where in anti-trust the Commission has eroded the strict neo-classical approach of controlling market power with the plethora of policy considerations.

4.127 Litigation and jurisprudential inferences will be extremely important in understanding the thrust of the new regime. The role of the Court has been instrumental in shaping many of the newly introduced concepts and, in the future, will be invaluable in interpreting the new regime and pronouncing on the compatibility of national provisions with *acquis communautaire*.

5

THE APPLICABILITY OF THE PUBLIC SECTOR RULES

A. Coverage and Scope of the Public Sector Directive

The Public Sector Directive[1] is applicable to the award of public contracts   **5.01**
between economic operators and contracting authorities. The term 'economic
operator' includes undertakings that are described as contractors, suppliers and
service providers and has been introduced in the new Public Sector Directive for
simplification purposes.[2] On the other hand, the concept of 'contracting authority' embraces a variety of organizations that fall within the remit of the state,
central or local government[3] and also bodies which are governed by public law.[4]

(1) Public contracts: types and categories

One of the most important ingredients for the applicability of the Public Sector   **5.02**
Directive is the existence of a public contract. What determines the nature of a
public contract is not the legal regime that governs its terms and conditions and
the relations between the parties. The crucial characteristic of a public contract
for the purpose of the Public Sector Directive is the makeup of the parties to that
contract. More specifically, according to, and for the purposes of, the Public
Sector Directive, public contracts[5] are contracts for pecuniary interest concluded
in writing between one or more economic operators and one or more contracting
authorities and having as their object the execution of works, the supply of
products, or the provision of services.

Public works contracts[6] are public contracts which have as their object either the   **5.03**
execution, or both the design and execution, of works, or the completion, by whatever means, of a work corresponding to the requirements specified by the contracting
authority. A work means the outcome of building or civil engineering works taken as
a whole which is sufficient of itself to fulfil an economic or technical function.

Public supply contracts[7] are public contracts having as their object the purchase,   **5.04**
lease, rental, or hire purchase, with or without option to buy, of products. A public

---

[1] *See* Directive 2004/18 [2004] OJ L134/114.
[2] *See* Art. 8, second indent, of the Public Sector Directive.
[3] The definition of contracting authorities has been uniformly maintained across the evolution
stages of public procurement regulation. Art. 9 of the Public Sector Directive repeats *verbatim* the
definition of contracting authorities previously found in the preceding Public Procurement
Directives and in particular the Public Supplies Directive 93/36/EC [1993] OJ L199/1, as amended
by 97/52/EC [1997] OJ L328/1 and Directive 2001/78/EC [2001] OJ L285/1; the Public Works
Directive 93/37/EC [1993] OJ L199/54, amended by Directive 97/52/EC [1997] OJ L328/1 and
Directive 2001/78/EC [2001] OJ L285/1; and the Public Services Directive 92/50/EEC [1992] OJ
L209/1, amended by 97/52/EC [1997] OJ L328/1 and Directive 2001/78/EC [2001] OJ L285/1.
[4] *See* Art. 9 second indent of the Public Sector Directive.
[5] *See* Art. 1(2)(a) of the Public Sector Directive.
[6] *See* Art. 1(2)(b) of the Public Sector Directive.
[7] *See* Art. 1(2)(c) of the Public Sector Directive.

contract having as its object the supply of products and which also covers, as an incidental matter, placement and installation operations, must be considered as a public supply contract.

5.05 Public service contracts[8] are public contracts, other than public works or supply contracts, having as their object the provision of services referred to in Annex II of the Directive. A public contract having as its object both products and services within the meaning of Annex II must be considered as a 'public service contract' if the value of the services in question exceeds that of the products covered by the contract. The Directive stipulates specific arrangements[9] for public service contracts listed in Annex II A. These contracts must be awarded as any other public contract covered by the Directive and, in particular, in accordance with Articles 23 to 55. However, for contracts which have as their object services listed in Annex II B, the Directive is applicable only[10] with respect to the setting of technical specifications (Article 23) and the requirement to file a report to the Commission after the award of the contract (Article 35(4). Mixed contracts[11] including services listed in Annex II A and services listed in Annex II B must be awarded as any other public contract covered by the Directive where the value of the services listed in Annex II A is greater than the value of the services listed in Annex II B. In the reverse scenario, contracts are awarded in accordance with Article 23 and Article 35(4) of the Directive. A public contract having as its object services within the meaning of Annex II, and including activities within the meaning of Annex I that are only incidental to the principal object of the contract, must be considered as a public service contract.

5.06 Public works concession[12] is a contract of the same type as a public works contract except for the fact that the consideration for the works to be carried out consists either solely in the right to exploit the work, or in this right together with payment.

5.07 Service concession[13] is a contract of the same type as a public service contract except for the fact that the consideration for the provision of services consists either solely in the right to exploit the service, or in this right together with payment.

5.08 A framework agreement[14] is an agreement between one or more contracting authorities and one or more economic operators, the purpose of which is to establish the terms governing contracts to be awarded during a given period, in particular with regard to price and, where appropriate, the quantity envisaged.

5.09 A dynamic purchasing system[15] is a completely electronic process for making commonly-used purchases, the characteristics of which, as generally available on the market, meet the requirements of the contracting authority, which is limited

---

[8] *See* Art. 1(2)(d) of the Public Sector Directive.   [9] *See* Art. 20 of the Directive
[10] *See* Art. 21 of the Directive   [11] *See* Art. 22 of the Directive
[12] *See* Art. 1(3) of the Public Sector Directive.   [13] *See* Art. 1(4) of the Public Sector Directive.
[14] *See* Art. 1(5) of the Public Sector Directive.   [15] *See* Art. 1(6) of the Public Sector Directive.

in duration and open throughout its validity to any economic operator which satisfies the selection criteria and has submitted an indicative tender that complies with the specification.

An electronic auction[16] is a repetitive process involving an electronic device for the presentation of new prices, revised downwards, or new values concerning certain elements of tenders, which occurs after an initial full evaluation of the tenders, enabling them to be ranked using automatic evaluation methods. Consequently, certain service contracts and certain works contracts having as their subject-matter intellectual performances, such as the design of works, may not be the object of electronic auctions. **5.10**

(2) The supply side: economic operators

The terms 'contractor', 'supplier', and 'service provider' mean any natural or legal person or public entity, or group of such persons and/or bodies, which offers on the market, respectively, the execution of works and/or a work, products, or services.[17] The term 'economic operator' covers equally the concepts of contractor, supplier, and service provider. It is used merely in the interest of simplification. An economic operator who has submitted a tender must be designated as a 'tenderer'. One which has sought an invitation to take part in a restricted or negotiated procedure or a competitive dialogue must be designated as a 'candidate'. **5.11**

(3) The demand side: contracting authorities

The term 'contracting authorities' means the state, regional or local authorities, bodies governed by public law, associations formed by one or several of such authorities, or one or several of such bodies governed by public law.[18] **5.12**

A body governed by public law means any organization which satisfies the following conditions in a cumulative manner. Firstly, the organization must be established for the specific purpose of meeting needs in the general interest which do not have an industrial or commercial character; secondly, it must have legal personality; and thirdly, it must be financed, for the most part, by the state, regional or local authorities, or other bodies governed by public law. Alternatively, and as part of the third criterion, a body governed by public law must be subject to management supervision by the state, regional or local authorities, or other bodies governed by public law, or it must have an administrative, managerial, or supervisory board, more than half of whose members are appointed by the state, regional or local authorities, or by other bodies governed by public law. **5.13**

---

[16] *See* Art. 1(7) of the Public Sector Directive.   [17] *See* Art. 1(8) of the Public Sector Directive.
[18] *See* Art. 1(9) of the Public Sector Directive.

5.14 Non-exhaustive lists of bodies and categories of bodies governed by public law which fulfil the three cumulative criteria for a body governed by public law are set out in Annex III of the Directive. member states must periodically notify the Commission of any changes to their lists of bodies and categories of bodies.

5.15 A central purchasing body is a contracting authority which acquires supplies or services which are intended for contracting authorities. It may also award public contracts or conclude framework agreements for works, supplies, or services intended for contracting authorities.[19]

(4) The principles governing the award of public contracts

5.16 Articles 2 and 3 cover the principles of awarding contracts. In particular, contracting authorities must treat economic operators equally and in a non-discriminatory manner and act in a transparent way.

5.17 Article 3 includes a non-discrimination clause for the cases of granting special or exclusive rights. Where a contracting authority grants special or exclusive rights to carry out a public service activity to an entity other than such a contracting authority, the act by which that right is granted must provide that, in respect of the supply contracts which it awards to third parties as part of its activities, the entity concerned must comply with the principle of non-discrimination on the basis of nationality.

5.18 Article 6 also provides for the obligation to observe confidentiality in accordance with the national law to which the contracting authority is subject. Contracting authorities must not disclose information forwarded to it by economic operators which they have designated as confidential; such information includes, in particular, technical or trade secrets and the confidential aspects of tenders. This obligation is without prejudice to the provisions of the Directive relevant to the advertising of awarded contracts and to the information to candidates and tenderers set out in Articles 35(4) and 41.

(5) The substantive applicability of the Directive

(a) Excluded contracts

5.19 The Directive does not apply to public contracts in the water, energy, transport, and postal services sectors[20] which are awarded under Directive 2004/17.[21] However, the Directive applies to public contracts in the utilities sectors insofar as the member state concerned takes advantage of the option referred to in the second subparagraph of Article 71 of the Utilities Directive, which stipulates deferral of the Directive's application for up to thirty-five months from the deadline of its implementation by member states (31 January 2006).

---

[19] *See* Art. 1(10) of the Public Sector Directive.   [20] *See* Art. 12 of the Public Sector Directive.
[21] *See* the Utilities Directive 2004/17 [2004] OJ L134/1.

The Directive also does not apply to public contracts for the principal purpose of **5.20** permitting the contracting authorities to provide or exploit public telecommunications networks or to provide to the public one or more telecommunications services.[22] For the purposes of the non-applicability of the Directive in the field of telecommunications, 'public telecommunications network' means the public telecommunications infrastructure which enables signals to be conveyed between defined network termination points by wire, by microwave, by optical means, or by other electromagnetic means;[23] a 'network termination point' means all physical connections and their technical access specifications which form part of the public telecommunications network and are necessary for access to, and efficient communication through, that public network;[24] 'public telecommunications services' means telecommunications services the provision of which the member states have specifically assigned, in particular, to one or more telecommunications entities;[25] 'telecommunications services' means services the provision of which consists wholly, or partly, in the transmission and routing of signals on the public telecommunications network by means of telecommunications processes, with the exception of broadcasting and television.[26]

The Directive does not apply to public contracts when they are declared to be secret **5.21** contracts, and contracts requiring special security measures, when their performance must be accompanied by special security measures in accordance with the laws, regulations or administrative provisions in force in the member state concerned, or when the protection of the essential interests of that member state so requires.[27]

The Directive also does not apply to public contracts awarded pursuant to **5.22** international rules[28] which are governed by different procedural rules and awarded through the following means:

(a) pursuant to an international agreement concluded in conformity with the Treaty between a member state and one or more third countries, and covering supplies or works intended for the joint implementation or exploitation of a work by the signatory states, or services intended for the joint implementation or exploitation of a project by the signatory states; all agreements must be communicated to the Commission, which may consult the Advisory Committee for Public Contracts referred to in Article 77;
(b) pursuant to a concluded international agreement relating to the stationing of troops and concerning the undertakings of a member state or a third country;
(c) pursuant to the particular procedure of an international organization.

---

[22] *See* Art. 13 of the Public Sector Directive.
[23] *See* Art. 1(15)(a) of the Public Sector Directive.
[24] *See* Art. 1(15)(b) of the Public Sector Directive.
[25] *See* Art. 1(15)(c) of the Public Sector Directive.
[26] *See* Art. 1(15)(d) of the Public Sector Directive.
[27] *See* Art. 14 of the Public Sector Directive.   [28] *See* Art. 15 of the Public Sector Directive.

(b) Specific exclusions

5.23 The Public Sector Directive does not apply to public service contracts for: (a) the acquisition or rental, by whatever financial means, of land, existing buildings or other immovable property, or concerning rights thereon; nevertheless, financial service contracts concluded at the same time as, before or after, the contract of acquisition or rental, in whatever form, must be subject to this Directive; (b) the acquisition, development, production, or co-production of programme material intended for broadcasting by broadcasters and contracts for broadcasting time; (c) arbitration and conciliation services; (d) financial services in connection with the issue, sale, purchase, or transfer of securities, or other financial instruments, in particular transactions by the contracting authorities to raise money or capital, and central bank services; (e) employment contracts; and (f) research and development services other than those where the benefits accrue exclusively to the contracting authority for its use in the conduct of its own affairs, on condition that the service provided is wholly remunerated by the contracting authority.[29]

5.24 The Directive does not apply to service concessions[30] or service contracts awarded on the basis of an exclusive right awarded by a contracting authority to another contracting authority or to an association of contracting authorities on the basis of an exclusive right which they enjoy pursuant to a published law, regulation, or administrative provision which is compatible with the Treaty.[31]

(c) Reserved contracts

5.25 Member states may reserve the right to participate in public contract award procedures to sheltered workshops, or provide for such contracts to be performed in the context of sheltered employment programmes, where most of the employees concerned are handicapped persons who, by reason of the nature or the seriousness of their disabilities, cannot carry on occupations under normal conditions.[32]

(6) The monetary applicability of the Directive

(a) Threshold for public contracts

5.26 The Directive applies to public contracts which have a value exclusive of value added tax (VAT) estimated to be equal to or greater than the following thresholds:[33]

(a) €162,000 for public supply and service contracts others than those covered by point (b), third indent, awarded by contracting authorities which are listed as central government authorities in Annex IV; in the case of public

---

[29] *See* Art. 16 of the Public Sector Directive. [30] *See* Art. 17 of the Public Sector Directive.
[31] *See* Art. 18 of the Public Sector Directive. [32] *See* Art. 19 of the Public Sector Directive.
[33] *See* Art. 7 of the Public Sector Directive.

supply contracts awarded by contracting authorities operating in the field of defence, this must apply only to contracts involving products covered by Annex V;

(b) €249,000

— for public supply and service contracts awarded by contracting authorities other than those listed in Annex IV,

— for public supply contracts awarded by contracting authorities which are listed in Annex IV and operate in the field of defence, where these contracts involve products not covered by Annex V,

— for public service contracts awarded by any contracting authority in respect of the services listed in Category 8 of Annex IIA, Category 5 telecommunications services the positions of which in the CPV[34] are equivalent to CPC reference No. 7524, 7525 and 7526 and/or the services listed in Annex II B;

(c) €6,242,000 for public works contracts.

(b) Subsidized contracts

Contracts subsidized by more than fifty per cent by contracting authorities are covered by the Directive.[35] In particular, the Directive applies to the award of: **5.27**

(a) contracts which are subsidized directly by contracting authorities by more than fifty per cent and the estimated value of which, net of VAT, is equal to or greater than €6,242,000:

— where those contracts involve civil engineering activities within the meaning of Annex I;

— where those contracts involve building work for hospitals, facilities intended for sports, recreation and leisure, school and university buildings, and buildings used for administrative purposes;

(b) service contracts which are subsidized directly by contracting authorities by more than fifty per cent and the estimated value of which, net of VAT, is equal to or greater than €249,000 and which are connected with a works contract as described the above category (a).

Member states must take the necessary measures to ensure that the contracting authorities awarding such subsidized contracts ensure compliance with the provisions of the Directive where that contract is awarded by one or more entities other **5.28**

---

[34] The Common Procurement Vocabulary (CPV) represents the reference nomenclature applicable to public contracts while ensuring equivalence with the other existing nomenclatures. *See* Regulation 2195/2002 on the Common Procurement Vocabulary (CVP) [2002] OJ L340, 16 December 2002. In the event of varying interpretations of the scope of the Utilities Directive, owing to possible differences between the CPV and NACE nomenclatures listed in Annex XII or between the CPV and CPC (provisional version) nomenclatures listed in Annex XVII, the NACE or the CPC nomenclature respectively takes precedence.   [35] *See* Art. 8 of the Public Sector Directive.

than themselves. In addition, member states must comply with the Directive in cases where they themselves award that contract for and on behalf of other contracting entities.

(c) Contract value calculation

5.29 The Directive provides for methods for calculating the estimated value of public contracts, framework agreements, and dynamic purchasing systems.[36] The calculation of the estimated value of a public contract must be based on the total amount payable, net of VAT, as estimated by the contracting authority. This calculation must take account of the estimated total amount, including any form of option and any renewals of the contract.[37] Where the contracting authority provides for prizes or payments to candidates or tenderers it must take them into account when calculating the estimated value of the contract. This estimate must be valid at the moment at which the contract notice is sent, as provided for in Article 35(2), or, in cases where such notice is not required, at the moment at which the contracting authority commences the contract awarding procedure.[38]

5.30 Contracting authorities are under an obligation to avoid subdividing works projects or proposing the purchase of a certain quantity of supplies or services in order to escape the monetary applicability of the Directive.[39]

5.31 With regard to public works contracts, calculation of the estimated value must take account of both the cost of the works and the total estimated value of the supplies necessary for executing the works and placed at the contractor's disposal by the contracting authorities.[40]

5.32 Where a proposed work or purchase of services may result in contracts being awarded at the same time in the form of separate lots, contracting authorities must take into account the total estimated value of all such lots. Where the aggregate value of the lots is equal to, or exceeds, the threshold stipulated in the Directive, in that case each lot must be awarded separately in accordance with the Public Sector Directive. However, the contracting authorities may waive such application in respect of lots the estimated value of which net of VAT is less than €80,000 for services or €1 million for works, provided that the aggregate value of those lots does not exceed twenty per cent of the aggregate value of the lots as a whole.

5.33 Where a proposal for the acquisition of similar supplies may result in contracts being awarded at the same time in the form of separate lots, account must be taken of the total estimated value of all such lots.

---

[36] *See* Art. 9 of the Public Sector Directive.   [37] *See* Art. 9(1) of the Public Sector Directive.
[38] *See* Art. 9(2) of the Public Sector Directive.   [39] *See* Art. 9(3) of the Public Sector Directive.
[40] *See* Art. 9(4) of the Public Sector Directive.

With regard to public supply contracts relating to the leasing, hire, rental, or hire purchase of products,[41] the value to be taken as a basis for calculating the estimated contract value must be as follows: **5.34**

(a) in the case of fixed-term public contracts, if that term is less than or equal to twelve months, the total estimated value for the term of the contract or, if the term of the contract is greater than twelve months, the total value including the estimated residual value;

(b) in the case of public contracts without a fixed term or the term of which cannot be defined, the monthly value multiplied by forty-eight.

For public supply or service contracts which are regular in nature or which are intended to be renewed within a given period,[42] the calculation of the estimated contract value must be based on the following: **5.35**

(a) either the total actual value of the successive contracts of the same type awarded during the preceding twelve months or financial year adjusted, if possible, to take account of the changes in quantity or value which would occur in the course of the twelve months following the initial contract;

(b) or the total estimated value of the successive contracts awarded during the twelve months following the first delivery, or during the financial year if that is longer than twelve months.

The choice of method used to calculate the estimated value of a public contract may not be made with the intention of excluding it from the scope of the Public Sector Directive. **5.36**

With regard to public service contracts,[43] the value to be taken as a basis for calculating the estimated contract value for insurance services must reflect the premium payable and other forms of remuneration; for banking and other financial services it must comprise the fees, commissions, interest, and other forms of remuneration; for design contracts it must include fees, commission payable, and other forms of remuneration. For service contracts which do not indicate a total price, in the case of fixed-term contracts, if that term is less than or equal to forty-eight months, the estimated contract value must reflect the total value for their full term; in the case of contracts without a fixed term or with a term greater than forty-eight months the estimated value must include the monthly value multiplied by forty-eight. **5.37**

With regard to framework agreements and dynamic purchasing systems, the value to be taken into consideration must be the maximum estimated value net of VAT of all the contracts envisaged for the total term of the framework agreement or the dynamic purchasing system.[44] **5.38**

---

[41] *See* Art. 9(6) of the Public Sector Directive.   [42] *See* Art. 9(7) of the Public Sector Directive.

[43] *See* Art. 9(8)(a)(b) of the Public Sector Directive.

[44] *See* Art. 9(9) of the Public Sector Directive.

(d) Revision of the thresholds

5.39 Revision of the thresholds will be undertaken by the Commission every two years from the entry into force of the Public Sector Directive.[45] The calculation of the value of these thresholds must be based on the average daily value of the euro, expressed in SDRs, over the twenty-four months terminating on the last day of August preceding the revision with effect from 1 January. The value of the thresholds thus revised must, where necessary, be rounded down to the nearest thousand euro so as to ensure that the thresholds in force provided for by the Agreement, expressed in SDRs, are observed. The value of the thresholds set in the national currencies of the member states which are not participating in monetary union is normally to be adjusted every two years from 1 January 2004 onwards. The calculation of such value must be based on the average daily values of those currencies expressed in euro over the twenty-four months terminating on the last day of August preceding the revision with effect from 1 January. The revised thresholds and their corresponding values in the national currencies must be published by the Commission in the *Official Journal of the European Union* at the beginning of the month of November following their revision.

5.40 The thresholds applicable to subsidized works contracts (Article 8(a)) and subsidized service contracts (Article 8(b)), to public works concessions (Article 56), to concession works contacts awarded by concessionaires which are not contracting authorities (Article 63(1)), and to design contests (Article 67(1)(a)), should be aligned at the same time as the revisions covering the other thresholds.[46]

B. Advertisement and publicity of public contracts

(1) Publication of notices

(a) Prior information notices (PINs)

5.41 Prior information notices are notices sent by contracting authorities for publication to the *Official Journal* or notices published by contracting authorities themselves on their buyer profile through the internet.[47]

Both prior information notices and notices on buyer profile must include the following information:[48]

(a) for public supplies contracts, and as soon as possible after the beginning of the budgetary year, the internet address of the contracts or the framework agreements by product area which they intend to award over the following twelve

---

[45] *See* Art. 78 of the Public Sector Directive.
[47] *See* Art. 35 of the Public Sector Directive.
[46] *See* Art. 78(2) of the Public Sector Directive.
[48] *See* Art. 35(1) of the Public Sector Directive.

months, where the total estimated value is equal to or greater than €750,000. The product area must be established by the contracting authorities by reference to the CPV nomenclature;

(b) for public services contracts, and as soon as possible after the beginning of the budgetary year, the estimated total value of the contracts or the framework agreements in each of the categories of services listed in Annex II A which they intend to award over the following twelve months, where such estimated total value is equal to or greater than €750,000;

(c) for public works contracts, and as soon as possible after the decision approving the planning of the works contracts or the framework agreements that the contracting authorities intend to award, the essential characteristics of the contracts or the framework agreements which they intend to award, the estimated value of which is equal to, or greater than, the threshold specified in Article 7 of the Public Sector Directive.

The notice of the publication for a prior indicative notice on a buyer profile must **5.42** contain the country and name of the contracting authority, the internet address of the 'buyer profile', and any CPV Nomenclature reference numbers.[49] The buyer profile may include[50] prior information notices, information on ongoing invitations to tender, scheduled purchases, contracts concluded, procedures cancelled, and any useful general information, such as a contact point, a telephone and a fax number, a postal address, and an e-mail address. Contracting authorities who publish a prior information notice on their buyer profiles must send the Commission, electronically, a notice of such publication.[51] Prior information notices may not be published on a buyer profile before the dispatch to the Commission of the notice of their publication in that form; they must mention the date of that dispatch.[52]

Contracting authorities should not publish notices and their contents at national **5.43** level before the date on which they are sent to the Commission for publication in the *Official Journal*. Notices published at national level must not contain information other than information contained in the notices dispatched to the Commission or published on a buyer profile. However, they must mention the date of dispatch of the notice to the Commission or its publication on the buyer profile.[53]

The publication of prior indicative notices is compulsory only where the **5.44** contracting authorities take the option of shortening the time limits for the receipt of tenders as laid down in Article 38(4) of the Directive. Also, in the exceptional

---

[49] *See* Annex VII A of the Public Sector Directive.

[50] *See* point 2(b) of Annex VIII of the Public Sector Directive.

[51] *See* the format and detailed procedures for sending notices indicated in point 3 of Annex VIII of the Public Sector Directive.

[52] *See* Art. 36(5) second indent of the Public Sector Directive.

[53] *See* Art. 36(5) of the Public Sector Directive.

cases of contracting authorities having recourse to negotiated procedures without the prior publication of a contract notice, the publication of prior information notices or notices on buyer profile is not required.

(b) Contract notices

5.45 Contracting authorities which wish to award a public contract or a framework agreement by open or restricted procedures, negotiated procedures with prior advertisement, or through the procedures of a competitive dialogue, must make known their intention by publishing a contract notice. Also, when contracting authorities wish to set up a dynamic purchasing system, they must publish a contract notice. Furthermore, when contracts are to be awarded based on a dynamic purchasing system, contracting authorities must publish a simplified contract notice.[54]

5.46 Notices must include the information required in Annex VII A of the Directive and, where appropriate, any other information deemed useful by contracting authorities for publicizing the award of public contracts in the standard format adopted by the Commission in accordance with the procedure referred to in Article 77(2) of the Directive. In particular, contracting authorities should provide the following information in contract notices for open and restricted procedures, competitive dialogues, and negotiated procedures with prior advertisement:

1. Their name, address, telephone and fax number, and email address.
2. An indication of whether the public contract is restricted to sheltered workshops, or whether its execution is restricted to the framework of protected job programmes.
3. The award procedure chosen and, where appropriate, the reasons for use of the accelerated procedure (in restricted and negotiated procedures); also, where appropriate, an indication of whether a framework agreement, or a dynamic purchasing system is involved; finally, where appropriate, an indication of whether the holding of an electronic auction will be held, in the event of open, restricted or negotiated procedures covered by Article 30(1)(a).
4. The form of the contract.
5. The place of execution or performance of the works, of delivery of products or of the provision of services.

---

[54] A simplified contract notice for use in a dynamic purchasing system must include the following information: the country, name and e-mail address of the contracting authority; publication reference of the contract notice for the dynamic purchasing system; the e-mail address at which the technical specification and additional documents relating to the dynamic purchasing system are available; the subject of contract and a description by reference number(s) of 'CPV' nomenclature; and the quantity or extent of the contract to be awarded the time frame for submitting indicative tenders. *See* Annex VII A of the Public Sector Directive.

6. Information about the work or service:
    (a) for public works contracts:
        i. a description of the nature and extent of the works and general nature of the work; an indication in particular of options concerning supplementary works, and, if known, the provisional timetable for recourse to these options as well as the number of possible renewals; an indication of the size of the different lots, if the work or the contract is subdivided into several lots; and a reference to nomenclature number(s);
        ii. information concerning the purpose of the work or the contract where the latter also involves the drawing-up of projects;
        iii. an indication, in the event of a framework agreement, of the planned duration of the framework agreement, the estimated total value of the works for the entire duration of the framework agreement, and, as far as possible, the value and the frequency of the contracts to be awarded.
    (b) for public supply contracts:
        i. a description of the nature of the products to be supplied, indicating in particular whether tenders are requested with a view to purchase, lease rental, hire or hire purchase, or a combination of these, nomenclature reference number; an indication of the quantity of products to be supplied, specifying in particular options concerning supplementary purchases and the provisional timetable for recourse to these options as well as the number of renewals; a reference to nomenclature number(s);
        ii. in the case of regular or renewable contracts during the course of a given period, an indication of the timetable for subsequent contracts for purchase of intended supplies;
        iii. in the event of a framework agreement, an indication of the planned duration of the framework agreement, the estimated total value of the supplies for the entire duration of the framework agreement, and, as far as possible, the value and the frequency of the contracts to be awarded.
    (c) for public service contracts:
        i. a reference to the category and description of service by nomenclature number(s); an indication of the quantity of services to be provided, and in particular any options concerning supplementary purchases and the provisional timetable for recourse to these options as well as the number of renewals; in the case of renewable contracts over a given period, an estimate of the time frame for subsequent public contracts for purchase of intended services; in the event of a framework agreement, an indication of the planned duration of the framework agreement, the estimated total value of the services for the entire duration of the

framework agreement, and, as far as possible, the value and the frequency of the contracts to be awarded;

    ii. an indication of whether the execution of the service is reserved by law, regulation, or administrative provision to a particular profession and a reference to the law, regulation, or administrative provision;

    iii. an indication of whether legal persons should indicate the names and professional qualifications of the staff to be responsible for the execution of the service.

7. In case the contracts are subdivided into lots, an indication of the possibility of tendering for one, for several, or for all the lots.

8. Any time limit for completion of works/supplies/services or duration of the works/supply/services contract; where possible, any time limit by which works will begin or any time limit by which delivery of supplies or services will begin.

9. An indication for admission or prohibition of variants.

10. An indication any particular conditions to which the performance of the contract is subject.

11. In open procedures, provision of:

    (a) name, address, telephone and fax number, and email address of the service from which contract documents and additional documents can be requested;

    (b) where appropriate, time limit for submission of such requests;

    (c) where appropriate, cost of and payment conditions for obtaining these documents;

    (d) time limit for receipt of tenders or indicative tenders where a dynamic purchasing system is being used (open procedures);

    (e) time limit for receipt of request to participate (restricted and negotiated procedures);

    (f) address where these have to be transmitted;

    (g) the language or languages in which they must be drawn up;

    (h) persons authorized to be present at the opening of tenders; and

    (i) date, time and place for such opening.

12. An indication for any deposit and guarantees required.

13. A reference to the main terms concerning financing and payment.

14. Where applicable, the legal form to be taken by the grouping of economic operators to whom the contract is to be awarded.

15. An indication of the selection criteria regarding the personal situation of economic operators that may lead to their exclusion, and required information proving that they do not fall within the cases justifying exclusion; an indication of the selection criteria and information concerning the economic operators' personal situation, information and any necessary formalities for assessment of the minimum economic and technical standards required of the

economic operator; an indication of any minimum level(s) of standards required.

16. In cases of framework agreements: a reference to the number and, where appropriate, proposed maximum number of economic operators who will be members of the framework agreement; and an indication of the duration of the framework agreement provided for, stating, if appropriate, the reasons for any duration exceeding four years.

17. In cases of a competitive dialogue or a negotiated procedure with the publication of a contract notice, an indication of a possible recourse to a staged procedure in order gradually to reduce the number of solutions to be discussed or tenders to be negotiated.

18. In cases of restricted procedures, a competitive dialogue, or negotiated procedures with the publication of a contract notice, when contracting authorities exercise the option of reducing the number of candidates to be invited to submit tenders, to engage in dialogue or to negotiate, an indication of the minimum and, if appropriate, the proposed maximum number of candidates, and a reference to objective criteria to be used to choose that number of candidates.

19. In cases of open procedures, an indication of the time frame during which the tenderer must maintain its tender.

20. In cases of negotiated procedures, a reference to names and addresses of economic operators already selected by the contracting authority.

21. A reference to the award criteria to be used for award of the contract: 'lowest price' or 'most economically advantageous tender'; in cases where criteria representing the most economically advantageous tender are selected, a description of their weighting in the event that such weighting does not appear in the specifications or in the descriptive document for competitive dialogue.

22. A reference of the name and address of the body responsible for appeal and, where appropriate, mediation procedures; an indication of precise information concerning deadlines for lodging appeals, or if need be the name, address, telephone number, fax number, and email address of the service from which this information may be obtained.

23. The date(s) of publication of the prior information notice; the date of dispatch of the notice.

24. An indication of whether the contract is covered by the reasons for publication in restricted and negotiated procedures for transmission indicated in Annex VIII, paragraph 3, or by other means. In such cases, the content of notices must be limited to approximately 650 words. In the event of recourse to the accelerated procedure set out in Article 30(1)(a).

The notices must be published no later than five days after they are sent. Notices **5.47** which are not transmitted by electronic means must be published not later than twelve days after they are sent, or, in the case of accelerated procedure referred to in Article 38(8), not later than five days after they are sent. Contracting authorities must be able to supply proof of the dates on which notices are dispatched. The Commission must give the contracting authority confirmation of the publication of the information sent, mentioning the date of that publication. Such confirmation must constitute proof of publication.

5.48 Contract notices must be published in full in an official language of the Community as chosen by the contracting authority, this original language version constituting the sole authentic text. A summary of the important elements of each notice must be published in the other official languages. The costs of publication of such notices by the Commission must be borne by the Community.

(c) Contract award notices

5.49 Contracting authorities which have awarded a public contract or concluded a framework agreement must send a notice of the results of the award procedure no later than forty-eight days after the award of the contract or the conclusion of the framework agreement.[55] In the case of framework agreements, contracting authorities are not bound to send a notice of the results of the award procedure for each contract based on that agreement. Contracting authorities must send a notice of the result of the award of contracts based on a dynamic purchasing system within forty-eight days of the award of each contract. They may, however, group such notices on a quarterly basis. In that case, they must send the grouped notices within forty-eight days of the end of each quarter. In the case of public contracts for services listed in Annex II B, the contracting authorities must indicate in the notice whether they agree to its publication. For such services contracts, the Commission must draw up the rules for establishing statistical reports on the basis of such notices and for the publication of such reports in accordance with the procedure laid down in Article 77(2) of the Directive.

5.50 Certain information on the contract award or the conclusion of the framework agreement may be withheld from publication where release of such information would impede law enforcement or otherwise be contrary to the public interest, would harm the legitimate commercial interests of economic operators, public or private, or might prejudice fair competition between them.

(2) Deadlines for receipt of requests to participate and for receipt of tenders

5.51 Contracting authorities should take into account the complexity of the contract and the time required for drawing up tenders, when determining the time limits for the receipt of tenders and requests to participate.[56]

---

[55] *See* Art. 35(4) of the Public Sector Directive.
[56] *See* Art. 38(1) of the Public Sector Directive.

In open procedures, the minimum time limit for the receipt of tenders must be fifty- **5.52**
two days from the date on which the contract notice was sent.[57] When contracting
authorities have published a prior information notice, the minimum time limit for
the receipt of tenders under open procedures may, as a general rule, be shortened to
thirty-six days.[58] The time limit must run from the date on which the contract notice
was sent in for publication. The shortened time limits should be permitted, provided
that the prior information notice has included all the information required for the
contract notice, insofar as that information is available at the time the notice is published, and that the prior information notice was sent for publication between fifty-
two days and twelve months before the date on which the contract notice was sent.
Where notices are drawn up and transmitted by electronic means, the time limits for
the receipt of tenders in open procedures may be shortened by seven days.[59]

The time limits for receipt of tenders referred to in open procedures may be **5.53**
reduced by five days where the contracting authority offers unrestricted and full
direct access by electronic means to the contract documents and any supplementary documents from the date of publication of the notice, specifying in the text of
the notice the internet address at which this documentation is accessible.[60] This
reduction may run concurrently with the shortened period provided for receipt of
tenders where notices are drawn up and transmitted by electronic means.

In restricted procedures, negotiated procedures with publication of a contract **5.54**
notice and the competitive dialogue:[61]

(a) the minimum time limit for receipt of requests to participate must be thirty-
seven days from the date on which the contract notice is sent;
(b) in the case of restricted procedures, the minimum time limit for the receipt of
tenders must be forty days from the date on which the invitation is sent.

When contracting authorities have published a prior information notice, the **5.55**
minimum time limit for the receipt of tenders under restricted procedures may be
shortened to twenty-two days.[62] The time limit must run from the date on which
the invitation to tender was sent in restricted procedures. The shortened time
limits should be permitted, provided that the prior information notice has
included all the information required for the contract notice, insofar as that
information is available at the time the notice is published and that the prior
information notice was sent for publication between fifty-two days and twelve
months before the date on which the contract notice was sent.

---

[57] *See* Art. 38(2) of the Public Sector Directive.
[58] *See* Art. 38(4) of the Public Sector Directive.
[59] *See* Art. 38(5) of the Public Sector Directive.
[60] *See* Art. 38(6) of the Public Sector Directive.
[61] *See* Art. 38(3) of the Public Sector Directive.
[62] *See* Art. 38(4) of the Public Sector Directive.

5.56   Where notices are drawn up and transmitted by electronic means, the time limit for the receipt of the requests to participate in restricted and negotiated procedures and the competitive dialogue may be shortened by seven days.[63]

5.57   The time limits for receipt of tenders referred to in restricted procedures may be reduced by five days where the contracting authority offers unrestricted and full direct access by electronic means to the contract documents and any supplementary documents from the date of publication of the notice, specifying in the text of the notice the internet address at which this documentation is accessible.[64] This reduction may run concurrently with the shortened period provided for receipt of tenders where notices are drawn up and transmitted by electronic means.

5.58   If, for whatever reason, the specifications and the supporting documents or additional information, although requested in good time, are not supplied within the time limits set in Articles 39 and 40 of the Directive, or where tenders can be made only after a visit to the site or after on-the-spot inspection of the documents supporting the contract documents, the time limits for the receipt of tenders must be extended so that all economic operators concerned may be aware of all the information needed to produce tenders.[65]

5.59   In the case of restricted procedures and negotiated procedures with publication of a contract notice, where urgency renders impracticable the time limits laid down in the Directive, contracting authorities may accelerate the award procedure[66] by specifying:

(a)   a time limit for the receipt of requests to participate which may not be less than fifteen days from the date on which the contract notice was sent, or less than ten days if the notice was sent by electronic means, in accordance with the format and procedure for sending notices; and

(b)   in the case of restricted procedures, a time limit for the receipt of tenders which must be not less than ten days from the date of the invitation to tender.

(3) Technical specifications

5.60   The technical specifications must be set out in the contract documentation, such as contract notices, contract documents, or additional documents.[67] Whenever possible, these technical specifications should be defined so as to take into account accessibility criteria for people with disabilities or designed for all users. Technical specifications must afford equal access for tenderers and not have the effect of

---

[63] *See* Art. 38(5) of the Public Sector Directive.
[64] *See* Art. 38(6) of the Public Sector Directive.
[65] *See* Art. 38(7) of the Public Sector Directive.
[66] *See* Art. 38(8) of the Public Sector Directive.   [67] *See* Art. 23 of the Public Sector Directive.

creating unjustified obstacles to the opening up of public procurement to competition.

Without prejudice to mandatory national technical rules, to the extent that they are compatible with Community law, the technical specifications must be formulated:[68]

5.61

(a) either by reference to technical specifications defined in Annex VI of the Public Sector Directive and, in order of preference, to national standards transposing European standards, European technical approvals, common technical specifications, international standards, other technical reference systems established by the European standardization bodies, or—when these do not exist—to national standards, national technical approvals, or national technical specifications relating to the design, calculation and execution of the works and use of the products. Each reference must be accompanied by the words 'or equivalent';

(b) or in terms of performance or functional requirements; the latter may include environmental characteristics. However, such parameters must be sufficiently precise to allow tenderers to determine the subject-matter of the contract and to allow contracting authorities to award the contract;

(c) or in terms of performance or functional requirements as mentioned in subparagraph (b), with reference to the specifications mentioned in subparagraph (a) as a means of presuming conformity with such performance or functional requirements;

(d) or by referring to the specifications mentioned in subparagraph (a) for certain characteristics, and by referring to the performance or functional requirements mentioned in subparagraph (b) for other characteristics.

Where a contracting authority makes use of the option of referring to the specifications defined in Annex VI of the Public Sector Directive and, in order of preference, to national standards transposing European standards, European technical approvals, common technical specifications, international standards, or other technical reference systems established by the European standardization bodies, it cannot reject a tender on the grounds that the products and services tendered for do not comply with the specifications to which it has referred, once the tenderer proves in his tender to the satisfaction of the contracting authority, by whatever appropriate means, that the solutions which he proposes satisfy in an equivalent manner the requirements defined by the technical specifications.[69] An appropriate means might be constituted by a technical dossier of the manufacturer or a test report from a recognized body.

5.62

---

[68] *See* Art. 23(3) of the Public Sector Directive.
[69] *See* Art. 23(4) of the Public Sector Directive.

5.63 Where a contracting authority prescribes in terms of performance or functional requirements, it may not reject a tender for works, products, or services which comply with a national standard transposing a European standard, with a European technical approval, a common technical specification, an international standard, or a technical reference system established by a European standardization body, if these specifications address the performance or functional requirements which it has laid down.[70] Within the tender documents, the tenderer must prove to the satisfaction of the contracting authority and by any appropriate means that the work, product, or service in compliance with the standard meets the performance or functional requirements of the contracting authority. An appropriate means might be constituted by a technical dossier of the manufacturer or a test report from a recognized body.

5.64 Where contracting authorities lay down environmental characteristics in terms of performance or functional requirements, they may use the detailed specifications, or, if necessary, parts thereof, as defined by European or (multi-) national eco-labels, or by any other eco-label, provided that those specifications are appropriate to define the characteristics of the supplies or services that are the object of the contract, that the requirements for the label are drawn up on the basis of scientific information, that the eco-labels are adopted using a procedure in which all stakeholders, such as government bodies, consumers, manufacturers, distributors, and environmental organizations can participate, and, finally, they are accessible to all interested parties.[71]

5.65 Contracting authorities may indicate that the products and services bearing the eco-label are presumed to comply with the technical specifications laid down in the contract documents; they must accept any other appropriate means of proof, such as a technical dossier of the manufacturer or a test report from a recognized body. Recognized bodies, within the meaning of the Directive, are test and calibration laboratories, and certification and inspection bodies which comply with applicable European standards. Contracting authorities must accept certificates from recognized bodies established in other member states.[72]

5.66 Unless justified by the subject-matter of the contract, technical specifications must not refer to a specific make or source, or a particular process, or to trade marks, patents, types, or a specific origin or production with the effect of favouring or eliminating certain undertakings or certain products. Such reference must be permitted on an exceptional basis, where a sufficiently precise and intelligible description of the subject-matter of the contract is not possible, and such reference must be accompanied by the words 'or equivalent'.[73]

---

[70] *See* Art. 23(5) of the Public Sector Directive.
[71] *See* Art. 23(6) of the Public Sector Directive.
[72] *See* Art. 23(7) of the Public Sector Directive.
[73] *See* Art. 23(8) of the Public Sector Directive.

(4) Variants

Contracting authorities may allow tenderers to submit variants, only where the **5.67** criterion for award is that of the most economically advantageous tender.[74] Contracting authorities must indicate in the contract notice whether or not they authorize variants, as variants should not be forwarded without prior authorization from the contracting authority. Contracting authorities authorizing variants must state in the contract documents the minimum requirements to be met by the variants and any specific requirements for their presentation. Only variants meeting the minimum requirements laid down by these contracting authorities must be taken into consideration. In procedures for awarding public supply or service contracts, contracting authorities which have authorized variants may not reject a variant on the sole ground that it would, if successful, lead to a service contract rather than a public supply contract, or a supply contract rather than a public service contract.

(5) Contractual performance

(a) Subcontracting

In the contract documents, the contracting authority may ask or may be required **5.68** by a member state to ask the tenderer to indicate in his tender any share of the contract he may intend to subcontract to third parties and any proposed subcontractors. This indication must be without prejudice to the question of the principal economic operator's liability.[75]

(b) Socio-economic conditions

Contracting authorities may lay down special conditions relating to the **5.69** performance of a contract, provided that these are compatible with Community law and are indicated in the contract notice or in the specifications. The conditions governing the performance of a contract may, in particular, concern social and environmental considerations.[76]

(c) Obligations relating to taxes, environmental protection, employment protection provisions, and working conditions

A contracting authority may state in the contract documents, or be obliged by a **5.70** member state to state, the body or bodies from which a candidate or tenderer may obtain the appropriate information on the obligations relating to taxes, to environmental protection, to the employment protection provisions, and to the

---

[74] *See* Art. 24 of the Public Sector Directive.   [75] *See* Art. 25 of the Public Sector Directive.
[76] *See* Art. 26 of the Public Sector Directive.

working conditions which are in force in the member state, region or locality in which the works are to be carried out or services are to be provided, and which must be applicable to the works carried out on site or to the services provided during the performance of the contract.[77]

5.71 A contracting authority must request the tenderers or candidates in the contract award procedure to indicate that they have taken account, when drawing up their tender, of the obligations relating to employment protection provisions and the working conditions which are in force in the place where the works are to be carried out or the service is to be provided.[78]

C. Qualitative Selection

(1) Reasons for automatic exclusion

(a) Personal situation of candidates or tenderers

5.72 Contracting authorities may exclude[79] from participation in a public contract any candidate or tenderer who has been the subject of a conviction by final judgment of which the contracting authority is aware for one or more of following reasons:[80]

(a) participation in a criminal organization, as defined in Article 2(1) of Council Joint Action 98/733/JHA;[81]

(b) corruption, as defined in Article 3 of the Council Act of 26 May 1997[82] and Article 3(1) of Council Joint Action 98/742/JHA[83] respectively;

(c) fraud within the meaning of Article 1 of the Convention relating to the protection of the financial interests of the European Communities;[84]

(d) money laundering, as defined in Article 1 of Council Directive 91/308/EEC of 10 June 1991 on prevention of the use of the financial system for the purpose of money laundering.[85]

5.73 In addition to the above reasons, contracting authorities may exclude an economic operator from participation in a contract where that economic operator:[86]

(a) is bankrupt or is being wound up, where his affairs are being administered by the court, where he has entered into an arrangement with creditors, or where

---

[77] *See* Art. 27(1) of the Public Sector Directive.
[78] *See* Art. 27(2) of the Public Sector Directive.
[79] *See* Art. 45 of the Public Sector Directive.
[80] *See* Art. 45(1) of the Public Sector Directive.   [81] [1998] OJ L351/1, 29 December 1998.
[82] [1997] OJ C195/1, 25 June 1997.   [83] [1998] OJ L358/2, 31 December 1998.
[84] [1995] OJ C316/48, 27 November 1995.
[85] [1991] OJ L166/77, 28 June 1991, as amended by Directive 2001/97/EC of the European Parliament and of the Council of 4 December 2001 ([2001] OJ L344/76, 28 December 2001).
[86] *See* Art. 45(2) of the Public Sector Directive.

he has suspended business activities or is in any analogous situation arising from a similar procedure under national laws and regulations;

(b) is the subject of proceedings for a declaration of bankruptcy, for an order for compulsory winding up or administration by the court, or of an arrangement with creditors or of any other similar proceedings under national laws and regulations;

(c) has been convicted by a judgment which has the force of *res judicata* in accordance with the format and procedure for sending notices; (b) and, in the case of restricted procedures, a time limit for the receipt of tenders which the contracting authorities can demonstrate;

(d) has not fulfilled obligations relating to the payment of social security contributions in accordance with the legal provisions of the country in which he is established or with those of the country of the contracting authority;

(e) has not fulfilled obligations relating to the payment of taxes in accordance with the legal provisions of the country in which he is established or with those of the country of the contracting authority;

(f) is guilty of serious misrepresentation in supplying the information required under this Section or has not supplied such information. Member states must specify, in accordance with their national law.

(b) Derogation

Member states may provide for derogation from the automatic exclusion grounds relating to participation in a criminal organization, corruption, fraud or money laundering for overriding requirements in the general interest.[87]   **5.74**

(c) Proof of the personal situation of candidates and tenderers

Sufficient evidence of the personal situation of candidates and tenderers in accordance with Article 45 can be provided by means of the production of an extract from the judicial record, or of an equivalent document issued by a competent judicial or administrative authority in the country of origin of the candidate or the tenderer, proving that none of the automatic exclusion grounds relating to participation in a criminal organization, corruption, fraud or money laundering is present.[88]   **5.75**

With regard to the requirements of evidence of payment of social security contributions and taxes in accordance with Article 45(2)(e) and (f), a certificate issued by the competent authority in the member state concerned is adequate proof.[89]   **5.76**

---

[87] *See* the second indent of Article 45(1) of the Public Sector Directive.
[88] *See* Art. 45(3)(a) of the Public Sector Directive.
[89] *See* Art. 45(3)(b) of the Public Sector Directive.

5.77 Where the country in question does not issue extracts from the judicial record or of an equivalent document or certificates, proof of the personal situation of candidates and tenderers may be provided by a declaration on oath or, in member states where there is no provision for declarations on oath, by a solemn declaration made by the person concerned before a competent judicial or administrative authority, a notary or a competent professional or trade body, in the country of origin or in the country whence that person comes. For these purposes, member states must designate the authorities and bodies competent to issue the documents, certificates, or declarations and inform the Commission, subject to data protection laws.

(d) Ex officio application

5.78 Contracting authorities, where they have doubts concerning the personal situation of such candidates or tenderers, may themselves apply to the competent authorities to obtain any information they consider necessary on the personal situation of the candidates or tenderers.[90] Where the information concerns a candidate or tenderer established in a State other than that of the contracting authority, the contracting authority may seek the cooperation of the competent authorities. Such requests must relate to legal and/or natural persons, including, if appropriate, company directors and any person having powers of representation, decision or control in respect of the candidate or tenderer.

(2) *Economic and financial standing*

5.79 Contracting authorities may request economic operators to prove their financial and economic standing for the performance of a contract.[91] Proof of the economic operator's economic and financial standing may, as a general rule, be furnished by appropriate statements from banks or, where appropriate, evidence of relevant professional risk indemnity insurance.[92] Contracting authorities may also request the presentation of balance-sheets or extracts from the balance-sheets, where publication of the balance-sheet is required under the law of the country in which the economic operator is established.[93]

5.80 In cases that bank statements or balance-sheets or extracts from the balance-sheets cannot be produced, a statement of the operator's overall turnover and, where appropriate, of turnover in the area covered by the contract will be sufficient. The period which such statement should cover must be for a maximum of the last

---

[90] *See* Art. 45(1) and, in particular, its second indent, of the Public Sector Directive.
[91] *See* Art. 47 of the Public Sector Directive.
[92] *See* Art. 47(1)(a) of the Public Sector Directive.
[93] *See* Art. 47(1)(b) of the Public Sector Directive.

three financial years. However, depending on the date on which an undertaking was set up or the economic operator started trading, the information provided on the turnovers should be acceptable.[94]

(a) Reliance on group and consortia

In cases where an economic operator is part of a group of companies, or belongs to a consortium especially formed to tender for the envisaged works, supplies, or services, contracting authorities may rely on the financial standing of other entities, regardless of the legal nature of the links which the economic operator has with them.[95] However, the operator which relies on the financial standing of group or consortia members must prove to the contracting authority that it will have at its disposal the resources necessary, for example, by producing an undertaking by those entities to that effect. Under the same conditions, a group of economic operators may rely on the economic and financial standing of participants in the group or of other entities.[96] **5.81**

Contracting authorities must specify, in the contract notice or in the invitation to tender, the type of reference they require for proof or evidence of economic and financial standing of economic operators, and which other additional references must be provided.[97] If, for any valid reason, the economic operator is unable to provide the references requested by the contracting authority, he may prove his economic and financial standing by any other document which the contracting authority considers appropriate.[98] **5.82**

(3) Technical and professional ability

Evidence of the technical and professional ability of economic operators may be requested by contracting authorities.[99] Such evidence may be furnished by a range of documentation provided by economic operators according to the nature, quantity, or importance, and use of the works, supplies, or services they intend to tender for. The contracting authority must specify, in the contract notice or in the invitation to tender, which references relevant to the technical and professional ability of economic operators it wishes to consider for evaluating the suitability to perform. In particular, the ability of economic operators to provide a service or a product or to execute the envisaged works may be evaluated with reference to their skills, efficiency, experience, and reliability. **5.83**

---

[94] *See* Art. 47(1)(c) of the Public Sector Directive.
[95] *See* Art. 47(2) of the Public Sector Directive.
[96] *See* Art. 47(3) of the Public Sector Directive.
[97] *See* Art. 47(4) of the Public Sector Directive.
[98] *See* Art. 47(5) of the Public Sector Directive.
[99] *See* Articles 46 and 48 of the Public Sector Directive.

(a) Previous experience

5.84 For works contracts,[100] evidence of technical ability may be provided by a list of the works carried out over the past five years, accompanied by certificates of satisfactory execution for the most important works. These certificates must indicate the value, date, and site of the works and must specify whether they were carried out according to the rules of the trade and properly completed. Where the recipient of the work is a contracting authority, such authority must submit these certificates to the contracting authority directly.

5.85 For service and supplies contracts, evidence of technical ability may be provided by a list of the principal deliveries supplied or the main services provided in the past three years, with the sums, dates, and recipients, whether public or private, of such supplies and services.[101] Evidence of delivery of supplies and services provided must be given by means of certificates issued or countersigned by the competent authority, where the recipient was a contracting authority itself. In cases where the recipient is a private purchaser, evidence must be provided by the purchaser's certification. In cases where the purchaser cannot provide any certification, a declaration by the economic operator should be sufficient evidence of previous experience relevant to its technical abilities.

(b) Technical expertise

5.86 The technical and professional expertise of economic operators could be furnished by documentation providing an indication of the technicians or technical bodies involved directly or indirectly with the economic operator.[102] Emphasis should be placed on those resources responsible for quality control. In cases of public works contracts, the technical and professional expertise of the economic operator can be proved by identifying those upon whom the contractor can call in order to carry out the works.

5.87 The technical capacity of economic operators can also be evidenced by means of a description of the technical facilities, measures, and systems used by the supplier or service provider for ensuring quality control. Relevant to this ground of technical capacity is a description of the operator's research and development facilities.

5.88 In services, works, and construction projects, the technical capacity of economic operators can be proved by a statement covering the average annual manpower of the service provider or the contractor and the number of managerial staff for the last three years. In addition, a statement of the tools, plant, or technical

---

[100] *See* Art. 48(2)(a)(i) of the Public Sector Directive.
[101] *See* Art. 48(2)(a)(ii) of the Public Sector Directive.
[102] *See* Art. 48(2)(a)(b) of the Public Sector Directive.

equipment available to the service provider or contractor for carrying out the contract could also be requested by contracting authorities.

(c) Professional expertise and suitability to pursue professional activities

Contracting authorities may request evidence of the educational and professional **5.89** qualifications of the service provider or contractor and, in particular, the educational and professional qualifications of the operators' managerial staff, as well as of those persons responsible for providing the services or managing the work.

Evidence of the suitability of economic operators to pursue professional activities **5.90** may be requested by contracting authorities.[103] In such cases, proof can be furnished by certified copies of the operator's enrolment on professional or trade registers prescribed in member states. In the absence of such documentation, evidence of suitability to pursue professional activities can be provided by a declaration on oath or a certificate as described in Annex IX A for public works contracts, in Annex IX B for public supply contracts, and in Annex IX C for public service contracts.

For the performance of public service contracts, insofar as candidates or tenderers **5.91** have to possess a particular authorization or to be members of a particular organization in order to be able to perform in their country of origin the service concerned, contracting authorities may require them to prove that they hold such authorization or membership.

(d) Reality checks

Contracting authorities may request reality checks where the products or services **5.92** to be supplied are complex or in exceptional circumstances they are procured for a specific purpose.[104] Reality checks can be carried out by the contracting authorities themselves or on their behalf by a competent official body of the country in which the supplier or service provider is established. The content and purpose of reality checks is to verify the production capacities of the supplier or the technical capacity of the service provider. The checks may also cover research and development facilities available to the economic operator, or measures, systems and procedures on quality control operating under that undertaking.

In cases of supplies contracts, contracting authorities may request samples, **5.93** descriptions, or photographs of the physical products.[105] The economic operator must be in a position to certify the authenticity of the products should the contracting authority request this. Such official recognition can be provided by

---

[103] *See* Art. 46 of the Public Sector Directive.
[104] *See* Art. 48(2)(d) of the Public Sector Directive.
[105] *See* Art. 48(2)(i) and (j) of the Public Sector Directive.

certificates drawn up by official quality control institutes or agencies of recognized competence attesting the conformity of products and clearly identifying them by reference to specifications or standards.

(e) Evidence of environmental management

5.94 For public works contracts and public services contracts, and only in appropriate cases, an indication of the environmental management measures that the economic operator will be able to apply when performing the contract may be requested by contracting authorities.[106] Should contracting authorities require the production of certificates drawn up by independent bodies attesting the compliance of the economic operator with certain environmental management standards, they must refer to the Eco-Management and Audit Scheme (EMAS). Alternatively, they could refer to environmental management standards based on the relevant European or international standards certified by bodies conforming to Community law.[107]

5.95 In the absence of EMAS or other European or international environmental standardization certificates, contracting authorities must recognize equivalent certificates from bodies established in member states or equivalent environmental management measures from economic operators.

(f) Reliance on group or consortia

5.96 In cases where an economic operator is part of a group of companies or belongs to a consortium especially formed to tender for the envisaged works, supplies, or services, contracting authorities may rely on the capacities of other entities, regardless of the legal nature of the links which the economic operator has with them.[108]

5.97 However, the economic operator must prove to the contracting authority that it will have at its disposal the resources necessary for the execution of the contract, for example, by producing an undertaking by those entities to place the necessary resources at the disposal of the economic operator. Under the same conditions, a group of economic operators may rely on the abilities of participants in the group or in other entities.

(g) Evidence of intended subcontracting

5.98 Contracting authorities may request economic operators to provide evidence of their intention to subcontract a proportion of the contract.[109]

---

[106] *See* Art. 48(2)(f) of the Public Sector Directive.
[107] *See* Art. 50 of the Public Sector Directive.
[108] *See* Art. 48(3) and (4) of the Public Sector Directive.
[109] Article 48(2)(i) of the Public Sector Directive.

(h) Quality assurance standards

In cases where contracting authorities require proof of quality assurance standards **5.99** of economic operators, such proof may be furnished by the production of certific-ates drawn up by independent bodies attesting the compliance of the economic operator with certain European series quality assurance standards.[110] In the event that the economic operator cannot produce such documentation, contracting authorities must recognize equivalent certificates from bodies established in member states and also accept other evidence of equivalent quality assurance measures from economic operators.

(4) Official lists of approved economic operators

Member states may introduce official lists of approved contractors,[111] suppliers, or **5.100** service providers in order to assist contracting authorities with the qualitative evaluation of tenderers and candidates in public procurement contracts.[112] Economic operators may ask at any time to be registered in an official list. They must be informed within a reasonably short period of time of the decision of the authority drawing up the list or of the competent certification body.

The conditions for registration in such lists must reflect the personal situation of **5.101** the candidate or tenderer to the extent of its participation in a criminal organiza-tion, corruption, fraud, money laundering, bankruptcy, winding up, compulsory administration, professional misconduct, serious misrepresentation, ability to pursue a professional activity, economic and financial standing, technical and professional capacity, quality assurance standards, and, where appropriate, envir-onmental management standards.[113] Registration in approved lists must not constitute a presumption of suitability of the registered undertakings, except for the conditions upon which their registration is based.

Economic operators belonging to a group and claiming resources made available **5.102** to them by the other companies in the group operators may apply for registration in an official list of approved undertakings.[114] In such cases, these operators must prove to the authority establishing the official list that they will have these resources at their disposal throughout the period of validity of the certificate attesting to their being registered in the official list, and that, throughout the same period, these companies continue to fulfil the qualitative selection requirements on which operators rely for their registration.

---

[110] *See* Art. 49 of the Public Sector Directive.   [111] *See* Art. 52(1) of the Public Sector Directive.
[112] Member states which have official lists or certification bodies as referred to in paragraph 1 must be obliged to inform the Commission and the other member states of the address of the body to which applications should be sent.
[113] *See* the provisions of Arts. 45(1), 45(2)(a) to (d) and (g), 46, 47(1), (4) and (5), 48(1), (2), (5) and (6), 49 and 50.   [114] Art. 52(2) of the Public Sector Directive.

5.103   Registration in official lists of approved economic operators can be demonstrated by the issue of a certificate which must state the references which enabled the registration in the list and the classification given in that list.[115] Economic operators registered on the official lists may be requested, for each contract they tender, to submit to the contracting authority such a certificate of registration issued by the competent authority. The information which can be deduced from registration on official lists or certification may not be questioned without justification by contracting authorities. For proof of payment of social security contributions and taxes, an additional certificate may be required of any registered economic operator whenever a contract is offered.

(5) Certification

5.104   Member states may introduce certification by certification bodies established in public or private law. Such certification bodies must comply with European certification standards.[116] For any registration of economic operators of other member states in an official list, or for their certification by the competent bodies, no further proof or statements can be required other than those requested of national economic operators. However, economic operators from other member states may not be obliged to undergo such registration or certification in order to participate in a public contract.[117] The contracting authorities must recognize equivalent certificates from bodies established in other member states and accept other equivalent means of proof relevant to the conditions required for registration or certification.

(6) Exclusion and rejection of economic operators

5.105   Candidates or tenderers who, under the law of the member state in which they are established, are entitled to provide the relevant service, must not be rejected solely on the ground that, under the law of the member state in which the contract is awarded, they would be required to be either natural or legal persons.[118] However, in the case of public service and public works contracts as well as public supply contracts covering in addition services and installation operations, legal persons may be required to indicate in the tender or the request to participate, the names and relevant professional qualifications of the staff to be responsible for the performance of the contract in question.

---

[115] *See* Art. 52(3) and (4) of the Public Sector Directive.
[116] *See* Art. 52(1) of the Public Sector Directive.
[117] Art. 52(4) of the Public Sector Directive.
[118] *See* Art. 4(1) of the Public Sector Directive.

(a) Verification of the suitability of participants

Contracting authorities may require candidates and tenderers to meet minimum **5.106** capacity levels.[119] The extent of the information referred to in these provisions laid down in Articles 47 and 48 and relating to the economic operators' financial and economic standing and their technical and professional capacity, as well as the minimum levels of ability required for a specific contract, must be related and proportionate to the subject matter of the contract. These minimum levels must be indicated in the contract notice.

(b) Group of economic operators

Groups of economic operators may submit tenders or put themselves forward as **5.107** candidates.[120] In order to submit a tender or a request to participate, these groups may not be required by the contracting authorities to assume a specific legal form; however, the group selected may be required to do so when it has been awarded the contract, to the extent that this change is necessary for the satisfactory performance of the contract.

D. Award Procedures

(1) Use of open, restricted, and negotiated procedures, and of competitive dialogue

Contracting authorities must award public contracts by applying principally **5.108** open or restricted procedures. In the specific circumstances expressly provided for in Article 29 of the Directive, contracting authorities may award their public contracts by means of the competitive dialogue. In the specific cases and circumstances referred to expressly in Articles 30 and 31 of the Directive, they may apply a negotiated procedure, with or without publication of the contract notice.[121]

(2) The choice of participants in award procedures

In restricted procedures, negotiated procedures with publication of a contract **5.109** notice, and in the competitive dialogue procedure, contracting authorities may limit the number of suitable candidates they will invite to tender, to negotiate or to conduct a dialogue with, provided a sufficient number of suitable candidates are available.[122] The contracting authorities must indicate in the contract notice

---

[119] *See* Art. 44 of the Public Sector Directive.
[120] Art. 4(2) of the Public Sector Directive.
[121] Art. 28 paragraph 2 of the Public Sector Directive.
[122] *See* Art. 44(3) of the Public Sector Directive.

the objective and non-discriminatory criteria or rules they intend to apply, the minimum number of candidates they intend to invite, and, where appropriate the maximum number.

5.110   In the restricted procedure, the minimum number of tenderers must be five. In the negotiated procedure with publication of a contract notice and the competitive dialogue procedure, the minimum number of candidates must be three. In any event, the number of candidates invited must be sufficient to ensure genuine competition. The contracting authorities must invite a number of candidates at least equal to the minimum number set in advance.[123] Where the number of candidates meeting the selection criteria and the minimum levels of ability is below the minimum number, the contracting authority may continue the procedure by inviting the candidate(s) with the required capabilities. However, when the number of candidates is below the minimum number, contracting authorities may not include other economic operators who did not request to participate, or candidates who do not have the required capabilities.

5.111   Where contracting authorities exercise the option of reducing the number of solutions to be discussed or of tenders to be negotiated, provided for in Articles 29(4) and 30(4) of the Directive, they must apply the award criteria stated in the contract notice, in the specifications or in the descriptive document.[124] In the final stage, the number of candidates invited to participate or tender must ensure genuine competition to the extent that there are enough solutions or suitable candidates.

(3) Open procedures

5.112   Open procedures, alongside restricted procedures, are the normal award procedures stipulated in the Directive, and contracting authorities must first have recourse to them for awarding public contracts.[125] The normal character of the open procedure does not mean that it is a mandatory award procedure. Rather, it indicates its priority over other procedures such as negotiated procedures or the competitive dialogue.

5.113   Open procedures are those award procedures where any interested economic operator may submit a tender.[126] After publishing a notice, contracting authorities must wait a minimum of fifty-two days from the date on which the contract notice was published for the receipt of tenders.[127] When contracting authorities have published a prior information notice (PIN), the minimum time limit for the

---

[123] Art. 44(3) second indent of the Public Sector Directive.
[124] *See* Art. 44(4) of the Public Sector Directive.
[125] Art. 28(2) of the Public Sector Directive.
[126] Art. 1(11)(a) of the Public Sector Directive.
[127] *See* Art. 38(2) of the Public Sector Directive.

receipt of tenders may, as a general rule, be shortened to thirty-six days. The time limit must run from the date on which the contract notice was sent in open procedures.[128]

The shortened time limit should be permitted on two conditions.[129] Firstly, the **5.114** contracting authorities must have dispatched the prior information notice for publication between fifty-two days and twelve months before the date on which the relevant contract notice was sent for publication. Secondly, the prior information notice has to include all the information required for the contract notice, insofar as that information is available at the time the prior information notice is published.

Where notices are drawn up and transmitted by electronic means, the time limits **5.115** for the receipt of tenders in open procedures may be shortened by seven days. The time limits for receipt of tenders may be reduced by further five days where the contracting authority offers unrestricted and full direct access by electronic means to the contract documents and any supplementary documents from the date of publication of the notice, specifying in the text of the notice the internet address at which this documentation is accessible.[130]

(a) Specifications, additional documents, and information

Where contracting authorities do not offer unrestricted and full direct access by **5.116** electronic means to the specifications and any supporting documents, the specifications and supplementary documents must be sent to economic operators within six days of receipt of the request to participate, provided that the request was made in good time before the deadline for the submission of tenders.[131]

Provided that it has been requested in good time, additional information relating **5.117** to the specifications and any supporting documents must be supplied by the contracting authorities or competent departments not later than six days before the deadline fixed for the receipt of tenders.[132]

(b) Extension of time limits

Contracting authorities may extend the time limits and deadlines applicable to **5.118** open procedures for the receipt of tenders if, for whatever reason, the specifications and the supporting documents or additional information, although requested in good time, are not supplied within six days of receipt of the request to

---

[128] Art. 38(4) of the Public Sector Directive.
[129] *See* Art. 38(4) of the Public Sector Directive.
[130] Art. 38(5) of the Public Sector Directive.
[131] Art. 39(1) of the Public Sector Directive.
[132] *See* Art. 39(2) of the Public Sector Directive.

participate.[133] In cases where additional information relating to the specifications and any supporting documents were requested but not provided within six days of receipt of the request to participate, the contracting authority may also extend the time limits for the receipt of the tenders.

5.119 Extension of time limits can be provided also where the submission of tenders is possible only after a visit to the site, or after on-the-spot inspection of the documents supporting the contract documents.

(4) Restricted procedures

5.120 Alongside open procedures, restricted procedures represent the norm in award procedures for public procurement contracts.[134] Restricted procedures are those procedures in which any economic operator may request to participate and whereby only those economic operators invited by the contracting authority may submit a tender.[135]

5.121 Contracting authorities using restricted procedures must set the minimum time limit for receipt of requests to participate to thirty-seven days from the date on which the contract notice is sent for publication.[136] The minimum time limit for the receipt of tenders must be forty days from the date on which the invitation is sent to the participant tenderers.[137]

5.122 When contracting authorities have published a prior information notice, the minimum time limit for the receipt of tenders may, as a general rule, be shortened to twenty-two days. The time limit must run from the date on which the invitation to tender was sent to the participants.[138] The shortened time limit should be allowed if contracting authorities have fulfilled two conditions. Firstly, the prior information notice has to include all the information required for the contract notice, insofar as that information is available at the time the notice is published. Secondly, the prior information notice must have been sent for publication between fifty-two days and twelve months before the date on which the contract notice was sent.

5.123 In cases where contracting authorities utilize electronic means to draw up and transmit notices in accordance with the format and procedures for transmission indicated in Annex VIII of the Directive, the time limit for the receipt of the requests to participate may be shortened by seven days.[139]

---

[133] *See* Art. 38(7) of the Public Sector Directive.
[134] Art. 28(2) of the Public Sector Directive.
[135] *See* Art. 1(11)(b) of the Public Sector Directive.
[136] Art. 38(3)(a) of the Public Sector Directive.
[137] *See* Art. 38(3)(b) of the Public Sector Directive.
[138] Art. 38(4) of the Public Sector Directive.   [139] Art. 38(5) of the Public Sector Directive.

In cases where the contracting authority offers unrestricted and full direct access **5.124** by electronic means to the contract documents and any supplementary documents from the date of publication of the notice, by specifying in the text of the notice the internet address at which this documentation is accessible, the time limit for receipt of tenders may be reduced by five days.[140]

The reduction of time limits for the receipt of the requests to participate in cases **5.125** where contracting authorities utilize electronic means to draw up and transmit notices, and the reduction of time limits for receipt of tenders in cases where contracting authorities offer unrestricted and full direct access by electronic means to the contract documents and any supplementary documents may run concurrently.

(a) Extension of time limits

Contracting authorities may extend the time limits and deadlines specified for the **5.126** receipt of tenders in restricted procedures if, for whatever reason, the specifications and the supporting documents or additional information, although requested in good time, are not supplied within the time limits set in Articles 38(4)(5) of the Directive.[141] Extension of time limits can be provided also where the submission of tenders is possible only after a visit to the site or after on-the-spot inspection of the documents supporting the contract documents.

(b) Accelerated restricted procedure on grounds of urgency

Where for reasons of urgency, contracting authorities cannot adhere to the time **5.127** limits specified in the Directive for the receipt of requests to participate and for the receipt of tenders respectively, an accelerated form of the restricted procedure may be used.[142]

Contracting authorities may stipulate a time limit for the receipt of requests to **5.128** participate which may not be less than fifteen days from the date on which the contract notice was sent, or less than ten days if the notice was sent by electronic means, in accordance with the format and procedure for sending notices laid down in Annex VIII. Contracting authorities may also stipulate a time limit for the receipt of tenders which must be not less than ten days from the date of the invitation to tender.

(c) Invitation to submit a tender under restricted procedures

Contracting authorities must simultaneously and in writing invite the selected **5.129** candidates to submit their tenders.[143] The invitation to the candidates should

---

[140] Art. 38(6) of the Public Sector Directive.   [141] Art. 38(7) of the Public Sector Directive.
[142] *See* Art. 38(8) of the Public Sector Directive.
[143] Art. 40(1) of the Public Sector Directive.

include a copy of the specifications and any supporting documents, or a reference to allow the invited parties to access by electronic means the specifications and the supporting documents.[144]

5.130 Where an entity other than the contracting authority responsible for the award procedure has the specifications and any supporting documents, the invitation must provide the address from which the specifications and the supporting documents may be requested and, where appropriate, the deadline for requesting such documents, and the sum payable for obtaining them, and any payment procedures.[145] The entity that is responsible for dispatching the relevant documentation, upon receipt of a request from economic operators that have been invited to tender, must send any documentation relevant to specifications and any supporting documents to the economic operators without delay.

5.131 Any additional information relevant to the specifications, or any supporting documents, must be sent by the contracting authority or the competent department not less than four days before the deadline fixed for the receipt of tenders, provided that it is requested in good time.[146]

(d) The content of the invitation to tender in restricted procedures

5.132 Apart from the copy of the specifications and any supporting documents, or a reference to allow the invited parties to access by electronic means the specifications and the supporting documents, contracting authorities must provide,[147] as minimum requirement, the following information in the invitation to submit tenders:

(a) a reference to the contract notice published;
(b) the deadline for the receipt of the tenders; the address to which the tenders must be sent and the language or languages in which the tenders must be drawn up;
(c) a reference to any documents or certificates to be submitted in support of the economic operator's personal situation, economic and financial standing, and technical and professional capacity according to Articles 44, 47 and 48 of the Directive, or documents in support of verifiable declarations by the tenderer in the case that official documentation and certification cannot be provided in accordance with Article 44.
(d) The relative weighting of criteria for the award of the contract or, where appropriate, the descending order of importance for such criteria, if they are not given in the contract notice, the specifications, or the descriptive document.

---

[144] Art. 40(2) of the Public Sector Directive.   [145] *See* Art. 40(3) of the Public Sector Directive.
[146] Art. 40(4) of the Public Sector Directive.
[147] *See* Art. 40(5) of the Public Sector Directive.

(5) The competitive dialogue

In cases of particularly complex contracts, contracting authorities may provide **5.133** that where contracting authorities consider that the use of the open or restricted procedure will not allow the award of the contract, the use of the competitive dialogue procedure is required.[148]

Competitive dialogue is a procedure in which any economic operator may request **5.134** to participate and whereby the contracting authority conducts a dialogue with the candidates admitted to that procedure, with the aim of developing one or more suitable alternatives capable of meeting its requirements, and on the basis of which the candidates chosen are invited to tender.[149]

A public contract is considered to be particularly complex where the contracting **5.135** authorities are not able to define objectively the technical means of the contract.[150] In particular, to formulate the technical specifications required for the performance of the contract, contracting authorities must take into account any mandatory national technical rules, to the extent that they are compatible with Community law.[151] In addition, the technical specifications must be formulated by sufficiently precise parameters having reference to the performance or functional requirements, including environmental characteristics, of the works, supplies, or services. The requirement of sufficient precision in the formulation of the technical specifications must be present in order to allow tenderers to determine the subject-matter of the contract and also to allow contracting authorities to award the contract. In such cases, where the technical specifications cannot be formulated with sufficient precision so they are capable of satisfying their needs or objectives of the contracting authority, the contract is deemed to be particularly complex.[152]

A public contract is also considered particularly complex in cases where contracting **5.136** authorities cannot determine the performance or functional requirements of a project in conformity with the technical standards defined in Annex VI of the Directive, and, in order of preference, national standards transposing European standards, European technical approvals, common technical specifications, international standards, or any equivalent standard.[153] In such cases, the inability to comply with the required technical standards precludes the contracting authority from determining the technical specifications necessary for the performance of

---

[148] *See* Art. 29(1) of the Public Sector Directive.
[149] Art. 1(11)(c) of the Public Sector Directive.
[150] *See* Art. 1(11)(c) second indent of the Public Sector Directive.
[151] Art. 23(3) of the Public Sector Directive.
[152] Art. 23(3)(b) of the Public Sector Directive.
[153] *See* Art. 23(3)(c) of the Public Sector Directive.

the contract and, as a consequence, the needs and objectives of the contracting authority cannot be met.[154] Therefore, the public contract is deemed to be particularly complex.

5.137   Finally, when contracting authorities cannot objectively specify the legal or the financial make-up of a project, the contract is deemed to be particularly complex.

(a) Conduct of the competitive dialogue

5.138   When contracting authorities wish to use the competitive dialogue as an award procedure, they must publish a notice for the contract setting out their needs and requirements.[155] The notice must define in clear and objective manner the needs and requirements to be achieved through the contract. Alternatively, a descriptive document may be used to stipulate the contracting authority's need and requirements. Contracting authorities may specify prices or payments to the participants in the dialogue.[156]

5.139   The preliminary phase of the competitive dialogue is to select a number of candidates with which contracting authorities may commence a dialogue with the aim of identifying the means best suited to meet the needs and requirements. The selection process should take place in accordance with the usual selection provisions found in Articles 44 to 52 of the Directive, covering, *inter alia*, the personal situation of the candidates, their suitability to pursue a professional activity, their economic and financial standing, and their technical and professional ability. The Directive does not specify the minimum number of candidates to be invited to participate in the competitive dialogue. However, the number of candidates should be adequate in order to provide sufficient competition and to identify enough solutions from which the solution which meets the needs and requirements of the contracting authority will emerge.

(b) Opening of the competitive dialogue

5.140   The most important requirement in this phase is the equal treatment of candidates by the contracting authority.[157] They may discuss all aspects of the contract with the chosen candidates. However, they must not provide information in a discriminatory manner which may give some candidates an advantage over others.

5.141   The opening of the competitive dialogue commences when contracting authorities, simultaneously and in writing, invite the selected candidates to take part in the dialogue.[158] The invitation to the candidates must include either a copy of

---

[154] Art. 23(3)(d) of the Public Sector Directive.
[155] *See* Art. 29(2) of the Public Sector Directive.
[156] Art. 29(8) of the Public Sector Directive.   [157] Art. 29(3) of the Public Sector Directive.
[158] *See* the requirements laid down in Article 40 of the Public Sector Directive.

the specifications or of the descriptive document and any supporting documents, or a reference in order to access by electronic means the specifications and any supporting documents.[159] Where an entity other than the contracting authority responsible for the award procedure has the specifications, the descriptive document or any supporting documents, the invitation must state the address from which those documents may be requested, and, if appropriate, the deadline for requesting such documents, and the sum payable for obtaining them, and any payment procedures.

The invitation to participate in the dialogue must contain also[160] a reference to the contract notice published; the date and the address set for the start of consultation, and the language or languages used; a reference to any additional documents to be submitted, either in support or supplementing of verifiable declarations by the participants that they meet minimum capacity levels required for the contract, levels which must be related to, and be proportionate to, the subject matter of the contract and previously indicated in the contract notice; the relative weighting of criteria for the award of the contract or, where appropriate, the descending order of importance for such criteria, if they are not given in the contract notice, the specifications, or the descriptive document.   **5.142**

The deadline for the receipt of the tenders, the address to which the tenders must be sent, and the language or languages in which the tenders must be drawn up must not appear in the invitation to participate in the dialogue but instead in the invitation to submit a tender.   **5.143**

In principle, contracting authorities may not reveal to the other participants the solutions proposed or other confidential information communicated by a candidate participating in the dialogue without that candidate's prior agreement.[161] The dialogue should be continued until the contracting authority can identify the solution or solutions, if necessary after comparing them, which are capable of meeting its needs.[162]   **5.144**

The dialogue with the selected candidates can take place in a single stage or in successive stages.[163] The reason for the successive stages in the competitive dialogue is to reduce the number of solutions to be discussed by the contracting authority and the candidates. When contracting authorities wish to have recourse to successive stages during the competitive dialogue, their intention must be mentioned in the contract notice or the descriptive document. In order to reduce   **5.145**

---

[159] Art. 40(2) of the Public Sector Directive.
[160] Art. 40(5) of the Public Sector Directive.
[161] *See* Art. 29(3) second indent of the Public Sector Directive.
[162] *See* Art. 29(5) of the Public Sector Directive.
[163] Art. 29(4) of the Public Sector Directive.

the solutions on offer during the competitive dialogue, contracting authorities must apply the award criteria in the contract notice or the descriptive document. Contracting authorities must ensure that the elimination of solutions proposed by candidates does not jeopardize a genuine competition, which is necessary for the final tendering stage of the competitive dialogue.[164]

(c) Closure of the competitive dialogue

5.146 When a particular solution or a number of solutions have been identified, the contracting authority must declare that the dialogue is concluded.[165] It must communicate its decision to all candidates who have participated and at the same time ask them to submit their final tenders on the basis of the solution or solutions presented and specified during the dialogue. The minimum number of candidates which could be invited to submit tenders is three.

(d) Submission of final tenders

5.147 The tenders submitted by the invited candidates must contain all the elements required and necessary for the performance of the project, as identified in the solution or the solutions during the dialogue between the contracting authorities and the candidates.[166]

5.148 These tenders may be clarified, specified and fine-tuned at the request of the contracting authority. However, such clarification, specification, fine-tuning or additional information may not involve changes to the basic features of the tender or the call for tender, variations in which are likely to distort competition or have a discriminatory effect.

5.149 For the assessment of the tenders, contracting authorities must apply the criteria specified in the contract notice or the descriptive document.[167] After the assessment exercise of the tenders, the contracting authority must identify the candidate that submitted the most economically advantageous tender in accordance with Article 53 of the Directive.

(e) Award of the contract

5.150 Contracting authorities may award the contract straightforwardly or seek clarifications of any aspects of the tender or commitments which were contained in the tender.[168] A public contract awarded under the procedures of the

---

[164] Art. 44(4) of the Public Sector Directive.
[165] *See* Art. 29(6) of the Public Sector Directive.
[166] *See* Art. 29(6) second indent of the Public Sector Directive.
[167] Art. 29(7) of the Public Sector Directive.
[168] Art. 29(7) second indent of the Public Sector Directive.

competitive dialogue must be based solely on the most economically advantageous tender as the award criterion. The candidate which submitted the most economically advantageous tender, at the request of the contracting authority, may be asked to clarify aspects of the tender or confirm commitments contained in the tender provided this does not have the effect of modifying substantial aspects of the tender or of the call for tender, and does not risk distorting competition or causing discrimination.

(6) Negotiated procedures

5.151 Negotiated procedures are the award procedures under which contracting authorities consult the economic operators of their choice and negotiate the terms of contract with one or more of these.[169] There are two types of negotiated procedures: negotiated procedures with prior publication of a contract notice; and negotiated procedures without prior publication of a contract notice.[170]

(a) Grounds for use of the negotiated procedure with prior publication of a contract notice

5.152 Contracting authorities may award their public contracts by negotiated procedure, after publication of a contract notice, in the following cases:[171]

(a) in the event of irregular tenders in response to an open or restricted procedure or a competitive dialogue insofar as the original terms of the contract are not substantially altered.

   i. in the event of submission of tenders which are unacceptable and have been rejected under national provisions compatible with the provisions of the Directive and, in particular, the nature of economic operators (Article 4); variants included in the tender (Article 24); subcontracting (Article 25); the obligations of economic operators relating to taxes, environmental protection, employment protection, and working conditions (Article 27); and provisions of Chapter VII of the Directive on the economic operator's personal situation, economic and financial standing, and technical and professional capacity.

(b) in exceptional cases, when the nature of the works, supplies, or services or the risks attached to the performance of the contract do not permit prior overall pricing;

(c) in the case of services, *inter alia*, services within category 6 of Annex II A (insurance services, and banking and investment services, except financial

---

[169] *See* Art. 1(11)(d) of the Public Sector Directive.
[170] Art. 38(8) of the Public Sector Directive.
[171] *See* Art. 31 of the Public Sector Directive.

services in connection with the issue, sale, purchase or transfer of securities or other financial instruments, and central bank services), and intellectual services such as services involving the design of works, insofar as the nature of the services to be provided is such that contract specifications cannot be established with sufficient precision to permit the award of the contract by selection of the best tender according to the rules governing open or restricted procedures;

(d) in respect of public works contracts, for works which are performed solely for purposes of research, testing or development, and not with the aim of ensuring profitability or recovering research and development costs.

(b) Accelerated negotiated procedures on grounds of urgency

5.153 Where for reasons of urgency, contracting authorities cannot adhere to the time limits specified in the Directive for the receipt of requests to participate and for the receipt of tenders respectively, an accelerated form of the negotiated procedure may be used.[172]

5.154 Contracting authorities may stipulate a time limit for the receipt of requests to participate which may not be less than fifteen days from the date on which the contract notice was sent, or less than ten days if the notice was sent by electronic means, in accordance with the format and procedure for sending notices indicated in Annex VIII of the Directive.

(c) Invitation to negotiate

5.155 In negotiated procedures with publication of a contract notice, contracting authorities must simultaneously, and in writing, invite the selected candidates to negotiate. The invitation to the candidates must include either a copy of the specifications and any supporting documents or a reference to accessing the specifications and any related documents, when they are made directly available by electronic means.[173] The invitation to negotiate must contain, as a minimum requirement, the following information:

(a) a reference to the contract notice published;

(b) the deadline for the receipt of the tenders; the address to which the tenders must be sent and the language or languages in which the tenders must be drawn up;

(c) a reference to any documents or certificates to be submitted in support of the economic operator's personal situation, economic and financial standing and technical and professional capacity according to Articles 44, 47 and 48 of the

---

[172] *See* the provisions laid down in Art. 38(8) of the Public Sector Directive.
[173] Art. 44 of the Public Sector Directive.

Directive, or documents in support of verifiable declarations by the tenderer in the case that official documentation and certification cannot be provided in accordance with Article 44.

(d) the relative weighting of criteria for the award of the contract or, where appropriate, the descending order of importance for such criteria, if they are not given in the contract notice, the specifications, or the descriptive document.

Where an entity other than the contracting authority responsible for the award **5.156** procedure has the specifications or any supporting documents, the invitation to negotiate must specify the address from which those specifications and those documents may be requested, and, if appropriate, the deadline for requesting such documents and any payment necessary for obtaining them.[174] Upon receipt of such a request, the entity that has the specifications or any supporting documents must dispatch them to the economic operators participating in the negotiations without delay.

Any additional information on the specifications or the supporting documents **5.157** must be sent by the contracting authority or the competent department at least six days before the deadline for the receipt of tenders, provided that such information is requested in good time. In the event of an accelerated negotiated procedure, that period must be four days.

(d) Conduct of negotiated procedures with prior publication

In negotiated procedures with publication of a contract notice the minimum time **5.158** limit for receipt of requests to participate must be thirty-seven days from the date on which the contract notice is sent to the *Official Journal*.[175] Where notices are drawn up and transmitted by electronic means in accordance with the format and procedures for transmission indicated in Annex VIII, the time limits for the receipt of tenders may be shortened by seven days.[176] In the case of negotiated procedures with publication of a contract notice where urgency renders impracticable the time limits specified above, contracting authorities may stipulate a time limit for the receipt of requests to participate which may not be less than fifteen days from the date on which the contract notice was sent, or less than ten days if the notice was sent by electronic means, in accordance with the format and procedure for sending notices described in Annex VIII of the Directive.[177]

During the negotiations with participants, contracting authorities must ensure **5.159** that all tenderers receive equal treatment. In particular, contracting authorities

---

[174] Art. 44(2) of the Public Sector Directive.
[175] Art. 38(3) of the Public Sector Directive.
[176] Art. 38(5) of the Public Sector Directive.
[177] Art. 38(8) of the Public Sector Directive.

must not provide any information in a discriminatory manner which may give some tenderers an advantage over others.[178]

5.160 Contracting authorities may provide for the negotiated procedure to take place in successive stages in order to reduce the number of tenders to be negotiated by applying the award criteria in the contract notice or the specifications. The contract notice or the specifications must indicate whether contracting authorities wish to use successive stages in the procedure.[179]

5.161 The outcome of the negotiated procedures with prior publication must lead to the adaptation of the tenders and offers submitted by the participants to the needs and requirements of the contracting authority, which must have been set in the contract notice, the specifications, and any additional documents.[180] Following this process, the contracting authority must seek out the best tender in accordance with Article 53(1) of the Directive, and award the contact based on either the most economically advantageous offer or the lowest price.

(e) Grounds for use of the negotiated procedure without prior publication of a contract notice

5.162 Contracting authorities may award public contracts by a negotiated procedure without prior publication of a contract notice in the following cases:[181]

1. *For public works contracts, public supply contracts and public service contracts:*
   (a) when no tenders or no suitable tenders or no applications have been submitted in response to an open procedure or a restricted procedure, provided that the initial conditions of contract are not substantially altered and on condition that a report is sent to the Commission if it so requests;
   (b) when, for technical or artistic reasons, or for reasons connected with the protection of exclusive rights, the contract may be awarded only to a particular economic operator;
   (c) insofar as is strictly necessary when, for reasons of extreme urgency brought about by events unforeseeable by the contracting authorities in question, the time limit for the open, restricted or negotiated procedures with publication of a contract notice cannot be complied with. The circumstances invoked to justify extreme urgency must not in any event be attributable to the contracting authority;
   (d) where they include in the negotiated procedure all of, and only, the tenderers which satisfy the selection and qualification criteria of Articles

---

[178] *See* Art. 30(3) of the Public Sector Directive.   [179] Art. 30(4) of the Public Sector Directive.
[180] *See* Art. 30(2) of the Public Sector Directive.
[181] *See* the requirements laid down in Art. 31 of the Public Sector Directive.

45 to 52 of the Directive, and have submitted acceptable tenders as a result of prior open or restricted procedure or competitive dialogue.

2. *For public supply contracts:*

    (a) when the products involved are manufactured purely for the purpose of research, experimentation, study or development; this provision does not extend to quantity production to establish commercial viability or to recover research and development costs;

    (b) for additional deliveries by the original supplier which are intended either as a partial replacement of normal supplies or installations, or as the extension of existing supplies or installations, where a change of supplier would oblige the contracting authority to acquire material having different technical characteristics which would result in incompatibility or disproportionate technical difficulties in operation and maintenance; the length of such contracts as well as that of recurrent contracts may not, as a general rule, exceed three years;

    (c) for supplies quoted and purchased on a commodity market;

    (d) for the purchase of supplies on particularly advantageous terms, from either a supplier which is definitively winding up its business activities, or the receivers or liquidators of a bankruptcy, an arrangement with creditors, or a similar procedure under national laws or regulations;

3. *For public service contracts*, when the contract concerned follows a design contest and must, under the applicable rules, be awarded to the successful candidate or to one of the successful candidates; in the latter case, all successful candidates must be invited to participate in the negotiations;

4. *For public works contracts and public service contracts:*

    (a) for additional works or services not included in the project initially considered or in the original contract but which have, through unforeseen circumstances, become necessary for the performance of the works or services described therein, on condition that the award is made to the economic operator performing such works or services:

    i. when such additional works or services cannot be technically or economically separated from the original contract without major inconvenience to the contracting authorities, or

    ii. when such works or services, although separable from the performance of the original contract, are strictly necessary for its completion.

    However, the aggregate value of contracts awarded for additional works or services may not exceed fifty per cent of the amount of the original contract;

    (b) for new works or services consisting in the repetition of similar works or services entrusted to the economic operator to whom the same contracting authorities awarded an original contract, provided that such works or services are in conformity with a basic project for which the original contract was awarded according to the open or restricted procedure. Contracting authorities wishing to apply negotiated procedures without prior publication of a notice for the possibility of awarding additional works to the successful candidate, must make their intention known in the contract notice that led to the award of the original contract under open or restricted procedures.

5.163 The total estimated cost of subsequent works or services must be taken into consideration by the contracting authorities when they calculate the contract value in accordance with the thresholds applicable under the provisions of Article 7 of the Directive. Negotiated procedure without prior publication of a notice can be used for the award of new works or services consisting in the repetition of similar works or services entrusted to the economic operator to whom the same contracting authorities awarded an original contract only during the three years following the conclusion of the original contract.

(7) Design contests

5.164 Design contests are those procedures which enable the contracting authority to acquire a plan or design selected by a jury after being put out to competition, with or without the award of prizes. The plan or design should be mainly in the disciplines of town and country planning, architecture and engineering, or data processing.[182]

(a) Scope and thresholds

5.165 The following contracting authorities can organize design contests:[183]

(a) contracting authorities which are listed as central government authorities in Annex IV of the Directive, starting from a threshold equal to or greater than €162,000;

(b) contracting authorities not listed in Annex IV of the Directive, starting from a threshold equal to or greater than €249,000;

(c) by all the contracting authorities, starting from a threshold equal to or greater than €249,000 where contests concern services in the field of research and development,[184] telecommunications services,[185] or services listed in Annex II B.[186]

---

[182] *See* Art. 1(11)(e) of the Public Sector Directive.

[183] *See* the provisions of Article 67 of the Public Sector Directive.

[184] *See* category 8 of Annex II A of the Directive for research and development services, except research and development services other than those where the benefits accrue exclusively to the contracting authority for its use in the conduct of its own affairs on condition that the service provided is wholly remunerated by the contracting authority.

[185] Telecommunication services capable of being awarded through design contests have positions which in the CPV are equivalent to reference No. CPC 7524, 7525 and 7526.

[186] Services described in Annex II B include the following: hotel and restaurant services; rail transport services; water transport services; supporting and transport services; legal services;

(b) Conduct of design contests

Contracting authorities which wish to carry out a design contest must make **5.166** known their intention by means of a contest notice. The usual advertisement and publicity requirements stipulated in Article 36 of the Directive apply to design contests.[187] The notices relating to organization of design contests must contain the following information:[188]

1. Name, address, fax number and email address of the contracting authority and those of the service from which the additional documents may be obtained.
2. Description of the project.
3. Type of contest: open or restricted.
4. In the event of an open contest: time limit for the submission of projects.
5. In the event of a restricted contest:
    (a) number of participants contemplated;
    (b) names of the participants already selected, if any;
    (c) criteria for the selection of participants;
    (d) time limit for requests to participate.
6. If appropriate, indicate that the participation is restricted to a specified profession.
7. Criteria which will be applied in the evaluation of the projects.
8. Names of any members of the jury who have already been selected.
9. Indicate whether the jury's decision is binding on the contracting authority.
10. Number and value of any prizes.
11. Payments to be made to all participants, if any.
12. Indicate whether any contracts following the contest will or will not be awarded to the winner or winners of the contest.

Design contests could be arranged as part of a procedure leading to the award of a **5.167** public service contract or as a competition with prizes or payments to participants.[189] The value of the public service contract subject to a design contest should be net of VAT, including any possible prizes and/or payments to participants. The total amount of the prizes and payments to the participants of a design contest, including the estimated value of the public services contract which might be subsequently concluded, should not exceed the stipulated thresholds.

---

personnel and placement supply services (except employment contracts); investigation and security services (except armoured services); education and vocational education services; health and social services; recreational, cultural, and sporting services; or other services (except contracts for the acquisition, development, production or co-production of programmes by broadcasting organizations and contracts for broadcasting time).

[187] Art. 69 of the Public Sector Directive.
[188] *See* the format and template of information required in Annex VII D of the Public Sector Directive.   [189] *See* Art. 67(2) of the Public Sector Directive.

5.168   After the conclusion of the design contest, contracting authorities must publish a notice of the results including the following information:[190] reference of the contest notice, description of the project, total number of participants, number of foreign participants, the winner(s) of the contest, and any prizes awarded to the winner(s).

5.169   The admission of participants to design contests must not be limited either by reference to the territory or part of the territory of a member state or on the grounds that, under the law of the member state in which the contest is organized, they would be required to be either natural or legal persons.[191] For the selection of competitors, where design contests are restricted to a limited number of participants, contracting authorities are obliged to lay down clear and non-discriminatory selection criteria. In any event, the number of candidates invited to participate must be sufficient to ensure genuine competition.

5.170   Contracting authorities cannot utilize design contests to award public contracts in the water, energy, transport, and postal services sectors (Article 12), contracts with the principal purpose of permitting the contracting authorities to provide or exploit public telecommunications networks or to provide to the public one or more telecommunications services (Article 13), secret contracts and contracts requiring special security measures (Article 14), and contracts awarded pursuant to international rules (Article 15).[192]

(c) Composition of the jury

5.171   The jury in a design contest should be composed exclusively of natural persons who are independent of participants in the contest.[193] Where a particular professional qualification is required from participants in a contest, at least a third of the members of the jury must have that qualification or an equivalent qualification.

(d) Decisions of the jury

5.172   The jury must be autonomous in its decisions or opinions. In its decision-making process, it examines the plans and projects submitted by the candidates anonymously and solely on the basis of the criteria indicated in the contest notice.[194] It records its ranking of projects in a report, signed by its members, made according to the merits of each project, together with its remarks and any points which may need clarification. Anonymity must be observed until the jury has reached its opinion or decision. Candidates may be invited, if need be, to answer questions which the jury has recorded in the minutes to clarify any aspects of the projects. The organizer of a design contest must keep complete minutes of the dialogue between jury members and candidates.

---

[190] *See* Art. 69(2) of the Public Sector Directive.
[191] Art. 66(2) of the Public Sector Directive.   [192] Art. 68 of the Public Sector Directive.
[193] Art. 73 of the Public Sector Directive.   [194] *See* Art. 74 of the Public Sector Directive.

(e) Communication between participants and the jury

Communications, exchanges and the storage of information relevant to a **5.173** design contest must ensure that the integrity and the confidentiality of all information communicated by the participants in a contest are preserved and that the jury ascertains the contents of plans and projects only after the expiry of the time limit for their submission.[195] For the electronic receipt of plans and projects, the Directive stipulates that the information relating to the specifications which is necessary for the presentation of plans and projects by electronic means, including encryption, must be available to the parties concerned. Member states may introduce or maintain voluntary arrangements for accreditation intended to improve the level of the certification service provided for such devices.[196]

(8) Framework agreements

A framework agreement is an agreement between one or more contracting **5.174** authorities and one or more economic operators, the purpose of which is to establish the terms and conditions governing contracts to be awarded during a given period, in particular with regard to price and, where appropriate, the quantity envisaged.[197]

(a) Conduct of framework agreements

Contracting authorities may not use framework agreements improperly or in **5.175** such a way as to prevent, restrict or distort competition.[198] The duration of a framework agreement may not exceed four years.[199] That period may be extended in exceptional circumstances which should be duly justified particularly by reference to the subject of the framework agreement.

The conclusion of a framework agreement should follow all the phases specified **5.176** in the Directive in relation to advertisement and publication, selection and qualification of economic operators, and award procedures.[200] Contracting authorities must select the parties to the framework agreement by applying the award criteria laid down in Article 53 of the Directive.

After the award of a framework agreement, individual contracts between the **5.177** contracting authority and the participant(s) to such a framework agreement must be awarded in accordance with specific procedures covering single-operator framework agreements and multi-operator framework agreements, respectively.[201]

---

[195] Art. 71(2) of the Public Sector Directive.   [196] Art. 71(3) of the Public Sector Directive.
[197] *See* the definition provided in Art. 1(5) of the Public Sector Directive.
[198] Art. 32(2) fifth indent of the Public Sector Directive.
[199] Art. 2(2) fourth indent of the Public Sector Directive.
[200] *See* Art. 32(2) of the Public Sector Directive.   [201] Art. 32(4) of the Public Sector Directive.

Those procedures may only be applied between the contracting authorities and the economic operators originally party to the framework agreement.

5.178 When awarding contracts based on a framework agreement, especially a single-operator framework agreement, the parties must ensure that no substantial amendments to the terms and conditions laid down in that framework agreement should be allowed.[202]

(b) Award of contracts-based framework agreements

5.179 Where a framework agreement is concluded with a single economic operator, contracts based on that agreement must be awarded within the limits of the terms laid down in the framework agreement.[203] For the award of those contracts, contracting authorities may consult the operator party to the framework agreement in writing, requesting it to supplement its tender as necessary.

5.180 Where a framework agreement is concluded with several economic operators, contracting authorities must ensure that the minimum number of operators to be included in the framework agreement is three, provided that a sufficient number of economic operators can satisfy the selection criteria and submit admissible tenders which meet the award criteria.[204]

5.181 Contracts based on framework agreements concluded with several economic operators may be awarded without re-opening any tendering/competition stage by application of the terms laid down in the framework agreement.[205]

5.182 Alternatively, in cases where the framework agreement does lay down all the terms and conditions of individual contracts, contracting authorities may stipulate that the parties to the framework agreement should compete on the basis of the same and, if necessary, more precisely formulated terms, and, where appropriate, other terms referred to in the specifications of the framework agreement. The reopening of competition should follow a specific procedure:

(a) for every contract to be awarded, contracting authorities must consult in writing the economic operators capable of performing the contract;

(b) contracting authorities must determine a time limit which is sufficiently long to allow tenders for each specific contract to be submitted, taking into account factors such as the complexity of the subject-matter of the contract, and the time needed to send in tenders;

(c) tenders must be submitted in writing, and their content must remain confidential until the stipulated time limit for reply has expired;

---

[202] Art. 32(3) of the Public Sector Directive.
[203] *See* the provisions laid down in Art. 32(3) of the Public Sector Directive.
[204] Art. 32(4) of the Public Sector Directive.
[205] Art. 32(4) second indent of the Public Sector Directive.

(d) contracting authorities must award each contract to the tenderer who has submitted the best tender on the basis of the award criteria set out in the specifications of the framework agreement.

(9) Dynamic purchasing systems

A dynamic purchasing system is a completely electronic process for making **5.183** commonly used purchases of products. The characteristics of such products should be such as to meet the requirements of contracting authorities by reference to their products' general availability in the market and their standardized specifications.[206] A dynamic purchasing system must have limited duration and be open throughout its validity to any economic operator which satisfies the selection criteria and has submitted an indicative tender that complies with the specification.[207] The costs of setting and running a dynamic purchasing system are borne by the contracting authority. No charges for the set-up costs or participating costs for the duration of the dynamic purchasing system may be billed to the interested economic operators or to parties to the system.[208]

(a) Setting up a dynamic purchasing system

In order to set up a dynamic purchasing system, contracting authorities must **5.184** follow the rules of the open procedure in all its phases up to the award of the contracts.[209]

Contracting authorities must:

(a) publish a contract notice with their clear intention to set up a dynamic purchasing system;
(b) indicate in the specifications, amongst other matters, the nature of the purchases envisaged under that system, as well as all the necessary information concerning the purchasing system, the electronic equipment used, and the technical connection arrangements and specifications;
(c) offer by electronic means, on publication of the notice and up to the expiry of the system, unrestricted, direct and full access to the specifications and to any additional documents, and they must indicate in the notice the internet address at which such documents may be consulted.

With a view to setting up the system and to awarding of contracts under that **5.185** system, contracting authorities must use solely electronic means.[210] The means of communication chosen must be generally available and under no circumstances

---

[206] *See* Art. 1(6) of the Public Sector Directive. [207] Art. 3(4) of the Public Sector Directive.
[208] Art. 33(7) second indent of the Public Sector Directive.
[209] Article 33(3) of the Public Sector Directive. [210] *See* Art. 42(2) to (5) of the Directive.

may restrict the economic operators' access to the tendering procedure. The tools to be used for communicating by electronic means, as well as their technical characteristics, must be non-discriminatory, generally available, and interoperable with the information and communication technology products in general use.[211]

5.186 Devices used for the electronic receipt of requests to participate, and devices used for the electronic transmission and receipt of tenders, must ensure the availability of information regarding the specifications necessary for the electronic submission of tenders and requests to participate, including any encryption requirements.[212] Member states may introduce or maintain voluntary accreditation schemes aiming at enhanced levels of certification service provision for these devices.

5.187 Such electronic devices must also conform to the requirements of Annex X of the Directive[213] and, in particular, they must guarantee, through technical means and appropriate procedures, that:

(a) electronic signatures relating to tenders, requests to participate and the forwarding of plans and projects comply with national provisions adopted pursuant to Directive 1999/93; contracting authorities may require that electronic tenders be accompanied by an advanced electronic signature;

(b) the exact time and date of the receipt of tenders, requests to participate and the submission of plans and projects can be determined precisely;

(c) that no person can have access to data transmitted before the time limits laid down;

(d) if data access prohibition is infringed, the infringement must be clearly detectable;

(e) only authorized persons may set or change the dates for opening data received;

(f) during the different stages of the contract award procedure or of the contest, access to all data submitted must be possible only through simultaneous action by authorized persons;

(g) simultaneous action by authorized persons must give access to data transmitted only after the prescribed date;

(h) data received and opened in accordance with these requirements must remain accessible only to authorized persons.

5.188 Under a dynamic purchasing system, communication and the exchange and storage of information must be carried out in such a way as to ensure that the integrity of data and the confidentiality of tenders and requests to participate are preserved, and that the contracting authorities examine the content of tenders

---

[211] *See* the provisions of Art. 42(4) of the Public Sector Directive.
[212] Art. 42(5) of the Public Sector Directive.
[213] *See* Annex X of the Directive on Requirements relating to devices for the electronic receipt of tenders, request for participation and plans and projects in contests.

and requests to participate only after the time limit set for submitting them has expired.[214] Tenderers or candidates to a dynamic purchasing system must submit in hard copy the documents, certificates, and declarations referred to in Articles 45 to 50 and Article 52, if they do not exist in electronic format, before expiry of the time limit laid down for submission of tenders or requests to participate.

(b) The conduct of dynamic purchasing systems

A dynamic purchasing system may not last for more than four years, except in duly justified exceptional cases. Contracting authorities may not resort to this system to prevent, restrict, or distort competition.[215] **5.189**

Admission into a dynamic purchasing system is subject to two requirements: a) meeting and satisfying the selection and qualification criteria, and b) submitting an indicative tender which complies with the specification or any possible additional documents.[216] Admittance to a dynamic purchasing system or the rejection of an economic operator's indicative tender must be communicated to the relevant economic operator at the earliest possible opportunity. Throughout the entire period of a dynamic purchasing system, contracting authorities must give any economic operator having met and satisfied the selection and qualification requirements, the possibility of submitting an indicative tender and of being admitted to the system. **5.190**

(c) The indicative tenders

In order to issue an invitation to tender to those economic operators admitted into a dynamic purchasing system, contracting authorities must publish a simplified contract notice inviting all interested economic operators to submit an indicative tender within fifteen days from the date on which the simplified notice was sent. Contracting authorities may not proceed with tendering until they have completed evaluation of all the indicative tenders received by that deadline.[217] **5.191**

Indicative tenders may be improved at any time provided that they continue to comply with the specification. Contracting authorities must complete the evaluation of indicative tenders within a maximum of fifteen days from the date of their submission.[218] However, they may extend the evaluation period provided that no invitation to tender is issued in the meantime. **5.192**

(d) The award of contracts under dynamic purchasing systems

Each specific contract awarded under a dynamic purchasing system must be the subject of an invitation to tender. Contracting authorities, after evaluating the **5.193**

---

[214] Art. 42(3) of the Public Sector Directive.   [215] Art. 33(7) of the Public Sector Directive.
[216] Art. 33(2) of the Public Sector Directive.   [217] Art. 33(5) of the Public Sector Directive.
[218] *See* Art. 33(4) first indent of the Public Sector Directive.

indicative tenders and admitting economic operators into the dynamic purchasing system, must invite tenders from those admitted to the system for each specific contract to be awarded under the system.[219]

5.194 A time limit for the submission of tenders must be set by contracting authorities. The evaluation of tenders should be based on the award criteria set out in the contract notice for the establishment of the dynamic purchasing system.[220] The award of contracts under a dynamic purchasing system must reflect the best tender on the basis of those criteria which may, if appropriate, be formulated more precisely in the invitation to tender extended to the economic operators admitted into the dynamic purchasing system.

(10) Electronic auctions

5.195 An electronic auction is a repetitive process involving an electronic device for the presentation of new prices, revised downwards, and/or new values concerning certain elements of tenders, which occurs after an initial full evaluation of the tenders, enabling them to be ranked using automatic evaluation methods. Consequently, certain service contracts and certain works contracts having as their subject matter intellectual performances, such as the design of works, may not be the object of electronic auctions.[221]

5.196 Contracting authorities may hold electronic auctions on the reopening of competition among the parties to a framework agreement, as well as on the opening for competition of contracts to be awarded under the dynamic purchasing system.[222] Contracting authorities which decide to hold an electronic auction must indicate their intention in the contract notice.

5.197 In open, restricted or negotiated procedures, contracting authorities may decide that the award of a public contract must be preceded by an electronic auction when the contract specifications can be established with precision.[223] The specifications must include, *inter alia*, the following details:[224]

(a) the features, the values for which will be the subject of electronic auction, provided that such features are quantifiable and can be expressed in figures or percentages;

(b) any limits on the values which may be submitted, as they result from the specifications relating to the subject of the contract;

---

[219] *See* Art. 33(5) of the Public Sector Directive.
[220] Art. 33(6) of the Public Sector Directive.
[221] Art. 1(7) of the Public Sector Directive.
[222] Art. 54(2) of the Public Sector Directive.
[223] Art. 54(2) first indent of the Public Sector Directive.
[224] Art. 54(3) of the Public Sector Directive.

(c) the information which will be made available to tenderers in the course of the electronic auction and, where appropriate, when it will be made available to them;

(d) the relevant information concerning the electronic auction process;

(e) the conditions under which the tenderers will be able to bid and, in particular, the minimum differences which will, where appropriate, be required when bidding;

(f) the relevant information concerning the electronic equipment used and the arrangements and technical specifications for connection.

(a) Organization of electronic auctions

Before proceeding with an electronic auction, contracting authorities must make **5.198** a full initial evaluation of the tenders in accordance with the award criteria set, and with the weighting attached to them for evaluation purposes.[225] All tenderers who have submitted admissible tenders must be invited simultaneously by electronic means to submit new prices and/or new values; the invitation must contain all relevant information concerning individual connection to the electronic equipment being used and must state the date and time of the start of the electronic auction. The electronic auction may take place in a number of successive phases. The electronic auction may not start sooner than two working days after the date on which invitations are sent out.

The invitation must also state the mathematical formula to be used in the electronic **5.199** auction to determine automatic re-rankings on the basis of the new prices or new values submitted by the participants.[226] That formula must incorporate the weighting of all the criteria fixed to determine the most economically advantageous tender, as indicated in the contract notice or in the specifications; for that purpose, any ranges must, however, be reduced beforehand to a specified value. Where variants are authorized, a separate formula must be provided for each variant.

Throughout each phase of an electronic auction, the contracting authorities must **5.200** instantaneously communicate to all tenderers at least sufficient information to enable them to ascertain their relative rankings at any moment. They may also communicate other information concerning other prices or values submitted, provided that that is stated in the specifications.

They may also at any time announce the number of participants in that phase of **5.201** the auction. However, they must not disclose the identities of the tenderers during any phase of an electronic auction.

---

[225] Art. 54(4) of the Public Sector Directive.
[226] *See* Art. 54(6) of the Public Sector Directive.

(b) Closure of electronic auctions

5.202 The closure of electronic auctions is the next phase that contracting authorities have to follow prior to the award of the contract. The closure of the auction is a necessary procedural requirement integral to the award of contracts in such award procedures and should be observed rigorously.[227]

5.203 There are three possible ways under which electronic auctions should be drawn to a close. Firstly, the indication of such closure could be stipulated in the invitation to take part in the auction, where contracting authorities clearly define the date and time of the closure in advance. Secondly, the action can be closed when participant to the auction do not furnish any more new prices or new values which meet the requirements concerning minimum differences stipulated by the contracting authority in the invitation to participate in the auction. In such an event, the contracting authorities must affirm in the invitation to take part in the auction the time which they will allow to elapse after receiving the last submission before they close the electronic auction. Thirdly, an electronic auction may be drawn to a close when the number of phases in the auction, which must be prescribed by contracting authorities in the invitation to take part in the auction, has been completed. The closure of an auction as a result of the elapse of its predetermined phases must be based on a clear indication of the timetable for each phase of the auction, which must also be stated in the invitation to take part in the auction.

5.204 After closing an electronic auction, contracting authorities must award the contract on the basis of the results of the electronic auction. Contracting authorities may not have improper recourse to electronic auctions nor may they use them in such a way as to prevent, restrict or distort competition, or to change the subject-matter of the contract, as put up for tender in the published contract notice and defined in the specification.[228]

(c) Award criteria in electronic auctions

5.205 Contracting authorities after the closure of an electronic auction must award the contract based on the following criteria:[229]

    i. either solely on prices when the contract is awarded to the lowest price;

    ii. or on prices or on the new values of the features of the tenders indicated in the specification when the contract is awarded to the most economically advantageous tender.

5.206 Contracting authorities must stipulate in the invitation to participate in the electronic auctions the criteria they will apply to the award of the contract. When

---

[227] *See* Art. 54(7) of the Public Sector Directive.
[228] Art. 54(8) of the Public Sector Directive.
[229] *See* the details specified in Art. 54(8) of the Public Sector Directive.

the contract is to be awarded on the basis of the most economically advantageous tender, the invitation to participate in an electronic auction must include the relative weighting of the criteria or factors that the contracting authority considers relevant for the evaluation process.[230]

(11) Public housing schemes

Contracting authorities may utilize a special award procedure for the award of **5.207** public contracts relating to the design and construction of subsidized housing schemes. A public housing scheme is a project which, due to its size and complexity and the estimated duration of the work involved, requires that planning be based from the outset on close collaboration within a team comprising representatives of the contracting authority, experts, and the contractor to be responsible for carrying out the works. The purpose of such special award procedure is to select the contractor most suitable for integration into the team.[231]

(a) Conduct of public housing schemes award

Contracting authorities must publish a contract notice in accordance with the **5.208** standard advertisement and publicity requirements stipulated in the Directive. In the contract notice, they must include a description of the works to be carried out as accurately as possible, in order to enable interested contractors to form a valid and realistic idea of the project.

They also need to include their envisaged requirements in relation to the personal situ- **5.209** ation of the candidates, their technical and professional capacity and their economic and financial standing in order to perform the public housing scheme contract.

(b) Award of public housing schemes

Where such a procedure is adopted for the award of public housing schemes, **5.210** contracting authorities must comply with the principles of transparency, equality and non-discrimination stipulated in Article 2 of the Directive. In addition, they must observe the rules on advertising and transparency, in particular the publication of notices (Article 35), the form and manner of publication of notices (Article 36), the time limits for receipt of requests to participate (Article 38), specifications, additional documents, and information in relation to open procedures (Article 39), rules applicable to information and communication with candidates and tenderers (Articles 41 and 42), and rules on the content of reports (Article 43).

Finally, before the selection of the successful operator which will be integrated into the **5.211** team responsible for delivering the public housing scheme, contracting authorities

---

[230] Art. 54(5) of the Public Sector Directive.
[231] *See* the provisions of Art. 34 of the Public Sector Directive.

must observe the provisions of the Directive relevant to the personal situation of the candidates or tenderers (Article 45), their suitability to pursue a professional activity (Article 46), their economic and financial standing (Article 47), their technical and professional ability (Article 48), their quality assurance standards (Article 49), and their environmental management standards (Article 50). Contracting authorities must also consider candidates who belong to official lists of approved economic operators established by member states or provide certification by bodies established under public or private law in accordance with Article 52 of the Directive.

(12) Public works concessions

(a) Scope and remit

5.212   Public works concession is a contract of the same type as a public works contract except for the fact that the consideration for the works to be carried out consists either solely in the right to exploit the work or in this right together with payment.[232] The Directive applies to all public works concession contracts concluded by contracting authorities where the value of the contracts is equal to or greater than €6,242,000. For the purposes of calculating the contract value, the rules applicable to public works contracts defined in Article 9 of the Directive apply.[233] The Directive does not apply to works concession contracts in the in the water, energy, transport, and postal services sectors (Article 12), contracts with the principal purpose of permitting the contracting authorities to provide or exploit public telecommunications networks or to provide to the public one or more telecommunications services (Article 13), secret contracts and contracts requiring special security measures (Article 14), and contracts awarded pursuant to international rules (Article 15).[234]

(b) The nature of the concessionaire

5.213   A concessionaire could be an undertaking which is a contracting authority in accordance with the provision of the Directive.[235] Where the concessionaire is a contracting authority, it must comply with the provisions laid down by this Directive for public works contracts in the case of works to be carried out by third parties. However, it is possible that the concessionaire could be an entity which is not a contracting authority. In such cases, the applicability of the Directive is extended to cover the procurement of the necessary works.[236]

5.214   Groups of undertakings which have been formed to obtain the concession or undertakings related to them must not be considered third parties.[237] The term

---

[232] Art. 1(3) of the Public Sector Directive.   [233] *See* Art. 56 of the Public Sector Directive.
[234] For the exclusions, *see* Art. 57(a)(b) of the Public Sector Directive.
[235] Art. 62 of the Public Sector Directive.   [236] Art. 63(1) of the Public Sector Directive.
[237] *See* the provisions of Art. 63(2) of the Public Sector Directive.

'related undertaking' means any undertaking over which the concessionaire can exert a dominant influence, whether directly or indirectly, or any undertaking which can exert a dominant influence on the concessionaire, or which, as the concessionaire, is subject to the dominant influence of another undertaking as a result of ownership, financial participation or the rules which govern it. A dominant influence on the part of an undertaking is presumed when, directly or indirectly in relation to another undertaking, it: (a) holds a majority of the undertaking's subscribed capital; (b) controls a majority of the votes attached to the shares issued by the undertaking; or (c) can appoint more than half of the undertaking's administrative, management or supervisory body.

The exhaustive list of such undertakings must be included in the application for **5.215** the concession. That list must be brought up to date following any subsequent changes in the relationship between the undertakings.[238]

(c) Advertisement and publicity of public works concessions

When contracting authorities wish to award a public works concession contract, **5.216** they must utilize the advertisement and publicity provisions stipulated in the Directive and must make known their intention by means of a notice.[239] Notices of public works concessions must contain the information referred to in Annex VII C and, where appropriate, any other information deemed useful by the contracting authority, in accordance with the standard forms adopted by the Commission pursuant to the procedure in Article 77(2) of the Directive.

Contract notices for the award of public works concessions must follow the **5.217** standards procedure stipulated within Article 36(2) to (8). In cases that the envisaged works concession contract is not covered by the Directive, contracting authorities may still publish the notice in accordance with Article 37 on the non-mandatory publication of notices.[240]

(d) Award procedures for public works concessions

The Public Sector Directive does not provide for a specific award procedure **5.218** envisaged for public works concession. Contracting authorities are free to select the standard procedures specified for the award of public contracts. However, contracting authorities must allow a time limit not less than fifty-two days from the date of dispatch of the notice for the presentation of applications for the concession.[241] In cases where dispatch of the notice was transmitted by electronic means, the time limit may be shortened by seven days according to Article 38(5).

---

[238] Art. 63(2) second indent of the Public Sector Directive.
[239] Art. 64 of the Public Sector Directive.   [240] Art. 64(3) of the Public Sector Directive.
[241] *See* Art. 59 of the Public Sector Directive.

5.219 Member states must ensure that public works concessionaires which are not contracting authorities apply the advertising rules defined in Article 64 when awarding works contracts to third parties where the value of such contracts is equal to or greater than €6,242,000. Works concessionaires which are not contracting authorities and which wish to award works contracts to third parties must use notices in accordance with the standard publication procedures stipulated in the Directive. Notices must contain the information referred to in Annex VII C and, where appropriate, any other information deemed useful by the works concessionaire, in accordance with the standard form adopted by the Commission in accordance with the procedure in Article 77(2). When recourse to negotiated procedures without notification is justified according to Article 31, the advertising of contract notices is not required. The values of contracts awarded by concessionaires which are not contracting authorities must be calculated in accordance with the rules applicable to public works contracts laid down in Article 9 of the Directive.

5.220 In works contracts awarded by a works concessionaire which is not a contracting authority, the time limit for the receipt of requests to participate, fixed by the concessionaire, must be not less than thirty-seven days from the date on which the contract notice was dispatched and the time limit for the receipt of tenders not less than forty days from the date on which the contract notice or the invitation to tender was dispatched.

(e) Subcontracting in concession contracts

5.221 The contracting authority may require the concessionaire to award contracts representing a minimum of thirty per cent of the total value of the work for which the concession contract is to be awarded, to third parties, at the same time providing the option for candidates to increase this percentage, this minimum percentage being specified in the concession contract. Also, the contracting authority may request the candidates for concession contracts to specify in their tenders the percentage, if any, of the total value of the work for which the concession contract is to be awarded which they intend to assign to third parties.[242]

(f) Additional works awarded to the concessionaire

5.222 Additional works which have not been included in the concession contract when initially considered but subsequently have, through unforeseen circumstances, become necessary for the performance of the work concession are allowed to be awarded by the contracting authority to the concessionaire[243] subject to the following conditions: a) the additional works cannot be technically or economically

---

[242] Art. 60 of the Public Sector Directive.   [243] *See* Art. 61 of the Public Sector Directive.

separated from the initial contract without major inconvenience to the contracting authorities, or b) when such works, although separable from the performance of the initial contract, are strictly necessary for its completion. The aggregate value of contracts awarded for additional works may not exceed fifty per cent of the amount of the original works concession contract.

E. Award Criteria

There are two criteria on which the contracting authorities must base the award **5.223** of public contracts:[244] (a) the most economically advantageous tender, or (b) the lowest price.

(1) The most economically advantageous tender

When the award is made to the tender most economically advantageous from the **5.224** point of view of the contracting authority, various criteria linked to the subject-matter of the public contract in question, for example, quality, price, technical merit, aesthetic and functional characteristics, environmental characteristics, running costs, cost-effectiveness, after-sales service and technical assistance, delivery date, and delivery period or period of completion, can be taken into consideration. The above listed criteria which constitute the parameters of the most economically advantageous offer are not exhaustive.[245]

For the purposes of defining what does constitute a most economically advant- **5.225** ageous offer, the contracting authority must specify in the contract notice or in the contract documents or, in the case of a competitive dialogue, in the descriptive document, the relative weighting which it gives to each of the criteria chosen to determine the most economically advantageous tender. Those weightings can be expressed by providing for a range with an appropriate maximum spread. Where, in the opinion of the contracting authority, weighting is not possible for demonstrable reasons, the contracting authority must indicate in the contract notice or contract documents or, in the case of a competitive dialogue, in the descriptive document, the criteria in descending order of importance.[246]

(2) The lowest price

When the lowest price has been selected as the award criterion, contracting **5.226** authorities must not refer to any other qualitative consideration when deliberating

---

[244] Art. 53 of the Public Sector Directive. [245] Art. 53(1)(a) of the Public Sector Directive.
[246] Art. 53(2) of the Public Sector Directive.

the award of a contract. The lowest price is a sole quantitative benchmark that is intended to differentiate the offers made by tenderers.[247] However, contracting authorities can reject a tender, if they regard the price attached to it as abnormally low.

(3) Abnormally low tenders

5.227   In cases where tenders appear to be abnormally low in relation to the goods, works, or services, the contracting authority must request in writing details of the constituent elements of the tender which it considers relevant before it rejects those tenders.[248]

5.228   The clarification details[249] may relate in particular to: (a) the economics of the construction method, the manufacturing process or the services provided; (b) the technical solutions chosen and/or any exceptionally favourable conditions available to the tenderer for the execution of the work, for the supply of the goods or services; (c) the originality of the work, supplies or services proposed by the tenderer; (d) compliance with the provisions relating to employment protection and working conditions in force at the place where the work, service, or supply is to be performed; and (e) the possibility of the tenderer obtaining state aid.

5.229   Where a contracting authority establishes that a tender is abnormally low because the tenderer has obtained state aid, the tender can be rejected on that ground alone only after consultation with the tenderer where the latter is unable to prove, within a sufficient time limit fixed by the contracting authority, that the aid in question was granted legally.[250] Where the contracting authority rejects a tender in these circumstances, it must inform the Commission of their decision.

(4) Informing candidates and tenderers

5.230   Upon receiving a request in writing from any candidate or tenderer concerned, contracting authorities must inform, as soon as possible, all candidates and tenderers concerned of their decisions reached in relation to the award of a public contract, the conclusion of a framework agreement, or the admittance of participants into a dynamic purchasing system.[251]

5.231   Contracting authorities must also inform the candidates and tenderers concerned of the grounds for any decision not to conclude a framework agreement, or not to award a contract for which there has been a call for competition, or not to implement a dynamic purchasing system.

---

[247] *See* Art. 53(1)(b) of the Public Sector Directive.
[248] Art. 55 of the Public Sector Directive.   [249] Art. 55(1) of the Public Sector Directive.
[250] Art. 55(3) of the Public Sector Directive.   [251] *See* Art. 41(1) of the Public Sector Directive.

On request from the party concerned and within fifteen days from receipt of a **5.232** written request, contracting authorities must inform[252] any unsuccessful candidate of the reasons for the rejection of his application, as well as of the reasons for the rejection of his tender, including reasons for not accepting specifications referred to in Article 23(4) and (5), the reasons for its decision that specifications offered by the tenderer do not meet the 'equivalence requirement' specified in Article 23(8), or its decision that the works, supplies, or services do not meet the performance or functional requirements. Contracting authorities must also inform any tenderer who has made an admissible tender of the characteristics and relative advantages of the tender selected, as well as the name of the successful tenderer or the parties to the framework agreement.

However, contracting authorities may decide to withhold certain information **5.233** regarding the contract award, the conclusion of framework agreements, or admittance to a dynamic purchasing system where the release of such information would impede law enforcement, would otherwise be contrary to the public interest, would prejudice the legitimate commercial interests of economic operators, whether public or private, or might prejudice fair competition between them.[253]

F. Monitoring Requirements

(1) Reports of contract awards

For every contract, framework agreement, and every establishment of a dynamic **5.234** purchasing system, the contracting authorities must draw up a written report which must include at least the following:[254]

(a) the name and address of the contracting authority, the subject-matter and value of the contract, framework agreement or dynamic purchasing system;
(b) the names of the successful candidates or tenderers and the reasons for their selection;
(c) the names of the candidates or tenderers rejected and the reasons for their rejection;
(d) the reasons for the rejection of tenders found to be abnormally low;
(e) the name of the successful tenderer and the reasons why his tender was selected, and, if known, the share of the contract or framework agreement which the successful tenderer intends to subcontract to third parties;
(f) for negotiated procedures, the circumstances referred to in Articles 30 and 31 which justify the use of these procedures;

---

[252] Art. 41(2) of the Public Sector Directive.   [253] Art. 41(3) of the Public Sector Directive.
[254] Art. 43 of the Public Sector Directive.

(g) as far as the competitive dialogue is concerned, the circumstances as laid down in Article 29 justifying the use of this procedure;

(h) if necessary, the reasons why the contracting authority has decided not to award a contract or framework agreement or to establish a dynamic purchasing system.

The contracting authorities must take appropriate steps to document the progress of award procedures conducted by electronic means. The report, or the main features of it, must be communicated to the Commission if it so requests.

(2) *Statistical obligations*

5.235 In order to permit assessment of the results of applying this Directive, member states must forward to the Commission[255] a statistical report addressing public supply, services and works contracts awarded by contracting authorities during the preceding year, by no later than 31 October of each year. The content of statistical report must include:[256]

(a) the number and value of awarded contracts covered by this Directive; the contract award procedures used; and for each of these procedures, works as given in Annex I and products and services as given in Annex II identified by category of the CPV nomenclature; and the nationality of the economic operator to which the contract was awarded;

(b) the number and total value of contracts awarded pursuant to derogations to the WTO GPA Agreement. As far as possible, the data referred to in point (a) above should be included in the statistical report.

5.236 Where the contracts have been concluded according to the negotiated procedure, the information provided must include the circumstances present for justifying use of the negotiated procedure and specify the number and value of contracts awarded by the member states and the country of origin of the successful contractor.[257]

---

[255] Art. 75 of the Public Sector Directive.
[256] Art. 76(1)(a) of the Public Sector Directive.
[257] *See* Art. 76(1)(b) of the Public Sector Directive.

6

THE APPLICABILITY OF THE UTILITIES RULES

A. Coverage and Scope of the Utilities Directive

The Utilities Directive[1] applies to the award for contracts between contractors, **6.01** suppliers, or service providers, and contracting entities. The terms 'contractor', 'supplier' or 'service provider' mean either a natural or a legal person, or a contracting entity, or a group of such persons or entities which offers on the market, respectively, the execution of works, products, or services. The term 'economic operator' covers equally the concepts of contractor, supplier. and service provider and it is used for simplification purposes.[2]

(1) Utilities contracts: types and categories

Supply, works, and service contracts in the utilities sectors are contracts for **6.02** pecuniary interest concluded in writing between, on the one hand, one or more of the contracting entities referred to in the Utilities Directive, and on the other hand, one or more contractors, suppliers, or service providers.[3]

Works contracts are contracts having as their object either the execution, or both **6.03** the design and execution, of works related to one of the activities within the meaning of Annex XII of the Directive, or a work, or the realization by whatever means of a work, corresponding to the requirements specified by the contracting entity.[4] A work means the outcome of building or civil engineering works taken as a whole which is sufficient of itself to fulfil an economic or technical function.

Supply contracts are contracts having as their object the purchase, lease, rental, or **6.04** hire-purchase, with or without the option to buy, of products. A contract having as its object the supply of products which also covers, as an incidental matter, placement and installation operations must be considered to be a supply contract.[5]

Service contracts are contracts with as an object the provision of services referred **6.05** to in Annex XVII of the Directive. A contract having as its object both products and services within the meaning of Annex XVII of the Directive is considered to be a service contract, if the value of the services in question exceeds that of the products covered by the contract.[6] A contract having as its object services within the meaning of Annex XVII of the Directive, and including activities within the meaning of Annex XII of the Directive that are only incidental to the principal object of the contract, must be considered to be a service contract.

The Utilities Directive stipulates specific arrangements[7] for service contracts listed in **6.06** Annex XVII A. These contracts must be awarded as any other contract covered by the

---

[1] *See* Directive 2004/17 [2004] OJ L134/1.   [2] *See* Art. 1(7) of the Utilities Directive.
[3] *See* Art. 1(2)(a) of the Utilities Directive.   [4] *See* Art. 1(2)(b) of the Utilities Directive.
[5] *See* Art. 1(2)(c) of the Utilities Directive.   [6] *See* Art. 1(2)(d) of the Utilities Directive.
[7] *See* Art. 31 of the Utilities Directive.

Directive and, in particular, in accordance with Articles 34 to 59. However, for contracts which have as their object services listed in Annex XVII B, the Directive is applicable only[8] with respect to the setting of technical specifications (Article 34) and the requirement to file a report to the Commission after the award of the contract (Article 43). Mixed contracts[9] including services listed in Annex XVII A and services listed in Annex XVII B must be awarded as any other public contract covered by the Directive where the value of the services listed in Annex XVII A is greater than the value of the services listed in Annex XVII B. In the reverse scenario, contracts are awarded in accordance with Article 34 and Article 43 of the Utilities Directive.[10]

6.07 A works concession is a contract of the same type as a works contract, except for the fact that the consideration for the works to be carried out consists either solely in the right to exploit the work, or in that right together with payment.[11] A service concession is a contract of the same type as a service contract, except for the fact that the consideration for the provision of services consists either solely in the right to exploit the service, or in that right together with payment.[12]

6.08 A framework agreement is an agreement between one or more contracting entities and one or more economic operators, the purpose of which is to establish the terms governing contracts to be awarded during a given period, in particular with regard to price and, where appropriate, the quantities envisaged.[13]

6.09 A dynamic purchasing system is a completely electronic process for making commonly-used purchases, the characteristics of which, as generally available on the market, meet the requirements of the contracting entity, which is limited in duration and open throughout its validity to any economic operator which satisfies the selection criteria and has submitted an indicative tender that complies with the specification.[14]

6.10 An electronic auction is a repetitive process involving an electronic device for the presentation of new prices, revised downwards, and/or new values concerning certain elements of tenders, which occurs after an initial full evaluation of the tenders, enabling them to be ranked using automatic evaluation methods.[15] Consequently, certain service contracts and certain works contracts having as their subject-matter intellectual performances, such as the design of works, may not be the object of electronic auctions.

6.11 Design contests are those procedures which enable the contracting entity to acquire, mainly in the fields of town and country planning, architecture,

---

[8] *See* Art. 32 of the Utilities Directive.   [9] *See* Art. 33 of the Utilities Directive.
[10] *See* Art. 1(2)(d), second indent, of the Utilities Directive.
[11] *See* Art. 1(3)(a) of the Utilities Directive.   [12] *See* Art. 1(3)(b) of the Utilities Directive.
[13] *See* Art. 1(4) of the Utilities Directive.   [14] *See* Art. 1(5) of the Utilities Directive.
[15] *See* Art. 1(6) of the Utilities Directive.

engineering, or data processing, a plan or design selected by a jury after having been put out to competition with or without the award of prizes.[16]

The Common Procurement Vocabulary (CPV) represents the reference nomen-   **6.12**
clature applicable to public and utilities contracts while ensuring equivalence with the other existing nomenclatures.[17]

(2) *The supply side: economic operators*

The terms 'contractor', 'supplier', and 'service provider' mean any natural or legal   **6.13**
person, or public entity, or group of such persons and/or bodies, which offers on the market, respectively, the execution of works and/or a work, products, or services.[18] The term 'economic operator' covers equally the concepts of contractor, supplier, and service provider. It is used merely in the interest of simplification.[19]
An economic operator who has submitted a tender must be designated a 'tenderer'.
One which has sought an invitation to take part in a restricted or negotiated procedure or a competitive dialogue must be designated a 'candidate'.[20]

Candidates or tenderers who, under the law of the member state in which they are   **6.14**
established, are entitled to provide the relevant service, must not be rejected solely on the ground that, under the law of the member state in which the contract is awarded, they would be required to be either natural or legal persons.[21] However, in the case of service and works contracts, as well as supply contracts, covering, in addition, services or installation operations, legal persons may be required to indicate, in the tender or the request to participate, the names and relevant professional qualifications of the staff to be responsible for the performance of the contract in question.[22]

Groups of economic operators may submit tenders or put themselves forward as   **6.15**
candidates. In order to submit a tender or a request to participate, these groups may not be required by the contracting entities to assume a specific legal form; however, the group selected may be required to do so when it has been awarded the contract, to the extent to which this change is necessary for the satisfactory performance of the contract.[23]

---

[16] *See* Art. 1(10) of the Utilities Directive.
[17] *See* Regulation 2195/2002 on the Common Procurement Vocabulary (CVP) [1992] OJ L340,16 December 2002. In the event of varying interpretations of the scope of the Utilities Directive, owing to possible differences between the CPV and NACE nomenclatures listed in Annex XII, or between the CPV and CPC (provisional version) nomenclatures listed in Annex XVII, the NACE or the CPC nomenclature respectively must take precedence.
[18] *See* Art. 1(7) of the Utilities Directive.
[19] *See* Art. 1(7), second indent, of the Utilities Directive.
[20] *See* Art. 1(7), third indent, of the Utilities Directive.
[21] *See* Art. 11(1) of the Utilities Directive.
[22] *See* Art. 11(1), second indent, of the Utilities Directive.
[23] *See* Art. 11(2) of the Utilities Directive.

6.16 Economic operators based in third countries which have concluded agreements within the World Trade Organisation must enjoy conditions as favourable as those which member states offer to operators based in countries which are signatories to the Government Procurement Agreement.[24]

(a) Economic operators and third countries

6.17 A special regime[25] under the Utilities Directive applies for supplies contracts that include products originating in third countries with which the European Union has not concluded either multilateral or bilateral agreements to enable comparable and effective access for Community undertakings to the markets of those third countries.

6.18 Where two or more tenders, after their evaluation in accordance with the award criteria, appear as equivalent, contracting entities must give preference to the tender that consist of products originating[26] in third countries, provided that the proportion of the products does not exceed fifty per cent. In order to assess the equivalence of tenders, if the price difference does not exceed three per cent, those tenders are considered equivalent by contracting entities.[27]

6.19 However, contracting entities may reject tenders for supplies where the proportion of the products originating in third countries exceeds fifty per cent of the total value of the products constituting the tender. Products include software used in telecommunications network equipment. In addition, preference must not be given to a tender when its acceptance would oblige the contracting entity to acquire equipment which has technical characteristics different from those of existing equipment, resulting in incompatibility, technical difficulties in operation and maintenance, or disproportionate costs.[28]

6.20 When, by virtue of a Decision adopted by the Council, the benefit of the provisions of the Utilities Directive are extended to third countries, products originating in those countries should not count towards determining the fifty per cent proportion of products originating in third countries required for the preferential treatment of tenders for supplies contracts.[29]

6.21 The progress made in multilateral or bilateral negotiations regarding access for Community undertakings to the markets of third countries in the activities covered by the Utilities Directive, the results which such negotiations may have achieved and the implementation in practice of all the agreements which have been concluded between third countries and the European Union are subjects of

---

[24] *See* Art. 12 of the Utilities Directive.   [25] *See* Art. 58 of the Utilities Directive.
[26] For the source of products and their origin from third countries, *see* Regulation 2913/92 establishing the Community Customs Code [1992] OJ L302/1, 19 October 1992, as last amended by Regulation 2700/2000 [2001] OJ L311/17, 12 December 2000.
[27] *See* Art. 58(3) of the Utilities Directive.   [28] *See* Art. 58(2) of the Utilities Directive.
[29] *See* Art. 58(4) of the Utilities Directive.

an annual report submitted by the Commission to the Council.[30] The Council, acting by a qualified majority on a proposal from the Commission, may amend the special regime under the Utilities Directive for supplies contracts that include products originating in third countries in the light of such developments.[31]

(b) Relations with third countries

In cases where third countries do not grant Community undertakings effective **6.22** access comparable to that granted by the European Community to undertakings from that country, or the same competitive opportunities as are available to national undertakings, and instead grant undertakings from other third countries more favourable treatment than Community undertakings, the Commission must approach the third country concerned in an attempt to remedy the situation.[32]

Member states must inform the Commission of any general difficulties, in law or **6.23** in fact, encountered and reported by their undertakings in securing the award of service contracts in third countries,[33] as well as of any difficulties, in law or in fact, encountered and reported by their undertakings and which are due to the non-observance of the international labour law conventions[34] related to Convention 87 on Freedom of Association and the Protection of the Right to Organise, Convention 98 on the Right to Organise and Collective Bargaining, Convention 29 on Forced Labour, Convention 105 on the Abolition of Forced Labour, Convention 138 on Minimum Age, Convention 111 on Discrimination (Employment and Occupation), Convention 100 on Equal Remuneration, and Convention 182 on Worst Forms of Child Labour.[35]

The Commission may at any time propose, on its own initiative or at the request of **6.24** a member state,[36] that the Council decide to suspend or restrict the award of service contracts to undertakings governed by the law of the third country in question; undertakings affiliated to the undertakings governed by the law of the third country and having their registered office in the Community but having no direct and effective link with the economy of a member state; or undertakings submitting tenders which have as their subject services originating in the third country in question.[37]

The Council may adopt a Decision by qualified majority, to suspend or restrict **6.25** the award of service contracts to undertakings governed by the law of the third country in question over a period to be laid down in the decision.[38]

---

[30] Such report should first be submitted in the second half of the first year following the entry into force of this Directive (Summer 2007). *See* Art. 58(5) of the Utilities Directive.

[31] *See* Art. 58(5) of the Utilities Directive.   [32] *See* Art. 59(3) of the Utilities Directive.

[33] *See* Art. 59(1) of the Utilities Directive.   [34] *See* Art. 59(4) of the Utilities Directive.

[35] *See* Annex XXIII of the Utilities Directive.

[36] *See* Art. 59(5), second indent, of the Utilities Directive.

[37] *See* Art. 59(5)(a) and (b) of the Utilities Directive.

[38] *See* Art. 59(1) of the Utilities Directive.

6.26 The Commission must report to the Council before 31 December 2005, and periodically thereafter, on the opening up of service contracts in third countries and on progress in negotiations with these countries on this subject, particularly within the framework of the WTO.[39]

(3) The demand side: contracting entities

6.27 For the purposes of the Utilities Directive, contracting entities include the state, regional or local authorities, bodies governed by public law, associations formed by one or several such authorities or one or several of such bodies governed by public law.[40]

6.28 A body governed by public law means any body which is established for the specific purpose of meeting needs in the general interest, which do not have an industrial or commercial character. A body governed by public law must also have legal personality and must be financed, for the most part, by the State, regional, or local authorities, or other bodies governed by public law.[41] With respect to the latter requirement, a body governed by public law may also be subject to management supervision by the state, regional, or local authorities, or by other bodies governed by public law or may have an administrative, managerial, or supervisory board, more than half of whose members are appointed by those bodies.

6.29 Contracting entities also include public undertakings. A public undertaking is any undertaking over which the contracting authorities may exercise directly or indirectly a dominant influence by virtue of their ownership of it, their financial participation therein, or the rules which govern it.[42]

6.30 Contracting authorities exercise dominant influence upon public undertakings when, directly or indirectly, in relation to an undertaking, they hold the majority of the undertaking's subscribed capital, or control the majority of the votes attaching to shares issued by the undertaking, or can appoint more than half of the undertaking's administrative, management, or supervisory body.

6.31 A central purchasing body[43] is a contracting authority within the meaning of the Utilities Directive,[44] or a contracting authority within the meaning of the Public Sector Directive,[45] which acquires supplies or services intended for contracting

---

[39] *See* Art. 59(2) of the Utilities Directive.   [40] *See* Art. 2(1)(a) of the Utilities Directive.
[41] *See* Art. 2(1)(a), second indent, of the Utilities Directive.
[42] *See* Art. 2(1)(b) of the Utilities Directive.   [43] *See* Art. 1(8) of the Utilities Directive.
[44] *See* Art. 2(1)(a) of the Utilities Directive
[45] *See* Art. 1(9) of the Public Sector Directive 2004/18/EC.

entities or awards public contracts or concludes framework agreements for works, supplies, or services intended for contracting entities.

The Utilities Directive also includes as contracting entities undertakings which, **6.32** although they are not contracting authorities or public undertakings themselves, operate on the basis of special or exclusive rights granted by a competent authority of a member state.[46] These special or exclusive rights are conveyed upon the relevant undertaking by a competent authority of a member state through means of legislative, regulatory, or administrative provisions which have as their objective to limit the exercise of activities covered by the Utilities Directive to one or more entities. The conferral of special or exclusive rights substantially affects the ability of other entities to carry out such activities in the market place.

(a) Lists of contracting entities

The non-exhaustive lists of contracting entities within the meaning of this **6.33** Directive are contained in Annexes I to X of the Utilities Directive. Member states must notify the Commission periodically of any changes to their lists.[47]

(4) Principles of awarding contracts in utilities

The Utilities Directive establishes three principles which cover the award of **6.34** contracts. In particular, contracting authorities must treat economic operators equally and in a non-discriminatory manner and act in a transparent way.[48]

The principle of confidentiality is also enshrined in the Utilities Directive, where **6.35** specific provisions[49] allow for discretion on the part of contracting entities to impose requirements with a view to protecting the confidential nature of information which they make available, in the context of provision of technical specifications to interested economic operators.

The Utilities Directive also provides for the obligation[50] to observe confidentiality **6.36** in accordance with the national law to which the contracting authority is subject. Contracting authorities must not disclose information forwarded to it by economic operators which they have designated as confidential; such information includes, in particular, technical or trade secrets and the confidential aspects of tenders. This obligation is without prejudice to the provisions of the Directive relevant to the advertising of awarded contracts and to the information to candidates and tenderers set out in Articles 43 and 49 of the Utilities Directive.

---

[46] *See* Art. 2(3) of the Utilities Directive.   [47] *See* Art. 8 of the Utilities Directive.
[48] *See* Art. 10 of the Utilities Directive.   [49] *See* Art. 13 of the Utilities Directive.
[50] *See* Art. 13(2) of the Utilities Directive.

(5) The substantive applicability of the Utilities Directive

(a) Activities covered

(i) The gas and heat sector

6.37 The provision of fixed networks or the operation of fixed networks in order to provide a service to the public in connection with the production, transport, or distribution of gas or heat, as well as the supply of gas[51] or heat to such networks,[52] are activities covered by the Utilities Directive. However, the supply of gas or heat to networks which provide a service to the public by a contracting entity fall outside[53] the remit of the Utilities Directive, when the production of gas or heat by the entity concerned is the unavoidable consequence of carrying out an activity unrelated to the activities covered by the Utilities Directive,[54] and when supply to the public network is aimed only at the economic exploitation of such production and amounts to less than twenty per cent of the entity's average turnover for the preceding three years.[55]

(ii) The electricity sector

6.38 The Utilities Directive applies to activities dealing with the provision of fixed networks[56] or the operation of fixed networks intended to provide a service to the public in connection with the production, transport, or distribution of electricity or the supply of electricity to such networks.[57] The supply of electricity to networks which provide a service to the public by a contracting entity is not covered[58] by the Directive when the production of electricity by the entity concerned takes place because its consumption is necessary for carrying out an activity unrelated to the activities covered by the Utilities Directive,[59] and also when supply to the public network depends only on the entity's own consumption and has not exceeded thirty per cent of the entity's total production of energy during the past three years.[60]

(iii) The water sector

6.39 The provision of fixed networks or the operation of fixed networks intended to provide a service to the public in connection with the production, transport, or distribution of drinking water[61] or the supply of drinking water to such networks are activities covered by the Utilities Directive.[62] In addition, the Utilities Directive applies to contracts or design contests awarded or organized by entities which pursue an activity related to the provision of fixed networks, or the operation of fixed

---

51 *See* Art. 3(1)(a) of the Utilities Directive.
52 *See* Art. 3(1)(b) of the Utilities Directive.
53 *See* Art. 3(2) of the Utilities Directive.
54 *See* Art. 3(2)(a) of the Utilities Directive.
55 *See* Art. 3(2)(b) of the Utilities Directive.
56 *See* Art. 3(3)(a) of the Utilities Directive.
57 *See* Art. 3(3)(b) of the Utilities Directive.
58 *See* Art. 3(4) of the Utilities Directive.
59 *See* Art. 3(4)(a) of the Utilities Directive.
60 *See* Art. 3(4)(b) of the Utilities Directive.
61 *See* Art. 4(1)(a) of the Utilities Directive.
62 *See* Art. 4(1)(b) of the Utilities Directive.

networks, in order to provide a service to the public in connection with the production, transport, or distribution of gas or heat, and which are connected with hydraulic engineering projects, irrigation, or land drainage,[63] provided that the volume of water to be used for the supply of drinking water represents more than twenty per cent of the total volume of water made available by such projects or irrigation or drainage installations, or are connected with the disposal or treatment of sewage.[64]

However, the supply of drinking water to networks which provide a service to the **6.40** public by a contracting entity is not covered by the Utilities Directive in cases where the production of drinking water by the entity concerned takes place because its consumption is necessary for carrying out an activity unrelated to the activities covered by the Utilities Directive,[65] and where supply to the public network depends only on the entity's own consumption and has not exceeded thirty per cent of the entity's total production of drinking water during the past three years.[66]

(iv) Transport services

The Utilities Directive applies to activities relating to the provision or operation of **6.41** networks providing a service to the public in the field of transport by railway, automated systems, tramway, trolley bus, bus, or cable.[67] A transport services network is a network where the service is provided under operating conditions laid down by a competent authority of a member state, such as conditions on the routes to be served, the capacity to be made available or the frequency of the service.[68]

The Directive does not apply to entities providing bus transport services to the **6.42** public which were excluded from the scope of the previous Utilities Directive 93/38 according to Article 2(4). In particular, where other entities are free to provide bus transport services to the public, either in general or in a particular geographical area, under the same conditions as those applied to the contracting entities, the Directive assumes that the relevant activities are performed in a sufficiently competitive market and specifically excludes them from its coverage. The exclusion of such activities in the bus transport sector from the remit of the new Utilities Directive is justified by reference to the effects of the competition which already exists in the relevant markets, and the need to prevent the existence of a multitude of specific arrangements applying to that sector.

(v) Postal services

The Utilities Directive applies to activities relating to the provision of postal **6.43** services[69] consisting of the clearance, sorting, routing, and delivery of postal

---

[63] *See* Art. 4(2)(a) of the Utilities Directive.   [64] *See* Art. 4(2)(b) of the Utilities Directive.
[65] *See* Art. 4(3)(a) of the Utilities Directive.   [66] *See* Art. 4(3)(b) of the Utilities Directive.
[67] *See* Art. 5(1) of the Utilities Directive.   [68] *See* Art. 5(2) of the Utilities Directive.
[69] *See* Art. 6(2)(b) of the Utilities Directive.

items. A postal item[70] is an item addressed in the final form in which it is to be carried, irrespective of weight. In addition to items of correspondence, such items also include, for instance, books, catalogues, newspapers, periodicals, and postal packages containing merchandise with or without commercial value, irrespective of weight. Postal services may comprise any postal services[71] which are, or may be, reserved on the basis of Article 7 of Directive 97/67/EC, as well as other postal services which may not be reserved on the basis of Article 7 of Directive 97/67/EC.

6.44 In addition to the postal services relating to the clearance, sorting, routing, and delivery of postal items, the Utilities Directive covers services ancillary[72] to postal services and, in particular, mail service management services (services both preceding and subsequent to dispatch, such as mailroom management services); added-value services linked to and provided entirely by electronic means (including the secure transmission of coded documents by electronic means, address management services, and transmission of registered electronic mail); services concerning postal items such as direct mail bearing no address; financial services including, in particular, postal money orders and postal giro transfers;[73] philatelic services; and, finally, logistics services (services combining physical delivery or warehousing with other non-postal functions), on condition that such services are provided by an entity which also provides postal services and that such logistics services are not directly exposed to competition on markets to which access is not restricted.[74]

(vi) Exploration for, or extraction of, oil, gas, coal, or other solid fuels

6.45 Activities relating to the exploitation of a geographical area for the purpose of exploring for oil, gas, coal, or other solid fuels or extracting oil, gas, coal, or other solid fuels are covered by the Utilities Directive.[75]

(vii) Ports and airports

6.46 The construction of airports and maritime or inland ports, or other terminal facilities to carriers by air, sea, or inland waterway are activities covered by the Utilities Directive.[76]

---

[70] *See* Art. 6(2)(a) of the Utilities Directive.
[71] *See* Art. 6(2)(b), second indent, of the Utilities Directive.
[72] *See* Art. 6(2)(c) of the Utilities Directive.
[73] *See* the services defined in category 6 of Annex XVII A and in Article 24(c) of the Utilities Directive.
[74] To decide whether an activity is directly exposed to competition, the criteria that must be used refer to the characteristics of the goods or services concerned, the existence of alternative goods or services, the prices, and the actual or potential presence of more than one supplier of the goods or services in question, and must be in conformity with the Treaty provisions on competition. *See* the conditions set out in Article 30(1) of the Utilities Directive.
[75] *See* Art. 7(a) of the Utilities Directive.   [76] *See* Art. 7(b) of the Utilities Directive.

(viii) Contracts covering several activities

A contract which is intended to cover several activities included within the remit **6.47** of the Utilities Directive must be subject to the rules applicable to the activity for which it is principally intended.[77] However, in cases where one of the activities covered by a contract falls within the scope of the Public Sector Directive 2004/18, and if it is objectively impossible to determine for which activity the contract is principally intended, the contract must be awarded in accordance with the provisions laid down in the Public Sector Directive.[78]

On the other hand, if one of the activities for which the contract is intended is **6.48** subject to the Utilities Directive and other activities are not covered by either the Utilities Directive or the Public Sector Directive, and if it is objectively impossible to determine for which activity the contract is principally intended, the contract must be awarded in accordance with the provisions laid down in Utilities Directive.[79]

(6) Activities excluded from the Utilities Directive

(a) Contracts awarded for purposes of resale or lease to third parties

The Utilities Directive does not apply to contracts awarded for purposes of resale **6.49** or lease to third parties, provided that the contracting entity enjoys no special or exclusive right to sell or lease the subject of such contracts, and other entities are free to sell or lease it under the same conditions as the contracting entity.[80]

The contracting entities must notify the Commission at its request of all the **6.50** categories of products or activities which they regard as excluded for purposes of resale or lease to third parties. The Commission, for information purposes and subject to any commercial confidentiality aspects pointed out by contracting entities, may periodically publish in the *Official Journal* lists of the categories of products and activities which it considers to be covered by this exclusion.[81]

(b) Contracts awarded for purposes other than the pursuit of an activity covered or for the pursuit of such an activity in a third country

The Utilities Directive does not apply to contracts which contracting entities **6.51** award for purposes other than the pursuit of their activities covered by the Utilities Directive or for the pursuit of such activities in a third country,[82] in conditions not involving the physical use of a network or geographical area within the Community. The contracting entities must notify the Commission at its

---

[77] *See* Art. 9 of the Utilities Directive.   [78] *See* Art. 9(2) of the Utilities Directive.
[79] *See* Art. 9(3) of the Utilities Directive.   [80] *See* Art. 19(1) of the Utilities Directive.
[81] *See* Art. 19(2) of the Utilities Directive.   [82] *See* Art. 20(1) of the Utilities Directive.

request of all the categories of such activities which they regard as excluded for the above purposes. The Commission, for information purposes and subject to any commercial confidentiality aspects pointed out by contracting entities, may periodically publish in the *Official Journal* lists of the categories of products and activities which it considers to be covered by this exclusion.[83]

(c) Contracts which are secret or require special security measures

6.52 Contracts which are declared to be secret by a member state are not covered by the Utilities Directive. These secret contracts must be performed on the basis of special security measures which should be in place in accordance with the laws, regulations, or administrative provisions in force in the member state concerned.[84] Alternatively, secret contracts could be awarded on the basis of the protection of the security interests of a member state.

(d) Contracts awarded pursuant to international rules

6.53 The Utilities Directive does not apply to contracts governed by different procedural rules and awarded pursuant to an international agreement[85] concluded in accordance with the Treaty between a member state and one or more third countries, and covering supplies, works, services, or design contests intended for the joint implementation or exploitation of a project by the signatory states;[86] the Utilities Directive is also inapplicable to contracts concluded pursuant to a signed international agreement relating to the stationing of troops and concerning the undertakings of a member state[87] or a third country, or contracts concluded pursuant to the particular procedure of an international organization.[88]

(e) Contracts awarded to an affiliated undertaking, to a joint venture, or to a contracting entity forming part of a joint venture

6.54 The Utilities Directive does not apply to contracts awarded by a contracting entity to an affiliated undertaking.[89] An affiliated undertaking is an undertaking the annual accounts of which are consolidated with those of the contracting entity in accordance with the requirements of the Seventh Council Directive[90] on consolidated accounts, or, in the case of entities not subject to that Directive,[91] any

---

[83] *See* Art. 20(2) of the Utilities Directive.   [84] *See* Art. 21 of the Utilities Directive.
[85] *See* Art. 22(a) of the Utilities Directive.
[86] All agreements covering supplies, works, services or design contests must be communicated to the Commission, which may consult the Advisory Committee for Public Contracts referred to in Art. 68 of the Utilities Directive.   [87] *See* Art. 22(b) of the Utilities Directive.
[88] *See* Art. 22(c) of the Utilities Directive.   [89] *See* Art. 23(2)(a) of the Utilities Directive.
[90] *See* Directive 83/349 [1983] OJ L193/1, 18 July 1983. Directive as last amended by Directive 2001/65/EC of the European Parliament and of the Council [2001] OJ L283/28 27 October 2001.
[91] *See* Art. 23(1) of the Utilities Directive.

undertaking over which the contracting entity may exercise, directly or indirectly, a dominant influence,[92] or which may exercise a dominant influence over the contracting entity, or which, in common with the contracting entity, is subject to the dominant influence of another undertaking by virtue of ownership, financial participation, or the rules which govern it.

The Utilities Directive does not apply to contracts awarded by a joint venture, **6.55** formed exclusively by a number of contracting entities for the purpose of carrying out activities covered by the Utilities Directive to an undertaking which is affiliated with one of these contracting entities.[93]

Types of contracts cover service contracts provided that at least eighty per cent of the **6.56** average turnover of the affiliated undertaking with respect to services for the preceding three years derives from the provision of such services to undertakings with which it is affiliated;[94] supplies contracts provided that at least eighty per cent of the average turnover of the affiliated undertaking with respect to supplies for the preceding three years derives from the provision of such supplies to undertakings with which it is affiliated;[95] works contracts provided that at least eighty per cent of the average turnover of the affiliated undertaking with respect to works for the preceding three years derives from the provision of such works to undertakings with which it is affiliated.[96]

When the turnover of an affiliated undertaking is not available for the past three **6.57** years, as a result of the date on which an affiliated undertaking was created or commenced activities, it will be sufficient for that undertaking to demonstrate the required turnover by means of financial projections.[97] Where more than one undertaking affiliated with the contracting entity provides the same or similar services, supplies, or works, the required turnover percentages must be calculated taking into account the total turnover deriving respectively from the provision of services, supplies, or works by those affiliated undertakings.[98]

The Utilities Directive is inapplicable to contracts awarded by a joint venture,[99] **6.58** formed exclusively by a number of contracting entities for the purpose of carrying out activities covered by the Utilities Directive, to one of these contracting entities, or by a contracting entity to such a joint venture of which it forms part, provided that the joint venture has been set up in order to carry out the activity

---

[92] According to Art. 2(1)(b) of the Utilities Directive, contracting authorities exercise dominant influence upon public undertakings when, directly or indirectly, in relation to an undertaking, they hold the majority of the undertaking's subscribed capital, or control the majority of the votes attaching to shares issued by the undertaking, or can appoint more than half of the undertaking's administrative, management, or supervisory body. [93] *See* Art. 23(2)(b) of the Utilities Directive.
[94] *See* Art. 23(3)(a) of the Utilities Directive.
[95] *See* Art. 23(3)(b) of the Utilities Directive. [96] *See* Art. 23(3)(c) of the Utilities Directive.
[97] *See* Art. 23(3), second indent, of the Utilities Directive.
[98] *See* Art. 23(3) third indent of the Utilities Directive.
[99] *See* Art. 23(4) of the Utilities Directive.

concerned over a period of at least three years and that the instrument setting up the joint venture stipulates that the contracting entities, which form it, will be part thereof for at least the same period.

6.59   The Commission may request[100] from member states notification of the names of affiliated undertakings or joint ventures concerned, the nature and value of the contracts involved and such proof as may be deemed necessary by the Commission that the relationship between the undertaking or joint ventures to which contracts are awarded and the contracting entity complies with the requirements of the Utilities Directive and, in particular, Article 23.

(f) Contracts relating to certain services excluded from the scope of this Directive

6.60   The Utilities Directive does not cover service contracts for: (a) the acquisition or rental, by whatever financial means, of land, existing buildings or other immovable property, or related real estate rights. Nevertheless, financial service contracts concluded at the same time as, before, or after, the contract of acquisition or rental, in whatever form, are covered by the Utilities Directive; (b) arbitration and conciliation services; (c) financial services in connection with the issue, sale, purchase, or transfer of securities or other financial instruments, in particular, transactions by the contracting entities to raise money or capital; (d) employment contracts; or (e) research and development services other than those where the benefits accrue exclusively to the contracting entity for its use in the conduct of its own affairs, on condition that the service provided is wholly remunerated by the contracting entity.[101]

(g) Service contracts awarded on the basis of an exclusive right

6.61   The Utilities Directive does not apply to service contracts awarded to an entity which is itself a contracting authority within the meaning of Article 2(1)(a)[102] or to an association of contracting authorities on the basis of an exclusive right which they enjoy pursuant to a published law, regulation, or administrative provision which is compatible with the Treaty.[103]

(h) Contracts awarded by certain contracting entities for the purchase of water and for the supply of energy or of fuels for the production of energy

6.62   The Utilities Directive does not apply to contracts for the purchase of water,[104] if awarded by contracting entities engaged in the provision of fixed networks or the

---

[100] *See* Art. 23(5) of the Utilities Directive.   [101] *See* Art. 24 of the Utilities Directive.

[102] For the purposes of the Utilities Directive, contracting entities include the state, regional, or local authorities, bodies governed by public law, associations formed by one or several such authorities, or one or several of such bodies governed by public law.

[103] *See* Art. 25 of the Utilities Directive.   [104] *See* Art. 26(a) of the Utilities Directive.

operation of fixed networks intended to provide a service to the public in connection with the production, transport, or distribution of drinking water, or the supply of drinking water to such networks.[105]

The Utilities Directive does not apply to contracts for the supply of energy or of **6.63** fuels for the production of energy,[106] if awarded by contracting entities engaged in the provision of fixed networks or the operation of fixed networks in order to provide a service to the public in connection with the production, transport, or distribution of gas or heat, as well as the supply of gas or heat to such networks;[107] the provision of fixed networks or the operation of fixed networks intended to provide a service to the public in connection with the production, transport, or distribution of electricity or the supply of electricity to such networks;[108] or the exploitation of a geographical area for the purpose of exploring for oil, gas, coal, or other solid fuels or extracting oil, gas, coal, or other solid fuels.[109]

(i) Contracts subject to special arrangements

The Kingdom of the Netherlands, the United Kingdom, the Republic of Austria **6.64** and the Federal Republic of Germany have established special arrangements for entities exploiting geographical areas for the purpose of exploring for or extracting oil, gas, coal, or other solid fuels by virtue of Decisions 93/676, 97/367, 2002/205 and 2004/73. The Utilities Directive does not apply to entities entity operating in the sectors covered by the special arrangements.[110] However, the member states concerned must ensure, by way of the conditions of authorization or other appropriate measures, that the excluded entities observe the principles of non-discrimination and competitive procurement in respect of the award of supplies, works, and service contracts, in particular as regards the information which they make available to economic operators concerning its procurement intentions.[111] These entities must communicate[112] to the Commission all relevant information relating to the contracts they award under the parameters of the special arrangement regime.[113]

(j) Reserved contracts

Member states may reserve the right to participate in contract award procedures **6.65** to sheltered workshops, or provide for such contracts to be performed in the

---

[105] *See* Art. 4(1) of the Utilities Directive.   [106] *See* Art. 26(b) of the Utilities Directive.
[107] *See* Art. 3(1) of the Utilities Directive.   [108] *See* Art. 3(3) of the Utilities Directive.
[109] *See* Art. 7(a) of the Utilities Directive.   [110] *See* Art. 27 of the Utilities Directive.
[111] *See* Art. 27(a) of the Utilities Directive.   [112] *See* Art. 27(b) of the Utilities Directive.
[113] *See* the conditions defined in Commission Decision 93/327 [1993] OJ L129/25, 27 May 1993, defining the conditions under which contracting entities exploiting geographical areas for the purpose of exploring for or extracting oil, gas, coal, or other solid fuels must communicate to the Commission information relating to the contracts they award.

context of sheltered employment programmes, where most of the employees concerned are disabled persons who, by reason of the nature or the seriousness of their disabilities, cannot carry on occupations under normal conditions.[114] The notice used to make the call for competition must make reference to the intention of contracting entities to reserve contracts for the specific requirements stipulated in Article 28 of the Utilities Directive.

(k) Contracts and framework agreements awarded by central purchasing bodies

6.66 Contracting entities which purchase works, supplies, or services from or through a central purchasing body do not have to follow the provisions of the Utilities Directive,[115] provided that the central purchasing body has complied with the relevant procurement regime laid down in the Utilities Directive or in the Public Sector Directive, where appropriate.[116]

(l) Contracts of an activity are directly exposed to competition

6.67 Contracts intended to enable a contracting entity to pursue an activity covered by the Utilities Directive do not fall within its remit if, in the member state in which the activity is performed, it is directly exposed to competition on markets to which access is not restricted.[117]

6.68 Access to a market is deemed not to be restricted[118] if the member state has implemented and applied specific provisions of Community legislation mentioned in Annex XI of the Utilities Directive regarding the opening up of the relevant markets and, in particular, in the sector of transport or distribution of gas or heat, Directive 98/30[119] concerning common rules for the internal market in natural gas; in the sector of production, transmission, or distribution of electricity, Directive 96/92[120] concerning common rules for the internal market in electricity; in the postal sector, Directive 97/67[121] on common rules for the development of the internal market of Community postal services and the improvement of quality of service; and, finally, in the exploration of gas or oil and in the extraction for gas or oil sectors, Directive 94/22[122] on the conditions for granting and using authorizations for the prospecting, exploration, and production of hydrocarbons. If free access to a given market cannot be presumed on the basis of compliance with the above legislation, then it must be demonstrated that access to the market in question is free *de facto* and *de jure*.[123]

---

[114] *See* Art. 28 of the Utilities Directive.   [115] *See* Art. 29(1) of the Utilities Directive.
[116] *See* Art. 29(2) of the Utilities Directive.   [117] *See* Art. 30(1) of the Utilities Directive.
[118] *See* Art. 30(3) of the Utilities Directive.   [119] *See* [1998] OJ L204/1, 21 July 1998.
[120] *See* [1997] OJ L27/20, 30 January 1997.
[121] *See* [1998] OJ L15/14, 21 January 1998, last amended by Directive 2002/39/EC [2002] OJ L176/21, 5 July 2002.   [122] *See* [1994] OJ L164/3, 30 June 1994.
[123] *See* Art. 30(3), second indent, of the Utilities Directive.

(i) Procedure for establishing whether an activity is directly exposed to competition

The question of whether an activity is directly exposed to competition must be **6.69** decided on the basis of criteria that are in conformity with the Treaty provisions on competition, such as the characteristics of the goods or services concerned, the existence of alternative goods or services, the prices, and the actual or potential presence of more than one supplier of the goods or services in question.[124]

(ii) Notification by member states

When a member state considers that an activity is directly exposed to competition, **6.70** it must notify the Commission and inform it of all relevant facts and, in particular, of any law, regulation, administrative provision, or agreement concerning compliance with the legislation regarding the opening up of the relevant markets as set out in Annex XI of the Utilities Directive. In addition to the above notification requirement, member states, where appropriate, must furnish a position adopted by an independent national authority that is competent in relation to the activity concerned in their territory.[125]

When an activity in a member state is already the subject of a notification procedure, **6.71** further requests concerning the same activity in the same member state, before the expiry of the period opened when the first notification was made to the Commission, are not considered as new procedures and they will not be treated in the context of the first request.[126]

(iii) Decision by the Commission

After the notification, the Commission can adopt a Decision[127] establishing the **6.72** fact that an activity is directly exposed to competition and, therefore, the Utilities Directive does not apply within a period of three months. For the adoption of a Decision, the Commission must allow a period of three months commencing on the first working day following the date on which it receives the notification or the request. However, this period may be extended once by a maximum of three months in duly justified cases, in particular, if the information contained in the notification or the request or in the documents justifying the alleged competitive environment of an activity is incomplete, or if the facts as reported are subjected to any substantive changes. This extension must be limited to one month where an independent national authority that is competent in the activity concerned has established the applicability of Article 30(1) of the Utilities Directive and, in particular, that the activity concerned is directly exposed to competition on markets to which access is not restricted.

---

[124] *See* Art. 30(2) of the Utilities Directive.   [125] *See* Art. 30(4) of the Utilities Directive.
[126] *See* Art. 30(6), second indent, of the Utilities Directive.
[127] *See* Art. 30(6) first indent of the Utilities Directive.

6.73   However, the inapplicability of the Directive is also presumed when that period has expired without the Commission adopting a decision.[128] Where free access to a given market is presumed on the basis of compliance with the legislation regarding the opening up of the relevant markets as set out in Annex XI of the Utilities Directive,[129] and where an independent national authority that is competent in the activity concerned has established that the relevant activity is directly exposed to competition on markets to which access is not restricted, the Utilities Directive is inapplicable if the Commission does not adopt a Decision declaring the inapplicability of Article 30(1) of the Utilities Directive.

6.74   The Commission may also begin the procedure for adoption of a Decision establishing that a given activity is directly exposed to competition on its own initiative.[130] In such a case, the Commission must inform the member state concerned.

(iv) Publicity requirements

6.75   The Commission must adopt detailed rules for applying the provisions referred to in Article 30 of the Utilities Directive concerning activities which are directly exposed to competition, prior to adopting a Decision. Such requirements include the publication of notices in the *Official Journal* which, for information purposes, state the date on which the three-month period required for the adoption of a Decision begins and, in case this period is extended, any extension granted.[131] In addition, the notice must contain any arrangements for forwarding positions adopted by an independent national authority that is competent in the activity concerned, and any relevant information which should be forwarded to the Commission to determine either compliance with the required legislation of opening up the relevant market in which an activity is performed or any *de facto* or *de jure* conditions which should be taken into account by the Commission in establishing whether an activity is directly exposed to competition.

(m) Works and service concessions

6.76   The Utilities Directive does not apply to works and service concessions[132] which are awarded by contracting entities carrying out one or more of the activities covered by the Utilities Directive and, in particular, activities including gas, heat and electricity, water, transport services, postal services, exploration for oil, gas or other solid fuels, extraction of oil, gas or other solid fuels, and provision of ports and airports referred to in Articles 3 to 7, where those concessions are awarded for carrying out those activities.

---

128   *See* Art. 30(4) of the Utilities Directive.
129   *See* Art. 30(3), first subparagraph, of the Utilities Directive.
130   *See* Art. 30(5) of the Utilities Directive.   131   *See* Art. 30(6) of the Utilities Directive.
132   *See* Art. 30(6), third indent, of the Utilities Directive.

(7) The monetary applicability of the Utilities Directive

(a) Contract thresholds

6.77 The Utilities Directive applies to contracts which have a value[133] excluding value added tax (VAT) estimated at:

(a) €499,000 in the case of supply and service contracts;
(b) €6,242,000 in the case of works contracts.

(b) Contract value calculation

6.78 The Directive provides for methods for calculating the estimated value of contracts, framework agreements and dynamic purchasing systems.[134] The calculation of the estimated value of a contract must be based on the total amount payable, net of VAT, as estimated by the contracting entity. This calculation must take account of the estimated total amount, including any form of option and any renewals of the contract.[135] Where the contracting entity provides for prizes or payments to candidates or tenderers it must take them into account when calculating the estimated value of the contract.

6.79 Contracting entities are under an obligation to avoid subdividing works projects or proposing the purchase of a certain quantity of supplies or services in order to circumvent the monetary applicability of the Directive.[136]

6.80 With regard to framework agreements and dynamic purchasing systems, the value to be taken into consideration must be the maximum estimated value net of VAT of all the contracts envisaged for the total term of the framework agreement or the dynamic purchasing system.[137]

6.81 With regard to works contracts, calculation of the estimated value must take account of both the cost of the works and the total estimated value of the supplies or services necessary for executing the works.[138] The value of supplies or services which are not necessary for the performance of a particular works contract may not be added to the value of the works contract when to do so would result in removing the procurement of those supplies or services from the scope of the Utilities Directive.

6.82 Where a proposed work or purchase of services may result in contracts being awarded at the same time in the form of separate lots, contracting entities must take into account the total estimated value of all such lots.[139] Where the aggregate

---

[133] *See* Art. 16 of the Utilities Directive.   [134] Art. 17 of the Utilities Directive.
[135] Art. 17(1) of the Utilities Directive.   [136] Art. 17(3) of the Utilities Directive.
[137] Art. 17(9) of the Utilities Directive.   [138] Art. 17(4) of the Utilities Directive.
[139] Art. 17(6) of the Utilities Directive.

value of the lots is equal to, or exceeds, the threshold stipulated in the Directive, in that case each lot must be awarded separately in accordance with the Utilities Directive. However, the contracting entities may waive such application in respect of lots the estimated value of which net of VAT is less than €80,000 for services or €1 million for works, provided that the aggregate value of those lots does not exceed twenty per cent of the aggregate value of the lots as a whole.

6.83 Where a proposal for the acquisition of similar supplies may result in contracts being awarded at the same time in the form of separate lots, account must be taken of the total estimated value of all such lots.

6.84 In the case of supply or service contracts which are regular in nature or which are intended to be renewed within a given period, the calculation of the estimated contract value must be based on the following:

(a) either the total actual value of the successive contracts of the same type awarded during the preceding twelve months or financial year, adjusted, if possible, to take account of the changes in quantity or value which would occur in the course of the twelve months following the initial contract; or

(b) the total estimated value of the successive contracts awarded during the twelve months following the first delivery, or during the financial year if that is longer than twelve months.

6.85 The basis for calculating the estimated value of a contract including both supplies and services must be the total value of the supplies and services, regardless of their respective shares. The calculation must include the value of the installation operations.

6.86 With regard to supply contracts relating to the leasing, hire, rental, or hire purchase of products,[140] the value to be taken as a basis for calculating the estimated contract value must be as follows:

(a) in the case of fixed-term contracts, if that term is less than or equal to twelve months, the total estimated value for the term of the contract or, if the term of the contract is greater than twelve months, the total value including the estimated residual value;

(b) in the case of contracts without a fixed term or the term of which cannot be defined, the monthly value multiplied by forty-eight.

6.87 With regard to service contracts,[141] the value to be taken as a basis for calculating the estimated contract value for insurance services must reflect the premium payable and other forms of remuneration. For banking and other financial services it must comprise the fees, commissions, interest, and other forms of

---

[140] Art. 17(6) of the Utilities Directive.   [141] Art. 17(8)(a)(b) of the Utilities Directive.

remuneration. For design contracts it must include fees, commission payable, and other forms of remuneration. For service contracts which do not indicate a total price, in the case of fixed-term contracts, if that term is less than or equal to forty-eight months, the estimated contract value must reflect the total value for their full term; in the case of contracts without a fixed term or with a term greater than forty-eight months, the estimated value must include the monthly value multiplied by forty-eight.

(c) Revision of the thresholds

Revision of the thresholds will be undertaken by the Commission every two years **6.88** from the entry into force of the Utilities Directive.[142] The calculation of the value of these thresholds must be based on the average daily value of the euro, expressed in SDRs, over the twenty-four months terminating on the last day of August preceding the revision with effect from 1 January. The value of the thresholds thus revised must, where necessary, be rounded down to the nearest thousand euro so as to ensure that the thresholds in force provided for by the Agreement, expressed in SDRs, are observed. The value of the thresholds set in the national currencies of the member states which are not participating in monetary union is normally to be adjusted every two years from 1 January 2004 onwards. The calculation of such value must be based on the average daily values of those currencies expressed in euro over the twenty-four months terminating on the last day of August preceding the revision with effect from 1 January. The revised thresholds and their corresponding values in the national currencies must be published by the Commission in the *Official Journal of the European Union* at the beginning of the month of November following their revision.

B. Publicity and advertisement

(1) Notices

(a) Periodic indicative notices

Periodic indicative notices are notices sent by contracting entities for publication **6.89** to the *Official Journal* or notices published by contracting entities themselves on their buyer profile through the internet.[143]

Both periodic indicative notices and notices on buyer profile must include the **6.90** following information:[144]

(a) for public supplies contracts, and as soon as possible after the beginning of the budgetary year, the estimated total value of the contracts or the framework

---

[142] *See* Art. 69 of the Utilities Directive.   [143] Art. 41 of the Utilities Directive.
[144] *See* Art. 41(1) of the Utilities Directive.

agreements by product area which they intend to award over the following twelve months, where the total estimated value is equal to or greater than €750,000. The product area must be established by the contracting entities by reference to the CPV nomenclature;

(b) for public services contracts, and as soon as possible after the beginning of the budgetary year, the estimated total value of the contracts or the framework agreements in each of the categories of services listed in Annex XVII A which they intend to award over the following twelve months, where such estimated total value is equal to or greater than €750 000;

(c) for public works contracts, and as soon as possible after the decision approving the planning of the works contracts or the framework agreements that the contracting entities intend to award, the essential characteristics of the contracts or the framework agreements which they intend to award, the estimated value of which is equal to or greater than the threshold specified in Article 16 of the Utilities Directive.

6.91 The notice of the publication for a prior indicative notice on a buyer profile must contain the country and name of the contracting authority, the internet address of the 'buyer profile' and any CPV Nomenclature reference numbers.[145] The buyer profile may include[146] periodic indicative notices, information on ongoing invitations to tender, scheduled purchases, contracts concluded, procedures cancelled, and any useful general information, such as a contact point, a telephone and a fax number, a postal address, and an e-mail address. Contracting entities which publish a periodic indicative notice on their buyer profiles must send the Commission, electronically, a notice of such publication.[147] Periodic indicative notices may not be published on a buyer profile before the dispatch to the Commission of the notice of their publication in that form; they must mention the date of that dispatch.[148]

6.92 Contracting entities should not publish notices and their contents at national level before the date on which they are sent to the Commission for publication in the *Official Journal*.[149] Notices published at national level must not contain information other than information contained in the notices dispatched to the Commission or published on a buyer profile. However, they must mention the date of dispatch of the notice to the Commission or its publication on the buyer profile.[150]

6.93 The publication of prior indicative notices is compulsory only where the contracting entities take the option of shortening the time limits for the receipt of

---

[145] *See* Annex XV A of the Utilities Directive.
[146] *See* point 2(b) of Annex XX of the Utilities Directive.
[147] *See* the format and detailed procedures for sending notices indicated in point 3 of Annex XX of the Utilities Directive.   [148] *See* Art. 36(5), second indent, of the Utilities Directive.
[149] *See* Art. 42(5) of the Utilities Directive.
[150] Art. 44, second indent, of the Utilities Directive.

tenders as laid down in Article 45 of the Utilities Directive. Also, in the exceptional cases of contracting entities having recourse to procedures without the prior publication of a contract notice, the publication of periodic indicative notices or notices on buyer profile is not required.

Contracting entities may publish, or arrange for the Commission to publish, **6.94** periodic indicative notices relating to major projects without repeating information previously included in a periodic indicative notice, provided that it is clearly pointed out that these notices are additional ones.[151]

Notices sent by contracting entities to the Commission must be sent either by **6.95** electronic means, in accordance with the format and procedures for transmission indicated in Annex XX of the Utilities Directive, or by other means.[152] Notices drawn up and transmitted by electronic means, in accordance with the format and procedures for transmission indicated in point 3 of Annex XX of the Utilities Directive, will be published within five days from dispatch. Notices which are not transmitted by electronic means will be published not later than twelve days after they are transmitted.[153] However, in exceptional cases, the contract notices utilized as a call for competition according to Article 42(1)(c) of the Utilities Directive must be published within five days in response to a request by the contracting entity, provided that the notice has been sent by fax.

(b) Notices on the existence of qualification system

Where contracting entities choose to set up a qualification system in accordance **6.96** with Article 53 of the Utilities Directive, the system must be the subject of a notice as referred to in Annex XIV, indicating the purpose of the qualification system and how to have access to the rules concerning its operation.[154] According to Annex XIV of the Utilities Directive, information to be included in the notice on the existence of a qualification system must comprise:

1. The name, address, telegraphic address, electronic address, telephone number, telex, and fax number of the contracting entity.
2. An indication, where appropriate, as to whether the contract is reserved for sheltered workshops or whether its performance is reserved in the context of sheltered employment programmes.
3. A statement on the purpose of the qualification system, including the description of the goods, services or works, or categories to be procured through the system by reference to nomenclature numbers.
4. A statement on the conditions to be fulfilled by the economic operators in view of their qualification pursuant to the system and the methods according

---

[151] *See* Art. 41(2) of the Utilities Directive.   [152] *See* Art. 44(3) of the Utilities Directive.
[153] *See* Art. 44(3), second indent, of the Utilities Directive.
[154] *See* Art. 41(3) of the Utilities Directive.

to which each of those conditions will be verified. Where the description of such conditions and verification methods is voluminous and based on documents available to interested economic operators, a summary of the main conditions and methods and a reference to those documents will be sufficient.

5. An indication of the period of validity of the qualification system and the formalities for its renewal.
6. A reference to the fact that the notice acts as the call for competition.
7. An address where further information and documentation concerning the qualification system can be obtained.
8. A reference concerning the name and address of the body responsible for appeal and, where appropriate, mediation procedures. In addition, precise information should be provided concerning time limits for lodging appeals, or the name, address, telephone number, fax number, and e-mail address of the service from which this information may be obtained.
9. An indication of award criteria, where known, for award of the contract. Criteria representing the most economically advantageous tender as well as their weighting or, where appropriate, the order of importance of these criteria, must be mentioned where they do not appear in the specifications or will not be indicated in the invitation to tender or to negotiate.
10. Any other relevant information.

6.97   Where the system is of duration greater than three years, the notice must be published annually. Where the system is of a shorter duration, an initial notice will be adequate.

(c) Notices used as a call for competition

6.98   In the case of supply, works, or service contracts, the call for competition may be made by means of a periodic indicative notice or by means of a notice on the existence of a qualification system or by means of a contract notice in accordance with Annex XXX of the Utilities Directive.[155]

6.99   When a call for competition is made by means of a periodic indicative notice, the notice must refer specifically to the supplies, works, or services which will be the subject of the contract to be awarded and must indicate that the contract will be awarded by restricted or negotiated procedure without further publication of a notice of a call for competition and invite interested economic operators to express their interest in writing.[156] The periodic indicative notice must be published not more than twelve months prior to the date on which the invitation to negotiate or submit a tender is sent for publication according to Article 47(5) of

---

[155] *See* Art. 42 of the Utilities Directive.   [156] *See* Art. 42(3) of the Utilities Directive.

292

the Utilities Directive. Moreover, the contracting entity must meet the time limits laid down in Article 45 with respect to the time limits for the receipt of requests to participate in award procedures and the time limits for the receipt of tenders.

When a call for competition is made by means of a notice on the existence of a **6.100** qualification system, tenderers in a restricted procedure or participants in a negotiated procedure must be selected from the qualified candidates in accordance with such a system.[157]

In particular, when a call for competition is made by means of a contract notice, **6.101** contracting entities should provide the following information in contract notices for open and restricted procedure and negotiated procedures with prior advertisement:[158]

1. Their name, address, telephone and fax number, and email address.
2. An indication of whether the public contract is restricted to sheltered workshops, or whether its execution is restricted to the framework of protected job programmes.
3. The award procedure chosen and, where appropriate, the reasons for use of the accelerated procedure (in restricted and negotiated procedures); also, where appropriate, an indication of whether a framework agreement, or a dynamic purchasing system is involved; finally, where appropriate, an indication of whether the holding of an electronic auction will be held, in the event of open, restricted or negotiated procedures covered by Article 30(1)(a).
4. The form of the contract.
5. The place of execution or performance of the works, of delivery of products or of the provision of services.
6. (a) For public works contracts:
    i. a description of the nature and extent of the works and general nature of the work; an indication in particular of options concerning supplementary works, and, if known, the provisional timetable for recourse to these options as well as the number of possible renewals; an indication of the size of the different lots, if the work or the contract is subdivided into several lots; and a reference to nomenclature number(s);
    ii. information concerning the purpose of the work or the contract where the latter also involves the drawing-up of projects;
    iii. an indication, in the event of a framework agreement, of the planned duration of the framework agreement, the estimated total value of the works for the entire duration of the framework

---

[157] *See* Art. 42(1)(b) of the Utilities Directive.   [158] *See* Art. 42(1)(c) of the Utilities Directive.

agreement and, as far as possible, the value and the frequency of the contracts to be awarded.

(b) for public supply contracts:

    i. a description of the nature of the products to be supplied, indicating in particular whether tenders are requested with a view to purchase, lease rental, hire or hire purchase, or a combination of these; an indication of the quantity of products to be supplied, specifying in particular options concerning supplementary purchases and the provisional timetable for recourse to these options as well as the number of renewals; and a reference to nomenclature number(s);

    ii. in the case of regular or renewable contracts during the course of a given period, an indication of the timetable for subsequent contracts for purchase of intended supplies,

    iii. in the event of a framework agreement, an indication of the planned duration of the framework agreement, the estimated total value of the supplies for the entire duration of the framework agreement and, as far as possible, the value and the frequency of the contracts to be awarded.

(c) for public service contracts:

    i. a reference to the category and description of service by nomenclature number(s); an indication of the quantity of services to be provided and, in particular, any options concerning supplementary purchases and the provisional timetable for recourse to these options as well as the number of renewals; in the case of renewable contracts over a given period, an estimate of the time frame for subsequent public contracts for purchase of intended services; in the event of a framework agreement, an indication of the planned duration of the framework agreement, the estimated total value of the services for the entire duration of the framework agreement, and, as far as possible, the value and the frequency of the contracts to be awarded;

    ii. an indication of whether the execution of the service is reserved by law, regulation, or administrative provision to a particular profession, and a reference to the law, regulation or administrative provision;

    iii. an indication of whether legal persons should indicate the names and professional qualifications of the staff to be responsible for the execution of the service.

7. In case the contracts are subdivided into lots, an indication of the possibility of tendering for one, for several or for all the lots.

8. Any time limit for completion of works/supplies/services or duration of the works/supply/services contract; where possible, any time limit by which works will begin or any time limit by which delivery of supplies or services will begin.

9. An indication for admission or prohibition of variants.
10. An indication any particular conditions to which the performance of the contract is subject.
11. In open procedures, provision of:
    (a) name, address, telephone and telefax number, and electronic address of the service from which contract documents and additional documents can be requested;
    (b) where appropriate, time limit for submission of such requests;
    (c) where appropriate, cost of and payment conditions for obtaining these documents;
    (d) time limit for receipt of tenders or indicative tenders where a dynamic purchasing system is being used (open procedures);
    (e) time limit for receipt of request to participate (restricted and negotiated procedures);
    (f) address where these have to be transmitted;
    (g) the language or languages in which they must be drawn up;
    (h) persons authorised to be present at the opening of tenders;
    (i) date, time, and place for such opening.
12. An indication of any deposit and guarantees required.
13. A reference to the main terms concerning financing and payment.
14. Where applicable, the legal form to be taken by the grouping of economic operators to whom the contract is to be awarded.
15. An indication of the selection criteria regarding the personal situation of economic operators that may lead to their exclusion, and required information proving that they do not fall within the cases justifying exclusion; an indication of the selection criteria and information concerning the economic operators' personal situation; information and any necessary formalities for assessment of the minimum economic and technical standards required of the economic operator; and an indication of any minimum level(s) of standards required.
16. In cases of framework agreements, a reference to the number and, where appropriate, proposed maximum number of economic operators who will be members of the framework agreement; and an indication of the duration of the framework agreement provided for, stating, if appropriate, the reasons for any duration exceeding four years.
17. In cases of negotiated procedures with the publication of a contract notice, an indication of a possible recourse to a staged procedure in order gradually to reduce the number of solutions to be discussed or tenders to be negotiated.
18. In cases of restricted procedures or negotiated procedures with the publication of a contract notice, when contracting entities exercise the option of reducing the number of candidates to be invited to submit tenders, to engage in dialogue or to negotiate, an indication of the minimum and, if

appropriate, the proposed maximum number of candidates and a reference to objective criteria to be used to choose that number of candidates.

19. In cases of open procedures, an indication of the time frame during which the tenderers must submit their tender.

20. In cases of negotiated procedures, a reference to names and addresses of economic operators already selected by the contracting authority.

21. A reference to the award criteria to be used for award of the contract: 'lowest price' or 'most economically advantageous tender'; in cases where criteria representing the most economically advantageous tender are selected, a description of their weighting in the event that such weighting does not appear in the specifications.

22. A reference of the name and address of the body responsible for appeal and, where appropriate, mediation procedures; an indication of precise information concerning deadlines for lodging appeals, or, if need be, the name, address, telephone number, fax number, and email address of the service from which this information may be obtained.

23. The date(s) of publication of the prior information notice; the date of dispatch of the notice.

24. An indication of whether the contract is covered by the WTO GPA Agreement.

6.102 Contract notices must be published in full in an official language of the Community as chosen by the contracting entity, this original language version constituting the sole authentic text. A summary of the important elements of each notice will be published in the other official languages.

6.103 When contracting entities wish to set up a dynamic purchasing system, they must publish a contract notice. Furthermore, when contracts are to be awarded based on a dynamic purchasing system, contracting entities must publish a simplified contract notice.[159]

6.104 Notices and their contents may not be published at national level before the date on which they are sent to the Commission. Notices published at national level must not contain information other than that contained in the notices dispatched to the Commission or published on a buyer profile, but must mention the date of dispatch of the notice to the Commission or its publication on the buyer profile. Periodic indicative notices may not be published on a buyer profile before the

---

[159] A simplified contract notice for use in a dynamic purchasing system must include the following information: the country, name, and e-mail address of the contracting authority; publication reference of the contract notice for the dynamic purchasing system; the e-mail address at which the technical specification and additional documents relating to the dynamic purchasing system are available; the subject of contract and a description by reference number(s) of 'CPV' nomenclature; the quantity or extent of the contract to be awarded; and the time frame for submitting indicative tenders. *See* Annex XIII D of the Utilities Directive.

dispatch to the Commission of the notice of their publication in that form; and they must mention the date of that dispatch.

(d) Contract award notices

Contracting entities which have awarded a contract or a framework agreement must, within two months of the award of the contract or framework agreement, send a contract award notice to the Commission.[160] In the case of contracts awarded under a framework agreement, contracting entities are not obliged to send a notice of the results of the award procedure for each contract based on that agreement. Contracting entities must send a contract award notice based on a dynamic purchasing system within two months after the award of each contract.[161] They may, however, group such notices on a quarterly basis. In that case, they must send the grouped notices within two months of the end of each quarter.[162]   **6.105**

The Commission must respect any sensitive commercial aspects which the contracting entities may point out when forwarding this information, concerning the number of tenders received, the identity of economic operators, or prices. Where contracting entities award a research and development service contract through procedures without a call for competition, they may limit information to be provided with reference to the research and development services.[163] In particular, they may, on grounds of commercial confidentiality, limit the information to be provided in the contract award notice concerning the nature and quantity of the services supplied. In cases where a research and development contract is awarded through negotiated procedures with prior notice, contracting entities must ensure that any information published under a contract award notice is similar in detail and description to the information contained in the notice of the call for competition.[164]   **6.106**

Contract award notices of contracts based on a qualification system must also contain information similar in detail and description with the information contained in the list of qualified service providers drawn up in accordance with Article 53(7) of the Utilities Directive.[165]   **6.107**

For contracts awarded for services listed in Annex XVII B of the Utilities Directive, contracting entities must indicate in the contract notice whether they agree to publication of a contract award notice.[166]   **6.108**

---

[160] *See* the content and conditions of such notices in Annex XVI of the Utilities Directive.
[161] *See* Art. 43 of the Utilities Directive.   [162] *See* Art. 43(1) of the Utilities Directive.
[163] *See* Art. 43(2) of the Utilities Directive.   [164] *See* Art. 43(3) of the Utilities Directive.
[165] *See* Art. 43(3), fourth indent, of the Utilities Directive.
[166] *See* Art. 43(4) of the Utilities Directive.

(2) Time limits for the receipt of requests to participate and for the receipt of tenders

6.109 In determining the time limits for requests to participate and the receipt of tenders, contracting entities must take particular account of the complexity of the contract and the time required for drawing up tenders.[167]

(a) Time limits for open procedures

6.110 When contracting entities wish to award a contract through open procedures, the minimum time limit for the receipt of tenders must be fifty-two days from the date on which the contract notice was sent for publication to the Commission.[168] Where notices are drawn up and transmitted by electronic means in accordance with the format and procedures for transmission indicated in Annex XX of the Utilities Directive, the time limits for the receipt of tenders in open procedures may be reduced by seven days.[169]

6.111 The time limits for the receipt of tenders in open procedures may be further reduced by five days where the contracting entity offers unrestricted and full direct access to the contract documents, and any supplementary documents, by electronic means from the date on which the notice used as a means of calling for competition is published, in accordance with Annex XX of the Utilities Directive. The notice should specify the internet address at which this documentation is accessible.[170]

6.112 If contracting entities have published a periodic indicative notice, the minimum time limit for the receipt of tenders in open procedures must be, as a general rule, not less than thirty-six days. In cases where the periodic indicative notice has included, in addition to the information required by Annex XV A, Part I, all the information required by Annex XV A, Part II, insofar as the latter information is available at the time the notice is published, and that the notice has been sent for publication between fifty-two days and twelve months before the date on which the contract notice referred to in Article 42(1)(c) is sent for publication, a reduced time limit for the receipt of tenders is permitted, provided that it will not be less than twenty-two days from the date on which the notice was sent.[171]

6.113 In open procedures, the cumulative effect of the reductions provided for the receipt of tenders may in no case result in a period for the receipt of tenders of less than fifteen days from the date on which the contract notice is sent. However, if the contract notice is not transmitted by fax or electronic means, the cumulative effect of the reductions may in no case result in a time limit for receipt of tenders

---

[167] *See* Art. 45 of the Utilities Directive.   [168] *See* Art. 45(1) of the Utilities Directive.
[169] *See* Art. 45(5) of the Utilities Directive.   [170] *See* Art. 45(6) of the Utilities Directive.
[171] *See* Art. 45(4) of the Utilities Directive.

in an open procedure of less than twenty-two days from the date on which the contract notice is transmitted.

In open procedures, where contracting entities do not offer unrestricted and full **6.114** direct access by electronic means in accordance with Article 45(6) of the Utilities Directive to the specifications and any supporting documents, the specifications and supporting documents must be sent to economic operators within six days of receipt of the request, provided that the request was made in good time before the time limit for the submission of tenders. Provided that it has been requested in good time, contracting entities must supply additional information relating to the specifications not later than six days before the time limit for the receipt of tenders.[172]

(b) Request to participate or negotiate

In restricted procedures with a prior call for competition, the time limit for the receipt **6.115** of requests to participate, in response to a contract notice used as a call for competition and published under Article 42(1)(c) of the Utilities Directive, must be no less than thirty-seven days from the date on which the notice was sent for publication.[173]

In negotiated procedures with a prior call for competition, the time limit for the **6.116** receipt of requests to negotiate in response to an invitation by contracting entities under Article 47(5) must be no less than thirty-seven days from the date on which the notice or invitation was sent for publication. If notices were sent for publication by means other than electronic means or fax, the time limit may be no less than twenty-two days; on the other hand, if notices are transmitted by electronic means or fax the time limit must be no less than fifteen days from the dispatch of the notice.[174]

Where notices are drawn up and transmitted by electronic means in accordance **6.117** with the format and procedures for transmission indicated in Annex XX of the Utilities Directive, the time limits for the receipt of requests to participate in restricted and negotiated procedures may be reduced by seven days.[175]

The cumulative effect of the reductions may in no case result in a time limit **6.118** for receipt of requests to participate, in response to a notice published under Article 42(1)(c), or in response to an invitation by the contracting entities under Article 47(5) of the Utilities Directive, of less than fifteen days from the date on which the contract notice or invitation is sent.[176]

(c) Receipt of tenders in restricted and negotiated procedures

The time limit for the receipt of tenders may be set by mutual agreement between **6.119** the contracting entity and the selected candidates, provided that all candidates

---

[172] *See* Art. 45(8) of the Utilities Directive.   [173] *See* Art. 45(3)(a) of the Utilities Directive.
[174] *See* Art. 45(3)(a), second indent, of the Utilities Directive.
[175] *See* Art. 45(5) of the Utilities Directive.   [176] *See* Art. 45(8) of the Utilities Directive.

have the same time to prepare and submit their tenders.[177] Where it is not possible to reach agreement on the time limit for the receipt of tenders, the contracting entity should determine a time limit which, as a general rule, must be at least twenty-four days and in no case must be less than ten days from the date of the invitation to tender.[178]

6.120 The time limits for the receipt of tenders in restricted and negotiated procedures may be further reduced by five days where the contracting entity offers unrestricted and full direct access to the contract documents and any supplementary documents by electronic means from the date on which the notice used as a means of calling for competition is published, in accordance with Annex XX of the Utilities Directive. The notice should specify the internet address at which this documentation is accessible.[179]

6.121 In restricted and negotiated procedures, the cumulative effect of the reductions to the time limits to submit tenders may in no case, except that of a time limit set by mutual agreement, result in a time limit for the receipt of tenders of less than ten days from the date of the invitation to tender.[180]

(d) Extensions to time limits for the receipt of tenders

6.122 If, for whatever reason, the contract documents and the supporting documents or additional information, although requested in good time, have not been supplied within the time limits set in Articles 46 and 47 of the Utilities Directive, or where tenders can be made only after a visit to the site or after on-the-spot inspection of the documents supporting the contract documents, the time limits for the receipt of tenders must be extended accordingly, except in the case of a time limit set by mutual agreement in accordance with paragraph 3(b), so that all economic operators concerned may be aware of all the information needed for the preparation of a tender.[181]

(3) Invitations to submit a tender or to negotiate

6.123 In restricted procedures and negotiated procedures, contracting entities must simultaneously and in writing invite the selected candidates to submit their tenders or to negotiate.[182] The invitation to the candidates must include either a copy of the specifications and any supporting documents,[183] or a reference to accessing the specifications and any supporting documents, when they are made directly

---

[177] *See* Art. 45(3)(b) of the Utilities Directive.   [178] *See* Art. 45(3)(c) of the Utilities Directive.
[179] *See* Art. 45(6) of the Utilities Directive.
[180] *See* Art. 45(8), second indent, of the Utilities Directive.
[181] *See* Art. 45(9) of the Utilities Directive.   [182] *See* Art. 47 of the Utilities Directive.
[183] *See* Art. 47(1) of the Utilities Directive.

available by electronic means in accordance with Article 45(6) of the Utilities Directive.[184]

Where the specifications or any supporting documents are held by an entity other **6.124** than the contracting entity responsible for the award procedure, the invitation must indicate the address from which those specifications and documents may be requested and, if appropriate, the closing date for requesting such documents, the sum payable for obtaining them, and any payment procedures.[185]

The additional information on the specifications or the supporting documents **6.125** must be sent by the contracting entity or the competent department not less than six days before the final date for the receipt of tenders, provided that it is requested in good time.[186] In addition, the invitation must include at least the following:[187]

(a) where appropriate, the time limit for requesting additional documents, as well as the amount and terms of payment of any sum to be paid for such documents;

(b) the final date for receipt of tenders, the address to which they are to be sent, and the language or languages in which they are to be drawn up;

(c) a reference to any published contract notice;

(d) an indication of any documents to be attached;

(e) the criteria for the award of the contract, where they are not indicated in the notice on the existence of a qualification system used as a means of calling for competition;

(f) the relative weighting of the contract award criteria or, where appropriate, the order of importance of such criteria, if this information is not given in the contract notice, the notice on the existence of a qualification system or the specifications.

When a call for competition is made by means of a periodic indicative notice,[188] **6.126** contracting entities must subsequently invite all candidates to confirm their interest on the basis of detailed information on the contract concerned before beginning the selection of tenderers or participants in negotiations. This invitation must include at least the following information:

(a) nature and quantity, including all options concerning complementary contracts and, if possible, the estimated time available for exercising these options for renewable contracts, the nature and quantity and, if possible, the estimated publication dates of future notices of competition for works, supplies, or services to be put out to tender;

---

[184] *See* Art. 47(2) of the Utilities Directive.
[185] *See* Art. 47(2), second indent, of the Utilities Directive.
[186] *See* Art. 47(3) of the Utilities Directive. [187] *See* Art. 47(4) of the Utilities Directive.
[188] *See* Art. 47(5) of the Utilities Directive.

(b) type of procedure: restricted or negotiated;

(c) where appropriate, the date on which the delivery of supplies, or the execution of works or services, is to commence or terminate;

(d) the address and closing date for the submission of requests for tender documents, and the language or languages in which they are to be drawn up;

(e) the address of the entity which is to award the contract and the information necessary for obtaining the specifications and other documents;

(f) economic and technical conditions, financial guarantees, and information required from economic operators;

(g) the amount and payment procedures for any sum payable for obtaining tender documents;

(h) the form of the contract which is the subject of the invitation to tender: purchase, lease, hire or hire-purchase, or any combination of these; and

(i) the contract award criteria and their weighting or, where appropriate, the order of importance of such criteria, if this information is not given in the indicative notice or the specifications or in the invitation to tender or to negotiate.

(4) Technical specifications

6.127　The technical specifications must be set out in the contract documentation, such as contract notices, contract documents, or additional documents.[189] Whenever possible these technical specifications should be defined so as to take into account accessibility criteria for people with disabilities or design for all users. Technical specifications must afford equal access for tenderers and not have the effect of creating unjustified obstacles to the opening up of public procurement to competition.

6.128　Without prejudice to mandatory national technical rules, to the extent that they are compatible with Community law, the technical specifications must be formulated:[190]

(a) either by reference to technical specifications defined in Annex XXI of the Utilities Directive and, in order of preference, to: national standards transposing European standards, European technical approvals, common technical specifications, international standards, other technical reference systems established by the European standardisation bodies, or—when these do not exist—to national standards, national technical approvals, or national technical specifications relating to the design, calculation, and execution of the works and use of the products. Each reference must be accompanied by the words 'or equivalent';

---

[189] Art. 34 of the Utilities Directive.　　[190] *See* Art. 34(3) of the Utilities Directive.

(b) or in terms of performance or functional requirements; the latter may include environmental characteristics. However, such parameters must be sufficiently precise to allow tenderers to determine the subject-matter of the contract and to allow contracting entities to award the contract;

(c) or in terms of performance or functional requirements as mentioned in subparagraph (b), with reference to the specifications mentioned in subparagraph (a) as a means of presuming conformity with such performance or functional requirements;

(d) or by referring to the specifications mentioned in subparagraph (a) for certain characteristics, and by referring to the performance or functional requirements mentioned in subparagraph (b) for other characteristics.

Where a contracting entity makes use of the option of referring to the specifica- **6.129**
tions defined in Annex XXI of the Utilities Directive and, in order of preference, to national standards transposing European standards, European technical approvals, common technical specifications, international standards, or other technical reference systems established by the European standardization bodies, it cannot reject a tender on the grounds that the products and services tendered for do not comply with the specifications to which it has referred, once the tenderer proves in his tender to the satisfaction of the contracting entity, by whatever appropriate means, that the solutions which he proposes satisfy in an equivalent manner the requirements defined by the technical specifications.[191] An appropriate means might be constituted by a technical dossier of the manufacturer or a test report from a recognized body.

Where a contracting entity prescribes, in terms of performance or functional **6.130**
requirements, it may not reject a tender for works, products, or services which comply with a national standard transposing a European standard, with a European technical approval, a common technical specification, an international standard, or a technical reference system established by a European standardization body, if these specifications address the performance or functional requirements which it has laid down.[192] Within the tender documents, the tenderer must prove to the satisfaction of the contracting entity and by any appropriate means that the work, product, or service in compliance with the standard meets the performance or functional requirements of the contracting entity. An appropriate means might be constituted by a technical dossier of the manufacturer or a test report from a recognized body.

Where contracting entities lay down environmental characteristics in terms of **6.131**
performance or functional requirements, they may use the detailed specifications or, if necessary, parts thereof, as defined by European or (multi-) national eco-labels,

---

[191] Art. 34(4) of the Utilities Directive.   [192] Art. 34(5) of the Utilities Directive.

or by any other eco-label, provided that those specifications are appropriate to define the characteristics of the supplies or services that are the object of the contract, that the requirements for the label are drawn up on the basis of scientific information, that the eco-labels are adopted using a procedure in which all stakeholders, such as government bodies, consumers, manufacturers, distributors, and environmental organizations can participate, and, finally, they are accessible to all interested parties.[193]

6.132 Contracting entities may indicate that the products and services bearing the eco-label are presumed to comply with the technical specifications laid down in the contract documents; they must accept any other appropriate means of proof, such as a technical dossier of the manufacturer or a test report from a recognised body. Recognised bodies, within the meaning of the Directive, are test and calibration laboratories, and certification and inspection bodies, which comply with applicable European standards. Contracting entities must accept certificates from recognized bodies established in other member states.[194]

6.133 Unless justified by the subject-matter of the contract, technical specifications must not refer to a specific make or source, or a particular process, or to trade marks, patents, types, or a specific origin or production with the effect of favouring or eliminating certain undertakings or certain products. Such reference must be permitted on an exceptional basis, where a sufficiently precise and intelligible description of the subject-matter of the contract is not possible, and such reference must be accompanied by the words 'or equivalent'.[195]

6.134 Any technical specifications regularly referred to in the supply, works, or service contracts of contracting entities, or the technical specifications which they intend to apply to specific contracts covered by periodic indicative notices within the meaning of Article 41(1) of the Utilities Directive, must be made available on request to interested economic operators. Where the technical specifications are based on documents available to interested economic operators, the inclusion of a reference to those documents is sufficient proof of the requirements stipulated in Article 35 of the Utilities Directive in relation to communication of technical specifications.

(5) Variants

6.135 Contracting entities may allow tenderers to submit variants only where the criterion for award is that of the most economically advantageous tender.[196] Contracting entities must indicate in the specifications whether or not they authorize variants. Contracting entities authorizing variants must state in the contract documents the

---

[193] *See* Art. 34(6) of the Utilities Directive.   [194] Art. 34(7) of the Utilities Directive.
[195] *See* Art. 34(8) of the Utilities Directive.   [196] Art. 36 of the Utilities Directive.

minimum requirements to be met by the variants and any specific requirements for their presentation. In procedures for awarding public supply or service contracts, contracting entities which have authorized variants may not reject a variant on the sole ground that it would, if successful, lead to a service contract rather than a public supply contract, or a supply contract rather than a public service contract.

(6) Contractual performance

(a) Subcontracting

In the contract documents, contracting entities may ask or may be required by a **6.136** member state to invite tenderers to indicate in their tender any share of the contract they may intend to subcontract to third parties and any proposed subcontractors. This indication must be without prejudice to the question of the principal economic operator's liability.[197]

(b) Socio-economic conditions

Contracting entities may lay down special conditions relating to the performance **6.137** of a contract, provided that these are compatible with Community law and are indicated in the contract notice or in the specifications. The conditions governing the performance of a contract may, in particular, concern social and environmental considerations.[198]

(c) Obligations relating to taxes, environmental protection, employment protection provisions, and working conditions

Contracting entities may state in the contract documents, or be obliged by a **6.138** member state to state, the body or bodies from which a candidate or tenderer may obtain the appropriate information on the obligations relating to taxes, to environmental protection, to the employment protection provisions, and to the working conditions which are in force in the member state, region, or locality in which the works are to be carried out or services are to be provided, and which must be applicable to the works carried out on site or to the services provided during the performance of the contract.[199]

A contracting entity must request the tenderers or candidates in the contract **6.139** award procedure to indicate that they have taken account, when drawing up their tender, of the obligations relating to employment protection provisions and the working conditions which are in force in the place where the works are to be carried out or the service is to be provided.[200]

---

[197] *See* Art. 37 of the Utilities Directive.   [198] Art. 38 of the Utilities Directive.
[199] Art. 39(1) of the Utilities Directive.   [200] Art. 39(2) of the Utilities Directive.

C. Qualification and Qualitative Selection

(1) Qualification systems

6.140 Contracting entities may resort to qualifications systems in order to select the economic operators to invite them to submit a tender or to negotiate the award of a contract. The Utilities Directive provides for discretion on the part of contracting entities to establish and operate a system of qualification of economic operators. The operation of such systems must be based on objective criteria and rules for qualification which are to be established by the contracting entity.[201]

6.141 Contracting entities which establish or operate such a system must ensure that economic operators are at all times able to request participation in the qualification system.[202] The criteria and rules for qualification must be made available to economic operators on request. The updating of these criteria and rules must be communicated to interested economic operators. Where a contracting entity considers that the qualification system of certain other entities or bodies meets its requirements, it must communicate to interested economic operators the names of such other entities or bodies.[203]

(a) Establishment of qualification systems

6.142 Qualification systems may involve different stages.[204]

(b) Qualification with reference to technical specifications

6.143 In qualifications systems, contracting entities may determine criteria and rules for the selection of candidates to be invited to tender or negotiate, which include technical specifications.[205] In such cases, the provisions of Article 34 of the Utilities Directive must apply.

6.144 The technical specifications must be set out in the contract documentation, such as contract notices, contract documents, or additional documents.[206] Whenever possible, these technical specifications should be defined so as to take into account accessibility criteria for people with disabilities or design for all users. Technical specifications must afford equal access for tenderers and not have the effect of creating unjustified obstacles to the opening up of public procurement to competition.

---

[201] *See* Art. 53 of the Utilities Directive.   [202] *See* Art. 53(1) of the Utilities Directive.
[203] *See* Art. 53(2) of the Utilities Directive.   [204] *See* Art. 53(2) of the Utilities Directive.
[205] *See* Art. 53(2), second indent, of the Utilities Directive.
[206] Art. 34 of the Utilities Directive.

Without prejudice to mandatory national technical rules, to the extent that **6.145** they are compatible with Community law, the technical specifications must be formulated:[207]

(a) either by reference to technical specifications defined in Annex XXI of the Utilities Directive and, in order of preference, to national standards transposing European standards, European technical approvals, common technical specifications, international standards, other technical reference systems established by the European standardization bodies or, when these do not exist, to national standards, national technical approvals, or national technical specifications relating to the design, calculation, and execution of the works and use of the products. Each reference must be accompanied by the words 'or equivalent';

(b) or in terms of performance or functional requirements; the latter may include environmental characteristics. However, such parameters must be sufficiently precise to allow tenderers to determine the subject-matter of the contract and to allow contracting entities to award the contract;

(c) or in terms of performance or functional requirements as mentioned in subparagraph (b), with reference to the specifications mentioned in subparagraph (a) as a means of presuming conformity with such performance or functional requirements;

(d) or by referring to the specifications mentioned in subparagraph (a) for certain characteristics, and by referring to the performance or functional requirements mentioned in subparagraph (b) for other characteristics.

Where a contracting entity makes use of the option of referring to the specifications **6.146** defined in Annex XXI of the Utilities Directive and, in order of preference, to national standards transposing European standards, European technical approvals, common technical specifications, international standards, or other technical reference systems established by the European standardization bodies, it cannot reject a tender on the grounds that the products and services tendered for do not comply with the specifications to which it has referred, once the tenderer proves in his tender to the satisfaction of the contracting entity, by whatever appropriate means, that the solutions which he proposes satisfy in an equivalent manner the requirements defined by the technical specifications.[208] An appropriate means might be constituted by a technical dossier of the manufacturer or a test report from a recognized body.

Where a contracting entity prescribes in terms of performance or functional **6.147** requirements, it may not reject a tender for works, products, or services which comply with a national standard transposing a European standard, with a European technical approval, a common technical specification, an international

---

[207] *See* Art. 34(3) of the Utilities Directive.   [208] Art. 34(4) of the Utilities Directive.

standard, or a technical reference system established by a European standardization body, if these specifications address the performance or functional requirements which it has laid down.[209] Within the tender documents, the tenderer must prove to the satisfaction of the contracting entity and by any appropriate means that the work, product, or service in compliance with the standard meets the performance or functional requirements of the contracting entity. An appropriate means might be constituted by a technical dossier of the manufacturer or a test report from a recognized body.

6.148 Where contracting entities lay down environmental characteristics, in terms of performance or functional requirements they may use the detailed specifications or, if necessary, parts thereof, as defined by European or (multi-) national eco-labels or by any other eco-label, provided that those specifications are appropriate to define the characteristics of the supplies or services that are the object of the contract, that the requirements for the label are drawn up on the basis of scientific information, that the eco-labels are adopted using a procedure in which all stakeholders, such as government bodies, consumers, manufacturers, distributors, and environmental organizations can participate, and, finally, they are accessible to all interested parties.[210]

6.149 Contracting entities may indicate that the products and services bearing the eco-label are presumed to comply with the technical specifications laid down in the contract documents; they must accept any other appropriate means of proof, such as a technical dossier of the manufacturer or a test report from a recognised body. Recognised bodies, within the meaning of the Directive, are test and calibration laboratories, and certification and inspection bodies, which comply with applicable European standards. Contracting entities must accept certificates from recognized bodies established in other member states.[211]

6.150 Unless justified by the subject-matter of the contract, technical specifications must not refer to a specific make or source, or a particular process, or to trade marks, patents, types, or a specific origin or production with the effect of favouring or eliminating certain undertakings or certain products. Such reference must be permitted on an exceptional basis, where a sufficiently precise and intelligible description of the subject-matter of the contract is not possible, and such reference must be accompanied by the words 'or equivalent'.[212]

6.151 Any technical specifications regularly referred to in the supply, works, or service contracts of contracting entities, or the technical specifications which they intend to apply to specific contracts covered by periodic indicative notices within the meaning of Article 41(1) of the Utilities Directive, must be made available on

---

[209] Art. 34(5) of the Utilities Directive.
[211] Art. 34(7) of the Utilities Directive.
[210] *See* Art. 34(6) of the Utilities Directive.
[212] *See* Art. 34(8) of the Utilities Directive.

request to interested economic operators.[213] Where the technical specifications are based on documents available to interested economic operators, the inclusion of a reference to those documents is sufficient proof of the requirements stipulated in Article 35 of the Utilities Directive in relation to communication of technical specifications.

The criteria and rules in relation to qualifications systems based on technical **6.152** specifications may be updated as required.[214]

(c) Qualification with reference to exclusion criteria

Contracting entities when establishing a qualification system, may utilize as **6.153** criteria the exclusion criteria listed in Article 45 of the Public Sector Directive 2004/18 and the terms and conditions set out within that provision.[215] Where contracting entities are also contracting entities within the meaning of Article 2(1)(a) of the Utilities Directive, viz. entities such as the state, regional, or local entities, bodies governed by public law, associations formed by one or several such entities, or one or several of such bodies governed by public law, it is mandatory to utilize as criteria for a qualification system those criteria and rules relevant to automatic exclusion grounds relating to participation in a criminal organization, corruption, fraud, or money laundering listed in Article 45(1) of Directive 2004/18.

In particular, the criteria and rules for qualification in relation to exclusion criteria **6.154** may include reasons for automatic exclusion of economic operators in relation to their personal situation.

(d) Personal situation of economic operators

Contracting entities may exclude[216] from participation in a public contract any **6.155** candidate or tenderer who has been the subject of a conviction by final judgment of which the contracting authority is aware for one or more of following reasons:[217]

(a) participation in a criminal organization, as defined in Article 2(1) of Council Joint Action 98/733/JHA;[218]
(b) corruption, as defined in Article 3 of the Council Act of 26 May 1997[219] and Article 3(1) of Council Joint Action 98/742/JHA[220] respectively;
(c) fraud within the meaning of Article 1 of the Convention relating to the protection of the financial interests of the European Communities;[221]

---

213 *See* Art. 35 of the Utilities Directive.
214 *See* Art. 53(2), second indent, of the Utilities Directive.
215 *See* Art. 53(3) of the Utilities Directive.   216 *See* Art. 45 of the Public Sector Directive.
217 Art. 45(1) of the Public Sector Directive.   218 [1998] OJ L351/1, 29 December 1998.
219 [1997] OJ C195/1, 25 June 1997.   220 [1998] OJ L358/2, 31 December 1998.
221 [1995] OJ C316/48, 27 November 1995.

(d) money laundering, as defined in Article 1 of Council Directive 91/308/EEC of 10 June 1991 on prevention of the use of the financial system for the purpose of money laundering.[222]

6.156 In addition to the above reasons, contracting entities may exclude an economic operator from participation in a contract where that economic operator:[223]

(a) is bankrupt or is being wound up, where his affairs are being administered by the court, where he has entered into an arrangement with creditors, where he has suspended business activities or is in any analogous situation arising from a similar procedure under national laws and regulations;

(b) is the subject of proceedings for a declaration of bankruptcy, for an order for compulsory winding up or administration by the court or of an arrangement with creditors or of any other similar proceedings under national laws and regulations;

(c) has been convicted by a judgment which has the force of *res judicata* in accordance with the legal provisions of the country of any offence concerning his professional conduct;

(d) has been guilty of grave professional misconduct proven by any means which the contracting entities can demonstrate;

(e) has not fulfilled obligations relating to the payment of social security contributions in accordance with the legal provisions of the country in which he is established or with those of the country of the contracting authority;

(f) has not fulfilled obligations relating to the payment of taxes in accordance with the legal provisions of the country in which he is established or with those of the country of the contracting entity;

(g) is guilty of serious misrepresentation in supplying the information required or has not supplied such information.

(e) Derogation

6.157 Member states may provide for derogation from the automatic exclusion grounds relating to participation in a criminal organization, corruption, fraud, or money laundering for overriding requirements in the general interest.[224]

(f) Proof of the personal situation of economic operators

6.158 Sufficient evidence of the personal situation of candidates and tenderers in accordance with Article 45 can be provided by means of the production of an

---

[222] [1991] OJ L166/77, 28 June 1991, as amended by Directive 2001/97/EC of the European Parliament and of the Council of 4 December 2001 [2001] OJ L344/76, 28 December 2001.

[223] Art. 45(2) of the Public Sector Directive.

[224] *See* the second indent of Article 45(1) of the Public Sector Directive.

extract from the judicial record or of an equivalent document issued by a competent judicial or administrative authority in the country of origin of the candidate or the tenderer proving that none of the automatic exclusion grounds relating to participation in a criminal organization, corruption, fraud, or money laundering is present:[225]

With regard to the requirements of evidence of payment of social security **6.159** contributions and taxes, a certificate issued by the competent authority in the member state concerned is adequate proof.[226]

Where the country in question does not issue extracts from the judicial record or **6.160** an equivalent document or certificates, proof of the personal situation of candidates and tenderers may be provided by a declaration on oath or, in member states where there is no provision for declarations on oath, by a solemn declaration made by the person concerned before a competent judicial or administrative authority, a notary or a competent professional or trade body, in the country of origin or in the country whence that person comes. For these purposes, member states must designate the entities and bodies competent to issue the documents, certificates, or declarations and inform the Commission, subject to data protection laws.

(g) Ex officio application

Contracting entities, where they have doubts concerning the personal situation of **6.161** such candidates or tenderers, may themselves apply to the competent entities to obtain any information they consider necessary on the personal situation of the candidates or tenderers.[227] Where the information concerns a candidate or tenderer established in a state other than that of the contracting entity, the contracting entity may seek the cooperation of the competent entities. Such requests must relate to legal and/or natural persons including, if appropriate, company directors and any person having powers of representation, decision, or control in respect of the candidate or tenderer.

(h) Qualification with reference to economic and financial capacity

In cases where contracting entities set as criteria and rules for qualification those **6.162** which include requirements relating to the economic and financial capacity, economic operators may, where necessary, rely on the capacity of other entities, irrespective of the legal nature or the link between them and those entities.[228]

However, in this case the economic operator which wishes to rely on the economic **6.163** and financial capacity of others must prove to the contracting entity that these

---

[225] Art. 45(3)(a) of the Public Sector Directive.
[226] Art. 45(3)(b) of the Public Sector Directive.
[227] *See* Art. 45(1) and in particular its second indent of the Public Sector Directive.
[228] *See* Art. 53(4) of the Utilities Directive.

resources will be available to it throughout the period of the validity of the qualification system.[229] Such proof can be furnished, for example, by producing an undertaking by those entities to that effect. Under the same conditions, a group of economic operators[230] may rely on the capacity of participants in the group or of other entities.

(i) Qualification with reference to technical and professional ability

6.164 Where the criteria and rules for qualification include requirements relating to technical or professional ability, economic operators may rely, where necessary, on the capacity of other entities, whatever the legal nature or the link between them and those entities.[231] In this case the economic operator must provide evidence to the contracting entity, by producing an undertaking of certificates from the entities it wishes to rely on for technical and professional ability qualification purposes, that the required resources will be available to it throughout the period of the validity of the qualification system. Similarly to qualification as to reference to economic and financial capacity, a group of economic operators may rely on the technical and professional abilities of participants in the group or of other entities.[232]

6.165 Contracting entities must keep written records of qualified economic operators. Such records may be divided into categories according to the type of contract for which the qualification is valid.[233]

(j) Operation of qualification systems

6.166 When establishing or operating a qualification system,[234] contracting entities must in particular observe the provisions of Article 41(3) concerning notices on the existence of a system of qualification. The qualification system must be the subject of a notice as referred to in Annex XIV, indicating the purpose of the qualification system and how to have access to the rules concerning its operation. According to Annex XIV of the Utilities Directive, information to be included in the notice on the existence of a qualification system must comprise:

1. The name, address, telegraphic address, electronic address, telephone number, telex, and fax number of the contracting entity.

---

[229] *See* Art. 53(4), second indent, and Article 54(5) of the Utilities Directive.

[230] *See* Art. 11 of the Utilities Directive; groups of economic operators may submit tenders or put themselves forward as candidates. In order to submit a tender or a request to participate, these groups may not be required by the contracting entities to assume a specific legal form; however, the group selected may be required to do so when it has been awarded the contract, to the extent to which this change is necessary for the satisfactory performance of the contract.

[231] *See* Art. 53(5) of the Utilities Directive.   [232] *See* Art. 54(6) of the Utilities Directive.

[233] *See* Art. 53(7) of the Utilities Directive.   [234] *See* Art. 53(8) of the Utilities Directive.

2. An indication, where appropriate, as to whether the contract is reserved for sheltered workshops or whether its performance is reserved in the context of sheltered employment programmes.

3. A statement on the purpose of the qualification system, including the description of the goods, services, or works or categories to be procured through the system by reference to nomenclature numbers.

4. A statement on the conditions to be fulfilled by the economic operators in view of their qualification pursuant to the system and the methods according to which each of those conditions will be verified. Where the description of such conditions and verification methods is voluminous, and based on documents available to interested economic operators, a summary of the main conditions and methods and a reference to those documents will be sufficient.

5. An indication of the period of validity of the qualification system and the formalities for its renewal.

6. A reference to the fact that the notice acts as the call for competition.

7. An address where further information and documentation concerning the qualification system can be obtained

8. A reference concerning the name and address of the body responsible for appeal and, where appropriate, mediation procedures. In addition, precise information should be provided concerning time limits for lodging appeals, or the name, address, telephone number, fax number, and e-mail address of the service from which this information may be obtained.

9. An indication of award criteria, where known, for award of the contract. Criteria representing the most economically advantageous tender as well as their weighting or, where appropriate, the order of importance of these criteria, must be mentioned where they do not appear in the specifications or will not be indicated in the invitation to tender or to negotiate.

10. Any other relevant information.

6.167 Where the system is of duration greater than three years, the notice must be published annually. Where the system is of a shorter duration, an initial notice will be sufficient.[235]

6.168 Contracting entities must also adhere to the requirements concerning the information to be delivered to economic operators having applied for qualification, laid down in Article 49(3), (4) and (5) of the Utilities Directive, when they operate a qualifications system.[236] More specifically, contracting entities which establish and operate a system of qualification must inform applicants of their decision as to qualification within a period of six months. If the decision will take longer than four months from the presentation of an application, contracting

---

[235] *See* Art. 41(3) of the Utilities Directive.   [236] *See* Art. 53(8) of the Utilities Directive.

entities must inform the applicant, within two months of the application, of the reasons justifying the longer period and of the date by which the operator's application will be accepted or refused.

6.169 Disqualified applicants whose qualification is refused must be informed of the contracting entity's decision and the reasons for refusal as soon as possible and under no circumstances more than fifteen days later than the date of the decision. The reasons must be based on the objective criteria for qualification referred to in Article 53(2) of the Utilities Directive, established by the contracting entity and referring to reasons and grounds for automatic exclusions relating to participation in a criminal organization, corruption, fraud, or money laundering, or criteria relevant to economic and financial standing, or criteria concerning technical and professional ability.[237]

6.170 Contracting entities which establish and operate a system of qualification may bring the qualification of an economic operator to an end only for reasons based on the criteria for qualification referred to in Article 53(2) of the Utilities Directive. Any intention to bring qualification to an end must be notified in writing to the economic operator beforehand, at least fifteen days before the date on which qualification is due to end, together with the reason or reasons justifying the proposed action.[238]

6.171 When operating a qualification system, contracting entities must also observe the requirements concerning the selection of participants when a call for competition is made by means of a notice on the existence of a qualification system in accordance with Article 51(2) of the Utilities Directive.[239] When a call for competition is made by means of a notice on the existence of a qualification system, and for the purpose of selecting participants in award procedures for the specific contracts which are the subject of the call for competition, contracting entities must qualify economic operators in accordance with the provisions of Article 53. In restricted or negotiated procedures,[240] They also need to apply to such qualified economic operators such criteria as those which may be based on the objective need of the contracting entity to reduce the number of candidates to a level which is justified by the need to balance the particular characteristics of the procurement procedure with the resources required to conduct it.[241] The number of candidates selected must, however, take account of the need to ensure adequate competition.

6.172 Finally, contracting entities operating qualification systems must respect the principle of mutual recognition[242] concerning administrative, technical or

---

[237] *See* Art. 49(4) of the Utilities Directive. [238] *See* Art. 49(5) of the Utilities Directive.
[239] *See* Art. 53(8) of the Utilities Directive. [240] *See* Art. 51(2)(b) of the Utilities Directive.
[241] *See* Art. 54(3) of the Utilities Directive. [242] *See* Art. 52 of the Utilities Directive.

financial conditions, certificates, tests, and evidence, as laid down in Article 52 of the Utilities Directive.

(2) *Mutual recognition*

Contracting entities must recognize equivalent certificates from bodies **6.173** established in other member states. They must also accept other evidence of equivalent quality assurance measures from economic operators. For works and service contracts, and only in appropriate cases, the contracting entities may require, in order to verify the economic operator's technical abilities, an indication of the environmental management measures which the economic operator will be able to apply when carrying out the contract.[243] In such cases, should the contracting entities require the production of certificates drawn up by independent bodies attesting the compliance of the economic operator with certain environmental management standards, they must refer to the EMAS or to environmental management standards based on the relevant European or international standards certified by bodies conforming to Community law or the relevant European or international standards concerning certification.[244]

When selecting participants for a restricted or negotiated procedure, in reaching their **6.174** decision as to qualification or when the criteria and rules are being updated, contracting entities must not impose administrative, technical, or financial conditions on certain economic operators which would not be imposed on others, or require tests or evidence which would duplicate objective evidence already available.[245]

Where they request the production of certificates drawn up by independent **6.175** bodies attesting the compliance of the economic operator with certain quality assurance standards, contracting entities must refer to quality assurance systems based on the relevant European standards series certified by bodies conforming to the European standards series concerning certification.[246]

(3) *Criteria for qualitative selection*

The criteria for qualitative selection of economic operators by contracting entities in **6.176** open, restricted, or negotiated procedures must be established in accordance with objective rules and criteria which are available to interested economic operators.[247]

In restricted or negotiated procedures, the criteria may be based on the objective **6.177** need[248] of the contracting entity to reduce the number of candidates to a level

---

[243] *See* Art. 52(2) of the Utilities Directive.   [244] *See* Art. 52(3) of the Utilities Directive.
[245] *See* Art. 52(1) of the Utilities Directive.
[246] *See* Art. 52(3), second indent, of the Utilities Directive.
[247] *See* Art. 54 of the Utilities Directive.   [248] *See* Art. 54(3) of the Utilities Directive.

which is justified by the need to balance the particular characteristics of the procurement procedure with the resources required to conduct it. However, the number of candidates selected must take into account of the need to ensure adequate competition.

6.178 The criteria may include the exclusion criteria relating to participation in a criminal organization, corruption, fraud, or money laundering, criteria referring to the economic and financial capacity of the economic operators, or criteria relating to the technical or professional abilities of economic operators.[249]

D. Award Procedures

(1) Use of open, restricted, and negotiated procedures

6.179 Contracting entities may choose any of the procurement procedures described in Article 1(9)(a), (b) or (c) of the Utilities Directive, namely open, restricted, and negotiated procedures, provided[250] that a call for competition has been made in accordance with Article 42 of the Utilities Directive. In the case of open procedures, any interested economic operator may submit a tender; in the case of restricted procedures, any economic operator may request to participate and only candidates invited by the contracting entity may submit a tender; and finally, in the case of negotiated procedures, the contracting entity consults the economic operators of its choice and negotiates the terms of the contract with one or more of these contractors.[251]

6.180 Contracting entities may use a procedure without prior call for competition in the following cases.[252]

(a) when no tenders or no suitable tenders or no applications have been submitted in response to a procedure with a prior call for competition, provided that the initial conditions of contract are not substantially altered;

(b) where a contract is purely for the purpose of research, experiment, study, or development, and not for the purpose of securing a profit or of recovering research and development costs, and insofar as the award of such contract does not prejudice the competitive award of subsequent contracts which do seek, in particular, those ends;

(c) when, for technical or artistic reasons, or for reasons connected with the protection of exclusive rights, the contract may be executed only by a particular economic operator;

---

[249] *See* Art. 54(4), (5) and (6) of the Utilities Directive.
[250] *See* Art. 40(3) of the Utilities Directive.   [251] *See* Art. 1(9) of the Utilities Directive.
[252] *See* Art. 40(3) of the Utilities Directive.

(d) insofar as is strictly necessary when, for reasons of extreme urgency brought about by events unforeseeable by the contracting entities, the time limits laid down for open procedures, restricted procedures, and negotiated procedures with a prior call for competition cannot be adhered to;

(e) in the case of supply contracts for additional deliveries by the original supplier, which are intended either as a partial replacement of normal supplies or installations or as the extension of existing supplies or installations, where a change of supplier would oblige the contracting entity to acquire material having different technical characteristics which would result in incompatibility or disproportionate technical difficulties in operation and maintenance;

(f) for additional works or services which were not included in the project initially awarded or in the contract first concluded but have, through unforeseen circumstances, become necessary to the performance of the contract, on condition that the award is made to the contractor or service provider executing the original contract when such additional works or services cannot be technically or economically separated from the main contract without great inconvenience to the contracting entities, or when such additional works or services, although separable from the performance of the original contract, are strictly necessary to its later stages;

(g) in the case of works contracts, for new works consisting in the repetition of similar works assigned to the contractor to which the same contracting entities awarded an earlier contract, provided that such works conform to a basic project for which a first contract was awarded after a call for competition; as soon as the first project is put up for tender, notice must be given that this procedure might be adopted and the total estimated cost of subsequent works must be taken into consideration by the contracting entities when they calculate the applicable contract value thresholds in accordance with the provisions of Articles 16 and 17 of the Utilities Directive;

(h) for supplies quoted and purchased on a commodity market;

(i) for contracts to be awarded on the basis of a framework agreement, provided that the framework agreement itself has been awarded in accordance with the Utilities Directive as provided in Article 14(2);

(j) for bargain purchases, where it is possible to procure supplies by taking advantage of a particularly advantageous opportunity available for a very short time at a price considerably lower than normal market prices;

(k) for purchases of supplies under particularly advantageous conditions from either a supplier definitively winding up his business activities or the receivers or liquidators of a bankruptcy, an arrangement with creditors or a similar procedure under national laws or regulations;

(l) when the service contract concerned is part of the follow-up to a design contest organized in accordance with the provisions of the Utilities Directive and must, in accordance with the relevant rules, be awarded to the winner or to one of the winners of that contest; in the latter case, all the winners must be invited to participate in the negotiations.

(2) Framework agreements

6.181 A framework agreement is an agreement between one or more contracting entities and one or more economic operators, the purpose of which is to establish the terms governing contracts to be awarded during a given period, in particular with regard to price and, where appropriate, the quantities envisaged.[253] Contracting entities may regard a framework agreement as a contract within the remit of the Utilities Directive.[254] Framework agreements should not be misused in order to hinder, limit, or distort competition.[255]

6.182 In cases where contracting entities have awarded a framework agreement in accordance with the Utilities Directive, the award of contracts based on that framework agreement may be pursued though an award procedure without prior call for competition.[256] Where a framework agreement has not been awarded in accordance with the provisions of the Utilities Directive, contracting entities must not utilize such award procedures.

E. Award Criteria

6.183 There are two criteria on which the contracting entities must base the award of contracts:[257] (a) the most economically advantageous tender, or (b) the lowest price.

(1) The most economically advantageous tender

6.184 When the award is made to the tender most economically advantageous from the point of view of the contracting authority, various criteria linked to the subject-matter of the public contract in question, for example, quality, price, technical merit, aesthetic and functional characteristics, environmental characteristics, running costs, cost-effectiveness, after-sales service and technical assistance, delivery date and delivery period, or period of completion, can be taken into consideration. The above listed criteria which constitute the parameters of the most economically advantageous offer are not exhaustive.[258]

6.185 For the purposes of defining what does constitute a most economically advantageous offer, the contracting authority must specify in the contract notice or in the contract

---

[253] *See* Art. 1(4) of the Utilities Directive.   [254] *See* Art. 14 of the Utilities Directive.
[255] *See* Art. 14(4) of the Utilities Directive.
[256] *See* Art. 14(2) and Article 40(3)(i) of the Utilities Directive.
[257] Art. 55 of the Utilities Directive.   [258] Art. 55(1)(a) of the Utilities Directive.

documents or, in the case of a competitive dialogue, in the descriptive document, the relative weighting which it gives to each of the criteria chosen to determine the most economically advantageous tender. Those weightings can be expressed by providing for a range with an appropriate maximum spread. Where, in the opinion of the contracting authority, weighting is not possible for demonstrable reasons, the contracting authority must indicate in the contract notice or contract documents or, in the case of a competitive dialogue, in the descriptive document, the criteria in descending order of importance.[259] The relative weighting or order of importance must be specified, as appropriate, in the notice used as a means of calling for competition, in the invitation to confirm the interest referred to in Article 47(5) of the Utilities Directive, in the invitation to tender or to negotiate, or in the specifications.

(2) The lowest price

When the lowest price has been selected as the award criterion, contracting **6.186** entities must not refer to any other qualitative consideration when deliberating the award of a contract. The lowest price is a sole quantitative benchmark that intends to differentiate the offers made by tenderers.[260] However, contracting entities can reject a tender, if they regard the price attached to it as abnormally low.

(3) Abnormally low tenders

In cases that tenders appear to be abnormally low in relation to the goods, works **6.187** or services, the contracting entity must request in writing details of the constituent elements of the tender which it considers relevant before it rejects those tenders.[261]

The clarification details[262] may relate in particular to: **6.188**

(a) the economics of the construction method, the manufacturing process or the services provided;
(b) the technical solutions chosen and/or any exceptionally favourable conditions available to the tenderer for the execution of the work, for the supply of the goods or services;
(c) the originality of the work, supplies, or services proposed by the tenderer;
(d) compliance with the provisions relating to employment protection and working conditions in force at the place where the work, service, or supply is to be performed;
(e) the possibility of the tenderer obtaining state aid.

---

[259] Art. 55(2) of the Utilities Directive.   [260] *See* Art. 55(1)(b) of the Utilities Directive.
[261] Art. 57 of the Utilities Directive.   [262] Art. 57(1) of the Utilities Directive.

6.189 Where a contracting entity establishes that a tender is abnormally low because the tenderer has obtained state aid, the tender can be rejected on that ground alone only after consultation with the tenderer where the latter is unable to prove, within a sufficient time limit fixed by the contracting entity that the aid in question was granted legally.[263] Where the contracting entity rejects a tender in these circumstances, it must inform the Commission of their decision.

(4) Dynamic purchasing systems

6.190 A dynamic purchasing system is a completely electronic process for making commonly-used purchases of products. The characteristics of such products should be such as to meet the requirements of contracting entities by reference to their products' general availability in the market and their standardized specifications.[264] A dynamic purchasing system must have limited duration and be open throughout its validity to any economic operator which satisfies the selection criteria and has submitted an indicative tender that complies with the specification. The costs of setting and running a dynamic purchasing system are borne by the contracting entity. No charges for the set-up costs or participating costs for the duration of the dynamic purchasing system may be billed to the interested economic operators or to parties to the system.[265]

(a) Setting up a dynamic purchasing system

6.191 In order to set up a dynamic purchasing system, contracting entities must follow the rules of the open procedure in all its phases up to the award of the contracts.[266] Contracting entities must:

(a) publish a contract notice with their clear intention to set up a dynamic purchasing system;

(b) indicate in the specifications, amongst other matters, the nature of the purchases envisaged under that system, as well as all the necessary information concerning the purchasing system, the electronic equipment used, and the technical connection arrangements and specifications;

(c) offer by electronic means, on publication of the notice and up to the expiry of the system, unrestricted, direct, and full access to the specifications and to any additional documents, and must indicate in the notice the internet address at which such documents may be consulted.

6.192 With a view to setting up the system and to awarding of contracts under that system, contracting entities must use solely electronic means.[267] The means of

---

[263] Art. 57(3) of the Utilities Directive.   [264] *See* Art. 1(7) of the Utilities Directive.
[265] Art. 15(7), second indent, of the Utilities Directive.
[266] Art. 15(3) of the Utilities Directive.   [267] *See* Art. 48(2) to (5) of the Directive.

communication chosen must be generally available and under no circumstances may restrict the economic operators' access to the tendering procedure. The tools to be used for communicating by electronic means, as well as their technical characteristics, must be non-discriminatory, generally available and interoperable with the information and communication technology products in general use.[268]

Devices used for the electronic receipt of requests to participate and devices used for the electronic transmission and receipt of tenders must ensure the availability of information regarding the specifications necessary for the electronic submission of tenders and requests to participate, including any encryption requirements.[269] Member states may introduce or maintain voluntary accreditation schemes aiming at enhanced levels of certification service provision for these devices. **6.193**

Such electronic devices must also conform to the requirements of Annex XXIV of the Utilities Directive[270] and, in particular, they must guarantee, through technical means and appropriate procedures, that: **6.194**

(a) electronic signatures relating to tenders, requests to participate, and the forwarding of plans and projects comply with national provisions adopted pursuant to Directive 1999/93; contracting entities may require that electronic tenders be accompanied by an advanced electronic signature;

(b) the exact time and date of the receipt of tenders, requests to participate and the submission of plans and projects can be determined precisely;

(c) that no person can have access to data transmitted before the time limits laid down;

(d) if data access prohibition is infringed, the infringement must be clearly detectable;

(e) only authorized persons may set or change the dates for opening data received;

(f) during the different stages of the contract award procedure or of the contest, access to all data submitted must be possible only through simultaneous action by authorized persons;

(g) simultaneous action by authorized persons must give access to data transmitted only after the prescribed date;

(h) data received and opened in accordance with these requirements must remain accessible only to authorized persons.

Under a dynamic purchasing system, communication and the exchange and storage of information must be carried out in such a way as to ensure that the **6.195**

---

[268] *See* the provisions of Article 48(4) of the Utilities Directive.

[269] Art. 48(5) of the Utilities Directive.

[270] *See* Annex XXIV of the Directive on Requirements relating to devices for the electronic receipt of tenders, request for participation, and plans and projects in contests.

integrity of data and the confidentiality of tenders and requests to participate are preserved, and that the contracting entities examine the content of tenders and requests to participate only after the time limit set for submitting them has expired.[271]

(b) The conduct of dynamic purchasing systems

6.196 A dynamic purchasing system may not last for more than four years, except in duly justified exceptional cases. Contracting entities may not resort to this system to prevent, restrict or distort competition.[272]

6.197 Admission into a dynamic purchasing system is subject to two requirements: a) meeting and satisfying the selection and qualification criteria, and b) submitting an indicative tender which complies with the specification or any possible additional documents.[273] Admittance to a dynamic purchasing system or the rejection of an economic operator's indicative tender must be communicated to the relevant economic operator at the earliest possible opportunity. Throughout the entire period of a dynamic purchasing system, contracting entities must give any economic operator having met and satisfied the selection and qualification requirements, the possibility of submitting an indicative tender and of being admitted to the system.

(c) The indicative tenders

6.198 In order to issue an invitation to tender to those economic operators admitted into a dynamic purchasing system, contracting entities must publish a simplified contract notice inviting all interested economic operators to submit an indicative tender within fifteen days from the date on which the simplified notice was sent. Contracting entities may not proceed with tendering until they have completed evaluation of all the indicative tenders received by that deadline.[274]

6.199 Indicative tenders may be improved at any time provided that they continue to comply with the specification. Contracting entities must complete the evaluation of indicative tenders within a maximum of fifteen days from the date of their submission.[275] However, they may extend the evaluation period provided that no invitation to tender is issued in the meantime.

(d) The award of contracts under dynamic purchasing systems

6.200 Each specific contract awarder under a dynamic purchasing system must be the subject of an invitation to tender. Contracting entities, after evaluating the

---

[271] Art. 48(3) of the Utilities Directive.   [272] Art. 15(7) of the Utilities Directive.
[273] Art. 15(2) of the Utilities Directive.   [274] Art. 15(5) of the Utilities Directive.
[275] *See* Art. 15(4), first indent, of the Utilities Directive.

indicative tenders and admitting economic operators into the dynamic purchasing system must invite tenders from those admitted to the system for each specific contract to be awarded under the system.[276]

A time limit for the submission of tenders must be set by contracting entities. The evaluation of tenders should be based on the award criteria set out in the contract notice for the establishment of the dynamic purchasing system.[277] The award of contracts under a dynamic purchasing system must reflect the best tender on the basis of those criteria which may, if appropriate, be formulated more precisely in the invitation to tender extended to the economic operators admitted into the dynamic purchasing system.   **6.201**

(5) *Electronic auctions*

An electronic auction is a repetitive process involving an electronic device for the presentation of new prices, revised downwards, and/or new values concerning certain elements of tenders, which occurs after an initial full evaluation of the tenders, enabling them to be ranked using automatic evaluation methods. Consequently, certain service contracts and certain works contracts having as their subject-matter intellectual performances, such as the design of works, may not be the object of electronic auctions.[278]   **6.202**

Contracting entities may hold electronic auctions on the opening for competition of contracts to be awarded under the dynamic purchasing system.[279] Contracting entities which decide to hold an electronic auction must indicate their intention in the contract notice.   **6.203**

In open, restricted, or negotiated procedures contracting entities may decide that the award of a public contract must be preceded by an electronic auction when the contract specifications can be established with precision.[280] The specifications must include, *inter alia*, the following details:[281]   **6.204**

(a) the features, the values for which will be the subject of electronic auction, provided that such features are quantifiable and can be expressed in figures or percentages;

(b) any limits on the values which may be submitted, as they result from the specifications relating to the subject of the contract;

(c) the information which will be made available to tenderers in the course of the electronic auction and, where appropriate, when it will be made available to them;

---

[276] *See* Art. 15(5) of the Utilities Directive.   [277] Art. 15(6) of the Utilities Directive.
[278] Art. 1(6) of the Utilities Directive.   [279] Art. 56(2) of the Utilities Directive.
[280] Art. 56(2) first indent of the Utilities Directive.   [281] Art. 56(3) of the Utilities Directive.

(d) the relevant information concerning the electronic auction process;

(e) the conditions under which the tenderers will be able to bid and, in particular, the minimum differences which will, where appropriate, be required when bidding;

(f) the relevant information concerning the electronic equipment used, and the arrangements and technical specifications for connection.

(a) Organization of electronic auctions

6.205 Before proceeding with an electronic auction, contracting entities must make a full initial evaluation of the tenders in accordance with the award criteria set and with the weighting attached to them for evaluation purposes.[282] All tenderers who have submitted admissible tenders must be invited simultaneously by electronic means to submit new prices and/or new values; and the invitation must contain all relevant information concerning individual connection to the electronic equipment being used and must state the date and time of the start of the electronic auction. The electronic auction may take place in a number of successive phases. The electronic auction may not start sooner than two working days after the date on which invitations are sent out.

6.206 The invitation must also state the mathematical formula to be used in the electronic auction to determine automatic re-rankings on the basis of the new prices or new values submitted by the participants.[283] That formula must incorporate the weighting of all the criteria fixed to determine the most economically advantageous tender, as indicated in the contract notice or in the specifications; for that purpose, any ranges must, however, be reduced beforehand to a specified value. Where variants are authorized, a separate formula must be provided for each variant.

6.207 Throughout each phase of an electronic auction, the contracting entities must instantaneously communicate to all tenderers at least sufficient information to enable them to ascertain their relative rankings at any moment. They may also communicate other information concerning other prices or values submitted, provided that that is stated in the specifications.

6.208 They may also at any time announce the number of participants in that phase of the auction. However, they must not disclose the identities of the tenderers during any phase of an electronic auction.

(b) Closure of electronic auctions

6.209 The closure of electronic auctions is the next phase that contracting entities have to follow prior to the award of the contract. The closure of the auction is a

---

[282] Art. 56(4) of the Utilities Directive.   [283] *See* Art. 56(6) of the Utilities Directive.

necessary procedural requirement integral to the award of contracts in such award procedures and should be observed rigorously.[284]

There are three possible ways under which electronic auctions should be drawn to a close. First, the indication of such closure could be stipulated in the invitation to take part in the auction, where contracting entities clearly define the date and time of the closure in advance. Secondly, the auction can be closed when participants to the auction do not furnish any more new prices or new values which meet the requirements concerning minimum differences stipulated by the contracting authority in the invitation to participate in the auction. In such an event, the contracting entities must affirm in the invitation to take part in the auction the time which they will allow to elapse after receiving the last submission before they close the electronic auction. Thirdly, an electronic auction may be drawn to a close when the number of phases in the auction, which must be prescribed by contracting entities in the invitation to take part in the auction, has been completed. The closure of an auction as a result of the elapse of its predetermined phases must be based on a clear indication of the timetable for each phase of the auction which must also be stated in the invitation to take part in the auction. **6.210**

After closing an electronic auction, contracting entities must award the contract on the basis of the results of the electronic auction. Contracting entities may not have improper recourse to electronic auctions nor may they use them in such a way as to prevent, restrict or distort competition or to change the subject-matter of the contract, as put up for tender in the published contract notice and defined in the specification.[285] **6.211**

(c) Award criteria in electronic auctions

Contracting entities after the closure of an electronic auction must award the contract based on the following criteria:[286] **6.212**

— either solely on prices when the contract is awarded to the lowest price;
— or on prices or on the new values of the features of the tenders indicated in the specification when the contract is awarded to the most economically advantageous tender.

Contracting entities must stipulate in the invitation to participate in the electronic auctions the criteria they will apply to the award of the contract. When the contract is to be awarded on the basis of the most economically advantageous tender, the invitation to participate in an electronic auction must include the relative weighting of the criteria or factors that the contracting authority considers relevant for the evaluation process.[287] **6.213**

---

[284] *See* Art. 56(7) of the Utilities Directive.   [285] Art. 56(8) of the Utilities Directive.
[286] *See* the details specified in Art. 54(8) of the Utilities Directive.
[287] Art. 54(5) of the Utilities Directive.

(6) Design contests

6.214 Design contests are those procedures which enable the contracting authority to acquire a plan or design selected by a jury after being put out to competition with or without the award of prizes. The plan or design should be mainly in the disciplines of town and country planning, architecture and engineering, or data processing.[288]

(a) Scope and thresholds

6.215 Design contests could be arranged as part of a procurement procedure leading to the award of a service contract or as a competition with prizes or payments to participants.[289] The value of the service contract subject to a design contest should be €499,000 net of VAT, including any possible prizes or payments to participants. The total amount of the prizes and payments to the participants of a design contest, including the estimated value of the services contract which might be subsequently concluded,[290] should not exceed the stipulated threshold of €499,000.

6.216 Design contests excluded[291] from the Utilities Directive include contests for service contracts which are organized for service contracts awarded for purposes other than the pursuit of an activity covered by the Utilities Directive, or service contracts awarded for purposes for the pursuit of an activity covered by the Utilities Directive in a third country;[292] contests for service contracts which are secret or require special security measures;[293] and, finally, contests for service contracts awarded pursuant to international rules.[294] Design contests organized as part of a procurement process of an activity which is directly exposed to competition[295] are also excluded from the Utilities Directive.

(b) Conduct of design contests

6.217 Contracting entities which wish to carry out a design contest must make known their intention by means of a contest notice.[296] The notices relating to organization of design contests must contain the following information:[297]

1. Name, address, fax number, and email address of the contracting entity and those of the service from which the additional documents may be obtained.
2. Description of the project.

---

[288] *See* Art. 1(10) of the Utilities Directive.
[289] *See* Art. 61(1) and (2) of the Utilities Directive.
[290] *See* Art. 40(3) of the Utilities Directive.   [291] *See* Art. 62 of the Utilities Directive.
[292] *See* Art. 20 of the Utilities Directive.   [293] *See* Art. 21 of the Utilities Directive.
[294] *See* Art. 22 of the Utilities Directive.
[295] *See* Arts. 30(1) and 30(4), second and third indent, and 30(5), fourth indent, of the Utilities Directive.   [296] *See* Art. 63 of the Utilities Directive.
[297] *See* the format and template of information required in Annex XVIII of the Utilities Directive.

3. Type of contest: open or restricted.
4. In the event of an open contest: time limit for the submission of projects.
5. In the event of a restricted contest:
   (a) number of participants contemplated;
   (b) names of the participants already selected, if any;
   (c) criteria for the selection of participants;
   (d) time limit for requests to participate.
6. If appropriate, indicate that the participation is restricted to a specified profession.
7. Criteria which will be applied in the evaluation of the projects.
8. Names of any members of the jury who have already been selected.
9. Indicate whether the jury's decision is binding on the contracting entity.
10. Number and value of any prizes.
11. Payments to be made to all participants, if any.
12. Indicate whether any contracts following the contest will or will not be awarded to the winner or winners of the contest.

6.218 After the conclusion of the design contest, contracting entities must publish a notice of the results including the following information:[298] reference of the contest notice, description of the project, total number of participants, number of foreign participants, the winner(s) of the contest, and any prizes awarded to the winner. The notice of the results of a design contest must be forwarded to the Commission by contracting entities within two months of the closure of the design contest, pointing out any sensitive commercial aspects which may concern the number of projects or plans received, the identity of the economic operators, and the prices tendered.

6.219 The admission of participants to design contests must not be limited either by reference to the territory or part of the territory of a member state or on the grounds that, under the law of the member state in which the contest is organized, they would be required to be either natural or legal persons.[299] For the selection of competitors, where design contests are restricted to a limited number of particip-ants, contracting entities are obliged to lay down clear and non-discriminatory selection criteria. In any event, the number of candidates invited to participate must be sufficient to ensure genuine competition.[300]

(c) Composition of the jury

6.220 The jury in a design contest should be composed exclusively of natural persons who are independent of participants in the contest.[301] Where a particular

---

[298] *See* Art. 63(2) of the Utilities Directive and Annex XIX.
[299] Art. 60(2) of the Utilities Directive.   [300] Art. 65(2) of the Utilities Directive.
[301] Art. 65(3) of the Utilities Directive.

professional qualification is required from participants in a contest, at least a third of the members of the jury must have that qualification or an equivalent qualification.

(d) Decisions of the jury

6.221 The jury must be autonomous in its decisions or opinions. In its decision making process, it examines the plans and projects submitted by the candidates anonymously and solely on the basis of the criteria indicated in the contest notice.[302] It records its ranking of projects in a report, signed by its members, made according to the merits of each project, together with its remarks and any points which may need clarification. Anonymity must be observed until the jury has reached its opinion or decision. Candidates may be invited, if need be, to answer questions which the jury has recorded in the minutes to clarify any aspects of the projects. The organizer of a design contest must keep complete minutes of the dialogue between jury members and candidates.

(e) Communication between participants and the jury

6.222 Communications, exchanges, and the storage of information relevant to a design contest must ensure that the integrity and the confidentiality of all information communicated by the participants in a contest are preserved, and that the jury ascertains the contents of plans and projects only after the expiry of the time limit for their submission.[303] For the electronic receipt of plans and projects, the Directive stipulates that the information relating to the specifications which is necessary for the presentation of plans and projects by electronic means, including encryption, must be available to the parties concerned. Member states may introduce or maintain voluntary arrangements for accreditation intended to improve the level of the certification service provided for such devices.[304]

F. Monitoring Requirements

(1) Information to be stored concerning awards

6.223 Contracting entities must keep appropriate information on each contract which must be sufficient to permit them at a later date to justify decisions taken in connection with:

(a) the qualification and selection of economic operators and the award of contracts;

---

[302] *See* Art. 66 of the Utilities Directive.   [303] Art. 64(2) of the Utilities Directive.
[304] Art. 64(3) of the Utilities Directive.

(b) the use of procedures without a prior call for competition by virtue of Article 40(3);

(c) the non-application of Chapters III to VI of this Title by virtue of the derogations provided for in Chapter II of Title I and in Chapter II of this Title.

Contracting entities must record and document the progress of award procedures **6.224** conducted by electronic means. The information must be kept for at least four years from the date of award of the contract so that the contracting entity will be able, during that period, to provide the necessary information to the Commission.

(a) Statistical obligations

Member states must ensure, in accordance with the arrangements to be laid down **6.225** under the procedure provided for in Article 68(2), that the Commission receives every year a statistical report concerning the total value, broken down by member state and by category of activity to which Annexes I to X refer, of the contracts awarded below the thresholds set out in Article 16 but which would be covered by this Directive were it not for those thresholds.

As regards the categories of activity to which Annexes II, III, V, IX and X refer, **6.226** member states must ensure that the Commission receives a statistical report on contracts awarded no later than 31 October 2004 for the previous year, and before 31 October of each year thereafter, in accordance with arrangements to be laid down under the procedure provided for in Article 68(2). The statistical report must contain the information required to verify the proper application of the Agreement.

The information required under the first subparagraph must not include **6.227** information concerning contracts for the research and development services listed in category 8 of Annex XVII A, for telecommunications services listed in category 5 of Annex XVII A whose CPV positions are equivalent to the CPC reference numbers 7524, 7525, and 7526, or for the services listed in Annex XVII B.

The arrangements under paragraphs 1 and 2 must be laid down in such a way as **6.228** to ensure that: (a) in the interests of administrative simplification, contracts of lesser value may be excluded, provided that the usefulness of the statistics is not jeopardized; and (b) the confidential nature of the information provided is respected.

(b) Monitoring mechanisms

In conformity with Council Directive 92/13 coordinating the laws, regulations **6.229** and administrative provisions relating to the application of Community rules on the procurement procedures of entities operating in the water, energy, transport and telecommunications sectors, member states must ensure implementation of this Directive by effective, available, and transparent mechanisms. For this purpose they may, among other things, appoint or establish an independent body.

Part III

PUBLIC PROCUREMENT AND THE EUROPEAN COURT OF JUSTICE

7

PUBLIC CONTRACTS AND CONTRACTING AUTHORITIES

Introductory Remarks: Public Procurement from
the Court's Perspective

7.01 The European Court of Justice has been instrumental in interpreting the public procurement legal framework. The Court has provided intellectual assistance to the efforts of European institutions in order to strengthen the three principles (non-discrimination, objectivity, and transparency) underlying the regulation of public procurement,[1] to eliminate discrimination and non-tariff barriers in the fields of technical standards (product specification and standardization) and the selection procedures (quantitative and qualitative suitability criteria). The jurisprudence of the Court also reflects on a strategic goal of the European judiciary: to vest the regime wherever possible with direct effect. Arming the public procurement rules with direct effect will enhance access to justice at national level, improve compliance, increase the quality of the regulatory regime, and, finally, streamline the public procurement process across the common market by introducing an element of uniformity. By conferring direct effect upon the Public Procurement Directives and inviting national courts to play a prominent role in future public procurement litigation, the Court has hinted towards its preference for a decentralized enforcement of the public procurement regime. However, the most important lesson law and policy makers have learnt from the Court's jurisprudence reflects on a *rule of reason approach* which propels public procurement regulation as an instrument of policy making at national and European levels.

A. Public Contracts

(1) The notion of public service concessions

7.02 The notion of a concession is based on the fact that no remuneration is paid by the granting entity to the concessionaire. The latter must, therefore, simply be given the right to economically exploit the concession, although this right may be accompanied by a requirement to pay some consideration to the grantor. The main distinctive feature of a concession includes three essential characteristics. First, the beneficiary of the service provided must be third parties rather than the awarding entity itself. Second, the subject of the service ceded must concern a

---

[1] *See* the recital of Directive 89/440, [1989] OJ L210/1, amending the original Works Directive 71/305 concerning co-ordination of procedures for the award of public works contracts, stating that '. . . it is necessary to improve and extend the safeguards in the directives that are designed to introduce transparency into the procedures and practices for the award of such contracts, in order to be able to monitor compliance with the prohibition of restrictions more closely and at the same time to reduce disparities in the competitive conditions faced by nationals of different member states'.

matter which is in the public interest. Finally, the concessionaire must assume the economic risk related to the performance of the service at issue.[2]

The Community legislature has viewed the absence of, at least full, consideration **7.03** passing from the granting entity to the concessionaire as constituting the essence of a concession. The Public Works Directive 93/37 defines a public works concession as a contract of the same type as public works contracts, except for the fact that consideration for the works to be carried out consists either solely in the right to exploit the construction or in this right together with payment.[3] The above characteristic represents a fundamental feature of a concession whose importance is not limited to those which are concerned with public works. This feature finds expression in the fact that the concessionaire itself must bear the principal, or at least the substantive, economic risk attaching to the performance of the service involved. If the national court is satisfied that the economic burden or risk has effectively been passed to the concessionaire by the grantor of the concession, then there must be a very strong presumption that the arrangement concluded between them amounts to a concession rather than a contract.

The single most important indication of whether economic risk is to be borne by **7.04** the concessionaire will emerge from examining the nature of the exploitation in which the supposed concession requires it to engage. *Arnhem and Rheden* provides a strong indication that the Court views the requirement to exploit the right ceded in order to obtain remuneration as the core of what constitutes a genuine concession.[4] Thus, where, for example, the public authorities effectively guarantee to indemnify the concessionaire against future losses, or where there is no effective exploitation by the concessionaire of the service whose performance is ceded, the arrangement at issue could not amount to a concession.[5]

However, there is no overriding definition of a public services concession. What **7.05** *Lottomatica* and *Arnhem and Rheden* reveal is that, where the remuneration is fixed or determinable, the arrangement should be viewed as contractual and falling, *prima facie*, within the scope of the relevant Procurement Directive. In *Lottomatica*, the Italian State had published a contract notice for the purported concession of the computerization of the Italian Lotto and maintained that, as a concession to carry out a public service, it was not covered by the Public Supplies

---

[2] *See* Case C-324/98 *Telaustria Verlags GmbH and Telefonadress GmbH v. Post & Telekom Austria AG*, judgment of 18 May 2000.

[3] *See* Art. 1(d) of the Public Works Directive 93/37 and the fifth recital in the preamble to that Directive.

[4] *See* Case C-360/96, *Arnhem and Rheden* [1998] ECR I-6821 paragraph 25. The Court implicitly agreed with the view of the Advocate General that an important feature of service concessions in the Community context is that the concessionaire automatically assumes the economic risk associated with the provision and management of the services that are the subject of the concession. *See* paragraph 26 of the Opinion provided by Advocate General La Pergola.

[5] *See* European Commission *Interpretative Communication of Community Law on Public Procurement Concessions* [2000] OJ C21/2, footnote 10.

Directive 77/62. The Court rejected this argument and held that the introduction of the computerized system in question does not involve any transfer of responsibilities to the concessionaire in respect of the various operations inherent in the lottery, and that it was common ground that the contract at issue related to the supply of an integrated computerized system including, in particular, the supply of certain foods to the administration. The fact that the system was to become the property of the administration at the end of the contractual relationship with the tenderer was irrelevant, because the price for the supply took the form of an annual payment in proportion to revenue.

7.06 It is, therefore, necessary in each case to look at a number of factors which will indicate whether in reality the arrangement amounts to a written contract for a pecuniary interest in respect of the provision of services. In the case of a concession, the beneficiary of the service must be a third party unconnected with the contractual relationship[6] and the concessionaire effectively must obtain at least a significant proportion of its remuneration not from the granting entity but from the exploitation of the service. Therefore, a case-by-case approach should be adopted to the question of whether a contract amounts to a concession or a service contract which takes account of all indicative factors, the most important of which is whether the supposed concession amounts to a conferral of a right to exploit a particular service as well as the simultaneous transfer of a significant proportion of the risk associated with that transfer to the concessionaire. The likelihood that the concessionaire will be able beneficially to exploit the concession would not suffice to permit a national court or tribunal to conclude that there is no economic risk. A national court or tribunal would need to be satisfied to a high degree of probability that the possibility of loss was minimal or even non-existent.

7.07 However, the requirement that the service ceded must be of public interest is more complicated. Under Community law, the service that is the subject of a service concession must also be in the general interest, so that a public authority is institutionally responsible for providing it. The fact that a third party provides the service means that the concessionaire replaces the authority granting the concession in respect of its obligations to ensure that the service is provided for the community.[7] Nevertheless, *Data-processing* held that the development of the data-processing systems for the performance of certain public activities, as well as the supply of such systems, was not in itself a public service activity, although they enabled the authorities to outsource their duties.[8]

7.08 It appears that the supposed relevance of the general interest nature of the service that is the subject of the concession derives from the definition proposed by the

---

[6] *See* Case C-360/96, *Arnhem and Rheden* [1998] ECR I-6821, paragraph 26.
[7] *See* Case C-360/96, *Arnhem and Rheden* [1998] ECR I-6821 paragraph 26 to 28.
[8] *See* Case C-3/88, *Commission v Italy (Data Processing)* [1989] ECR 4035, paragraph 26.

Commission in both its initial and amended proposals for a procurement Directive concerning public service contracts, where it referred, at Article 1(h) in both cases, to the transfer by an awarding authority of the execution of a service to the public lying within its responsibility.[9] Although it is likely that there will be a public interest in most of the services that are awarded under a public service concession arrangement between a contracting authority and a private or a public undertaking, the Court held that the notion of a service to the public under a public service concession arrangement should not be construed as the same with the notion of general interest[10] or as a service of general economic interest in the sense in which that notion has been interpreted for the purposes of applying Article 90 of the EC Treaty (now Article 86 EC).[11] It should rather refer to the fact that the typical intended beneficiaries of a genuine public service concession will be third-party members of the general public or a particular category of that general public.

(2) *The exclusion of public service concessions from the public procurement rules*

The legislative history of the Public Services Directive 92/50, as well as from **7.09** consideration of the overall scope of the all Public Procurement Directives, reveals that the Council did not wish to include concessions within the material scope of the Community instruments on public procurement. The Council rejected the Commission's proposal to include concessions within the scope of the Public Services Directive 92/50.[12] The initial rationale given by the Commission for their inclusion focused on a coherent regime between the public works and public services regimes so public service concessions should be covered equally by the Public Services Directive in the same way as public works concessions are regulated by the Public Works Directives. However, during the legislative process, the Council decided to eliminate all references to public service concession from the proposal.[13] The Commission also failed to include public service concessions in its

---

[9] *See* [1991] OJ C23/1 and [1991] OJ C250/4.

[10] *See* Case C-324/98, *Telaustria Verlags GmbH and Telefonadress GmbH v. Post & Telekom Austria AG*, judgment of 18 May 2000.

[11] *See* Case C-67/96 *Albany International v. Stichting Bedrijfspensioenfonds Textielindustrie* [1999] ECR I-4532, paragraphs 102 to 107.

[12] *See* Proposal for Council Directive relating to the coordination of procedures on the award of public service contracts, COM (90) 372 final [1991] OJ C23/1. Special rules dealing with the situation where a concessionaire is a contracting authority were set out in Article 3 of the Proposal. *See* also the amended proposal for Council Directive relating to the coordination of procedures on the award of public service contracts, COM (91) 322 final [1991] OJ C250/4.

[13] *See* Document No. 4444-92-ADD-1 of 25 February 1992. The Council felt that the differences between the various national laws on such concessions were too great so that the impact of adopting the proposal would not be the same in all member states. That opposition appears to have been motivated by the fact that in some member states concessions were only granted by public or administrative acts which would therefore have fallen outside the Commission's proposed definition

proposal for the initial Utilities Directive 90/531, as well as the consolidated Utilities Directive 93/38.[14] The Council rejected such inclusion on the grounds that public service concessions in the water, gas and electricity sectors were not uniformly regulated in the member states.[15]

7.10   The Court has also explicitly recognized that public service concessions were not regulated by the Utilities Directives.[16] It also maintained that a literal interpretation of the notion of public service concessions would not permit written agreements, where the consideration is obtainable whether wholly by exploitation or partly by both exploitation and payment from the awarding entity, to fall within the scope of Public Procurement Directives. Even if the legislative history of public service concessions were to be overlooked, a contextual construction of the notion of *contracts for pecuniary interest concluded in writing*, which would be necessary to trigger the applicability of the Public Procurement Directives, would exclude concessions.[17]

7.11   However, public service concessions should not be viewed as falling outside the scope of European Union Law, although they are excluded from the public procurement rules. Even if public service concessions fall outside the scope of the Public Procurement Directives, the awarding authorities are bound to respect the Treaty and, in particular, Articles 52 and 59 of the EC Treaty (now, after amendment, Articles 43 EC and 49 EC) which preclude all direct and indirect discrimination based on nationality. In other words, contracting authorities must respect the principle of equal treatment between tenderers. They must also ensure that no conditions are imposed on the tenderer that would amount to an infringement of Article 30 of the EC Treaty (now, after amendment, Article 28 EC) on the principle of free movement of goods. Entities awarding public service concessions are also under a more general obligation, which it appears derive from the objectives underlying Articles 30, 52 and 59 of the EC Treaty, to ensure the transparency of the award procedures.[18] *Unitrans Scandinavia* concerned the obligations affecting a body other than a contracting authority, but upon which special or exclusive rights to engage in a public service activity have been granted by such an authority,

---

which was based on concessions being granted pursuant to consensual contracts governed by private law. This was recognized by the Commission itself in its communication to the European Parliament concerning the common position; *see* SEC (2) 406 final of 5 March 1992.

[14]   *See* Proposal for a Council Directive amending Directive 90/531/EEC on the procurement procedures of entities operating in the water, energy, transport and telecommunications sectors, COM (91) 347 final [1991] OJ C337/1.

[15]   *See* point 10 of Council Document No. 5250/90 of 22 March 1990, MAP 7, PRO-COOP 28.

[16]   *See* Case C-360/96, *Arnhem and Rheden* [1998] ECR I-6821, paragraph 26.

[17]   *See* Case C-324/98, *Telaustria Verlags GmbH and Telefonadress GmbH v. Post & Telekom Austria AG*, judgment of 18 May 2000.

[18]   *See* Case C-275/98, *Unitrans Scandinavia and Others v. Ministeriet for Fødevarer, Landbrug og Fiskeri* [1999] ECR I-564, paragraph 42.

when that body awards public supply contracts to third parties. The Court held that the principle of non-discrimination on grounds of nationality cannot be interpreted restrictively, and that principle implies, in particular, an obligation of transparency in order to enable the contracting authority to satisfy itself that it has been complied with.

The Court also considered that substantive compliance with the principle of non- **7.12** discrimination on grounds of nationality requires that the award of concessions respect a minimum degree of publicity and transparency. However, the publicity and transparency requirements for the award of public service concessions should not necessarily be equated with publication.[19] Thus, if the awarding entity addresses itself directly to a number of potential tenderers, and assuming the latter are not all or nearly all undertakings having the same nationality as that entity, the requirement of transparency would be respected. Transparency, in this context, is therefore concerned with ensuring the fundamental fairness and openness of the award procedures, particularly as regards potential tenderers who are not established in the member state of the awarding authority. It does not however require the awarding entity to apply by analogy the provisions of the most relevant of the Public Procurement Directives.

(3) Vertical procurement

A functional approach to the concept of contracting authority under the Public **7.13** Procurement Directives[20] might imply that the public procurement rules do not apply to a contracting authority which is a prospective supplier to another contracting authority. If a contracting authority, while trading as a supplier, subcontracts certain services to a third party, the selection of that subcontractor may well be based on non-economic considerations, and it is also quite possible that, at some stage in the process, public funds will be used.[21] The fact that the matter of the subcontracting does not fall within the remits of the activities of the contracting authority[22] and might be also subject to competition[23] is immaterial.

Mannesmann Anlagenbau Austria[24] made no distinction between public contracts **7.14** awarded by a contracting authority for the purposes of fulfilling its task of meeting

---

[19] *See* Case C-324/98, *Telaustria Verlags GmbH and Telefonadress GmbH v. Post & Telekom Austria AG*, judgment of 18 May 2000.

[20] *See* Case C-31/87 *Beentjes* [1988] ECR 4635, paragraph 11; and Case C-360/96 *BFI Holding* [1998] ECR I-6821, paragraph 62.

[21] *See* Case C-126/03, *Commission of the European Communities v. Federal Republic of Germany*, judgment of 18 November 2004 and the Opinion of Advocate General paragraph 28.

[22] *See* Cases C-107/98, *Teckal* [1999] ECR I-8121, and C-399/98, *Ordine degli Architetti and Others* [2001] ECR I-5409.

[23] *See* Case C-360/96, *BFI Holding*, and Joined Cases C-223/99 and C-260/99, *Agorà and Excelsior* [2001] ECR I-3605. [24] *See* Case C-44/96 [1998] ECR I-73.

needs in the general interest, and those which are unrelated to that task. It is imma-terial that the activity in question may be unrelated to the body's task in the general interest, or may not involve any public funds. Where, under the terms of the Public Procurement Directives, a body ranks as a contracting authority, the Directives require the conduct of award procedures. Accordingly, that rule applies even where the contracting authority itself is trading as a supplier on the market, and subcon-tracting certain parts of a contract to a third party. It is, after all, entirely possible that non-economic considerations might be involved in the selection of a subcontractor, just as it is possible that public funds might be used in the course of the operation.

7.15 Contracting authorities are free to set up legally independent entities if they wish to offer services to third parties under normal market conditions. If such entities aim to make profit, bear the losses related to the exercise of their activities, and perform no public tasks, they are not to be classified as public bodies and hence not as contracting authorities for the purposes of the Public Procurement Directives. Their activities will therefore not be subject to the provisions of the Public Procurement Directives. A body which aims to make a profit and bears the losses associated with the exercise of its activity will not normally become involved in an award procedure on conditions which are not economically justified.[25]

7.16 It could be argued that the Public Procurement Directives do not require 'tenders within tenders'. Article 7 of the Utilities Directive 93/38 excludes contracts awarded for the purposes of resale or hire to third parties from the scope of that Directive by virtue of the fact that the purchase of the goods occurs in principle in a context of free competition, and the ensuing commercial discipline prevents a contracting authority from favouring particular tenderers on non-economic grounds. However, this provision cannot be applied by analogy to supplies, works, or services public procurement contracts, as the relevant provisions stipulated in the Public Supplies, Works and, Services Directives respectively establish a divid-ing line between their regimes and the regime of the Utilities Directive[26] and do not extend the possibility of vertical procurement to contracting authorities in the public sector.[27]

(4) Subcontracting

7.17 A provision in an invitation to tender which prohibits recourse to subcontracting for material parts of the contract is contrary to the Public Procurement

---

[25] *See* Case C-18/01, *Korhonen and Others* [2003] ECR I-5321, paragraph 51.

[26] *See* Art. 1(a)(ii) of the Public Services Directive 92/50 and the equivalent Articles in Council Directive 93/36 coordinating procedures for the award of public supply contracts [1993] OJ L199/1, and Directive 93/37 coordinating procedures for the award of public works contracts [1993] OJ L199/54.

[27] *See* Case C-126/03, *Commission of the European Communities v. Federal Republic of Germany*, judgment of 18 November 2004.

Directives.[28] On the contrary, all Directives envisage the possibility for a tenderer to subcontract a part of the contract to third parties, as that provision states that the contracting authority may ask that tenderer to indicate in its tender any share of the contract which it may intend to subcontract.[29] Furthermore, with regard to the qualitative selection criteria, all Public Procurement Directives make express provision for the possibility of providing evidence of the technical capacity of the service provider by means of an indication of the technicians or technical bodies involved, whether or not belonging directly to the undertaking of that service provider, and which the latter will have available to it, or by indicating the proportion of the contract which the service provider may intend to subcontract.

The Court ruled[30] that a tenderer cannot be eliminated from a procedure for the **7.18** award of a public service contract solely on the ground that the tenderer proposes, in order to carry out the contract, to use resources which are not its own but belong to one or more other entities. This means that it is permissible for a service provider which does not itself fulfil the minimum conditions required for participation in the procedure for the award of a public service contract to rely, vis-à-vis the contracting authority, on the standing of third parties upon whose resources it proposes to draw if it is awarded the contract. However, according to the Court, the onus rests on a service provider which relies on the resources of entities or undertakings with which it is directly or indirectly linked, with a view to being admitted to participate in a tendering procedure, to establish that it actually has available to it the resources of those entities or undertakings which it does not itself own and which are necessary for the performance of the contract.[31]

Nevertheless, the Public Procurement Directives do not preclude a prohibition or **7.19** a restriction on the use of subcontracting for the performance of essential parts of the contract precisely in the case where the contracting authority has not been in a position to verify the technical and economic capacities of the subcontractors when examining the tenders.[32]

(5) Procurement and state aids

Preference schemes have been indissolubly linked with regional development **7.20** policies, but their interpretation by the Court has always been restrictive.[33]

---

[28] *See* Case C-176/98, *Holst Italia* [1999] ECR-I-8607.

[29] *See* Case C-314/01, *Siemens AG Österreich, ARGE Telekom & Partner and Hauptverband der österreichischen Sozialversicherungsträger*, judgment of 18 March 2004.

[30] *See* Case C-176/98, *Holst Italia*, [1999] ECR-I-8607, paragraphs 26 and 27.

[31] *See* Case C-176/98, *Holst Italia*, [1999] ECR-I-8607, paragraph 29.

[32] *See* Case C-314/01, *Siemens AG Österreich, ARGE Telekom & Partner and Hauptverband der österreichischen Sozialversicherungsträger*, judgment of 18 March 2004.

[33] *See* Case 84/86, *Commission v. Hellenic Republic*, not reported; Case C-21/88, *Dupont de Nemours Italiana SpA v. Unita Sanitaria Locale No.2 di Carrara*, judgment of 20 March 1990,

It appears that the Court has experimented with the question of the compatibility between state aids and free movement of goods in a number of cases where, initially, it was held that the two regimes are mutually exclusive, to the extent that the principle of free movement of goods could not apply to measures relating to state aids.[34] The acid test for such mutual exclusivity was the prior notification of such measures to the European Commission. However, the Court departed from such a position, when it applied free movement of goods provisions to a number of cases concerning state aids, which had not been notified to the Commission.[35] Surprisingly, the Court also brought notified state aids measures under the remit of the provision of free movement of goods and reconsidered the whole framework of the mutual exclusivity of states aids and free movement of goods.[36]

(6) Procurement and services of general interest

7.21　State aids jurisprudence has revealed the catalytic position of public procurement in the process of determining whether subsidies or state financing of public services represent state aids. Public procurement rules have served as a yardstick to determine the nature of an undertaking in its contractual interface when delivering public services.

7.22　The application of the state aid approach creates a *lex and policy lacuna* in the treatment of funding of services of general economic interest and normal services. In fact, it presupposes that the services of general economic interest emerge in a different market, where the state and its emanations act in a public function. Such markets are not susceptible to the private operator principle,[37] which has been relied upon by the Commission and the European Courts[38] to determine the

---

[1990] ECR 889; Case C-351/88, *Laboratori Bruneau Slr v. Unita Sanitaria Locale RM/24 di Monterotondo*, judgment of 11 July 1991; Case C-360/89, *Commission v. Italy* [1992] ECR I-3401; Case C- 362/90, *Commission v. Italy*, judgment of 31 March 1992.

[34] *See* Case C-74/76, *Ianelli & Volpi Spa v. Ditta Paola Meroni* [1977] 2 CMLR 688.

[35] *See* Case C-18/84, *Commission v. France* [1985] ECR 1339; Case 103/84, *Commission v. Italy* [1986] ECR 1759; also Case C-244/81, *Commission v. Ireland* [1982] ECR 4005.

[36] *See* Bovis, 'Public Procurement as an Instrument of Industrial Policy in the European Union', in T. Lawton (ed.), *Industrial Policy and Competitiveness in Europe* (MacMillan Publishers, 1998), Chapter 7; Fernadez-Martin and Stehmann, *Product Market Integration versus Regional Cohesion in the Community*, op. cit.

[37] *See* 'Communication of the Commission to the Member States Concerning Public Authorities' Holdings in Company Capital', *Bulletin EC*, 9-1984, point 3.5.1. The Commission considers that such an investment is not aid where the public authorities effect it under the same conditions as a private investor operating under normal market economy conditions. *See also* Commission Communication to the member states on the application of Articles 92 and 93 of the EEC Treaty and of Article 5 of Commission Directive 80/723/EEC to public undertakings in the manufacturing sector [1993] OJ C307/3, point 11.

[38] *See* in particular Case 234/84, *Belgium v. Commission* [1986] ECR 2263, paragraph 14; Case C-142/87, *Belgium v. Commission* ('*Tubemeuse*') [1990] ECR I-959, paragraph 26; and Case C-305/89, *Italy v. Commission* ('*Alfa Romeo*') [1991] ECR I-1603, paragraph 19.

borderline between market behaviour and state intervention. European jurisprudence distinguishes the economic nature of state intervention and the exercise of
public powers. The application of the private operator principle is confined to the
economic nature of state intervention[39] and is justified by the principle of equal
treatment between the public and private sectors.[40] Such treatment requires that
intervention by the state should not be subject to stricter rules than those applicable to private undertakings. The non-economic character of state intervention[41]
renders immaterial the test of private operator, for the reason that profitability,
and thus the *raison d'être* of the private investment, is not present. It follows that
services of general economic interest cannot be part of the same demand and
supply equation, as other normal services the state and its organs procure.[42] Along
the above lines, a convergence emerges between public procurement jurisprudence and the state aid approach in the light of the reasoning behind the *BFI*[43]
and *Agora*[44] cases. Services of general economic interest are *sui generis*, having as
main characteristics the lack of industrial and commercial character, where the
absence of profitability and competitiveness are indicative of the relevant market
place. As a rule, the procurement of such services should be subject to the rigour
and discipline of public procurement rules and in analogous ratione, classified as
state aid, in the absence of the competitive award procedures. In consequence, the
application of the public procurement regime reinforces the character of services
of general interest as non-commercial or industrial and the existence of public
markets.[45]

---

[39] For example, where the public authorities contribute capital to an undertaking (Case 234/84,
Belgium v. Commission [1986] ECR 2263; Case C-142/87, *Belgium v. Commission* [1990] ECR
I-959; Case C-305/89, *Italy v. Commission* [1991] ECR I-1603), grant a loan to certain undertakings
(Case C-301/87, *France v. Commission* [1990] ECR I-307; Case T-16/96, *Cityflyer Express v.
Commission* [1998] ECR II-757), provide a state guarantee (Joined Cases T-204/97 and T-270/97,
EPAC v. Commission [2000] ECR II-2267), sell goods or services on the market (Joined Cases 67/85,
68/85 and 70/85 *Van der Kooy and Others v. Commission* [1988] ECR 219; Case C-56/93 *Belgium v.
Commission* [1996] ECR I-723; Case C-39/94, *SFEI and Others* [1996] ECR I-3547), or grant facil-
ities for the payment of social security contributions (Case C-256/97, *DM Transport* [1999] ECR
I-3913), or the repayment of wages (Case C-342/96, *Spain v. Commission* [1999] ECR I-2459).
[40] *See* Case C-303/88, *Italy v. Commission* [1991] ECR I-1433, paragraph 20; Case C-261/89,
Italy v. Commission [1991] ECR I-4437, paragraph 15; and Case T-358/94, *Air France v Commission*
[1996] ECR II-2109, paragraph 70.
[41] For example where the public authorities pay a subsidy directly to an undertaking (Case
310/85, *Deufil v. Commission* [1987] ECR 901), grant an exemption from tax (Case C-387/92,
Banco Exterior [1994] ECR I-877; Case C-6/97, *Italy v. Commission* [1999] ECR I-2981; Case
C-156/98, *Germany v. Commission* [2000] ECR I-6857) or agree to a reduction in social
security contributions (Case C-75/97, *Belgium v. Commission* [1999] ECR I-3671; Case T-67/94,
Ladbroke Racing v. Commission [1998] ECR II-1)
[42] *See* the analysis in the Joined Cases C-278/92 to C-280/92, *Spain v. Commission* [1994] ECR
I-4103.   [43] *See* Case C-360/96, *Gemeente Arnhem Gemeente Rheden v. BFI Holding BV*, op. cit.
[44] Cases C-223/99, *Agora Srl v. Ente Autonomo Fiera Internazionale di Milano* and C-260/99,
Excelsior Snc di Pedrotti Runa & C v. Ente Autonomo Fiera Internazionale di Milano, op. cit.
[45] *See* Bazex, *Le droit public de la concurrence*, (RFDA, 1998); Arcelin, *L'Enterprise en Droit Interne
et Communautaire de la Concurrence*, (Paris: Litec, 2003); Guézou, 'Droit de la Concurrence et Droit

7.23   The compensation approach relies heavily upon the real advantage theory to determine the existence of any advantages conferred to undertakings through state financing. Thus, the advantages given by the public authorities and threat to distort competition are examined together with the obligations on the recipient of the aid. Public advantages thus constitute aid only if their amount exceeds the value of the commitments the recipient enters into. The compensation approach treats the costs offsetting the provision of services of general interest as the base line over which state aids should be considered. That base line is determined by the market price, which corresponds to the given public/private contractual interface and is demonstrable through the application of public procurement award procedures. The real advantage theory runs contrary to the apparent advantage theory which underlines Treaty provisions[46] and the approach that relies on the economic effects and the nature of the measures in determining the existence of state aids. The borderline of the market price, which will form the conceptual base above which state aids would appear, is not always easy to determine, even with the presence of public procurement procedures. The state and its organs as contracting authorities (state emanations and bodies governed by public law) have wide discretion to award public contracts under the public procurement rules.[47] Often, price plays a secondary role in the award criteria. In cases when the public contract is awarded to the lowest price, the element of *market price* under the

---

des Marchés Publics: Vers une Notion Transverale de Mise en Libre Concurrence', *Contrats Publics*, Mars 2003.

[46]   According to Advocate General Léger in his Opinion on the *Altmark* case, the apparent advantage theory occurs in several provisions of the Treaty, in particular in Article 92(2) and (3), and in Article 77 of the EC Treaty (now Article 73 EC). Article 92(3) of the Treaty provides that aid may be regarded as compatible with the common market if it pursues certain objectives such as the strengthening of economic and social cohesion, the promotion of research and the protection of the environment.

[47]   According to Article 26 of Directive 93/36, Article 30 of Directive 93/37, Article 34 of Directive 93/38 and Article 36 of Directive 92/50, two criteria provide the conditions under which contracting authorities award public contracts: *the lowest price* or the *most economically advantageous offer*. The first criterion indicates that, subject to the qualitative criteria and financial and economic standing, contracting authorities do not rely on any other factor than the price quoted to complete the contract. The Directives provide for an automatic disqualification of an 'obviously abnormally low offer'. The term has not been interpreted in detail by the Court and serves rather as an indication of a 'lower bottom limit' of contracting authorities accepting offers from the private sector tenderers. *See* Case 76/81, *SA Transporoute et Travaux v. Minister of Public Works*, [1982] ECR 457; Case 103/88, *Fratelli Costanzo SpA v. Comune di Milano* [1989] ECR 1839; Case 296/89, *Impresa Dona Alfonso di Dona Alfonso & Figli snc v. Consorzio per lo Sviluppo Industriale del Comune di Monfalcone*, judgment of 18 June 1991. In Case C-94/99, *ARGE Gewässerschutzt* the Court ruled that directly or indirectly subsidised tenders by the state or other contracting authorities or even by the contracting authority itself can be legitimately part of the evaluation process, it did not elaborate on the possibility of rejection of an offer, which is appreciably lower than those of unsubsidised tenderers by reference to the of abnormally low disqualification ground. *See* paragraphs 26 *et seq.* of the Court's judgment. Although the case has relevance in the fields of selection and qualification procedures and award criteria, the Court made no references to previous case law regarding state aids in public procurement, presumably because the *Dupont de Nemours* precedence is still highly relevant.

compensation approach could be determined. However, when the public contract is to be awarded by reference to the most economically advantageous offer,[48] the market price might be totally different than the price the contracting authority wish to pay for the procurement of the relevant services. The mere existence of public procurement procedures cannot, therefore, reveal the necessary element of the compensation approach: the market price which will determine the 'excessive' state intervention and introduce state aids regulation.

An indication of the application of the compensation approach is reflected in the **7.24** *Stohal*[49] case, where an undertaking could provide commercial services and services of general interest, without any relevance to the applicability of the public procurement rules. The rationale of the case runs parallel with the real advantage theory, up to the point of recognizing the different nature and characteristics of the markets under which normal (commercial) services and services of general interest are provided. The distinction begins where, for the sake of legal certainty and legitimate expectation, the activities of undertakings of dual capacity are equally covered by the public procurement regime and the undertaking in question is considered as *contracting authority* irrespective of any proportion or percentage between the delivery of commercial services and services of general interest. This finding might have a significant implication for the compensation approach in state aids jurisprudence: irrespective of any costs offsetting the costs related to the provision of general interest, the entire state financing could be viewed under the state aid approach.

Finally, the *quid pro quo* approach relies on the existence of a direct and manifest **7.25** link between state financing and services of general interest, existence indicative through the presence of a public contract concluded in accordance with the provisions of the Public Procurement Directives. Apart from the obvious criticism the *quid pro quo* approach has received, its interface with public procurement appears as the most problematic facet in its application. The procurement of public services does not always reveal a public contract between a contracting authority and an undertaking.

(7) Needs in general interest

Although the Public Procurement Directives do not define the term 'needs' in the **7.26** general interest in a contract covered by their provisions, the term is an

---

[48] The meaning of 'the most economically advantageous offer' includes a series of factors chosen by the contracting authority, including price, delivery or completion date, running costs, cost-effectiveness, profitability, technical merit, product or work quality, aesthetic and functional characteristics, after-sales service and technical assistance, commitments with regard to spare parts and components and maintenance costs, and security of supplies. The above list is not exhaustive.

[49] C-44/96, *Mannesmann Anlangenbau Austria AG et al. v. Strohal Rotationsdurck GesmbH*, op. cit. *See also* the analysis of the case by Bovis, in [1999] 36 CMLR 205–225.

autonomous concept of Community law[50] and represents a notion which must be assessed independently without reference to the national legal systems of the member states. The Court declared that the term 'needs' in the general interest must be appraised objectively, without regard to the legal forms of the provisions in which those needs are mentioned.[51] Having regard to the principle of legal certainty, it would be unacceptable that the same activity may be regarded either as being in the general interest depending on the member state in which it is exercised. Terms of Community law must be interpreted by reference to national concepts only in those exceptional cases in which reference is expressly or implicitly made to definitions laid down by the legal systems of the member states.[52] The need for uniform application of Community law and the principle of equality require that the terms of a provision of Community law which makes no express reference to the law of the member states for the purpose of determining its meaning and scope must normally be given an autonomous and uniform interpretation throughout the Community. That interpretation must take into account the context of the provision and the purpose of the legislation in question.[53]

7.27　The Commission has taken the view that the term 'needs' in the general interest must be defined solely on the basis of national law. It is thus for each member state, when determining the aims of its public policy, to determine what constitutes general interest and, in each individual case, the legal and factual situation of the body concerned must be examined in order to assess whether or not there is a need in the general interest. For these purposes, the Commission relies on *Mannesmann Anlagenbau Austria*,[54] in which the Court based its finding that the Austrian state printing office was established for the purpose of meeting needs in the general interest, not having an industrial or commercial character, on the relevant national provisions and on *BFI Holding*, in which the Court ruled, on the basis of, in particular, the list set out in Annex I to Directive 93/37, that the removal and treatment of household refuse is one of the services which a member state may require to be carried out by public authorities or over which it wishes to retain a decisive influence.

7.28　The Court held that the absence of competition is not a condition which must necessarily be taken into account in defining a 'body governed by public law'.[55] The requirement that there should be no private undertakings capable of meeting the needs for which the body financed by the state, regional, or local authorities, or other

---

[51] *See* Case C-360/96, *Gemeente Arnhem Gemeente Rheden v. BFI Holding BV* [1998] ECR 6821.
[52] *See* Case C-327/82, *Ekro* [1984] ECR 107 and Case C-273/90, *Meico-Fell* [1991] ECR I-5569.
[53] *See* Case C-287/98, *Linster and Others* [2000] ECR I-6917, paragraph 43, and Case C-357/98, *Yiadom* [2000] ECR I-9265, paragraph 26.
[54] *See* Case C-44/96, *Mannesmann Anlangenbau Austria AG et al. v. Strohal Rotationsdurck GesmbH* [1998] ECR 73.　　　　[55] *See* C-360/96, *BFI Holding* paragraph 47.

bodies governed by public law, was set up would be liable to render meaningless the term 'body governed by public law'. However, the Court stated that the existence of competition is not entirely irrelevant to the question whether a need in the general interest is other than industrial or commercial. The existence of significant competition, and, in particular, the fact that the entity concerned is faced with competition in the marketplace, may be indicative of the absence of a need in the general interest not having an industrial or commercial character. The existence of significant competition is, in itself, not sufficient to justify the conclusion that there is no need in the general interest, not having an industrial or commercial character, The national court must assess whether or not there is such a need, taking account of all the relevant legal and factual circumstances, such as those prevailing at the time of establishment of the body concerned and the conditions under which it exercises its activity.

(8) Contracts financing public services

There are three approaches under which the European judiciary and the **7.29** Commission have examined the financing of public services: the *state aids* approach, the *compensation* approach, and the *quid pro quo* approach. The above approaches reflect not only conceptual and procedural differences in the application of state aid control measures within the common market, but also raise imperative and multi-faceted questions relevant to the state funding of services of general interest.

The state aids approach[56] examines state funding granted to an undertaking for **7.30** the performance of obligations of general interest amounts to State aid within the meaning of Article 87(1) EC[57] which may however be justified under Article 86(2) EC,[58] provided that the conditions of that derogation are fulfilled and, in particular, if the funding complies with the principle of proportionality. The state aids approach provides for the most clear and legally certain procedural and conceptual framework to regulate state aids, since it positions the European Commission in the centre of that framework.

The compensation approach[59] reflects upon a 'compensation' being intended to **7.31** cover an appropriate remuneration for the services provided or the costs of

---

[56] *See* Case C-387/92, [1994] ECR I-877; Case T-106/95, *FFSA and Others v Commission* [1997] ECR II-229; Case C-174/97 P, [1998] ECR I-1303; Case T-46/97, [2000] ECR II-2125.

[57] Art. 87(1) EC defines state aid as 'any aid granted by a Member state or through State resources in any form whatsoever which distorts or threatens to distort competition by favoring certain undertakings or the production of certain goods . . ., in so far as it affects trade between member states'.

[58] Art. 86(2) EC stipulates that 'Undertakings entrusted with the operation of services of general economic interest . . . shall be subject to the rules contained in this Treaty, in particular to the rules on competition, insofar as the application of such rules does not obstruct the performance, in law or in fact, of the particular tasks assigned to them. The development of trade must not be affected to such an extent as would be contrary to the interests of the Community'.

[59] *See* Case 240/83, [1985] ECR 531; Case C-53/00, judgment of 22 November 2001; Case C-280/00, judgment of 24 July 2003.

providing those services. Under that approach state funding of services of general interest amounts to state aid within the meaning of Article 87(1) EC, only if, and to the extent that, the economic advantage which it provides exceeds such an appropriate remuneration or such additional costs. European jurisprudence considers that state aids exist only if, and to the extent that, the remuneration paid, when the state and its organs procure goods or services, exceeds the market price.

7.32 The *quid pro quo* approach distinguishes between two categories of state funding; in cases where there is a direct and manifest link between the state financing and clearly-defined public service obligations, any sums paid by the state would not constitute state aid within the meaning of the Treaty. On the other hand, where there is no such link or the public service obligations were not clearly defined, the sums paid by the public authorities would constitute state aids.

(a) The state aid approach and public procurement

7.33 The application of the state aid approach creates a *lex and policy lacuna* in the treatment of funding of services of general economic interest and other services, which is filled by the application of the public procurement regime. In fact, it presupposes that the delivery of services of general economic interest emerge and take place in a different market, where the state and its emanations act in a public function. Such markets are not susceptible to the private operator principle[60] which has been relied upon by the Commission and the European Courts[61] to determine the borderline between market behaviour and state intervention. The state aids approach runs parallel with the assumption that services of general interest emerge and their delivery takes place within distinctive markets, which bear little resemblance with private markets in terms of competitiveness, demand and supply substitutability, structure, and even regulation.

7.34 European jurisprudence distinguishes the economic nature of state intervention and the exercise of public powers.[62] The application of the private operator principle is confined to the economic nature of state intervention[63] and is justified

---

[60] *See* the 'Communication of the Commission to the Member States concerning Public Authorities' Holdings in Company Capital', *Bulletin EC*, 9-1984, point 3.5.1. The Commission considers that such an investment is not aid where the public authorities effect it under the same conditions as a private investor operating under normal market economy conditions. *See also* Commission Communication to the member states on the application of Articles 92 and 93 of the EEC Treaty and of Article 5 of Commission Directive 80/723/EEC to public undertakings in the manufacturing sector [1993] OJ C307/3, point 11.

[61] *See* in particular Case 234/84, *Belgium v. Commission* [1986] ECR 2263, paragraph 14; Case C-142/87, *Belgium v. Commission* ('*Tubemeuse*') [1990] ECR I-959, paragraph 26; and Case C-305/89, *Italy v. Commission* ('*Alfa Romeo*') [1991] ECR I-1603, paragraph 19.

[62] *See* Joined Cases C-278/92 to C-280/92, *Spain v. Commission* [1994] ECR I-4103.

[63] For example where the public authorities contribute capital to an undertaking (Case 234/84, *Belgium v. Commission* [1986] ECR 2263; Case C-142/87, *Belgium v. Commission* [1990] ECR I-959; Case C-305/89, *Italy v. Commission* [1991] ECR I-1603), grant a loan to certain undertakings

by the principle of equal treatment between the public and private sectors.[64] That principle requires that intervention by the state should not be subject to stricter rules than those applicable to private undertakings. The non-economic character of state intervention[65] renders immaterial the test of private operator, for the reason that profitability, and thus the *raison d'être* of the private investment, is not present.

It follows that services of general economic interest cannot be part of the same **7.35** demand/supply equation, as are other normal services the state and its organs procure.[66] Along the above lines, a convergence emerges between public procurement jurisprudence and the state aid approach in the light of the reasoning behind the *BFI*[67] and *Agora*[68] cases. Services of general economic interest are *sui generis*, having as main characteristics the lack of industrial and commercial character, where the absence of profitability and competitiveness are indicative of the relevant market place. As a rule, the procurement of such services should be subject to the rigor and discipline of public procurement rules and in analogous ratione, classified as state aid, in the absence of the competitive award procedures. In consequence, the application of the public procurement regime reinforces the character of services of general interest as non-commercial or industrial and the existence of *marches publics*.[69]

Of interest is the latest case, *Chronopost*,[70] where the establishment and maintenance **7.36** of a public postal network such as the one offered by the French *La Poste* to its

---

(Case C-301/87, *France v. Commission* [1990] ECR I-307; Case T-16/96, *Cityflyer Express v. Commission* [1998] ECR II-757), provide a state guarantee (Joined Cases T-204/97 and T-270/97, *EPAC v. Commission* [2000] ECR II-2267), sell goods or services on the market (Joined Cases 67/85, 68/85 and 70/85, *Van der Kooy and Others v. Commission* [1988] ECR 219; Case C-56/93, *Belgium v. Commission* [1996] ECR I-723; Case C-39/94, *SFEI and Others* [1996] ECR I-3547), or grant facilities for the payment of social security contributions (Case C-256/97, *DM Transport* [1999] ECR I-3913), or the repayment of wages (Case C-342/96 *Spain v. Commission* [1999] ECR I-2459).

[64] *See* Case C-303/88, *Italy v. Commission* [1991] ECR I-1433, paragraph 20; Case C-261/89, *Italy v. Commission* [1991] ECR I-4437, paragraph 15; and Case T-358/94, *Air France v. Commission* [1996] ECR II-2109, paragraph 70.

[65] For example where the public authorities pay a subsidy directly to an undertaking (Case 310/85, *Deufil v. Commission* [1987] ECR 901), grant an exemption from tax (Case C-387/92, *Banco Exterior* [1994] ECR I-877; Case C-6/97, *Italy v. Commission* [1999] ECR I-2981; Case C-156/98, *Germany v. Commission* [2000] ECR I-6857) or agree to a reduction in social security contributions (Case C-75/97, *Belgium v. Commission* [1999] ECR I-3671; Case T-67/94, *Ladbroke Racing v. Commission* [1998] ECR II-1)

[66] *See* the analysis in the Joined Cases C-278/92 to C-280/92, *Spain v. Commission* [1994] ECR I-4103.

[67] *See* Case C-360/96, *Gemeente Arnhem Gemeente Rheden v. BFI Holding BV*, op. cit.

[68] Cases C-223/99, *Agora Srl v. Ente Autonomo Fiera Internazionale di Milano* and C-260/99, *Excelsior Snc di Pedrotti Runa & C v. Ente Autonomo Fiera Internazionale di Milano*, op. cit.

[69] *See* Bazex, op. cit. (n. 45); Arcelin, op. cit. (n. 45); op. cit. (n. 45).

[70] *See* Joined Cases C-83/01 P, C-93/01 P, and C-94/01, *Chronopost and Others* [2003] OJ C200/4; *see also* the earlier judgment of the CFI Case T-613/97, *Ufex and Others v. Commission* [2000] ECR II-4055.

subsidiary *Chronopost* was not considered as a 'market network'. The Court arrived at this reasoning by using a market analysis, which revealed that under normal conditions it would not have been rational to build up such a network with the considerable fixed costs necessary in order to provide third parties with the kind of assistance at issue in that case. Therefore, the determination of a platform under which the normal remuneration a private operator incurs would have constituted an entirely hypothetical exercise. As the universal network offered by *La Poste* was not a 'market network', there were no specific and objective references available in order to establish what normal market conditions should be. On the one hand, there was only one single undertaking, i.e. *La Poste*, that was capable of offering the services linked to its network, and none of the competitors of *Chronopost* had ever sought access to the French Post Office's network. Consequently, objective and verifiable data on the price paid within the framework of a comparable commercial transaction did not exist. The Commission's solution of accepting a price that covered all the additional costs, fixed and variable, specifically incurred by *La Poste* in order to provide the logistical and commercial assistance, and an adequate part of the fixed costs associated with maintaining the public postal network, represented a sound way in order to exclude the existence of state aid within the meaning of Article 87(1) EC. The *Chronopost* ruling approached the private investor principle from state aid regulation, by indirectly accepting the state aid approach and therefore the existence of sui generis markets within which services of general interest emerge and are delivered and which cannot feasibly be compared with private ones.

(b) The compensation approach and public procurement

7.37 The compensation approach relies heavily upon the real advantage theory to determine the existence of any advantages conferred to undertakings through state financing.[71] Thus, under the real advantage theory, the advantages given by the public authorities and threat to distort competition are examined together with the obligations on the recipient of the aid. Public advantages thus constitute aid only if their amount exceeds the value of the commitments the recipient enters into. The compensation approach treats the costs offsetting the provision of services of general interest as the base line over which state aids should be considered. That base line is determined by the market price, which corresponds to the given public/private contractual interface, and is demonstrable through the application of public procurement award procedures. The application of the compensation approach reveals a significant insight into the financing of services of general interest. A quantitative distinction emerges, over and above which state aids exist. The compensation approach introduces an applicability threshold of state aids regulation, and that threshold is the perceived market price, terms, and conditions for the delivery of the relevant services.

---

[71] *See* Evans, *European Community Law of State Aid* (Oxford: Clarendon Press, 1997).

An indication of the application of the compensation approach is reflected in the   **7.38**
Stohal [72] case, where an undertaking could provide commercial services and services
of general interest, without any relevance to the applicability of the public procurement rules. The rationale of the case runs parallel with the real advantage theory, up
to the point of recognizing the different nature and characteristics of the markets
under which normal (commercial) services and services of general interest are provided. The distinction begins where, for the sake of legal certainty and legitimate
expectation, the activities of undertakings of dual capacity are equally covered by the
public procurement regime and the undertaking in question is considered as the
contracting authority irrespective of any proportion or percentage between the
delivery of commercial services and services of general interest. This finding might
have a significant implication for the compensation approach in state aids jurisprudence: irrespective of any costs offsetting the costs related to the provision of general
interest, the entire state financing could be viewed under the state aid approach.

Nevertheless, the real advantage theory upon which the compensation approach   **7.39**
seems to rely runs contrary to the apparent advantage theory which underlines
Treaty provisions[73] and the so-called 'effects approach'[74] adopted by the Court in
determining the existence of state aids. The real advantage theory seems to underpin the *quid pro quo* approach and it also creates some conceptual difficulties in
reconciling jurisprudential precedent in state aids regulation.

(c) The *quid pro quo* approach and public procurement

The *quid pro quo* approach appears to define state aids no longer by reference   **7.40**
solely to the effects of the measure, but by reference to criteria of a purely formal
or procedural nature. This means that the existence of a procedural or a substantive link between the state and the service in question lifts the threat of state aids
regulation, irrespective of any effect the state measure has on competition.
However, the Court considers that, to determine whether a state measure constitutes aid, only the effects of the measure are to be taken into consideration,
whereas other elements[75] typifying a measure are not relevant during the stage of

---

[72] C-44/96, *Mannesmann Anlangenbau Austria AG et al. v. Strohal Rotationsdurck GesmbH*, op.
cit. *See also* the analysis of the case by Bovis, in [1999] 36 CMLR, 205–225.

[73] According to Advocate General Léger in his Opinion on the *Altmark* case, the apparent advantage
theory occurs in several provisions of the Treaty, in particular in Art. 92(2) and (3), and in Art. 77 of
the EC Treaty (now Art. 73 EC). Art. 92(3) of the Treaty provides that aid may be regarded as
compatible with the common market if it pursues certain objectives such as the strengthening of
economic and social cohesion, the promotion of research, and the protection of the environment.

[74] *See* Case C-173/73, *Italy v. Commission* [1974] ECR 709; *Deufil v. Commission*, [1987] ECR
901; Case C-56/93, *Belgium v. Commission* [1996] ECR I-723; Case C-241/94, *France v.
Commission* [1996] ECR I-4551; Case C-5/01, *Belgium v. Commission* [2002] ECR I-3452.

[75] For example, the form in which the aid is granted, the legal status of the measure in national
law, the fact that the measure is part of an aid scheme, the reasons for the measure, the objectives of
the measure and the intentions of the public authorities, and the recipient undertaking.

determining the existence of aid, because they are not liable to affect competition. However, the relevance of these elements may appear when an assessment of the compatibility of the aid[76] with the derogating provisions of the Treaty takes place.

7.41 The application of the *quid pro quo* approach amounts to introducing such elements into the actual definition of aid. The presence of a direct and manifest link between the state funding and the public service obligations amounts to the existence of a public service contract awarded after a public procurement procedure. In addition, the clear definition of public service obligations amounts to the existence of laws, regulations, or contractual provisions which specify the nature and content of the undertaking's obligations. The borderline of the market price, which will form the conceptual base above which state aids would appear, is not always easy to determine, even with the presence of public procurement procedures. The state and its organs as contracting authorities (state emanations and bodies governed by public law) have wide discretion to award public contracts under the public procurement rules.[77] Often, price plays a secondary role in the award criteria. In cases when the public contract is awarded to the lowest price,[78] the element of *market price* under the compensation approach could be determined. However, when the public contract is to be awarded by reference to the most economically advantageous offer,[79] the market price might be totally different than the price that the contracting authority wishes to pay for the

---

[76] For example, certain categories of aid are compatible with the common market on condition that they are employed through a specific format. *See* Commission Notice 97/C 238/02 on Community Guidelines on State Aid for Rescuing and Restructuring Firms in Difficulty [1997] OJ C283.

[77] According to Art. 26 of Directive 93/36, Art. 30 of Directive 93/37, Art. 34 of Directive 93/38 and Art. 36 of Directive 92/50, two criteria provide the conditions under which contracting authorities award public contracts: *the lowest price* or the *most economically advantageous offer*. The first criterion indicates that, subject to the qualitative criteria and financial and economic standing, contracting authorities do not rely on any other factor than the price quoted to complete the contract. The Directives provide for an automatic disqualification of an 'obviously abnormally low offer'. The term has not been interpreted in detail by the Court and serves rather as an indication of a 'lower bottom limit' of contracting authorities accepting offers from the private sector tenderers. *See* Case 76/81, *SA Transporoute et Travaux v. Minister of Public Works* [1982] ECR 457; Case 103/88, *Fratelli Costanzo SpA v. Comune di Milano* [1989] ECR 1839; Case 296/89, *Impresa Dona Alfonso di Dona Alfonso & Figli snc v. Consorzio per lo Sviluppo Industriale del Comune di Monfalcone*, judgment of 18 June 1991.

[78] An interesting view of the lowest price representing market value benchmarking is provided by Case C-94/99, *ARGE Gewässerschutzt*, op. cit, where the Court ruled that directly or indirectly subsidised tenders by the state or other contracting authorities or even by the contracting authority itself can be legitimately part of the evaluation process, although it did not elaborate on the possibility of rejection of an offer which is appreciably lower than those of unsubsidised tenderers by reference to the of abnormally low disqualification ground.

[79] The meaning of 'the most economically advantageous offer' includes a series of factors chosen by the contracting authority, including price, delivery or completion date, running costs, cost-effectiveness, profitability, technical merit, product or work quality, aesthetic and functional characteristics, after-sales service and technical assistance, commitments with regard to spare parts and components and maintenance costs, and security of supplies. The above list is not exhaustive.

procurement of the relevant services. The mere existence of public procurement procedures cannot, therefore, reveal the necessary element of the compensation approach: the market price which will determine the 'excessive' state intervention and introduce state aids regulation.

Finally, the *quid pro quo* approach relies on the existence of a direct and manifest **7.42** link between state financing and services of general interest, existence indicative through the presence of a public contract concluded in accordance with the provisions of the Public Procurement Directives. Apart from the criticism it has received concerning the introduction of elements into the assessment process of state aids, the interface of the *quid pro quo* approach with public procurement appears as the most problematic facet in its application. The procurement of public services does not always reveal a public contract between a contracting authority and an undertaking.

The *quid pro quo* approach appears to define state aids no longer by reference solely **7.43** to the effects of the measure, but by reference to criteria of a purely formal or pro-cedural nature. This means that the existence of a procedural or a substantive link between the state and the service in question lifts the threat of state aids regulation, irrespective of any effect the state measure has on competition. However, the Court considers that to determine whether a state measure constitutes aid, only the effects of the measure are to be taken into consideration, whereas other elements[80] typify-ing a measure are not relevant during the stage of determining the existence of aid, because they are not liable to affect competition. However, the relevance of these elements may appear when an assessment of the compatibility of the aid[81] with the derogating provisions of the Treaty takes place. The application of the *quid pro quo* approach amounts to introducing such elements into the actual definition of aid. Its first criterion suggests examining whether there is a direct and manifest link between the state funding and the public service obligations. In practice, this amounts to requiring the existence of a public service contract awarded after a pub-lic procurement procedure. Similarly, the second criterion suggests examining whether the public service obligations are clearly defined. In practice, this amounts to verifying that there are laws, regulations, or contractual provisions which specify the nature and content of the undertaking's obligations.

Although the public procurement regime embraces activities of the *state*, which **7.44** covers central, regional, municipal, and local government departments, as well as *bodies governed by public law*, and public utilities, in-house contracts are not

---

[80] For example, the form in which the aid is granted, the legal status of the measure in national law, the fact that the measure is part of an aid scheme, the reasons for the measure, the objectives of the measure, and the intentions of the public authorities and the recipient undertaking.

[81] For example, certain categories of aid are compatible with the common market on condition that they are employed through a specific format. *See* Commission Notice 97/C 238/02 on Community Guidelines on State Aid for Rescuing and Restructuring Firms in Difficulty [1997] OJ C283.

subject to its coverage. The existence of dependency, in terms of overall control of an entity by the state or another contracting authority, renders the public procurement regime inapplicable. Dependency presupposes a control similar to that which the state of another contracting authority exercises over its own departments. The 'similarity' of control denotes lack of independence with regard to decision-making. The Court in *Teckal*[82] concluded that a contract between a contracting authority and an entity, in which the former exercises a control similar to that which exercises over its own departments and, at the same time, that entity carries out the essential part of its activities with the contracting authority, is not a public contract, irrespective of that entity being a contracting authority or not. The similarity of control as a reflection of dependency reveals another facet of the thrust of contracting authorities: the non-applicability of the public procurement rules for in-house relationships.

7.45 Along the same line of argument, contracts to affiliated undertakings escape the applicability of the Directives. Article 6 of the Services Directive provides for the inapplicability of the Directive to service contracts which are awarded to an entity which is itself a contracting authority within the meaning of the Directive, on the basis of an exclusive right which is granted to the contracting authority by a law, regulation, or administrative provision of the member state in question. Article 13 of the Utilities Directive provides for the exclusion of certain contracts between contracting authorities and affiliated undertakings. For the purposes of Article 1(3) of the Utilities Directive, an affiliated undertaking is one the annual accounts of which are consolidated with those of the contracting entity, in accordance with the requirements of the Seventh Company Law Directive.[83] These are service contracts that are awarded to a service provider which is affiliated to the contracting entity, and service contracts that are awarded to a service provider which is affiliated to a contracting entity participating in a joint venture formed for the purpose of carrying out an activity covered by the Directive.[84]

---

[82] *See* Case C-107/98, *Teckal Slr v. Comune di Viano*, judgment of 18 November 1999.

[83] *See* Council Directive 83/349 [1983] OJ L193/1.

[84] The explanatory memorandum accompanying the text amending the Utilities Directive (COM (91) 347-SYN 36 1) states that this provision relates, in particular, to three types of service provision within groups. These categories, which may not or may not be distinct, are: the provision of common services such as accounting, recruitment, and management; the provision of specialised services embodying the know-how of the group; and the provision of a specialised service to a joint venture. The exclusion from the provisions of the Directive is subject, however, to two conditions: the service provider must be an undertaking affiliated to the contracting authority and, at least eighty per cent of its average turnover arising within the European Community for the preceding three years derives from the provision of the same or similar services to undertakings with which it is affiliated. The Commission is empowered to monitor the application of this Article and require the notification of the names of the undertakings concerned and the nature and value of the service contracts involved.

In addition, the connection between the state and entities which operate in the **7.46** utilities sector and have been privatised is also weak to sustain the presence of a public procurement contract for the delivery of services of general interest. Privatised utilities could be, in principle, excluded from the procurement rules when a genuinely competitive regime[85] within the relevant market structure would rule out purchasing patterns based on non-economic considerations.

(d) The *Altmark* case

The European Court of Justice, as well as the Court of First Instance has **7.47** approached the subject of financing services of general interest from different perspectives. These perspectives show a degree of inconsistency but they shed light on the demarcation of competitiveness and protection with respect to the financing of public services. Also, the inconsistent precedent has opened a most interesting debate focusing on the role and remit of the state within the common market and its relation with the provision and financing of services of general interest. The conceptual link between public procurement and the financing of services of general interest reveals the policy implications and the interplay of jurisprudence between public procurement and state aids. The three approaches used by the Courts to construct the premises upon which the funding of public service obligations, services of general interest, and services for the public at large could be regarded as state aids, utilize public procurement in different ways. On the one hand, under the state aids and compensation approaches, public procurement sanitizes public subsidies as legitimate contributions towards public service obligations and services of general interest. From procedural and substantive viewpoints, the existence of public procurement award procedures, as well as the existence of a public contract between the state and an undertaking, reveals the necessary links between the markets where the state intervenes in order to provide services of general interest. In fact, both approaches accept the *sui generis* characteristics of public markets and the role the state and its organs play within such markets. On the other hand, the *quid pro quo* approach relies on public procurement to justify the clearly-defined and manifest link between the funding and the delivery of a public service obligation. It assumes that, without these procedural and substantive links between public services and their financing, the financing of public services is state aids.

In most cases, public procurement connects the activities of the state with the **7.48** pursuit of public interest. The subject of public contracts and their financing relates primarily to services of general interest. Thus, public procurement

---

[85] The determination of a genuinely competitive regime is left to the utilities operators themselves. *See* Case C-392/93, *The Queen and HM Treasury, ex parte British Telecommunications Plc* [1993] OJ C287/6. This is perhaps a first step towards self-regulation which could lead to the disengagement of the relevant contracting authorities from the public procurement regime.

indicates the necessary link between state financing and services of general interest, a link which takes state aids regulation out of the equation. The existence of public procurement, and the subsequent contractual relations ensuing from the procedural interface between the public and private sectors, neutralizes state aids regulation. In principle, the financing of services of general interest, when channelled through public procurement, reflects market value. However, it should be maintained that the safeguards of public procurement reflecting genuine market positions are not robust, and the foundations upon which a quantitative application of state aids regulation is based are not stable. The markets within which the services of general interest emerged and were delivered reveal little evidence of similarities and do not render meaningful any comparison with private markets, where competitiveness and substitutability of demand and supply feature. The approach adopted by the European judiciary indicates the presence of *marchés publics, sui generis* markets where the state intervenes in pursuit of public interest. State aids regulation could be applied, as a surrogate system of public procurement, to ensure that distortions of competition do not emerge as a result of the inappropriate financing of services.

7.49   However, the debate of the delineation between market forces and protection in the financing of public services took a twist. The Court in *Altmark*,[86] followed a hybrid approach between the compensation and the *quid pro quo* approaches. It ruled that where subsidies are regarded as compensation for the services provided by the recipient undertakings in order to discharge public service obligations, they do not constitute state aids. Nevertheless for the purpose of applying that criterion, national courts should ascertain that four conditions are satisfied: firstly, the recipient undertaking is actually required to discharge public service obligations and those obligations have been clearly defined; secondly, the parameters on the basis of which the compensation is calculated have been established beforehand in an objective and transparent manner; thirdly, the compensation does not exceed what is necessary to cover all or part of the costs incurred in discharging the public service obligations, taking into account the relevant receipts and a reasonable profit for discharging those obligations; and fourthly, where the undertaking which is to discharge public service obligations is not chosen in a public procurement procedure, the level of compensation needed has been determined on the basis of an analysis of the costs which a typical undertaking, well run and adequately provided with appropriate means so as to be able to meet the necessary public service requirements, would have incurred in discharging those obligations, taking into account the relevant receipts and a reasonable profit for discharging the obligations.

---

[86] *See* Case C-280/00, *Altmark Trans GmbH, Regierungsprδsidium Magdeburg et Nahverkehrsgesellschaft Altmark GmbH, Oberbundesanwalt beim Bundesverwaltungsgericht*, (third party), judgment of 24 July 2003.

The first criterion which requires the existence of a clear definition of the **7.50** framework within which public service obligations and services of general interest have been entrusted to the beneficiary of compensatory payments runs consistently with Article 86(2) EC jurisprudence, where an express act of the public authority to assign services of general economic interest[87] is required. However, the second criterion which requires the establishment of the parameters on the basis of which the compensation is calculated in an objective and transparent manner departs from existing precedent,[88] as it establishes an *ex post* control mechanism by the member states and the European Commission. The third criterion, that the compensation must not exceed what is necessary to cover the costs incurred in discharging services of general interest or public service obligations, is compatible to the proportionality test applied in Article 86(2) EC. However, there is an inconsistency problem, as the European judiciary is rather unclear to the question whether any compensation for public service obligations may comprise a profit element.[89] Finally, the fourth criterion which establishes a comparison of the cost structures of the recipient on the one hand, and of a private undertaking, well run and adequately provided to fulfil the public service tasks, in the absence of a public procurement procedure, inserts elements of subjectivity and uncertainty that will inevitably fuel more controversy.

The four conditions laid down in *Altmark* are ambiguous. In fact they represent **7.51** the hybrid link between the compensation approach and the *quid pro quo* approach. The Court appears to accept unequivocally the parameters of the compensation approach (*sui generis* markets, remuneration over and above normal market prices for services of general interest), although the link between the services of general interest and their legitimate financing requires the presence of public procurement, as procedural verification of competitiveness and cost

---

[87] *See* Case 127/73, *BRT v. SABAM* [1974] ECR 313, para. 20; Case 66/86, *Ahmed Saeed Flugreisen v. Commission* [1989] ECR 803, para. 55.

[88] The standard assessment criterion applied under Article 86(2) EC only requires for the application of Article 87(1) EC to frustrate the performance of the particular public service task, allowing for the examination being conducted on an *ex post facto* basis. *See* also the *ratione* behind the so-called 'electricity judgments' of the ECJ of 23 October 1997; Case C-157/94, *Commission v. Netherlands* [1997] ECR I-5699; Case C-158/94, *Commission v. Italy* [1997] ECR I-5789; Case C-159/94, *Commission v. France* [1997] ECR I-5815 and C-160/94, *Commission v. Spain* [1997] ECR I-5851; a great deal of controversy exists as to whether the material standard of the frustration of a public service task under Article 86(2) EC had lost its strictness. *See* Magiera, *Gefährdung der öffentlichen Daseinsvorsorge durch das EG-Beihilfenrecht?* FS für Dietrich Rauschning, 2000.

[89] *See* Opinion of Advocate General Lenz, delivered on 22 November 1984, in Case 240/83, *Procureur de la République v. ADBHU* [1985] ECR 531 (536). Advocate General Lenz in his Opinion held that the indemnities granted must not exceed annual uncovered costs actually recorded by the undertaking, taking into account a reasonable profit. However, the Court In the *ADBHU* case did not allow for the permissibility of taking into account such a profit element. Interestingly, the approach of the Court of First Instance on Art. 86(2) EC has never allowed any profit element to be taken into account, but instead focused on whether without the compensation at issue being provided the fulfilment of the specific public service tasks would have been jeopardized.

authentication of market prices. However, the application of the public procurement regime cannot always depict the true status of the market. Furthermore, the condition relating to the clear definition of an undertaking's character in receipt of subsidies to discharge public services in an objective and transparent manner, in conjunction with the costs attached to the provision of the relevant services, could give rise to major arguments across the legal and political systems in the common market. The interface between public and private sectors in relation to the delivery of public services is in an evolutionary state across the common market. Finally, the concept of 'reasonable profit' over and above the costs associated with the provision of services of general interest could complicate matters more, since they appear as elements of subjectivity and uncertainty.

(9) Delineation of public service contracts

7.52 A question often arises whether the purpose of a contract is relevant in determining the applicable regime and, in particular, whether, for the award of a contract with a single object but which is composed of several services, those services must be classified individually in the categories provided for in Annex I A and I B to Directive 92/50, in order to determine the regime applicable to the contract in accordance with Articles 8–10 of the Directive, or whether, on the contrary, the main purpose of the contract must be identified, in which case the ancillary services are governed by the same regime as the service relating to the main purpose. The Court held that the determination of the regime applicable to public service contracts, composed partly of services falling within Annex I A to Directive 92/50 and partly of services falling within Annex I B to the Directive, does not depend on the main purpose of those contracts and is to be made in accordance with the unequivocal test laid down by Article 10 of that Directive.[90]

7.53 The 21st recital in the preamble to Directive 92/50 states that the application of its provisions in full must be limited, for a transitional period, to contracts for services where its provisions will enable the full potential for increased cross-border trade to be realized, the contracts for other services during that period being subject only to monitoring. To that end, Directive 92/50 makes a distinction between contracts for services referred to in Annex I A, which under Article 8 are awarded in accordance with the provisions of Titles III to VI, and those for services referred to in Annex I B, which under Article 9 are subject to the provisions of Articles 14 and 16. In Article 10, Directive 92/50 also provides that contracts which have as their object services listed in both Annex I A and Annex I B are to be awarded in accordance with the provisions of Titles III to VI where the value of the services

---

[90] *See* Case C-411/00, *Felix Swoboda GmbH v. Österreichische Nationalbank*, judgment of 14 November 2002.

listed in Annex I A exceeds the value of the services listed in Annex I B, and, where this is not the case, only in accordance with Articles 14 and 16.

The argument that the main purpose of a contract determines the regime **7.54** applicable to it cannot be accepted, according to the Court. The Public Services Directive does not contain any definition of what constitutes the main purpose of a contract, whilst Article 10 explicitly acknowledges, on the contrary, that a contract may have as its purpose the provision of different services falling under different Annexes to the Directive. In that respect, the Court in *Tögel* held that the references in the Annexes to Directive 92/50 to the CPC nomenclature were binding. It is thus contrary to the purpose of the Directive to classify a contract composed of several services, referred to in different sections of the CPC nomenclature, according to only one of those services. The judgment in *Gestion Hotelera Internacional*,[91] in which the Court laid down the principle that the main purpose of the contract determined which Directive was applicable to a given contract, provides little support. *Gestion Hotelera Internacional* is rather irrelevant in determining the applicable regime within the Public Services Directive insofar as, firstly, its purpose was to determine whether a contract constituted a contract for works or a contract of another type and, secondly, the criterion adopted by the Court in that judgment was the merely incidental nature of repair work in relation to the main purpose of the contract based on the express definition of public works contracts in accordance with the Public Works Directives. If, in the context of that judgment, the Court had taken the view that the determining factor for distinguishing between contracts for works and contracts for services was the predominant nature of a service in terms of value, it would have clearly so ruled, referring to Article 10 of Directive 92/50 and not to the 16th recital in the preamble thereto, which provides that, when those works are incidental rather than forming the object of a contract, they do not justify treating the contract as a public works contract.

It follows from those provisions that, in the context of Directive 92/50, the **7.55** argument that the main purpose of a contract determines the regime applicable to it cannot be accepted. Firstly, Directive 92/50 itself states, in the 7th recital in the preamble, that, for the application of procedural rules and for monitoring purposes, the field of services is best described by subdividing it into categories corresponding to particular positions of a common classification, in this case the CPC nomenclature. In paragraph 37 of the judgment in *Tögel*, the Court held that the reference made in Annexes I A and I B to Directive 92/50 to the CPC nomenclature was binding. Secondly, Article 10 of Directive 92/50 provides an unequivocal test for the determination of the regime applicable to a contract

---

[91] *See* Case C-331/92, *Gestion Hotelera Internacional SA v. Communidad Autonoma de Canarias* [1994] ECR 1-1329.

composed of several services, which is based on the comparison of the value of the services referred to in Annex I A to the Directive with the value of the services referred to in Annex I B.

7.56 A further question arises whether, in the award of a contract having one purpose but composed of several services, the classification of those services in Annexes I A and I B to Directive 92/50 deprives the Directive of its effectiveness.[92] This question also leads to uncertainty whether there is an obligation on the part of the contracting authority, if, as a result of that classification, the value of the services falling within Annex I B exceeds that of the services falling within Annex I A, to separate the services referred to in Annex I B from the contract in question and to award separate contracts in respect of them. The Court maintained that, regarding the award of a contract with a single object but composed of several services, the classification of those services in Annexes I A and I B to Directive 92/50, far from depriving it of its effectiveness, is in accordance with the system laid down by the Directive. When, following the classification thus made by reference to the CPC nomenclature, the value of the services falling within Annex I B exceeds the value of the services falling within Annex I A, there is no obligation on the part of the contracting authority to separate from the contract in question the services referred to in Annex I B and to award separate contracts in respect of them.

7.57 The classification of services in Annexes I A and I B to Directive 92/50, even in the context of a contract with a single object, is in accordance with the system provided for by the Directive as it appears, *inter alia*, in the 7th and 21st recitals in the preamble and in Articles 8 and 10, which envisage the application of the Directive on two levels. Directive 92/50 must be interpreted as in no way requiring the separate award of a contract for the services referred to in Annex I B thereto when, in accordance with the classification made by reference to the CPC nomenclature, the value of those services exceeds, for the contract in question, the value of the services referred to in Annex I A. To require such a separation in that case would effectively deprive Article 10 of Directive 92/50 of any purpose.[93] Under the second sentence of Article 10 of the Directive the contract is subject only to Articles 14 and 16.

7.58 It would be the same if the contracting authority artificially grouped in one contract services of different types without there being any link arising from a joint purpose or operation, with the sole purpose of increasing the proportion of the services referred to in Annex I B to Directive 92/50 in the contract and thus of avoiding, by way of the second sentence of Article 10, the application of its

---

[92] *See* Case C-411/00, *Felix Swoboda GmbH v. Österreichische Nationalbank*, judgment of 14 November 2002.

[93] *See* the Opinion of the Advocate General, paragraph 55, in Case C-411/00, *Felix Swoboda GmbH v. Österreichische Nationalbank*, judgment of 14 November 2002.

provisions in full. Moreover, that conclusion is supported by the wording of Article 7(3) of Directive 92/50, from which it is clear that the choice of the valuation method is not to be made with the intention of avoiding the application of the Directive. Although that Article relates to a different situation (the artificial splitting up of the contract), the purpose which inspires it (the concern to avoid any risk of manipulation) also precludes a contracting authority from artificially grouping different services in the same contract solely in order to avoid the application in full of the Directive to that contract.

The classification of services in Annexes I A and I B to Directive 92/50 is primarily **7.59** a question of fact for the contracting authority to determine, subject to review by the national courts which eventually must decide the regime applicable to the contract forming the object of the procedure at issue in the main proceedings on the basis of Article 10 of Directive 92/50, in particular by verifying that the services which make up that contract and the reference numbers of the CPC nomenclature correspond. In any case, Category 20 of Annex I B to Directive 92/50 cannot be interpreted as also including land transport services themselves, as they are explicitly covered by Category 2 of Annex I A to the Directive.

(10) Inter-administrative agreements as public contracts

Exclusion of agreements between legally distinctive contracting authorities from **7.60** the public procurement rules is contrary to the principles of the Directives.[94] In *Commission v. Spain*, national law excluded from its scope cooperation agreements concluded either between the general state administration and the social security, autonomous communities, local bodies, their autonomous bodies and any other public body, or between public bodies themselves. The Spanish government maintained that inter-administrate agreements are the normal way for bodies governed by public law to establish relations between each other, and asserted that those relations are marginal to the concept of a contract. Furthermore, it suggested that the principle enshrined in Article 6 of the Public Services Directive 92/50 is implicitly included in the other Directives on public contracts. Article 6 of the Public Services Directive provides for the inapplicability of the Directive to service contracts which are awarded to an entity which is itself a contracting authority within the meaning of the Directive on the basis of an exclusive right which is granted to the contracting authority by a law, regulation or administrative provision of the member state in question.

The Commission argued that exclusion of inter-administrative agreements from **7.61** the framework of the Public Procurement Directives constitutes an incorrect

---

[94] *See* Case C-84/03, *Commission of the European Communities v. Kingdom of Spain*.

transposition of the Directives, as inter-administrative agreements are of the same kind as the public contracts covered by them, and that this exclusion is not found in Directives 93/36 and 93/37. The Commission relied on the definition of a contract set out in Article 1(a) of Directives 93/36 and 93/37 and the case-law of the Court, according to which, in order to show the existence of a contract, it must be determined whether there has been an agreement between two separate persons.[95]

7.62   The Court held that, according to the definitions given in Article 1(a) of Directives 93/36 and 93/37, public supply or public works contracts are contracts for pecuniary interest concluded in writing between a supplier or a contractor and a contracting authority within the meaning of Article 1(b) of the Directives, for the purchase of products or the performance of a certain type of works. In accordance with Article 1(a) of Directive 93/36, it is sufficient, in principle, if the contract was concluded between a local authority and a person legally distinct from it. The position can be otherwise only in the case where the local authority exercises over the person concerned a control which is similar to that which it exercises over its own departments and, at the same time, that person carries out the essential part of its activities with the controlling local authority or authorities.[96]

7.63   Having regard to the fact that the elements constituting the definition of a contract in Directives 93/36 and 93/37 are identical, except for the purpose of the contract in question, the approached adopted in *Teckal* must be applied to inter-administrative agreements covered by Directive 93/37. Consequently, if national law excludes, *a priori*, from the scope of the Public Procurement Directives relations between public authorities, their public bodies, and non-commercial bodies governed by public law, whatever the nature of those relations, such law constitutes an incorrect transposition of the Public Procurement Directives 93/36 and 93/37.

B. Contracting Authorities

(1) The public nature of public procurement

7.64   The remit and thrust of public procurement legislation relies heavily on the connection between contracting authorities and the state. Compliance procedures brought by the European Commission against member states are a good indication of determining contracting authorities under public procurement law. If the state can be held responsible under Article 169 EC (now Article 226 EC) not only for breaches of EC law committed by the central or local government, but also for breaches by other public entities and bodies over which it exercises a

---

[95] *See* Case C-107/98, *Teckal* [1999] ECR I-8121, paragraph 49.
[96] *See* Case C-107/98, *Teckal* [1999] ECR I-8121, paragraph 50.

certain degree of control, that responsibility denotes a degree of connection between the state and the entities in question sufficient to characterize these entities as contracting authorities for the purposes of the Public Procurement Directives.[97] A comprehensive and clear definition of the term 'contracting authorities', a factor that determines the applicability of the relevant rules, is probably the most important element of the public procurement legal framework. The structure of the Directives is such as to embrace the purchasing behaviour of all entities which have a close connection with the state. These entities, although not formally part of the state, disperse public funds in pursuit or on behalf of public interest. The Directives describe as contracting authorities the *state*, which covers central, regional, municipal, and local government departments, as well as *bodies governed by public law*. Provision has been also made to cover entities which receive more than fifty per cent subsidies by the state or other contracting authorities.

However, that connection might be weak to cover entities which operate in the **7.65** utilities sector and have been privatised. The *Foster* principle[98] established that state accountability could not embrace privatized enterprises.[99] The enactment of the Utilities Directives[100] brought under the procurement framework entities operating in the water, energy, transport, and telecommunications sectors. A wide range of these entities are covered by the term 'bodies governed by public law', which is used by the Utilities Directives for the contracting entities operating in the relevant sectors.[101] Interestingly, another category of contracting authorities under the Utilities Directives includes 'public undertakings'.[102] The term indicates any undertaking over which the state may exercise direct or indirect dominant influence by means of ownership, or by means of financial participation, or by means of laws and regulations, which govern the public undertaking's operation. Dominant influence can be exercised in the form of a majority holding of the undertaking's subscribed capital, in the form of majority controlling of the undertaking's issued shares, or, finally, in the form of the right to appoint the majority of the undertaking's management board. Public undertakings cover utilities operators which have been granted exclusive rights of exploitation of a service. Irrespective of their ownership, they are subject to the Utilities Directive in as much as the *exclusivity* of their operation precludes other entities from entering the relevant market under substantially the same competitive conditions. Privatised utilities could, in principle,

---

[97] *See* Case 24/91, *Commission v. Kingdom of Spain*, [1994] CMLR 621; Case 247/89, *Commission v. Portugal* [1991] ECR I-3659;

[98] *See* Case 188/89, *Foster v British Gas* [1990] ECR-1313, in which the European Court of Justice ruled that a Directive capable of having direct effect could be invoked against a body which is subject to the *control* of the State and has been delegated special powers.

[99] This was the view of Advocate General Lenz in Case 247/89, *Commission v. Portugal* [1991] ECR I 3659.   [100] EC Directive 90/531, as amended by EC Directive 93/38 [1993] OJ L199.

[101] *See* Art. 1(1) of Directive 93/38.   [102] *See* Art. 1(2) of Directive 93/38.

be excluded from the procurement rules when a genuinely competitive regime within the relevant market structure would rule out purchasing patterns based on non-economic considerations. The determination of a genuinely competitive regime is left to the utilities operators themselves. This is perhaps a first step towards self-regulation which could lead to the disengagement of the relevant contracting authorities from the public procurement regime.[103]

(2) *The functional dimension of contracting authorities*

7.66 Although the term 'contracting authorities' appears rigorous and well defined, public interest functions are dispersed through a range of organizations which, *stricto sensu*, could not fall under the ambit of the term 'contracting authorities', since they are not formally part of the state, nor are all criteria for the definition of bodies governed by public law present. This is particularly the case of non-governmental organizations (NGOs) which operate under the auspices of the central or local government and are responsible for public interest functions.[104] The Court addressed the *lex lacuna* through its landmark case *Beentjes*.[105] The Court diluted the rigorous definition of contracting authorities for the purposes of public procurement law, by introducing a *functional dimension* of the state and its organs. In particular, it considered a 'local land consolidation committee' with no legal personality, but with its functions and compositions specifically governed by legislation, as part of the state. The Court interpreted the term 'contracting authorities' in *functional terms* and considered the local land consolidation committee, which depended on the relevant public authorities for the appointment of its members and the supervision of its operations, and which had as its main task the financing and award of public works contracts, as falling within the notion of state, even though it was not part of the state administration in *formal terms*.[106] The Court held that the aim of the public procurement rules, as well as the attainment of freedom of establishment and freedom to provide services would be jeopardised if the public procurement provisions were to be held inapplicable solely because entities, which were set up by the state to carry out tasks entrusted to by legislation, were not formally part of its administrative organization.

7.67 The Court in two recent cases applied the functionality test, when it was requested to determine the nature of entities which could not meet the criteria of

---

[103] *See* Case C-392/93, *The Queen and HM Treasury, ex parte British Telecommunications Plc* [1993] OJ C287/6.

[104] *See* Bovis, 'Public Entities Awarding Procurement Contracts under the Framework of EC Public Procurement Directives', *Journal of Business Law*, 1 (1993), 56–78.

[105] Case 31/87, *Gebroeders Beentjes BV v. State of Netherlands* [1988] ECR 4635.

[106] The formality test and the relation between the state and entities under its control was established in Cases C-249/81, *Commission v. Ireland* [1982] ECR 4005; C-36/74 *Walrave and Koch v. Association Union Cycliste International et. al* (1974) ECR 1423.

bodies governed by public law, but had a distinctive public interest remit. In *Teoranta*,[107] a private company established according to national legislation to carry out the business of forestry and related activities, was deemed as falling within the notion of the state. The company was set up by the state and was entrusted with specific tasks of public interest, such as managing national forests and woodland industries, as well as providing recreation, sporting, educational, scientific, and cultural facilities. It was also under decisive administrative, financial, and management control by the state, although the day-to-day operations were left entirely to its board. The Court accepted that, since the state had at least indirect control over the *Teoranta's* policies, in functional terms the latter was part of the state. In the *Vlaamese Raad*,[108] the Flemish Parliament of the Belgian federal system was considered part of the 'federal' state. The Court held that the definition of the state encompasses all bodies which exercise legislative, executive, and judicial powers, at both regional and federal levels. The Raad, as a legislative body of the Belgian state, although under no direct control by it, was held as falling within the definition of the state and thus being regarded as a contracting authority. The fact that the Belgian Government did not, at the time, exercise any direct or indirect control relating to procurement policies over the *Vlaamese Raad* was considered immaterial on the grounds that a state cannot rely on its own legal system to justify non-compliance with EC law and particular Directives.[109]

The functional dimension of contracting authorities has exposed the Court's **7.68** departure from the formality test, which has rigidly positioned an entity under state control on *stricto sensu* traditional public law grounds. Functionality, as an ingredient of assessing the relationship between an entity and the state demonstrates, in addition to the elements of management or financial control, the importance of constituent factors such as the intention and purpose of establishment of the entity in question. Functionality depicts a flexible approach in the applicability of the Procurement Directives, in a way that the Court through its precedence established a pragmatic approach as to the nature of the demand side of the public procurement equation.

(3) Bodies governed by public law

The latter category is subject to a set of cumulative criteria[110] in order to be **7.69** classified as contracting authorities for the purposes of the Directives. In

---

[107] *See* Cases C-353/96, *Commission v. Ireland* and C-306/97, *Connemara Machine Turf Co Ltd v. Coillte Teoranta*, judgment of 17 December 1998.
[108] *See* Case C-323/96, *Commission v Kingdom of Belgium*, judgment of 17 September 1998.
[109] For a similar approach, *see also* Case C-144/97, *Commission v France* [1998] ECR 1-613.
[110] *See* Art. 1(b) of Directive 93/37.

particular, 'bodies governed by public law': i) must be established for the specific purpose of meeting needs in the general public interest not having an industrial or commercial character; ii) must have legal personality; and iii) must be financed, for the most part, by either the state, or regional or local authorities, or other bodies governed by public law, or subject to management supervision by these bodies, or having an administrative or supervisory board, more than half of whose members are appointed by the state, regional, or local authorities, or by other bodies governed by public law. There is a list of such bodies in Annex I of Directive 93/37 which is not an exhaustive one, in the sense that member states are under an obligation to notify the Commission of any changes to that list. The term 'bodies governed by public law' provided the opportunity to the Court to elaborate on each of the cumulative criteria and shed light on their constituent elements. The Court's jurisprudence has revealed the following thematic areas.

(4) The dependency test

7.70 To assess the existence of the third criterion of bodies governed by public law, the Court assumed that there is a close dependency of these bodies on the State, in terms of corporate governance, management supervision and financing.[111] These dependency features are alternative, thus the existence of one satisfies the third criterion. The Court held in *OPAC*[112] that management supervision by the state or other contracting authorities entails not only administrative verification of legality or appropriate use of funds or exceptional control measures, but also the conferring of significant influence over management policy, such as the narrowly circumscribed remit of activities, the supervision of compliance, as well as the overall administrative supervision. Of interest and high relevance, is the Court's analysis and argumentation relating to the requirements of management supervision by the state and other public bodies, where it maintained that entities entrusted to provide social housing in France are deemed to be bodies governed by public law, thus covered by the Public Procurement Directives.

7.71 The Court (and the Advocate General) drew an analogy amongst the dependency features of bodies governed by public law on the state. Although the corporate governance and financing feature are quantitative (the state must appoint more than half of the members of the managerial or supervisory board or it must finance for the most part the entity in question), the exercise of management supervision is a qualitative one. The Court held that management supervision by the state denotes dependency ties similar to the financing or governance control of the entity concerned.

---

[111] This type of dependency resembles the Court's definition in its ruling on state controlled enterprises in Case 152/84, *Marshall v. Southampton and South West Hampshire Area Health Authority* [1986] ECR 723.

[112] *See* Case C-237/99, *Commission v. France*, judgment of 1 February 2001.

Receiving public funds from the state or a contracting authority is an indication **7.72** that an entity could be a body governed by public law. However, this indication is not an absolute one. The Court, in the *University of Cambridge* case,[113] was asked whether: i) awards or grants paid by one or more contracting authorities for the support of research work; ii) consideration paid by one or more contracting authorities for the supply of services comprising research work; iii) consideration paid by one or more contracting authorities for the supply of other services, such as consultancy or the organization of conferences; and iv) student grants paid by local education authorities to universities in respect of tuition for named students, constitute public financing for the university.

The Court held that only specific payments made to an entity by the state or other **7.73** public authorities have the effect of creating or reinforcing a specific relationship or subordination and dependency. The funding of an entity within a framework of general considerations indicates that the entity has close dependency links with the state or other contracting authorities. Thus, funding received in the form of grants or awards paid by the state or other contracting authorities, as well as funding received in the form of student grants for tuition fees for named students, constitutes public financing. The rationale for such approach lies in the lack of any contractual consideration between the entity receiving the funding and the state or other contracting authorities, which provide it in the context of the entity's public interest activities. The Court drew an analogy with public financing received by an entity with the receipt of subsidies.[114] However, if there is a specific consideration for the state to finance an entity, such as a contractual nexus, the Court suggested that the dependency ties are not sufficiently close to merit the entity financed by the state meeting the third criterion of the term 'bodies governed by public law'. Such relationship is analogous to the dependency that exists in normal commercial relations formed by reciprocal contracts which have been negotiated freely between the parties. Therefore, funding received by Cambridge University for the supply of services for research work, or consultancies or conference organization, cannot be deemed as public financing. The existence of a contract between the parties, apart from the specific considerations for funding, indicates supply substitutability, in the sense that the entity receiving the funding faces competition in the relevant markets.

The Court stipulated that the proportion of public finances received by an entity, **7.74** as one of the alternative features of the third criterion of the term 'bodies governed by public law' must exceed fifty per cent to enable it to meet that criterion. For

---

[113] *See* Case C-380/98, *The Queen and HM Treasury, ex parte University of Cambridge*, judgment of 3 October 2000.

[114] *See* paragraph 25 of the Court's judgment, as well as the Opinion of the Advocate General in paragraph 46.

assessment purposes of this feature, there must be an annual evaluation of the (financial) status of an entity for the purposes of being regarded as a contracting authority.

7.75 Dependency, in terms of overall control of an entity by the state or another contracting authority, presupposes a control similar to that which the state or another contracting authority exercises over its own departments. The 'similarity' of control denotes lack of independence with regard to decision-making. The Court in *Teckal*,[115] concluded that a contract between a contracting authority and an entity, in which the former exercises a control similar to that which it exercises over its own departments and where, at the same time, that entity carries out the essential part of its activities with the contracting authority, is not a public contract, irrespective of whether or not that entity is a contracting authority. The similarity of control as a reflection of dependency reveals another facet of the thrust of contracting authorities: the non-applicability of the public procurement rules for in-house relationships.

(5) Management supervision of bodies governed by public law

7.76 The close dependency of a body governed by public law on the state, regional or local authorities, or other bodies governed by public law, is recognized in case law of the Court.[116] More specifically, as regards the criterion of management supervision, the Court has held that that supervision must give rise to dependence on the public authorities equivalent to that which exists where one of the other alternative criteria is fulfilled, namely where the body in question is financed, for the most part, by the public authorities or where the latter appoint more than half of the members of its administrative, managerial, or supervisory organs, enabling the public authorities to influence their decisions in relation to public contracts.[117]

7.77 The criterion of managerial supervision cannot be regarded as being satisfied in the case of mere review since, by definition, such supervision does not enable the public authorities to influence the decisions of the body in question in relation to public contracts. That criterion is, however, satisfied where the public authorities supervise not only the annual accounts of the body concerned but also its conduct from the point of view of proper accounting, regularity, economy, efficiency, and expediency, and where those public authorities are authorized to inspect the business premises and facilities of that body and to report the results of those

---

[115] *See* Case C-107/98, *Teckal Slr v. Comune di Viano*, judgment of 18 November 1999.
[116] *See* Case C-380/98, *The Queen and HM Treasury, ex parte University of Cambridge* [2000] ECR 8035, paragraph 20, and Case C-237/99, *Commission v. France* [2001] ECR 934, paragraph 44.
[117] *See* Case C-237/99, *Commission v. France*, paragraphs 48 and 49.

inspections to a regional authority which holds, through another company, all the shares in the body in question.[118]

(6) *Commerciality and needs in the general interest*

Commerciality and its relationship with needs in the general interest is perhaps **7.78** the most important theme that has emerged from the Court's jurisprudence in relation to the remit of bodies governed by public law as contracting authorities. In fact, the theme sets out to explore the interface between profit-making and public interest, as features which underpin the activities of bodies governed by public law.

The criterion of specific establishment of an entity to meet needs in the general **7.79** interest having non-commercial or industrial character has attracted the attention of the Court in some landmark cases.[119] The above criterion appears as the first of the three cumulative criteria for bodies governed by public law. The Court drew its experience from jurisprudence in the public undertakings field, as well as case law relating to public order to define the term 'needs in the general interest'.[120] The Court approached the above concept by a direct analogy of the concept 'general economic interest', as defined in Article 90(2) EC.[121] The concept 'general interest' denotes the requirements of a community (local or national) in its entirety, which should not overlap with the specific or exclusive interest of a clearly-determined person or group of persons.[122] However, the problematic concept of the *specificity* of the establishment of the body in question was approached by reference to the reasons and the objectives behind its establishment. Specificity of the purpose of an establishment does not mean exclusivity, in the sense that other types of activities can be carried out without escaping classification as a body governed by public law.[123]

On the other hand, the requirement of non-commercial or industrial character of **7.80** needs in the general interest has raised some difficulties. The Court had recourse

---

[118] *See* Case C-373/00 *Adolf Truley GmbH and Bestattung Wien GmbH* [2003] ECR I-1931.

[119] *See* Cases C-223/99, *Agora Srl v. Ente Autonomo Fiera Internazionale di Milano*, and C-260/99, *Excelsior Snc di Pedrotti runa & C v. Ente Autonomo Fiera Internazionale di Milano*, judgment of 10 May 2001; C-360/96, *Gemeente Arnhem Gemeente Rheden v. BFI Holding BV*, judgment of 10 November 1998; C-44/96, *Mannesmann Anlangenbau Austria AG et al. v. Strohal Rotationsdurck GesmbH*, judgment of 15 January 1998.

[120] *See* the Opinion of Advocate-General Léger, point 65, of the *Strohal* case.

[121] *See* Case C-179/90, *Merci Convenzionali Porto di Gevova* [1991] ECR 1-5889; General economic interest as a concept represents 'activities of direct benefit to the public', point 27 of the Opinion of Advocate General van Gerven.

[122] *See* Valadou, 'La Notion de Pouvoir Adjudicateur en Matière de Marchés de Travaux', *Semaine Juridique*, 3, Ed. E. (1991), 33.

[123] *See* Case C-44/96, *Mannesmann Anlangenbau Austria*, op. cit.

to case law and legal precedence relating to public undertakings, where the nature of industrial and commercial activities of private or public undertakings was defined.[124] The industrial or commercial character of an organization depends much upon a number of criteria that reveal the thrust behind the organization's participation in the relevant market. The state and its organs may act either by exercising public powers or by carrying out economic activities of an industrial or commercial nature by offering goods and services on the market. The key issue is the organization's intention to achieve profitability and pursue its objectives through a spectrum of commercially motivated decisions. The distinction between the range of activities which relate to public authority and those which, although carried out by public persons, fall within the private domain, is drawn most clearly from case law and judicial precedence of the Court concerning the applicability of competition rules of the Treaty to the given activities.[125]

7.81 The Court in *BFI* [126] had the opportunity to clarify the element of non-commercial or industrial character. It considered that the relationship of the first criterion of bodies governed by public law is an integral one. The non-commercial or industrial character is a criterion intended to clarify the term 'needs in the general interest'. In fact, it is regarded as a category of needs of general interest. The Court recognised that there might be needs of general interest which have an industrial and commercial character, and it is possible that private undertakings can meet needs of general interest which do not have industrial and commercial character. The acid test for needs in the general interest not having an industrial or commercial character is that the state or other contracting authorities choose themselves to meet these needs or to have a decisive influence over their provision.

7.82 In the *Agora* case[127] the Court indicated that if an activity which meets general needs is pursued in a competitive environment, there is a strong indication that the entity, which pursues it is not a body governed by public law. The reason can be found in the relationship between competitiveness and commerciality. Market forces reveal the commercial or industrial character of an activity, irrespective the latter meeting the needs of general interest or not. However, market competitiveness as well as profitability cannot be absolute determining factors for the commerciality or the industrial nature of an activity, as they are not sufficient to exclude the possibility that a body governed by public law may choose to be guided by considerations other that economic ones. The absence of competition

---

[124] For example, *see* Case 118/85 *Commission v. Italy* [1987] ECR 2599, para 7, where the Court had the opportunity to elaborate on the distinction of activities pursued by public authorities.

[125] *See* Case C-364/92, *SAT Fluggesellschaften* [1994] ECR 1-43; also Case C-343/95, *Diego Cali et Figli* [1997] ECR 1-1547.

[126] *See* Case C-360/96, *Gemeente Arnhem Gemeente Rheden v. BFI Holding BV*, op. cit.

[127] *See* Case C-223/99, *Agora Srl v. Ente Autonomo Fiera Internazionale di Milano*, op. cit.

is not a condition necessarily to be taken into account in order to define a body governed by public law, although the existence of significant competition in the marketplace may be indicative of the absence of a need in the general interest, which does not carry commercial or industrial elements. The Court reached this conclusion by analysing the nature of the bodies governed by public law contained in Annex 1 of the Works Directive 93/37 and verifying that the intention of the state to establish such bodies has been to retain decisive influence over the provision of the needs in question.

(7) The dual capacity of contracting authorities

The dual capacity of an entity as a public service provider and a commercial **7.83** undertaking respectively, and the weighting of the relevant activity in relation to the proportion of its output, should be the decisive factor in determining whether an entity is a body governed by public law. This argument appeared for the first time before the Court in the *Strohal*[128] case. The Austrian Government suggested that, only if the activities in pursuit of the 'public services obligations' of an entity supersede its commercial thrust, could the latter be considered as a body covered by public law and a contracting authority. In support of its argument that the relevant entity (*Österreichische Staatsdruckerei*) is not a body governed by public law, the Austrian Government maintained that the proportion of public interest activities represents no more than fifteen to twenty per cent of its overall activities.[129]

In practice, the argument put forward implied a selective application of the Public **7.84** Procurement Directives in the event of dual capacity entities. This sort of application is not entirely unjustified as, on a number of occasions,[130] the Public Procurement Directives themselves utilize thresholds or proportion considerations in order to include or exclude certain contracts from their ambit. For example, the relevant provisions stipulating the thresholds for the applicability of the public procurement rules as well as the provisions relating to the so-called 'mixed contracts', where the proportion of the value of the works or the supplies element in a public contract determines the applicability of the relevant Directive and, finally, the relevant provisions which embrace the award of works contracts subsidised *directly* by more than fifty per cent by the state within the scope of the Directive.

However, the Court ruled out a selective application of the Directives in the case of **7.85** dual capacity contracting authorities based on the principle of legal certainty.

---

[128] *See* Case C-44/96, *Mannesmann Anlangenbau Austria. v. Strohal Rotationsdurck GesmbH,* op. cit.

[129] For a comprehensive analysis of the case, see the annotation by Bovis in CMLR 36 (1999), 205–225.

[130] *See* Art. 3(1) of Directive 93/37; Art. 5(1) of Directive 93/36; Art. 14 of Directive 93/38; Art. 7(1) of Directive 92/50; Art. 6(5) of Directive 93/37; and Art. 2(1)(2) of Directive 93/37.

It substantiated its position on the fact that only the purpose for which an entity is established is relevant in order to classify it as body governed by public law and not the division between public and private activities. Thus, the pursuit of commercial activities by contracting authorities is incorporated with their public interest orientation aims and objectives, without taking into account their proportion and weighting in relation to the total activities dispersed, and contracts awarded in pursuit of commercial purposes fall under the remit of the Public Procurement Directives. The Court recognised the fact that, by extending the application of public procurement rules to activities of a purely industrial or commercial character, an onerous constraint would be probably imposed upon the relevant contracting authorities, which may also seem unjustified on the grounds that public procurement law, in principle, does not apply to private bodies, which carry out identical activities.[131] The above situation represents a considerable disadvantage in delineating the distinction between private and public sector activities and their regulation, to the extent that the only determining factor appears to be the nature of the organization in question. The Court suggested that this disadvantage could be avoided by selecting the appropriate legal instrument for the objectives pursued by public authorities. As the reasons for the creation of a body governed by public law would determine the legal framework which would apply to its contractual relations, those responsible for establishing it must restrict its thrust in order to avoid the undesirable effects of that legal framework on activities outside their scope.

7.86 The Court in *Strohal* established dualism, to the extent that it specifically implied that contracting authorities may pursue a dual range of activities: to procure goods, works and services destined for the public, as well as participate in commercial activities. They can pursue other activities in addition to those which meet needs of general interest not having an industrial and commercial character. The proportion between activities pursued by an entity, which on the one hand aim to meet needs of general interest not having an industrial or commercial character and, on the other, commercial activities, is irrelevant for the characterization of that entity as a body governed by public law. What is relevant is the intention of establishment of the entity in question, which reflects on the 'specificity' requirement. Also, specificity does not mean exclusivity of purpose. Specificity indicates the intention of establishment to meet general needs. Along these lines, ownership or financing of an entity by a contracting authority does not guarantee the condition of establishment of that entity to meet needs of general interest not having industrial and commercial character.

---

[131] *See* Bovis, *The Liberalisation of Public Procurement in the European Union and its Effects on the Common Market* (Ashgate, 1998), Chapter 1, 16 *et seq.*

(8) The connection of contracting authorities with private undertakings

There is considerable risk of circumventing the Public Procurement Directives, if **7.87** contracting authorities award their public contracts via private undertakings under their control, which cannot be covered by the framework of the Directives. Under the domestic laws of the member states, there is little to prevent contracting authorities from acquiring private undertakings in an attempt to participate in market activities. In fact, in many jurisdictions the socio-economic climate is very much in favour of public–private sector partnerships, in the form of joint-ventures or in the form of private financing of public projects. A classic example of such an approach is the view of the UK Government in relation to the involvement of the private sector in delivering public services. A number of government documents have eulogised the so-called *Private Finance Initiative (PFI)*, which attempts to create a framework between the public and private sectors working together in delivering public services.[132] Unfortunately, the Public Procurement Directives have not envisaged such a scenario, where avoidance of the rules could be based on the fact that the entities which award the relevant contracts cannot be classified as contracting authorities within the meaning of the Directives.

The Court, prior to the *Stohal* case, did not have the opportunity to examine such **7.88** corporate relationships and the effect that public procurement law has upon them. Even in *Strohal*, the Court did not rule directly on the subject, but instead it provided the necessary inferences for national courts, in order to ascertain whether such relations between public and private undertakings aim at avoiding the application of the Public Procurement Directives. Indeed, national courts, in litigation before them, must establish *in concreto* whether a contracting authority has established an undertaking in order to enter into contracts for the sole purpose of avoiding the requirements specified in public procurement law. Such conclusions must be beyond doubt based on the examination of the actual purpose for which the undertaking in questions has been established. The rule of thumb is the connection between the nature of a project, and the aims and objectives of the undertaking which awards it. If the realization of a project does not contribute to the aims and objectives of an undertaking, then it is assumed that the project in question is awarded 'on behalf' of another undertaking, and, if the latter beneficiary is a contracting authority under the framework of public procurement law, then the relevant Directives should apply. The Court followed the *Strohal* line in

---

[132] *See*, in particular, Department of Environment *Working Together—Private Finance and Public Money* (Department of Environment, 1993). Private Finance Panel and HM Treasury, *Private Opportunity, Public Benefit—Progressing the Private Finance Initiative* (Private Finance Panel and HM Treasury, 1995).

Teckal,[133] where the exercise of a similar control over the management of an entity by a contracting authority prevents the applicability of the Directives.

7.89 The dual capacity of contracting authorities is irrelevant to the applicability of public procurement rules. If an entity is a contracting authority, it must apply public procurement rules irrespective of the pursuit of general interest needs or the pursuit of commercial activities. Also, if a contracting authority assigns the rights and obligations of a public contract to an entity which is not a contracting authority, that entity must follow public procurement rules. The contrary would be acceptable if the contract fell within the remit of the entity, which is not a contracting authority, and the contract was entered into on its behalf by a contracting authority.

7.90 Dualism's irrelevance for the applicability of public procurement represents a safeguard for the *acquis communautaire*. Dualism could be viewed as recognition of contractualized governance, where the demarcation between public and private activities of the public sector has become difficult to define, as well as a counterbalance of commerciality. If commercialism might shield the activities of a contracting authority from the application of public procurement rules, dualism provides for the necessary inferences to subject dual capacity entities to the *acquis communautaire*.

(9) Transfer of undertakings and public procurement

7.91 The relevance of the Acquired Rights Directive[134] to the public procurement regime became clear when contracting authorities started *testing the market* in an attempt to define whether the provision of works or services from a commercial operator could be cheaper than that from the in-house team. This is the notion of *contracting out*, an exercise which aims at achieving potential savings and efficiency gains for contracting authorities. The application of the transfer of undertakings rules in contracting out cases has the important consequence that the external bidder (if successful) must engage the authority's former employees on the same conditions as they enjoyed under the authority itself.

7.92 The initial Directive proclaimed its inapplicability in cases where the undertaking was not in the nature of a commercial venture; this proviso was interpreted as exclusive of contracting out by government. The impact of the Transfer of Undertakings Directive in the context of public procurement was felt in a landmark decision of the Court,[135] which maintained that the Directive does not permit such a limitation. Thus it became apparent that contracting out by government and other public authorities was covered, and a transfer of an undertaking may take place where the government contracts out to the private sector a

---

[133] *See* Case C-107/98, *Teckal Slr v Comune di Viano*, op. cit
[134] Directive 77/62 [1977] OJ C61/26, as amended by Directive 98/50 [1998] OJ L132 and consolidated by Directive 2001/23 [2001] OJ L82/16.
[135] Case C 29/91, *Dr Sophie Redmond Stichting v. Bartol* [1992] IRLR 369.

function previously carried out in-house[136] and vice versa, viz. where the contracting authority takes back in-house a service formerly contracted out. The circumstances under which a transfer of an undertaking through contracting out occurs depend upon the transfer retaining its identity.[137] However, the 'retention of identity' test can only be satisfied when the undertaking transferred represents *substantially the same* or *similar activities*,[138] as well as if it relates to a *stable economic entity*.[139] The existence of a contractual link or relation between the parties to a transfer of an undertaking is not a decisive criterion to establish the applicability of the Directive.[140]

Serious concerns have been raised over the compatibility of the public procure- **7.93** ment and the transfer of undertakings regimes.[141] It appeared that there was a clear antithesis between the drivers of two regimes in achieving savings on the one hand, whilst protecting employees on the other. However, the *Liikenne*[142] case confirmed the compatibility of the two regimes.[143] The Court's jurisprudence relating to the applicability of transfer of undertakings to public procurement has positioned transfers amongst contractual terms and conditions of a contract, thus obliging contracting authorities to inform tenderers appropriately, so the latter can factor all relevant financial consequences to their bid.

(10) Private law entities as contracting authorities

An entity which is governed by private law, but which nevertheless meets all the **7.94** requirements of bodies governed by public law laid down in the first, second and third indents of the second subparagraph of Article 1(b) of Directives 93/36 and 93/37, is considered a contracting authority for the purposes of the Public Procurement Directives. In *Commission v Spain*,[144] the Commission argued that national law which excludes from the scope of the Public Procurement Directives private entities which may fulfil the requirements of contracting authorities is in default with public procurement *acquis*. The Commission argued that the scope

---

[136] Case C-382/92, *Commission v. United Kingdom* [1994] ECR 1.

[137] Case 24/85, *Spijkers v. Gebroders Benedik Abbatoir CV* [1986] ECR 1-1123, Case C 209/91, *Rask v. ISS Kantinservice* [1993] ECR 1. Case C 392/92, *Schmidt v. Spar und Leihkasse der fruherer Amter Bordersholm, Kiel und Cronshagen* [1994] ECR 1-1320.

[138] Case C 392/92, *Schmidt v. Spar und Leihkasse der fruherer Amter Bordersholm, Kiel und Cronshagen* [1994] ECR 1-1320.

[139] Case C-48/94, *Rygaard v. Stro Molle Akustik*, judgment of 19 September 1995.

[140] *See* Case C-324/86, *Tellerup*, judgment of 10 February 1998.

[141] *See* the analysis of Bovis, 'The Compatibility of Socio-economic Policies with Competitive Tendering: The Case of Contract Compliance and Transfer of Undertakings', in Collins, Davies and Rideout (eds.) *Legal Regulation of the Employment Relations*, (Kluwer, 2000), Chapter 21.

[142] *See* Case C-172/99, judgment of 25 January 2001, points 21 to 22.

[143] *See* also the conclusions of Advocate General Léger in Case C-172/99, in particular paragraphs 28 to 37, and also paragraph 22 of the judgment in this case.

[144] *See* Case C-84/03, *Commission of the European Communities v. Kingdom of Spain*.

ratione personae of the codified law does not coincide with that of Directives 93/36 and 93/37, insofar as the national law applies exclusively to bodies subject to a public law regime for the purposes of Spanish law, while the legal form of the body at issue falls outside the definition of 'body governed by public law' set out in the Public Procurement Directives. The Commission asserted that the concept 'body governed by public law' is a Community-wide concept of autonomous nature. The Commission maintained that, according to the Court's jurisprudence,[145] a body governed by public law must be understood as a body which fulfils the three cumulative conditions set out in the second subparagraph of Article 1(b) of Directive 93/37, and that the definition of a contracting authority in Article 1 of Directives 93/36 and 93/37 must be interpreted in functional terms.[146]

7.95 The Spanish Government suggested that a literal interpretation of the definition of body governed by public law does not allow the inclusion of private entities within the scope of the Public Procurement Directives. It argued that Directives 93/36 and 93/37 do not include commercial companies under public control in that definition. In support of its arguments, it relied on the Utilities Directive 93/38, which distinguishes between the notion of 'body governed by public law', which is the same in the public contracts Directives, and 'public undertaking', whose definition corresponds to the definition of public commercial company. Furthermore, the Spanish Government submitted that a genuine delimitation of the definition of the term 'body governed by public law' may be made only after defining needs in the general interest and, in particular, needs not having an industrial or commercial character, by means of a detailed examination of the entity in question on a case-by-case basis.

7.96 The Court held that the definition of 'body governed by public law', represents a concept of Community law which must be given an autonomous and uniform interpretation throughout the Community, and is defined in functional terms exclusively under the three cumulative conditions in the second subparagraph of Article 1(b) of Directives 93/36 and 93/37.[147] In order to determine whether a private law body is to be classified as a body governed by public law it is only necessary to establish whether the body in question satisfies the three cumulative conditions laid down in the second subparagraph of Article 1(b) of Directives 93/36 and 93/37, since an entity's private law status does not constitute a criterion for precluding it from being classified as a contracting authority for the purposes of the Public Procurement Directives.[148]

---

[145] *See* Case C-44/96, *Mannesmann Anlagenbau Austria*, [1998] ECR I-73, paragraphs 17 to 35.
[146] *See* Case 31/87, *Beentjes* [1988] ECR 4635 and Case C-360/96, *BFI Holding* [1998] ECR I-6821.
[147] *See* Case 44/96, *Mannesmann Anlagenbau Austria and Others*, paragraphs 20 and 21; Case C-470/99, *Universale-Bau and Others* [2002] ECR I-11617, paragraphs 51 to 53; Case C-214/00, *Commission v. Spain* [2003] ECR I-4667, paragraphs 52 and 53; and Case C-283/00, *Commission v. Spain* [2003] ECR I-11697, paragraph 69.
[148] *See* Case C-214/00, *Commission v. Spain*, paragraphs 54, 55 and 60.

The Court has also stated that that interpretation does not amount to a disregard   **7.97**
for the industrial or commercial character of the general interest needs which the
body concerned satisfies, since that factor is necessarily taken into consideration
in order to determine whether or not it satisfies the condition laid down in the first
indent of the second subparagraph of Article 1(b) of Directives 93/36 and
93/37.[149] Furthermore, that conclusion is not invalidated by the want of an
express reference in Directives 93/36 and 93/37 to the specific category of 'public
undertakings' which is used in Directive 93/38.[150]

(11) Semi-public undertakings as contracting authorities

In *Staad Halle*,[151] a question arose as to whether, where a contracting authority   **7.98**
intends to conclude with a company governed by private law, legally distinct from
the authority and in which it has a majority capital holding and exercises a certain
control, a contract for pecuniary interest relating to services within the material
scope of Directive 92/50, it is always obliged to apply the public award procedures
laid down by that Directive. In other words, the question prompted the criteria
and their references under which mere participation of a contracting authority,
even in a minority form, in the shareholding of a private company with which it
concludes a contract to be a ground for the applicability of the Public
Procurement Directives. The Court held that, where a contracting authority
intends to conclude a contract for pecuniary interest relating to services within the
material scope of Directive 92/50 with a company legally distinct from it, in
whose capital it has a holding, together with one or more private undertakings,
the public award procedures laid down by that Directive must always be applied.

The Court maintained that the obligation to apply the Public Procurement   **7.99**
Directives in the case of semi-public undertakings is confirmed by the fact that, in
Article 1(c) of Directive 92/50 the term 'service provider', that is, a tenderer for
the purposes of the application of that Directive, also includes a public body
which offers services.[152]

Any exception to the application of that obligation must consequently be inter-   **7.100**
preted strictly. Thus the Court has held, concerning recourse to a negotiated procedure without the prior publication of a contract notice, that Article 11(3) of
Directive 92/50, which provides for such a procedure, must, as a derogation from
the rules intended to ensure the effectiveness of the rights conferred by the EC
Treaty in relation to public service contracts, be interpreted strictly, and that the

---

[149] *See* Case C-283/00, *Commission v. Spain*, paragraph 75.
[150] *See* Case C-283, *Commission v. Spain*, paragraph 76.
[151] *See* Case C-26/03, *Stadt Halle, RPL Recyclingpark Lochau GmbH v. Arbeitsgemeinschaft Thermische Restabfall- und Energieverwertungsanlage TREA Leuna*.
[152] *See* Case C-94/99, *ARGE* [2000] ECR I-11037, paragraph 28.

burden of proving the existence of exceptional circumstances justifying the derogation lies on the person seeking to rely on those circumstances.[153]

7.101　The Court has held that, in the spirit of opening up public contracts to the widest possible competition, the Public Procurement Directives are applicable in the case where a contracting authority plans to conclude a contract for pecuniary interest with an entity which is legally distinct from it, whether or not that entity is itself a contracting authority.[154] It is relevant to note that the other contracting party in that case was a consortium consisting of several contracting authorities, of which the contracting authority in question was also a member. A public authority which is a contracting authority has the possibility of performing the tasks conferred on it in the public interest by using its own administrative, technical, and other resources, without being obliged to call on outside entities not forming part of its own departments. In such a case, there can be no question of a contract for pecuniary interest concluded with an entity legally distinct from the contracting authority. There is, therefore, no need to apply the Community rules in the field of public procurement.

7.102　The Court's case law does not exclude other circumstances in which a call for tenders is not mandatory even though the other contracting party is an entity legally distinct from the contracting authority. That is the case where the public authority which is a contracting authority exercises over the separate entity concerned a control which is similar to that which it exercises over its own departments, and that entity carries out the essential part of its activities with the controlling public authority or authorities.[155] It should be noted that, in the case cited, the distinct entity was wholly owned by public authorities. By contrast, the participation, even as a minority, of a private undertaking in the capital of a company in which the contracting authority in question is also a participant excludes in any event the possibility of that contracting authority exercising over that company a control similar to that which it exercises over its own departments.

7.103　In this respect, it must be observed, firstly, that the relationship between a public authority which is a contracting authority and its own departments is governed by considerations and requirements proper to the pursuit of objectives in the public interest. Any private capital investment in an undertaking, on the other hand, follows considerations proper to private interests and pursues objectives of a different kind. Secondly, the award of a public contract to a semi-public company without calling for tenders would interfere with the objective of free and undistorted competition and the principle of equal treatment of the persons concerned,

---

[153] *See* Joined Cases C-20/01 and C-28/01, *Commission v. Germany* [2003] ECR I-3609, paragraph 58.
[154] *See* Case C-107/98, *Teckal* [1999] ECR I-8121, paragraphs 50 and 51.
[155] *See* Case C-107/98, *Teckal* [1999] ECR I-8121, paragraph 50.

referred to in Directive 92/50, in particular, in that such a procedure would offer a private undertaking with a capital presence in that undertaking an advantage over its competitors.

(12) State commercial companies as contracting authorities

Sociedad Estatal de Infraestruturas y Equipamientos Penitenciarios SA (SIEPSA), a **7.104** private company under the control of the Spanish Government did not follow the provisions of the Public Procurement Directives in connection with the call for tenders for the execution of works for the *Centro Educativo Penitenciario Experimental de Segovia* (Experimental Educational Prison, Segovia). The question which arose in Case C-283/00, *Commission v Spain*, was whether such private companies under state control should be considered as contracting authorities for the purposes of the Public Procurement Directives.[156]

The Spanish Government argued that SIEPSA was not to be considered as a **7.105** contracting authority on the grounds that commercial companies under public control, such as SIEPSA, are not included within the notion of bodies governed by public law. That argument was based on the fact that the Utilities Directive 93/38 draws a distinction between the concept of a body governed by public law, identical in all Public Procurement Directives, and the concept of a public undertaking, the definition of which corresponds to that of a public commercial company. The Spanish Government noted that the Community legislature was aware that many undertakings in the private sector, although possessing the form of a public undertaking, specifically pursue a wholly commercial object, despite their dependency on the state, and operate on the market in accordance with the rules of free competition and in conditions of equality with other private undertakings strictly for the purpose of making profits. That is why the legislature confined the Directive's ambit to bodies cumulatively satisfying the three conditions set out in Article 1(b) thereof.

While acknowledging that SIEPSA fulfils the two last conditions under Article **7.106** 1(b) of the Directive, the Spanish Government argued that SIEPSA possesses the attributes of a commercial company, given that its objects and tasks are typically commercial, and that it therefore meets general interest needs of a commercial character, which does not meet the first criterion of that provision. In addition, referring to the list in Part V of Annex I to the Directive, which contains the categories of Spanish bodies governed by public law that meet the criteria laid down in the second paragraph of Article 1(b) of that Directive, the Spanish Government asserted that SIEPSA does not belong to any of those categories, since it is not an

---

[156] *See* Case C-283/00, *Commission of the European Communities v. Kingdom of Spain.*

independent body and since it is not subject to the Spanish laws on public procurement.

7.107 The exclusion of companies such as SIEPSA from the scope *ratione personae* of the Public Procurement Directives, according to the Spanish Government, is accounted for by the circumstance that, in the Spanish legal order, it is generally the task of public bodies governed by private law, a category consisting of commercial companies under public control, such as SIEPSA, to meet general interest needs, which explains why they are under public control, but those needs are commercial or industrial in nature for, if that were not so, they could not be the object of a commercial company. The Spanish Government stated that the principal task entrusted to SIEPSA, namely, the building of new prisons suited to the needs of society, consists of a general interest requirement of a commercial character, which serves the ultimate purpose of contributing to prison policy, which is also in the general interest. SIEPSA was created in order to carry out all actions which prove necessary to the proper management of the programmes and transactions provided for in the plan for financing and constructing prisons, either by its own resources or through the resources of other undertakings. Its attributes are those of a typical commercial company, it even being governed by commercial law, without prejudice to the exceptions provided for in the areas of budget, accounts, and financial audit. In order to attain those objectives, SIEPSA performs transactions which must, in the Spanish Government's submission, be objectively classified as commercial, such as locating and acquiring buildings to be fitted out as new prisons, and the development and execution of preparatory and construction works.

7.108 The Spanish Government observed that, in carrying on those activities, SIEPSA makes a profit, and that the performance of those operations with a view to generating profits is a typically commercial activity which can be successfully carried out only by a company subject to the commercial rules of the private sector with which it must necessarily engage. It goes on to say that that company's activity cannot be treated as administrative, since its objective is to acquire financial means or resources like any contractor, and that is so, even though, in the final analysis, those resources are applied for other general interest purposes.

7.109 The Spanish Government argued that, whether or not SIEPSA is subject to market competition, it carries on activities which are commercial in nature. According to the case law of the Court,[157] the absence of competition is not a condition necessarily to be taken into account in defining a body governed by public law and, therefore, an entity such as SIEPSA cannot fall within the notion of a contracting authority used by the Public Procurement Directives. The fact that

---

[157] *See* Case C-360/96, *BFI Holding* [1998] ECR I-6821, paragraph 47.

state commercial companies such as SIEPSA are regulated by private law is not so much the cause as the consequence of their actual nature. It states in this regard that that a company is not commercial in character because it is governed by private law, but that it is precisely the commercial character of its activity that confers on it the attributes it possesses and results in its being governed by private law. The Spanish Government submitted that it is the only view that respects the autonomous definition of the criterion of the non-industrial or commercial character of needs in the general interest.[158] It contended that, since the state serves the general interest and since it has a majority shareholding in state commercial companies, it is logical to suppose that those companies will always serve the general interest to a greater or lesser extent. If, in order for the body to be classified as a contracting authority, it were sufficient that it should perform tasks in the general interest, such as contributing to the imposition of criminal penalties, then the condition that those tasks should not be industrial or commercial in character would be meaningless.

The Spanish Government concluded that SIEPSA ought to receive the same treatment as undertakings supplying gas, electricity, or water, sectors which satisfy essential social requirements and which are, in most cases, in the hands of private undertakings which also pursue broader objectives in the general interest. **7.110**

The Commission considered that SIEPSA fulfils all the conditions laid down in Article 1(b) of the Directive and that it is, therefore, a contracting authority for the purposes of that Directive. The Commission noted that, when implementing Community Directives in domestic law, the member states are required to respect the meaning of the words and concepts used in those measures, in order to guarantee uniform interpretation and application of Community legislation in the various member states. As a result, the Spanish authorities are bound to give the expression 'body governed by public law', used in the Directive, the meaning it has under Community law. Thus, according to the Commission, if SIEPSA is excluded from the ambit of the Community rules on the award of public procurement contracts by virtue of national law, the Public Procurement Directives have not been properly implemented into Spanish law. **7.111**

The Commission claimed that the functional interpretation of the notion of 'contracting authority' and, therefore, of 'body governed by public law' adopted in the established case law of the Court implies that the latter notion includes commercial companies under public control, provided that they fulfil the conditions laid down in the second paragraph of Article 1(b) of the Directive. As regards the distinction drawn by the Utilities Directive 93/38 between the definitions of a 'body governed by public law' and a 'public undertaking', the Commission **7.112**

---

[158] *See* Case C-360/96, *BFI Holding* [1998] ECR I-6821, paragraphs 32 and 36.

stated that that Directive does not clarify the concept of a body governed by public law, which is identical in all Public Procurement Directives, but extends the scope *ratione personae* of the provisions of Community law relating to public procurement to the utilities sectors which are excluded from Directives 93/36, 93/37, and 92/50, in order to cover certain bodies carrying on significant activity in those sectors, namely, public undertakings and those which enjoy special or exclusive rights granted by the authorities. In addition, the concept of a public undertaking has always been different from that of a body governed by public law, in that bodies governed by public law are created specifically to meet needs in the general interest, having no industrial or commercial character, whereas public undertakings act to satisfy needs of an industrial or commercial character.

7.113 The Commission also disproved the Spanish Government's interpretation which makes the concept of body governed by public law dependent on the lists contained in Annex I to the Directive in respect of every member state, with the result that a Community concept comes to have different meanings, depending on the way in which the various lists in Annex I were drawn up. According to the Commission, the interpretation favoured by the Spanish Government runs counter to the primary object of the Directive, as set out in the second recital in the preamble thereto, and is also contrary to the third paragraph of Article 1(b) thereof, according to which the lists are to be as exhaustive as possible. The Commission stressed the point that that expression cannot be understood to mean anything other than that the lists are not exhaustive and that that interpretation has been confirmed by the Court in *BFI Holding* case.[159] From that it can be deduced that, if state companies do not appear, directly or indirectly, in the list of bodies governed by public law in Part V of Annex I to the Directive, it does not mean that they fall outside the concept defined in the second paragraph of Article 1(b) for the purposes of being considered as contracting authorities. So far as the conditions laid down in the second paragraph of Article 1(b) of the Directive are concerned, the Commission observed that this provision makes no mention of the set of rules, whether public or private, under which bodies governed by public law have been formed, or of the legal form chosen, but rather refers to other standards, including the purpose for which the bodies in question were created.

7.114 The Commission submitted that SIEPSA was established for the specific purpose of meeting needs in the general interest, not having an industrial or commercial character, namely to contribute to the implementation of state prison policy through the management of programmes and actions contained in the plan for paying off the costs of and establishing prisons approved by the Council of Ministers. The concept of general interest is closely linked to public order and the institutional operation of the state and even to the very essence of the state, in as

---

[159] *See* Case C-360/96, *BFI Holding* [1998] ECR I-6821, paragraph 50.

much as the state holds the monopoly of power in the penal sphere consisting of the imposition of penalties depriving persons of their liberty, and does not possess an industrial or commercial character.[160]

The Commission disagreed with the Spanish Government's argument that **7.115** companies which, like SIEPSA, operate on the market subject to the principles of free competition in the same way as private undertakings and for the same purpose of making profits, have a purely commercial object and by that token fall outside the ambit of the Community Directives on public procurement. In particular, it referred by way of example to the award of works contracts for the construction of public prisons or the sale of the state's prison properties, which are two of SIEPSA's company objects and which cannot be regarded as activities subject to market competition. Furthermore, the Commission submitted that, even if it should be conceded that SIEPSA carries on activity subject to free competition, that fact does not mean that it cannot be regarded as a contracting authority.[161]

The Commission claimed that the Spanish Government's argument that all **7.116** SIEPSA's activities are commercial is without substance. First, it stated that, contrary to the claims made by the Spanish Government, SIEPSA's activity cannot be compared with private sector activity. It explained that that company does not offer prisons on the penal establishments market (there is no such market) but rather acts as the representative of the state administration in order to assist the latter in a task of a typically state nature: the construction, management, and selling of prison properties. On this subject, the Commission noted that, as is clear from the company's statutes, in carrying out its tasks SIEPSA follows Directives issued by the general management of the prison administration, and real property is sold and the sums so realised are used in accordance with the Directives issued by the general management of state assets. Secondly, the Commission observed that the Spanish Government separates the need to build prisons (from which it infers that it is of general interest and possessed of a commercial character) from the ultimate purpose, which is to contribute to penal policy (which it classifies as being in the general interest). It stated that this separation, as well as being artificial in that the two needs are closely linked, is inconsistent with the reasoning followed by the Court in other cases, in which it has declared that the collection and treatment of waste (*BFI Holding*) or the printing of official administrative documents (*Mannesmann Anlagenbau Austria*) are needs in the general interest, not having an industrial or commercial character, without separating those activities from their ultimate purpose: public health and environmental protection, on the one hand, and public order and the institutional operation of the State, on the other. Finally, the Commission claimed that, even if SIEPSA's objective were profit, that aim

---

[160] *See* Case C-44/96, *Mannesmann Anlagenbau Austria* [1998] ECR I-73, paragraph 24.
[161] *See* Case C-360/96, *BFI Holding* [1998] ECR I-6821, paragraph 47.

would not prevent the company from meeting needs in the general interest not having an industrial or commercial character. While the pursuit of profit may be a distinguishing feature of the company's activities, it is not stated in the text of the Directive that this goal makes it impossible to consider that the general interest needs to meet which SIEPSA was created have no industrial or commercial character. The Commission added that it is debatable whether the pursuit of profit is an object for a state company such as SIEPSA, which is wholly funded out of public resources, and which was created for the purpose of drawing up and implementing a plan for paying off the costs of and establishing prisons. It is obvious to the Commission that, in such a sphere, making a profit is not a factor which a member state would consider of prime importance.

7.117 The Court held that, in order to be defined as a body governed by public law within the meaning of the second paragraph of Article 1(b) of the Directive, an entity must satisfy the three cumulative conditions set out therein, requiring it to be a body established for the specific purpose of meeting needs in the general interest not having an industrial or commercial character, to possess legal personality, and to be closely dependent on the state, regional, or local authorities or other bodies governed by public law.[162]

7.118 The crucial point to determine whether SIEPSA is a contracting authority is whether or not the needs in the general interest to meet which SIEPSA was specifically created are commercial in character. In *Commission v. Spain* the Court rejected the Spanish Government's arguments based on the fact that, under the Spanish applicable legislation, commercial companies under public control such as SIEPSA are excluded from the ambit *ratione personae* of both the Spanish rules and the Community rules on public procurement. More specifically, in order to determine whether that exclusion constitutes correct transposition of the concept of contracting authority, the Court referred to the scope of the concept of body governed by public law employed by the Public Procurement Directives.[163] In that context the Court noted that, in accordance with established case law, in light of the dual purpose of opening up competition and of transparency pursued by the Public Procurement Directives, that concept must be given a functional and broad interpretation.[164]

7.119 The Court has held that for the purposes of settling the issue of the classification of an entity governed by public law within the meaning of the second paragraph of Article 1(b) of the Directive, it is necessary to establish only whether or not the body concerned fulfils the three conditions set out in that provision, for that

---

[162] *See* Case 44/96, *Mannesmann Anlagenbau Austria*, paragraphs 20 and 21, and Case C-214/00, *Commission v. Spain* [2003] ECR I-0000, paragraph 52.
[163] *See Commission v. Spain*, paragraphs 48, 50 and 51.
[164] *See Commission v. Spain*, paragraphs 48, 50 and 51.

body's status as a body governed by private law does not constitute a criterion capable of excluding it from being classified as a contracting authority for the purposes of the Directive.[165] In addition, the Court has stated that this interpretation, the only one capable of maintaining the full effectiveness of the Directive, does not disregard the industrial or commercial character of the general interest needs which the body concerned is intended to meet, for that aspect is necessarily taken into consideration for the purpose of determining whether or not that body satisfies the condition laid down in the first indent of the second paragraph of Article 1(b) of the Directive.[166] Nor is that conclusion invalidated by the want of an express reference in the Directive to the specific category of public undertakings which is, however, used in the Utilities Directive 93/38. The Utilities Directive was adopted for the purpose of extending the application of the Community rules regulating public procurement to the water, energy, transport, and telecommunications sectors which were not covered by other Directives. From that point of view, by employing the concepts of public authorities, on the one hand, and public undertakings, on the other, the Community legislature adopted a functional approach similar to that adopted in Directives 92/50, 93/36 and 93/37. It was thus able to ensure that all the contracting entities operating in the sectors regulated by Directive 93/38 were included in its ambit *ratione personae*, on condition that they satisfied certain criteria, their legal form and the rules under which they were formed being in this respect immaterial.

With regard to the relevance of the Spanish Government's argument that SIEPSA **7.120** does not fall within any of the categories of Spanish bodies governed by public law listed in Annex I to the Directive, the Court has held that that list is in no way exhaustive, as its accuracy varies considerably from one member state to another.[167] The Court concluded that, if a specific body does not appear in that list, its legal and factual situation must be determined in each individual case in order to assess whether or not it meets a need in the general interest.

With regard to the concept of needs in the general interest, not having an indus- **7.121** trial or commercial character, the Court has held that concept is one of Community law and must accordingly be given an autonomous and uniform interpretation throughout the Community, the search for which must take account of the background to the provision in which it appears and of the purpose of the rules in question.[168] Needs in the general interest, not having an industrial or commercial character, within the meaning of Article 1(b) of the Community Directives coordinating the award of public contracts are generally needs which

---

[165] *See Commission v. Spain*, paragraphs 54 and 55.
[166] *See Commission v. Spain*, paragraphs 56 and 58.
[167] *See* Case C-373/00, *Adolf Truly* [2003] ECR I-0000, paragraph 39.
[168] *See* Case C-373/00, *Adolf Truly* [2003] ECR I-0000, paragraphs 36, 40 and 45.

are satisfied otherwise than by the supply of goods and services in the marketplace and which, for reasons associated with the general interest, the state chooses to provide itself or over which it wishes to retain a decisive influence.[169] The case law makes it clear that, in determining whether or not there exists a need in the general interest, not having an industrial or commercial character, account must be taken of relevant legal and factual circumstances, such as those prevailing when the body concerned was formed and the conditions in which it carries on its activity, including, *inter alia*, lack of competition on the market, the fact that its primary aim is not the making of profits, the fact that it does not bear the risks associated with the activity, and any public financing of the activity in question.[170] The Court found in *Korhonen* that, if the body operates in normal market conditions, aims at making a profit, and bears the losses associated with the exercise of its activity, it is unlikely that the needs it aims at meeting are not of an industrial or commercial nature.

7.122   To determine whether or not the needs in the general interest that SIEPSA is designed to meet are other than industrial or commercial in character, the Court maintained that an intrinsic link between such needs and the public order of the state in question must be established. That intrinsic link is to be seen, in particular, in the decisive influence wielded by the state over the carrying through of the tasks entrusted to SIEPSA. The Court held that there is no market for the goods and services offered by SIEPSA in the planning and establishment of prisons. Activities such as paying off the costs of, and establishment of prisons, which are among SIEPSA's primary objectives, are not subject to market competition. That company cannot, therefore, be regarded as a body which offers goods or services on a free market in competition with other economic agents. Even the argument which the Spanish Government forwarded, that SIEPSA carries on its activities for profit, cannot support the fact that it would appear inconceivable that the pursuit of such profit should be in itself the company's chief aim.

7.123   The Court went further to declare that it seems unlikely that state controlled companies such as SIEPSA should themselves have to bear the financial risks related to their activities. If fact, the state would take all necessary measure to protect the financial viability of such entities, such as measures to prevent compulsory liquidation. In those circumstances, it is possible that, in a procedure for the award of public contracts, an entity such as SIEPSA should allow itself to be guided by other than purely economic considerations. Therefore, in order to safeguard against such a possibility, it is essential to apply the Public Procurement Directives.[171] The Court concluded that the needs in the general interest to meet

---

[169] *See Adolf Truly*, paragraph 50, and Case C-18/01, *Korhonen* [2003] ECR I-0000, paragraph 47.
[170] *See Adolf Truly*, paragraph 66, and *Korhonen*, paragraphs 48 and 59.
[171] *See Adolf Truley*, paragraph 42, and *Korhonen*, paragraphs 51 and 52.

which the company was specifically established possess a character which is other than industrial or commercial. It follows that a body such as SIEPSA must be treated as a body governed by public law for the purposes of the second paragraph of Article 1(b) of the Directive and, therefore, as a contracting authority for the purposes of the first paragraph thereof.

(13) Private companies as contracting authorities

Companies governed by private law established for the specific purpose of meeting needs in the general interest which do not have an industrial or commercial character, have legal personality, and are financed for the most part by public authorities or other entities governed by public law or are subject to supervision by the latter, or have an administrative, managerial, or supervisory board more than half of whose members are appointed by public authorities or other entities governed by public law, are considered as contracting authorities for the purposes of the Public Procurement Directives. **7.124**

The Court stated, in connection with the second subparagraph of Article 1(b) of Directive 93/37, that, in order to be defined as a body governed by public law within the meaning of that provision, an entity must satisfy the three cumulative conditions set out therein, according to which it must be a body established for the specific purpose of meeting needs in the general interest, not having an industrial or commercial character, which has legal personality, and is closely dependent on the state, regional, or local authorities or other bodies governed by public law.[172] Moreover, the Court has repeatedly held that, in the light of the dual objective of opening up competition and transparency pursued by the Directives on the coordination of the procedures for the award of public contracts, the term 'contracting authority' must be interpreted in functional terms.[173] The Court has also stated that, in the light of that dual purpose, the term 'body governed by public law' must be interpreted broadly.[174] The Court, for the purposes of settling the question whether various private law entities could be classified as bodies governed by public law, has proceeded in accordance with settled case law and merely ascertained whether those entities fulfilled the three cumulative conditions set out in the second subparagraph of Article 1(b) of Directives 92/50, 93/36, and 93/37, considering that the method in which the entity concerned has been set up was irrelevant in that regard.[175] **7.125**

---

[172] *See* Case C-44/96, *Mannesmann Anlagenbau Austria* [1998] ECR I-73, paragraphs 20 and 21.
[173] *See* Case C-237/99, *Commission v. France* [2001] ECR I-939, paragraphs 41 to 43, and Case C-470/99, *Universale-Bau and Others* [2002] ECR I-11617, paragraphs 51 to 53.
[174] *See* Case C-373/00, *Adolf Truley* [2003] ECR-1931, paragraph 43.
[175] *See*, in particular, *Mannesmann Anglagenbau Austria and Others*, paragraphs 6 and 29; Case C-360/96, *BFI Holding* [1998] ECR I-6821, paragraphs 61 and 62; and Case C-237/99, *Commission v. France*, paragraphs 50 and 60.

7.126 It is apparent from the jurisprudence of the Court that an entity's private law status does not constitute a criterion for precluding it from being classified as a contracting authority. Furthermore, it should be pointed out that the effectiveness of the Public Procurement Directives would not be fully preserved if the application of those Directives to an entity which fulfils the three aforementioned conditions could be excluded solely on the basis of the fact that, under the national law to which it is subject, its legal form and rules which govern it fall within the scope of private law.

7.127 In the light of those considerations, it is not possible to interpret the term 'body governed by public law' used in the second subparagraph of Article 1(b) of Directives 92/50, 93/36, and 93/37 as meaning that member states may automatically exclude commercial companies under public control from the scope *ratione personae* of those Directives. Furthermore, it cannot be maintained that to reach that conclusion is to disregard the industrial or commercial character of the needs in the general interest which those companies meet, because that aspect is necessarily taken into consideration for the purpose of determining whether or not the entity concerned meets the condition set out in the first indent of the second subparagraph of Article 1(b) of Directives 92/50, 93/36, and 93/37. Nor is that conclusion invalidated by the lack of an express reference, in the Public Services, Supplies, and Works Directives 92/50, 93/36, and 93/37 respectively, to the specific category of public undertakings which is nevertheless used in the Utilities Directive 93/38.

(14) Entities meeting needs of general interest retrospectively

7.128 A question arose before the Court as to whether an entity which was not established for the specific purpose of meeting needs in the general interest, not having an industrial or commercial character, but which has subsequently taken responsibility for such needs, which it has subsequently been actually meeting, fulfils the condition required by the first indent of the second subparagraph of Article 1(b) of Directive 93/37 so as to be capable of being regarded as a body governed by public law within the meaning of that provision. In the dispute in the main proceedings, it emerged *Entsorgungsbetriebe Simmering GesmbH* (EBS) took over the operation of the main sewage treatment plant, under a contract made in 1985 with the city of Vienna. It was not disputed that the company satisfies a need in the general interest not having an industrial or commercial character. However, its treatment as a body governed by public law within the meaning of the second subparagraph of Article 1(b) of Directive 93/37 depends on the answer to be given to the question whether the condition set out in the first indent of that provision precludes an entity from being regarded as a contracting authority where it was not established for the purposes of satisfying needs in the general interest having a character other than industrial or commercial, but has undertaken such tasks as a result of a subsequent change in its sphere of activities.[176]

EBS submitted that it cannot be regarded as a body governed by public law within **7.129** the meaning of the second subparagraph of Article 1(b) of Directive 93/37, on the ground that it is clear from the actual wording of the first indent of that provision that the sole deciding factor is the task which it was given at the date of its establishment. It adds that the fact that it has, subsequently, taken responsibility for tasks in the general interest having a character other than industrial or commercial does not affect its status since it continues to carry out industrial and commercial assignments. The Commission maintained that EBS cannot be regarded as a contracting authority within the meaning of Article 1(b) of Directive 93/37, because the change in its activities stems neither from an amendment to that effect of its objects as defined in its statutes, nor from a legal obligation.

In contrast, the applicants in the main proceedings *(Universale-Bau AG)*, as well as the **7.130** Austrian and Netherlands Governments as intervening parties, argued that it is EBS's current activity which is to be taken into consideration and not its purpose at the date of its establishment. They asserted that a different interpretation would mean that, notwithstanding the fact that an entity corresponded as a matter of fact to the definition of contracting authority in Directive 93/37, it would not be required, in awarding public works contracts, to observe the requirements of that Directive. In addition, they maintained that a functional interpretation of the term 'contracting authority' is the only one capable of preventing possible evasion, since, otherwise, Directive 93/37 could easily be circumvented by transferring tasks in the general interest having a character other than industrial or commercial, not to an entity newly established for that purpose, but to an existing one which previously had another object.

The Court has held that the purpose of coordinating at Community level the **7.131** procedures for the award of public contracts is to eliminate barriers to the freedom to provide services and goods and, therefore, to protect the interests of traders established in a member state who wish to offer goods or services to contracting authorities established in another member state.[177] The aim of Directive 93/37 is to avoid both the risk of preference being given to national tenderers or applicants whenever a contract is awarded by the contracting authorities, and the possibility that a body financed or controlled by the state, regional, or local authorities, or other bodies governed by public law, may choose to be guided by considerations other than economic ones.[178]

---

[176] *See* Case C-470/99, *Universale-Bau AG, Bietergemeinschaft Hinteregger & Söhne Bauges.mbH Salzburg, ÖSTU-STETTIN Hoch- und Tiefbau GmbH, and Entsorgungsbetriebe Simmering GesmbH.*

[177] *See* Case C-380/98, *University of Cambridge* [2000] ECR I-8035, paragraph 16, and Case C-237/99, *Commission v. France* [2001] ECR I-939, paragraph 41.

[178] *See,* in particular, *University of Cambridge,* paragraph 17, and C-237/99 *Commission v. France,* paragraph 42.

7.132 The Court has therefore held that it is in the light of those objectives that the concept of 'body governed by public law' in the second subparagraph of Article 1(b) of Directive 93/37 must be interpreted in functional terms.[179] Thus, in *Mannesmann Anlagenbau Austria*, in relation to the treatment of an entity which had been established for the specific purpose of meeting needs in the general interest not having an industrial or commercial character, but which also carried on commercial activities, the Court held that the condition laid down in the first indent of the second subparagraph of Article 1(b) of Directive 93/37 does not entail that the body concerned may be entrusted only with meeting needs in the general interest, not having an industrial or commercial character. In particular, the Court has held that it is immaterial that, in addition to the specific task of meeting needs in the general interest, the entity concerned is free to carry out other activities, but, on the other hand, decided that it is a critical factor that it should continue to attend to the needs which it is specifically required to meet. For the purposes of deciding whether a body satisfies the condition set out in the first indent of the second subparagraph of Article 1(b) of Directive 93/37, it is necessary to consider the activities which it actually carries on. In that regard, it should be pointed out that the effectiveness of Directive 93/37 would not be fully upheld if the application of the scheme of the Directive to a body which satisfies the conditions set out in the second subparagraph of Article 1(b) thereof, could be excluded owing solely to the fact that the tasks in the general interest having a character other than industrial or commercial which it carries out in practice were not entrusted to it at the time of its establishment.

7.133 The same concern to ensure the effectiveness of the second subparagraph of Article 1(b) of Directive 93/37 also militates against drawing a distinction according to whether the statutes of such an entity were, or were not, amended to reflect actual changes in its sphere of activity. In addition, the wording of the second subparagraph of Article 1(b) of Directive 93/37 contains no reference to the legal basis of the activities of the entity concerned.

7.134 The Court considered appropriate to point out that, in relation to the definition of the expression 'body governed by public law' in the second subparagraph of Article 1(b) of Directive 92/50, which is in terms identical to those contained in the second subparagraph of Article 1(b) of Directive 93/37, the Court has already held that the existence or absence of needs in the general interest not having an industrial or commercial character must be appraised objectively, the legal form of the provisions in which those needs are mentioned being immaterial in that regard.[180]

7.135 The Court regarded as irrelevant that fact that the extension of the sphere of activities of EBS did not give rise to an amendment to the provisions of its statutes

---

[179] *See* Case C-237/99, *Commission v. France*, paragraph 43.
[180] *See* Case C-360/96, *BFI Holding* [1998] ECR I-6821, paragraph 63.

concerning its objects. Although EBS's assumption of responsibility for needs in the general interest not having an industrial or commercial character has not been formally incorporated in its statutes, it is none the less set out in the contracts which EBS made with the city of Vienna and is, therefore, capable of being objectively established.

The Court concluded that a body which was not established to satisfy specific **7.136** needs in the general interest not having an industrial or commercial character, but which has subsequently taken responsibility for such needs, which it has since actually satisfied, fulfils the condition required by the first indent of the second subparagraph of Article 1(b) of Directive 93/37 so as to be capable of being regarded as a body governed by public law within the meaning of that provision, on condition that the assumption of responsibility for the satisfaction of those needs can be established objectively.

(15) *Private entities for industrial and commercial development as contracting authorities*

A question was referred to the Court as to whether a limited company established, **7.137** owned, and managed by a regional or local authority may be regarded as meeting a specific need in the general interest, not having an industrial or commercial character, where that company's activity consists in acquiring services with a view to the construction of premises intended for the exclusive use of private under-takings, and whether the assessment of whether that condition is satisfied would be different, if the building project in question were intended to create favourable conditions on that local authority's territory for the exercise of business activi-ties.[181] Taitotalo is a limited company whose capital is wholly owned by the town of Varkaus (Finland), and whose objects are to buy, sell, and lease real property and shares in property companies, and to organise and supply property mainten-ance services and other related services needed for the management of those prop-erties and shares. The company's board has three members, who are officials of the town of Varkaus, appointed by the general meeting of the company's shareholders, at which the town has a hundred per cent of the voting rights.

The Court found that a limited company established, owned, and managed by a **7.138** regional or local authority meets a need in the general interest, within the mean-ing of the second subparagraph of Article 1(b) of Council Directive 92/50/EEC of 18 June 1992 relating to the coordination of procedures for the award of public service contracts, where it acquires services with a view to promoting the develop-ment of industrial or commercial activities on the territory of that regional or local

---

[181] *See* Case C-18/01, *Arkkitehtuuritoimisto Riitta Korhonen Oy, Arkkitehtitoimisto Pentti Toivanen Oy, Rakennuttajatoimisto Vilho Tervomaa and Varkauden Taitotalo Oy.*

authority. To determine whether that need has no industrial or commercial character, the national court must assess the circumstances which prevailed when that company was set up and the conditions in which it carries on its activity, taking account in particular of the fact that it does not aim primarily at making a profit, the fact that it does not bear the risks associated with the activity, and any public financing of the activity in question. The fact that the premises to be constructed are leased only to a single undertaking is not capable of calling into question the lessor's status of a body governed by public law, where it is shown that the lessor meets a need in the general interest not having an industrial or commercial character.

7.139 Taitotalo considered that its activity is not intended to meet needs in the general interest and, in any event, has an industrial or commercial character. It submitted that its sole object is to promote the conditions for the exercise of the activities of specific undertakings, not for the exercise generally of economic activity in the town of Varkaus, while the fact that it is owned and financed by a contracting authority is of no relevance, since, in the case in the main proceedings, it meets industrial or commercial needs. Taitotalo stated, in particular, that it acquired at market price the land needed for the building works at issue in the main proceedings, and that the financing of the project will be taken in hand essentially by the private sector, by means of bank loans secured by mortgages. The leasing of premises for industrial or commercial use cannot in any case be regarded as within the prerogatives which by their very nature are part of the exercise of public powers.[182]

7.140 According to the arguments submitted by the Finnish Government, Taitotalo's activity typically appears among those which respond to a need in the general interest with no industrial or commercial character. Firstly, Taitotalo's primary aim is not to generate profits by its activity but to create favourable conditions for the development of economic activities on the territory of the town of Varkaus, which fits in perfectly with the functions which regional and local authorities may assume by virtue of the autonomy guaranteed to them by the Finnish constitution. Secondly, the objective of Directive 92/50 would be compromised if such a company were not regarded as a contracting authority within the meaning of the Directive, as municipalities might in that case be tempted to establish, in their traditional sphere of activity, other undertakings whose contracts would be outside the scope of the Directive.

7.141 Finally, while not excluding the possibility that Taitotalo's activity may meet a need in the general interest because of the stimulus it gives to trade and the development of business activities in the territory of the town of Varkaus, the Austrian

---

[182] *See* Case C-44/96, *Mannesmann Anlagenbau Austria and Others* [1998] ECR I-73; Case C-237/99, *Commission v. France* [2001] ECR I-939.

Government and the Commission, as intervening parties, stated that, in view of the incomplete information available, they are unable to assess the extent to which that need has an industrial or commercial character. They therefore invited the national court to perform that assessment itself, examining in particular the competition position of Taitotalo and whether it bears the risks associated with its activity.

The Court held that the second subparagraph of Article 1(b) of Directive 92/50 **7.142** draws a distinction between needs in the general interest not having an industrial or commercial character and needs in the general interest having an industrial or commercial character.[183] To give a useful answer to the questions put, it must first be ascertained whether activities such as those at issue in the main proceedings in fact meet needs in the general interest, and then, if necessary, it must be determined whether such needs have an industrial or commercial character. As regards the question whether the activity at issue in the main proceedings meets a need in the general interest, it appears from the order for reference that Taitotalo's principal activity consists in buying, selling, and leasing properties and organising and supplying property maintenance services and other related services needed for the management of those properties. The operation carried out by Taitotalo in the main proceedings consists, more precisely, in acquiring design and construction services in connection with a building project relating to the construction of several office blocks and a multi-storey car park. That operation, which followed from the town of Varkaus's decision to create a technological development centre on its territory, and Taitotalo's stated intention to buy the land from the town once the site has been parcelled out, and to make the newly-constructed buildings available to firms in the technology sector, is an activity capable of meeting a need in the general interest.

The Court held in a similar case[184] whether a body whose objects were to carry on **7.143** and facilitate any activity concerned with the organization of trade fairs, exhibitions, and conferences could be regarded as a body governed by public law within the meaning of Article 1(b) of Directive 92/50, that activities relating to the organization of such events meet needs in the general interest, in that an organizer of those events, in bringing together manufacturers and traders in one geographical location, is not acting solely in the individual interest of those manufacturers and traders, who are thereby afforded an opportunity to promote their goods and merchandise, but is also providing consumers who attend the events with information that enables them to make choices in optimum conditions. The resulting stimulus to trade may be considered to fall within the general interest. Similar considerations may be put forward *mutatis mutandis* with respect to the activity at

---

[183] *See, inter alia, BFI Holding*, paragraph 36, and *Agorà and Excelsior*, paragraph 32
[184] *See Agorà and Excelsior*, paragraphs 33 and 34.

issue in the main proceedings, in that it is undeniable that, in acquiring design and construction services in connection with a building project relating to the construction of office blocks, Taitotalo is not acting solely in the individual interest of the undertakings directly concerned by that project but also in that of the town of Varkaus. Activities such as those carried on by Taitotalo in the case in the main proceedings may be regarded as meeting needs in the general interest, in that they are likely to give a stimulus to trade and the economic and social development of the local authority concerned, since the location of undertakings on the territory of a municipality often has favourable repercussions for that municipality in terms of creation of jobs, increase of tax revenue, and improvement of the supply and demand of goods and services.

7.144 A more difficult question, on the other hand, is whether such needs in the general interest have a character which is not industrial or commercial. While the Finnish Government submitted that those needs have no industrial or commercial character, in that Taitotalo aims not so much to make a profit as to create favourable conditions for the location of undertakings on the territory of the town of Varkaus, Taitotalo put forward the contrary argument, on the ground that it provides services precisely for commercial undertakings, and that the financing of the building project in question is borne essentially by the private sector.

7.145 The Court has maintained that needs in the general interest, not having an industrial or commercial character, within the meaning of Article 1(b) of the Community Directives relating to the coordination of procedures for the award of public contracts, are generally needs which are satisfied otherwise than by the availability of goods and services in the market place and which, for reasons associated with the general interest, the state chooses to provide itself or over which it wishes to retain a decisive influence.[185] It cannot be excluded that the acquisition of services intended to promote the location of private undertakings on the territory of a particular local authority may be regarded as meeting a need in the general interest whose character is not industrial or commercial. In assessing whether or not such a need in the general interest is present, account must be taken of all the relevant legal and factual elements, such as the circumstances prevailing at the time when the body concerned was established and the conditions under which it exercises its activity. In particular, it must be ascertained whether the body in question carries on its activities in a situation of competition, since the existence of such competition may, as the Court has previously held, be an indication that a need in the general interest has an industrial or commercial character.[186]

7.146 However, it also follows from the wording of that judgment that the existence of significant competition does not of itself permit the conclusion that there is no

---

[185] *See BFI Holding*, paragraphs 50 and 51, *Agorà and Excelsior*, paragraph 37, and *Adolf Truley*, paragraph 50.　　　　　　　　　　　　　　[186] *See BFI Holding*, paragraphs 48 and 49.

need in the general interest not having an industrial or commercial character.[187] The same applies to the fact that the body in question aims specifically to meet the needs of commercial undertakings. Other factors must be taken into account before reaching such a conclusion, in particular, the question of the conditions in which the body in question carries on its activities. If the body operates in normal market conditions, aims to make a profit, and bears the losses associated with the exercise of its activity, it is unlikely that the needs it aims to meet are not of an industrial or commercial nature. In such a case, the application of the Public Procurement Directives would not be necessary, moreover, because a body acting for profit and itself bearing the risks associated with its activity will not normally become involved in an award procedure on conditions which are not economically justified. The purpose of those Directives is to avert both the risk of preference being given to national tenderers or applicants whenever a contract is awarded by the contracting authorities and the possibility that a body financed or controlled by the state, regional, or local authorities, or other bodies governed by public law may choose to be guided by other than economic considerations.[188]

The Court considered that there are few differences between companies such as Taitotalo and limited companies owned by private operators, in that they bear the same economic risks as the latter and may similarly be declared bankrupt, but the regional and local authorities to which they belong rarely allow such a thing to happen and will, if appropriate, recapitalise those companies so that they can continue to look after the tasks for which they were established, essentially the improvement of the general conditions for the pursuit of economic activity in the local authority area in question. The Court also held that while it is not impossible that the activities of companies such as Taitotalo may generate profits, the making of such profits can never constitute the principal aim of such companies, since, under Finnish law, they must always aim primarily to promote the general interest of the inhabitants of the local authority area concerned. In such conditions, and having regard to the fact mentioned by the national court that Taitotalo received public funding for carrying out the building project at issue in the main proceedings, it appears probable that an activity such as that pursued by Taitotalo in this case meets a need in the general interest not having an industrial or commercial character. The Court asserted that it is for the national court to assess the circumstances which prevailed when that body was set up and the conditions in which it carries on its activity, including in particular whether it aims at making a profit and bears the risks associated with its activity. **7.147**

The fact that the activity at issue represents only a minor part of Taitotalo's activities, would be of no relevance to the description of the entity as a contracting **7.148**

---

[187] *See Adolf Truley*, paragraph 61.

[188] *See* Case C-380/98, *University of Cambridge* [2000] ECR I-8035, paragraph 17; Case C-470/99, *Universale-Bau and Others* [2002] ECR I-11617, paragraph 52; and *Adolf Truley*, paragraph 42.

authority, insofar as that company continues to look after needs in the general interest. The status of a body governed by public law is not dependent on the relative importance, within that body's activity, of the meeting of needs in the general interest not having an industrial or commercial character.[189] The Court reached the conclusion that a limited company established, owned, and managed by a regional or local authority meets a need in the general interest, within the meaning of the second subparagraph of Article 1(b) of Directive 92/50, where it acquires services with a view to promoting the development of industrial or commercial activities on the territory of that regional or local authority. To determine whether that need has no industrial or commercial character, the national court must assess the circumstances which prevailed when that company was set up and the conditions in which it carries on its activity, taking account in particular of the fact that it does not aim primarily at making a profit, the fact that it does not bear the risks associated with the activity, and any public financing of the activity in question.

The question as to whether the fact that the offices to be constructed are leased only to a single undertaking would not affect the lessor's status as a body governed by public law, where it is shown that the lessor meets a need in the general interest not having an industrial or commercial character.

---

[189] *See Mannesmann Anlagenbau Austria and Others*, paragraphs 25, 26 and 31; *BFI Holding*, paragraphs 55 and 56; and *Adolf Truley*, paragraph 56.

8

SELECTION AND QUALIFICATION

A. Technical Standards

The Court has approached very proactively the discriminatory use of specification **8.01** requirements and standards.[1] It established the 'equivalent standard' doctrine, where contracting authorities are prohibited from introducing technical specifications or trade marks which mention products of a certain make or source, or a particular process which favours or eliminate certain undertakings, unless these specifications are justified by the subject and nature of the contract and on condition that they are only permitted if they are accompanied by the words 'or equivalent'.

National technical standards, industrial product and service specifications, and **8.02** their harmonization were considered priority areas for the internal market programme. The European Commission's *White Paper for the Completion of the Internal Market* stipulated for a number of Directives to be adopted and implemented with a view to eliminating discrimination based on the description of

---

[1] *See* Case C-45/87, *Commission v. Ireland* [1988] ECR 4929; also Case C-359/93, *Commission v. The Netherlands*, judgment of 24 January 1995.

national standards. The rules on technical standards and specifications have been brought in line with the new policy which is based on the mutual recognition of national requirements, where the objectives of national legislation are essentially equivalent, and on the process of legislative harmonization of technical standards through non-governmental standardization organizations (CEPT, CEN, CENELEC).[2] However, persistence of contracting authorities to specify their procurement requirements by reference to national standards poses obstacles in the public sector integration.[3] The European Commission has been for some time aware of the most notable examples of circumvention of the policy on standards and specifications.[4] These include the exclusive familiarity of national suppliers with technical data existing in a particular member state, over-specification by contracting authorities in order to exclude potential bidders, and, finally, favouritism and discrimination by contracting authorities as a result of the availability of technical standards and specifications to certain suppliers only.

8.03 Standardization and specification can act as a non-tariff barrier in public procurement contracts in two ways: firstly, contracting authorities may use apparently different systems of standards and specifications as an excuse for disqualification of tenderers. It should be maintained here that the description of the intended supplies, works, or services to be procured is made by reference to the Common Product Classification, the NACE (General Industrial Classification of Economic Activities within the European Communities), and the Common Procurement Vocabulary (CPV); however, this type of description is of generic nature and does not cover industrial specifications and standardization requirements. Secondly, standardization and specification requirements can be restrictively defined in order to exclude products or services of a particular origin, or narrow the field of competition amongst tenderers. National standards are not only the subject of domestic legislation, which, of course, need to be harmonized and mutually recognised across the common market. One of the most significant aspects of standardization and specification appears to be the operation of voluntary standards, which are mainly specified at industry level. The above category is rather difficult to harmonize, as any approximation and mutual recognition relies on the willingness of the industry in question. Voluntary standards and specifications are used quite often in the utilities sector, where the relevant procurement requirements are complex and cannot be specified solely by reference to 'statutory' standards, thus leaving a considerable margin of discretion in the hands of the

---

[2] *See* Art. 7 of Directive 88/295. *See White Paper on Completing the Internal Market*, paras. 61–79; also Council Resolution of 7 May 1985 [1985] OJ C136, on a new approach in the field of technical harmonization and standards.

[3] *See* the Documents of the Advisory Committee for the Opening up of Public Procurement, *Policy Guidelines on the Obligation to refer to European Standards*, CCO/91/67 final.

[4] *See* the report of the Advisory Committee for the Opening up of Public Procurement, *Standards for Procurement*, CCO/92/02.

contracting authorities, which may abuse it during the selection and qualification stages of the procurement process.

The European Court of Justice has condemned discriminatory use of specification **8.04** requirements and standards. In the Irish *Dundalk* pipeline case,[5] the Commission had received complaints that Ireland had not complied with the Public Works Directive 71/305 and in particular Article 10 of Directive 71/305. This provision prohibits member states from introducing into the contractual clauses relating to a given contract, technical specifications, unless they are justified by the subject of the contract, which mention products of a specific make or source or a particular process which favour or eliminate certain undertakings. Such indications are only permitted if they are accompanied by the words 'or equivalent' where the authorities awarding contracts are unable to give sufficiently precise and intelligible specifications of the subject of the contract. In the *Dundalk* case, the invitation to tender referred to technical specifications which could only be adhered to by national contractors. Furthermore, there were not justified by the subject of the contract.

In another case, the Commission brought the Netherlands before the European **8.05** Court of Justice[6] for a failure to observe the Supplies Directive and, in particular, to specify, without discriminatory descriptions, the required goods for procurement. The *Neerlands Inkoopcentrum NV* had published a notice in the *Official Journal* for the procurement of a meteorological data processing system, which it specified with a particular trade mark, without using the term 'equivalent'. The Court, following its previous case law,[7] reiterated that Article 7(6) of the Supplies Directive 77/62 (as amended by Article 8 of Directive 89/295) intends to eliminate discriminatory description of supplies by utilization of particular trade marks, unless accompanied by the words 'or equivalent', and only in cases where reference to a particular trade mark is necessary for the description of the product in question. The Court of Justice also pronounced the compulsory and unconditional character of point 7 of Annex III to the Supplies Directive 77/62, which requires indication of authorised persons, date, time, and place for the opening of tenders, in order to allow tenderers to identify their competitors and enable them to ensure that their offers are being evaluated in a transparent and equal manner.

B. Selection and Qualification

The relevant provisions of the Procurement Directives relating to the qualitative **8.06** selection and qualification criteria refer to the technical ability and knowledge of

---

[5] Case 45/87, *Commission v. Ireland* [1988] ECR 4929.
[6] Case C-359/93, *Commission v. The Netherlands*, judgment of 24 January 1995.
[7] Case 45/87, *Commission v. Ireland* [1988] ECR 4929.

tenderers, where proof may be furnished by evidence of educational or professional qualifications, previous experience in performing public contracts, and statements on the contractor's expertise.[8] The references, which the tenderers may be required to produce, must be specified in the notice or invitation to tender. The rules relating to technical capacity and eligibility of tenderers represent an exhaustive list and are capable of producing direct effect.[9] The *Transporoute* legacy paved the way for the Court to elaborate on forms of selection and qualification, such as registration in lists of recognized contractors. Such lists exist in member states, and tenderers may use their registration in them as an alternative means of proving their technical suitability, also before contracting authorities of other member states. *CEI-Bellini* followed the same line,[10] although it conferred discretion on contracting authorities to request further evidence of technical capacity, other than the mere certificate of registration in official lists of approved contractors, on the grounds that such lists might not be referring to uniform classifications.

8.07   *Ballast Nedam I*[11] took qualitative selection and qualification criteria a step further. The Court ruled that a holding company which does not itself carry out works may not be precluded from registration on an official list of approved contractors, and consequently, from participating in tendering procedures, if it shows that it actually has available to it the resources of its subsidiaries necessary to carry out the contracts, unless the references of those subsidiaries do not themselves satisfy the qualitative selection criteria specified in the Directives. *Ballast Nedam II*[12] conferred an obligation on the authorities of member states, which are responsible for the compilation of lists of approved contractors, to take into account evidence of the technical capacity of companies belonging to the same group, when assessing the parent company's technical capacity for inclusion into the list, provided the holding company establishes that it has available to it the resources of the companies belonging to the group that are necessary to carry out public contracts. *Holst Italia*,[13] by analogy, applied the *Ballast* principle to undertakings that belong to the same group structure but do not have the status of a holding company and the requisite availability of the technical expertise of its subsidiaries. The Court held that, with regard to the qualitative criteria relevant to the economic, financial, and technical standing, a tenderer may rely on the standing of other entities, regardless of the legal nature of the links which it has with them,

---

[8]   *See* Art. 27 of Directive 93/37, Art.31 of Directive 93/38 and Art. 22 of Directive 92/50.

[9]   *See* Case 76/81, *SA Transporoute et Travaux v. Minister of Public Works* [1982] ECR 457.

[10]   *See* Case C-27/86, *Constructions et Enterprises Industrielles SA (CEI) v. Association Intercommunale pour les Autoroutes des Ardennes*; Case C-28/86, *Ing. A. Bellini & Co. SpA v. Regie de Bâtiments* and Case C-29/86, *Ing. A. Bellini & Co. SpA v. Belgian State* [1987] ECR 3347.

[11]   *See* Case C-89/92, *Ballast Nedam Groep NV v. Belgische Staat* [1994] 2 CMLR.

[12]   *See* Case C-5/97, *Ballast Nedam Groep NV v. Belgische Staat*, judgment of 18 December 1997.

[13]   *See* Case C-176/98, *Holst Italia v Comune di Cagliari*, judgment of 2 December 1999.

provided that it is able to show that it actually has at its disposal the resources of those entities which are necessary for performance of a public contract.

However, for the purposes of assessing the financial and economic standing of contractors, an exception to the exhaustive (and directly applicable) nature of technical capacity and qualification rules has been made. Evidence of financial and economic standing may be provided by means of references including: i) appropriate statements from bankers; ii) the presentation of the firm's balance sheets or extracts from the balance sheets where these are published under company law provisions; and iii) a statement of the firm's annual turnover and the turnover on construction works for the three previous financial years. The non-exhaustive character of the list of references in relation to the contractors' economic and financial standing was recognised by Court in the *CEI-Bellini* case,[14] where the value of the works which may be carried out at any one time may constitute a proof of the contractors' economic and financial standing. The contracting authorities are allowed to fix such a limit, as the provisions of the public procurement Directives do not aim at delimiting the powers of member states, but at determining the references or evidence which may be furnished in order to establish the contractors' financial and economic standing. Of interest is the recent case *ARGE*,[15] where even the receipt of aid or subsidies incompatible with the Treaty by an entity may be a reason for disqualification from the selection process, as an obligation to repay an illegal aid would threaten the financial stability of the tenderer in question. **8.08**

The Court also maintained[16] that the examination of a contractor's suitability based on its technical capacity and qualifications and its financial and economic standing may take place simultaneously with the award procedures of a contract.[17] However, the two procedures (the suitability evaluation and bid evaluation) are totally distinct processes, which shall not be confused.[18] **8.09**

C. References as a Selection Criterion

A question arose[19] as to whether Directive 93/36 precludes contracting authorities, in a procedure to award a public supply contract, from taking account of the **8.10**

---

[14] *See Bellini* case, op. cit.
[15] *See* Case C-94/99, *ARGE Gewässerschutzt v. Bundesministerium für Land- und Forstwirtschaft*, paragraph 30, judgment of 7 December 2000.
[16] Case 31/87, *Gebroeders Beentjes BV v. State of Netherlands* [1988] ECR 4635.
[17] *See* Case 28/86, *Bellini*, op.cit.
[18] *See* Case C-71/92, *Commission v. Spain*, judgment of 30 June 1993. Also, *Beentjes*, op. cit at paragraphs 15 and 16, where the simultaneous application of selection of tenderers and award procedures is not precluded, on condition that the two are governed by different rules.
[19] *See* Case C-315/01, *Gesellschaft für Abfallentsorgungs-Technik GmbH (GAT) and Österreichische Autobahnen und Schnellstraßen AG (ÖSAG)* [2003] ECR I-6351.

number of references relating to the products offered by the tenderers to other customers, not as a criterion for establishing their suitability for carrying out the contract, but as a criterion for awarding the contract. The Court held that the Public Procurement Directives preclude any reference obtained by a contracting authority in relation to products or services offered by tenderers to other customers from being a criterion for awarding the contract. Such references may only serve as a criterion for establishing their suitability for carrying out the contract.

8.11   The Court maintained that the examination of the suitability of contractors to deliver the products which are the subject of the contract to be awarded, and the awarding of the contract, are two different operations in the procedure for the award of a public works contract. Article 15(1) of the Public Supplies Directive 93/36 provides that the contract is to be awarded after the supplier's suitability has been verified,[20] although the Public Procurement Directives do not rule out the possibility that examination of the tenderer's suitability and the award of the contract may take place simultaneously, provided that the two procedures are governed by different rules.[21] Article 15(1) of the Directive provides that the suitability of tenderers is to be verified by the contracting authority in accordance with the criteria of economic and financial standing and of technical knowledge or ability referred to in Articles 22, 23, and 24 of the Directive. The purpose of these Articles is not to delimit the power of the member states to fix the level of financial and economic standing and technical knowledge required in order to take part in procedures for the award of public works contracts, but to determine the references or evidence which may be furnished in order to establish the suppliers' financial or economic standing and technical knowledge or ability.[22]

8.12   The Court reiterated that, as far as the criteria which may be used for the award of a public contract are concerned, Article 26(1) of Directive 93/36 provides that the authorities awarding contracts must base their decision either on the lowest price only or, when the award is made to the most economically advantageous tender, on various criteria according to the contract involved, such as price, delivery date, running costs, cost-effectiveness, quality, aesthetic and functional characteristics, technical merit, after-sales service, and technical assistance. The Court maintained that, as is apparent from the wording of that provision, in particular the use of the expression "for example" in relation to the factors comprising the most economically advantageous offer, the criteria which may be accepted as criteria for the award of a public contract to what is the most economically advantageous tender are not listed exhaustively.[23] However, although Article 26(1) of Directive 93/36

---

[20] *See* Case C-31/87, *Beentjes* [1988] ECR 4635, paragraph 15.
[21] *See* Case C-31/87, *Beentjes* [1988] ECR 4635, paragraph 16.
[22] *See* Case C-31/87, *Beentjes* [1988] ECR 4635, paragraph 17.
[23] *See* Case C-19/00, *SIAC Construction* [2001] ECR I-7725, paragraph 35; Case C-513/99, *Concordia Bus Finland* [2002] ECR I-7213, paragraph 54.

leaves it to the contracting authority to choose the criteria on which it intends to base its award of the contract, that choice may relate only to criteria aimed at identifying the offer which is the most economically advantageous.[24] However, the fact remains that the submission of a list of the principal deliveries effected in the past three years, stating the sums, dates, and recipients (public or private) involved, is expressly included among the references or evidence which, under Article 23(1)(a) of Directive 93/36, may be required to establish the suppliers' technical capacity. Furthermore, a simple list of references, such as that called for in the invitation to tender at issue in the main proceedings, which contains only the names and number of the suppliers' previous customers, without other details relating to the deliveries effected to those customers, cannot provide any information to identify the offer which is the most economically advantageous within the meaning of Article 26(1)(b) of Directive 93/36, and therefore cannot in any event constitute an award criterion within the meaning of that provision. The Court therefore concluded that contracting authorities are precluded from taking account of the number of references relating to the products offered by the tenderers to other customers as a criterion for awarding the contract, but not as a criterion for establishing their suitability for carrying out the contract.

D. Location of Contractors as Selection Criterion

In *Gesellschaft für Abfallentsorgungs-Technik GmbH (GAT)*,[25] a further question **8.13** arose as to whether the location of the contractor can play any role in the selection and qualification stage or the award stage of public contracts. The national law asked the Court whether the principle of equal treatment under the Public Procurement Directives precludes a criterion for the award of a public supply contract, according to which a tenderer's offer may be favourably assessed only if the product which is the subject of the offer is available for inspection by the contracting authority within a radius of 300 kilometers of the premises of the contracting authority. The Court maintained that such a criterion cannot constitute a criterion for the award of the contract. It forwarded two reasons. Firstly, it is apparent from Article 23(1)(d) of Directive 93/36 that, for public supply contracts, the contracting authorities may require the submission of samples, descriptions, or photographs of the products to be supplied as references or evidence of the suppliers' technical capacity to carry out the contract concerned. Secondly, a criterion such as that which is the subject of Question 4 cannot serve to identify the most economically advantageous offer within the meaning of

---

[24] *See Beentjes*, paragraph 19, *SIAC Construction*, paragraph 36, and *Concordia Bus Finland*, paragraph 59.
[25] *See* Case C-315/01, *Gesellschaft für Abfallentsorgungs-Technik GmbH (GAT) and Österreichische Autobahnen und Schnellstraßen AG (ÖSAG)* [2003] ECR I-6351.

Article 26(1)(b) of Directive 93/36, and, therefore, cannot, in any event, constitute an award criterion within the meaning of that provision.

E. Market Testing and Selection of Undertakings that Assist in the Preparation of Public Contracts

8.14 The Belgian *Conseil d'État* asked the Court whether the Public Procurement Directives prevent an undertaking which has participated in the preparatory stages of a public contract from being precluded from submitting a tender for that public contract, where that undertaking has not been given an opportunity to prove that its previous involvement with the preparation of the contract has not distorted competition amongst the tenderers.[26]

8.15 *Fabricom*, the claimant in the main proceedings before national courts, argued that the relevant Belgian laws[27] contravened Community law and, in particular, that they were contrary to the principle of non-discrimination.[28] That principle is applicable to all tenderers, including those who have participated in the preparatory stage of the contract. The latter should be excluded from participating in a public contract only if it appears clearly and specifically that, by such participation alone, they have gained an advantage which distorts normal competition. Thus, in Fabricom's submission, the irrefutable presumption set out in the national legislation has an effect which is disproportionate to the objective which they pursue, namely to ensure fair competition between tenderers. According to case law,[29] Community law on public procurement precludes a particular tender being eliminated as a matter of course and on the basis of a criterion which is applied automatically. The exclusion of an undertaking in the particular case of participation in preparatory works must be preceded by a full and differentiated examination of the kind of preparatory works concerned, in particular as regards access to the contract specifications. Exclusion is possible only if the undertaking has obtained, through its preparatory activity, specific information relating to the contract which gives it a competitive advantage.[30]

8.16 On the other hand, the Commission contended that the provisions of Belgian law seek to avoid possible discrimination and a competitive advantage to the person who has participated in the preparatory works when he submits his tender for the same contract. If the person who carries out the preparatory work could also be

---

[26] *See* Joined Cases C-21/03 and C-34/03, *Fabricom SA v. État Belge*, judgment of 3 March 2005.
[27] *See* Arts. 26 and 32 of the Royal Decree of 25 March 1999.
[28] *See* Case C-324/98, *Telaustria and Telefonadress* [2000] ECR I-10745.
[29] *See* Joined Cases C-285/99 and C-286/99, *Lombardini and Mantovani* [2001] ECR I-9233.
[30] Those were the arguments of the Austrian and Finnish Governments, which intervened in the Joined Cases C-21/03 and C-34/03, *Fabricom SA v. État Belge*, judgment of 3 March 2005.

the successful tenderer, he might steer the preparation of the public contract in a direction favourable to him.

The Court held that the duty to observe the principle of equal treatment lies at the **8.17** very heart of the Public Procurement Directives, which are intended in particular to promote the development of effective competition in the fields to which they apply, and which lay down criteria for the award of contracts which are intended to ensure such competition.[31] Furthermore, the principle of equal treatment requires that comparable situations must not be treated differently, and that different situations must not be treated in the same way, unless such treatment is objectively justified.[32] The Court held that a person who has been instructed to carry out research, experiments, studies, or development in connection with works, supplies, or services relating to a public contract (hereinafter 'a person who has carried out certain preparatory work') is not necessarily in the same situation as regards participation in the procedure for the award of that contract as a person who has not carried out such works. A person who has participated in certain preparatory works may be at an advantage when formulating his tender on account of the information concerning the public contract in question which he has received when carrying out that work. However, all tenderers must have equality of opportunity when formulating their tenders.[33]

The Court, furthermore, maintained that a person may be in a situation which **8.18** may give rise to a conflict of interests in the sense that he may, without even intending to do so, where he himself is a tenderer for the public contract in question, influence the conditions of the contract in a manner favourable to himself. Such a situation would be capable of distorting competition between tenderers. Taking account of the situation in which a person who has carried out certain preparatory work may find himself, therefore, it cannot be maintained that the principle of equal treatment requires that that person be treated in the same way as any other tenderer. The difference in treatment established by a national rule which consists in prohibiting, in all circumstances, a person who has carried out certain preparatory works from participating in a procedure for the award of the public contract in question is not objectively justified. Such a prohibition could be disproportionate. Equal treatment for all tenderers is ensured where there is a procedure whereby an assessment is made, in each specific case, of whether the fact of carrying out certain preparatory works has conferred on the person who carried out that work a competitive advantage over other tenderers. Such a measure is less restrictive for a person who has carried out certain preparatory work.

---

[31] *See* Case C-513/99, *Concordia Bus Finland* [2002] ECR I-7213, paragraph 81.
[32] *See* Case C-434/02, *Arnold André* [2004] ECR I-2902, paragraph 68, and Case C-210/03, *Swedish Match* [2004] ECR I-1620, paragraph 70.
[33] *See* Case C-87/94, *Commission v Belgium* [1996] ECR I-2043, paragraph 54.

8.19   In that regard, the Court held that such a national rule does not afford a person who has carried out certain preparatory work any possibility to demonstrate that the principles of equal treatment and non-discrimination, as well as the competition envisaged amongst the participants in a public contract, is not jeopardized. The Court held that such a rule goes beyond what is necessary to attain the objective of equal treatment for all tenderers, as it may have the consequence that persons who have carried out certain preparatory works are precluded from the award procedure, even though their participation in the procedure entails no risk whatsoever for competition between tenderers.

8.20   The Court concluded that, on the grounds of the proportionality and objectivity principles, national laws cannot preclude an undertaking which has been instructed to carry out research, experiments, studies, or development in connection with public works, supplies, or services to apply to participate in or to submit a tender for those works, supplies, or services and, in particular, where that undertaking is not given the opportunity to prove that, in the circumstances of the case, the experience which he has acquired was not capable of distorting competition. The Court expanded its conclusions to cover even public undertakings which have previously assisted other contracting authorities in the preparation of specifications related to public contracts. The Court relied on previous jurisprudence[34] and established that the Public Procurement Directives apply equally to contracts between contracting authorities and private undertakings, and contracting authorities and undertakings in which public authorities have an interest.

F. Exclusion of a Tenderer who Participates in the Preparatory Stages of a Public Contract

8.21   However, in the *Fabricom* case, the Advocate General took a different view.[35] He established in hierarchical form the principles which underlie public procurement legislation and he referred to the principles of European law which influence the interpretation of such legislation. He established that the fundamental principles of the public procurement *acquis* include the principle of objectivity and the principle of transparency. However, in an interesting interpretation, he positioned the principle of competition as the ultimate objective of the European Public Procurement Directives.[36] Thus, he hierarchically transposed the underlying principles of specific European rules (the public procurement legislation) within

---

³⁴ *See* Case C-107/98, *Teckal* [1999] ECR I-4973.

³⁵ *See* the Opinion of Advocate General Léger in Joined Cases C-21/03 and C-34/03, *Fabricom SA v Belgian State*, delivered on 11 November 2004.

³⁶ *See* Case 103/88, *Fratelli Costanzo* [1989] ECR 1839, paragraph 18; Joined Cases C-285/99 and C-286/99, *Lombardini and Mantovani* [2001] ECR I-9233; Case 31/87 *Beentjes* [1988] ECR 4635.

an etymological interpretation and content analysis of the wording, scheme and objectives of the Directives.[37] His teleological interpretation revealed that, although the Directives provide no specific rules governing the inability of undertakings to participate in tendering procedures, and, in particular, to exclude an undertaking which has previously participated in the preparation and planning of a public contract, there is a need to ensure that contracting authorities do not discriminate amongst tenderers when they evaluate their submissions and respective offers. The Advocate General maintained that the Public Procurement Directives allow contracting authorities to request or to receive advice for the purpose of drawing up the specifications for public contracts from private undertakings, provided that competition is not distorted.[38] Consequently the Directives view the preparatory work of private undertakings prior to the tendering procedure for a public contract, not as grounds for ineligibility to participate in the tendering procedures, but as a condition to allow them to do so provided that competition amongst all potential tenderers is not distorted.

Since the Public Procurement Directives provide for discretion on that part of member states to implement in detail provisions at national level in relation to the award of public contracts, such discretion should be delimited by the objectives of the Directives themselves and also the general principles of Community Law.[39] The freedom of member states to transpose the Public Procurement Directives in their domestic legal systems must always observe the principle of equal treatment, which implies an obligation of transparency as a means of verification of compliance with such principles.[40] Therefore, if national provisions seek to exclude an undertaking which has previously participated in the preparation of a public contract, such provisions attempt to safeguard the fundamental objective of effective competition of public procurement. The Advocate General posed the same question at to whether such a national provision may serve at the same time the principle of equal treatment. **8.22**

The Court has held that the equal treatment principle lies in the heart of the Public Procurement Directives.[41] Accordingly, the system whereby tenderers **8.23**

---

[37] *See* Case C-208/98, *Berliner Kindl Brauerei* [2000] ECR I-1741; Case C-372/98, *Cooke* [2000] ECR I-8683; and Case C-341/01, *Plato Plastik Robert Frank* [2004] ECR I-4673.

[38] *See* the 10th recital in the preamble to Directive 97/52 and the 13th recital in the preamble to Directive 98/4 which state that contracting authorities may request advice for the purpose of drawing up public contracts, provided that that does not distort competition. Directive 97/52 has amended the Public Supplies, Works, and Services Directives respectively to take into account the obligations of the Government Procurement Agreement arising out of the WTO. Directive 98/4 amended the Utilities Directive to accommodate public contacts concluded within the framework of the WTO.

[39] *See* Joined Cases 27/86 to 29/86, *CEI and Others* [1987] ECR 3347, paragraph 15.

[40] *See* Case C-275/98, *Unitron Scandinavia and 3-S* [1999] ECR I-8291, paragraph 31; *Telaustria and Telefonadress*, op. cit., paragraph 61; and Case C-59/00, *Vestergaard* [2001] ECR I-9505.

[41] *See* Case C-243/89, *Commission v Denmark* [1993] ECR I-3353, paragraph 33.

participate on an equal basis must provide that any undertaking which wishes to be awarded a public contract must be aware beforehand that participation for preparatory work for the contract in question may have the effect of excluding the undertaking from the tendering procedures. Consequently, account must be taken of the aim of guaranteeing effective competition and balancing compliance with the principle of equality. This is where the Advocate General positioned the principle of effective competition on an uncompromised pedestal within the public procurement *acquis*. He, therefore, considered that, firstly the principle of competition must be preserved, secondly, the equality principle must be complied with, and, thirdly, the application of the above principles should be subject to the principle of proportionality.

8.24 He considered that any national provision ruling on ineligibility of an undertaking which has previously participated in the preparation of a contract, seeks to prevent a situation in which competition is distorted on the ground of the information held by the undertaking as a result of his participation in the preparation of the contract in question. He held that it is virtually impossible to envisage any means of ensuring that the information and experience required during the preparatory stage will not provide for an advantage on the part of an undertaking when that undertaking submits a tender for the same contract. The knowledge acquired by the undertaking is for the most part subjective, not demonstrable, and difficult to identify. Thus, in the interest of legal certainty, in the interest of transparency, and, foremost, in the interest of competition, it is necessary to prevent any possibility of a privileged position of an undertaking when participating in public procurement procedures. The Advocate General took a different view from that of the Court and concluded that ineligibility of undertakings based on the need to preserve competition serves not only principles of Community law but also corresponds to an objective of general interest.[42] He concluded that the Public Procurement Directives do not preclude national rules which exclude undertakings which have previously assisted contracting authorities in the drafting of the specifications of a public contract.

G. Connection of Tenderers with Undertakings that Assisted in the Preparation of Tenders

8.25 *Fabricom* revealed another question as to whether a contracting authority is allowed to exclude a tenderer which appears to have connections with undertakings that have carried out certain preparatory works from the procurement procedures for the

---

[42] *See* paragraph 44 of the Opinion of Advocate General Léger in Joined Cases C-21/03 and C-34/03, *Fabricom SA v Belgian State*, delivered on 11 November 2004; also Case C-280/93, *Germany v Council* [1994] ECR I-4973.

award of the relevant contract, even though, when questioned on that point by the contracting authority, the undertaking can prove that it has not obtained an unfair advantage capable of distorting the normal conditions of competition.[43]

The provisions of the Belgian legislation provided that any undertaking **8.26** connected to a person who has been instructed to carry out preparatory work in connection with the public contract in question may reverse the presumption that it has a competitive advantage by providing information on which it may be established that dominant influence has not affected the contract. However, the awarding authority is not subject to any time limits and may, at any time, and thus up to the end of the award procedure, eliminate the undertaking on account of the unfair advantage which it is presumed to have gained, if the evidence provided by the undertaking is deemed insufficient. That meant that the undertaking concerned would be aware of its ineligibility at the same time of the contracting authority adopting a decision to award the contract. In such a situation, a connected undertaking is unable to obtain a declaration by a court, if necessary, that in the particular case the presumption of exclusion equivalent to a reduction in competition is inapplicable, before the contract is awarded. However, it follows from the Review Directive and the Court's case law that the member states must ensure remedies whereby the procedure or decision to award the contract by the contracting authority can be suspended.[44] Therefore, the decision to exclude a connected undertaking must be notified before the decision awarding the public contract and such advance notice must be sufficient to enable that undertaking, if it considers it appropriate, to bring an action and have the exclusion decision annulled if the relevant conditions are met. By allowing the decision to be taken to eliminate a connected undertaking which would wish to tender up to the end of the procedure for examination of the tenders, in such a manner that a review can be sought only at a stage where the infringements can no longer be rectified, as the public contract has been awarded in the meantime, and at a stage where the applicant is only able to obtain damages, the effectiveness of the Review Directive is severely compromised.

The Court held that the possibility that the contracting authority might delay, **8.27** until the procedure has reached a very advanced stage, taking a decision as to whether an undertaking connected with a person who has carried out certain preparatory works may participate in the procedure or submit a tender, when that authority has before it all the information which it needs in order to take that decision, deprives that undertaking of the opportunity to rely on the Community rules on the award of public contracts as against the awarding authority for a period which is solely within that authority's discretion and which, where

---

[43] *See* Joined Cases C-21/03 and C-34/03, *Fabricom SA v État Belge*, judgment of 3 March 2005, paragraph 41.　　　　[44] *See* Case C-81/98, *Alcatel Austria and Others* [1999] ECR I-7671.

necessary, may be extended until a time when the infringements can no longer be usefully rectified. Such a situation is obviously contrary to public procurement *acquis* and capable of depriving the Public Procurement Directives and, in particular, the Remedies Directives 89/665 and 92/13 of all practical effect, as they are susceptible of giving rise to an unjustified postponement of the possibility for those concerned to exercise the rights conferred on them by the Public Procurement Directives.

H. Reliance of Tenderers on Other Sources

8.28 The Court reiterated[45] that a service provider which, with a view to being admitted to participate in a tendering procedure, intends to rely on the resources of entities or undertakings with which it is directly or indirectly linked must establish that it actually has available to it the resources of those entities or undertakings which are necessary for the performance of the contract but which it does not itself own.[46]

I. Substitution of Consortia Members

8.29 National law[47] which precluded the substitution of a member of a consortium which has been awarded a public contract was at the heart of the question[48] referred to the Court as to the possibility of excluding a tenderer, in the form of a consortium, from award procedures for public works contracts. Such substitution, which is always subject to approval by the contracting authority, is provided for only at the stage when the works are being carried out, that is to say the phase which follows signature of the contract between the contractor and the contracting authority and not at a stage prior to award of the contract.

8.30 The Greek Ministry for the Environment, Planning and Public Works issued a notice of an invitation to tender, announcing the first stage (pre-selection stage) of an international tendering procedure for the appointment of a contractor for the planning and construction, self-financing, and operation of an underground railway for Thessaloniki. At that stage, the awarding body selected eight groups of companies which had declared an interest, including the appellant consortium. Subsequently, the bid documentation for the second stage of the tendering

---

   45 *See* Case C-126/03, *Commission v Germany*, judgment of 18 November 2004.

   46 *See* Case C-176/98, *Holst Italia* [1999] ECR I-8607, paragraph 29; Case C-399/98, *Ordine degli Architetti and Others* [2001] ECR I-5409, paragraph 92; and Case C-314/01, *Siemens and ARGE Telekom & Partner*, judgment of 18 March 2004, paragraph 44.

   47 *See* Law No. 1418/1984 (23 A) on public works and related matters, and Presidential Decree 609/1985 (223 A).

   48 *See* Case C-57/01, *Makedoniko Metro and Mikhaniki* [2003] ECR I-1091.

procedure was approved, including the supplementary notice and the contract specifications. At that stage, technical proposals, financial studies, and economic and financial proposals were submitted by, among others, the consortium Makedoniko Metro in its original form, and the consortium Thessaloniki Metro (Bouygues). At the pre-selection stage, the members of the initial Makedoniko consortium were the undertakings *Mikhaniki AE, Fidel SpA, Edi-Sta-Edilizia Stradale SpA and Teknocenter-Centro Servizi Administrativi-SRL*. In the second stage of the tendering procedure in question, that is, after the pre-selection stage and invitation to tender, the consortium was enlarged by the addition of the undertaking *AEG Westinghouse Transport Systems GmbH*. In that form, the consortium submitted a bid and under that composition it was nominated as provisional contractor.

After negotiations had commenced between the Greek authorities and the **8.31** consortium in its enlarged format, Makedoniko Metro enlarged its composition by adding *ABB Daimler-Benz Transportation (Deutschland) GmbH* in its members. Two years into negotiations with the Greek authorities and responding to rumours that members of the Fidel Group of the consortium had become insolvent and gone into liquidation, Makedoniko Metro informed the Greek authorities of the situation and the change in its composition to include different members than those which it had when it qualified as provisional contractor and started negotiations (*Mikhaniki AE, Adtranz and Transurb Consult*).

The Minister for the Environment, Planning and Public Works, acting for the **8.32** awarding authority, found that Makedoniko Metro had substantially departed from the provisions of the tender documentation, terminated the negotiations and, having considered that the negotiations had failed, called for negotiations with the second consortium (*Thessaloniki Metro Bouygues*), which was the next candidate for provisional contractor. As a result, the Makedonico Metro appealed to the Greek Council of State and applied for the awarding authority's decision to break off negotiations to be set aside. The Council of State considered that a change in the composition of a consortium was only permissible prior to submission of bids. Thus, the consortium was not entitled, in its altered composition, to apply for the decision to be set aside. Also, in its action before the Administrative Court of First Instance, Athens, Makedoniko, together with the other undertakings in the consortium, sought a declaration that the state was liable to pay the sums specified in the statement of claim by way of damages and financial compensation for the non-material losses suffered by them as a result of the above unlawful act and omission. That claim was dismissed by the Administrative Court of First Instance, Athens, on the ground that, in the new composition in which the consortium had brought the action, it was not entitled to claim compensation. Makedoniko Metro appealed against the judgment to the Administrative Court of Appeal, Athens, claiming misinterpretation and misapplication of the relevant provisions in the judgment under appeal, and asked that a reference for a preliminary ruling be made to the Court of Justice of the European Communities on the interpretation of the relevant Community provisions.

8.33 Makedoniko Metro argued that the enlargement of the consortium and subsequent substitution of one its members are typical events for a complex public works contract that takes a number of years to conclude, and the latest change in the composition of the consortium was irrelevant to the ability of the consortium to perform the terms and condition of the contract. The change in the composition of the consortium can neither result in such a consortium losing its status as tenderer as a result, nor in the consortium or its members being deprived of their interest in the award, or of the possibility of bringing an action to enforce the rights to which they are entitled under Community law. The Greek authorities, by excluding the consortium from further negotiations jeopardized its chances to win the contract and violated the Public Procurement Directives, as well as the principle of the freedom to provide services.

8.34 The Greek Government maintained that the Public Procurement Directives are silent as to a change in the composition of a consortium. The national law did not permit a change in composition during negotiations with the tenderer which has provisionally been selected as contractor. The only subject of negotiations with the prospective successful contractor is the final terms of the contract to be awarded and not the identity of the contractor, which is not negotiable. Therefore, the Greek law legitimately provided that the identity of a provisionally selected contractor may not change.

8.35 The Commission argued that the Works Directive contains no express provisions concerning a change in the composition of a consortium after the submission of tenders. Article 21 merely provides that groups of contractors which submit tenders may not be required to assume a specific legal form prior to the award. It is therefore, left to the national legislature, or the individual contracting authority, to regulate the details. This applies also to public works concessions. The Commission presumed that the principle of equal treatment of tenderers would be undermined if a contracting authority could, for the benefit of one tenderer, unilaterally change the terms which are fixed in the tender documentation as not being open to variation, without reopening the whole award procedure. This would otherwise prevent the other tenderers from benefiting from the change. Therefore, the Public Procurement Directives do not allow a public contracting authority to continue to negotiate with a bidder whose composition has changed, contrary to national law or to the terms of the contract documentation. However, the Commission regarded that a change in the composition of a consortium that is in breach of national law or the contract documentation does not affect the exercise of rights which the consortium could claim on the basis of the Legal Remedies

Directive, in particular, the right to claim damages. Under Article 1(1) of the Remedies Directive, only infringements of Community law and national rules implementing that law may be reviewed. This provision does not, therefore, require member states to provide for procedures to allow review of decisions which have been taken in the context of an award procedure and which infringe rules that do not implement the Public Procurement Directives.

The Court held that, in the context of Article 234 EC, it has no jurisdiction to rule **8.36** either on the interpretation of provisions of national laws or regulations or on their conformity with Community law. It may, however, supply the national court with an interpretation of Community law that will enable that court to resolve the legal problem before it.[49] It is for the Court alone, where questions are formulated imprecisely, to extract from all the information provided by the national court and from the documents in the main proceedings the points of Community law which require interpretation, having regard to the subject-matter of those proceedings.[50]

The Greek Government argued that under specific circumstances a contracting **8.37** authority may refrain from awarding a contract.[51] The Court found such argument weak as, in that case, the award procedure ended without the contract being awarded, because the contracting authority had opted for a material other than that stipulated in the tender notice, which meant a change in the subject-matter of the contract. The Court maintained the discretion which underlies the implementation of the Public Procurement Directives and the relative freedom given to the member states. The remit of the Directives is to coordinate national procedures for the award of public works contracts and not the creation of a complete system of Community rules.[52]

The Court recognized that express rules on consortia are provided only in **8.38** Article 21 of the Public Works Directive, which does not expressly regulate changes in the composition of a consortium. However, that provision deals only with specific legal problems in connection with consortia. It thus affords them the right to submit tenders. Further, whilst it prohibits any requirement that consortia assume a particular legal form for the purpose of tendering, it does permit such requirement in the event of the award of a contract. Therefore, incomplete harmonization and the existence of only selective rules on consortia leave member states free to regulate other related matters as they see fit in accordance with their internal legal systems. This includes rules as to the composition of a consortium, such as the legal consequences of changes in its composition.

---

[49] *See* Case C-17/92, *Distribuidores Cinematográficos* [1993] ECR I-2239, paragraph 8; Case C-107/98 *Teckal* [1999] ECR I-8121, paragraph 33.

[50] *See* Case C-168/95 *Arcaro* [1996] ECR I-4705, paragraph 21, and Case C-107/98 *Teckal* [1999] ECR I-8121, paragraph 34.

[51] *See* Case C-27/98, *Fracasso and Leitschutz* [1999] ECR I-5697.

[52] *See* Joined Cases C-285/99 and C-286/99, *Impresa Lombardini* [2001] ECR I-9233, paragraph 33.

8.39   However, the Court positioned two obstacles in the member states' freedom to implement aspects of public procurement law which have not been expressly provided for in the relevant Directives. The principles of transparency and competition as recognized by the Court underpin the entire public procurement *acquis.*[53] The Court has declared that the aim of the Directives is to abolish restrictions on the freedom of establishment and the freedom to provide services in respect of public works contracts in order to open up such contracts to genuine competition between undertakings in the member states.[54] The Court has also pronounced on the requirement that contracting authorities observe the principle of non-discrimination of tenderers, which equates to the principle of equal treatment.[55]

8.40   The Court has also stated that the prohibition of discrimination implies an obligation of transparency, as a means of verification of compliance in order to allow the contracting authority to ensure that the prohibition has been observed.[56] The Court suggested that, even in the case where the principle of equal treatment cannot be observed within the Public Procurement Directives, its surrogate principle of equality, which is recognized as a general principle of European law prevails.[57]

8.41   The Court found that the equal treatment obligation prescribed in the Public Procurement Directives, as well as the principle of equality, would be breached, however, if the contracting authority unilaterally departed from its own rules concerning changes in the composition of consortia, particularly if it were to negotiate with a tenderer whose tender did not match the terms advertised. To that extent, an infringement of Community law can flow from the infringement of a national prohibition.

8.42   The freedom and discretion of member states to implement public procurement law in their own legal systems is also curtailed by primary Community law, in particular the fundamental freedoms and the competition provisions addressed to the state, including legislation on state aid.[58] In this context, it must be generally noted that the fundamental freedoms do not prohibit only direct or indirect discrimination, but also rules applicable without distinction which disproportionately inhibit any of the fundamental freedoms. From the application of primary

---

[53] *See* the preamble to the Public Works Directive 93/37, second and tenth recitals.

[54] *See* Joined Cases C-285/99 and C-286/99, *Impresa Lombardini* [2001] ECR I-9233, paragraph 34; see also Case C-399/98, *Ordine degli Architetti* [2001] ECR I-5409, paragraph 52.

[55] *See* Joined Cases C-285/99 and C-286/99, *Impresa Lombardini* [2001] ECR I-9233, paragraph 37.

[56] *See Impresa Lombardini*, paragraph 38; *see also* Case C-275/98 *Unitron Scandinavia and 3-S* [1999] ECR I-8291, paragraph 31.

[57] *See* the Opinion of Advocate General in Case C-57/01, *Makedoniko Metro and Mikhaniki* [2003] ECR I-1091, paragraph 65.

[58] *See* Case C-243/89, *Commission v Denmark* [1993] ECR I-3353, Case C-328/96, *Commission v Austria* [1999] ECR I-7479, and Case C-225/98, *Commission v France* [2000] ECR I-7445.

Community law to the public procurement *acquis* two further legal principles have emerged and developed in case law.[59] First, the principles of equivalence according to which the rules of national law must not be less favourable than those of corresponding domestic provisions. Secondly, the principle of effectiveness which obliges member states not to make the exercise of rights conferred by the system of Community law virtually impossible or excessively difficult.

The Court examined the question referred to it by considering the relevant **8.43** contract for the Thessaloniki metro as a public works contract and also as a concession contract. If the contract at issue were a public works contract within the meaning of Directive 93/37, the Court found that the Directive would apply as provided in Articles 4 to 6. The only provision of Directive 93/37 dealing with groups of contractors is Article 21. That is confined, firstly, to stating that tenders may be submitted by groups of contractors and, secondly, to preventing them from being required to assume a specific legal form before the contract has been awarded to the group selected. Article 21 makes no provision about the composition of such groups. Rules about their composition are thus a matter for the member states. The same is true *a fortiori* if the contract at issue in the main proceedings is a public works concession within the meaning of Directive 93/37. The Court concluded that, from Article 3(1) of the Directive, Article 21 does not even apply to public works concessions. The Court held that Directive 93/37 does not preclude national rules which prohibit a change in the composition of a group of contractors taking part in a procedure for the award of a public works contract or a public works concession which occurs after submission of tenders.

The Court also reiterated that Article 1(1) of Directive 89/665 requires member **8.44** states to take the measures necessary to ensure that, as regards contract award procedures falling within the scope of the relevant Community Directives, decisions taken by the contracting authorities may be reviewed effectively and as rapidly as possible on the grounds that such decisions have infringed Community law in the field of public procurement or national rules implementing that law. The Court ruled that member states are also required, under Article 1(3), to ensure that the review procedures are available at least to any person having, or having had, an interest in obtaining a particular public supply or public works contract and who has been, or risks being, harmed by an alleged infringement.

The Court found that the Greek authorities legitimately regarded that **8.45** Makedoniko Metro had departed substantially from the requirements laid down for the contract and terminated negotiations with the consortium. For the purpose of ascertaining whether the exclusion decision is covered by the expression decisions taken by the contracting authorities in Article 1(1) of Directive 89/665,

---

[59] *See* Cases C-261/95, *Palmisani* [1997] ECR I-4025, paragraph 27, and C-453/99, *Courage* [2001] ECR I-6297.

the Court reiterated that the term 'decisions taken by contracting authorities' encompasses decisions taken by contracting authorities which are made subject to the Community law rules on public contracts.[60] The Court extended the application of the general principles of Community law, and the principle of equal treatment in particular to the public procurement procedures governing the award of public contracts[61] and thus, embraced by analogy a decision taken in the context of a procedure for the award of a public contract to fall within the Public Procurements Directives, even in the absence of express provisions stipulating its coverage. The Court also held that the national court should be empowered to decide issues of *locus standi* in accordance with prior examination of the factual circumstances of the case in question.

---

[60] *See* Case C-92/00, *Hospital Ingenieure* [2002] ECR I-5553, paragraph 37.
[61] *See* Case C-324/98, *Telaustria and Telefonadress* [2000] ECR I-10745, paragraph 60, and Case C-92/00, *Hospital Ingenieure* [2002] ECR I-5553, paragraph 47.

9

AWARD PROCEDURES AND CRITERIA

A. Award Procedures

The process of liberalizing public procurement relies to a great extent on the **9.01** principle of objectivity in the award of public contracts. The Court had the opportunity to reflect on award procedures under the relevant Directives and subject the negotiated procedures, particularly those without prior advertisement, to a restrictive interpretation. According to the Procurement Directives, negotiated procedures without prior notification shall be used restrictively *inter alia '. . . when for technical or artistic reasons or reasons connected with the protection of exclusive rights the services could only be procured by a particular provider . . . and . . . in cases of extreme urgency brought about by events unforeseeable by the contracting authority.'*

The Court reinforced its restrictive interpretation of the above two reasons to **9.02** which contracting authorities might be allowed to have recourse and maintained their exceptional character rather than their prohibitive use, and the onerous obligation of contracting authorities to justify them.

9.03 The alleged existence of technical or artistic reasons, or reasons connected with the protection of exclusive rights, which reveal a particular contractor or service provider for a contracting authority to negotiate without prior advertisement attracted the attention of the Court in two instances.[1] The Court rejected the existence of exclusive rights in both cases and regarded the abuse of this provision as contrary to the right of establishment and freedom to provide services which are based on the principle of equal treatment, and prohibit, not only overt discrimination on grounds of nationality, but also all covert forms of discrimination, which, by the application of other criteria of differentiation, lead to the same result. Interestingly, the Court elucidated that exclusive rights might include contractual arrangements such as know-how and intellectual property rights (Case 199/85, *Commission v. Italy*).

9.04 Urgency reasons brought by unforeseen events to contracting authorities received similarly restrictive interpretation.[2] The Court maintained the need for a justification test based on the proportionality principle (Case 199/85, *Commission v. Italy*), as well as the existence of a causal link between the alleged urgency and the unforeseen events.[3]

(1) Negotiated procedures without prior publicity

9.05 The central issue in *Commission v. Italy*[4] was the utilization of negotiated procedures without prior advertisement and an assessment of the conditions stipulated in the relevant Directives, in particular whether, in the case of new works consisting of the repetition of similar earlier works, it is permissible and, if so, subject to what conditions, for a negotiated procedure to be conducted without prior publication of a contract notice.

9.06 The rules governing negotiated procedures without prior publication are defined restrictively in Article 7(3) and (4) of Directive 93/37. Negotiated procedures without prior publication are allowed when, for technical or artistic reasons, or for reasons connected with the protection of exclusive rights, the works may only be carried out by a particular contractor; insofar as is strictly necessary when, for reasons of extreme urgency brought about by events unforeseen by the contracting authorities in question, the time limit laid down for the open, restricted, or

---

[1] *See* Cases C-199/85, *Commission v. Italy* [1987] ECR 1039; also C-3/88, *Commission v. Italy* [1989] ECR 4035.

[2] *See* C-199/85, *Commission v. Italy* op. cit; C-3/88, *Commission v Italy*, op. cit. C-24/91, *Commission v. Spain*, [1994] CMLR 621; C-107/92, *Commission v. Italy*, judgment of 2 August 1993; C-57/94, *Commission v. Italy*, judgment of 18 May 1995; C-296/92, *Commission v. Italy*, judgment of 12 January 1994.

[3] *See* Case C-107/92, *Commission v. Italy*, judgment of 2 August 1993.

[4] *See* Case C-385/03, *Commission v. Italy*, 14 September 2004.

negotiated procedures cannot be kept. The circumstances invoked to justify extreme urgency must not in any event be attributable to the contracting authorities; for new works consisting of the repetition of similar works entrusted to the undertaking to which the same contracting authorities awarded an earlier contact, provided that such works conform to a basic project for which a first contract was awarded. This procedure may only be adopted during the three years following the conclusion of the original contract and subject to notice which should be given in the original invitation to tender.

The Court reiterated the exceptional character of negotiated procedures by reference to Article 7(4) of Directive 93/37 which provides that, in principle, public works contracts are to be awarded by the open procedure or the restricted procedure—and *not*, therefore, by the negotiated procedure. Only in exceptional cases is it permissible to use the negotiated procedure without prior publication of a contract notice. These cases are listed exhaustively in Article 7(3) of the Directive.[5] **9.07**

(2) Use of negotiated procedure for technical reasons

Under Article 7(3)(b) of Directive 93/37, negotiated procedures without prior publication may be allowed when, for technical or artistic reasons, or for reasons connected with the protection of exclusive rights, the works may only be carried out by a particular contractor. The definition of the condition that the works may 'only be carried out by a particular contractor' should be interpreted restrictively. According to the Court's case law, that constitutes derogation and should therefore apply only where there exist exceptional circumstances.[6] Contracting authorities cannot justify the use of negotiated procedures without prior publicity by simply invoking technical constraints in non-specific terms.[7] Instead they must explain in detail why, in the circumstances of the case, technical reasons made it absolutely necessary for the contract to be awarded to a particular contractor. The burden of proof of the existence of exceptional circumstances lies on the person seeking to rely on them.[8] In the absence of such a justification, contracting authorities might abuse the negotiated procedures without prior publicity in **9.08**

---

[5] *See* Case C-323/96, *Commission v. Belgium* [1998] ECR I-5063, paragraph 34.

[6] *See* Case C-57/94, *Commission v. Italy* [1995] ECR I-1249, paragraph 23. *See* also case C-318/94 *Commission v. Germany* [1996] ECR I-1949, paragraph 13. Similarly Advocate General Jacobs at paragraph 64 of his Opinion of 23 March 2000 in Case C-337/98 *Commission v. France* [2000] ECR I-8377, 8379.

[7] In case C-385/03, *Commission v. Italy*, the Italian Government stated that the competent authority wished to forestall any damage to or deterioration of the works already completed, and to avoid difficult questions as to the respective liability of a number of contractors. Those arguments were rejected by the Court.

[8] *See* Case C-57/94 *Commission v. Italy* [1995] ECR I-1249, paragraph 23.

order to avoid calls for tender, and thus subverting the general purpose of the Public Procurement Directives.

(3) Extreme urgency as a reason for negotiated procedure

9.09 Under Article 7(3)(c) of Directive 93/37 negotiated procedures without prior publicity may be allowed insofar as is strictly necessary when, for reasons of extreme urgency brought about by events unforeseen by the contracting authorities in question, the time-limit laid down for the open, restricted or negotiated procedures cannot be kept. The circumstances invoked to justify extreme urgency must not in any event be attributable to the contracting authorities. The Court maintained that the wording of the relevant provision ('strictly necessary', 'extreme urgency', and 'events unforeseen') attach strict conditions to any reliance on it and must be construed narrowly.[9] The extreme urgency to conclude a contract by negotiated procedures without prior publicity must not be attributed to the contracting authority. Thus, organisational issues and internal considerations on the part of the contacting authority cannot justify any urgency requirements. The burden of proof of the existence of extreme urgency not attributable to the contracting authority and exceptional circumstances lies on the contracting authority itself.[10]

(4) Repetition of similar works within three years

9.10 Under Article 7(3)(e) of Directive 93/37 negotiated procedures without prior publicity may be allowed for new works consisting of the repetition of similar works entrusted to the undertaking to which the same contracting authorities awarded an earlier contact, provided that such works conform to a basic project for which a first contract was awarded. This procedure may only be adopted during the three years following the conclusion of the original contract and subject to notice which should be given in the original invitation to tender. The Court held that, in the light of a comparison of the language versions of that provision, the expression 'conclusion of the original contract' must be understood as meaning the time when the original contract was entered into and not as referring to the completion of the works to which the contract relates. As the Court has consistently held,[11] all language versions of a Community provision must be, in principle, recognised as having the same weight. It follows that the correct

---

[9] *See* Case 199/85, *Commission v. Italy* [1987] ECR 1039, paragraph 14. *See also* Case C-318/94, *Commission v. Germany* [1996] ECR I-1949, paragraph 13.

[10] *See* Case C-57/94, *Commission v. Italy* [1995] ECR I-1249, paragraph 23.

[11] *See* Cases C-296/95, *EMU Tabac and Others* [1998] ECR I-1605, paragraph 36, and C-257/00, *Givane and Others* [2003] ECR I-345, paragraph 36.

starting-point for the three-year period should be determined, not by considering a single language version in isolation, but on the basis of an overview of all language versions. That interpretation is confirmed by the objective of the provision in question and its place in the scheme of the Directive. First, as it is a derogating provision which falls to be strictly interpreted, the interpretation which restricts the period during which the derogation applies must be preferred rather than that which extends it. That objective is met by the interpretation which takes the starting point as being the date on which the original contract is entered into rather than the, necessarily later, date on which the works which are its subject-matter are completed. Secondly, legal certainty, which is desirable where procedures for the award of public procurement contracts are involved, requires that the date on which the period in question begins can be defined in a certain and objective manner. While the date on which a contract is entered into is certain, numerous dates may be treated as representing the completion of the works and thus give rise to a corresponding level of uncertainty. Moreover, while the date on which the contract is entered into is clearly established at the outset, the date of completion of the works, whatever definition is adopted, may be altered by accidental or voluntary factors for so long as the contract is being carried out.

(5) Grounds for use of negotiated procedures

In *Commission v. Spain*,[12] the use of negotiated procedures based on grounds not   **9.11**
provided by the Directives was examined. The Commission took the view that the Spanish law has authorised the use of the negotiated procedure in two cases, namely for the award of contracts following procedures declared unsuccessful and the award of supply contracts for uniform goods.

First, the ground concerning the award of contracts following unsuccessful   **9.12**
procedures was examined and was deemed to contravene the exhaustive list of grounds for the use of negotiated procedures stipulated in the Public Procurement Directives. The national law provided that contracting authorities may also have recourse to negotiated procedures, insofar as it has not been possible to award the contract during an open or restricted procedure or where the candidates were not allowed to tender, provided that there were no modifications of the original con-ditions of the contract apart from the price, which cannot be increased by more than ten per cent. In the Commission's view, by permitting an increase of the ori-ginal tender price of up to ten per cent in relation to the earlier open or restricted procedures, the national law contravened Directives 93/36 and 93/37, since they allow a substantial alteration of one of the original conditions of the contract,

---

[12] *See* Case C-84/03, *Commission of the European Communities v. Kingdom of Spain.*

namely the price. The Commission maintained that the list of cases in respect of which the negotiated procedure may be used is limited. The interpretation of the concept of 'non-substantial alteration' must therefore be restrictive. The Spanish Government asserted that for the purposes of legal certainty, the Spanish legislature transformed the vague notion of 'substantial modifications to the original conditions of the contract' into a well-defined notion, since in the wording of the Public Procurement Directives, there is no indication as to which price modifications must be regarded as substantial and which do not merit such a classification.

9.13 The Court ruled that the negotiated procedure is exceptional in nature and, therefore, must be applied only in cases which are set out in an exhaustive list.[13] It held that Articles 6(3)(a) of Directive 93/36 and Article 7(3)(a) of Directive 93/37 exhaustively list the cases in which the negotiated procedure may be used without prior publication of a tender notice. The derogations from the rules intended to ensure the effectiveness of the rights conferred by the Treaty in connection with public works contracts must be interpreted strictly.[14] To prevent the Directives at issue being deprived of their effectiveness, the member states cannot, therefore, provide for the use of the negotiated procedure in cases not provided for in Directives 93/36 and 93/37, or add new conditions to the cases expressly provided for by those Directives which make that procedure easier to use. The Court held that the national law has added a new condition to the provisions of Directives 93/36 and 93/37 which is capable of undermining both their scope and their exceptional character. Such a condition cannot be regarded as a non-substantial alteration of the original terms of the contracts as provided for in Article 6(3)(a) of Directive 93/36 and Article 7(3)(a) of Directive 93/37.

9.14 Secondly, the ground concerning the award of supply contracts for uniform goods, as a justification for the use of negotiated procedures, was also deemed in contravention to the Public Procurement Directives. The Spanish law provided that the negotiated procedure may be used without prior publication of a tender notice in respect of goods whose uniformity has been held to be necessary for their common use by the administration. The use of that procedure was possible in so far as the type of goods has been chosen in advance and independently, pursuant to a call for tenders.

9.15 The Commission submitted that the award of supply contracts for uniform goods disregards the provisions of Article 6(2) and (3) of Directive 93/36, which sets out in an exhaustive manner the cases in which the negotiated procedure may be applied. The Spanish Government contended that the calls for tenders seeking to determine the type of uniform goods are similar to framework contracts and do

---

[13] The Court referred to the twelfth recital in the preamble to Directive 93/36 and the eighth recital in the preamble to Directive 93/37.

[14] *See* Case C-57/94, *Commission v Italy* [1995] ECR I-1249, paragraph 23, and Case C-318/94, *Commission v Germany* [1996] ECR I-1949, paragraph 13.

not differ in any way from the tendering procedures following a contract under a framework agreement, although framework agreements are not covered by the Public Supplies Directive 93/36.

The Court reiterated that the negotiated procedure may be used only in the cases **9.16** exhaustively listed in Article 6(2) and (3) of Directive 93/36, whereas Article 6(4) of that Directive states that 'in all other cases, the contracting authorities shall award their supply contracts by the open procedure or by the restricted procedure'. The Court found that the provision at issue concerning the award of supply contracts for uniform goods, did not correspond either to the case mentioned in Article 6(2) of Directive 93/36 or to one of the five situations listed in Article 6(3) in which the use of a negotiated procedure without prior publication of a tender notice is expressly permitted. It also stated that the concept of framework agreement does not come within the scope of those exceptions. The Court repeated its consistent jurisprudence that the provisions which authorise derogations from the rules intended to ensure the effectiveness of the rights conferred by the Treaty in the field of public supply contracts must be strictly interpreted.[15] The Court concluded that the law at issue, to the extent that it authorises use of the negotiated procedure without prior publication of a tender notice for the procedures involving goods whose uniformity has been held to be necessary for their common use by the public authorities, provided that the choice of the type of goods has been made in advance, pursuant to a call for tenders, constitutes an incorrect transposition of Article 6(2) and (3) of Directive 93/36.

(6) Justifications for use of negotiated procedures

The Municipality of Bockhorn in Lower Saxony concluded a contract for the **9.17** collection of its waste water for a term of at least thirty years from 1997 with the energy distribution undertaking *Weser-Ems AG* without recourse to the Public Procurement Directives. Also the City of Braunschweig, also in Lower Saxony, concluded a contract with *Braunschweigsche Kohlebergwerke* for residual waste disposal by thermal processing for a period of thirty years from 1999. The Commission brought two actions[16] under Article 226 EC for declarations that, by failing to invite tenders for the award of the contract, Germany had failed to observed the relevant provisions of the Public Services Directive 92/50 in relation to the publication and advertisement of contracts[17] and those provision in relation to the award of public contracts by negotiated procedures without prior advertisement.[18]

---

[15] *See* Case C-71/92, *Commission v. Spain* [1993] ECR I-5923, paragraph 36.
[16] *See* Joined Cases, C-20/01 and C-28/01, *Commission of the European Communities v. Federal Republic of Germany.*
[17] *See* Art. 8 in conjunction with Art. 15(2) and Art. 16(1) of Directive 92/50 [1992] OJ L209/1.
[18] *See* Arts. 8 11(3)(b) of Directive 92/50.

9.18   The German government and the municipality of Bockhorn did not contest the applicability of the relevant public procurement provisions in relation to the advertisement of the contract with *Weser-Ems AG*. The Court therefore pronounced on Germany's failure to observe the Public Services Directive. However, the competent authorities of the City of Braunschweig took the view that Directive 92/50 applied, but relied on Article 11(3) thereof to release them from their obligation to publish a contract notice, and awarded the contract by a negotiated procedure. They argued that the conditions on which Article 11(3)(b) of Directive 92/50 applied were met, since for technical reasons thermal treatment of waste could be entrusted only to *Braunschweigsche Kohlebergwerke*. It had been an essential criterion of the award of the contract that the incineration facilities were close to the City of Braunschweig in order to avoid transport over longer distances. Furthermore, the city authorities justified the choice of the award procedure at issue by an argument based on the guarantee that waste would be disposed of.

9.19   The German government argued that only *Braunschweigsche Kohlebergwerke* was in a position to satisfy the quite lawfully selected criterion that the waste disposal facility should be close to the relevant region. The criterion was not automatically discriminatory, since it was not impossible that undertakings established in other member states would be able to meet the requirement. The German government submitted that a contracting authority is entitled to take account of environmental criteria in its considerations relating to the award of a public contract when it determines which type of service it is proposing to acquire.

9.20   The Commission submitted that the criteria allowing a negotiated procedure to be used without publication of a prior contract notice, as provided for in Article 11(3)(b) of Directive 92/50, were not met. Neither the location of the undertaking selected, on account of its proximity to the place where the services were to be provided, nor the fact that award of the contract was urgent, provides a basis for the application of that provision in this instance. The Commission argued that the principle, provided for in Article 130r(2) of the EC Treaty (now, after amendment, Article 174 EC), that environmental damage should as a priority be rectified at source, should be read in the light of that provision as a whole, according to which environmental protection requirements must be integrated into the definition and implementation of other Community policies. Article 130r(2) does not provide that Community environmental policy is to take precedence over other Community policies in the event of a conflict between them. Nor, in the context of a procedure for the award of public contracts, can ecological criteria be used for discriminatory ends. As to the argument that the contracting authority justified its choice of the award procedure at issue by an argument based on the guarantee that waste would be disposed of, the Commission maintained that the City's argument refuted the argument that the procedure had been chosen on account of environmental considerations and the proximity of the waste disposal facility.

The Court declared that the argument forwarded by the German Government **9.21** that *Braunschweigsche Kohlebergwerke* was actually the only undertaking to which the contract could be awarded, and that a further award procedure would not affect that outcome, could not be accepted. It stated that the provisions of Article 11(3) of Directive 92/50, which authorize derogations from the rules intended to ensure the effectiveness of the rights conferred by the Treaty in relation to public service contracts, must be interpreted strictly, and that the burden of proving the existence of exceptional circumstances justifying a derogation lies on the person seeking to rely on those circumstances.[19] Article 11(3)(b) of Directive 92/50 cannot apply unless it is established that, for technical or artistic reasons, or for reasons connected with the protection of exclusive rights, only one undertaking is actually in a position to perform the contract concerned. Since no artistic reason, or any reason connected with the protection of exclusive rights, has been put forward in this instance, it is appropriate solely to ascertain whether the reasons relied on by the German Government are capable of constituting technical reasons for the purposes of Article 11(3)(b).

The Court maintained that a contracting authority may take account of criteria **9.22** relating to environmental protection at the various stages of a procedure for the award of public contracts.[20] Therefore, it is not impossible that a technical reason relating to the protection of the environment may be taken into account in an assessment of whether the contract at issue may be awarded to a given supplier. However, the procedure used where there is a technical reason of that kind must comply with the fundamental principles of Community law, in particular the principle of non-discrimination as it follows from the provisions of the Treaty on the right of establishment and the freedom to provide services.[21] The risk of a breach of the principle of non-discrimination is particularly high where a contracting authority decides not to put a particular contract out to tender.

The Court noted, also, that in the absence of any evidence to that effect, the **9.23** choice of thermal waste treatment cannot be regarded as a technical reason substantiating the claim that the contract could be awarded to only one particular supplier. Secondly, the argument regarding the proximity of the waste disposal facility as a necessary consequence of the City of Braunschweig's decision that residual waste should be treated thermally, is not borne out by any evidence and cannot therefore be regarded as a technical reason justifying the use of negotiated procedures without prior publicity. The Court held that the German Government did not prove that the transport of waste over a greater distance would necessarily constitute a danger to the environment or to public health.

---

[19] *See* Case C-318/94, *Commission v Germany* [1996] ECR I-1949, paragraph 13.
[20] *See* Case C-513/99, *Concordia Bus Finland* [2002] ECR I-7213, paragraph 57.
[21] *See* Case C-513/99, *Concordia Bus Finland* [2002] ECR I-7213, paragraph 63.

The Court finally concluded that the fact that a particular supplier is close to the contracting authority's area can likewise not amount, on its own, to a technical reason for justifying the use of negotiated procedures without prior publicity in accordance with Article 11(3)(b) of Directive 92/50.

(7) Causality of condition justifying the use of negotiated procedures

9.24 The Court pointed out that Article 11(3)(d) of Directive 92/50, as a derogation from the rules intended to ensure the effectiveness of the rights conferred by the EC Treaty in relation to public service contracts, must be interpreted strictly and that the burden of proving the existence of exceptional circumstances justifying a derogation lies on the person seeking to rely on those circumstances.[22] The application of Article 11(3) of the Directive is subject to three cumulative conditions. It requires the existence of an unforeseeable event, extreme urgency rendering the observance of time limits laid down by other procedures impossible, and a causal link between the unforeseeable event and the extreme urgency.[23] The Court maintained that where the causality link is not present, accelerated restricted procedures should be used.[24]

(8) Restricted procedures and weighting of criteria

9.25 A question arose[25] as to whether, in the context of a restricted procedure, a contracting authority which has laid down in advance the rules as to the weighting of the criteria for selecting the candidates who will be invited to tender, is obliged to state them in the contract notice or the tender documents. The relevant contracting authority had instead deposited the documents specifying those methods with a notary.

9.26 The applicants in the main proceedings before the national court claimed that the procedure followed by the contracting authority not to reveal to the candidates either the detailed rules of the scoring procedure or the importance of the different criteria for ranking the applications to take part is incompatible with the principles of transparency and objectivity. They claimed that the respective importance of the different ranking criteria must, in any event, appear in the contract notice, so as to exclude any arbitrariness in the contracting authority's

---

[22] *See* Joined Cases C-20/01 and C-28/01, *Commission v. Germany* [2003] ECR I-3609, paragraph 58.

[23] *See* Case C-107/92, *Commission v. Italy* [1993] ECR I-4655, paragraph 12, and Case C-318/94, *Commission v Germany* [1996] ECR I-1949, paragraph 14.

[24] *See* Case C-24/91, *Commission v. Spain* [1992] ECR I-1989, paragraph 14; Case C-107/92, *Commission v. Italy* [1993] ECR I-4655, paragraph 13.

[25] *See* Case C-470/99, *Universale-Bau and Others* [2002] ECR I-11617.

decision and to enable the candidates to scrutinise the lawfulness thereof and to make use of their right of review.

The contracting authority submitted that a procedure such as depositing with a **9.27** notary documents specifying the detailed rules for evaluating the applications to take part is sufficient guarantee of compliance with the principles of non-discrimination and objectivity. They submitted that, whilst it is clear from the principles of non-discrimination and objectivity that the contracting authority must prescribe in advance the procedure which it will use to choose the candidates and that such method of selection may not be subsequently changed, these principles do not require the contracting authorities to divulge the precise details of the rules for evaluating the candidatures. The contracting authority maintained that it had set out the principal criteria for ranking the applications to take part in the order of their importance, and that it was precisely to encourage lawful and fair competition that it did not make known in advance to the candidates the precise detailed rules for evaluating the applications.

The Court held that in the context of a restricted procedure, contracting author- **9.28** ities which have laid down in advance the rules for weighting the criteria for selecting the candidates who will be invited to tender, are obliged to state them in the contract notice or tender documents. The Court maintained that the Public Procurement Directives contain no specific provision relating to the requirements for prior advertisement concerning the criteria for selecting the candidates who will be invited to tender in the context of a restrictive procedure.[26] The Public Procurement Directives have as their prime aim simply to coordinate national procedures for the award of public works contracts, although it does not lay down a complete system of Community rules on the matter.[27] The Directives nevertheless aim to abolish restrictions on the freedom of establishment and on the freedom to provide services in respect of public works contracts in order to open up such contracts to genuine competition between undertakings in the member states.[28] The Court reiterated that the criteria and conditions which govern public contracts must be given sufficient publicity by the contracting authorities.[29]

The Court reiterated that the principle of equal treatment, which underlies the **9.29** Public Procurement Directives on procedures for the award of public contracts, implies an obligation of transparency in order to enable verification that it has been complied with.[30] That obligation of transparency which is imposed on the

---

[26] *See* Case C-470/99, *Universale-Bau and Others* [2002] ECR I-11617, paragraph 87.
[27] *See* Joined Cases C-285/99 and C-286/99, *Lombardini and Mantovani* [2001] ECR I-9233, paragraph 33.
[28] *See* Joined Cases C-285/99 and C-286/99, *Lombardini and Mantovani* [2001] ECR I-9233, paragraph 34. [29] *See* Case 31/87, *Beentjes* [1988] ECR 4635, paragraph 21.
[30] *See* Case C-324/98, *Telaustria and Telefonadress* [2000] ECR I-10745, paragraph 61, and Case C-92/00, *HI* [2002] ECR I-5553, paragraph 45.

contracting authority consists in ensuring, for the benefit of any potential tenderer, a degree of advertising sufficient to enable the services market to be opened up to competition and the impartiality of procurement procedures to be reviewed.[31] The Court held that the procedure for awarding a public contract must comply, at every stage, particularly that of selecting the candidates in a restricted procedure, both with the principle of the equal treatment of the potential tenderers and the principle of transparency so as to afford all tenderers equality of opportunity in formulating the terms of their applications to take part in the award procedures.[32]

9.30 The Court maintained that the Public Procurement Directives require advertising requirements in respect of both the criteria for selecting candidates and those for awarding the contract.[33] Thus, in relation, first, to the selection criteria, Article 7(2) of Directive 93/37, which concerns negotiated procedures, requires that the candidates are to be selected according to known qualitative criteria. Secondly, in relation to the award criteria for both negotiated and restricted procedures,[34] the public procurement rules provide that they form part of the minimum information which must be mentioned in the letter of invitation to tender, if they do not already appear in the contract notice. Similarly, for all types of procedure, where the award of the contract is made to the most economically advantageous tender, Article 30(2) of Directive 93/37, which applies both to the open procedure and the restricted and negotiated procedures, imposes on the contracting authority the obligation to state in the contract documents or in the contract notice all the criteria it intends to apply to the award, where possible in descending order of their importance. The Court stated that where the contracting authority has set out a ranking in their order of importance of the criteria for the award which it intends to use, it may not confine itself to a mere reference thereto in the contract documents or in the contract notice, but must, in addition, inform the tenderers of the ranking which it has used.

9.31 With respect to the Utilities Directive 90/531 and in particular Article 27(2), the terms of which are substantially the same as those of Article 30(2) of Directive 93/37, the requirement thus imposed on the contracting authorities is intended precisely to inform all potential tenderers, before the preparation of their tenders, of the award criteria to be satisfied by these tenders and the relative importance of those criteria, thus ensuring the observance of the principles of equal treatment of tenderers and of transparency.[35]

---

[31] *See* Case C-324/98, *Telaustria and Telefonadress* [2000] ECR I-10745, paragraph 62.
[32] *See* Case C-87/94, *Commission v. Belgium* [1996] ECR I-2043, paragraph 54.
[33] *See* the 10th and 11th recitals in the preamble of the Public Works Directive 93/37.
[34] *See* Art. 13(2)(e) of the Public Works Directive 93/97.
[35] *See* Case C-87/94, *Commission v Belgium* [1996] ECR I-2043, paragraphs 88 and 89.

The Court finally concluded that, in the context of a restricted procedure, if the **9.32** contracting authority has laid down, prior to the publication of the contract notice, the rules for the weighting of the selection criteria it intends to use, it is obliged to bring them to the prior knowledge of the candidates.

B. Award Criteria

(1) Award criteria

Two criteria laid down in the Public Procurement Directives provide the **9.33** conditions under which contracting authorities award public contracts: the lowest price or the most economically advantageous offer.[36]

The first criterion indicates that, subject to the qualitative criteria and financial **9.34** and economic standing, contracting authorities do not rely on any other factor than the price quoted to complete the contract. The tenderer who submits the cheapest offer must be awarded the contract. It should be mentioned that the Directives provide for an automatic disqualification of an 'obviously abnormally low offer'. The term has not been interpreted in detail by the Court and serves rather as an indication of a 'lower bottom limit'.[37] The Court, however, pronounced on the direct effect of the relevant provision requiring contracting authorities to examine the details of the tender before deciding the award of the contract. The contracting authorities are under a duty to seek from the tenderer an explanation for the price submitted, or to inform him that his tender appears to be abnormally low, and to allow a reasonable time within which to submit further details, before making any decision as to the award of the contract.

The debate over the terminology of 'obviously abnormally low' tenders surfaced **9.35** when the Court held[38] that rejection of a contract based on mathematical criteria without giving the tenderer an opportunity to furnish information is inconsistent with spirit of the Public Procurement Directives. The Court, following previous case law,[39] ruled that the contracting authorities must give an opportunity to tenderers to furnish explanations regarding the genuine nature of their tenders, when those tenders appear to be abnormally low. Unfortunately, the Court did not proceed to an analysis of the wording 'obviously'. It rather seems that the term 'obviously' indicates the existence of precise and concrete evidence as to the

---

[36] *See* Art. 26 of Directive 93/36, Art. 30 of Directive 93/37, Art. 34 of Directive 93/38 and Art. 36 of Directive 92/50.

[37] Case 76/81, *SA Transporoute et Travaux v. Minister of Public Works* [1982] ECR 457.

[38] *See* Case 103/88, *Fratelli Costanzo SpA v. Comune di Milano* [1989] ECR 1839; Case 296/89, *Impresa Dona Alfonso di Dona Alfonso & Figli snc v. Consorzio per lo Sviluppo Industriale del Comune di Monfalcone*, judgment of 18 June 1991.

[39] Case 76/81, *Transporoute*, [1982] ECR 417, op. cit.

abnormality of the low tender. On the other hand, the wording 'abnormally' implies a quantitative criterion left to the discretion of the contracting authority. However, if the tender is just 'abnormally' low, it could be argued that it is within the discretion of the contracting authority to investigate the genuine offer of a tender. *Impresa Lombardini* [40] followed the precedence established by *Transporoute* and maintained the unlawfulness of mathematical criteria used as an exclusion of a tender which appears abnormally low. Nevertheless, it held that such criteria may be lawful if used for determining the abnormality of a low tender, provided an *inter partes* procedure between the contracting authority and the tenderer that submitted the alleged abnormal low offer offers the opportunity to clarify the genuine nature of that offer. Contracting authorities must take into account all reasonable explanations furnished and avoid limiting the grounds on which justification of the genuine nature of a tender should be made. Both the wording and the aim of the Public Procurement Directives direct contracting authorities to seek explanation and reject unrealistic offers, informing the Advisory Committee. [41] In *ARGE*, [42] the rejection of a tender based on the abnormally low pricing attached to it got a different twist in its interpretation. Although the Court ruled that directly or indirectly subsidised tenders by the state or other contracting authorities, or even by the contracting authority itself, can be legitimately part of the evaluation process, it did not elaborate on the possibility of rejection of an offer which is appreciably lower than those of unsubsidised tenderers by reference to the abnormally low offer disqualification ground. In *ARGE* the Court adopted a literal interpretation of the Directives and concluded that, if the legislature wanted to preclude subsidized entities from participating in tendering procedures for public contracts, it should have said so explicitly in the relevant Directives. [43] Although the case has relevance in the fields of selection and qualification procedures and award criteria, the Court made no references to previous case law regarding state aids in public procurement, presumably because the *Dupont de Nemours* precedence is still highly relevant.

9.36 On the other hand, the meaning of 'the most economically advantageous offer' includes a series of factors chosen by the contracting authority, including price, delivery or completion date, running costs, cost-effectiveness, profitability, technical merit, product or work quality, aesthetic and functional characteristics, after-sales service and technical assistance, commitments with regard to spare parts and components and maintenance costs, and security of supplies. The above

---

[40] Case C-285/99 and 286/99, *Impresa Lombardini SpA v ANAS*, judgment of 27 November 2001.

[41] The Advisory Committee for Public Procurement was set up by Decision 77/63 ([1977] OJ L13/15) and is composed of representatives of the member states belonging to the authorities of those states and has as its task to supervise the proper application of Public Procurement Directives by member states.`   [42] *See* Case C-94/99, *ARGE Gewässerschutzt*, op. cit.

[43] *See* paragraphs 26 *et seq.* of the Court's judgment.

list is not exhaustive and the factors listed therein serve as a guideline for contracting authorities in the weighted evaluation process of the contract award. The Court reiterated the flexible and wide interpretation of the relevant award criterion[44] and had no difficulty in declaring that contracting authorities may use the most economically advantageous offer as award criterion by choosing the factors which they want to apply in evaluating tenders,[45] provided these factors are mentioned, in hierarchical order or descending sequence, in the invitation to tender or the contract documents,[46] so tenderers and interested parties can clearly ascertain the relative weight of factors other than price for the evaluation process. However, factors, which have no strict relevance in determining the most economically advantageous offer by reference to objective criteria do involve an element of arbitrary choice and therefore should be considered as incompatible with the Directives.[47]

(2) Social considerations as award criteria

The most economically advantageous offer as an award criterion has provided the **9.37** Court for the opportunity to balance the economic considerations of public procurement with policy choices. Although in numerous instances the Court has maintained the importance of the economic approach[48] to the regulation of public sector contracts, it has also recognised the relative discretion of contracting authorities to utilise non-economic considerations as award criteria. In *Beentjes*,[49] the Court ruled that social policy considerations and, in particular, measures aimed at combating long-term unemployment, could only be part of the award criteria of public contracts, especially in cases where the most economically advantageous offer is selected. The Court accepted that the latter award criterion contains features that are not exhaustively defined in the Directives, therefore there is discretion conferred on contracting authorities to specify what would be the most economically advantageous offer for them. However, contracting authorities cannot refer to such measures as a selection criterion and disqualify candidates which could not meet the relevant requirements. The selection of tenderers is a process which is based on an exhaustive list of technical and financial requirements expressly stipulated in the relevant Directives, and the insertion of contract compliance as a selection and qualification requirement, would be

---

[44] Case 31/87, *Gebroeders Beentjes v. The Netherlands*, op. cit, paragraph 19.
[45] Case C-324/93, *R. v. The Secretary of State for the Home Department, ex parte Evans Medical Ltd and Macfarlan Smith Ltd*, judgment of 28 March 1995, where the national court asked whether factors concerning continuity and reliability as well as security of supplies fall under the framework of the most economically advantageous offer, when the latter is being evaluated.
[46] *See* paragraph 22 of *Beentjes*.   [47] *See* paragraph 37 of *Beentjes*.
[48] *See* Cases C-380/98, *Cambridge University*, at paragraph 17, C-44/96, *Strohal*, paragraph 33; C-360/96, *BFI*, paragraphs 42 and 43; C-237/99, *OPAC*, paragraphs 41 and 42.
[49] *See* Case 31/87, *Gebroeders Beentjes BV v. The Netherlands* [1989] ECR 4365.

considered *ultra vires*. The Court held that a contractual condition relating to the employment of long-term unemployed persons is compatible with the Public Procurement Directives, if it has no direct or indirect discriminatory effect on tenders from other member states. Furthermore, such a contractual condition must be mentioned in the tender notice.[50] Rejection of a contract on the grounds of a contractor's inability to employ long-term unemployed persons has no relation to the checking of the contractors' suitability on the basis of their economic and financial standing and their technical knowledge and ability. The Court maintained that measures relating to employment could be utilised as a feature of the award criteria, only when they are part of a contractual obligation of the public contract in question, and on condition that they do not run contrary to the fundamental principles of the Treaty. The significance of that qualification has revealed the Court's potential stance over the issue of contract compliance in public procurement.

9.38   In the recent case *Nord-pas-de-Calais*, the Court considered whether a condition linked to a local project to combat unemployment could be considered as an award criterion of the relevant contract. The Commission alleged that the French Republic has infringed Article 30(1) of Directive 93/37 purely and simply by referring to the criterion linked to the campaign against unemployment as an award criterion in some of the disputed contract notices. Under Article 30(1) of Directive 93/37, the criteria on which contracting authorities are to base the award of contracts are the lowest price only or, when the award is made to the most economically advantageous tender, various criteria according to the contract, such as price, period for completion, running costs, profitability, and technical merit.

9.39   The Court held that the most economically advantageous offer does not preclude all possibilities for the contracting authorities to use as a criterion a condition linked to the campaign against unemployment, provided that this condition is consistent with all the fundamental principles of Community law, in particular the principle of non-discrimination deriving from the provisions of the Treaty on the right of establishment and the freedom to provide services.[51] Furthermore, even if such a criterion is not in itself incompatible with Directive 93/37, it must be applied in conformity with all the procedural rules laid down in that Directive, in particular the rules on advertising.[52] The Court therefore accepted the employment considerations as an award criterion, part of the most economically advantageous offer, provided it is consistent with the fundamental principles of Community law, in particular the principle of non-discrimination, and it is advertised in the contract notice.

---

[50] *See* Case 28/86, *Bellini* [1987] ECR 3347.   [51] *See Beentjes*, paragraph 29.
[52] *See*, to that effect, paragraph 31 of the judgment, where the Court stipulated that an award criterion linked to the campaign against unemployment must be expressly mentioned in the contract notice so that contractors may become aware of its existence.

(3) Environmental considerations as award criteria

In *Concordia*,[53] the Court was asked *inter alia* whether environmental considerations **9.40** such as low emissions and noise levels of vehicles could be included amongst the factors of the most economically advantageous criterion, in order to promote certain types of vehicles that meet or exceed certain emission and noise levels. The Court followed the *Beentjes* principle, and established that contracting authorities are free to determine the factors under which the most economically advantageous offer is to be assessed, and that environmental considerations could be part of the award criteria, provided they do not discriminate over alternative offers, as long as they have been clearly publicized in the tender or contract documents. However, the inclusion of such factors in the award criteria should not prevent alternative offers that satisfy the contract specifications being taken into consideration by contracting authorities. Clearly the Court wanted to exclude any possibility of environmental considerations being part of selection criteria or disguised as technical specifications, capable of discriminating against tenderers that could not meet them. Criteria relating to the environment, in order to be permissible as additional criteria under the most economically advantageous offer must satisfy a number of conditions, namely they must be objective, universally applicable, strictly relevant to the contract in question, and clearly contribute an economic advantage to the contracting authority.[54]

(4) Ecological criteria

A question arose as to whether, under Article 36(1) of Directive 92/50 or Article **9.41** 34(1)(a) of Directive 93/3 which define the most economically advantageous offer as an award criterion, the inclusion of a reduction of the nitrogen oxide emissions or the noise level of the vehicles in such a way that, if those emissions or that noise level is below a certain ceiling, may result in additional points being awarded for the comparison of tenders.[55]

The Court considered that in public procurement the criteria for the decision **9.42** must always be of an economic nature. If the objective of the contracting authority is to satisfy ecological or other considerations, it should have recourse to procedures other than public procurement procedures. The Commission contended that the criteria for the award of public contracts which may be taken into consideration when assessing the economically most advantageous tender must satisfy four conditions. They must be objective, apply to all the tenders, be strictly linked to the subject-matter of the contract in question, and be of direct economic advantage to the contracting authority. On the other hand, it was submitted

---

[53] *See* Case C-513/99, *Concordia Bus Filandia v. Helsingin Kaupunki et HKL-Bussiliikenne,* op. cit.
[54] *See* the analysis in the opinion of the Advocate General, paragraphs 77 to 123.
[55] *See* Case C-513/99, *Concordia Bus Finland* [2002] ECR I-7213.

before the Court that it is permissible to include ecological factors in the criteria for the award of a public contract. The Public Procurement Directives and, in particular Article 36(1)(a) of Directive 92/50 and Article 34(1)(a) of Directive 93/38, list merely as examples factors which the contracting authorities may take into account when awarding public contracts.[56] Thus the protection of the environment could well be included amongst the factors which determine the most economically advantageous offer. In addition, reference was made to Article 6 EC, which requires environmental protection to be integrated into the other policies of the Community. Finally, the protection of the environment could have direct economic links with policies associated with health and social affairs in the member states.

9.43   It also emerged that the award criteria based on the most economically advantageous offer may introduce two essential restrictions. Firstly, the criteria chosen by the contracting entity must relate to the contract to be awarded and make it possible to determine the most economically advantageous tender for it. Secondly, the criteria must be directly linked to the subject-matter of the contract, must have effects which can be measured objectively, must be quantifiable at the economic level, and must be capable of guiding the discretion of the contracting entity on an objective basis without including elements of arbitrary choice.

9.44   The Court held that, in order to determine whether and under what conditions the contracting authority may, in accordance with Article 36(1)(a), take into consideration criteria of an ecological nature, the criteria which may be used as criteria for the award of a public contract to the economically most advantageous tender are not listed exhaustively.[57] Secondly, the Court maintained that Article 36(1)(a) cannot be interpreted as meaning that each of the award criteria used by the contracting authority to identify the economically most advantageous tender must necessarily be of a purely economic nature. It cannot be excluded that factors which are not purely economic may influence the value of a tender from the point of view of the contracting authority. That conclusion is also supported by the wording of the provision, which expressly refers to the criterion of the aesthetic characteristics of a tender. In the light of Article 130r(2) EC and Article 6 EC, which lay down that environmental protection requirements must be integrated into the definition and implementation of Community policies and activities, the Court concluded that Article 36(1)(a) of Directive 92/50 does not exclude the possibility for the

---

[56]   Art. 36(1)(a) of Directive 92/50 and Art. 34(1)(a) of Directive 93/38 provides that the criteria on which the contracting authority may base the award of contracts may, where the award is made to the economically most advantageous tender, be various criteria relating to the contract, such as, for example, quality, technical merit, aesthetic and functional characteristics, technical assistance and after-sales service, delivery date, delivery period or period of completion, or price.

[57]   *See* Case C-19/00, *SIAC Construction* [2001] ECR I-7725, paragraph 35.

contracting authority of using criteria relating to the preservation of the environment when assessing the economically most advantageous tender.

However, that does not mean that any criterion of that nature may be taken into consideration by contracting authorities. While Article 36(1)(a) of Directive 92/50 leaves it to the contracting authority to choose the criteria on which it proposes to base the award of the contract, that choice may, however, relate only to criteria aimed at identifying the economically most advantageous tender.[58] Since a tender necessarily relates to the subject-matter of the contract, it follows that the award criteria which may be applied in accordance with that provision must themselves also be linked to the subject-matter of the contract. The Court has held that, in order to determine the economically most advantageous tender, the contracting authority must be able to assess the tenders submitted and take a decision on the basis of qualitative and quantitative criteria relating to the contract in question.[59] It is also clear that an award criterion having the effect of conferring on the contracting authority an unrestricted freedom of choice as regards the award of the contract to a tenderer would be incompatible with Article 36(1)(a) of Directive 92/50.[60]

9.45

The criteria adopted to determine the economically most advantageous tender must be applied in conformity with all the procedural rules laid down in Directive 92/50, in particular the rules on advertising. It follows that, in accordance with Article 36(2) of that Directive, all such criteria must be expressly mentioned in the contract documents or the tender notice, where possible in descending order of importance, so that operators are in a position to be aware of their existence and scope.[61] Such criteria must comply with all the fundamental principles of Community law, in particular the principle of non-discrimination as it follows from the provisions of the Treaty on the right of establishment and the freedom to provide services.[62]

9.46

The Court concluded that, where the contracting authority decides to award a contract to the tenderer who submits the economically most advantageous tender, it may take criteria relating to the preservation of the environment into consideration, provided that they are linked to the subject-matter of the contract, do not confer an unrestricted freedom of choice on the authority, are expressly mentioned in the contract documents or the tender notice, and comply with all the fundamental principles of Community law, in particular the principle of non-discrimination.

9.47

---

[58] *See Beentjes*, paragraph 19, *Evans Medical and Macfarlan Smith*, paragraph 42, and *SIAC Construction*, paragraph 36.

[59] *See* Case 274/83, *Commission v. Italy* [1985] ECR 1077, paragraph 25.

[60] *See Beentjes*, paragraph 26, and *SIAC Construction*, paragraph 37.

[61] *See Beentjes*, paragraphs 31 and 36, and Case C-225/98 *Commission v. France* [2000] ECR I-7445, paragraph 51.

[62] *See Beentjes*, paragraph 29, and *Commission v. France*, paragraph 50.

9.48 The Court also found that the principle of equal treatment does not preclude taking into consideration criteria concerned with the protection of the environment because the contracting entity's own transport undertaking is one of the few undertakings that actually perform the terms and conditions of the contract. The principle of equal treatment is not breached even if following a procedure for the award of a public contract, only one tender remains,[63] or even in a case where only a comparatively small number of tenderers are able to satisfy the award criteria. It appears, however, that there is a limit to the permissibility of certain minimum ecological standards where the criteria applied restrict the market for the services or goods to be supplied to the point where there is only one tenderer remaining.[64]

(5) Variants

9.49 The obligation to set out the minimum specifications required by a contracting authority in order to take variants into consideration is not satisfied where the contract documents merely refer to a provision of national legislation requiring an alternative tender to ensure the performance of work which is qualitatively equivalent to that for which tenders are invited, without further specifying the comparative parameters on the basis of which such equivalence is to be assessed.[65]

9.50 According to the Public Procurement Directives,[66] where the criterion for the award of the contract is that of the most economically advantageous tender, contracting authorities may take account of variants which are submitted by a tenderer and meet the minimum specifications required by the contracting authorities. Contracting authorities must state in the contract documents the minimum specifications to be respected by the variants and any specific requirements for their presentation, and they must indicate in the tender notice if variants are not permitted. Contracting authorities may not reject the submission of a variant on the sole grounds that it has been drawn up with technical specifications defined by reference to national standards transposing European standards, to European technical approvals, or to common technical specifications referred to in the Public Procurement Directives.[67]

9.51 Where the contracting authority has not excluded the submission of variants, it is under an obligation to set out in the contract documents the minimum specifications

---

[63] *See* Case C-27/98, *Fracasso and Leitschutz* [1999] ECR I-5697, paragraphs 32 and 33.

[64] *See* Case 45/87, *Commission v. Ireland* [1988] ECR 4929.

[65] *See* Case C-421/01, *Traunfellner GmbH and Österreichische Autobahnen und Schnellstraßen Finanzierungs-AG (Asfinag)*

[66] *See* Art. 19 of the Public Works Directive 93/37 and the equivalent provisions in all Public Procurement Directives.

[67] *See* Art. 10(2) or by reference to national technical specifications referred to in Art. 10(5)(a) and (b) of the Public Works Directive 93/37 and the equivalent provisions in all Public Procurement Directives.

with which those variants must comply. Consequently, a reference made in the contract documents to a provision of national legislation cannot satisfy the requirements of transparency and equal treatment of tenderers wishing to forward a variant bid.[68] Tenderers may be deemed to be informed in the same way of the minimum specifications with which their variants must comply in order to be considered by the contracting authority only where those specifications are set out in the contract documents. This involves an obligation of transparency designed to ensure compliance with the principle of equal treatment of tenderers, which must be complied with in any procurement procedure governed by the Directive.[69]

A question arose as to whether a contracting authority can reject an alternative **9.52** tender which differs from a tender conforming to the contract specifications in that it proposes different technical specifications, without specifying the comparative parameters to be used to assess the equivalence of all tenders.[70] The Court asserted that that consideration of variants is subject to fulfilment of the requirement that the minimum specifications with which those variants must comply be set out in the contract documents, and that a mere reference in those documents to a provision of national legislation is insufficient to satisfy that requirement. Variants may not be taken into consideration where the contracting authority has failed to comply with the requirements with respect to the statement of the minimum specifications, even if they have not been declared inadmissible in the tender notice. The Court held that award criteria based on the most economically advantageous offer can apply only to variants which have been properly taken into consideration by a contracting authority.

(6) Criteria related to the subject matter of the contract

A question arose as to whether a contracting authority can apply and under what **9.53** conditions, in its assessment of the most economically advantageous tender for a contract for the supply of electricity, a criterion requiring that the electricity supplied be produced from renewable energy sources.[71] In principle, that question referred to the possibility of a contracting authority to lay down criteria that pursue advantages which cannot be objectively assigned a direct economic value, such as advantages related to the protection of the environment. The Court held that that each of the award criteria used by the contracting authority to identify the most economically advantageous tender must not necessarily be of a purely

---

[68] *See* Case 31/87, *Beentjes* [1988] ECR 4635, paragraph 35, and Case C-225/98, *Commission v. France* [2000] ECR I-7445, paragraph 73.

[69] *See* Case C-19/00, *SIAC Construction* [2001] ECR I-7725, paragraphs 41 and 42.

[70] *See* Case C-421/01, *Traunfellner GmbH and Österreichische Autobahnen und Schnellstraßen Finanzierungs-AG (Asfinag)*

[71] *See* Case C-448/01, *EVN AG, Wienstrom GmbH and Republik Österreich*, judgment of 4 December 2003.

economic nature.[72] The Court therefore accepted that, where the contracting authority decides to award a contract to the tenderer who submits the most economically advantageous tender, it may take into consideration ecological criteria, provided that they are linked to the subject-matter of the contract, do not confer an unrestricted freedom of choice on the authority, are expressly mentioned in the contract documents or the tender notice, and comply with all the fundamental principles of Community law, in particular the principle of non-discrimination.[73] The Court concluded that the Public Procurement Directives do not preclude a contracting authority from applying, in the context of the assessment of the most economically advantageous tender for a contract for the supply of electricity, a criterion requiring that the electricity supplied be produced from renewable energy sources, provided that that criterion is linked to the subject-matter of the contract, does not confer an unrestricted freedom of choice on the authority, is expressly mentioned in the contract documents or the contract notice, and complies with all the fundamental principles of Community law, in particular the principle of non-discrimination.

9.54 The criterion requiring that the electricity supplied be produced from renewable energy sources had a number of characteristics which posed further questions as to their compatibility with public procurement *acquis*. In particular, the criterion that the electricity supplied should be produced from renewable energy sources had a weighting of forty-five per cent; it was not accompanied by requirements which permit the accuracy of the information contained in the tenders to be effectively verified, and could not necessarily achieve the objective pursued; it did not impose a defined supply period; and it required tenderers to state how much electricity they can supply from renewable energy sources to a non-defined group of consumers, and allocated the maximum number of points to whichever tenderer stated the highest amount, where the supply volume is taken into account only to the extent that it exceeded the volume of consumption to be expected in the context of the contract to which the invitation to tender relates.

9.55 With regard to the criterion that the that the electricity supplied should be produced from renewable energy sources had a weighting of forty-five per cent, the question posed was whether a consideration such as the protection of the environment which is not capable of being assigned a direct economic value, could have such a significant influence on the award decision. The Court held that it is open to the contracting authority when choosing the most economically advantageous tender to choose the criteria on which it proposes to base the award of contract, provided that the purpose of those criteria is to identify the most economically advantageous tender, and that they do not confer on the contracting authority an

---

72 *See* Case C-513/99, *Concordia Bus Finland* [2002] ECR I-7123, paragraph 55.
73 *See* Case C-513/99, *Concordia Bus Finland* [2002] ECR I-7123, paragraph 69.

unrestricted freedom of choice as regards the award of the contract to a tenderer.[74] Such criteria must be applied in conformity with both the procedural rules and the fundamental principles laid down in Community law.[75] The Court maintained that contracting authorities are free not only to choose the criteria for awarding the contract but also to determine the weighting of such criteria, provided that the weighting enables an overall evaluation to be made of the criteria applied in order to identify the most economically advantageous tender.

With reference to the award criterion requiring that the electricity supplied be **9.56** produced from renewable energy sources and its relative weighting of forty-five per cent in the evaluation process of determining the most economically advantageous offer, the Court held that the use of renewable energy sources for producing electricity is useful for protecting the environment insofar as it contributes to the reduction in emissions of greenhouse gases which are amongst the main causes of climate change which the European Community and its member states have pledged to combat.[76] Therefore, the importance of the objective pursued by that criterion justified its weighting of forty-five per cent and did not present an obstacle to an overall evaluation of the criteria applied in order to identify the most economically advantageous tender.

The award criterion requiring that the electricity supplied be produced from **9.57** renewable energy sources was not accompanied by requirements which permit the accuracy of the information contained in the tenders to be effectively verified, and, as a result, it was deemed that it could not necessarily serve the objective pursued. That posed a serious question as to the compatibility of such a criterion with public procurement rules. The Court held that an award criterion which is not accompanied by requirements which permit the information provided by the tenderers to be effectively verified is contrary to the principles of Community law in the field of public procurement and particularly the principle of equal treatment, which underlies[77] the Public Procurement Directives and implies that tenderers must be in a position of equality both when they formulate their tenders and when those tenders are being assessed by the contracting authority.[78] More specifically, that means that when tenders are being assessed, the award criteria must be applied objectively and uniformly to all tenderers.[79] The principle of equal treatment also implies an obligation of transparency in order to enable verification that it has been complied with, which consists in ensuring, *inter alia*, review of the impartiality of

---

[74] *See* Case 31/87, *Beentjes* [1988] ECR 4635, paragraphs 19 and 26; Case C-19/00, *SIAC Construction* [2001] ECR I-7725, paragraphs 36 and 37; and *Concordia Bus Finland*, paragraphs 59 and 61.

[75] *See Beentjes*, paragraphs 29 and 31, and *Concordia Bus Finland*, paragraphs 62 and 63.

[76] *See* Case C-379/98, *PreussenElektra* [2001] ECR I-2099, paragraph 73.

[77] *See* Case C-470/99, *Universale-Bau and Others* [2002] ECR I-11617, paragraph 91, and Case C-315/01, *GAT* [2003] ECR I-0000, paragraph 73.

[78] *See SIAC Construction*, paragraph 34.   [79] *See SIAC Construction*, paragraph 44.

procurement procedures.[80] Objective and transparent evaluation of the various tenders depends on the contracting authority, relying on the information and proof provided by the tenderers, being able to verify effectively whether the tenders submitted by those tenderers meet the award criteria. The Court concluded that, where a contracting authority lays down an award criterion indicating that it neither intends, nor is able, to verify the accuracy of the information supplied by the tenderers, it infringes the principle of equal treatment, because such a criterion does not ensure the transparency and objectivity of the tender procedure. However, the fact that an award criterion such as the requirement to supply electricity from renewable energy sources is not objectively verifiable cannot be regarded as incompatible with public procurement law simply because it does not necessarily achieve the objective pursued, insofar as it is not necessarily capable of helping to increase the amount of electricity produced from renewable energy sources.

9.58   The fact that in the invitation to tender the contracting authority omitted to determine the period in respect of which tenderers had to state the amount of electricity from renewable energy sources which they could supply, would result in an infringement of the principles of equal treatment and transparency if that omission made it difficult or even impossible for tenderers to interpret the exact scope of the criterion in question in a uniform manner. The Court held that it is for the national courts to determine the clarity of formulation of award criteria constituting the most economically advantageous offer to satisfy the requirements of equal treatment and transparency of procedures for awarding public contracts.

9.59   With regard to the requirement of the award criterion consisting in the allocation of points for the total amount of electricity from renewable energy sources in excess of the volume expected through the particular contract in question, the Court held that such a requirement is incompatible with the Community legislation on public procurement. The fact that the amount of electricity in excess of the expected annual consumption is decisive to the determination of the most economically advantageous offer is liable to confer an advantage on tenderers who, owing to their larger production or supply capacities, are able to supply greater volumes of electricity than other tenderers. That criterion is thus liable to result in unjustified discrimination against tenderers whose tender is fully able to meet the requirements linked to the subject-matter of the contract. Such a limitation on the circle of economic operators in a position to submit a tender would have the effect of thwarting the objective of opening up the market to competition pursued by the Directives coordinating procedures for the award of public supply contracts.

9.60   The Court maintained that a criterion relating to the reliability of supplies is a legitimate factor in determining the most economically advantageous offer for a

---

[80]   *See Universale-Bau and Others*, paragraphs 91 and 92.

contracting authority.[81] However, the capacity of tenderers to provide the largest amount of electricity possible from renewable sources in excess of the amount laid down in the invitation to tender cannot legitimately be given the status of an award criterion. The award criterion applied did not relate to the service which is the subject-matter of the contract, namely the supply of an amount of electricity to the contracting authority corresponding to its expected annual consumption as laid down in the invitation to tender, but to the amount of electricity that the tenderers have supplied, or will supply, to other customers. An award criterion that relates solely to the amount of electricity produced from renewable energy sources in excess of the expected annual consumption, as laid down in the invitation to tender, cannot be regarded as linked to the subject-matter of the contract. The applicants in the main proceedings submitted that the award criterion in question is in fact a disguised selection criterion inasmuch as it concerns the tenderers' capacity to supply as much electricity as possible from renewable energy sources and, in that way, ultimately relates to the tenderers themselves.

9.61 The Court concluded that Community legislation on public procurement does not preclude a contracting authority from applying, in the context of the assessment of the most economically advantageous tender for a contract for the supply of electricity, an award criterion with a weighting of forty-five per cent which requires that the electricity supplied be produced from renewable energy sources. The fact that this criterion does not necessarily serve to achieve the objective pursued is irrelevant in that regard. On the other hand, public procurement law does preclude such a criterion where it is not accompanied by requirements which permit the accuracy of the information contained in the invitation to tender document to be effectively verified, and it contains factors for its assessment which are not directly linked to the subject matter of the procurement in question.

(7) The lowest offer

9.62 The Public Procurement Directives provide for an automatic disqualification of an 'obviously abnormally low offer'. The term has not been interpreted in detail by the Court and serves rather as an indication of a 'lower bottom limit'.[82] The Court, however, pronounced on the direct effect of the relevant provision requiring contracting authorities to examine the details of the tender before deciding the award of the contract. The contracting authorities are under duty to seek from the tenderer an explanation for the price submitted or to inform him that his tender appears to be abnormally low and to allow a reasonable time within which to submit further details, before making any decision as to the award of the contract.

---

[81] *See* Case C-448/01, *EVN AG, Wienstrom GmbH and Republik Österreich*, judgment of 4 December 2003, paragraph 70.

[82] *See* Case C-76/81, *SA Transporoute et Travaux v. Minister of Public Works* [1982] ECR 457.

9.63 The debate over the terminology of 'obviously abnormally low' tenders surfaced when the Court held[83] that rejection of a contract based on mathematical criteria without giving the tenderer an opportunity to furnish information is inconsistent with spirit of the Public Procurement Directives. The Court following previous case law[84] ruled that the contracting authorities must give an opportunity to tenderers to furnish explanations regarding the genuine nature of their tenders, when those tenders appear to be abnormally low. Unfortunately, the Court did not proceed to an analysis of the wording 'obviously'. It rather seems that the term 'obviously' indicates the existence of precise and concrete evidence as to the abnormality of the low tender. On the other hand, the wording 'abnormally' implies a quantitative criterion left to the discretion of the contracting authority. However, if the tender is just 'abnormally' low, it could be argued that it is within the discretion of the contracting authority to investigate the genuine offer of a tender. *Impresa Lombardini*[85] followed the precedence established by *Transporoute* and maintained the unlawfulness of mathematical criteria used as an exclusion of a tender which appears abnormally low. Nevertheless, it held that such criteria may be lawful if used for determining the abnormality of a low tender, provided an *inter partes* procedure between the contracting authority and the tenderer that submitted the alleged abnormal low offer offers the opportunity to clarify the genuine nature of that offer. Contracting authorities must take into account all reasonable explanations furnished and avoid limiting the grounds on which justification of the genuine nature of a tender should be made. Both the wording and the aim of the Public Procurement Directives direct contracting authorities to seek explanation and reject unrealistic offers, informing the Advisory Committee.[86] In *ARGE*,[87] the rejection of a tender based on the abnormally low pricing attached to it got a different twist in its interpretation. Although the Court ruled that directly or indirectly subsidised tenders by the state or other contracting authorities or even by the contracting authority itself can be legitimately part of the evaluation process, it did not elaborate on the possibility of rejection of an offer which is appreciably lower than those of unsubsidised tenders by reference to the of abnormally low disqualification ground.[88]

---

[83] *See* Case C-103/88, *Fratelli Costanzo SpA v. Comune di Milano* [1989] ECR 1839; Case 296/89, *Impresa Dona Alfonso di Dona Alfonso & Figli snc v. Consorzio per lo Sviluppo Industriale del Comune di Monfalcone*, judgment of 18 June 1991.

[84] *See* Case C- 76/81, *Transporoute* [1982] ECR 417, op.cit.

[85] *See* Case C-285/99 and 286/99 *Impresa Lombardini SpA v ANAS*, judgment of 27 November 2001.

[86] The Advisory Committee for Public Procurement was set up by Decision 77/63 ([1977] OJ L13/15) and is composed of representatives of the member states belonging to the authorities of those states and has as its task to supervise the proper application of Public Procurement Directives by member states.   [87] *See* Case C-94/99, *ARGE Gewässerschutzt*, op. cit.

[88] In *ARGE* the Court adopted a literal interpretation of the Directives and concluded that if the legislature wanted to preclude subsidized entities from participating in tendering procedures for public contracts, it should have said so explicitly in the relevant Directives. *See* paragraphs 26 *et seq.* of the Court's judgment. Although the case has relevance in the fields of selection and qualification procedures and award criteria, the Court made no references to previous case law regarding state aids in public procurement, presumably because the *Dupont de Nemours* precedence is still highly relevant.

Part IV

ENFORCEMENT AND COMPLIANCE AT NATIONAL LEVEL

10

PUBLIC PROCUREMENT AND PUBLIC–PRIVATE PARTNERSHIPS

A. Introductory Remarks

From a constitutional point of view, the state is under an obligation to provide a **10.01** range of services to the public in the form of, for example, general infrastructure, healthcare, education, housing, transport, energy, defence, social security, and policing. Traditionally, the state either in its own capacity or through delegated monopolies and publicly controlled enterprises has engaged in market activities in order to serve public interest.

The concept of the state encapsulates an entrepreneurial dimension to the extent **10.02** that it deploys wealth as policy instrument (*dominium*).[1] However, although entering into transactions with a view to providing goods, services, and works to the public, this type of action by the state does not resemble the commercial

---

[1] *See* Daintith, 'The Executive Power Today: Bargaining and Economic Control in The Changing Constitution', in Jowell and Oliver (eds.), *The Changing Constitution* (Oxford University Press, 1985), where reference is made to the distinction between *dominium* and *imperium* (the use of force by way of regulatory or criminal law) as two ways of policy implementation by the state.

characteristics of entrepreneurship, in as much as the aim of the state's activities is not the maximization of profits[2] but the observance of public interest.

10.03 Such participation by the state in the relevant market takes place on behalf of the public and the society as a whole,[3] and the whole process has been described as *corporatism*.[4] In fact, *corporatism* has been seen as a market phenomenon which has created a specific forum for the supply and demand sides. This forum is known as *public markets*.[5] Public markets, in contrast to private ones, are the forum where *public interest*[6] substitutes *profit maximisation*.[7] *Corporatism* has also revealed the dimension of the state as a service provider to the public and that notion has always been linked with the procurement and subsequent state ownership of the relevant assets. As a process of public sector management, corporatism has primarily been delivered through competitive tendering in order to satisfy the needs for accountability and transparency. Alongside the above objectives, competitive tendering has also represented a procedural delivery system for corporatism which has aimed, at least in principle, at introducing a balanced equilibrium in the

---

[2] The industrial or commercial character of an organization depends much upon a number of criteria that reveal the thrust behind the organization's participation in the relevant market. The state and its organs may act either by exercising public powers or by carrying economic activities of an industrial or commercial nature by offering goods and services on the market. *See* for example, Case 118/85, *Commission v. Italy* [1987] ECR 2599, para 7, where the European Court of Justice had the opportunity to elaborate on the distinction of activities pursued by public authorities and activities of commercially oriented undertakings. The key issue is the organization's intention to achieve profitability and pursue its objectives through a spectrum of commercially motivated decisions. The distinction between the range of activities which relate to public authority and those which, although carried out by public persons, fall within the private domain is drawn most clearly from case law and judicial precedence of the ECJ concerning the applicability of competition rules of the Treaty to the given activities. *See* Cases C-364/92, *SAT Fluggesellschaften* [1994] ECR 1-43 and C-343/95, *Diego Cali et Figli* [1997] ECR 1-1547.

[3] The origins of such activities can be found in Rousseau, *The Social Contract*, where a core range of obligations is undertaken by the state on behalf of its subjects. This is perhaps the first attempt to contractualize the state/society relationship.

[4] *See* Harrison, *Corporatism and the Welfare State* (Aldershot: Gower, 1984) Chapter 1.

[5] *See* Flamme et Flamme, 'Enfin l' Europe des Marchés Publics', *Actualité Juridique—Droit Administratif*, November 20, 1989, 653.

[6] The concept 'public interest' denotes the requirements of a community (local or national) in its entirety which should not overlap with the specific or exclusive interest of a clearly determined person or group of persons. *See* Valadou, 'La Notion de Pouvoir Adjudicateur en Matière de Marchés de Travaux', *Semaine Juridique*, 3 Ed. E. (1991), 33. Also, the European Court of Justice has approached the above concept of public interest by a direct analogy of the concept 'general economic interest', as defined in Art. 90(2) EC, which refers to public undertakings). *See* Case C-179/90, *Merci Convenzionali Porto di Gevova* [1991] ECR 1-5889, where the notion of general economic interest as a concept represents 'activities of direct benefit to the public'.

[7] Apart from the above fundamental differentiating factor, a number of striking variances distinguish private from public markets. These variances focus on structural elements of the relevant market place, competitiveness, demand conditions, supply conditions, the production process, and, finally, pricing and risk. They also provide for an indication as to the different methods and approaches employed in their regulation. *See* Bovis, *The Liberalisation of Public Procurement and its Impact on the Common Market* (Ashgate: Dartmouth Publishing International, 1998), 5–11.

supply and demand public procurement equation. Thus, the public and private sectors transact through an institutionalized structure which aims at replicating a regime of competition similar to that which exists in private markets.[8] Private markets are generally structured as a result of competitive pressures originating in the buyer/supplier interaction and their configuration can vary from monopoly or oligopoly to perfect competition, whereas public markets reveal a different picture, their structure being based upon a monopsony or oligopsony character.

Due to their different integral nature and structure, private and public markets require different control and regulation. Whereas the weaponry for the control of private markets is dominated by anti-trust law and policy, public markets are *fora* where the structural and behavioural remedial tools of competition law have limited applicability, mainly due to the fact that anti-trust often clashes, *ipso facto*, with the monopolistic structures which exist in public markets. The control of private markets through anti-trust law and policy reveals a set of rules of negative nature; contemporary anti-trust is ill-disposed towards cartels and abuse of dominance, thus undertakings must *restrain* their activities to an acceptable range which is pre-determined[9] by the competent authorities. On the other hand, public markets require a set of regulatory rules that have positive character, and the sort of regulation envisaged aims at creating an appropriate environment which would facilitate *market access*.[10] **10.04**

Irrespective of the different control and regulation private and public markets require, as a result of the difference in their integral nature and structure, the rationale behind the process of regulating public markets can be summarised as the attempt to establish an effectively competitive regime, similar to that envisaged for the operation of private markets.[11] The accomplishment of such objective could bring about two types of beneficial effects for the supply and demand equation and enhance the image of corporatism. On the one hand, competition in public markets could benefit the supply side of the equation (the industry), by means of optimal allocation of resources, rationalization of production and supply, promotion of mergers and acquisitions, and elimination of sub-optimal firms **10.05**

---

[8] Corporatism has been deemed as an important instrument of industrial policy of a state, in particular where procurement systems have been utilized with a view to promoting structural adjustment policies and favour 'national champions'. *See* Bovis, 'The Choice of Policies and the Regulation of Public Procurement in the European Community' in Lawton (ed) *European Industrial Policy and Competitiveness: Concepts and Instruments* (Macmillan Publishers, 1998).

[9] Although anti-trust rules are of negative nature, by no means they can be deemed static. Perceptions concerning cartels and abusive dominant behaviour change in line with contemporary socio-economic parameters.

[10] *See* Bovis, 'The Regulation of Public Procurement as an element in the Evolution of European Economic Law', *European Law Journal*, 4/2 (June 1998), 220 *et seq.*

[11] The adverse effects of concerted practices in tendering procedures on competition in the common market were recognizedrecognised by the European Court of Justice in case *Cooperative Vereniging ' "Suiker Unie" ' UA v. Commission*, [1975] ECR 1663.

and creation of genuinely competitive industries. On the other hand, corporatism operating through a genuinely competitive regime has been also deemed to yield substantial purchasing savings for the public sector.[12]

10.06 The integration of the public sector management through a liberalized public procurement regime underpins the concept of corporatism. The opening-up of traditional public procurement has envisaged a competitive regime which would instigate the convergence of prices for goods, works and services destined for the public sector. Savings could materialize as a result of the elimination of preferential purchasing patterns and discriminatory procurement decisions which often tend to favour sub-optimal 'national champions' at the expense of competitive industries.

(1) From corporatism to contractualized governance

10.07 If one accepts the fact that the introduction of elements of competition in public markets through competitive tendering would have desirable effects for corporatism, a question which might arise is to what extent private markets can be entrusted with the delivery of public services, and, as a consequence, if the concept of corporatism is compatible with them. As mentioned previously, private markets operate under the laws of demand and supply and the private sector is profit orientated. A first step from corporatism towards government by contract appears to be the process of privatization. Privatization, as a process of transfer of public assets and operations to private hands, on grounds of market efficiency and competition, as well as responsiveness to customer demand and quality considerations, is often accompanied by simultaneous regulation by the state, in the form of a legal framework within which privatized industries will pursue public interest functions. It is not entirely clear that the process of privatization would reclaim public markets and transform them to private ones. One should never underestimate the fact that the control of operations related to public interest remains within the competence of the state in the form of the regulatory regime, thus maintaining strong public market characteristics. The extent to which the market freedom of a privatized entity could be curtailed by regulatory frameworks deserves a complex and thorough analysis, which exceeds by far the remit of this publication. However, it could be maintained that, through the privatization process, the previously clear-cut distinction between public and private markets becomes blurred, as a new marketplace emerges. This type of market embraces strong public law elements to the extent that it is regulated by the state with a view

---

[12] *See* European Commission, *The Cost of Non-Europe, Basic Findings, Vol. 5, Part. A; The Cost of Non-Europe in Public Sector Procurement*, Official Publications of the European Communities (Luxembourg, 1988). The European Commission has claimed that the regulation of public procurement through the newly established regime and the resulting elimination of non-tariff barriers arising from discriminatory and preferential purchasing patterns of Member Sates could bring about substantial savings of €20 billion or 0.5% of GDP to the (European) public sector.

to observing public interest in the relevant operations. The economic freedom and the risks associated with such operations are also subject to regulation, a fact which implies that the above regulatory framework incorporates more than mere procedural rules. This marketplace reveals a transformation from traditional *corporatism* to a public management system where *governance is dispersed through contract* under terms and conditions determined by the state.

Alongside privatization, the notion of *contracting out* represents a further depar- **10.08**
ture from the premises of traditional corporatism. The notion of *contracting out* is an exercise which aims at achieving potential savings and efficiency gains for contracting authorities, when they *test the market* in an attempt to define whether the provision of works or the delivery of services from a commercial operator could be cheaper than that from the in-house team. Contracting out differs from privatization to the extent that the former represents a transfer of undertaking only, whereas the latter denotes transfer of ownership. Contracting out depicts a price-discipline exercise by the state, against the principle of *insourcing*, where, the self-sufficient nature of corporatism resulted in budgetary inefficiencies and poor quality of deliverables to the public. Contracting out uses competitive tendering, which is the procedural mechanism for the delivery of corporatism as the Trojan Horse in an attempt to maximise outsourcing in the delivery of public service.

Both the privatization and contracting out processes resemble the *principle of* **10.09**
outsourcing, which is often utilised in restructuring exercises in the private sector. Outsourcing introduces elements of contractualization in the production process, as subcontracting takes over from the in-house operation in the production chain. Government by contract, along the same lines, introduces the principle of out-sourcing in the dispersement of public service, but the *contractualized govern-ance*[13] appears far more stringent than private sector outsourcing by virtue of its regulation. Furthermore, apart from operational savings, outsourcing in the pri-vate sector would normally spread the risk factor amongst the operations in the production chain. If the subcontractor could not deliver according to the expecta-tions, the main operator could switch to an alternative with no major implica-tions. Outsourcing, therefore, introduces an element of flexibility in the production process. It remains to be seen whether contractualized governance or government by contract conforms to the same parameters (savings, risk sharing, and flexibility) as private sector outsourcing.

The integral characteristics of privately financed projects reveal the degree that the **10.10**
state and its organs are prepared to drift away from *traditional corporatism*[14]

---

[13] For an analysis of the concept, see Bovis, op. cit. (n. 7).
[14] *See* Birkinshaw, 'Corporatism and Accountability in Corporatism and the Corporate State', in N. O'Sullivan and A. Cox (eds.), *The Corporate State: Corporatism and the State Tradition in Western Europe* (Edward Elgar, 1988).

towards *contractualized governance*. The degree of departure from traditional corporatism also reflects the state's perception vis-à-vis its responsibilities towards the public. A shift towards contractualized governance would indicate the departure from the assumption that the state embraces both roles of asset owner and service deliverer. It should also insinuate the shrinkage of the state and its organs and the need to define a range of core activities that are not to be contractualized.[15]

B. The Emergence of the Private Finance Initiative

10.11   The Private Finance Initiative (PFI) represents a process of public sector management which envisages the utilization of private finances in the delivery of public services and the provision of public infrastructure. The Private Finance Initiative has arrived in times when the role and the responsibilities of the state are being redefined and also has been seen as part of a process of slimming the state down to a bare minimum of fiscal responsibilities towards the public. The state then assumes a regulatory role in the marketplace where the private sector is elevated to a service deliverer. The principal benefit from such exercise could be that the public sector does not have to commit its own, often scarce, capital resources in delivering public services. Other reasons put forward for involving private finances in delivering public services include quality improvement, innovation, management efficiency, and effectiveness, elements that are often underlying the private sector entrepreneurship. Consequently, the public sector would receive value for money in the delivery of services to the public, whereas it could also be maintained that through this process the state manages public finances in a better way, to the extent that capital resources could be utilized in priority areas.

10.12   When the Private Finance Initiative was launched in 1992, it did not receive the envisaged response from either the public or the private sectors. The initial approach to privately financed projects by the public sector represented a disguised tendering for their financing, and as such it revealed a number of procedural and commercial inadequacies in the whole process. Policymakers incorrectly assumed that the mere private financing of projects could enhance their quality and value for money, as well as transform the often ill-fated traditional public procurement process into a supply chain system of advanced structure and

---

[15] For example, defence, policing, or other essential or core elements of governance. It is maintained here that activities related to *imperium* (the use of force by way of regulatory or criminal law) could not be the subject of contractualized governance. A useful analysis for such argument is provided in Case C-44/96, *Mannesmann Anlangenbau Austria AG et al. v. Strohal Rotationsdurck GesmbH*, judgment of 15 January 1998, where the notions of public security and safety are used to described a range of activities by the state which possess the characteristic of 'public service obligations'. For a commentary of the case, see Bovis, 'Redefining Contracting Authorities under the EC Public Procurement Directives: An Analysis of the Case C-44/96, Mannesmann Anlangenbau Austria AG et al. v. Strohal Rotationsdurck GesmbH', *Common Market Law Review*, Autumn 1998.

entrepreneurial flair. The Private Finance Initiative was wrongfully conceived as a *panacea* for the limitations of the traditional public procurement process,[16] which was blamed for inefficiencies and poor value for money.[17]

In principle, privately financed projects destined for the public sector have been **10.13** an option in the UK public procurement process since the eighties, where the government, with great deal of caution, allowed the conclusion of a limited number of contracts. The government applied the so-called *Ryrie Rules* in the process of allowing private finances to be used in public projects, subject to two strict conditions. The first one concerned the cost-effective nature of the privately financed delivery in comparison with a publicly funded alternative. To reach such a conclusion, contracting authorities should have established a public sector comparator, whereby the privately financed delivery model could be tested and compared against the traditional publicly funded one. The second condition for the government to give clearance for a privately finance project related to the compulsory substitution of publicly funded schemes with the privately funded ones. In other words, private finances were conceived as an exclusive alternative method in delivering public services and not as a complementary one.

Meeting the two conditions of the *Ryrie Rules* was not an easy exercise for public **10.14** authorities, particularly in attempting to establish the cost-effective nature of a privately financed project versus a publicly funded alternative and its value for money. Quite often the rationale behind such comparisons was founded upon unsound grounds. For example, in order to achieve a meaningful comparison, the two delivery models should be benchmarked against a set of *variable parameters* (e.g. technical merit, quality of deliverables, aesthetic reasons, maintenance facilities, warranties, and, last but not least, overall price). This was not always the case, as the specifications of the project were firmly predetermined from the outset by the public authority in question and the pricing of a project evolved around them. Hence, the only *variable parameter* to compare the two delivery models unfolded around pricing. The procurement of privately financed projects was a disguised tendering for their financing, and as such it was bound to have very limited impact upon the procurement process. There was little chance that the private sector could beat the privileged position governments enjoy in the financial markets and raise the capital required to finance a service or an infrastructure project in more preferable terms. Furthermore, the private sector would normally require extra levels of capital return for the deferred payment facility that the public sector would use for repayments during the life of the contract. In the light of the above considerations, it is not a surprise that only a handful of

---

[16] *See*, Thomas, 'Private Finance Initiative—Government by Contract', *European Public Law*, 3/4 (December 1997), 519 *et seq.*

[17] A number of reasons which have been put forward include *inter alia* poor specification design, wrong contractual risk allocation, poor control systems for contractual performance, and bad planning and delivery processes.

privately financed projects were concluded, particularly complex projects of massive scale and of multi-national dimension.

10.15 Against this background and bearing in mind the recently imposed restraints on public expenditure, for example, prudence in Public Sector Borrowing Requirement (PSBR), EMU convergence criteria, the Private Finance Initiative was given a new lease of life when the 1997 Labour Government committed itself, in principle, to the concept and, as a consequence, public authorities in the United Kingdom have been required to explore all potential ways of involving private finances in their public procurement process prior to committing their own funds.

10.16 There are two broad categories under which privately financed projects can be classified. The first one covers the so-called *financially free-standing ones*, where it is expected that the private sector designs, builds, finances, and then operates an asset. The recovery of its costs is guaranteed by direct charges on the users of the service which the particular asset provides. These projects are often described as *concession contracts*, where the successful contractor is granted an exclusive right over a period of time to exploit the asset that it has financed, designed, and built. The state and its authorities may also contribute, in financial terms, to the repayments in order to render the project viable or the service charge to the end users acceptable. The second category of privately financed projects embraces projects which have as their object the provision of services by the private sector to the public, in conjunction with, and subject to, the relevant investment in assets that are necessary to deliver the required service to the public. In such cases, the private sector provider is reimbursed by a series of future payments by the contracting authority, payments which depend upon the successful delivery of those services in accordance with certain specified quality standards.

10.17 Privately financed projects have two constituent elements which are prerequisites for their completion: i) a genuine allocation of contractual risk, and ii) value for money for the public sector. The first element represents the integral balance of contractual relationships. Under traditional public procurement transactions, a widespread assumption indicates that contractual relationships are based upon a disproportionate risk allocation amongst the parties. Although in traditional public procurement systems, the demand side appears the dominant part in the equation, when it comes to risk allocation, the roles appear reversed.[18] Risk allocation

---

[18] The structure of public markets reveals that in the supply/demand equation, the dominant part appears to be the demand side (the state and its organs as purchasers), which initializes demand through an institutionalized purchasing system, whereas the supply side (the industry) fights for access to the relevant markets. Although this is normally the case, one should not exclude the possibility of market oligopolization and the potential manipulation of the demand side. These advanced market structures can occur more often in the future, as a result of the well established trends of industrial concentration. *See* Bovis, op. cit. (n. 7); Also, Konstadacopoulos, 'The Linked Oligopoly Concept in the Single European Market, *Public Procurement Law Review*, 4 (1995), 213.

is a much misunderstood concept in contractual relationships in general, but particularly in public purchasing transactions it has never been properly addressed.[19] Risk allocation is the result of negotiations between the parties and is normally expected to reflect the pricing element of contractual arrangements between them. Thus, risk and pricing operate in an analogous relation within a contract. The more risk a party resumes, the higher the price to be paid by the other party, and *vice versa*.

In traditional public procurement transactions the demand side inevitably undertakes too much risk, as a result of its practices.[20] The award of publicly funded contracts takes place predominately by reference to *the lowest price*, which constitutes one of the two permissible award criteria under the procurement rules (the other being the criterion of *the most economically advantageous offer*). When contracting authorities award their contracts by reference to pricing, this would normally reflect the amount of risk they are prepared to resume.[21] **10.18**

There is not any golden rule as to what represents an acceptable risk transfer in a contract, the latter being private or public, for risk allocation primarily reflects the parties' perception of a transaction with reference to their own criteria. These criteria are often influenced by a range of parameters such as speculation, fear, and certainty, as well as by a number of qualitative attributes of the parties, for example, sound forecasting and planning, and market intelligence. **10.19**

On the other hand, value for money as the second constituent element of a privately financed project should reflect a benchmarked comparison between public and privately financed models of service delivery. The comparison should not only take into account factors such as quality or technical merit, but mainly aspects of sound supply chain management reflecting efficiency gains, in the sense that the conclusion of a privately financed project would resemble to a large extent **10.20**

---

[19] Normally in a public contract, risk assessment includes contractual elements which are associated with the design or construction of a project, the required investment and financing, planning and operational matters, maintenance, residualization, obsolescence, political/legal aspects, industrial relations, usage volumes, and, finally, currency transactions.

[20] A number of impact assessment studies of the procurement regime upon the demand and supply sides have revealed the disproportionate risk allocation amongst the parties. *See* European Commission, *The Use of Negotiated Procedures as a Non-Tariff Barrier in Public Procurement*, CC 9364 (Brussels, 1995). In this study, the author investigated on behalf of the European Commission the award patterns of public contracts in six EC member states. The results showed the overall preference of contracting authorities towards *the lowest price* award criterion. Even in cases where *the most economically advantageous offer* was used for the award of a public contract, contracting authorities prioritized the price given by tenderers amongst the other parameters (technical reasons, aesthetic reasons, quality of deliverables, after sales service, or maintenance).

[21] In another impact assessment study undertaken on behalf of the European Commission, (*The Opening-up of Public Procurement to Foreign Direct Investment* in the European Community, CC 93/79 (Brussels, 1995)), the author examined the impact of the public procurement regime upon foreign direct investment. Investment patterns towards industries doing business with the public sector showed a considerable link between the 'low risk' assessments of the public contracts of these industries.

a contractual arrangement between private parties. Value-for-money as an element in a PFI deal is a precursor of best purchasing practice by contracting authorities and also reflects the underlying competitive elements which are necessary in order to meet the accountability and transparency standards and principles.[22]

(1) The intellectual origins of the Private Finance Initiative

10.21 The origins of the Private Finance Initiative could be traced to the attempts to moderate the widespread dissatisfaction from traditional public procurement methods. The nexus of contractual relations between public authorities and the private sector has been often criticised for not giving the best value for money. The criticism has been primarily directed towards three elements of the process: i) adversarial contractual relations as a result of compulsory competitive tendering, ii) inefficient risk allocation, and iii) poor contractual performances resulting in delayed and over-budgeted completions.

10.22 Competitive tendering in public procurement has been reproached for creating a confrontational environment, where the antagonizing relations which emanate from the tendering and contract award processes are often reflected in the performance stage of the contract. Public procurement procedures which are based upon a win-to-win process have been deemed to deprive significant elements one can expect in the delivery of public services. For example, competitive tendering has been dissociated with innovation and quality. Also, as a result of inefficiently written specifications upon which the tender should be constructed, the deliverables often differ dramatically from contractual expectations.

10.23 On the other hand, risk allocation is probably the most crucial element in contractual relations that affects pricing as well as the overall contractual framework. Risk represents the level of financial exposure of a party prior to, or after the conclusion of a contract, or during its performance. In traditional public procurement, the risk allocation tends to favour the supply side, which mainly assumes the risks related to the tendering process. During the performance stage of the contract and up to its completion, the demand side could, usually, shift a considerable amount of risk by requesting from the supply side performance or defects bonds or other means of financial guarantees.

10.24 Finally, traditional procurement methods have often revealed a picture of poor contracts management as a result of inefficient control systems operated by public authorities. Poor contracts management have resulted in abysmally out-of-control

---

[22] In its policy statement *Public Sector Comparators and Value for Money*, February 1998, the HM Treasury Taskforce has set out the role of comparators in public procurement, stressing the importance of the value for money principle. The comparators are indices which help to distinguish between the lowest cost and the best value for money for public authorities, and also their use as an exercise of financial management and a means of demonstrating savings to public authorities.

contractual performances with all the financial consequences attributed to the delayed completions of the projects.

Competitive tendering, amongst other things, has been deemed responsible for **10.25** cyclical demand structures in public purchasing, a situation where the supply side (the industry) responds to the demand side (public authorities) through cycles of institutionalized bureaucracy (tender submission, selection, evaluation, and contract award processes). The demand side has institutionalized the procurement process, by imposing a disciplinarian compartmentalization of the relevant processes (advertisement, expression of interest, selection, qualification, tender, and contract award).

The institutionalization of the procurement process intends to facilitate the main **10.26** objectives of the European public procurement rules: the establishment of the principles of transparency and competitiveness in the award of public contracts and the achievement of savings for the public sector. The bureaucratic system which supports traditional public procurement uses the effects of transparency as leverage for value for money results. The fact that more suppliers are aware of a forthcoming public contract and the fact that interesting suppliers are aware that their rivals are informed about it, indicates two distinctive parameters which are relevant to savings and value for money. The first parameter focuses on value for money for the demand side and reveals the possibility for contracting authorities to compare prices and quality. The second parameter has an effect on the supply side of the equation (the suppliers) which amongst other things cannot longer rely on lack of price comparisons when serving the public sector. Openness in public procurement, by definition, results in price competition and the benefits for contracting authorities appear achievable. The institutionalized nature of the public of the procurement process also reflects the relative balance of powers in the demand/supply equation.

However, the traditional public procurement process often suffers from unneces- **10.27** sarily repetitive functions (in particularly the advertisement, selection, and qualification processes) which can be cost ineffective and pose a considerable financial burden on the demand side. In addition, the institutionalized process of public procurement may pose a question over long-term savings and value for money considerations. Price competition, as a result of the awareness of forthcoming public contracts, represents a rather static effect in the value for money process. The fact that more and more interested suppliers are aware and do submit tenders, in the long run, appears rather as a burden. If transparency and the resulting price competitiveness are based on a *win-to-win* process, the potential benefits for contracting authorities could easily be counterbalanced by the administrative costs in tender evaluation and replies to unsuccessful tenders. Furthermore, the risk management factor is much higher in a win-to-win purchasing scenario. Price competitiveness also represents some threats for contracting authorities, to the extent that quality of deliverables as well as the delivery process itself could be jeopardized, if contracting authorities deal with different and unknown contractors. It could thus be argued here that price competitiveness, as a trade effect potentially beneficial for the demand side of the public purchasing equation, has a static character. It seems that it does not take into account medium- or long-term purchasing patterns, as well as counter effects of competition. Two elements deserve further analysis here:

10.28 The first raises questions over the aggregate economic loss through transparent competitive purchasing patterns. For example, if a large number of interested suppliers submit their offer to a particular contracting authority, two types of costs should be examined. Firstly, the cost which is attributed to the response and tendering stage of the procurement process. Human and capital resources are directed by the suppliers towards the preparation of documents and the submission of the offers. If one of these suppliers wins the contract, the remaining would have suffered an unrecoverable loss. If that aggregate loss exceeds the benefit/saving accomplished by the contracting authority by following transparent and competitive purchasing patterns, value for money has not been achieved. Secondly, along the same lines, the evaluation and selection process during tendering represents a considerable administrative cost for the contracting authorities. If the principle of transparency complements the principle of equal treatment, contracting authorities should give the same attention to all interested suppliers that have submitted a response. Downsizing the list through evaluation and assessment based on stipulated criteria is by no means an inexpensive exercise. Human and capital resources have to be directed by contracting authorities towards meeting that cost. If the latter exceeds the potential savings achieved through the competitive tendering route, then value for money is unaccomplished.

10.29 The second element that deserves attention relates to the definition of price competitiveness in public purchasing as well as its interrelation with anti-trust law and policy. A question which arises in price competitive tendering patterns is: *What would be the lowest offer contracting authorities can accept?* If the maximization of savings is the only achievable objective in the public procurement process, the transparent/competitive pattern cannot guarantee and evaluate safeguards in relation to under-priced offers. If the supply side responds to the perpetuated competitive purchasing pattern by lowering prices, contracting authorities could face a dilemma: where to stop. It should be mentioned here that the European rules provide for an automatic disqualification of an 'abnormally low offer'. The term has not been interpreted in detail by the judiciary at European and domestic levels and serves rather as a 'lower bottom limit'.[23] Also, when an offer appears low,

---

[23] Case 76/81, *SA Transporoute et Travaux v. Minister of Public Works* [1982] ECR 457; Case No. 104/75, *SA SHV Belgium v. La Maison Ideale et Societe Nationale du Logement*, before the Belgian *Conseil d'Etat*, judgment of 24 June 1986 of the Belgian *Conseil d'Etat*.

contracting authorities may request clarifications from the tenderer in question. Contracting authorities face a dilemma in evaluating and assessing low offers other than abnormal ones. It is difficult for them to identify dumping or predatory pricing disguised behind a low offer for a public contract. In addition, even if there is an indication of anti-competitive price fixing, the European public procurement rules do not provide for any kind of procedure. The suspension of the award procedures (or even the suspension of the conclusion of the contract itself) would be unlikely without a thorough and exhaustive investigation by the competent anti-trust authorities.

Against this background, the Private Finance Initiative was originally construed as **10.30** the process that could bring the public and private sectors closer and break the mistrust which has surrounded traditional public procurement. The Private Finance Initiative should not be conceived as a capital facility to the state and its organs in the process of delivering public services. It should not been seen as a borrowing exercise by the public sector, as the latter can acquire capital in much more preferential terms than any private person. The Private Finance Initiate should be rather conceived as a process of involving the private sector in the delivery of public services. As such, the Private Finance Initiative attempts to introduce a contractual element in the delivery of public services, to the extent that private sector, as a contractual party undertakes the responsibility to provide not only an asset but to deliver its associated functions to the public. Therefore, the Private Finance Initiative has contributed in changing the traditionally acquisitorial nature of public sector contracts by inserting a service delivery element.

One of the most important attractions of the Private Finance Initiative has been **10.31** the ability of public authorities to classify the relevant transactions as exempted from the Public Sector Borrowing Requirement (PSBR), thus by-passing centrally controlled budgetary allocations and cash limits in the public sector spending. In such a way, the Private Finance Initiative represented a viable solution to cash-stranded public authorities, which could, independently, proceed and strike deals that otherwise would not have been materialized. Furthermore, the public spending relating to the repayments of the privately financed transactions would not appear as public debt. By taking privately financed transactions out of the PSBR balance sheet, the government may implicitly have attempted to liberalize public purchasing from budgetary constraints and public spending capping. It could be also argued that such an attempt could indicate the beginning of the end to the institutionalized decision making process and control of public procurement imposed under the European (and domestic) public procurement regime.

The paramount implication of not classifying privately financed projects as public **10.32** debt could be that such purchasing would not fall under the annual comprehensive spending review of the government. In fact, non-inclusion of PFI deals in the

PSBR could transform the structure of public markets[24] by reversing the roles and the relative importance of the demand and supply sides. Indeed, it was originally suggested[25] that the private sector should initiate demand by exploring the overall potential and delivery options and then introducing the plan to the relevant public authority. Such a scenario could also mean dismantling of public markets and the elevation of private markets[26] as the forum for the pursuit of public interest.

(2) The procedural delivery of the Private Finance Initiative

10.33 The Private Finance Initiative is proclaimed[27] to represent an evolution in the public sector management and a step forward in achieving real value for money in public purchasing. Numerous guidance notes have been issued by government departments[28] in an attempt to provide for a framework of smooth procedural delivery process. However, a number of difficult issues arise when a privately financed contract is examined under the spectrum of the European Public Procurement Directives.[29] Notwithstanding the fact that a PFI project is privately financed, it will be paid by public funds, thus compliance with the European

---

[24] The structure of public markets often reveals a monopsony/oligopsony character. In terms of its origins, demand in public markets is institutionalized and operates mainly under budgetary considerations rather than price mechanisms. It is also based on fulfilment of tasks (pursuit of public interest) and it is single for many products. Supply also has limited origins, in terms of the establishment of close ties between the public sector and industries supplying it and there is often a limited product range. Products are rarely innovative and technologically advanced and pricing is determined through tendering and negotiations. The purchasing decision is primarily based upon the life-time cycle, reliability, price, and political considerations. Purchasing patterns follow tendering and negotiations and often purchases are dictated by policy rather than price/quality considerations.

[25] *See Working Together—Private Finance and Public Money*, Department of the Environment, 1993.

[26] Private markets are generally structured as a result of competitive pressures originating in the buyer/supplier interaction and their configuration can vary from monopoly/oligopoly to perfect competition. Demand arises from heterogeneous buyers with a variety of specific needs. It is based on expectations and is multiple for each product. Supply, on the other hand, is offered through various product ranges, where products are standardized using known technology, but constantly improved through research and development processes. The production process is based on mass-production patterns and the product range represents a large choice including substitutes, whereas the critical production factor is cost level. The development cycle appears to be short- to medium-term and finally, the technology of products destined for the private markets is evolutionary. Purchases are made when an acceptable balance between price and quality is achieved. Purchase orders are multitude and at limited intervals. Pricing policy in private markets is determined by competitive forces and the purchasing decision is focused on the price-quality relation. The risk factor is highly present.

[27] A number of government documents have eulogized the Private Finance Initiative. *See* in particular, *Working Together—Private Finance and Public Money*, Department of Environment, 1993. *Private Opportunity, Public Benefit—Progressing the Private Finance Initiative*, Private Finance Panel and HM Treasury, 1995.

[28] *See* the *Guidelines for Smoothing the Procurement Process*, Private Finance Panel and HM Treasury, 1996. Also *A Step by Step Guide to PFI*, HM Treasury, 1997.

[29] The European Public Procurement Directives include the Supplies Directive 93/36 [1993] OJ L199/1, the Works Directive 93/37 [1993] OJ L199/54, the Utilities Directive 93/38 [1993] OJ L199/84, and, finally, the Services Directive 92/50 [1992] OJ L209/1.

public procurement rules is of paramount importance. It would be naive for contracting authorities to ignore the spirit and the wording of the Directives. It could also be embarrassing for them if litigation before domestic courts or the European Court of Justice concerning the award procedures of a privately financed project is initiated. Clearly, there is a great deal of uncertainty in relation to the compatibility of the European public procurement rules and the Private Finance Initiative. The situation has not yet been clarified by the European Commission, which seems to sit in the background waiting for the domestic government to determine any issues of compatibility.

It appears that two major issues in a privately financed project may cause **10.34** considerable friction between the European Commission and contracting authorities. The first one relates to the contractual nature of the privately financed transaction, when viewed through the spectrum of the European Public Procurement Directives. The second issue is concerned with the process of contract award, and in particular the type of procedures that contracting authorities may use in order to conclude a private financed project.

(3) *The contractual nature of a PFI project*

A privately financed project can be classified as a 'public services contract' or as a **10.35** 'public works contract' depending upon the nature of the deliverables. It could also be considered as a 'mixed contract', where both services and construction work are parts of the project. Finally, it can be characterised as a 'concession contract'. The contractual nature of a PFI project is crucial in its procedural delivery and detrimental in complying with the relevant European procurement rules, as it triggers the applicability of different Directives and requirements stipulated therein.

(4) *The services/works dilemma*

In order to classify a PFI project as public works or public services contract, three **10.36** significant factors should be taken into account:

 i) the intention of the contracting authority;
 ii) the description of the contract's specification and standardization;
 iii) the issue of ownership of the asset to be privately financed.

The intention of the contracting authority to procure a privately financed project **10.37** is the starting point in deciding whether the relevant contract is a public works or services one. In many cases, contracting authorities perceive a PFI project as the vehicle for the provision of a service to the public. However, they do not distinguish between the facilities provision and the provision of the necessary infrastructure. Clearly, prior to any procedural steps towards the procurement process, the contracting authority should have in place a plan of action (establish business needs, appraise options, create a business case and project reference, evaluate market soundings, and create a project team)[30] which will determine whether the project is a works or a services contract. To facilitate the contracting authority's decision on the subject, reference to the definitions of works or services contracts according to the relevant European Directives is crucial.[31] It is, therefore, up to the contracting authority to identify the generic contractual nature of the project.

10.38 The extent to which the description of the contract's specification and standardization requirements emerge from the contracting authority's intention to procure a privately financed project reflects the disposition of the contracting authority towards the classification of the project as a works or a services contract. Contracting authorities must provide an accurate description of the contractual specifications using non-discriminatory standards. The contractual specifications are the competitive benchmark amongst the private sector candidates/tenderers. Under-specification, which is normally the case in PFI projects, raises serious questions over the contractual nature of a privately financed project. Furthermore, apart from their competitive benchmark use, specifications are the core part of the contract itself. Under-specified PFI projects tend to appear as services contracts, as the service element of the contract takes the predominant part in the equation.[32] Under-specification at the preliminary level of the procurement process of a PFI project is usually rectified by negotiating the specifications with the preferred bidder prior to the conclusion of the contract. This sort of practice appears questionable in terms of its legality[33] and the value for money aspect for the contracting authority.[34]

10.39 The question of ownership of the asset to be privately financed also plays a crucial role in determining the contractual nature of the project. If the asset remains in

---

[30] These stages represent the necessary steps that a contracting authority should take before publicizing its intention to procure a PFI project. *See A Step-by-Step Guide to the PFI Procurement Process*, Private Finance Executive Panel, 1997.

[31] According to Art. 1(a) of the Works Directive 93/37, a works contract refers to the execution, by whatever means, of a work corresponding to the requirements specified by the contracting authority. According to Article 1(a) of Services Directive 92/50, a services contract refers to the provision of a service by a service provider to a contracting authority.

[32] Interestingly, the Services Directive 92/50 allows the use of negotiated procedures in cases where specifications of a contract cannot be drawn (Article 11(2)(c)).

[33] If the contract specifications were negotiated with a sole contractor, other tenderers/candidates are discriminated against. Contract specifications cannot be part of any award procedures, particularly the negotiated ones. *See* Bovis, *EC Public Procurement Law* (Longman, European Law Series, 1997), 63–66.

[34] Contract specifications affect essentially the price of the contract. There is no real element of competition in the process when the contracting authority cannot compare other offers with the offer of the preferred bidder.

the ownership of the contracting authority, the objective of the contract is to finance, design, and build the asset. This contractual nexus reveals in a large number of cases a works contract. In cases where a service element (maintenance or operation) is part of the contract, this represents an ancillary component which should be looked at separately if it exceeds certain thresholds. On the other hand, if the ownership of the asset which will be privately financed is retained by the contractor, the objective of the contract is to finance, design, build, and operate the asset for a given period, with or without an option to transfer it to the contracting authority at the end of the contract. Such contractual arrangement often reveals a services contract.

10.40 The consequences of the classification of a PFI project as a 'public services contract' or as a 'public works contract' are reflected in the advertisement and publicity requirements and the award procedures. The financial threshold for advertisement and publicity requirements in the *Official Journal* for services contracts is considerably lower (€200,000) than the threshold of works contracts (€5 million). However, certain public services contracts need not to be advertised Community-wide.[35] With reference to the award procedures, the utilization of negotiated procedures appears more flexible in public services contracts, where their specification requirements cannot be set by the contracting authority in advance.[36] Nevertheless, this option is not available for public works contracts.

(5) *The case of mixed contracts*

10.41 Special attention is required in cases of 'mixed contracts', where works and services are part of the project. The distinguishing factor here is the 'incidental purpose test', where works or services are considered incidental to the main objective of the contract.[37] The concept of incidental purpose was developed by the European Court of Justice in the absence of specific and explicit rules in the Public Works Directive regarding public projects where works and services form an integral part of the contract.

10.42 However, in many PFI projects, both works and services are often indistinguishable elements of the contract, in the sense that they form a contractual package which cannot be split in a commercially viable way. In such cases, the incidental purpose test provides little help. The very fact that a public project is privately

---

[35] Services which are included in Part B of the Services Directive 92/50: hotel and restaurant services, rail transport services, water transport services, supporting and auxiliary transport services, legal services, personnel placement and supply services, investigation and security services, education and vocational education services, health and social services, recreational, cultural, and sporting services.   [36] *See* Art. 11(2)(c) of the Services Directive 92/50.

[37] *See* Case C-331/92, *Gestion Hotelera Internacional SA v. Communidad Autonoma de Canarias* [1994] ECR 1-1329.

financed reveals an element of a service to be provided to the contracting authority from the outset. The majority of privately financed contracts envisage management and operational services in addition to the procurement of construction works. They are obviously a 'mixed type' of public contracts; however, their classification as public services or public works contracts requires further elaboration. It appears rather difficult to decide the incidental purpose of the works or the services involved in a PFI project. Unfortunately, the ECJ did not clarify the constituents of the term 'incidental', so the contractual nature of a 'mixed type' public contract could be assessed. It has been suggested[38] that the value of the works or the services could be used as the decisive criterion in describing a mixed public contract as a public services or public works contract. However, in PFI projects the contractual elements of works and services are closely interdependent and their pricing is mutually affected. Their potential split would result in an artificial outcome, as the value of the works element without the service element would not reflect commercially realistic figures.

10.43 The danger in classifying a mixed contract as a services contract appears to be the potential contravention of the Public Works Directive. Even if the services contract is properly advertised and awarded according with the relevant European Directive, its award could be linked with the award of a works contract outside the framework of the Works Directives. In many PFI projects the services element tends to be overstressed. It then emerges that a privately financed public service contract is a disguised public works contract. This appears as an unsatisfactory outcome and such course of action by contracting authorities is legally questionable before domestic courts or the ECJ.

10.44 In deciding the contractual nature of a PFI mixed type project, the threshold test represents the safest option for contracting authorities, when a realistic split of the contractual elements can be achieved. In cases where the ownership of an asset is vested with the contractor, the value of the operation and management element of the contract should be counterbalanced with the residual value of the asset after a certain period of time, when an option to transfer the asset to the contracting authority is exercised. If the operation and management (services) element exceeds the residual value of the asset (which represents the construction costs minus depreciation), there is a strong indication that the project is a public services contract. On the other hand, when ownership of an asset remains with the contracting authority, the value of the operation and management element of the contract during its life should be compared with the construction costs, when these are completed. Again, if the services element exceeds in value the works element, the project is a services contract.

---

[38] This line of argument was put forward by the European Commission in its submissions in the *Gestion Hotelera* case.

(6) The case of concession contracts

The classification of a PFI project as a concession contract depends very much **10.45** upon the repayment method to the contractor by the contracting authority. The definition of a 'public works concession contract' under the Procurement Directives covers an agreement between a contractor and a contracting authority concerning either the execution or both the execution and design of a work, and for which remunerative considerations consist, at least partly, in the right of the *concessionaire* to exploit exclusively the finished construction works for a period of time.[39] Public works concessions which are privately financed are often *financially free standing* projects, where the contractor finances, designs, builds, and then operates an asset, and recovers its costs by direct charges on the users of the service which the asset provides. There is usually an option to transfer the asset to the contracting authority by the end of the concession period or at break points during the life of the concession.

The Public Works Directive has adopted a special, mitigated regime for the award **10.46** of concession contracts.[40] The provisions of the Directive only apply to concession contracts when the value is at least €5 million. There are no rules given as to the way in which the contract value must be calculated. For the award of concession contracts, contracting authorities must apply similar rules on advertising to the advertising rules concerning open and restricted procedures for the award of every works contract. Also, the provisions on technical standards and on criteria for qualitative selection of candidates and tenderers do apply to the award of concession contracts. The Directive does not prescribe the use of specific award procedures for concession contracts. The Directive presupposes that concession contracts should be awarded in two rounds, such as in the case of restricted procedures or negotiated procedures for ordinary works contracts. Nothing, however, prevents contracting authorities from applying a one-round open procedure. The Directive contains no rules on the minimum number of candidates which have to be invited to negotiate or to submit a tender. It would seem that a contracting authority may limit itself to selecting only one single candidate, provided the intention to award a concession contract has been adequately published. A contracting authority may under no circumstances refrain from publicising a notice in the *Official Journal* indicating its intention to proceed with the award of a concession works contract.[41]

Contracting authorities awarding the principal concession contract may impose **10.47** contractual obligations upon the concessionaire to subcontract at least thirty per cent of the total work provided for by the principal contract to third parties. Such

---

[39] Art. 1(d) of the Works Directive 93/37.   [40] Art. 3 of the Works Directive 93/37.
[41] *See* Bovis, op. cit. (n. 33), 67–68.

subcontracting arrangements by the concessionaire, even if they are not contracting authorities themselves, should be pursued in accordance with the advertisement, selection and qualification criteria and award procedures of public works contracts, if their value exceeds €5 million. Exceptions to this requirement apply in a limited number of cases where negotiated procedures without prior advertisement are allowed,[42] and in the case of subcontracting works to affiliated undertakings[43] of the concessionaire.

10.48 Interestingly, public service concessions, although included in the draft Public Services Directive,[44] have been excluded from its final the provisions and as a consequence, their award falls outside the thrust of EU public procurement rules. The exclusion of service concessions falls short of the aspirations to regulate concession contracts for the public sector under the Works Directive and breaks the consistency in the two legal instruments. The reasons for the exclusion of service concessions from the regulatory regime of public procurement could be attributed to the different legal requirements in member states to delegate powers to services *concessionaires*. The delegation of services by public authorities to private undertakings in some member states runs contrary to their constitutional provisions regarding state monopolies, public security, and defence matters.[45]

10.49 Concession contracts under European public procurement law represent a grey area. Their regulation appears, *prima facie*, to be incompatible with the main principles of the liberalization of public procurement, but eventually the requirement imposed on concessionaires to subcontract principal contracts to third parties, at least up to thirty per cent of their total value, attempts to bring the whole regime in conformity with the Community's policy on the opening up of the public sector contracts. However, the relaxed language of their regulation cannot guarantee legal certainty. It is rather unfortunate that private undertakings whose construction projects are subsidized from the state by more than fifty per cent must comply with the Public Procurement Directives,[46] whereas concessionaires would not even be declared to be obliged not to discriminate on grounds of nationality when they themselves contract out construction work to third parties.

(7) The award procedures for PFI

10.50 Public contracts can be awarded by virtue of three types of procedures: open, negotiated or restricted procedures. Open procedures are those where every

---

[42] *See* Art. 7(3) of the Works Directive 93/37.
[43] *See* Art. 3(4) of the Works Directive 93/37. An affiliated undertaking is one over which the concessionaire exercises dominant influence directly or indirectly or vice versa or both the concessionaire and its affiliated undertaking are part of another undertaking which exercises directly or indirectly dominant influence over them.
[44] *See* COM (90) 372 final, SYN 293 and COM (91) 322 final, SYN 293.
[45] *See* Bovis, op. cit. (n. 7). [46] *See* Art. 2 of the Works Directive 93/37.

interested supplier, contractor, or service provider may submit an offer. Restricted procedures are those procedures for the award of public contracts whereby only those contractors invited by the contracting authority may submit tenders. The selection of the winning tender usually takes place in two rounds. In the first round, all interested contractors may submit their interest and the contracting authority selects, from the candidates, those who will be invited to tender. In principle, the minimum number of candidates to be selected is five. In the second round, bids are submitted and the successful tender is selected. Negotiated procedures are such procedures for the award of public contracts whereby contracting authorities consult contractors of their choice and negotiate the terms of the contract with one or more of them. There are two types of negotiated procedures: i) negotiated procedures with prior notification, and ii) negotiated procedures without prior notification. Negotiated procedures with prior notification provide for selection of candidates in two rounds. In the first round, all interested contractors may submit their tenders and the contracting authority selects, from the candidates, those who will be invited to negotiate. In the second round, negotiations with various candidates take place and the successful tender is selected. In principle, the minimum number of candidates to be selected is three, provided that there are a sufficient number of suitable candidates. Negotiated procedures without prior notification may be conducted in one single round. Contracting authorities are allowed to choose whichever contractor they want, begin negotiations directly with this contractor and award the contract to him. These procedures should be used only in exceptional situations.

The Public Procurement Directives stipulate that open procedures, where possible, **10.51** should constitute the norm. Although contracting authorities can freely opt for open or restricted procedures, the latter should be justified by reference to the nature of the products or services to be procured and the balance between contract value and administrative costs associated with tender evaluation. A more rigorous set of conditions apply for the use of negotiated procedures. When negotiated procedures with prior notification are used, they must be justified on grounds of irregular or unacceptable tenders received as a result of a previous call. Negotiated procedures without prior notification are restrictively permitted in absence of tenders, when the procurement involves manufactured products or construction works purely for research and development, when for technical or artistic reasons or reasons connected with the protection of exclusive rights a particular supplier or contractor is selected, in cases of extreme urgency brought by unforeseeable events not attributable to the contracting authorities, when additional deliveries and supplies or works would cause disproportionate technical operational and maintenance difficulties.

All negotiations with candidates or tenderers on fundamental aspects of contracts, **10.52** in particular on prices, are prohibited in open and restricted procedures;

discussions with candidates or tenderers may be held, but only for the purpose of clarifying or supplementing the content of their tenders or the requirements of the contracting authorities and provided this does not involve discriminatory practices.[47] The need for such a prohibition is clear, since the possibility to negotiate may allow the contracting authority to introduce subjective appraisal criteria. The European Court of Justice has condemned post-tender negotiations[48] and a Declaration on the above subject has been made by the European Council and the Commission of the European Communities.[49] It should also be clear that the selection process must be completely distinguished from the award process. Quite often, contracting authorities appear to fuse the two basic processes of the award of public procurement contracts. This runs contrary to legal precedence of the European Court of Justice.[50]

10.53 In contrast with the above background, when contracting authorities award PFI projects classified as public works or public services contracts, they have been urged to have recourse to negotiated procedures.[51] The official line adopted is that a privately financed project could meet all the conditions imposed by the European public procurement rules for allowing the negotiated procedures to be used in contract awards and form a sort of precedence for future projects. Negotiated procedures for public works and services contracts with prior notification shall be used in the following cases: in the event of irregular tenders as a result of open or restricted procedures; in cases where the works are carried out purely for the purpose of research and development; in exceptional cases where the nature of the service does not permit overall pricing; and in cases where the contract specification of the services to be procured is not possible. On the other hand, negotiated procedures without prior notification can be used in the following cases: in the absence of tenders responding to open or restricted procedures; when, for technical or artistic reasons or reasons connected with the protection of exclusive rights, the services could only be procured by a particular contractor or service provider; in cases of extreme urgency brought about by events unforeseeable by the contracting authority; when design contests are awarded, provided the contracting authority negotiates with all participants; when additional services have to be awarded to a prior contract which had not been foreseen at the time of its award, and which cannot be separated from the main contract without great inconvenience to the contracting authority, and the additional works or services must not exceed fifty per cent of the value of main contract; and when repetitive

---

[47] *See* for example Art. 24 of the Supplies Directive 93/36.

[48] *See* Case C-243/89, *Commission v. Denmark*, judgment of 22 June 1993.

[49] *See* European Commission, *Declaration on the Use of Post-tender Negotiations* [1994] OJ L 111/114.

[50] *See* Case 31/87, *Gebroeders Beentjes v. Netherlands* [1988] ECR 4635. Also Case C-71/92, *Commission v. Spain*, judgment of 30 June 1993.

[51] *See* Private Finance Panel, *Private Opportunity, Public Benefit*, 1995.

or similar services to a main contract are awarded within three years of its award and subject to the main contract being awarded through either open or restricted procedures.

It should be maintained here that the European institutions never looked **10.54** favourably at the use of negotiated procedures by contracting authorities. The European Court of Justice has always been very reluctant in accepting the use of negotiated procedures, particularly without prior advertisement.[52] In a number of notable cases[53] before it relating to improper use of the award procedures, the Court has maintained the exceptional character of negotiated procedures and the extremely onerous obligation of contracting authorities to justify them. In fact, in every case relating to the justification of the negotiated procedures, the Court has condemned the relevant authorities for breaching the Procurement Directives. It might be construed from the case law of the Court of Justice that the particular procedure stipulated by the rules requires some sort of clearance prior to its utilization. This is not, however, the case, as the only form of official notification by contracting authorities when the use of negotiated procedures takes place after the award of the contract in question, where a notice containing the reasons for having recourse to negotiation should be communicated to the European Commission. This rather reinforces the exceptional character of the negotiated procedures rather than their prohibitive nature.

(8) Publicity requirements

The Public Procurement Directives have established a regime which *inter alia* **10.55** provides a mechanism for all the information needed to the relevant parties or the public in relation to the award of public contracts. Contracting authorities are under explicit obligation to furnish timely a range of information on their own initiative[54] or upon request.[55] This obligation is, in principle, extended to all PFI

---

[52] *See* the analysis of the relevant case law in Bovis, op. cit. (n. 33).

[53] *See* Case C-199/85, *Commission v. Italy* [1987] ECR 1039; Case 31/87, *Gebroeders Beenjes v. The Netherlands* [1988] ECR 4635; Case 3/88, *Commission v. Italy* [1989] ECR 4035; Case 24/91, *Commission v. Kingdom of Spain* [1994] CMLR 621; Case 107/92, *Commission v. Italy*, judgment of 2 August 1993; Case C 324/93, *R. v. Secretary of State for the Home Department, ex parte Evans Medical Ltd and Macfarlan Smith Ltd*, judgment of 28 March 1995; Case C-57/94, *Commission v. Italy*, judgment of 18 May 1995; Case 296/92, *Commission v. Italy*, judgment of 12 January 1994.

[54] After a contract award, contracting authorities are obliged to publish a Contract Award Notice (CAN) in the *Official Journal*. This is a form of formal notification of the award of the contract, of the successful tenderer, and the price of its offer, as well as the reasons for its selection.

[55] Any eliminated candidate from the selection process has the right to ask the contracting authority for the reasons for his rejection, and any tenderer whose bid has been rejected has the right to ask for the reasons and for the name of the successful tenderer. The contracting authority must provide the information requested within fifteen days of receiving the request. Contracting authorities must also inform candidates or tenderers who so request of the grounds for their decision to cancel an award procedure.

projects that are awarded under the procurement rules. However, practice has shown that very little information concerning the award of a PFI contract sees the light of publicity, often being described as '*commercially confidential*'. The onus is on the public authority to meet these publicity requirements, although the private sector appears extremely reluctant in allowing vital information regarding contractual structures, financial arrangements, technical specifications, or pricing to be in the public domain. Given the fact that a PFI project is substantially more complicated than a conventional public procurement equivalent, the argument of essential or confidential information being made public appears a valid one.

10.56 The Freedom of Information Act in the United Kingdom has implications for the publicity of PFI contracts, implications which mirror the obligations of contracting authorities stipulated in the Public Procurement Directives. In particular, a statutory obligation to make public certain information is proposed. This obligation covers information relating to reasons for rejection or disqualification and pricing. The appropriate publicity requirements will be included in the individual contracts between public authorities and contractors. The above obligation is intended to apply to all government departments, local authorities, the National Health Service, and all other public bodies, while it will also be extended to the privatised utilities and private organizations which perform public interest functions under contractual arrangements with the state. An exemption for confidentially commercial information will apply, provided *substantial harm* to a party can be demonstrated.

C. The Development of Public–Private Partnerships at European Level

10.57 The term public–private partnership is not defined at European Union level. Public–private partnerships denote a contractual format between public authorities and private sector undertakings. Such relations aim at delivering infrastructure projects, as well as many other schemes in areas covering transport, public health, education, public safety, and waste management and water distribution, and have the following characteristics: the relatively long duration of the relationship; the funding source for the project; the strategic role of the private sector in the sense that it is expected that to provide input into different stages of the project such as design, completion, implementation, and funding; and, finally, the distribution of risks between the public and private sectors and the expectation that the private sector will assume substantial risk.

10.58 Public authorities in the member states often have recourse to public–private partnership arrangements to facilitate mainly infrastructure projects. Budget constraints confronting national governments and the widespread assumption that private sector know-how will benefit the delivery of public services appear as the main policy drivers[56] for selecting a public–private partnership route. Also, the accounting treatment of public–private partnership contracts benefits national governments as the assets involved in a public–private partnership should be classified as non-government assets, and therefore recorded off balance sheet for public accountancy purposes,[57] subject to two conditions: i) that the private partner bears the construction risk, and ii) that the private partner bears at least one of either availability or demand risk. However, it is necessary to assess whether a public–private partnership option offers real value added compared with the conclusion of traditional public contracts.[58]

At European level, as part of the Initiative for Growth, the Council has approved **10.59** a series of measures designed to increase investment in the infrastructure of the trans-European transport networks and also in the areas of research, innovation, and development,[59] as well as the delivery of services of general interest.[60] European Community law does not lay down any special rules covering the award or the contractual interface of public–private partnerships. Nevertheless, such arrangements must be examined in the light of the rules and principles resulting from the European Treaties, particularly as regards the principles of freedom of establishment and freedom to provide services (Articles 43 and 49 of the EC Treaty),[61] which encompass in particular the principles of transparency, equality of treatment, proportionality, and mutual recognition[62] and the Public Procurement Directives.[63] The Commission has already taken initiatives under

---

[56] *See* Communication from the Commission of 23 April 2003, Developing the Trans-European Transport Network: Innovative Funding Solutions—Interoperability of Electronic Toll Collection Systems, COM (2003) 132, and the Report of the high-level group on the trans-European transport network of 27 June 2003.

[57] *See* Eurostat (Statistical Office of the European Communities) press release STAT/04/18 of 11 February 2004.

[58] *See* Communication from the Commission to the Council and to the Parliament 'Public finances in EMU 2003', published in the *European Economy No. 3/2003* (COM (2003) 283 final).

[59] Conclusions of the Presidency, Brussels European Council, 12 December 2003.

[60] COM (2003) 270 final.

[61] The rules on the internal market, including the rules and principles governing public contracts and concessions, apply to any economic activity, i.e. any activity which consists in providing services, goods, or carrying out works in a market, even if these services, goods, or works are intended to provide a 'public service', as defined by a member state.

[62] *See Interpretive Communication of the Commission on Concessions in Community Law* [2000] OJ C121, 29 April 2000.

[63] i.e. Directives 92/50/EEC, 93/36/EEC, 93/37/EEC, and 93/38/EEC, relating to the coordination of procedures for the award respectively of public service contracts, public supply contracts, public works contracts, and contracts in the water, energy, transport, and telecommunications sectors. These Directives will be replaced by Directive 2004/18/EC of the European Parliament and of Council of 31 March 2004 relating to the coordination of procedures for the award of public works, supply and services contracts, and Directive 2004/17/EC of the European Parliament and of the Council of 31 March 2004 relating to the coordination of procedures for the award of contracts in the water, energy, transport and postal services sectors, which will be published in the near future

public procurement law to deal with the award of public–private partnerships. In 2000 it published an *Interpretive Communication on Concessions and Community Public Procurement Law*,[64] in which it defined, on the basis of the rules and principles derived from the Treaty and applicable secondary legislation, the outlines of the concept of concession in Community law and the obligations incumbent on the public authorities when selecting the economic operators to whom the concessions are granted.

10.60   The *Green Paper on Public Private Partnerships* distinguishes two major formats of public private partnerships: the contractual formant, also described as the concession model, and the institutional format which is often described as the 'joint-venture model'.

(1)   The contractual public–private partnership

10.61   The contractual model of a public–private partnership reflects on a relation between public and private sectors based solely on contractual links. It involves different interfaces where tasks and responsibilities can be assigned to the private partner, including the design, funding, execution, renovation, or exploitation of a work or service. In this category, concession contracts and arrangements such as the private finance initiative or arrangements of similar contractual nexus create the link between public and private sectors.

10.62   There are few provisions of secondary legislation which coordinate the procedures for the award of contracts designated as concession contracts in Community law. In the case of works concessions, there are only certain advertising obligations, intended to ensure prior competition by interested operators, and an obligation regarding the minimum time limit for the receipt of applications.[65] The contracting authorities are free to decide how to select the private partner, although in so doing they must nonetheless guarantee full compliance with the principles and rules resulting from the Treaty. The rules governing the award of services concessions apply only by reference to the principles resulting from Articles 43 and 49 of

---

in the *Official Journal*. Moreover, in certain sectors, and particularly the transport sector, the organization of a PPP may be subject to specific sectoral legislation. *See* Regulation (EEC) No. 2408/92 of the Council on access of Community air carriers to intra-Community air routes, Council Regulation (EEC) No. 3577/92 applying the principle of freedom to provide services to maritime transport within Member States, Council Regulation (EEC) No. 1191/69 on action by Member States concerning the obligations inherent in the concept of a public service in transport by rail, road and inland waterway, as amended by Regulation (EEC) No 1893/91, and the amended proposal for a Regulation of the European Parliament and of the Council on action by Member States concerning public service requirements and the award of public service contracts in passenger transport by rail, road and inland waterway (COM (2002) 107 final).

[64]   op. cit. (n. 62).
[65]   *See* Art. 3(1) of Directive 93/37/EEC, and Arts. 56 to 59 of Directive 2004/18/EC.

the Treaty, in particular the principles of transparency, equality of treatment, proportionality, and mutual recognition.[66]

The Community law applicable to the award of concessions is derived primarily **10.63** from general obligations which involve no coordination of the legislation of member states. In addition, although the member states are free to do so, very few have opted to adopt national laws to lay down general and detailed rules governing the award of works or services concessions.[67] Thus, the rules applicable to the selection of a concessionaire by a contracting body are, for the most part, drawn up on a case-by-case basis. This situation may present problems for Community operators. The lack of coordination of national legislation could in fact be an obstacle to the genuine opening up of such projects in the Community, particularly when they are organized at transnational level. The legal uncertainty linked to the absence of clear and coordinated rules might in addition lead to an increase in the costs of awarding such projects. Moreover, it could be argued that the objectives of the internal market might not be achieved in certain situations, owing to a lack of effective competition on the market.

On the other hand, the rules applicable to the award of public private partnerships **10.64** in the format of a public works contracts or public services contracts[68] are contained in the Public Sector Directives,[69] where a contracting authority must normally have recourse to the open or restricted procedure to choose its private partner. By way of exception, and under certain conditions, recourse to the negotiated procedure is sometimes possible. In this context, the Commission has pointed out that the derogation under Article 7(2) of Directive 93/37/EEC, which provides for recourse to negotiated procedure in the case of a contract when 'the nature of the works or the risks attaching thereto do not permit prior overall pricing', is of limited scope. This derogation is to cover solely the exceptional situations in which there is uncertainty *a priori* regarding the nature or scope of the work to be carried out, but is not to cover situations in which the uncertainties

---

[66] Although the Commission had proposed that services concessions be included in Directive 92/50/EEC, in the course of the legislative process the Council decided to exclude them from the scope of that Directive. In the *Telaustria* case, the Court stated that '*[the] obligation of transparency which is imposed on the contracting authority consists in ensuring, for the benefit of any potential tenderer, a degree of advertising sufficient to enable the services market to be opened up to competition and the impartiality of procurement procedures to be reviewed*'. *See* Case C-324/98. *See also* ruling of 30 May 2002, also Case C-358/00, *Deutsche Bibliothek* ECR. I-4685. These principles are also applicable to other state acts entrusting an economic service to a third party, as for example the contracts excluded from the scope of the Directives owing to the fact that they have a value below the threshold values laid down in the secondary legislation (Order of the Court of 3 December 2001, Case C-59/00, *Vestergaard* [2000] ECR. I-9505), or so-called non-priority services.

[67] Spain (Law of 23 May 2003 on works concessions), Italy (Merloni law of 1994, as amended) and France (Sapin law of 1993) have nonetheless adopted such legislation.

[68] i.e. those listed in Annex IA of Directive 92/50/EEC and Annex XVIA of Directive 93/38/EEC.   [69] i.e. Directives 93/37/EEC, 92/50/EEC, and 2004/18/EC.

result from other causes, such as the difficulty of prior pricing owing to the complexity of the legal and financial package put in place.[70]

10.65 Since the adoption of Directive 2004/18/EC, a new procedure known as 'competitive dialogue' may apply when awarding particularly complex contracts.[71] The competitive dialogue procedure is launched in cases where the contracting body is objectively unable to define the technical means that would best satisfy its needs and objectives or in cases where it is objectively unable to define the legal and/or financial form of a project. This new procedure will allow the contracting bodies to open a dialogue with the candidates for the purpose of identifying solutions capable of meeting these needs. At the end of this dialogue, the candidates will be invited to submit their final tender on the basis of the solution or solutions identified in the course of the dialogue. These tenders must contain all the elements required and necessary for the performance of the project. The contracting authorities must assess the tenders on the basis of the pre-stated award criteria. The tenderer who has submitted the most economically advantageous tender may be asked to clarify aspects of it or confirm commitments featuring therein, provided this will not have the effect of altering fundamental elements in the tender or invitation to tender, of falsifying competition, or of leading to discrimination.

10.66 The competitive dialogue procedure should provide the necessary flexibility in the discussions with the candidates on all aspects of the contract during the set-up phase, while ensuring that these discussions are conducted in compliance with the principles of transparency and equality of treatment, and do not endanger the rights which the Treaty confers on economic operators. It is underpinned by the belief that structured selection methods should be protected in all circumstances, as these contribute to the objectivity and integrity of the procedure leading to the selection of an operator. This in turn guarantees the sound use of public funds and reduces the risk of practices that lack transparency and strengthens the legal certainty necessary for such projects. In addition, the new Directives make clear the benefit to contracting authorities of formulating the technical specifications in terms of either performance or functional requirements. New provisions will thus give the contracting bodies more scope to take account of innovative solutions during the award phase, irrespective of the procedure adopted.[72]

---

[70] For example, it may apply when the works are to be carried out in a geologically unstable or archaeological terrain and for this reason the extent of the necessary work is not known when launching the tender procedure. A similar derogation is provided for in Art. 11(2) of Directive 92/50, and in Art. 30(1)(b) of Directive 2004/18/EC.   [71] Art. 29 of Directive 2004/18/EC.
[72] Art. 23 of Directive 2004/18/EC and Art. 34 of Directive 2004/17/EC.

(2) The institutional public–private partnership

10.67 The joint venture model of public–private partnerships involves the establishment of an entity held jointly by the public partner and the private partner.[73] The joint entity thus has the task of ensuring the delivery of a work or service for the benefit of the public. Direct interface between the public partner and the private partner in a forum with a legal personality allows the public partner, through its presence in the body of shareholders and in the decision-making bodies of the joint entity, to retain a relatively high degree of control over the development of the projects, which it can adapt over time in the light of circumstances. It also allows the public partner to develop its own experience of running the service in question, while having recourse to the support of a private partner. An institutional public–private partnership can be put in place, either by creating an entity held jointly by the public sector and the private sector, or by the private sector taking control of an existing public undertaking.

10.68 The law on public contracts and concessions does not of itself apply to the transaction creating a mixed-capital entity. However, when such a transaction is accompanied by the award of tasks through an act which can be designated as a public contract, or even a concession, it is important that there be compliance with the rules and principles arising from this law (the general principles of the Treaty or, in certain cases, the provisions of the Directives).[74] The selection of a private partner called on to undertake such tasks while functioning as part of a mixed entity can therefore not be based exclusively on the quality of its capital contribution or its experience, but should also take account of the characteristics of its offer—the most economically advantageous—in terms of the specific services to be provided. Thus, in the absence of clear and objective criteria allowing the contracting authority to select the most economically advantageous offer, the capital transaction could constitute a breach of the law on public contracts and concessions.

10.69 In this context, the transaction involving the creation of such an entity does not generally present a problem in terms of the applicable Community law when it constitutes a means of executing the task entrusted under a contract to a private partner. However, the conditions governing the creation of the entity must be clearly laid down when issuing the call for competition for the tasks which one wishes to entrust to the private partner. Also, these conditions must not discriminate against or constitute an unjustified barrier to the freedom to provide services or to freedom of establishment, or be disproportionate to the desired objective.

---

[73] The member states use different terminology and schemes in this context (for example, the *Kooperationsmodell*, joint PPPs, joint ventures).

[74] It is worth noting that the principles governing the law on public contracts and concessions apply also when a task is awarded in the form of a unilateral act (for example, a legislative or regulatory act).

10.70   However, in certain member states, national legislation allows the mixed entities, in which the participation by the public sector involves the contracting body, to participate in a procedure for the award of a public contract or concession even when these entities are only in the course of being incorporated. In this scenario, the entity will be definitively incorporated only after the contract has actually been awarded to it. In other member states, a practice has developed which tends to confuse the phase of incorporating the entity and the phase of allocating the tasks. Thus the purpose of the procedure launched by the contracting authority is to create a mixed entity to which certain tasks are entrusted.

10.71   Such solution does not appear to offer satisfactory solutions in terms of the provisions applicable to public contracts and concessions.[75] In the first case, there is a risk that the effective competition will be distorted by a privileged position of the company being incorporated, and consequently of the private partner participating in this company. In the second case, the specific procedure for selecting the private partner also poses many problems. The contracting authorities encounter certain difficulties in defining the subject-matter of the contract or concession in a sufficiently clear and precise manner in this context, as they are obliged to do. The Commission has frequently noted that the tasks entrusted to the partnership structure are not clearly defined and that, in certain cases, they even fall outside any contractual framework.

10.72   This in turn raises problems not only with regard to the principles of transparency and equality of treatment, but even risks prejudicing the general interest objectives which the public authority wishes to attain. It is also evident that the lifetime of the created entity does not generally coincide with the duration of the contract or concession awarded, and this appears to encourage the extension of the task entrusted to this entity without a true competition at the time of this renewal. In addition, it should be pointed out that the joint creation of such entities must respect the principle of non-discrimination in respect of nationality in general and the free circulation of capital in particular.[76] Thus, for example, the public authorities cannot normally make their position as shareholder in such an entity contingent on excessive privileges which do not derive from a normal application of company law.[77]

---

[75] When planning and arranging such transactions, the test involving the use of the standard forms—which include the elements indispensable for a well-informed competition,—also demonstrate how difficult it can be to find an adequate form of advertising to award tasks falling within the scope of the law on public contracts or concessions.

[76] Participation in a new undertaking with a view to establishing lasting economic links is covered by the provisions of Art. 56 relating to the free movement of capital. *See* Annex I of Directive 88/361/EEC, adopted in the context of the former Art. 67, which lists the types of operations which must be considered as movements of capital.

[77] *See* judgments of the Court of 4 June 2002, Case C-367/98, *Commission v. Portugal* ECR I-4731; Case C-483/99, *Commission v. France* ECR I-4781; and judgments of 13 May 2003, Case C-463/00, *Commission v. Spain* ECR. I-4581; Case C-98/01, *Commission v. United Kingdom* Rec. I-4641. On the possible justifications in this framework, *see* judgment of the Court of 4 June 2002, Case C-503/99, *Commission v. Belgium* ECR I-4809.

On the other hand, the creation of an institutional public private partnership may **10.73** also lead to a change in the body of shareholders of a public entity. In this context, it should first be emphasised that the changeover of a company from the public sector to the private sector is an economic and political decision which, as such, falls within the sole competence of the member states.[78] Community law on public contracts is not as such intended to apply to transactions involving simple capital injections by an investor in an enterprise, whether this latter be in the public or the private sector. Such transactions fall under the scope of the provisions of the Treaty on the free movement of capital,[79] implying in particular that the national measures regulating them must not constitute barriers to investment from other member states.[80] Nevertheless, the provisions on freedom of establishment within the meaning of Article 43 of the Treaty must be applied when a public authority decides, by means of a capital transaction, to cede to a third party a holding conferring a definite influence in a public entity providing economic services normally falling within the responsibility of the state.[81]

When public authorities grant an economic operator a definite influence in a **10.74** business under a transaction involving a capital transfer, and when this transaction has the effect of entrusting to this operator tasks falling within the scope of the law on public contracts which had been previously exercised, directly or indirectly, by the public authorities, the provisions on freedom of establishment require compliance with the principles of transparency and equality of treatment, in order to ensure that every potential operator has equal access to performing those activities which had hitherto been reserved.

The phenomenon of public–private partnerships represents a genuine attempt to **10.75** introduce the concept of contractualized governance in the delivery of public services. Although the public sector has always depended upon traditional corporatism to disperse public services, there is mounting evidence that the role and the involvement of the state in the above process is under constant review. The private finance initiative can be described as an institutionalized mechanism in engaging the private sector in the delivery of public services, not only through the financing but mainly through the operation of assets. The private sector assumes a direct responsibility in serving the public interest, as part of its contractual obligations vis-à-vis the public sector. The motive and the intention behind such approach focus on the benefits which would follow as a result of the private sector's involvement in the delivery of public services. Efficiency gains, qualitative improvement,

---

[78] This follows from the neutrality principle of the Treaty in relation to ownership rules, recognized by Art. 295 of the Treaty.   [79] *See* Art. 56 ff. of the EC Treaty.

[80] *See* Communication of the Commission on certain legal aspects concerning intra-EU investment [1997] OJ C220/15, 19 July 1997.

[81] *See*, on these lines, the judgment of the Court of 13 April 2000, Case C-251/98, *Baars* ECR I-2787.

innovation, value for money and flexibility appear as the most important ones, whereas an overall better allocation of public capital resources sums up the advantages of privately financed projects.

10.76 Both the private finance initiative and the phenomenon of public–private partnerships do not alter the character of the contractual relationship between the private and public sectors, for such character is predominately determined by other factors attributed to the legal order in question. The contractual relationship between the private and public sectors is not merely determined by the fact that one party to the agreement is a public authority, but mainly by reference to the appropriate forum for access to justice, or the relevant remedial availability.[82] Under both traditional corporatism and contractualized governance, the contractual nexus between the private and public sectors maintains the same characteristics, which are influenced by the disposition of the relevant legal and judicial system. What the Private Finance Initiative does change is the thrust of that contractual relationship. The integral nature of corporatism evolves around the notion of public ownership of assets destined to serve public interest. The Private Finance Initiative brings an end to the notion of public ownership and instead introduces the concept of service delivery in the relevant contractual relationship between private and public sectors. The private sector is no longer a supplier to the public sector but rather a partner through a concession. It seems that there is a quasi-agency relationship between the private and public sectors, in the sense that the former provides the relevant infrastructure and in fact delivers public services on behalf of the latter. Where corporatism was always delivered under considerable budgetary constraints, a fact that reflects not only the relative balance of powers between the demand and supply sides and the risk allocation factor in their contractual arrangements but mainly the adversarial environment and the compromised quality of the deliverables, contractualized governance appears to prioritize the value for money principle, which has primarily qualitative attributes.

10.77 Both corporatism and contractualized governance should be delivered through a system that guarantees accountability, openness, and competitiveness. Such a system for the delivery of public services is encapsulated in the European public procurement regime, which is expected to be the most appropriate delivery process for public–private partnerships. Contractual award arrangements are entirely covered by the Public Procurement Directives, which provide for a disciplined, transparent, and relatively swift system for the award of public procurement contracts.[83] What remains is the development of comprehensive guidelines for the deployment

---

[82] *See* the FIDE Congress on *The Application in the Member States of the Directives on Public Procurement*, Madrid 1990.

[83] One the most notorious features of the existing PFI process is the abysmally lengthy negotiation stage and the prolonged pre-contractual arrangements. This represents a considerable (recoverable) cost which would be reflected in the final deal. *See Financial Times*, 24 July 1998, where it was

of private finances in the delivery of public services[84] and the embedding of relevant legislation[85] that empowers public authorities to contractualize their governance. The public–private partnership regime needs to benefit from a simplification and standardization process, so a kind of routine similar to that reigning the award of traditional public procurement contracts can assist the demand and supply sides in delivering more privately financed deals. However, the relative volume of public–private partnerships projects is not the critical factor in determining its success. It is rather the value for money element that is expected to crop up through the involvement of private entrepreneurship in the delivery of public services.

public–private partnerships as a concept-tool of public sector management have, **10.78** in theory, a promising future. In reality, they should be benchmarked against traditional publicly funded systems, both in qualitative and quantitative terms. Only then one can assess with reasonable confidence their merits and impact upon the delivery of public services.

---

reported that lengthy negotiations due to the lack of clear guidelines and standard contractual forms presented a serious deterrent factor in concluding PFI contracts. The average PFI gestation period is eighteen months compared with eight months in traditional public procurement contracts.

[84] A serious set back for the Private Finance Initiative in the United Kingdom was the report of the Accounting Standards Board (*The Tweedie Report—September 1998*) which criticised the practice of the HM Treasury not to include PFI deals in the Public Sector Borrowing Requirement (PSBR) balance sheet. The report condemned such practices and urged the government, for the sake of legal certainty and good public sector management and accounting to issue new guidelines for future PFI projects and treat them in the same way as traditional public procurement spending.

[85] Prior to 1997, there was considerable uncertainty as to the legal position of the parties to a privately financed project. The relevant legislation did not provide *in concreto* for the rights and obligations of the private sector and threatened with *ultra vires* agreements concluded between certain public authorities (local authorities and health trusts) and the private sector. It was unclear whether these authorities had explicit or implied powers to enter into such contracts, a situation which left privately financed transactions *in limbo*. As a consequence, the National Health Service (Private Finance) Act 1997 and the Local Government (Contracts) Act 1997 have been enacted in order to clear all legal obstacles. Both Acts have introduced a 'clearance system' where the relevant authorities must certified a prospective PFI deal with the government, checking not only its *vires* but the whole commercial viability and procedural delivery mechanism of a privately financed contract.

11

ENFORCEMENT AND COMPLIANCE

A. The Remedies Directives

(1) The principles and remit

11.01 The enactment of the Remedies Directives has brought a different dimension into the application of public procurement rules. Such dimension relies on the decentralized compliance and enforcement of the substantive regime. Directive 89/665[1] on the coordination of the laws, regulations, and administrative provisions relating to the application of review procedures to the award of public supply and public works contracts and Directive 92/13[2] coordinating the laws,

---

[1] *See* [1989] OJ L395/33.
[2] *See* [1992] OJ L76/14.

regulations, and administrative provisions relating to the application of Community rules on the procurement procedures of entities operating in the water, energy, transport and telecommunications sectors require member states to introduce effective remedies and means of enforcement to suppliers, contractors and service providers who believe that they have been harmed by an infringement of the substantive procurement rules.

Existing arrangements at both national and Community levels for ensuring the **11.02** application of the substantive public procurement rules have been inadequate in ensuring compliance with the relevant Community provisions. Their inadequacy is highlighted in their inability to correct infringements and ensure an efficient application of the award procedures by contracting authorities. The absence or inadequacy of effective remedies at national level has a detrimental effect in the opening-up of public procurement by deterring undertakings from participating in award procedures for public contract and submitting tenders. The opening-up of public procurement to community-wide competition demands also a substantial increase of the levels of transparency at national level regarding the availability of redress to the supply side of the public procurement equation (tenderers and participants). Such increased levels of transparency must be accompanied by non-discriminatory measures introduced within national legal systems which provide interested parties, at least, the same treatment in public procurement litigation, as in other forms of litigation.

The Remedies Directives are based on three fundamental principles; the principle **11.03** of effectiveness, the principle of non-discrimination, and the principle of procedural autonomy.

(2) The principle of effectiveness

In both Remedies Directives, effective review of decisions or acts of contracting **11.04** authorities is the essential requirement of compliance with the substantive public procurement rules. The principle of effectiveness includes two individual features: firstly, the swift resolution of disputes, and, secondly, the enforceability of decisions. In particular, Article 1 of Directive 89/665 (Public Sector Remedies Directive) and Article 1 of Directive 92/13 (Utilities Remedies Directive) stipulate that member states must take any measures necessary to ensure that decisions taken by the contracting authorities may be reviewed effectively and as rapidly as possible and can be effectively enforced[3] on the grounds that such decisions have infringed Community law in the field of public procurement or national implementing laws.

---

[3] *See* Art. 2(7) of Directive 89/665 and Art. 2(8) of Directive 92/13.

(3) The principle of non-discrimination

11.05 There is an explicit obligation conferred on member states to avoid introducing review procedures for decisions of contracting authorities and utilities, as well as procedures for the recovery of damages which differ, in a discriminatory context, from review procedures for other administrative acts and procedures for the recovery of damages under national law.[4]

(4) The principle of procedural autonomy

11.06 The Remedies Directives leave member states with wide discretion as to the creation of the appropriate forum to receive complaints and legal actions against decisions of contracting authorities and utilities, as well as action for damages in public procurement cases.[5]

B. Litigation *Fora* in National Legal Orders

(1) Pre-judicial stages in review procedures

11.07 The Court stated[6] that, even though Article 1(3) of Directive 89/665 expressly allows member states to determine the detailed rules according to which they must make the review procedures provided for in that Directive available to any person having or having had an interest in obtaining a particular public contract, and who has been or risks being harmed by an alleged infringement, it none the less does not authorize them to give the term interest in obtaining a public contract an interpretation which may limit the effectiveness of that Directive.[7] However, a person who has participated in a contract award procedure, but subsequently failed to initiate pre-judicial proceedings, such as conciliation or mediation proceedings, to settle a contested act or decision of a contracting authority, must not be regarded as having lost his interest in obtaining the contract and therefore being precluded from lodging an action to contest the legality of the contract awarding decision or any decision of the contracting authority. The fact that access to the review procedures provided for by the Directive is made subject to prior referral to a pre-judicial stage such as conciliation or mediation would be contrary to the objectives of establishing fast and effective review mechanisms under the Remedies Directives.

---

[4] *See* Art. 1(2) of Directive 89/665 and Art. 1(2) of Directive 92/13.
[5] *See* Art. 2(2) of Directive 89/665 and Art. 2(2) of Directive 92/13.
[6] *See* Case C-230/02, *Grossmann Air Service, Bedarfsluftfahrtunternehmen GmbH & Co. KG and Republik Österreich*, judgment of 12 February 2004.
[7] *See* Case C-410/01, *Fritsch, Chiari & Partner and Others* [2003] ECR I-11547, paragraphs 31 and 34.

In another case,[8] The national court sought clarification from the European **11.08** Court of Justice to ascertain whether Article 1(3) of Directive 89/665 precludes an undertaking which has participated in a public procurement procedure from being considered as having lost its interest in obtaining that contract on the ground that, before bringing a review procedure under that Directive, it failed to initiate a pre-judicial dispute resolution such as conciliation. The Court examined whether, under the framework of Directive 89/665, it is necessary to make a tenderer's interest in obtaining a specific contract, and therefore its right to have access to the review procedures established by that Directive, dependent on the condition that it has beforehand exhausted pre-judicial review procedures. The Court maintained that Directive 89/665 is intended to strengthen the existing mechanisms, both at national and Community level, to ensure the effective application of Community rules on public procurement, in particular at a stage when infringements can still be remedied. To that effect, Article 1(1) of the Remedies Directive 89/665 requires member states to guarantee that unlawful decisions of contracting authorities can be subjected to effective and swift judicial review.[9]

The Court found that making access to the review procedures provided for by **11.09** Directive 89/665 conditional on prior application to a body which has not judicial character such as a conciliation commission, is contrary to the aims and objectives of the Remedies Directive and, in particular, the objective of speed and effectiveness in judicial review of acts or decisions of contracting authorities. Firstly, prior application to a non-judicial body which has the aim to conciliate disputes arising between contracting authorities and aggrieved tenderers inevitably has the effect of delaying the introduction of the review procedures which Directive 89/665 requires member states to establish. Secondly, a non-judicial review body such as a conciliation commission has none of the powers which Article 2(1) of Directive 89/665 requires member states to grant the bodies responsible for carrying out those review procedures, so that referral to it does not ensure the effective application of the Community Directives on public procurement.

(2) The Republic of Austria

(a) Remedies at federal level

At federal level, two administrative bodies have been set up to deal with procure- **11.10** ment complaints: the *Vergabekontrollkommission* (Commission for the Control of Award Procedures) and the *Bundesvergabeamt* (Public Procurement Agency). These bodies are funded by the Federal Ministry of Economic Affairs. However,

---

[8] See Case C-410/01, *Fritsch, Chiari & Partner, Ziviltechniker GmbH and Others and Autobahnen- und Schnellstraßen-Finanzierungs-AG (Asfinag)* [2003] ECR I-11547;
[9] See Case C-470/99, *Universale-Bau and Others* [2002] ECR I-11617, paragraph 74.

they are legally independent from the Ministry and are not bound by any government orders as regards their decisions on procurement matters. The Control Commission has a mediation function, while the Public Procurement Agency has powers of decision and is a court within the meaning of Article 234 of the EC Treaty, for the purposes of referring a case to the European Court of Justice for preliminary ruling. The chairman and the vice-chairmen of the Public Procurement Agency must be judges. On the other hand, the chairman and vice-chairmen of the Control Commission do not have to be judges, but they must not have any links with contracting authorities or tenderers. The tenure of appointment of all the members of the Control Commission and the Public Procurement Agency is five years.

11.11 *Locus standi* at federal level is afforded to a *tenderer* (a firm or person who submits a tender) or a *candidate* (someone who has sought an invitation to take part in restricted or negotiated procedures) who may launch a complaint before the Control Commission. Also, Chambers of Commerce and other associations (*Interessenvertretungen*) have *locus standi* before the Control Commission to initiate mediation procedures on behalf of particular undertakings. Such bodies may not, however, file a motion for a review procedure before the Public Procurement Agency. A contracting authority may ask the Control Commission for a legal opinion on the applicability of public procurement law.

11.12 An application to the Public Procurement Agency by interested candidates or tenderers who believe that their rights have been infringed is allowed only when they have previously tried to reach an amicable settlement of the case before the Control Commission. If a settlement was actually agreed, or if the alleged violation did not have any impact on the award, the complaint to the Public Procurement Agency will be rejected. A favourable ruling by the Public Procurement Agency is a pre-condition for any action for damages in the civil courts.

(b) Remedies at state level

11.13 A diverse range of judicial *fora* and remedies systems at state level has been created by Austria. Most have provided for review by a single body, rather than the two-stage system which is established at federal level.

11.14 However, Upper Austria has opted for a two-stage system, where first instance hearings are directed to the State Government of Upper Austria and second instance hearings are directed to the administrative tribunal of Upper Austria. In Upper Austria, complainants have to resort to the State Government before they can appeal to the Independent Administrative Senate. Lower Austria requires at least mediation before the state government of Lower Austria as a precondition for filing a complaint with the administrative tribunal of Lower Austria.

The states of Carinthia, Burgenland, Upper Austria, and Lower Austria have **11.15** declared their administrative tribunals (*Unabhängige Verwaltungssenate*) competent to hear cases from complainants who claim that a contracting authority of the relevant state did not comply with the law. In Burgenland, a specialized chamber of the Independent Administrative Senate hears public procurement cases.

The other states have established specialized administrative bodies to hear public **11.16** procurement cases. The states of Vorarlberg, Tyrol, and Vienna have established authorities which have similar features. The chairman of the body has to be a civil judge from a federal court,[10] while half of the other members are appointed by the Chambers of Commerce and the Chamber of Civil Engineers, and the other half by state administrative authorities. The chairman is appointed by the State Government.

In the State of Salzburg, the same requirements for the composition of the **11.17** administrative bodies apply, except that the presiding judge is not a civil judge from a federal court, but a member of the administrative tribunal of Salzburg (*Unabhängiger Verwaltungssenat Salzburg*).

The State of Styria has adopted a different structure. The administrative body to **11.18** control award procedures is composed by members from the Court of Auditors for Styria and, for its organizational and budgetary requirements, it relies on the Court of Auditors. However, neither the Court of Auditors nor the Styria State Government has any influence over its rulings.

Locus standi at state level depends on various degrees of admissibility requirements **11.19** which are employed by Austrian states for tenderers and candidates to lodge a complaint with the relevant administrative review body. For example, in the State of Vienna a rejected candidate may only bring an action if he can prove that he ought to have been admitted to the award procedures had the contracting authority complied with the law, and, in addition, that the contract would have been awarded to him if the contracting authority had complied with the law. In the State of Salzburg, the complainant must prove that the contested decision has a decisive impact on the award procedure. In the States of Burgenland, Salzburg, Tyrol, Vorarlberg and Upper Austria, recourse to the administrative body is only allowed after prior notification of the alleged illegality has been given to the contracting authority.

In Lower Austria, a candidate or tenderer may only raise a complaint with the **11.20** administrative tribunal if he first underwent a mediation procedure and if this

---

[10] In the State of Tyrol there is a requirement that only a member of the administrative body has to be a judge, and not necessarily the chairman. The Constitutional Court of Austria held that the review body of Tyrol did not comply with Art. 2(8) of Remedies Directive 89/665. The case has been referred to the European Court of Justice, Case C-103/97, [1997] OJ C142/10.

procedure was unsuccessful. In Upper Austria, the complainant must first file its complaint with the State Government of Upper Austria, which gives a binding decision thereon. If that decision is negative, the complainant may appeal to the administrative tribunal of Upper Austria. In Carinthia, after the contract in question has been awarded, it is not necessary for the complainant to bring its complaint before the administrative tribunal of Carinthia. The action for damages may be lodged directly with the civil courts, which are not bound by any decision of the administrative tribunal. The court has to decide for itself whether the contracting authority has violated a public procurement provision.

11.21   The time limit to initiate a compliant at state level varies significantly. In the State of Vienna, the law distinguishes between the various causes on which the complaint is based. If the bid of a tenderer was rejected or if a candidate were excluded from a restricted or negotiated procedure, the complaint has to be filed within two weeks after notification of the rejection or, in the case of an accelerated procedure, within three days after notification. If the provisions of the tender documents or the invitation to tender do not comply with the State Procurement Act of Vienna, the complaint has to be filed at least two weeks before the end of the time limit for the award procedure, but, in the case of an accelerated procedure this period is reduced to one week. If the complaint is filed after the award has been made, the time limit for the complaint is two weeks after the award has been published in the *Official Journal*. If there is no publication, the time limit is six months after the award has been made.

11.22   In the State of Lower Austria, where the administrative tribunal is asked to ascertain if the contracting authority complied with the law, the complaint has to be filed within four weeks after the complainant becomes aware of the award (or six months if the complainant does not have knowledge if it). The application for an interim measure has to be made within one month after knowledge of the allegedly illegal act.

11.23   In the State of Upper Austria, the motions for both claims, annulment, and interim measures, have to be filed within two weeks after the authority's report on the alleged illegality is received by the complainant. In the absence of such a report, the motions have to be filed two weeks after the date on which the contracting authority should have submitted such a report (two weeks after initial notification by the claimant). The contract must not be awarded during the period beginning with the notification by the tenderer to the contracting authority of an alleged violation and ending with the date for filing a complaint. After the award has been made, the complaint has to be filed within six weeks, starting from the date the complainant learned of the award. In the States of Salzburg, Carinthia, Burgenland and Vorarlberg, the complaint (including any application for an interim order) has to be filed within two weeks after the contracting authority's report on the alleged illegality is received by the complainant. After the award has been made, the complaint has to be filed within two weeks after the complainant has had knowledge of the award (or, in Burgenland and Vorarlberg, within 6 months if he had no such knowledge). In the State of Carinthia, the contracting authority is prohibited from awarding the contract within four weeks of it receiving notice of the complaint. A contract awarded within this four-week period would be null and void. In the State of Tyrol, a complaint against a rejection of a bid has to be brought within twenty days after the rejection has been received. If a complaint is brought during a restricted or negotiated procedure, the complainant has to seek recourse within half of the application period. If the complaint is launched after the award, the time limit is two weeks after the publication of the award.

Rights of appeal vary from state to state. In the States of Tyrol, Vorarlberg and **11.24** Vienna, the right of appeal mirrors that at federal level, in that the State Control Commission is a collegial body with judicial character and its decisions cannot be appealed to the administrative courts. A complaint may only be lodged with the Constitutional Court on the grounds of a violation of the Austrian Constitution. In all of the other states, on the other hand, decisions of the relevant review body are subject to rights of appeal to the administrative courts.

(c) The role of the Control Commission

The role of the Control Commission is to receive complaints from aggrieved **11.25** tenderers and subsequently make recommendations. However, the Control Commission cannot make decisions which have legally binding nature; its purpose is merely to act as a mediator and to give non-binding opinions. The precise function of the Control Commission evolves around opinions and guidance given to contracting authorities to assist them with the legality of existing practices in contract awards and to guide them for their future procurement practices.

The Control Commission, before a contract award is made, may mediate between **11.26** candidates or tenderers and contracting authorities after it has receive a claim from the candidates or tenderers that the contracting authority in question did not comply with the provisions of the Federal Procurement Act. In cases where the contracting authority intends to award the contract to a tenderer, the authority may ask the Control Commission for an opinion to determine the legality of the intended award. Also, when a contract award has been made, the contracting authority may ask the Control Commission for an opinion on the execution of the contract.

The mediation function of the Control Commission is the most important **11.27** function it performs. At first, the Control Commission must try to facilitate an amicable settlement between the complainant and the contracting authority. Upon receipt of a complaint, the Control Commission must notify the contracting authority involved. Such notification has significant importance; the award of the contract is suspended and the contracting authority must refrain from awarding the contract within four weeks beginning from the date of the notification. A contract concluded within this period is null and void, unless the complaint is dismissed for lack of jurisdiction or the parties reach an amicable settlement in the meantime. In cases where mediation between the parties cannot produce an amicable settlement, the Control Commission has to make a recommendation for a decision, which is not binding.

11.28 Complaints before the Control Commission involve a rather informal procedure. The procedure is a mediation procedure designed to reach an amicable settlement between tenderers and candidates, on the one hand, and contracting authorities on the other hand. The complaint may be launched either in writing or submitted orally to records kept by the Control Commission. The contracting authority is obliged to hand over the relevant records and to give the Control Commission any necessary additional information. If the authority fails to comply with a demand to see certain documents, the Control Commission may deem the allegations of the complainant to be true.[11]

11.29 After the complaint is found admissible, a hearing will take place. The procedural rules are laid down by the competent body of the Control Commission with a view to facilitating an amicable settlement. If no settlement can be reached within two weeks, the Control Commission will make a non-binding recommendation.

11.30 There is no strict time limit for launching a complaint with the Control Commission. Under the Federal Procurement Act, a complainant has to lodge his complaint as soon as possible after learning of the alleged violation of the public procurement rules. However, since the contracting authority may award the contract for as long as it has not been notified of a pending action with the Control Commission, it is in the interests of any aggrieved party to initiate promptly any mediation procedure. The Control Commission must deliver its decision within two weeks of receiving a complaint.

(d) The Austrian Public Procurement Agency

11.31 The Public Procurement Agency has two competencies. First, during the award procedure, it may annul decisions of the contracting authority and may issue interim measures. Secondly, after the award of the contract, it may, on request of an aggrieved tenderer, decide whether the contracting authority has unlawfully failed to award the contract to the most economically advantageous tender and, on request of the contracting authority, whether the claimant would not have had

---

[11] *See* §106 of the *Bundesgesetz, mit dem das Bundesvergabegesetz geändert wird* Act, *Federal Law Gazette*, 1996/776.

a realistic chance of winning the contract, had the contracting authority complied with the law.

A complaint may be brought before the Agency prior to the award of the contract only if a mediation procedure has first taken place before the Control Commission, or if the Control Commission either fails to act within two weeks or declares itself incompetent to decide on the matter in question. In other words, a complainant has to attempt to reach an amicable settlement before the Control Commission. If a tender is rejected, and the complainant claims that the rejection was illegal, it is presumed that the award procedure is still pending.   **11.32**

A complaint to the Public Procurement Agency has to be filed within two weeks of the Control Commission giving its recommendation. However, the complaint is inadmissible if an amicable settlement has been reached before the Control Commission. Such a settlement precludes the Agency from ruling on the complaint, unless the complainant shows that the contracting authority has failed to adhere to the settlement. For complaints brought before the Public Procurement Agency after the award of the contract in question, the time limit is six weeks, starting from the day on which the complainant is aware of the award.   **11.33**

The procedure before the Public Procurement Agency is governed by the Code on General Administrative Procedure.[12] The Public Procurement Agency is bound by principles of due process, fairness, equality and justice. The application may either be filed in writing or submitted orally to the Public Procurement Agency. The application has to indicate the procurement procedure in question, the contracting authority, the facts including the interest of the complainant in the award, the damage incurred or impending, reasons for the alleged illegality, and the remedy claimed. In the case of an application before the award of the contract, it is also necessary to supply the recommendation of the Control Commission or evidence that the Control Commission denied its competence or failed to act within two weeks. The same procedural requirements apply to applications for interim measures. An interim measure may be issued in the general review procedure. It has to be issued within five days.   **11.34**

The Public Procurement Agency has to ascertain the relevant facts and to collate the evidence. The contracting authority is obliged to hand over the relevant records and to give the Public Procurement Agency any necessary additional information. If the authority fails to produce requested information, the Agency may draw adverse conclusions. The compliance of public contracting authorities with their obligation to supply requested information is safeguarded by special government orders and disciplinary actions which are applicable to public authorities. In addition, contracting   **11.35**

---

[12] *See* Art. II § 2(c) *Einführungsgesetz zu den Verwaltungsverfahrensgesetzen, Federal Law Gazette,* 1992/121.

entities in the utilities sectors may be penalized for failing to supply requested information by way of a fine under a separate administrative procedure.

11.36 A complaint to the Public Procurement Agency prior to the award has to be filed within two weeks after the complainant learns of the decision of the Control Commission.[13] If the complaint is filed after the award has been made, the time limit is six weeks, starting from the day the complainant is aware of the award.[14] Prior to the award of the contract, the Public Procurement Agency has two months within which to lay down a ruling upon an application for annulment. Where the complainant seeks an interim order, the Agency must render its decision within five days. Once the contract has been concluded, the time limit for the Agency's decision is six months. The judge is bound to respect these motions and determinations and may not deviate from them.

11.37 Appeals against decisions issued by the Public Procurement Agency are not permitted,[15] as the Agency makes decisions in first and final instance. Due to the fact that the Public Procurement Agency is a collegial agency with judicial character, complaints against its decisions to the Administrative Court are not allowed under principles of constitutional law. A complaint to the Constitutional Court would be possible, only if the Public Procurement Agency was in violation of the Austrian Constitution, for example, by violating the principles of due process of law or equity. The Austrian code on the execution of administrative acts (*Verwaltungsvollstreckungsgesetz*) applies to the decisions of the Public Procurement Agency, including interim orders. In the event that such rulings are violated by a contracting authority, they can be immediately executed by means of financial or penal penalties.

(3) Belgium

11.38 The nature of the decision or the nature of the act that is challenged determines the legal forum where procurement disputes are settled in Belgium. A fundamental distinction exists between the *Conseil d'Etat* (the administrative court in Belgium) and the ordinary civil courts. The *Conseil d'Etat* can set aside administrative decisions taken in a procurement procedure prior to the award of a contract, including an award decision or any other detachable act (*acte detachable*) from the contract itself. It can also make interim suspension orders, and impose daily fines. The *Conseil d'Etat* lacks the power to award damages.

---

[13] *See* § 115(2) of the *Bundesgesetz, mit dem das Bundesvergabegesetz geändert wird* Act, *Federal Law Gazette*, 1996/776.

[14] *See* § 115(4) of the *Bundesgesetz, mit dem das Bundesvergabegesetz geändert wird* Act, *Federal Law Gazette*, 1996/776.

[15] *See* §99(2) of the *Bundesgesetz, mit dem das Bundesvergabegesetz geändert wird* Act, *Federal Law Gazette*, 1996/776.

Once a contract is awarded, it is considered to be a matter of private law which **11.39**
may only be challenged before the ordinary civil courts. Any action for damages
should be brought before the ordinary civil courts of first instance. Such courts
may, under general principles, award damages to an aggrieved tenderer, who need
not prove fault if the contested decision has already been annulled by the *Conseil
d'Etat*. Although the civil courts may, in principle, grant interim measures and
set aside orders in public procurement cases, they usually decline to do so on the
basis that the award decision is a matter within the discretion of the contracting
authority, which is subject to the judicial review of the *Conseil d'Etat*, and the
complainant has no subjective right to the contract.

The rules allocating jurisdiction between the *Conseil d'Etat* and the ordinary courts **11.40**
can raise complex issues, particularly where interim orders are sought. The same
dispute is sometimes litigated simultaneously before both the *Conseil d'Etat* and
the ordinary courts. The complex relationship between the *Conseil d'Etat* and the
ordinary courts which often leads the plaintiff to pursue separate but complementary actions, including applications for interim measures, before both legal *fora* in
relation to the same dispute, suggest that, if the *Conseil d'Etat* orders the suspension
of an award decision, then the plaintiff can request the ordinary court to suspend
the execution of the (concluded) contract in question. In the *CCN* case,[16] both the
Flemish Chambers of the *Conseil d'Etat* and the Brussels Court of Appeal appeared
to recognize that rejected tenderers may otherwise have no effective remedy and
that damages are not always adequate compensation. A similar line was taken
by the *Conseil d'Etat* (Flemish chamber) in the more recent *Strukton* case.[17] However,
there has not yet been a ruling in the ordinary courts where a concluded contract has
been set aside at the request of a third party such as an aggrieved tenderer.

(4) Denmark

The *Klagenævnet for Udbud*[18] (the Complaints Board) is the competent forum to **11.41**
deal with all complaints regarding infringements of Community law in the field
of public procurement as well as the Danish implementing legislation. Members
of the Board are appointed by the Minister for Business and Industry.

---

[16] *See Conseil d'Etat* decisions of 13 Otober 1992 (suspension, Case No. 40,734), 1 June 1993
(annulment, Case No. 43,019) and 22 February 1994 (second proceeding, Case No. 46,174),
all published in *Conseil d'Etat* decision reports. *Decisions of Brussels Court of Appeal* of 25 March
1993 (Entreprise et Droit, 1993), 232; 22 April 1993 (Entreprise et Droit, 1993), 241; and
31 August 1993.
[17] *See NV Strukton de Meyer v Maatschappij voor het Intercommunal Vervoerte Brussel*, decision of
the Brussels Court of Appeal of 18 December 1996, Case No. 63,634.
[18] The Complaints Board has been established by virtue of the Remedies Act (Act No. 206 of
25 March 1995 which entered into force on 31 March 1995), while detailed rules of procedure are
laid down in Order No. 26 of 23 January 1996 (the Complaints Board Order), which consolidates
Orders No. 912 of 18 December 1991 and No. 72 of 30 January 1992.

11.42   The Complaints Board does not have jurisdiction for cases concerning infringements committed by awarding authorities who exploit a geographical area with the purpose of extracting natural resources.[19] Such cases fall within the exclusive jurisdiction of the Maritime and Commercial Court[20] and must be dealt with as a matter of urgency. The Complaints Board is not competent with regard to claims for damages,[21] which can be brought only before the ordinary civil courts, and with regard to the imposition of fines,[22] which is a matter only for the Public Prosecutor and the ordinary courts.

11.43   The competence of the Complaints Board for public procurement cases is not exclusive. Complainants are free to bring their complaints before the ordinary courts without first having approached the Complaints Board. Claims for interim injunctions, as well as enforcement matters, may be brought before ordinary civil courts (the Bailiff's Court).

11.44   Complaints may be brought before the Complaints Board by any person or entity having legal interest in as much as the complainants must be individually and materially affected by the alleged infringement. Trade organizations and public bodies have *locus standi* which is not conditional upon the display of a specific legal interest.[23] The Secretariat of the Competition Council has also been granted general legal standing before the Complaints Board. The Complaints Board may allow third parties who have a legal interest in a pending case to intervene in support of one of the parties.[24]

11.45   Civil cases, such as claims for damages, are generally heard by the City Court at first instance, or special cases concerning previously unsettled questions of law or cases involving claims exceeding €67,000 can be brought directly before the High Court.[25]

(5) Finland

11.46   The Competition Council (*Kilpailuneuvosto*) has jurisdiction to deal with public procurement complaints and to challenge the legality of decisions of contracting authorities. The Competition Council is also the appellate body dealing with competition issues in Finland. The majority of the Council's members represent

---

[19]   *See* Art. 5(1) of the Remedies Act, which refers to offshore awarding authorities.
[20]   *See* Art. 6(4) of the Remedies Act.   [21]   *See* Art. 5(2) of the Remedies Act.
[22]   *See* Art. 6(1) of the Remedies Act.
[23]   The Minister for Business and Industry grants *locus standi* to trade organizations and public bodies listed in an annex to the Complaints Board Order.
[24]   *See* Art. 4(2) of the Remedies Act.
[25]   *See* Arts. 226 and 227 of the Administration of Justice Act.

economic entities and the body has special expertise in procurement issues. The Competition Council handles cases in a manner comparable to a court.

The County Administrative Courts are also competent, in accordance with **11.47** Finnish administrative law, to hear actions against municipal and state authorities when they act as contracting authorities under the remit of the Public Procurement Directives.

Any claim for damages must be made in an ordinary court of first instance, since **11.48** the Competition Council and County Administrative Courts do not have the power to decide upon and award damages. The Finnish Ministry of Trade and Industry also has jurisdiction to receive informal complaints from aggrieved tenderers. Upon receiving such a complaint, the Ministry may request information from awarding entities (public sector and utilities) regarding the award procedure in question. The Ministry may then give recommendations and instructions concerning the procedure and regarding interpretation of the Act.

(6) France

The relevant forum for adjudicating public procurement disputes in France **11.49** relates to the distinction under French law between matters subject to administrative law and thus reserved for the exclusive jurisdiction of the administrative courts, and those for which the ordinary civil courts are competent. In France, the majority of the contracts covered by the public procurement rules are awarded by public entities, either directly or indirectly through persons or corporate bodies acting on their behalf, and these contracts do relate to the implementation of public services. However, a significant proportion of contracts covered by the public procurement rules fall within the jurisdiction of the civil courts.

Depending on whether a contract is considered to be administrative in nature, the **11.50** competent *fora* are the *Tribunaux Administratifs*, the *Cours Administratives d'Appel* and the *Conseil d'Etat* (the Supreme Court for administrative cases). The president of the *Tribunal Administratif* or his delegate has powers to adjudicate on certain matters of urgency, through expedited proceedings (*procédures en référé*). A contract is considered an administrative contract when: (i) it is concluded by a public authority such as the state, a *département*, a *commune*, or their public administrative organs, or a private person or corporation contracting on behalf of such an entity; and (ii) the object of the contract is a public service or the contract contains clauses which one would not usually find in contracts between private persons.

For non-administrative contracts the competent *fora* are the *Tribunaux de Grande* **11.51** *Instance*, the *Tribunaux de Commerce*, the *Cours d'Appel* and the *Cour de Cassation* (the Supreme Court for civil and commercial cases). The president of the *Tribunal de Grande Instance* or of the *Tribunal de Commerce* or their respective delegates has powers to adjudicate on certain matters of urgency, through expedited proceedings (*procédures en référé*).

(7) Germany

11.52 The German legal order provides for a review system consisting of a voluntary review procedure at the Procurement Review Body (*Vergabeprüfstelle*). The Federal Government and the *Länder* are allowed to set up Procurement Review Bodies, which often are administrative bodies that supervise the legality of activities of other contracting authorities (*Rechtsaufsicht*). The function of the *Vergabeprüfstelle* is to facilitate amicable resolution in disputes and consultation with the parties to the award procedures for public contracts. On the federal level a Procurement Review Body operates under the auspices of the Ministry of Economic Affairs.

11.53 There is no requirement to exhaust review proceedings before the *Vergabeprüfstelle* in order to proceed to review procedures at the Procurement Chamber (*Vergabekammer*) as the review body of first instance and review procedure at the Procurement Division at the Court of Appeal (*Vergabesenat des Oberlandesgerichtes*) as a review body of second instance.

11.54 *The Procurement Chambers:* Both the Federal Government and the *Länder* Governments have set up independent Procurement Chambers (*Vergabekammer*) as a review body of first instance. These Chambers have exclusive competence for reviewing award procedures and claims against contracting authorities. The Federal Government establishes the Procurement Chambers at the Federal Competition Office. Each Federal Procurement Chamber has three members, at least two of whom, including the Chairman, must be civil servants qualified for higher administrative service and with good knowledge in the field of public procurement, and at least one of whom, preferably the Chairman, must be a judge or qualified to hold judicial office. The non-civil servant member should have practical experience in that area. Their term of engagement is five years. The *Länder*, when establishing their State Procurement Chambers, must also ensure the participation of at least one member who is a judge or qualified to hold judicial office with particular expertise in public procurement.

11.55 *The Procurement Division at the Court of Appeal:* Each Court of Appeal in Germany has set up a specialized Procurement Division (*Vergabesenat des Oberlandesgerichts*), which has the role to review the legality of decisions taken by the Procurement Chambers of first instance, as well as whether the Procurement Chambers have fully complied with their obligation to establish the relevant facts and apply the relevant public procurement provisions. Pending the award of a contract, the Procurement Division may take a new decision replacing the decision of the Procurement Chamber, or may instruct the Procurement Chamber to adopt a new decision, taking into consideration the grounds of the successful appeal. After the contract in question has been awarded, the Procurement Division can issue only declaratory decisions.

The civil courts: The Procurement Chamber and the Procurement Division lack   **11.56** any powers to award damages. Actions for damages are directed to civil courts. For claims with a value of more than €10,000 the competent courts are the district courts (*Landgerichte*). For claims of lower value, an action for damages has to be directed to the local courts (*Amtsgerichte*).

(8) Greece

A complainant against a contracting authority must firstly exhaust non-judicial   **11.57** remedies before being entitled to pursue any remedies before administrative or civil courts. Non-judicial remedies include formal complaints before the Ministry of Public Works or such other public authority as provided for by specific laws, which is competent to supervise the contracting authorities. Any person who has participated in an award procedure, including any stages regarding selection, sub-mission of tenders, and evaluation of offers, or who has been excluded from such procedure or any individual stages, may launch a complaint to the above author-ities seeking a review of the award procedure. The time limit for the compulsory non-judicial complaint differs depending on the stage reached in the award procedure. Any complaint referring to the tender specifications must be filed within a period corresponding to half of the period allowed for submission of bids. Complaints alleging irregularities in the bid procedure or opposing the selection of other participants may be submitted until one working day following the day on which the bids are first opened for evaluation by the contracting authority.

A complaint is subject to the jurisdiction of the administrative courts when it con-   **11.58** cerns a contract which has been awarded by the Greek state or a public authority and if the contract directly affects the public interest. Assuming this is the case, one of two branches of the administrative courts may have jurisdiction, depending on the nature of the act being challenged. If the complainant seeks the annulment of an administrative act, such as an award decision, the complainant must file his action for annulment before the *Symvoulion Epikratias* (the supreme administra-tive court). Interim measures may be sought from the Injunction Committee of the *Symvoulion Epikratias*. Where the complainant seeks to recover damages from the authority, or seeks to annul a public contract, rather than an act leading to the award of such a contract, the action must be brought before the administrative court of first instance.

If the public tender and the contract award procedures are organized by, or for the   **11.59** benefit of, an enterprise or legal entity which is owned or controlled by the state, but is otherwise subject to private law, any subsequent litigation is subject to the jurisdiction of the civil courts. Under the Greek rules of private law which include contractual and non-contractual liability, the complainant may only bring an action for damages against the contracting authority and not an action for the annulment of the award decision, as the civil courts have no relevant jurisdiction to annul administrative acts. In principle, the complainant could also seek an interim order.

(9) Ireland

11.60 The Procurement Directives have been implemented into Irish law through a series of Statutory Instruments. The provisions on enforcement laid down in Remedies Directives 89/665 and 92/13 have been implemented by Statutory Instruments No. 309/1994 and No. 104/1993 respectively. The Remedies Directives have been transposed largely by reference rather than by repeating or reiterating the provisions of those Directives. It is therefore the provisions of the Remedies Directives themselves which largely govern the availability of remedies in Ireland in the field of public procurement.

11.61 The competent forum to receive cases in the field of public procurement is the High Court in Ireland. Cases are heard by the High Court in the Four Courts in Dublin but, on occasion, a judge of the High Court may hear cases on circuit in the other major towns in Ireland.

(10) Italy

11.62 The powers to grant remedies in the field of procurement are conferred on separate systems of courts which are responsible for different aspects of the review procedure. On the one hand, under the traditional system of Italian administrative law, they are entrusted to the administrative courts. On the other hand, Article 13 of Law 142/92 has granted the power to award damages to the ordinary courts.

11.63 Administrative courts have the powers to grant interim measures and to set aside unlawful decisions, and include the *Tribunali Amministrativi Regionali* at first instance, and the *Consiglio di Stato* (Council of State) on appeal. The *Tribunali Amministrativi Regionali* have a general jurisdiction over the legitimacy of administrative measures which violate legitimately protected interests (*interessi legittimi*) and have the exclusive power to annul an unlawful administrative act.

11.64 The *Tribunali Amministrativi Regionali* have territorial jurisdiction based on the regional divisions of the country. Their composition comprises at least five administrative judges and a President and their seat is in each regional capital, although there may be other locations where some decentralized sections of the *Tribunali* operate.

Ordinary courts have jurisdiction in actions for the award damages. In addition, **11.65** they have jurisdiction to deal with cases involving administrative matters and in particular breach of individual rights (*diritti soggettiri*), as opposed to legitimately protected interests, which fall under the jurisdiction of *Tribunali Amministrativi Regionali*. Their powers are limited to declaring an administrative act illegitimate and refraining from applying it in a particular case. The organizational system of ordinary courts comprises, at first instance, *Giudici di Pace* (Justice of the Peace) and *Preture* and Tribunals; the Courts of Appeal at second instance; and the Court of Cassation as the final and last court of judicial review of, strictly, legal matters.

(11) Luxembourg

Actions dealing with public procurement contracts awarded by public authorities **11.66** must be brought before the President of the Administrative Tribunal (*Tribunal administratif*).[26]

Actions dealing with public procurement contracts awarded by private sector **11.67** utilities must be lodged before the President of the District Tribunal (*Tribunal d'arrondissement*). These Tribunals are competent to grant interim orders and annulment orders. The District Tribunal is also competent to grant dissuasive payment orders as against private sector utilities in accordance with Article 2.1c of Remedies Directive 92/13.

Actions for damages, even as against public authorities, must be made in the **11.68** District Tribunal, as under Luxembourg law, the administrative courts have no power to award damages.

The Tender Commission (*la Commission des Soumissions*) within the Ministry of **11.69** Public Works has been established as an adjudication body which oversees the procurement practices of public authorities and utilities[27] and is composed of representatives of public authorities and of professionals.[28] Before resorting to litigation in Administrative or District Tribunals, aggrieved tenderers may complain to the Tender Commission. Complaints may be lodged with the Commission by the contracting authority, an aggrieved tenderer or a professional body. An aggrieved tenderer may submit a complaint directly to the minister who has authority over the contracting authority or the utility in question, and who

---

[26] Prior to 1996, the *Conseil d'Etat* had jurisdiction over public procurement contracts awarded by public authorities.

[27] *See* Art. 36(6) of the Act on State Accountancy, as amended by the Public Procurement Act of 4 April 1974, which provides that the Tender Commission shall guarantee the correct application of the legislation on public procurement.

[28] *See* Arts. 44, 45 and 46 of Regulation of 2 January 1989, on the functions and procedure of the Tender Commission.

may refer the case to the Commission. The Commission may be asked to intervene even when the decision to award a public procurement has already been taken.

11.70 The Tender Commission has a conciliation function. It may issue advisory opinions which are normally complied with, although these are not binding and cannot be challenged in judicial review proceedings. Its principal role is to facilitate an amicable settlement for a dispute and avoid unnecessary litigation. In its capacity as an administrative adjudication body of non-contentious matters, the Commission is bound to respect due legal process and the right of defence whenever a decision is taken, and, in particular, the requirements that administrative acts always have to be reasoned and that access to files and documents must be available to the interested parties. The procedure before the Tender Commission is not an admissibility pre-requisite for future litigation before the Administrative or District Tribunal.

(12) The Netherlands

11.71 Any infringements of the Procurement Directives and implementing laws in the Netherlands can be challenged before an ordinary civil court or a special arbitration tribunal. In most cases, such arrangements pre-exists the Remedies Directives. Directive 89/665 has been partially implemented by Article 6.2 of *Besluit aanbesteding van werken* (the Regulation on the Procurement of Works). This Article stipulates that only central government authorities have to apply the *Uniform Aanbestedingsreglement* (Uniform Regulation of Procurement)[29] when awarding works contracts within the scope of the Works Directive. Any dispute arising therein[30] will be dealt with by arbitration before the *Raad van Arbitrage voor de Bouwbedrijven in Nederland* (Arbitration Board for the Building Industry in the Netherlands). Other public authorities may voluntarily declare the Regulation on the Procurement of Works applicable to a procurement procedure, even if the procedure falls outside the scope of the Works Directive. The *Raad van Arbitrage* is also competent to hear disputes arising from such award procedures. There are no national measures implementing Directive 92/13 for the provision of remedies in the utilities sectors, as specific implementation measures are not necessary because the existing remedies available before the ordinary civil courts already satisfy the requirements of the Remedies Directives.

11.72 An action for a breach of public procurement rules against a contracting authority may be brought before the relevant District Court.

11.73 Where the *Raad van Arbitrage* is competent to deal with cases, where the *Uniform Aanbestedingsreglement* (Uniform Regulation of Procurement) applies either

---

[29] *See* the *Uniform Aanbestedingsreglement EG* 1991.
[30] *See* paragraph 67 of the *Uniform Aanbestedingsreglement EG* 1991.

compulsorily or voluntarily, actions concerning alleged infringements of the procurement rules must be brought, at first instance, before the *Raad van Arbitrage.*

(13) Portugal

Complaints regarding an award procedure for public contracts may be first **11.74** brought before the contracting authority itself, which has certain adjudicating powers to resolve amicably and in a non-judicial manner any dispute arising from the award procedure in question. A complaint may also be lodged to higher authority which supervises the contracting authority *(recurso hierárquico)* if the original complaint is not satisfactorily resolved within fifteen days.

A formal complaint must be lodged with the contracting authority within eight **11.75** days from the time the complainant is aware of any violation of the public procurement rules which affect his position in an award procedure. The complaint must take the form of a written application addressed to the contracting authority. The authority is under an obligation to deal with the complaint within fifteen days. If the complaint is not resolved or if the authority ignores it, it is deemed to be refused after the elapse of the fifteen-day period. Conversely, if the authority accepts the complaint, it may remedy the infringement in question and, if necessary, annul any act or measure already taken pursuant to that infringement. A complaint does not suspend the award procedure for the public contract in question. The refusal of a complaint regarding a procurement procedure must be the subject of a hierarchical appeal before the matter can proceed to the courts.[31] An appeal against the refusal of a complaint to a contracting authority must be made to the higher authority which has supervising responsibilities over the contracting authority in question. Hierarchical appeals must be submitted within eight days from the notification to the complainant of the refusal of his complaint to the contracting authority. Where the contracting authority has ignored the original complaint and its refusal is assumed after the expiry of the fifteen-day period, the hierarchical appeal must be lodged within eight days of the expiry of the fifteen-day time limit. The hierarchical appeal should take the form of a written application addressed to the supervising authority.

If the hierarchical appeal is successful, the contracting authority must conform to **11.76** the decision of its supervisory authority and, accordingly, remedy the infringement in question. If necessary, the contracting authority must also revoke or annul any acts or measures that have been taken pursuant to the infringement. On the other hand, if the hierarchical appeal is refused, the matter may proceed to the competent administrative for review. Hierarchical appeals do not produce any suspensory effects on the award procedure for the public contract.

---

[31] *See* Decree 405/93 implementing the Public Works Directives in Portugal.

11.77 Under Portuguese law, a special stage of the award procedure of public contracts is the *acto público do concurso* (public session).[32] The public session is the stage when the bids and tenders are opened publicly and the participants are admitted or excluded. The public session is organized by a Committee composed of at least three members, one of them being appointed as President. The tenderers taking part in the award procurement procedure are invited to attend the public session. Any excluded tenderer may file a complaint if they wish to contest its exclusion from the list of accepted tenderers, or if they wish to contest the inclusion of certain tenderers, or if they wish to contest the refusal of its tender, and, finally, if they wish to contest the acceptance of another bidder's tender. Such a complaint must be addressed verbally or in writing by the complainant to the Committee during the public session. If the aggrieved party fails to make such a complaint immediately, no further appeal, either a hierarchical appeal or an action before the administrative courts, will be possible.

11.78 The decisions of the Committee in the *acto público do concurso* (public session) may be subject to hierarchical appeals to the appropriate administrative authority.[33] A hierarchical appeal must be made before any further appeal could be taken to the administrative courts. Hierarchical appeals for decisions taken during the public session do have suspensive effects. This implies that the award procedures are suspended and the award of the contract in question is blocked until all the hierarchical appeals filed against decisions of the Committee, pursuant to complaints submitted by the bidders during the public session, are decided upon by the appropriate administrative authority.

11.79 An aggrieved tenderer must file its appeal with the appropriate authority which supervises the Committee for the *acto público do concurso* (public session) within five days following receipt of a certified copy of the minutes of the public session. This hierarchical appeal is presumed as refused if no decision is notified to the appellant within a period of fifteen days for works contracts disputes, or ten days for supplies and services contracts disputes, from the date of filing the appeal. If the hierarchical appeal is successful, the infringement or irregularity concerned will be remedied and if necessary, the award procedures will be annulled.

11.80 After exhausting the pre-judicial proceedings and provided the alleged breach has not been rectified, an application may be brought before the administrative courts. Actions should be brought before the *Supremo Tribunal Administrativo* (Administrative Supreme Court), when the authority which supervises the contracting authority is the Portuguese Government, the regional governments of the autonomous regions of Azores and Madeira, or a Commander-in-Chief of the

---

[32] *See* Decree 405/93 and Decree 55/95, implementing the substantive procurement rules in Portugal.   [33] *See* Art. 95(3) of Decree 405/93 and Art. 64(1) of Decree 55/95.

Portuguese army. For all other public authorities awarding contracts under the public procurement rules, the competent forum to bring actions against decisions of contracting authorities is the *Tribunais Administrativos de Circulo* (Administrative Circle Courts).

In Portugal, the decisions of administrative authorities taken during procurement **11.81** procedures are subject of the exclusive jurisdiction of the administrative courts. The Decrees implementing the substantive public procurement rules (Decrees 405/93 and 55/95) place two specific limitations on the availability of remedies. Firstly, the infringement in question must have been the subject of a formal complaint followed by a hierarchical appeal, neither of which has succeeded in resolving the matter. Secondly, actions may only be brought before administrative courts in respect of the final decision of the public tender.[34] This requirement indicates that only the final contract award decision can be challenged before administrative courts and not any interim decisions taken during the award procedure. Any infringements or irregularities that have occurred in the course of the award procedure, such as a decision to exclude a particular bidder, provided that they had a direct influence on the final award decision, may be part of the appeal procedures.[35]

(14) Spain

Under Spanish law, persons wishing to oppose acts and decisions taken by an **11.82** administrative body must, as a general rule, firstly appeal directly either to the administrative body itself or to the superior authority which supervises that body. Once the preliminary administrative phase has been exhausted, a complainant in a procurement case may bring an action against the contracting authority in the Spanish administrative courts. The competence of the administrative courts to which the action should be addressed will depend on the nature of the administrative body and its contested decision. Actions against decisions taken by the Council of Ministers and bodies of the central government should normally be brought before the *Sala Tercera del Tribunal Supremo* (Third Chamber of the Supreme Court) or the *Sala de lo Contencioso-Administrativo de la Audiencia Nacional* (Chamber of Contentious Administrative Matters of the National Audience). Actions against the decisions of local or regional administrative authorities should generally be brought before the *Salas de lo Contencioso-Administrativo de los Tribunales Superiores de Justicia* (Chambers of Contentious Administrative Matters of the Superior Courts of Justice) in the relevant region.

An aggrieved tenderer who is affected by an alleged infringement of the procure- **11.83** ment rules must, as a first step, file a formal complaint with the contracting

---

[34] *See* Art. 55 of Decree 405/93 implementing the Public Works Directive in Portugal.
[35] *See* Art. 55(2) of Decree 405/93 implementing the Public Works Directive in Portugal.

authority in question. The complaint should be lodged either with the contracting authority itself or with the superior administrative body which supervises the contracting authority. It is usually the latter which is competent to adjudicate on the administrative complaint. In cases where there is no supervisory administrative authority to adjudicate the complaint, such as the case where the contested decision is taken by the Council of Ministers or a minister of the central Government, it is possible for the complainant to take action directly before the competent administrative courts without first having to go through the administrative complaints phase.

11.84 An administrative complaint can be brought by any person whose rights or legitimate interests may be affected by the contested administrative decision. Any person who has participated, or would have liked to have participated, in any stage of a contract award procedure will generally be recognized as having *locus standi* to lodge a complaint. The time limit for filing the complaint is generally one month from the date of notification or publication of the contested decision, or from the date the complainant becomes aware of the fact that a specific act such as an award decision has taken place without such publication.

11.85 The administrative complaint before the contracting authority or its supervisory authority does not have any suspensive effect and nor does it oblige the contracting authority to suspend the implementation of the contested act or decision. However, it is possible for the complainant to request a provisional suspension. The adjudicating authority, in order to decide whether to grant a suspension of the act awarding a public contract, must balance the likelihood of damage which the suspension may cause to the public interest with the interests of the applicant or the interests of third parties. In principle, the suspension of the awarding decision would be granted where implementation of the contested act may cause harm which is impossible or at least difficult to rectify (*perjuicios de imposible o difícil reparación*). If the authority fails to respond within thirty days of the request for suspension, the contested act is deemed to be suspended.

11.86 In Spain, administrative bodies are extremely reluctant to grant requests for suspension of administrative acts when dealing with administrative complaints. As a consequence, the lodging of an administrative appeal will not delay implementation of the contested decision. In a public procurement case, the administrative complaint will not prevent the contracting authority from continuing with the award process and ultimately adopting the award decision and subsequently concluding the contract.

11.87 After the launch of the administrative complaint by an aggrieved tenderer, the authority has a further three months within which to decide either to accept the complaint and rectify its procedure accordingly or to reject the complaint. A reasoned decision of the authority must be notified to the complainant. If the authority fails to notify a decision, the complaint will be deemed to have been implicitly rejected. When the authority explicitly rejects the complaint, the preliminary administrative phase is brought to an end. The complainant may then take action before the administrative courts with a view to review the decision of the contracting authority.

(15) Sweden

In Sweden, jurisdiction for actions against decisions of contracting authorities is vested in the competent *Länsrätt* (County Administrative Court). Actions for damages have to be brought before the competent *Tingsrätt* (District Court). **11.88**

The *Nämnden för Offentlig Upphandling* (National Board for Public Procurement) has been established and given responsibility for the overall supervision of public procurement procedures which are subject to the Public Procurement Act. Its supervisory capacity has the objective to monitor the legitimate application of award procedures for public contacts in Sweden and ensure compliance of public authorities and utilities with the letter and spirit if the rules. An important role in the *Nämnden's* function is to provide the Swedish government and the European Commission with information on the application of public procurement legislation in the country. For such purposes, it may request the submission of information in relation to award procedures of contracting authorities, conduct on-site visits to contracting authorities and undertakings participating in award procedures for public contracts, collate statistical and monitoring data, including case law arising from litigation before Swedish courts, and assess the performance of contracting authorities and utilities in their respective procurement policies. Finally, the *Nämnden* has authority to advise contracting authorities and utilities, as well as private undertakings, on the interpretation and application of the rules related to public procurement. However, its advice does not produce any legally binding effects. **11.89**

(16) United Kingdom

The United Kingdom has implemented the Public Procurement Directives by way of Statutory Instruments. The Public Works Directives have been implemented through the Public Works Contracts Regulations 1991;[36] the Public Services Directive has been implemented through the Public Services Contracts Regulations 1993;[37] the Public Supplies Directives have been implemented through the Public **11.90**

---

[36] *See* SI 1991/2680.   [37] *See* SI 1993/3228.

Supplies Contracts Regulations 1995;[38] and the Utilities Directives have been implemented through the Utilities Contracts Regulations 1996.[39]

11.91 The relevant forum to deal with public procurement cases in the United Kingdom is the High Court in England and Wales or the High Court in Northern Ireland or the Court of Session in Scotland.

C. Remedies Available in National Legal Orders

(1) Interim measures

11.92 The Remedies Directives require member states to ensure that interim measures are available to aggrieved tenderers and candidates in procurement award procedures. The most important function of interim measures in public procurement is the ability to suspend an award procedure, particularly prior to the conclusion of the contract in question. Such possible suspension is a demonstrable factor of the ability of aggrieved tenderers to review the actions and the behaviour of contracting authorities and utilities, without necessarily having recourse to an action for damages, which, in all member states, appears as the only possible remedy available after the conclusion of the contract.

11.93 Suspension of the award procedure aims at the possible annulment of the act which has awarded a public contract, or any other act or measure of a contracting authority or a utility which forms part of the procurement process for the award of such contracts. It is widely accepted that a public contract, once concluded, it is not subject to any set aside or annulment actions. For this reason, without interim orders, an aggrieved tenderer or candidate would be left with very few options to challenge an alleged infringement of the procurement rules which has a detrimental impact upon his right to participate and tender for public contracts.

11.94 Under Article 2(4) of Directive 89/665 and Article 2(4) of Directive 92/13, member states have discretion in allowing the competent judicial or administrative authorities to take into account the likely consequences of the interim measures upon the parties to the dispute and to balance their respective interests in contrast to the public interest at large. For these purposes, the courts in most member states apply a balance of interests test, where the complainant may have to show, *prima facie*, that he is likely to suffer serious and possibly irreparable harm if interim measures are not granted. Furthermore, that harm must outweigh the inconvenience or any harm or damages which the interim order would cause both to the awarding authority and to the public interest at large. The complainant might also have to show that the harm which he is likely to suffer, if the interim

---

[38] *See* SI 1995/201.   [39] *See* SI 1996/2911.

order is not granted, could not be adequately compensated through financial damages.

(2) *Interim measures from the Court's jurisprudence*

(a) Obligation to allow sufficient time between contract award and contract conclusion

The Court investigated[40] the obligations required by the Remedies Directives **11.95** 89/665/EEC and 92/13/EEC to transpose legislation at domestic level relating to the award of public contracts and provide for a procedure whereby all unsuccessful tenderers may have the award decision set aside. The Court took the view that the provisions of Article 2(1)(a) and (b) of Directive 89/665 require member states to provide for a review procedure so that an applicant may set aside a decision of a contracting authority to award a public contract to a third party, prior to the conclusion of the contract. That right of review for tenderers must be independent of the possibility for them to bring an action for damages once the contract has been concluded.[41]

According to the Court's analysis, a legal system of a member state that makes it **11.96** impossible to contest the award decision because of the award decision and the conclusion of the contract occurring at the same time, deprives interested parties of any possible review in order to have an unlawful award decision set aside or to prevent the contract from being concluded. Complete legal protection requires that it be possible for unsuccessful tenderers to examine in sufficient time the validity of the award decision. A reasonable period must elapse between the time when the award decision is communicated to unsuccessful tenderers and the conclusion of the contract, in order, in particular, to allow an application to be made for interim measures prior to the conclusion of the contract. Complete legal protection also presupposes an obligation to inform tenderers of the award decision. The decision of the contracting authority which is notified only to the person to whom the contract is awarded may, as a general rule, not be contested as unsuccessful tenderers have not become aware of that decision. National legislation relating to access to administrative documents which merely requires that tenderers be informed only as regards decisions which directly affect them cannot offset the failure to require that all tenderers be informed of the contract award decision prior to conclusion of the contract, so that a genuine possibility to bring an action is available to them. The effect of such national legislation is to preclude the possibility of an action to have the award decision set aside and, consequently, is

---

[40] *See* Case C-212/02, *Commission of the European Communities v. Republic of Austria*, judgment of 24 June 2004.
[41] *See* Case C-81/98, *Alcatel Austria and Others* [1999] ECR I-7671, paragraph 43.

incompatible with the public procurement rules. Member states are therefore required to put in place appropriate procedures to enable unlawful decisions or acts of contracting authorities to be set aside and, in accordance with Articles 1(3) of Directives 89/665 and 92/13, to ensure that review procedures are available at least to any person having an interest in obtaining a public contract. That effectiveness depends not only on the existence of a sufficiently long interval in which tenderers may react to the award decision but also on the obligation to keep tenderers informed of the award decision.

(b) Admissibility requirements of interim measures

11.97 The Court examined[42] review procedures under the Remedies Directive 89/665/EEC and, in particular, interim measures and the possibility of applying for interim measures after an action to set aide or annul an act or a decision of a contracting authority has been initiated. The Commission claimed that the scope *ratione materiae* of Directive 89/665 has been improperly reduced since the Spanish review provisions,[43] precluded a challenge to certain unlawful decisions taken by contracting authorities. In particular, national law limited the possibility of appealing against procedural acts, or administrative measures which do not bring administrative proceedings to an end. The Court stated that the Remedies Directive does not provide for any derogation in that regard.[44] In support of its argument, the Commission referred to Articles 1(1), 2(1)(b) and 8 of Directive 89/665, from which it follows that it must be ensured that any allegedly illegal measure may be reviewed effectively and, in particular, as rapidly as possible.

11.98 The Commission maintained that the wording of the provisions of the Remedies Directive such as 'any allegedly illegal measure' refers to all types of act alleged to be illegal, not only to definitive acts. Furthermore, the expression 'reviewed effectively and . . . as rapidly as possible' supports the conclusion that the possibility of seeking review of procedural acts is one of the best means of ensuring the effectiveness and rapidity of review procedures, since to wait for the outcome of the contract award procedure is the best way of weakening, or even undermining, the effectiveness and speediness of the review procedures envisaged by Directive 89/665.

11.99 The Spanish Government contended the Commission's interpretation of the term 'procedural act'. It considered that a procedural act, by definition, does not cause any harm to the interested party but is, at most, a preparatory step to

---

[42] *See* Cases C-214/00, *Commission of the European Communities v. Kingdom of Spain* [2003] ECR I-4667; C-236/95, *Commission v. Greece* [1996] ECR I-4459.

[43] *See* Art. 107 of Law 30/1992 and Art. 25(1) of Law 29/1998, which stipulate that procedural acts are not open to administrative appeal or administrative appeal proceedings unless they decide, directly or indirectly, the substance of the case, make it impossible to continue the procedure, make it impossible to put up a defence, or cause irreparable harm to legitimate rights or interests.

[44] *See* Case C-81/98, *Alcatel Austria and Others* [1999] ECR I-7671.

a decision which will be favourable or unfavourable to him. Thus, a procedural act does not imply the adoption of a position but is part of a procedure initiated in order to reach a decision. In that regard, the Spanish Government states that, if an act which appears to be a procedural act entailed *per se* the adoption of a position, it would cease to be a procedural act in the strict sense and would be reviewable. The Spanish Government claimed that the national provisions concerning the possibility of challenging procedural acts are not specific to the award of public contracts, but apply equally to all procedures. The Government pointed out that this device, which seeks to avoid procedures being paralyzed by successive claims and appeals at the stage of preparatory measures which do not yet definitively affect the rights of those concerned, is not only found within the Spanish legal system but it is also common to all the legal systems of the member states.[45]

The Court maintained that the national laws[46] did not allow judicial review of **11.100** procedural acts, are not open to administrative appeal or administrative appeal proceedings unless they decide, directly or indirectly, the substance of the case, make it impossible to continue the procedure, make it impossible to put up a defence, or cause irreparable harm to legitimate rights or interests. Therefore, those provisions have the effect of excluding procedural acts from the scope *ratione materiae* of Directive 89/665, unless they fulfil one of the above-mentioned conditions. Since Directive 89/665 does not expressly define the scope of the term 'decisions taken by contracting authorities', the question of whether procedural acts which do not fulfil one of the above-mentioned conditions constitute decisions in respect of which the member states must provide review procedures within the meaning of Directive 89/665, must be examined in the light of the aims of the Directive. In that regard, the Court pointed out that the sixth recital in the preamble and Article 1(1) of Directive 89/665 seek to ensure that adequate procedures exist in all the member states to permit the setting aside of decisions taken by contracting authorities in infringement of Community law on the award of public contracts or of national rules transposing that law, and also the compensating of persons harmed by such an infringement. The review procedures to which the Remedies Directive refers must be conducted effectively and as rapidly as possible, and must be available to any person having, or having had, an interest in obtaining a particular public contract and who has been, or risks being, harmed by an alleged infringement.

---

[45] The Spanish Government points out that that conception of precluding the review of procedural acts is embedded in Community case law. *See* Case C-282/95, *P. Guérin automobiles v. Commission* [1997] ECR I-1503. The Court has also held that the preparatory nature of the act against which the action is brought is one of the grounds of inadmissibility of an action for annulment, and that that is a ground which the Court may examine of its own motion, *See* Case 346/87, *Bossi v. Commission* [1989] ECR 303.

[46] *See* Art. 107 of Law 30/1992 and Art. 25(1) of Law 29/1998.

11.101 The Court found that the Spanish legislation enabled interested parties to bring actions against not only definitive acts but also procedural acts, if they decide, directly or indirectly, the substance of the case, make it impossible to continue the procedure or to put up a defence, or cause irreparable harm to legitimate rights or interests and, as a result, that legislation provided adequate judicial protection for individuals harmed by infringements of the relevant rules of Community law or of the national rules transposing that law.

11.102 The Commission also argued that the national provisions which transpose Article 2(1)(a) of Directive 89/665 into Spanish law,[47] do not provide for an urgent procedure independent of the lodging of an appeal, designed to suspend the procedure for the award of a public contract or the implementation of any decision adopted by the contracting authorities, and, in particular, do not provide any opportunity for applying for interim measures in the absence of an appeal on the merits. The Court has pointed out that it must be possible to adopt, independently of any prior action, any interim measures.[48]

11.103 The Commission claimed that, in administrative appeals, the only interim measure which may be adopted is suspension of operation. Secondly, in administrative appeal proceedings, the court hearing the application for interim relief tends not to adopt measures other than suspension of operation. The Commission stated that, according to Spanish case law, interim measures cannot relate to the substance, because they must not anticipate the outcome of the main proceedings. However, the rule that interim measures must be neutral as regards the substance of the main proceedings has the consequence that, contrary to the requirements of Article 2(1)(a) of Directive 89/665, the court hearing the application for interim relief cannot take all the measures necessary to correct an infringement.

11.104 The Spanish Government did not dispute that both the rules of administrative procedure and the rules governing administrative appeal proceedings have the effect that the adoption of an interim measure is linked to the prior lodging of an appeal and cannot, under any circumstances, be requested separately. However, it argued that, although interim measures may be requested and granted even before an appeal is lodged, that requirement does not imply that those measures are independent of the latter, since the person concerned is required to lodge such an appeal against the act he considers unlawful within a period of ten days of notification of the decision granting the measures requested. He must then request confirmation of those measures and, if he does not lodge the appeal within the time limit, the interim measures will automatically lapse.

---

[47] *See* Art. 111 of Law 30/1992 and Arts. 129 to 136 of Law 29/1998.
[48] *See* Case C-236/95, *Commission v. Greece* [1996] ECR I-4459, paragraph 11.

With regards to the suspension effects of legal proceedings, the Spanish Government **11.105**
claimed that administrative appeal proceedings are not initiated by application,
but by a simple written document which must indicate the act challenged or allege
inertia on the part of the authority, and in which the interested party may request
suspension of the operation of the contested act without necessarily having to lodge
a separate application. Once an appeal is lodged, the court will ask the authority to
forward the administrative file and it is only after the applicant in the review proceedings is in possession of the case file that the time limit within which he must
formulate his application and set out the grounds for review will begin to run.

The Court, in order to ascertain whether the Spanish legislation was consistent **11.106**
with Directive 89/665, referred to the fifth recital in the preamble to the Remedies
Directive, which stipulates the short duration of the procedures for the award of
public contracts, meaning that infringements of the relevant rules of Community
law or national rules transposing that law which mar those procedures need to be
dealt with urgently. For these purposes, Article 2(1)(a) of the Remedies Directive
requires member states to empower the review bodies to take, at the earliest
opportunity and by way of interlocutory procedures, interim measures with the
aim of correcting the alleged infringement or preventing further damage to the
interests concerned, including measures to suspend or to ensure the suspension of
the procedure for the award of a public contract or the implementation of any
decision taken by the contracting authorities.

In *Commission v Greece*,[49] which concerned the compliance with Directive **11.107**
89/665 of national legislation which restricted interim judicial protection to proceedings for suspension of the operation of an administrative act, and made the
suspension conditional on bringing an action for the annulment of the contested
act, the Court had the opportunity to define the scope of the obligations arising
in that regard under that Directive. In particular, it found that, under Article 2 of
Directive 89/665, the member states are under a duty more generally to empower
their review bodies to take, independently of any prior action, any interim measures, including measures to suspend or to ensure the suspension of the procedure
for the award of the public contract in question.[50] The Court found that, although
the Spanish legislation provides for the possibility of adopting positive interim
measures, it nevertheless cannot be regarded as a system of interim judicial protection which is adequate to remedy effectively any infringements that might have
been committed by the contracting authorities, since, as a general rule, it requires
proceedings on the merits to be brought beforehand as a condition for the
adoption of an interim measure against a decision of a contracting authority. That
finding is not affected by the fact that, where suspension is sought by way of legal

---

[49] *See* Case C-236/95, *Commission v. Greece* [1996] ECR I-4459.
[50] *See* Case C-236/95 *Commission v Greece* [1996] ECR I-4459, paragraph 11.

proceedings, this may be done merely by a written document and the application initiating the proceedings may be formulated after the request for grant of the interim measure, since the requirement that that formality be completed before-hand cannot be regarded as consistent with the requirements of Directive 89/665. Consequently, member states, by making the possibility of interim measures being granted in relation to decisions adopted by contracting authorities subject to the need to appeal against the decision of the contracting authority first, are in breach of Articles 1 and 2 of Directive 89/665.

(3) Interim measures in the Republic of Austria

11.108   A complainant in a procurement case at federal level may apply to the Public Procurement Agency for an interim order suspending the entire procurement procedure or part of it, such as the award of the contract, or ordering any measure to prevent the complainant from suffering damage. The admissibility of such application for interim measures is granted provided that the complainant has first exhausted the option for mediation before the Control Commission. In cases where an amicable settlement has not been reached, the application for interim measures must be launched within two weeks of the date on which the com-plainant learns of the Control Commission's recommendation. An amicable set-tlement precludes the issue of interim measures, unless the applicant demonstrates that the contracting authority has failed to adhere to that settlement.

11.109   Interim measures are only available during the award procedure. The Public Procurement Agency has to issue a decision concerning interim measures within five days. Once the contract in question has been entered into, interim measures are not available. Under the Federal Procurement Act, the contract is deemed to be formally concluded as soon as the contracting authority gives the successful tenderer written notice that his tender has been accepted. A contracting authority is precluded from awarding any contract within four weeks of being notified that a complaint has been lodged with the Control Commission. Also, an award can-not be made during the period of two weeks within which the Control Commission has to give a decision. Should the contracting authority award a con-tract within the first four weeks, starting from the date it receives notification of the motion for a procedure before the Control Commission, the contract con-cluded between the authority and the successful tenderer is null and void.[51] However, an unsatisfactory result may arise when a contracting authority awards a contract after the elapse of the four weeks from the date when the authority receives notice, but in violation of an interim order. If the successful tenderer had

---

[51]   *See* § 109(8) of the *Bundesgesetz, mit dem das Bundesvergabegesetz geändert wird* Act, Federal Law Gazette 1996/776.

not been made aware of the interim order, the contract concluded, although in violation of the interim order, may not be annulled.

The interim order may suspend the entire award procedure, annul certain **11.110** decisions of the contracting authority, or take any other appropriate steps to prevent and rectify damage caused to the complainant. The maximum length of an interim measure is two months,[52] which is the same time limit for the Public Procurement Agency to annul a decision of a contracting authority. Consequently, an interim order will remain in force for so long as the Agency has not yet decided on the merits.

The applicant for an interim measure has to prove that his interests are harmed by **11.111** the contested act of the contracting authority. The Public Procurement Agency has to balance the interests of the contracting authority, of the complainant, and of the other tenderers or candidates, by considering and taking into account any possible negative effects which may arise from the granting of interim measures. The Public Procurement Agency has to pay special attention to any public interest in the prompt execution of the award procedure. However, the burden of proof for establishing such a public interest consideration lies on the contracting authority.

(4) Interim measures in Belgium

A complainant may apply to the *Conseil d'Etat* for interim measures in order to **11.112** suspend a contract award procedure or the effects of a particular decision taken in the course of that procedure. The action before the *Conseil d'Etat* must relate to a decision whose legal effects adversely affect the interests of the applicant, such as one excluding the applicant from the award procedure (an *acte détachable*).

Usually, interim measures have the result of suspending the administrative deci- **11.113** sion in question, but there are other injunctions granted by the *Conseil d'Etat* which include specific action on behalf of the contracting authority (such as an obligation to invite the complainant to take part in the further stages of the award procedure, or an obligation to accord the same treatment to the complainant as that which the other candidates had enjoyed in the period between the challenged decision and the injunction, and an obligation prohibiting the contracting authority from notifying its award decision).

A complainant seeking interim measures must establish that *prima facie* there is a **11.114** case which raises a serious cause, in that serious harm would result from the immediate execution of the decision under challenge, and this harm could not easily be rectified. In addition, the applicant must prove that the balance of interests rest in

---

[52] *See* § 116(5) of the *Bundesgesetz, mit dem das Bundesvergabegesetz geändert wird* Act, Federal Law Gazette 1996/776.

favour of granting the interim order, taking into account all the probable consequences of the suspension for all interests of the other parties. Interim measures will be refused if any negative consequences exceed the benefits arising from granting such measures.

11.115   The French Chambers of the *Conseil d'Etat* regard that the harm that a complainant suffers or risks suffering, as a result of a breach in a procurement procedure, will very rarely be sufficiently serious and irreparable. Given the financial nature of that harm, the complainant can be adequately compensated in damages before civil courts. In contrast, the Flemish Chambers of the *Conseil d'Etat* have been much more willing to recognize the serious harm which can result from an infringement in the procurement process. Its various judgments have referred to matters such as the risk of losing highly specialized personnel, loss of commercial prestige and reputation, and prejudice to the chance of being chosen for later projects, and reveal the preventive nature of interim proceedings, given the great difficulty in obtaining any further relief once the contract has been concluded.

11.116   The registrar notifies a copy of the request for suspension or any other request for interim measures to the Auditor (who plays a role similar to that of an Advocate General before the European Court of Justice), to the defendant, and to any other parties likely to have an interest in the outcome of the case. Within eight days from the notification of the request, the defendant authority sends its file to the registrar together with any observations. Copies are forwarded to the applicant, the intervening parties and the Auditor.

11.117   Within eight days from the receipt of the file, the Auditor drafts a report relating the facts and the arguments of the case, and states his opinion on the merits of the request. On the basis of this report, the President of the *Conseil d'Etat* fixes a date for the hearing. If the request is manifestly inadmissible, the hearing should take place within ten days from the transmission of the report. In all other cases, the ruling of the *Conseil d'Etat* should take place within forty-five days from the submission of the suspension request.

11.118   However, none of these time limits are compulsory. In practice, given the number of requests submitted to the *Conseil d'Etat*, the time for an interim ruling averages between four and six months. In cases of extreme urgency, which are assessed at the discretion of the President with regard to the circumstances of the case, the President may convene the parties '*à son hotel*'. The suspension order must be confirmed by a second decision delivered within forty-five days from the date of the first.

11.119   The parties must be heard, except in cases where the urgency is such that the parties or some of them cannot be heard before the suspension decision. In such a case, the parties shall be convened within three days from that decision, although a delay beyond three days is not sanctioned. Interim measures are not usually available once a contract has been concluded. After that point, the harm caused by a procurement breach may never be regarded as sufficiently serious and irreparable to justify suspension, leaving an action for damages as the only remedy. A complainant may, therefore, find itself without any interim remedy, particularly given that a contract is regarded as having been concluded upon the notification of the award decision to all tenderers.

Interim orders are also available, at least in theory, from the ordinary civil courts, **11.120** which tend to apply very similar tests as the ones applied by the *Conseil d'Etat*. In practice, however, the civil courts are reluctant to grant interim orders suspending administrative decisions in the field of public procurement. The procedure is commenced by the notification of a summons by the process server. The period of summons is usually at least two days. Generally, the case will be pleaded by way of short debates (*débats succincts*), at the interlocutory hearing or within a very short time lag. The exchange of conclusions is not compulsory but is generally used in most cases. Interim proceedings can proceed rapidly and rulings can be laid down very shortly after the opening of the procedure. In cases of extreme urgency, the President may rule without hearing the defendant. The extent of his decision is strictly limited to what the urgency requires. Both sides will subsequently be given an opportunity to present their case, leading to a new decision. Rulings of the President of an ordinary court in interim proceedings can be appealed to the President of the Court of Appeal. The filing of an appeal does not suspend the execution of the first interim ruling.

(5) *Interim measures in Denmark*

Interim measure can be instigated before the Complaints Board. The Complaints **11.121** Board has the power to suspend an ongoing award procedure if it finds that there has been an unlawful act. Even in the absence of such a finding, the Complaints Board may suspend a procedure where this is deemed necessary or where such a suspension is specifically provided for by law. The remedy of suspension is mainly intended for cases in which a contract award has not been made and, in particular, where a contract has been awarded without prior publication and in the absence of a competitive tendering procedure. In such cases, the Complaints Board may deal with the question as a matter of urgency. The factors to be taken into account when considering whether to grant suspension are, primarily, the gravity of the infringement and consequences of suspension. The Complaints Board will carry out an overall assessment of the interests involved in the case. It is accepted, under general principles of Danish law on interim measures, that the applicant must establish the likelihood of his claim being upheld at the final trial and the probability that the purpose of his action will be lost unless interim measures, such as a suspension order, are granted. The Complaints Board has granted a limited number of interim orders, a fact that indicates the restrictive stance of the Board towards the principles allowing the granting of interim measures. The Complaints Board does not have jurisdiction to annul concluded contracts between contracting authorities and undertakings and is reluctant to interfere with the rights of third parties arising under a concluded contract, since it is an administrative body whose decisions are directed solely towards awarding authorities. The normal remedy in such cases should be the award of damages to the injured party before ordinary courts. The Complaints Board will decide a case before it regarding an application for interim measures within approximately two months.

11.122 Interim measures can be brought before civil courts in Denmark.[53] The Bailiff's Court may issue a prohibitory injunction if the complainant establishes that the defendant will, or is likely to perform, an act which infringes the complainant's rights. The complainant must also establish that it is probable that the purpose of his action will be lost unless an interim measure is granted. Such an injunction will not be granted if it appears that the normal rules on penalties and compensation afford sufficient protection to the complainant. An application for interim relief is likely to be rejected if there is an obvious discrepancy between the complainant's interest in relief and the harm which this will inflict upon the defendant. The Bailiff's Court has jurisdiction to suspend the performance of a concluded contract, provided that the general conditions under Danish law for obtaining an injunction are fulfilled. Nevertheless, an injunction would probably not be available where the concluded contract has already been substantially performed. In the Bailiff's Court, the decision on injunctions may be returned within a few weeks following the submission of an application.

(6) Interim measures in Finland

11.123 The Competition Council may decide upon applications for interlocutory or interim measures and suspension orders, even for public procurement contracts the value of which is below the thresholds stipulated in the Directives.[54] Interlocutory injunctions may, in particular, prohibit the application of a specific clause in the tender documents or of a procedure which infringes public procurement rules. The Competition Council may, also as an interim measure, oblige contracting authorities to correct any infringement of award procedures and impose fines for failure to do so.

11.124 The Competition Council may order that a decision taken by a contracting authority must not be implemented, or that the procedure for an award of a contract must be suspended, while the proceedings are pending before the Competition Council. There is also a possibility of imposing fines for failure

---

[53] *See* Art. 642 of the Administration of Justice Act (*Lov om Rettens Pleje*).
[54] *See* Art. 10 of the Act on Public Procurement.

of contracting authorities to observe the interim measures granted by the Competition Council.

The Competition Council is required to take into consideration the probable **11.125** consequences of the measures for all interests likely to be harmed, including the public interest. The Council may decide not to grant interim measures where the negative consequences could exceed the benefits.

The Competition Council does not have jurisdiction to deal with a complaint **11.126** from aggrieved tenderers, once the contract has been concluded. The conclusion of the contract entails signature of the relevant documents by the parties, but, more importantly, an agreement on the detailed terms and conditions, financial, and contractual performance. The only remedy available in such cases is an action for damages and the right for a compensatory payment before ordinary courts.

(7) *Interim measures in France*

Interim and annulment orders are only available as regards public contracts falling **11.127** within the scope of Remedies Directive 89/665. They are not generally available as against utilities under the measures implementing Remedies Directive 92/13. An alternative system of penalty fines applies to utilities.

Interim and annulment orders may be brought before the French administrative **11.128** courts. A complainant in a procurement dispute concerning an administrative contract may, before that contract has been entered into, apply to the president of the *Tribunal Administratif* in respect of a breach of the procurement rules. The president has the powers to take certain preventative measures.[55] The president may order the contracting authority to comply with its obligations to observe public procurement rules and, at the same time, suspend the award of the contract or the execution of any related decision. He may also nullify such decisions and cancel clauses or conditions intended to be included in the contract.

The nature of such an action is preventative, as it attempts to address a complaint **11.129** before the conclusion of the contract. The action must be filed before the contract is signed, whether it is an action for interim measures or one for a final annulment of decisions or draft contractual clauses. After the contract is signed, there is no longer any scope for such intervention and the judge does not have competence to adjudicate the case. The proceedings follow an expedited procedure known as a *procédure en référé*. The powers of a judge ruling on *référé* are generally limited to interim measures. However, under the provisions implementing Directive 89/665,

---

[55] *See* Law No. 92-10 gives the president the power to take certain preventative measures, by stipulating that Article L 22 of the *Code des Tribunaux Administratifs et des Cours Administratives d'Appel* applies in relation to procurement infringements.

the judge's powers are more extensive than usual, as he may also declare an administrative act null and void. A decision rendered *en la forme des référés*, confirms that the procedure is an expedited one that generally applies in emergency cases. The decision is not a typical *ordonnance de référé*, which is provisional in nature and may subsequently be reversed by the court of which the *juge des référés* is a member, when that court is called upon to adjudicate the case on its merits (*jugement au fond*). Under a *procédure en référé*, the judgment is final and binding. The nature of such actions and the character of these procedures reflect on their restrictive application.

11.130   Interim and annulment orders may also be brought before French civil courts. Interim and annulment orders are also available in the civil courts in respect of contracts which are caught by the EU procurement rules but which have a non-administrative nature.[56] A complainant may, prior to the contract being signed, seek an interim order. Such an order would instruct the contracting authority to comply with its obligations and may suspend the award procedure or the execution of any decision relating to that procedure. The complainant may also seek the annulment of such decisions or the cancellation of clauses or conditions intended to be incorporated into the contract, where these are contrary to the procurement rules. Such an action has to be brought before the president of the competent civil court, who must follow the *procédure en référé* applicable to administrative courts.

11.131   An application for interim measures before either the administrative or civil courts is made by submitting a written request to the administrative court or a writ of summons (*assignation*) before the civil courts. The application is then heard by the court's president, who should deliver his ruling within twenty days of the application being submitted. The time is only indicative, although the *Conseil d'Etat* requires the *juge des référés* to expedite the case in the shortest possible time, observing the due legal process and in particular the adversarial principles.

11.132   For actions regarding interim orders, the decision of the president of the lower court (*juge des référés*) is not subject to a full right of appeal on its merits to the *Cours d'Appel*. This does not preclude a party from filing a *pourvoi en cassation* before the *Cour de Cassation*, provided this is done within 15 days (instead of the ordinary time limit of 2 months). The purpose of such a *pourvoi* is limited to a review of the legality of the decision itself, which may be cancelled only if it contravenes certain basic legal principles to which any judgment must conform. The facts and merits of a claim cannot be discussed again in the *Cour de Cassation*. Similarly, an order by the *juge des référés* imposing a provisional penalty fine upon a utility is not subject to a full right of appeal. However, a full right of appeal to the

---

[56] Law No. 92-10 as amended by Article 11.1 of law No. 91.3, implementing the EU procurement rules for public works contracts and is also applicable to public supplies and services contracts.

Cour d'Appel does exist where the judge decides to convert a provisional penalty fine into a final penalty.

(8) Interim measures in Germany

In proceedings before the Procurement Chamber, the suspension of a public **11.133** procurement award procedure is automatic. Such a suspension is realized by the simple notification of the complainant's application to the contracting authority for reviewing the award procedure. The contracting authority is obliged to respect this suspensive effect and has to refrain from awarding the contract for a period of two weeks after the Procurement Chamber issues its final decision.

A contracting authority may contest the suspensory effect of the proceedings **11.134** before the Procurement Chambers and apply to the Procurement Chamber for permission to award the contract. When considering such an application for permission to award the contract, the Procurement Chamber is obliged to apply a balance of interests test, by balancing the interests of aggrieved tenderers and the public interest to avoid unreasonable delays in the award of contracts. On grounds of public interests, the suspensory character of the proceedings before the Procurement Chambers can be overruled and the contract in question may be awarded. In such cases, the contracting authority may award the contract two weeks after this decision, unless the complainant appeals to the Procurement Division at the Court of Appeal and applies for the restoration of the suspensory effect. A direct appeal against the Chamber's decision to lift the suspensory effect of the procedures before the Procurement Chambers is not permissible. An appeal to civil courts to lift the suspensory effect is not admissible, as the Procurement Chambers have exclusive competence as a review body of first instance in public procurement cases and the automatic suspensory regime is explicitly stipulated in the *Gesetzgegen Wettbewerbsbeschränkungen*.

(9) Interim measures in Greece

A complainant may apply to the Injunction Committee of the *Symvoulion* **11.135** *Epikratias* for an interim order provisionally suspending an administrative act taken during the course of a procurement award procedure. Such an application must be accompanied by a request for the act in question to be annulled. In considering an application for an interim order, the Injunction Committee will verify the admissibility of the application for annulment by ensuring its timely submission and that it concerns an administrative act which has legal effects. An application for interim orders has to be lodged at the *Symvoulion Epikratias* in the form of a judicial document. The hearing usually takes place within two weeks. Both parties are given the opportunity to present oral and written arguments at the hearing before the Injunction Committee. The procedure is rapid and the judgment is usually issued within a few days of the hearing. In cases of extreme urgency, the Injunction Committee may grant a provisional injunction, which is valid until the date of the Committee's definitive ruling on the application for an interim order.

11.136   The Committee does not, however, examine in detail the merits of the application itself, nor does it examine in depth the legality of the act being challenged. The Committee will simply consider whether the contested act is obviously legal or unlawful. In the first instance, it will reject the application for an interim order, even if irreparable damage may occur. On the other hand, if the challenged act is obviously unlawful, the Committee will grant interim measures. The determining feature in such cases is the likelihood of specific, direct, and irreparable damage, material or moral, to the complainant. Such damage must be either proven by the complainant or admitted by the contracting authority. Pecuniary damage is usually deemed to be reparable, since the complainant may file an action against the authority for damages before civil courts. The only exception is where the financial damage is likely to cause bankruptcy of the complainant.

11.137   Even where irreparable damage is established, the Injunction Committee may refuse to grant an interim order if this would be harmful to the public interest or when the interests of a third party may be seriously prejudiced.

11.138   The burden of proof rests on the complainant applying for an interim order. Three requirements must be met cumulatively. Firstly, the complainant must establish that *prima facie* serious evidence exists which shows the contested administrative act of the contracting authority infringes the relevant procurement rules; secondly, that the complainant may suffer serious harm as a consequence of the said act; and, thirdly, that such harm to the complainant is greater than the damage which might be caused to the interests of the public or third parties if the interim order were to be granted. Interim relief is only available in cases where the contract between the contracting authority and an undertaking has not been concluded.

11.139   Interim measures are, in principle, available in proceedings before the civil courts. In procurement cases, such an order would provide for the protection of the complainant's interests, in particular through a provisional suspension of the award procedure.

(10) Interim measures in Ireland

11.140   A complainant may apply to the High Court in Ireland for an interim order or an injunction which aims at suspending the award procedure for the contract in question or the implementation of any decision taken by the contracting authority. An application for an interim order must be brought at the earliest opportunity.

In practice, an interim order will not be admissible if the contract has been concluded. Interim measures remedies may be sought by any person having, or having had, an interest in obtaining a particular public or utility contract and who has been, or risks being, harmed by an alleged infringement. Therefore, an action could be brought by any party which participated in an award procedure or who would have liked to have participated in such a procedure. Applications for interim orders should be made at the earliest opportunity. It is not clear what time limits should apply, but a complainant should observe the three-month time limit within which applications for judicial review may be made, particularly as a complainant seeking relief under the Statutory Instruments may also decide to seek judicial review.

A complainant who seeks an interim measure such as an injunction must submit an application (summons) to the Court together with a supporting affidavit (sworn statement). This may initially be dealt with by the Court before the summons and affidavit are served on the other party (*ex parte*), but will then be dealt with at a subsequent hearing at which the other party may be present (*inter partes*). A claim for an interim injunction will not normally involve oral evidence but will, instead, involve lawyers making submissions to the judge on the basis of the affidavit evidence. The applicant for an injunction will be required to give an undertaking to the Court that he will pay damages for any loss suffered by the defendant if, at the final hearing of the proceedings, the applicant for the injunction loses the case.
11.141

The general principles governing the availability of interim orders in Irish law will also apply in procurement cases. The court, in dealing with an application of interim measures, may take into account the probable consequences of the measures for all interests likely to be harmed, as well as the public interest, and may decide not to grant such measures where their negative consequences could exceed their benefits. The general rule in Ireland is that the award of an interim order must be ancillary to a main, substantive action. In order to obtain an interim order, the complainant must firstly show that he has an arguable case in the substantive action. In other words, his case must be capable of serious argument but not necessarily one which the judge considers would have a better than fifty per cent chance of success.
11.142

The decision to grant an interim order depends on whether the complainant can satisfy the High Court that he has established a *prima facie* case and, if the injunction were not granted, damages would then provide an adequate remedy to the complainant. Conversely, if damages would not provide an adequate remedy, the complainant must prove that the balance of interest benefits his side. However, the Court will refuse to grant an interim order suspending the award procedure if that action would cause serious harm to the public interest, which outweighs any harm, prejudice, or damage likely to be inflicted to the complainant. Interim measures can be sought and obtained almost immediately in the High Court in
11.143

cases of urgency. The applicant is required to set out the urgent circumstances in the affidavit setting out the application.

(11) Interim measures in Italy

11.144 In procurement cases, interim orders have to be sought from the administrative courts and in particular the *Tribunali Amministrativi Regionali*.[57]

The Italian implementing legislation does not expressly provide for the *locus standi* of complainants. However, the basic principle of Italian procedure requires that an applicant must show an interest in obtaining a particular supply or public works contract, and must have been, or risks being, harmed by an alleged infringement. An *actio popularis* brought by a person who was not affected by the contested measure is inadmissible. An action brought by an organization representing contractors who did not take part in the procurement procedure and, therefore, were not affected by the contested measure is inadmissible.

11.145 The principles and procedures governing the availability and award of interim orders reveal that a complainant has to demonstrate the existence of a *prima facie* case and the risk of serious and irreparable injury, even though a risk of reparable injury is sufficient ground for the *Tribunali* to grant an interim suspension of an administrative act. The availability of interim measures is extended to cases where the administration refuses to adopt an act, or where the interim order granted forces the contracting authority to adopt an act such as the inclusion of a bidder in the selection and qualification process of a tender. As a consequence, the nature of interim measures available under the jurisdictional remit of the *Tribunali* embraces relief which, in addition to the suspension of an administrative act, provides any appropriate provisional relief which the judge deems fit to prevent imminent and irreparable injury to the applicant.[58]

11.146 A balance of interests test is applied by the *Tribunali* in order to determine the likelihood of any harm to the public interest, which may result from a suspension of an act and the subsequent delay in an award procedure, and the preservation of the individual interests of the complainant. The time limit for bringing applications for interim measures and annulment actions before the administrative courts is sixty days from the communication of the measure to the applicant.

11.147 The application for an interim order is usually contained in the application to set aside the contested administrative act, but can also be brought before the

---

[57] *See* Art. 21 of Law No. 1034 of 1971: *Legge di Tribunali Amministrativi Regionali*.

[58] The extension of interim measures under the jurisdiction of the *Tribunali* is influenced by an application, by analogy, of Article 700 of the Italian Code on Civil Procedure, which provides that, in cases of imminent and irreparable injury and where there are no specific provisional remedies available, ordinary courts may grant appropriate provisional relief in order to render effective any future judgment.

Tribunali Amministrativi Regionali separately. It is served upon the public authority which issued the contested measure or the State Attorney (*Avvocatura dello Stato*) in the case of public ministries, and upon any interested parties. The application must be lodged within sixty days of the communication of the measure to the applicant. The *Tribunali* decides in chambers and without a public hearing, but the lawyers representing the parties usually request to be heard. Any decision should be expected within two to three months.

(12) Interim measures in Luxembourg

An application for interim relief can be lodged before the Administrative Tribunals **11.148** for public procurement contracts awarded by public authorities and before the District Tribunals for contracts in the private sector utilities sectors.[59] Any interested party who considers that Community law has been violated in a public procurement procedure may request the President of the Administrative Tribunal to award interim measures.[60] Such a request may be lodged at any time before the conclusion of the contract in question.

The President Administrative Tribunal or District Tribunal may order interim **11.149** measures to correct the alleged infringement of Community law or to prevent further damage to the interests concerned, including measures to suspend or to ensure the suspension of the award procedure until the public authority has corrected the violation of public procurement rules.[61] In considering whether to order interim measures, the President may take into account the probable consequences of the measures for all interests likely to be harmed, as well as the public interest, and may decide not to grant such measures where their negative consequences could exceed their benefit.[62] A decision not to grant interim measures must not prejudice any other claim of the person seeking these measures.

Where interim measures are refused, reasons should be given for such a decision. **11.150** Interim measures in administrative jurisdiction within the Luxembourg system are considered exceptional, as they have been introduced by virtue of compliance with the Remedies Directives on Public Procurement. The *Conseil d'Etat* and the Administrative Tribunals are reluctant to adopt other than a restrictive approach in cases of summary proceedings such as interim measures, even though individual interests may be jeopardized. The general philosophy is that the administrative judge will annul or suspend administrative decisions only if it is strictly necessary or if the decision taken is manifestly unlawful.

---

[59] The power of the Administrative Tribunals to award interim measures was introduced into the Luxembourg legal system by the 1993 Act implementing Directive 89/665. Similar powers were granted to the District Tribunals, as regards private sector utilities, by the 1997 Act.

[60] *See* Art. 1 of the 1993 Act.   [61] *See* Art. 2 of the 1993 Act.

[62] *See* Art. 3 of the 1993 Act.

11.151   For utilities which operate in the public sector, the President of the Administrative Tribunal has the same powers to grant interim suspension orders and set aside orders as those when dealing with contracting authorities from the public sector. For utilities which are private entities, powers to grant interim orders are vested with the President of the District Tribunal, sitting as a judge of summary proceedings. This civil judge is given the power to award interim orders and set aside orders, suspending the award procedure or modifying or deleting technical specifications.[63] The President of the District Tribunal is also empowered to order dissuasive payments upon the private utility, if a wrongful or illegal clause, which would cause damage, is not modified or deleted.[64] The President of the District Tribunal may also initiate the conciliation procedure provided by the Remedies Directive for utilities.[65]

(13) Interim measures in The Netherlands

11.152   Interim measures are available before the President of the District Court and the President of the *Raad van Arbitrage*, pursuant to interlocutory proceedings, which must be distinguished from accelerated proceedings, on the substance of the case. The latter are available before the civil courts, provided the President grants leave, if the complainant establishes *prima facie* that the matter is urgent.

11.153   In procurement cases before the *Raad van Arbitrage*, interlocutory proceedings are granted automatically upon the complainant requesting accelerated proceedings. However, interim measures are not generally requested before the *Raad van Arbitrage*, because a ruling on the substance of the case can be obtained relatively swiftly.

11.154   Complainants may apply to the District Court or the *Raad van Arbitrage* for an interim order suspending a contract award procedure, on the ground that an infringement of the procurement rules has occurred.

11.155   The President of the District Court or the *Raad van Arbitrage* might suspend the award procedure, order that the procurement procedure be terminated and recommenced in conformity with the procurement rules, order the re-admission of a tenderer who has been unfairly excluded from the tendering procedure, and, finally, order the contracting authority to refrain from awarding the contract to an undertaking. In principle, the President of the District Court or the *Raad van Arbitrage* can suspend or set aside a contract which has been entered into but not yet performed.

---

[63] *See* Art.s 2.1(a) and 2.1(b) of Utilities Remedies Directive 92/13.
[64] *See* Art. 2.1(c) of Directive 92/13.
[65] *See* Art.s 9 to 11 of Directive 92/13.

In principle, a balance of interest test will be employed to demonstrate the urgency **11.156** of the case and the potential harm to public interest, even if the complainant suffers irreparable harm. However, in public procurement cases a probable cause of harm inflicted to individual interest would be sufficient to justify the grant of interim measures without a detailed application of the balance of interests or a concrete demonstration of the possible irreparable harm to the complainant.

(14) Interim measures in Portugal

Interim measures before administrative courts to suspend a decision of a con- **11.157** tracting authority awarding a public contract are exceptional under Portuguese law. The commencement of an action for annulment of the contracting authority's decision does not suspend the procurement process and cannot prevent the implementation of the decision by concluding the relevant contract.

A special proceeding may be instituted before the administrative court in order to **11.158** suspend the implementation of a decision of a contracting authority, which is under appeal. The applicant must show *prima facie* that the substantive appeal before the administrative court is legitimate and, in addition, must demonstrate that the implementation of the decision will cause irreparable damage (*prejuízo de difícil reparação*), while any suspension order will not seriously damage any public interest.

If the suspension is granted, it must be duly notified to the contracting authority, **11.159** in order to prevent the implementation or enforcement of the decision until the administrative court has taken a final decision on the subject matter. The contracting authority may nevertheless initiate or proceed with the implementation of its decision, while the appeal is pending, if it can show urgency on grounds of public interest. If the refusal to suspend the decision is not duly justified by the authority, the administrative court may, at the request of the complainant, reinstate the required suspension.

Administrative courts approach restrictively the concept of damage that is **11.160** difficult to remedy (*prejuízo de difícil reparação*), although, in principle, irreparable damages do exist. In practical terms, it is extremely difficult to obtain suspension of an award or exclusion decision, because the administrative courts are inclined to consider that, in the event of annulment, the appellant can always be duly indemnified through an award of damages.

(15) Interim measures in Spain

A complainant before the administrative courts may apply for the grant of an **11.161** interim order suspending the implementation of the contested administrative decision. In public procurement cases, the suspension may relate to any administrative act or decision taken at any stage of the award procedure. The court may grant such a suspension if the execution of the decision would cause damage which is impossible or difficult to remedy (*perjuicios de imposible o difícil reparación*). The complainant needs to establish that, if the contested act is not suspended, damages which are impossible or very difficult to remedy would be inflicted upon him, in as much as the contract will be awarded and subsequently concluded to a third party.

11.162 Once the suspension has been requested from the court, the Government Attorney, who represents the administration, the parties, and any joined parties, must be heard by the court within five days.[66] After the Government Attorney has delivered his report, or once fifteen days have elapsed without such a report being received, the court will give its ruling. If the Government Attorney opposes the suspension on the basis of harm to the public interest, the court may not grant a suspension without giving prior notice to the Ministry or authority which issued the contested act. On the other hand, if the suspension of the act is ordered, the court may demand a bond or any other financial guarantee from the complainant to cover the possibility of damage being caused to the public interest or to a third party. Such financial guarantees may consist of a deposit of funds with the court. The administrative court would decide an application for interim measures within three months.

11.163 Administrative courts in Spain have adopted a restrictive approach in relation to interim measures and, in particular, orders regarding the suspension of administrative acts awarding public contracts. In principle, a balance of interest test would be applied by the courts, determining any irreparable damage which the award of the contract in question may cause to the aggrieved tenderer and the harm which would be inflicted upon the public interest by virtue of a delay in completing the subject mater of the public contract. Quite often, the balance tips towards the public interest, as the courts regard the potential harm to the public at large from a delayed completion of a public contract far superior to any damage on individual interests, even if that damage is irreparable.

11.164 Spanish courts tend to view an aggrieved tenderer's interests as purely economic ones, thus any violation of a procedural rule which leads to the award of a public contract could be subsequently well rectified through an award for damages before the competent forum. Thus, the requirement that the applicant for interim measures and, in particular, an order to suspend an administrative act which awards a public contract, must show and prove harm which is impossible or

---

[66] *See* Art. 123 of the *Ley Reguladora de la Jurisdicción Contencioso-Adminitrativa*, which regulates appeal proceedings before the administrative courts once the non-judicial remedies have been exhausted.

at least difficult to rectify (*perjuicios de imposible o difícil reparación*) cannot be easily met. In theory, and if a suspension order is granted, the court may demand a bond or any other financial guarantee from the complainant in order to ensure that adequate compensation will be provided to the contracting authority for any damages caused to the public interest or to third parties, in the event that the administrative court rules against the complainant on the substantive merits of the case to annul the administrative act which awards the public contract in question.

(16) Interim measures in Sweden

Interim measures are available before the competent *Länsrätt* (County Administrative Court),[67] prior to the conclusion of the contract. The conclusion of the contract serves as the deadline for an application for interim relief against an allegedly unlawful decision of a contracting authority during the award procedure for a public contract.[68] The Public Procurement Act originally provided that interim orders were not available after the contracting authority had taken its award decision, even in cases where the contract had not been concluded. However, a ruling of the Supreme Administrative Court (*Regeringsrätten*) stipulated that interim measures must be available to aggrieved tenderers throughout the procurement process, including the award stage, and up to the conclusion of the contract.[69]   **11.165**

An applicant for a suspension order must establish that there is an infringement of public procurement rules relating to the award procedures for the relevant contract. However, it is not necessary to ascertain that there is a *prima facie* case, as far as the substantive part of the litigation (the annulment of the awarding act) is concerned. The application for suspension must demonstrate that the aggrieved tenderer is likely to suffer serious damage, unless the suspension order is granted. The *Länsrätt* will apply a balance of interest test by comparing the damage or harm which the order would cause to the contracting authority and the damage which the complainant will allegedly suffer if the order is rejected. The balance of interest test will reveal the economic importance to either party arising from the suspension of the award process. The public interest could be considered when applying the test. There are no express time limits within which actions for interim orders must be decided. In practice, an application for interim measures is usually decided within two weeks. Orders deciding interim measures are not subject to appeal.   **11.166**

---

[67] *See* Art. 7:2, Lag 1997:1068.   [68] *See* Art. 7.1 Lag 1997:1068.
[69] *See Regeringsrätten* (Supreme Administrative Court) RÅ 1996 ref. 50.

(17) Interim measures in the United Kingdom

11.167 An aggrieved tenderer may ask the court to issue an interim order or injunction which suspends a decision or an act of a contracting authority awarding a public contract, or suspends the implementation of any decision or action taken by the contracting authority during the award procedure. Interim measures are available prior to the conclusion of the contract between the contracting authority and an undertaking. After the conclusion of the contract, the only remedy available is damages.

11.168 Applications for interim measures orders such as injunctions or suspension orders commence by a summons application to the court, in conjunction with a supporting affidavit or a sworn statement. The application may be dealt with by the court before the summons and affidavit are served on the other party (*ex parte*) or after the summons and affidavit have been served on the other party (*inter partes*). A claim for an interim injunction will not normally involve oral evidence but will, instead, involve legal submissions to the judge on the basis of the affidavit evidence. The summons for interim measures may be issued prior to, simultaneously with, or after, the issue of a writ. The applicant will usually have to give an undertaking that he will compensate the contracting authority for damages for any loss suffered if, at the final hearing of the proceedings, the application for the injunction is rejected. Similar procedures apply in relation to interim injunctions in the context of judicial review proceedings.

11.169 The complainant must first show that there is a *prima facie* legitimate case with serious chances of success in its substantive stage. The complainant also has the burden of proving that the balance of interests are leaning towards his case. The court will examine, *inter alia* the potential effect of the interim order on the part of the contracting authority, as well as the impact upon public interest and public services. The court will also explore the likelihood of a potential action for damages as a more appropriate redress method to rectify the aggrieved tenderer's alleged harm.

D. Set Aside and Annulment

11.170 The Remedies Directives also stipulate that national courts or administrative tribunals must be given the power to set aside or annul acts of contracting authorities. Such orders aim at nullifying the decision of the contracting authority, or a utility which awards a contract, prior to its conclusion. A set aside or annulment order cannot attack the contract itself, as the latter represents a pact between the contracting authority and a third party. In most legal orders, a set aside or annulment order will be reached after application of a balance of interest test. However, many legal systems rely predominantly on the mere lawfulness of the administrative act of the contacting authority or the utility, and do not involve any test which weights interests and potential harm and damages.

(1) Set aside and annulment orders from the Court's jurisprudence

(a) Meaning and content of decisions for review

The Court examined the level of judicial protection afforded to third parties **11.171** having an interest under the Remedies Directive 89/665/EEC and verified that any remedies available to them against decisions taken by contracting authorities extends also to decisions taken outside a formal award procedure and decisions prior to a formal call for tenders,[70] in particular, the decision on whether a particular contract falls within the personal and material scope of the Public Procurement Directives. The national court asked whether Article 1(1) of Directive 89/665 could be interpreted as meaning that the member states' obligation to ensure that effective and rapid remedies are available against decisions taken by contracting authorities extends also to decisions taken outside a formal award procedure and decisions prior to a formal call for tenders, in particular the decision on whether a particular contract falls within the material scope of Public Procurement Directives, and from what moment during a procurement procedure the member states are obliged to make a remedy available to a tenderer, candidate, or an interested party.

The Court examined the scope of the concept 'decisions taken by the contracting **11.172** authorities' stipulated in Article 1(1) of Directive 89/665 on the basis of the wording of the relevant provisions of the Directive and the objective of effective and rapid judicial protection pursued by it. Although that concept is not expressly defined in the Remedies Directive, the wording of Article 1(1) of Directive 89/665 provided ample confidence in assuming that every decision of a contracting authority falling under the Community rules in the field of public procurement and liable to infringe them is subject to the judicial review provided for in Article 2(1)(a) and (b) of that Directive.[71] It thus embraces generally the decisions of a contracting authority without distinguishing between those decisions according to their content or time of adoption. In addition, The Court ascertained that Article 2(1)(b) of Directive 89/665 provides for the possibility of annulling unlawful decisions of the contracting authorities in relation to the technical and other specifications, not only in the invitation to tender, but also in any other document relating to the award procedure in question. That provision can therefore

---

[70] *See* Case C-26/03, *Stadt Halle, RPL Recyclingpark Lochau GmbH v Arbeitsgemeinschaft Thermische Restabfall und Energieverwertungsanlage TREA Leuna*, judgment of 11 January 2005;

[71] *See* Case C-92/00 *Hospital Ingenieure* [2002] ECR I-5553, paragraph 37; Case C-57/01 *Makedoniko Metro and Mikhaniki* [2003] ECR I-1091, paragraph 68.

include documents containing decisions of the contracting authority taken at a stage prior to the call for tenders.

11.173 That broad meaning of the concept of a decision taken by a contracting authority is confirmed by the Court's case law. The Court has already held that Article 1(1) of Directive 89/665 does not lay down any restriction with regard to the nature and content of the decisions it refers to.[72] Nor may such a restriction be inferred from the wording of Article 2(1)(b) of that Directive.[73] Moreover, a restrictive interpretation of the concept of a decision amenable to review would be incompatible with the provision in Article 2(1)(a) of that Directive which requires the member states to make provision for interim relief procedures in relation to any decision taken by the contracting authorities.[74] In line with this broad interpretation of the concept of a decision amenable to review, the Court has held that the contracting authority's decision prior to the conclusion of the contract as to the tenderer to whom the contract will be awarded must, in all cases, be open to review, regardless of the possibility of obtaining an award of damages once the contract has been concluded.[75]

11.174 The Court has also held that a contracting authority's decision to withdraw an invitation to tender for a public service contract must be open to a review procedure.[76] *A contrario*, a contracting authority's decision not to initiate an award procedure may be regarded as the counterpart of its decision to terminate such a procedure. Where a contracting authority decides not to initiate an award procedure on the ground that the contract in question does not fall within the scope of the relevant Community rules, such a decision constitutes the very first decision amenable to judicial review.[77] Therefore, any act of a contracting authority adopted in relation to a public service contract and capable of producing legal effects constitutes a decision amenable to review within the meaning of Article 1(1) of Directive 89/665, regardless of whether that act is adopted outside a formal award procedure or as part of such a procedure.

11.175 The approach under which an act or a decision of a contracting authority does not require judicial protection because it falls outside the framework of a formal award procedure is incorrect according to the Court, as the effect of such approach would be to make the application of the Public Procurement Remedies Directive optional, at the option of contracting authorities, even though that application is

---

[72] *See* Case C-81/98 *Alcatel Austria and Others* [1999] ECR I-7671, paragraph 35.
[73] *See* Case C-81/98 *Alcatel Austria and Others* [1999] ECR I-7671, paragraph 32.
[74] *See* Case C-92/00 *Hospital Ingenieure* [2002] ECR I-5553, paragraph 49.
[75] *See* Case C-81/98 *Alcatel Austria and Others* [1999] ECR I-7671, paragraph 43.
[76] *See* Case C-92/00 *Hospital Ingenieure* [2002] ECR I-5553, paragraph 55.
[77] *See* the Opinion of Advocate-General Stix-Hackl, point 23 in case C-26/03, *Stadt Halle, RPL Recyclingpark Lochau GmbH v Arbeitsgemeinschaft Thermische Restabfall und Energieverwertungsanlage TREA Leuna*, delivered on 23 September 2004.

mandatory where the relevant conditions are satisfied. Such an option could lead to the most serious breach of Community law in the field of public procurement on the part of a contracting authority, as it would substantially reduce the effective and rapid judicial protection aimed at by the Remedies Directives, and would interfere with the objectives of free movement of services and open and undistorted competition.

On the other hand, decisions or acts of contracting authorities which constitute a **11.176** mere preliminary study of the market, or which are purely preparatory and form part of the internal reflections of the contracting authority with a view to a public award procedure, are not amendable to review.

The Court also elaborated on the availability of the Remedies Directive **11.177** 89/665/EEC in relation to the scope of reviewing judicially a decision of a contracting authority to withdraw an invitation to tender.[78] The Court determined that the decision of the contracting authority to withdraw the invitation to tender for a public service contract should be open to a review procedure, and should be capable of being annulled, on the ground that it has infringed Community law on public contracts or national rules implementing that law. The Remedies Directives preclude national legislation from limiting review of the legality of the withdrawal of an invitation to tender to mere examination of whether it was arbitrary. The determination of the time to be taken into consideration for assessing the legality of the decision by the contracting authority to withdraw an invitation to tender is a matter for national law, provided that the relevant national rules are not less favourable than those governing similar domestic actions, and that they do not make it practicably impossible or excessively difficult to exercise rights conferred by Community law.

The national court (*Vergabekontrollsenat*) requested clarification from the **11.178** European Court of Justice asking whether Article 1(1) of Directive 89/665 requires the decision of the awarding authority to withdraw the invitation to tender for a public service contract to be open to review proceedings, and to annulment in appropriate cases, on the ground that it infringed Community law on public contracts or the national rules transposing that law. In that respect, whereas Article 2(1)(b) of Directive 89/665 delimits the scope of the Directive, it does not define the unlawful decisions of which annulment may be sought, confining itself to listing measures which member states are required to take for the purposes of the review proceedings referred to in Article 1 of the Remedies Directive.[79]

---

[78] *See* Case C-92/00, *Hospital Ingenieure Krankenhaustechnik Planungs- GmbH (HI) and Stadt Wien*, ECR [2002] I-5553.

[79] *See* Case C-81/98 *Alcatel Austria and Others* v *Bundesministerium für Wissenschaft und Verkehr* [1999] ECR I-7671, paragraphs 30 and 31.

11.179 The Austrian Government and the Commission maintained that member states are required to establish procedures allowing review proceedings to be brought against the withdrawal of an invitation to tender for a public service contract if that withdrawal is governed by Directive 92/50. In that respect, they considered that such withdrawal falls exclusively under national legal rules and, therefore, does not fall within the scope of Directive 89/665.

11.180 In particular, the Commission states that, in its proposal for a Council Directive 87/C 230/05 coordinating the laws, regulations and administrative provisions relating to the application of Community rules on procedures for the award of public supply and public works contracts,[80] it expressly proposed that the obligation of member states to establish review procedures should extend, not only to decisions taken by the contracting authorities in breach of Community law, but also to those infringing national legal rules. However, in the course of the legislative process, the obligation to establish a review mechanism was limited to its present scope, so as to cover only decisions which infringe 'Community law on public contracts or the national rules which transpose that law'.

11.181 The Austrian Government argued that the conclusion that the decision to withdraw an invitation to tender does not constitute a decision within the meaning of Directive 89/665 is confirmed by Article 2(1)(b) of that Directive, which exclusively concerns decisions which the contracting authority adopts during the procedure for the award of a public contract, whereas a decision to withdraw an invitation to tender brings such a procedure to an end. Thus, where an invitation to tender is withdrawn unlawfully, the national legislature is required, under Directive 89/665, only to ensure that the candidates and tenderers are given a right to damages.

11.182 The Court as a preliminary observation reiterated that Article 1(1) of Directive 89/665 places an obligation on member states to lay down procedures enabling review of decisions taken in a tender procedure on the ground that those decisions infringed Community law on public contracts or national rules transposing that law. It follows that, if a decision taken by a contracting authority in a procedure for awarding a public contract is made subject to the Community law rules on public contracts, and is therefore capable of infringing them, Article 1(1) of Directive 89/665 requires that this decision be capable of forming the subject-matter of an action for annulment.

11.183 Therefore, in order to determine whether a decision of a contracting authority to withdraw an invitation to tender for a public service contract may be regarded as one of those decisions in respect of which member states are required, under Directive 89/665, to establish annulment action procedures, the Court examined

---

[80] *See* [1987] OJ C230/6.

whether such a decision falls within Community law rules on public contracts. In that respect, the Court noted that the provisions found in the Public Procurement Directives which provide, *inter alia*, that, where the contracting authorities have decided to abandon an award procedure,[81] they also stipulate that contracting authorities must inform candidates and tenderers of the reasons for their decision as soon as possible.

The Court has defined the scope of the obligation to notify reasons for abandon- **11.184** ing the award of a contract in the context of the Public Works Directive 93/37,[82] where it held that public procurement rules[83] do not provide that the option of the contracting authority to decide not to award a contract put out to tender is limited to exceptional cases or must necessarily be based on serious grounds.[84] It follows that, although a contracting authority is required to notify candidates and tenderers of the grounds for its decision if it decides to withdraw the invitation to tender for a public contract, there is no implied obligation on that authority to carry the award procedure to its conclusion.

However, even though, apart from the duty to notify the reasons for the withdrawal **11.185** of the invitation to tender, the public procurement rules contain no specific provision concerning the substantive or formal conditions for that decision, the fact remains that the latter decision is still subject to fundamental rules of Community law, and, in particular, to the principles laid down by the EC Treaty on the right of establishment and the freedom to provide services. In that regard, the Court has consistently held that the purpose of coordinating at Community level the procedures for the award of public contracts is to eliminate barriers to the freedom to provide services and goods, and, therefore, to protect the interests of traders established in a member state who wish to offer goods or services to contracting authorities established in another member state.[85]

The Court's case law also demonstrates that the principle of equal treatment, **11.186** which underlies the Directives on procedures for the award of public contracts, implies in particular an obligation of transparency in order to enable verification that it has been complied with.[86] In that respect, it should be noted that the duty to notify reasons for a decision to withdraw an invitation to tender is dictated

---

[81] *See* Art. 12(2) of the public services Directive 92/50 and Article 8(2) of the public works Directive 93/37 relating specifically to the decision to withdraw an invitation to tender.

[82] *See* [1993] OJ L199/54.

[83] In particular Art. 8(2) of Directive 93/37.

[84] *See* Case C-27/98, *Fracasso and Leitschutz v. Salzburger Landesregierung* [1999] ECR I-5697, paragraphs 23 and 25.

[85] *See* Case C-380/98, *University of Cambridge* [2000] ECR I-8035, paragraph 16; Case C-19/00, *SIAC Construction* [2001] ECR I-7725, paragraph 32.

[86] *See* Case C-275/98 *Unitron Scandinavia and 3-S v. Ministeriet for Fødevarer, Landbrug og Fiskeri* [1999] ECR I-8291, paragraph 31; Case C-324/98, *Telaustria and Telefonadress v. Telekom Austria* [2000] ECR I-10745, paragraph 61.

precisely by concern to ensure a minimum level of transparency in the contract-awarding procedures to which that Directive applies, and hence compliance with the principle of equal treatment. Even though the Public Procurement Directives do not specifically govern the detailed procedures for withdrawing an invitation to tender for a public contract, the contracting authorities are nevertheless required, when adopting such a decision, to comply with the fundamental rules of the Treaty in general, and the principle of non-discrimination on the ground of nationality.[87]

11.187　Since the decision of a contracting authority to withdraw an invitation to tender for a public service contract is subject to the relevant substantive rules of Community law, the Court concluded that it also falls within the rules laid down by Directive 89/665 in order to ensure compliance with the rules of Community law on public contracts. That finding is corroborated, firstly, by the wording of the provisions of Directive 89/665. The Court pointed out that the provision in Article 1(1) of that Directive does not lay down any restriction with regard to the nature and content of the decisions referred to therein.[88] Nor can such a restriction be inferred from the wording of Article 2(1)(b) of that Directive.[89] Moreover, a restrictive interpretation of the category of decisions in relation to which member states must ensure the existence of review procedures would be incompatible with Article 2(1)(a) of the same Directive, which requires member states to make provision for interim relief procedures in relation to any decision taken by the contracting authorities.

11.188　The Court held that the general frameworks of Directive 89/665 requires a broad interpretation, insofar as Article 2(5) of that Directive authorizes member states to provide that, where damages are claimed on the ground that a decision by the contracting authority was taken unlawfully, the contested decision must first be set aside. To accept that member states are not required to lay down review procedures for annulment in relation to decisions withdrawing invitations to tender would amount to authorizing them, by availing themselves of the option provided for in the provision mentioned in the paragraph above, to deprive tenderers adversely affected by such decisions, adopted in breach of the rules of Community law, of the possibility of bringing actions for damages. Any other interpretation would undermine the effectiveness of Directive 89/665. As the first and second recitals in its preamble show, that Directive is designed to reinforce existing arrangements at both national and Community level for ensuring effective application of Community Directives on the award of public contracts, in particular

---

[87]　*See* Case C-324/98, *Telaustria Verlags GmbH and Telefonadress GmbH v Post & Telekom Austria AG*, paragraph 60, concerning the conclusion of public service concessions.

[88]　*See* Case C-81/98 *Alcatel Austria and Others* [1999] ECR I-7671, paragraph 35.

[89]　*See* Case C-81/98 *Alcatel Austria and Others* [1999] ECR I-7671, paragraph 32.

at the stage where infringements can still be rectified, and it is precisely in order to ensure compliance with those Directives that Article 1(1) of Directive 89/665 requires the member states to establish effective review procedures that are as rapid as possible.[90] The full attainment of the objective pursued by Directive 89/665 would be compromised if it were lawful for contracting authorities to withdraw an invitation to tender for a public service contract without being subject to the judicial review procedures designed to ensure that the Directives laying down substantive rules concerning public contracts and the principles underlying those Directives are genuinely complied with.

The Court concluded that the decision to withdraw an invitation to tender for **11.189** a public service contract is one of those decisions in relation to which member states are required, under Directive 89/665, to establish review procedures for annulment, for the purposes of ensuring compliance with the rules of Community law on public contracts and national rules implementing that law.

The national court also asked the European Court of Justice whether Directive **11.190** 89/665 precludes national rules from limiting review of the legality of the withdrawal of an invitation to tender to mere examination of whether that decision was arbitrary. The Court held that Directive 89/665 provides for the coordination of existing mechanisms in member states in order to ensure the full and effective application of the Directives laying down substantive rules concerning public contracts, and does not expressly define the scope of the remedies which the member states must establish for that purpose. Therefore, the question of the extent of the judicial review exercised in the context of the national review procedures covered by Directive 89/665 must be examined in the light of the aims and objectives of the Remedies Directive. In that respect, the latter requires member states to establish review procedures that are appropriate, in the event of procedures for the award of public contracts being unlawful. Therefore, the Court maintained that, with reference to the aim of strengthening remedies pursued by Directive 89/665, and in the absence of indications to the contrary, the scope of the judicial review to be exercised in the context of the review procedures referred to therein cannot be interpreted restrictively.

Even in cases where the relevant national legislation gives the contracting author- **11.191** ities a wide discretion in relation to the withdrawal of invitations to tender, the national courts must be able, pursuant to Directive 89/665, to verify the compatibility of a decision to withdraw an invitation to tender with the relevant rules of Community law. In those circumstances, the Court held that neither the letter nor the spirit of Directive 89/665 allow for discretion on the part of member states to reduce the review of the legality of a decision of a contracting authority to

---

[90] *See* Case C-81/98 *Alcatel Austria and Others* [1999] ECR I-7671, paragraph 33 and 34.

withdraw an invitation to tender to a mere examination of the arbitrariness of such decision. The Court, therefore, concluded that Directive 89/665 precludes national legislation from limiting the review of the legality of the withdrawal of an invitation to tender to mere examination of whether that withdrawal was arbitrary.

(b) Impact of the theory of detachable acts

11.192 The Court covered the review procedures concerning the award of public contracts under the Remedies Directive 89/665/EEC, and the effects of a decision by a contracting authority to award a public contract based on grounds which are incompatible with Community law upon the legality and validity of the contract itself.[91] The national court (Austrian *Bundesvergabeamt*) sought to ascertain whether Article 2(7) of Directive 89/665, which provided for effective enforcement of decisions annulling or setting aside acts or decisions of contracting authorities which award or lead to the award of public contracts, allows for a contract concluded at the end of an award procedure, the proper conduct of which is affected by the incompatibility with Community law of a provision in the invitation to tender, must be treated as void if the applicable national law declares contracts that are illegal to be void.

11.193 The Court maintained that, if a clause in the invitation to tender, such as a prohibition on the part of the successful tenderer to have recourse to subcontracting in order to perform the contract in question, is in fact contrary to the Public Procurement Directives, it would then be a matter for the legal systems of member states to take the measures necessary to ensure that decisions taken by the contracting authorities may be reviewed effectively and as rapidly as possible in the case where those decisions may have infringed Community law on public procurement in accordance with Articles 1(1) and 2(7) of Directive 89/665.

11.194 It follows that, in the case where a clause in the invitation to tender is incompatible with Community rules on public procurement, the national legal system of the member state in question must provide for the possibility of relying on that incompatibility in the review procedures referred to in Directive 89/665. However, the Court did not pronounce on the potential effect of such incompatibility on the legality and validity of a concluded contract, indicating the fact that, in most cases, the principle *pact servanta sunt* as applied in the jurisprudence of member states will be sufficient to save the concluded contract from nullity, even in the event of it being awarded on erroneous or illegal grounds.

11.195 The Court also discussed the review proceedings under the Remedies Directive 89/665/EEC for unlawful decisions of contracting authorities. It examined the

---

[91] *See* Case C-314/01, *Siemens AG Österreich, ARGE Telekom & Partner and Hauptverband der österreichischen Sozialversicherungsträger, judgment of 18 March 2004.*

possibility of annulment of a decision or an act of a contracting authority only in the case of material influence on the outcome of the tender procedure, and pronounced on the significance of the illegality of an award criterion and, as a consequence, the obligation of the contracting authority to cancel the invitation to tender.[92]

The national court requested clarification from the European Court of Justice on whether Article 2(1)(b) of Directive 89/665 precludes a provision of national law, which makes the annulment in review proceedings of an unlawful decision by a contracting authority dependent on proof that the unlawful decision materially influenced the outcome of the procurement procedure, and whether the answer to that question must differ if the proof of that influence derives from the examination by the review body of whether the ranking of the tenders actually submitted would have been different had they been re-evaluated disregarding the unlawful award criterion. The object of the review proceedings before the European Court of Justice related, *inter alia*, to the annulment of the invitation to tender in its entirety, and the annulment of a series of individual conditions in the contract documents, and of a number of decisions of the contracting authority relating to the requirements established by the award and selection criteria used in that tender procedure. **11.196**

The Court found, in the light of the information provided by the national court (the Austrian *Bundesvergabeamt*), that all the decisions whose annulment was sought in the main proceedings had a decisive effect on the outcome of the tender procedure. On the other hand, the Court declined to provide a ruling on the question of the annulment of a series of individual conditions in the contract documents, and of a number of decisions of the contracting authority relating to the requirements established by the award and selection criteria used in that tender procedure, since it considered such question as hypothetical and, accordingly, inadmissible. **11.197**

However, the Court elaborated on the requirement of contracting authorities to cancel the invitation to tender if it transpires in review proceedings under Article 1 of Directive 89/665 that a decision relating to one of the award criteria laid down by that authority is unlawful. According to the Bundesvergabeamt, if it is assumed that the review of the effects of unlawful decisions relating to award criteria is contrary to Community law, the only alternative where such a decision is unlawful seems to be cancellation of the invitation to tender, since otherwise the tender procedure would be carried out on the basis of weighting of criteria which was neither laid down by the authority nor known by the tenderers. **11.198**

---

[92] *See* Case C-448/01, *EVN AG, Wienstrom GmbH and Republik Österreich, judgment of 4 December 2003.*

11.199   The Austrian Government submitted that Community law does not recognise an express obligation to cancel invitations to tender, just as the Directives on public procurement do not lay down a tendering obligation, and concludes that it is for the member states, acting in accordance with the principles of Community law, to lay down rules determining whether, where a decision relating to an award criterion is recognized to be unlawful, the contracting authority is obliged to cancel the invitation to tender. On the other hand, the Commission considered that, if after the tenders have been submitted or opened, the review body declares a decision relating to an award criterion unlawful, the contract cannot be awarded on the basis of the invitation to tender and the only option is to cancel the invitation to tender. Any amendment to the criteria would have an effect on the evaluation of the tenders, whereas the tenderers would no longer have the possibility of adapting their tenders, prepared at a completely different time and in different circumstances and on the basis of different criteria. The only option would therefore be to start the entire tender procedure afresh.

11.200   The Court noted that a finding that a decision relating to an award criterion is unlawful does not always lead to the annulment of that decision. As a result of the option granted to member states under Article 2(6) of Directive 89/665 providing that, after the conclusion of a contract following its award, the powers of the body responsible for the review procedures are to be limited to awarding damages to any person harmed by an infringement, where the review proceedings are instituted after the conclusion of the contract and the member state concerned has made use of the option, if the review body finds that a decision relating to an award criterion is unlawful, it may not annul that decision, but only award damages. Nevertheless, prior to the conclusion of the relevant contract, the situation appears different. The question focuses on whether Community legislation on public procurement requires the contracting authority to cancel an invitation to tender, where it transpires in review proceedings under Article 1 of Directive 89/665 that a decision relating to one of the award criteria laid down by that authority is unlawful and it is therefore annulled by the review body.

11.201   The Court has held that the principles of equal treatment and transparency of tender procedures imply an obligation on the part of contracting authorities to interpret the award criteria in the same way throughout the procedure.[93] As far as the award criteria themselves are concerned, it is *a fortiori* clear that they must not be amended in any way during the tender procedure. As a consequence, where a national review body annuls a decision relating to an award criterion, the contracting authority cannot validly continue the tender procedure leaving aside that criterion, since that would be tantamount to amending the criteria applicable to the procedure in question. Therefore, the Court pronounced that there is

---

[93] *See* Case C-19/00 *SIAC Construction*, paragraph 43.

a requirement on contracting authorities to cancel an invitation to tender, if it transpires in review proceedings under Article 1 of Directive 89/665 that a decision relating to one of the award criteria laid down by a contracting authority is unlawful and it is therefore annulled by the review body.

(c) *Locus standi* and interest to review acts

The Court stated[94] that the persons to whom review procedures must be available include, at least, any person having, or having had, an interest in obtaining a public contract who has been, or risks being, harmed by an alleged infringement.[95] The formal capacity of tenderer or candidate is not thus required. **11.202**

The Court also dealt with the scope of review procedures for the award of public contracts under Articles 1(3) and 2(1)(b) of the Remedies Directive 89/665/EEC and, in particular, the persons to whom review procedures must be available.[96] The case provided a definition of 'interest in obtaining a public contract', as a condition for *locus standi* under the Remedies Directive. **11.203**

The national court asked the European Court of Justice whether Articles 1(3) and 2(1)(b) of Directive 89/665 must be interpreted as precluding a person from being regarded, once a public contract has been awarded, as having lost his right of access to the review procedures provided for by the Directive if he did not participate in the award procedure for that contract on the ground that he was not in a position to supply all the services for which bids were invited because there were allegedly discriminatory specifications in the documents relating to the invitation to tender, but he did not seek review of those specifications before the contract was awarded. **11.204**

The Court maintained that an assessment of an aggrieved tenderer's interest in reviewing a decision or an act of a contracting authority should be examined on the fact that he did not participate in the contract award procedure, as well as the fact that he did not appeal against the invitation to tender before the award of the contract. **11.205**

(d) The failure to participate in the contract award procedure

In accordance with Article 1(3) of Directive 89/665, the member states are required to ensure that the review procedures provided for are available at least to **11.206**

---

[94] *See* C-26/03, *Stadt Halle, RPL Recyclingpark Lochau GmbH v Arbeitsgemeinschaft Thermische Restabfall und Energieverwertungsanlage TREA Leuna*, judgment of 11 January 2005.

[95] *See* Case C-212/02 *Commission v Austria* [2004] ECR I-0000, paragraph 24.

[96] *See* Case C-230/02, *Grossmann Air Service, Bedarfsluftfahrtunternehmen GmbH & Co. KG and Republik Österreich*, judgment of 12 February 2004.

any person having, or having had, an interest in obtaining a particular public contract and who has been, or risks being, harmed by an alleged infringement of the Community law on public procurement or national rules transposing that law. It follows that member states are not obliged to make those review procedures available to any person wishing to obtain a public contract, but instead, require that the person concerned has been, or risks being, harmed by the alleged infringement.[97]

11.207 In that sense, participation in a contract award procedure may, in principle, with regard to Article 1(3) of Directive 89/665, validly constitute a condition which must be fulfilled before the person concerned can show an interest in obtaining the contract at issue or that he risks suffering harm as a result of the allegedly unlawful nature of the decision to award that contract. If he has not submitted a tender, it will be difficult for such a person to show that he has an interest in challenging that decision or that he has been harmed, or risks being harmed, as a result of that award decision. However, where an undertaking has not submitted a tender because there were allegedly discriminatory specifications in the documents relating to the invitation to tender, or in the contract documents, which have specifically prevented it from being in a position to provide all the services requested, it would be entitled to seek review of those specifications directly, even before the procedure for awarding the contract concerned is terminated.

11.208 The Court maintained that, on the one hand, it would be too much to require an undertaking allegedly harmed by discriminatory clauses in the documents relating to the invitation to tender to submit a tender before being able to avail itself of the review procedures provided for by Directive 89/665 against such specifications in the award procedure for the contract at issue, even though its chances of being awarded the contract are non-existent by reason of the existence of those specifications. On the other hand, it is clear from the wording of Article 2(1)(b) of Directive 89/665 that the review procedures to be organized by the member states in accordance with the Directive must, in particular, set aside decisions taken unlawfully, including the removal of discriminatory technical, economic, or financial specifications. It must, therefore, be possible for an undertaking to seek review of such discriminatory specifications directly, without waiting for the contract award procedure to be terminated.

(e) **Absence of proceedings against the invitation to tender**

11.209 The national court sought to ascertain whether Article 1(3) of Directive 89/665 must be interpreted as meaning that it precludes a person who, not only has not participated in the award procedure for a public contract, but has not sought any

---

[97] *See* Case C-249/01, *Hackermüller* [2003] ECR I-6319, paragraph 18.

review of the decision of the contracting authority determining the specifications of the invitation to tender either, from being regarded as having lost his interest in obtaining the contract and, therefore, the right of access to the review procedures provided for by the Directive.

The European Court of Justice examined the absence of proceedings against the **11.210** invitation to tender in the light of the purpose of Directive 89/665 and, in particular, its intentions to strengthen the existing mechanisms, both at national and Community level, to ensure the effective application of Community Directives relating to public procurement, in particular, at a stage when infringements can still be remedied. To that effect, Article 1(1) of that Directive requires member states to guarantee that unlawful decisions of contracting authorities can be subjected to effective review which is as swift as possible.[98]

It must be pointed out that, the fact that a person does not seek review of a decision **11.211** of the contracting authority determining the specifications of an invitation to tender which in his view discriminate against him, insofar as they effectively disqualify him from participating in the award procedure for the contract at issue, but awaits notification of the decision awarding the contract and then challenges it before the body responsible, on the ground specifically that those specifications are discriminatory, indicates a conduct which is incompatible with the spirit and objective of the Remedies Directive 89/665. Such conduct, insofar as it may delay, without any objective reason, the commencement of the review procedures which member states were required to institute by Directive 89/665, impairs the effective implementation of the Community Directives on the award of public contracts.

In those circumstances, a refusal to acknowledge the interest in obtaining the **11.212** contract in question and, therefore, the right of access to the review procedures provided for by Directive 89/665 of a person who has not participated in the contract award procedure, or sought review of the decision of the contracting authority laying down the specifications of the invitation to tender, does not impair the effectiveness of that Directive.

Therefore, once a public contract has been awarded, an aggrieved tenderer may be **11.213** regarded as having lost his right of access to the review procedures provided for by the Directive, if he did not participate in the award procedure for that contract on the ground that he was not in a position to supply all the services for which bids were invited because there were allegedly discriminatory specifications in the documents relating to the invitation to tender, but he did not seek review of those specifications before the contract was awarded.

---

[98] *See* Case C-81/98 *Alcatel Austria and Others* [1999] ECR I-7671, paragraphs 33 and 34, Case C-470/99 *Universale-Bau and Others* [2002] ECR I-11617, paragraph 74, and Case C-410/01 *Fritsch, Chiari & Partner and Others* [2003] ECR I-6413, paragraph 30.

11.214 The Court examined the material scope of Article 1(3) of the Remedies Directive 89/665/EEC with a view to determining the persons to whom review procedures must be available and providing a definition of 'interest in obtaining a public contract'.[99]

11.215 The Court pointed out that, the fact that Article 1(3) of Directive 89/665 expressly allows member states to determine the detailed rules according to which they must make the review procedures available to any person having, or having had, an interest in obtaining a particular public contract, and who has been, or risks being, harmed by an alleged infringement, none the less does not authorize them to give the term 'interest in obtaining a public contract' an interpretation which may limit the effectiveness of that Directive.[100] Thus, Article 1(3) of Directive 89/665 precludes an undertaking which has participated in a public procurement procedure from being considered as having lost its interest in obtaining that contract on the ground that, before bringing review procedures for setting aside or annulling an act or a decision of a contracting authority, it failed to exhaust pre-judicial proceedings.

11.216 The Court examined the scope of Article 1(3) of the Remedies Directive 89/665 in respect of review procedures concerning the award of public contracts and the *locus standi* of persons that are eligible to bring such review procedures before the competent national forum.[101]

11.217 The Court pointed out that, under Article 1(3) of Directive 89/665, member states are required to ensure that the review procedures laid down by the Directive are available at least to any person having, or having had, an interest in obtaining a particular public contract and who has been, or risks being, harmed by an alleged infringement of the Community law on public procurement or the national rules implementing that law. Therefore, it is apparent that the provision does not oblige the member states to make those review procedures available to any person wishing to obtain a public contract but allows them to require, in addition, that the person concerned has been, or risks being, harmed by the infringement he alleges. The Court concluded that Article 1(3) of Directive 89/665 does not preclude the review procedures laid down by the Directive being available to persons wishing to obtain a particular public contract only if they have been, or risk being, harmed by the infringement they allege.

11.218 The national court also sought to ascertain whether a tenderer seeking to contest the lawfulness of the decision of the contracting authority not to consider his bid

---

[99] *See* Case C-410/01, *Fritsch, Chiari & Partner, Ziviltechniker GmbH and Others and Autobahnen- und Schnellstraßen-Finanzierungs-AG (Asfinag)*, ECR [2003] I-11547.

[100] *See* Case C-470/99 *Universale-Bau and Others* [2002] ECR I-11617, paragraph 72.

[101] *See* C-249/01, *Werner Hackermüller and Bundesimmobiliengesellschaft mbH (BIG), Wiener Entwicklungsgesellschaft mbH für den Donauraum AG (WED)*, ECR [2003] I-6319.

as the best bid may be refused access to the review procedures laid down by Directive 89/665, on the ground that his bid should have been eliminated at the outset by the contracting authority for other reasons and that, therefore, he neither has been, nor risks being, harmed by the unlawfulness which he alleges.

The Court reiterated that Directive 89/665 is intended to strengthen the existing **11.219** mechanisms, both at national and Community level, to ensure the effective application of the Directives relating to public procurement, in particular, at a stage when infringements can still be remedied. To that effect, Article 1(1) of that Directive requires member states to guarantee that unlawful decisions of contracting authorities can be subjected to effective review which is as swift as possible.[102] The full achievement of the objective of Directive 89/665 would be compromised, if it were permissible for a body responsible for the review procedures provided for by the Directive to refuse access to them to a tenderer alleging the unlawfulness of the decision by which the contracting authority had not considered its bid as being the best bid, on the ground that the same contracting authority was wrong not to eliminate that bid even before making the selection of the best bid. The Court pointed out that, there can be no doubt that a decision by which the contracting authority eliminates the bid of a tenderer even before making that selection, is a decision of which it must be possible to seek review under Article 1(1) of Directive 89/665, since that provision applies to all decisions taken by contracting authorities which are subject to the rules of Community law on public procurement,[103] and makes no provision for any limitation as regards the nature and content of those decisions.[104] Therefore, if the tenderer's bid had been eliminated by the contracting authority at a stage prior to that of the selection of the best bid, he would have had to be allowed, as a person who has been, or risks being, harmed by that decision to eliminate his bid, to challenge the lawfulness of that decision by means of the review procedures provided for by Directive 89/665.

In those circumstances, if a review body were to refuse access to those procedures **11.220** to a tenderer, the effect would be to deny him, not only his right to seek review of the decision he alleges to be unlawful, but also the right to challenge the validity of the ground for exclusion raised by that body to deny him the status of a person who has been, or risks being, harmed by the alleged unlawfulness. Admittedly, if, in order to mitigate that situation, the tenderer is afforded the right to challenge the validity of that ground of exclusion in the review procedure he instigates in order to challenge the lawfulness of the decision by which the contracting

---

[102] *See* Case C-81/98 *Alcatel Austria and Others* [1999] ECR I-7671, paragraphs 33 and 34, and Case C-470/99 *Universale-Bau and Others* [2002] ECR I-11617, paragraph 74.

[103] *See* Case C-92/00 *Hospital Ingenieure* [2002] ECR I-5553, paragraph 37, and Case C-57/01 *Makedoniko Metro and Michaniki* [2003] ECR I-1091, paragraph 68.

[104] *See* Case C-81/98 *Alcatel Austria and Others* [1999] ECR I-7671, paragraph 35 and Case C-92/00 *Hospital Ingenieure* [2002] ECR I-5553, paragraph 49.

authority did not consider his bid as being the best bid, it is possible that, at the end of that procedure, the review body may reach the conclusion that the bid should actually have been eliminated at the outset and that the tenderer's application should be dismissed on the ground that, in the light of that circumstance, he neither has been, nor risks being, harmed by the infringement he alleges. However, if the contracting authority has not taken a decision to exclude the tenderer's bid at the appropriate stage of the award procedure, the method of proceeding described in the previous paragraph must be regarded as the only one likely to guarantee the tenderer the right to challenge the validity of the ground for exclusion, on the basis of which the review body intends to conclude that he neither has been, nor risks being, harmed by the decision he alleges to be unlawful and, accordingly, to ensure the effective application of the Community Directives on public procurement at all stages of the award procedure.

11.221 The Court concluded that Article 1(3) of Directive 89/665 does not permit a tenderer to be refused access to the review procedures laid down by the Directive to contest the lawfulness of the decision of the contracting authority not to consider his bid as the best bid, on the ground that his bid should have been eliminated at the outset by the contracting authority for other reasons and that, therefore, he neither has been, nor risks being, harmed by the unlawfulness which he alleges. In the review procedure thus open to the tenderer, he must be allowed to challenge the ground of exclusion on the basis of which the review body intends to conclude that he neither has been, nor risks being, harmed by the decision he alleges to be unlawful.

(f) Time limits to enact review proceedings

11.222 In an interesting case,[105] the national court asked whether Directive 89/665 precludes national legislation which provides that any application for review of the decision of a contracting authority must be commenced within a specific time limit, and that any irregularity in the award procedure relied upon in support of such application must be raised within the same period.

11.223 The Court noted that, whilst the objective of Directive 89/665 is to guarantee the existence, in all member states, of effective remedies for infringements of Community law in the field of public procurement or of the national rules implementing that law, so as to ensure the effective application of the Directives on the coordination of public procurement procedures, it contains no provision specifically covering time limits for the applications for review which it seeks to establish. It is, therefore, for the internal legal order of each member state to establish such time limits. However, since there are detailed procedural rules governing the

---

[105] *See* Case C-470/99, *Universale-Bau AG, Bietergemeinschaft* ECR [2002] I-11617.

remedies intended to protect rights conferred by Community law on candidates and tenderers harmed by decisions of contracting authorities, they must not compromise the effectiveness of Directive 89/665.

The Court reiterated that Directive 89/665 is intended to strengthen the existing   **11.224**
mechanisms, both at national and Community levels, to ensure the effective application of the Directives relating to public procurement, in particular at a stage when infringements can still be corrected. To that effect, Article 1(1) of that Directive requires member states to guarantee that unlawful decisions of contracting authorities can be subjected to effective review which is as swift as possible. The full implementation of the objective sought by Directive 89/665 would be undermined if candidates and tenderers were allowed to invoke, at any stage of the award procedure, infringement of the rules of public procurement, thus obliging the contracting authority to restart the entire procedure in order to correct such infringements. Moreover, the setting of reasonable limitation periods for bringing proceedings must be regarded as satisfying, in principle, the requirement of effectiveness under Directive 89/665, since it is an application of the fundamental principle of legal certainty.[106] The Court found that Directive 89/665 does not preclude national legislation which provides that any application for review of a contracting authority's decision must be commenced within a time limit laid down to that effect, and that any irregularity in the award procedure relied upon in support of such application must be raised within the same period, provided that the time limit in question is reasonable.

In another case,[107] the national court asked the European Court of Justice what   **11.225**
time is to be taken into consideration for assessing the legality of the decision by the contracting authority to withdraw an invitation to tender. The Court maintained that, in the absence of specific Community rules governing the decisive moment for the purposes of assessing the legality of the decision to withdraw an invitation to tender, it is for the domestic legal system of each member state to determine the decisive moment for the purposes of assessing the legality of the withdrawal decision, provided that the relevant national rules are not less favourable than those governing similar domestic actions (principle of equivalence), and that they do not make it practicably impossible or excessively difficult to exercise rights conferred by Community law (principle of effectiveness).[108] The Court pronounced that determination of the time to be taken into consideration for assessing the legality of the decision by the contracting authority to withdraw

---

[106] *See* Case C-261/95 *Palmisani* [1997] ECR I-4025, paragraph 28, and Case C-78/98 *Preston and Others* [2000] ECR I-3201, paragraph 33.

[107] *See* C-92/00, *Hospital Ingenieure Krankenhaustechnik Planungs- GmbH (HI) and Stadt Wien*, ECR [2002] I-5553.

[108] *See* Case C-390/98 *Banks* v *Coal Authority and Secretary of State for Trade and Industry* [2001] ECR I-6117, paragraph 121; Case C-453/99 *Courage and Crehan* [2001] ECR I-6297, paragraph 29.

an invitation to tender is a matter for national law, provided that the relevant national rules are not less favourable than those governing similar domestic actions and that they do not make it practicably impossible or excessively difficult to exercise rights conferred by Community law.

(2) *Set aside and annulment orders in the Republic of Austria*

11.226   A complainant may apply to the Public Procurement Agency for an order annulling any of the decisions taken by a contracting authority in the course of an award procedure. For an annulment order to be available, the complainant will need to show that his legal rights, whether procedural or material, have been infringed; the contested decision will have a decisive impact on the outcome of the award procedure; and, finally, a mediation procedure was previously conducted before the Control Commission and did not lead to an agreed settlement. However, the Public Procurement Agency is not bound by any opinion given by the Control Commission during the mediation procedure.

11.227   At federal level, the annulment order can relate to any decision taken during the course of the award procedure. This arrangement is essentially the same at state level in seven of the nine Austrian regions. However, in the States of Carinthia and Vienna, a more restricted regime applies. In Carinthia, not every decision of a contracting authority may be contested. Only discriminatory specifications of an economic or technical nature contained in the tender, non-admission to a closed or negotiated procedure, or the unjustified dismissal of a tenderer may be subject to an annulment order. In Vienna, the legislation is even more restrictive. The only decisions that may be contested are technical or economic specifications in the invitation to tender which have a discriminatory effect, and the dismissal of a tenderer in a negotiated or closed procedure who complies with the specifications in the invitation to tender.

11.228   Although decisions of contracting authorities taken during an award procedure can be annulled or set aside, a signed contract cannot be annulled or suspended, even if the contract was concluded unlawfully. The Public Procurement Agency has no power to annul a contract, and under the legal principle of *pacta sunt servanta*, such power is reserved to the civil courts.

11.229   Annulment of a concluded contract is reserved to the parties of that contract and not to any aggrieved tenderers or third parties. Reasons for annulment of a concluded contract include possible infringements and violations of any aspect of law. The contracting authority may seek annulment of the contract awarded if the successful tenderer has committed a crime to obtain the award. Clauses of the tender documents, or the invitation to tender, violating fundamental principles such as the non-discrimination principle are null and void in respect of the contract awarded. The successful tenderer is not obliged to adhere to such a contract and does not need to apply to a court for its annulment.

(3) *Set aside and annulment orders in Belgium*

Complainants can request the *Conseil d'Etat* to annul any administrative decision taken in the course of an award procedure. A decision may be found to be unlawful on a number of grounds, such as a manifest error in the authority's assessment of tenders having regard to its selection criteria, or an unjustified use of the negotiated award procedure. A further ground is where the contracting authority is guilty of *détournement de pouvoir* (abuse of power), such as a deliberate policy of bias towards a particular contractor, for example, on political grounds. **11.230**

The *Conseil d'Etat* is generally willing to suspend or annul an administrative action before the contract is concluded, although the benefit of such a ruling is limited to the fact that it constitutes proof of fault in any subsequent tort action for damages in the ordinary courts. **11.231**

For an action to suspend or annul an administrative action before the award of a public contract before the *Conseil d'Etat*, a complainant must establish an injury or an interest. A complainant must show that the decision has caused him a prejudice (either material or moral), so that the suspension or annulment of the challenged decision will confer a material or moral advantage to him. The annulment of an *acte détachable* has consistently been held in case law to grant at least a moral advantage. **11.232**

Locus standi before the *Conseil d'Etat* in procurement cases is reserved to applicants who have a sufficient interest by having submitted a tender or at least showed an intention to do so. Group actions by associations of individuals are not possible. An applicant who did not participate in the contract award procedure can also have the necessary interest in challenging the award decision, if such an interest arises when the contract was not properly advertised, when the contracting authority has decided unlawfully to apply the negotiated procedure, or when the complainant was unfairly excluded from the award procedure. A rejected candidate has an interest in requesting the annulment of a final award decision even if he did not submit the lowest or most economically advantageous tender. The complainant is not therefore required to prove that, in the absence of the infringement, the contract would necessarily have been awarded to him. **11.233**

Actions for interim measures or set aside orders before the *Conseil d'Etat* must be initiated by a written petition filed within sixty days following the date on which the decision in question is published or notified. If there is no obligation to publish or notify the administrative act, the sixty day period starts immediately following the day when the party concerned first became aware of the administrative **11.234** decision. The date to take into consideration is the date on which the candidate became aware of the decision itself and not when he first knew of the elements which made it invalid. When a candidate asks the contracting authority to give reasons for its choice, such a request suspends the time limit if it is filed within the sixty day period from the date of notification of his rejection. Where the defendant authority claims that the complainant has not respected the sixty day period, the authority has the burden of proof. For his part, the rejected candidate who files a petition before the *Conseil d'Etat* must have behaved in a diligent way and taken steps to obtain information about the exact contents of the authority's decision.

11.235 The procedure for obtaining an annulment of an administrative act involves the exchange of pleadings including the request by the applicant, the response by the defendant, the applicant's reply, the report of the Auditor, and a final '*mémoire*' for each party. The *Conseil d'Etat* can request investigations, such as the designation of an expert. Interested parties are allowed to intervene. The parties are heard through their pleadings and the Auditor via his opinion. The *Conseil d'Etat* then gives its decision. The time for a decision for annulment amounts is between two and three years. However, an accelerated procedure[109] can shorten the period to the same lengths of a decision to suspend an administrative act. When the Auditor considers that the request is manifestly well founded, he immediately makes his report and the parties are convened by the President for the hearing within ten days from the submission of the Auditor's report. The President then gives his decision without delay.

11.236 There is no right of appeal from the decisions of the *Conseil d'Etat*, which is the highest administrative authority in Belgium. Judgments of the *Conseil d'Etat* have *res judicata* authority. They operate *erga omnes*, with respect to the parties, third parties and courts and tribunals. The annulled decision is held never to have been made. The administrative authority is obliged to enforce the judgment with all its consequences. Its enforcement is submitted to the control of the *Conseil d'Etat*. The res judicata authority of the judgment is of a public order (*ordre public*) nature. This signifies that any infringement of it is a serious matter and may be invoked by any third party and not just by the parties directly concerned.

11.237 A suspension judgment allows the administration to withdraw its suspended decision and to replace it. However, the administration may decide to wait for the final judgment on the merits. The suspension judgment operates *erga omnes*, so that it is also binding on third parties, such as the preferred tenderer, but is only effective *ex nunc* (from the date of the order). The enforcement obligation of the administrative authority will depend on the reason for annulment, the nature of the annulled decision, and the vested rights of the applicant and those of third parties.

---

[109] *See* Art. 94 of the Rules of Procedure of the *Conseil d'Etat*.

In most cases, a new decision will be taken under a new procedure. While the administration usually tries to comply fully with annulment judgments, it can sometimes refuse to do so. The violation of the *res judicata*, being of a public order nature, is sanctioned in different ways. The applicant can lodge a new appeal directed either against the act made in violation of the annulment judgment or against the implied decision to disobey that judgment.

The failure to comply with the judgment within a reasonable period renders the **11.238** administrative authority liable. A new request for annulment can be accompanied by a request for suspension, for interim measures and even for daily fines. The controlling authority (*autorité de tutelle*) can also require the recalcitrant authority to execute the decision. If required, the *Conseil d'Etat* can impose daily fines.

(4) Set aside and annulment orders in Denmark

The Complaints Board can annul unlawful decisions leading to the award of a **11.239** public contract and even annul the entire award procedure.[110] Such annulment may occur prior to the conclusion of the contract. Grounds for annulment include a failure to advertise a relevant contract, discrimination in favour of a particular tenderer and the application of unlawful criteria or criteria that had not been previously specified. Also, the alleged infringement must be of certain gravity and must have had a direct effect on the award decision. This reflects the general principle of Danish administrative law that infringements only lead to annulment if they are likely to have had a direct effect on the final decision. However, the burden of proof that the infringement did not have such an effect lies upon the contracting authority.

The Complaints Board takes into account the interests of all parties involved **11.240** when deciding whether to grant the annulment order, having in mind that certain degree of administrative discretion must be afforded to the contracting authorities. The Complaints Board cannot annul a contract which has already been entered into. However, its reluctance to interfere with the rights of third parties under a concluded contract does not preclude the Board from annulling an unlawful award decision, even though it cannot determine the effect of such annulment upon the concluded contract.

There are not any specific time limits within which actions must be brought **11.241** before the Complaints Board, although complainants are in practice under a general obligation to take action within a reasonable time. According to the general Danish rules on the statute of limitations, claims elapse after five years from the time when the complainant first became able to bring his claim before

---

[110] *See* Art. 5(1) of the Remedies Act.

the courts. A complaint brought before the Complaints Board suspends this five-year period with respect to the lodging of that complaint before the ordinary courts.

11.242 The procedure before the Complaints Board is governed by the same principles, laid down in the Administration of Justice Act, which apply with respect to the ordinary courts. Thus, actions are instituted by a written claim (writ of summons) which must contain an indication of the claim, a brief review of the facts supporting the claim and an indication of any documents put forward in support of the claim. The defendant's reply must contain the same type of information as the claim. In most cases, the parties will submit at least one further brief each, before the exchange of written pleadings is closed. It is a fundamental principle before the ordinary courts that the actual deliberations of the parties be conducted orally. However, before the Complaints Board, oral pleadings will only be made if the parties so request and the Chairman of the Complaints Board consents to such a procedure. Unless one of the parties objects, requests for oral pleadings are normally accepted. Otherwise the decision of the Complaints Board will be based solely upon the written pleadings. For applications for annulment orders, decisions of the Complaints Board are delivered in approximately eight months, although this may be reduced where there is urgency. Decisions of the Complaints Board cannot be appealed to any other administrative forum. The decisions of the Board are final and binding unless appealed to the ordinary courts within eight weeks from the date when the complainant was notified of the Board's decision.[111] Fines may be imposed on awarding authorities who intentionally or by gross negligence ignore decisions issued by the Complaints Board or the ordinary courts.[112]

11.243 Ordinary courts in Denmark have jurisdiction to annul unlawful administrative acts, provided such acts had or are likely to have a direct effect on the final decision of the award of a public contract. In exceptional circumstances the ordinary courts may even annul a concluded contract. This competency to annul a concluded contract is compatible with the general principle of Danish law, that the courts may set aside contracts concluded in contravention of mandatory statutory rules.

(5) Set aside and annulment orders in Finland

11.244 The Competition Council has the power to set aside or to annul decisions of contracting authorities either in their entirety or in part,[113] provided the contract has not been concluded. A set aside order may also prohibit a contracting authority

---

[111] *See* Art. 5(4) of the Remedies Act.

[112] *See* Art. 13(b) of the Remedies Act. This provision was inserted into the Remedies Act in 1995 in response to concerns raised by the European Commission to facilitate proper implementation of Art. 2(8) of Directive 92/13 which requires that the decisions of review bodies can be properly enforced. [113] *See* Art. 9 of the Act on Public Procurement.

from applying a particular provision in the tender documents or applying an unlawful procedure *in toto*. *Locus standi* is reserved for any a person who has a legal interest in challenging the wrongful procurement procedure. In practice, an action may be bought by any person having, or having had, an interest in obtaining a particular contract and who has been, or risks being, harmed by an alleged infringement.[114] Proceedings before the Competition Council may be also brought by state authorities, which have granted subsidies to certain type of works contracts.[115] The Ministry of Trade and Industry and the Ministry of Finance may, under certain circumstances, also institute proceedings before the Competition Council. Before commencing an action for interim or set aside orders before the Competition Council, the complainant must first have given prior written notice to the contracting authority of the alleged infringement and of his intention to seek review. The purpose of the notice requirement is to give the contracting authority an opportunity to rectify any defects in the award procedure. The complainant has to demonstrate that such written notice was given.

A complainant before the Competition Council should institute proceedings by way of a written application. The application must set out the grounds for the action and the remedy sought. The contracting authority is then asked to submit its response to the claim. The Competition Council may ask the parties to submit additional written pleadings. The Competition Council may hold oral hearings in which it hears evidence from the parties and any other witnesses or experts. The Council may, under the threat of a fine, oblige the parties to be present at a hearing and to provide documentation. In some cases, the parties are then asked to provide final pleadings in writing. A special feature which improves the rapid availability of interim measures is the power whereby the presiding judge of the Competition Council may, in urgent matters, rule on interim measures in the absence of the other members of the Competition Council. The rulings of the presiding judge are confirmed or cancelled in a later session of the full Competition Council. Interim measures may be granted even before the response of the contracting authority is heard, in cases where the effectiveness of such measures would otherwise be jeopardized. **11.245**

The Competition Council may order the contracting authority to correct an unlawful procedure. However, it does not have the power to correct a decision made by a contracting authority or to order that a contract be made with a particular undertaking. The Competition Council may impose a conditional fine in order to secure compliance with its rulings. A conditional fine is not necessary in relation to any set aside order of a decision of a contracting authority, as the set **11.246**

---

[114] *See* Arts. 9 and 9(a) of the Act on Public Procurement, which correspond to Art. 1(3) of the Remedies Directives.   [115] *See* Art. 9a and Art. 5(4) of the Act on Public Procurement.

aside order automatically nullifies the authority's decision. Legal proceedings before the Competition Council have to be initiated in principle before the contract in question has been signed.[116] The conclusion of the contract does not prevent an application being made to the Competition Council, provided it is launched within fourteen days from having been informed of the contract award decision.

11.247 There is a right to appeal a decision of the Competition Council before the Supreme Administrative Court.[117] The time limit for submitting an appeal is thirty days. No leave to appeal is required. Judgments of the County Administrative Courts can also be appealed to the Supreme Administrative Court within thirty days. No leave to appeal is required when the case concerns a decision by a municipal authority.

(6) Set aside and annulment orders in France

11.248 A complainant in a procurement dispute concerning an administrative contract may, before that contract has been entered into, apply to the president of the *Tribunal Administratif* in respect of a breach of the procurement rules. Any person having a personal interest in being awarded the contract under an award procedure under dispute and who is potentially harmed by the alleged infringement of the procurement rules has *locus standi*, although this does not necessarily imply that the applicant must have actually participated in the award procedures. The state representative in a *département* also has standing to bring an action if the contract in question is concluded or to be concluded by a regional or local authority. The public prosecutor has the right to bring such an action in cases where the European Commission has notified the government, in accordance with the corrective mechanism under the Remedies Directives, that a clear and manifest infringement has been committed, or that the Commission intends to bring infringement proceedings against the state under Article 234 of the EC Treaty.

11.249 The complainant is under an obligation to give prior notice to the authority of his intention to commence proceedings in actions for interim or annulment orders against public authorities before administrative or civil courts. The notice must take the form of a written request addressed to the contracting authority and asking that the authority complies with its obligations under the procurement rules. The notice must go into detail regarding the complainant's arguments and must expressly seek to persuade the authority to take the necessary measures in order to comply with its obligations under the procurement rules. The authority has ten days to reply to the notice, a period which is a necessary admissibility requirement

---

[116] *See* Art. 9 of the Act on Public Procurement.
[117] *See* Art. 12 of the Act on Public Procurement.

for the action. Failing that, the complainant may submit his application to the president of the competent court.

In cases where, during the ten-day period, a contracting authority accelerates the **11.250** concluding of a contract, to prevent an interim order—since such orders can be made only before the contract is signed—the applicant may be able to benefit from other remedies available under ordinary *référés* proceedings, as a judge has general powers to prescribe interim measures in order to prevent any imminent prejudice or to prevent manifestly unlawful conduct. Another option would be for the complainant to argue and prove that the acceleration of the conclusion of the contract during the period pending for the enactment of interim measures constitutes an abuse of law, resulting in a *détournement de pouvoir* or *détournement de procedure* and, therefore, that there are grounds for the annulment of the administrative act or decision of the contracting authority.

The president has the powers to take certain preventative measures.[118] The presi- **11.251** dent may order the contracting authority to comply with its obligations to observe public procurement rules and at the same time suspend the award of the contract or the execution of any related decision. He may also nullify such decisions and cancel clauses or conditions intended to be included in the contract. The nature of such an action is preventative as it attempts to address a complaint before the conclusion of the contract. The action must be filed before the contract is signed, whether it is an action for interim measures or one for a final annulment of decisions or draft contractual clauses. After the contract is signed, there is no longer any scope for such intervention and the judge does not have competence to adjudicate the case. No specific time limit is laid down in the legislation implementing the Remedies Directives. The only significant time constraint is that any action for an interim order, annulment order, or an order for penalty fines must be brought before the contract in question is entered into by being signed by the parties. This reflects the preventive nature of these remedies, which all seek (provisionally or finally) to restrain the contracting authority from signing a contract or from incorporating unlawful contractual clauses into a contract.

As regards actions for annulment orders, the decision of the president of the lower **11.252** court (*juge des référés*) is not subject to a full right of appeal on its merits to the *Cours d'Appel*. This does not preclude a party from filing a *pourvoi en cassation* before the *Cour de Cassation*, provided this is done within fifteen days (instead of the ordinary time limit of two months). The purpose of such a *pourvoi* is limited to a review of the legality of the decision itself, which may be cancelled only if it contravenes certain basic legal principles to which any judgment must conform.

---

[118] *See* Law No. 92-10 gives the president the power to take certain preventative measures, by stipulating that Art. L 22 of the *Code des Tribunaux Administratifs et des Cours Administratives d'Appel* applies in relation to procurement infringements.

The facts and merits of a claim cannot be discussed again in the *Cour de Cassation*. Similarly, an order by the *juge des référés* imposing a provisional penalty fine upon a utility is not subject to a full right of appeal. However, a full right of appeal to the *Cour d'Appel* does exist where the judge decides to convert a provisional penalty fine into a final penalty. A failure of public authorities to comply with judgments of administrative courts could, prompt the matter being referred to the *Médiateur de la République* (a type of ombudsman).

(7) Set aside and annulment orders in Germany

11.253 Provided the contract in question has not been concluded, a complainant may apply to the Procurement Chamber for the set aside or the annulment of unlawful acts taken by the contracting authority in the course of an award procedure. The Procurement Chamber examines the lawfulness of the contested award procedure upon an application by any person concerned. In particular, the Chamber examines whether any of the procurement rules applicable have been infringed. Any breach of the procurement rules, irrespective of being particularly serious or concerning essential legal provisions, gives rise to the finding that the award procedure is unlawful. Any violations of rules which aim at protecting the rights of participants in award procedures indicate that the award procedure is unlawful.

11.254 Any person who has an interest in a relevant contract or who claims a violation of his rights by infringement of procurement rules or who suffered, or could probably suffer, damages by the alleged infringement of procurement rules may initiate a review procedure before the Procurement Chamber in respect of an alleged infringement of the procurement rules, provided he did not become aware of that infringement during the award procedure. The Procurement Chamber may intervene only upon application, but not *ex officio*, even if it has reasons to believe that the procurement rules have been violated. The applicant has the right to appeal against a Chamber's decision to the Procurement Division at the Court of Appeal. *Locus standi* is also reserved for contracting authorities and any bidder whose interests were seriously affected by a decision of the contracting authority. Third parties who did not participate in the original procurement procedure do not have *locus standi* before the Procurement Chamber or the Procurement Division. The Procurement Chamber has to examine the compatibility and compliance of the award procedure in question with the applicable rules.[119] It may request from the contracting authority all relevant information it deems necessary for the purposes of factual and legal assessment. The parties of the procedure must be heard. The Procurement Chamber may set time limits to the parties after which further statements of the parties may be disregarded. In principle, the decision is

---

[119] *See* Art.s §§ 107–115 of *Gesetzgegen Wettbewerbsbeschränkungen*.

to be taken on the basis of an oral hearing, but, if the parties agree, a decision on the basis of submitted documents is possible.

There is no time limit for bringing a complaint before the Procurement Chamber. **11.255**
Complainants nevertheless have an interest in acting swiftly, since the powers of the Procurement Chamber are merely declaratory once the contract in question has been awarded. The suspensory effect of the procedures before the Procurement Chamber, any interim measures or annulment orders are only available if the complainant intervenes before the contract is concluded.

The Procurement Chamber may order the contracting authority to take adequate **11.256**
measures in order to annul unlawful measures or to adopt measures which restore the lawfulness of the award procedures. When the contract has been concluded, neither the Procurement Chamber nor the Procurement Division at the Court of Appeal have jurisdiction to set it aside or annul it. If a contracting authority enters into or awards the contract, before the Procurement Chamber has had the opportunity to act, that Chamber will in all cases be limited to a mere declaratory decision, which has legal significance in a subsequent case for action for damages. Due to the exclusive competence of the Procurement Chamber as a review body of first instance, there is no recourse to the administrative courts to annul a concluded contract between a contracting authority and an undertaking. However, in principle, civil courts may annul a contract which has been concluded in contravention to the suspension of the award procedures,[120] which is regarded as a breach of an express legal prohibition.

The decision of the Procurement Chamber contains a finding of whether the **11.257**
rights of the complainant have been violated and the appropriate measures to be taken in order to put an end to the violation and avoid any further damages. The Procurement Chamber is not bound by the application of the complainant, to the extent that it can order any measures it deems necessary to restore the lawfulness of the award procedure. A legal notice informing the complainant about the possibility of appeal against this decision and the competent review body *(Procurement Division at the Court of Appeal)* must be attached to the decision.

The Procurement Chamber has to deliver its final decision on the substantive **11.258**
application within five weeks after receiving an application. In extraordinary cases with factual or legal difficulties the Chairman of the Chamber can extend the time limit. If the Chamber does not deliver its decision within that time limit, the application is considered as rejected. The complainant is nevertheless entitled to appeal against it. Even though there is no express time limit for the decisions about interim measures (permission to award the contract immediately), the Chamber has to reach a decision within shorter period than the five week period

---

[120] *See* Art. § 134 BGB *Bürgerliches Gesetzbuch* (German Civil Code).

stipulated for the delivery of its judgments. The decisions of a Procurement Chamber may be appealed within two weeks before the Procurement Division at the Court of Appeal. Although a decision taken by a Procurement Chamber is an administrative act (*Verwaltungsakt*), its legality cannot be reviewed by the administrative courts because of the exclusive competence of the Procurement Chamber for reviewing public procurement award procedures.

11.259 An appeal against a final decision issued by a Procurement Chamber may only be submitted to the Procurement Division within two weeks after notification of the Chamber's decision to the complainant.[121] The procedure before the Procurement Division at the Court of Appeal[122] follows the normal rules which regulate civil procedures in the organization of justice.[123] The parties involved in the procedure of Procurement Division at the Court of Appeal must be the same parties involved in the review procedure of the first instance before a Procurement Chamber[124] and must be represented by a lawyer who is admitted to a German court. An appeal to the Procurement Division at the Court of Appeal suspends[125] the decision of the Procurement Chamber. Depending on whether there have been applications concerning the suspension of the award procedure, or decisions granting or denying the suspension of the award procedure during the first instance procedures before the Procurement Chamber, the suspension of the award procedure continues until the final decision the Procurement Division at the Court of Appeal. The decisions to be taken by the Procurement Division at the Court of Appeal depend on whether the contracting authority has brought an application for a preliminary decision on the award of the contract together with the appeal. In this case, the Procurement Division may allow the contracting authority to continue the award procedure or award the contract in question, after taking into account the prospect of success of the pending appeal or after applying a balance of interests test.

11.260 In its decision, the Procurement Division also has to explain the lawfulness or unlawfulness of the award procedure. The Procurement Division at the Court of Appeal may confirm the Procurement Chamber's decision, or annul it and then replace it by its own substantive decision, or order the Procurement Chamber to adopt a new decision taking into account the legal guidelines of the Procurement Division at the Court of Appeal. The decisions of the Procurement Division must contain, *inter alia*, the names of the members of the Division and of the parties, the finding and the reasons upon which the decision is based. The Procurement Division decides by an absolute majority of its members, and the decision has to be sent to the parties without undue delay. Since the Procurement Division at the

---

121 *See* Art. § 117 of *Gesetzgegen Wettbewerbsbeschränkungen*.
122 *See* Art. § 120 of *Gesetzgegen Wettbewerbsbeschränkungen*.
123 *See* Zivilprozeßordnung—ZPO (German Civil Procedure Code).
124 *See* Art. § 119 of *Gesetzgegen Wettbewerbsbeschränkungen*.
125 *See* Art. § 118 of *Gesetzgegen Wettbewerbsbeschränkungen*.

Court of Appeal is an integrated part of the ordinary Court of Appeal, it is considered as a court of last instance and is eligible to refer questions to the European Court of Justice under Article 234 of the EC Treaty.

There is no time limit to deliver a decision by the Procurement Division at the Court **11.261** of Appeal, although the average time is ten months. There is also no time limit for the decisions on the applications (to restore the suspensive effect or to allow the immediate award of the contract) that can be lodged as recourse against the Chamber's interim decisions to allow or prohibit the immediate award of the contract. But the Procurement Division is obliged to deliver its ruling to allow the award of the contract within five weeks after the application for that permission. There is no appeal to the decisions of the Procurement Division at the Court of Appeal.

Article 20 III of the German Constitution obliges the administration to act in a **11.262** lawful manner (*Gesetzmäßigkeit der Verwaltung*). Decisions of the Procurement Chambers are administrative acts (*Verwaltungsakte*).[126] They are addressed to the complainant and have to include the necessary information for judicial review by the Procurement Division at the Court of Appeals.[127] However, their enforcement rests within the remit of German administrative law, which provides for the enforcement of the *Verwaltungsakt* according to the provisions of the relevant federal or state enforcement law.[128] The enforcement of a decision of a Procurement Chamber falls within the competence of the relevant *Verwaltungsvollstreckungsgesetz*, which may allow for *substitute performance* (*Ersatzvornahme*) or a periodic penalty payment (*Zwangsgeld*) in those cases where a party refuses to observe the decision of the Procurement Chamber. Decisions of the Procurement Division at the Court of Appeal are considered as court judgments and may be enforced in the same way as a judgment following a civil court proceeding for damages[129] before the *Amts* or *Landgerichte*. Decisions of the Procurement Chamber or the Procurement Division at the Court of Appeals on the legality of a public procurement award procedure have a binding effect on the judge in a civil law procedure for the recovery of damages.[130]

(8) *Set aside and annulment orders in Greece*

Administrative courts have jurisdiction in cases where annulment of the **11.263** award decision itself or an unlawful administrative act taken during a contract

---

[126] *See* Art. § 114 III of *Gesetz gegen Wettbewerbsbeschränkungen*.

[127] *See* § 61 of *Gesetz gegen Wettbewerbsbeschränkungen*.

[128] *See Verwaltungsvollstreckungsgesetz des Bundes*, (VwVG), and *Verwaltungsvollstreckungsgesetze der Länder* (LVwVG).

[129] The enforcement of civil judgments is governed by Article §§ 704, 724, 750 ZPO *Zivilprozeßordnung* (German Civil Procedure Code).

[130] *See* Art. § 124 of *Gesetz gegen Wettbewerbsbeschränkungen*.

award procedure is sought. A set aside order is usually successful when a breach of the procurement rules occurs. Such breach usually provides adequate grounds for annulment of the award decision. When a contract has been concluded on the basis of the unlawful award decision, the annulment of that award decision has the effect of rendering the contract itself null and void. However, a concluded contract can only be set aside or annulled if the contract has been declared null and void by a final court decision. An application for annulment has to contain the specific grounds for the annulment. Additional grounds may also be presented in a separate document which must be filed at least fifteen days prior to the hearing. An action for set aside or annulment of a decision awarding a contract may last for two years.

11.264   *Locus standi* to challenge administrative decisions before administrative courts is reserved to complainants who must have a personal, direct, and legitimate interest in the decision in question. Jurisprudence shows that such interest is met when the applicant is a candidate who participated in an award procedure and, as a consequence, has a legitimate interest in challenging the award decision of the contracting authority. However, persons who did not participate in an award procedure for a public contract do not fulfil the requirements of a personal, direct, and legitimate interest to contest the decision of the contracting authority. The time limit for bringing an action for annulment in the administrative courts is sixty days from the date on which the contested act is published or notified. In the absence of publication or notification, the sixty days starts to run from the date on which the complainant became aware of the contested act. Should the authority fail to respond to the complaint, the sixty-day time limit begins to run three months after the filing of that complaint. In practice, the obligatory non-judicial phase frequently has the effect of delaying the commencement of an action in the *Symvoulion Epikratias* by a period of three months. The statute of limitation for commencing actions in the civil courts is five years.

11.265   Decisions of the administrative courts of first instance can be appealed to the Administrative Court of Appeal, within thirty days from the delivery of the Court's decision. The final rulings of the Administrative Court of Appeal or the *Symvoulion Epikratias* can be appealed to the *Symvoulion Epikratias* (Appeals Section) within sixty days of the delivery of the Court's decision. A judgment of an administrative court which annuls an administrative act is directly enforceable against the authority in question, as is an interim order laid down by the Injunction Committee of the *Symvoulion Epikratias* or by a civil court.

(9) Set aside and annulment orders in Ireland

11.266   The Irish High Court has the power to set aside unlawful decisions taken in a procurement procedure. The court may also order the amendment of any documents relating to the award procedure, such as the invitation to tender in order to remove discriminatory specifications. The court clearly has the power to make such orders prior to the contract in question being entered into and is likely to apply a balance of interests test similar to the one applied when assessing applications for interim order.

The rules of the High Court specify that an application for leave to apply for judi- **11.267** cial review must be made promptly and in any event within three months from the date when grounds for the application first arose (or six months where the relief sought is *certiorari*) unless the court considers that there is good reason for extending the period. It appears that a court would extend the three-month period where there is some delay between the occurrence of the breach and the time when the application could reasonably be expected to become aware of that breach. For instance, where the breach consists of a failure to advertise a relevant contract, the time limit might only start to run from the date when the complainant knew, or could reasonably be expected to have known, that the contracting authority had awarded a contract without properly advertising it.

When a public contract within the remit of the Public Sector Directives, after its **11.268** award, has been concluded between the contracting authority and an undertaking, the High Court may declare such contract, or any provision of such contract, to be void.[131] The court may also declare that the contract may have effect only subject to such variation as the court determines, including any variation required to protect the interests of party to the contract who is not responsible for the infringement, such as a third party to whom the contract has been awarded. Finally the court may make such other order concerning the validity of the contract or any provision of it. For contracts in the utilities sectors,[132] the High Court does not have authority to declare contracts void or subject to variation or to make any other order concerning the validity of the contract. It may therefore be implied that set aside and amendment orders are not available against utilities once the contract in question has been entered into.

A party may wish to proceed by making an application for *judicial review*, in **11.269** addition, or as an alternative, to proceedings brought pursuant to the Remedies Directives. The following remedies are available in judicial review proceedings: an order restraining the decision-making body from acting outside its jurisdiction (*prohibition*); quashing the decision and requiring it to reconsider the matter (*certiorari*); an order requiring the body to carry out its judicial or other public duty (*mandamus*); the granting of an injunction; and, depending on the type of claim, an award of damages against the decision-making body.

---

[131] *See* SI 1994/309.   [132] *See* SI 1993/104.

11.270 The applicant for judicial review must first seek leave of the High Court to commence proceedings. Any application for leave must be made promptly and, in any event, within three months from the date when the grounds for the application first arose (or six months where the relief sought is *certiorari*), unless the High Court considers that there is a good reason for extending the period. An applicant is required to demonstrate an arguable case. If leave is granted, the applicant is directed to proceed by way of an originating Notice of Motion in most cases. The defendant is usually given a relatively short period after service, usually four weeks, within which to file opposition papers. In practice, the time limit can be extended for a further two months, by consent, in order to allow the defendant to prepare its affidavits. The substantive application will be heard by a judge of the High Court, usually in public. Judicial review proceedings are usually determined by reference to affidavit evidence, without some of the other formal procedures which apply in ordinary civil cases. In certain cases, other formal procedures, such as discovery of documents may apply, by agreement of the parties or by order of the Court.

11.271 Decisions of the High Court may be appealed to the Supreme Court of Appeal. In some cases, the leave of the High Court judge or the Supreme Court of Appeal is may be needed. Appeals may only be brought on a point of law; an appeal does not involve a re-hearing of the High Court action. The appeal will usually be heard by three (or, exceptionally, five) judges of the Supreme Court. In the event that a contracting authority or utility fails to observe the terms of an interim order or a set aside order, the officers of that body would be in contempt of court. In the first instance, they are likely to be required to attend the court in order to explain the contempt and to rectify it. If the relevant officers failed to do so, they would face the risk of committal to prison.

(10) Set aside and annulment orders in Italy

11.272 The *Tribunali Amministrativi Regionali* are competent to review the acts and measures, both in form and in substance, of administrative bodies, and have jurisdiction over any dispute involving the legality of an administrative measure which violates a legitimately protected interest. A set aside order can be granted based on three specific grounds: a) incompetence, where an administrative organ exceeds its organizational and jurisdictional competence; b) violation of the law; and c) excess of power, which includes grounds such as an incorrect factual evaluation, illogical, insufficient or contradictory reasoning, and unequal or discriminatory treatment. For the *locus standi* before the *Tribunali* an applicant must show an interest in commencing proceedings. This principle seems to satisfy the requirements laid down in Article 1(3) of the Remedies Directive, where review procedures must be available to any person having, or having had, an interest in obtaining a particular supply or public works contract, and who has been, or risks being, harmed by an alleged infringement. An *actio popularis* brought by a person who was not affected by the contested measure is inadmissible. An action brought by an organization representing contractors who did not take part in the procurement procedure and therefore were not affected by the contested measure is inadmissible.

The *Tribunali* may annul *in toto* or in part the administrative measure in cases of **11.273** violation of the law or excess of power. Furthermore, it may annul the administrative measure and refer the matter to the competent authority in cases of incompetence, and, finally, order payment of costs by the public authority at fault. The *Tribunali* has the power to set aside the award decision of a contracting authority and simultaneously award the contract to the aggrieved tenderer, if is satisfied that the contract would have been awarded to him in the absence of the breach. In exceptional cases, the *Tribunali* have jurisdiction to review the merits of an administrative act and to adopt a decision which replaces the contested administrative measure.[133]

The *Tribunali* do not have jurisdiction over a concluded contract between a **11.274** contracting authority and one or more undertakings. A concluded contract is not an administrative contract and is governed by the rules of private law. In principle, an aggrieved tenderer may rely upon Article 1418 of the Civil Code, which provides that a contract is void if it is contrary to mandatory rules. On this ground, it is arguable that the infringement of the procurement rules affects the validity of the contract and enables the disappointed bidder to institute judicial proceedings before the ordinary courts, claiming the nullity of the contract. Furthermore, under Article 1425 of the Civil Code, a public authority may rely before ordinary courts upon infringements in the award procedure for the purposes of annulling the contract on grounds that its contractual freedom and choice were restricted by the violation of the (procedural) public procurement rules. However, a claim for damages before ordinary court appears as the only realistic and viable remedy, once a public procurement contract is concluded.

An application before the *Tribunali Amministrativi Regionali* to set aside an **11.275** administrative act is commenced by serving a *ricorso* (equivalent to an application for judicial review) upon the public authority which issued the contested measure or the State Attorney *(Avvocatura dello Stato)* in the case of public ministries, and upon any interested parties. The application must be lodged within sixty days of the communication of the measure to the applicant.

---

[133] Such jurisdiction is exceptional and strictly limited by law to specific subject matters, which include public loan agreements, the establishment of institutions of public education institutions, and state expenditure in the field of public health. *See* Art. 67 of Law No. 1034 of 1971: *Legge di Tribunali Amministrativi Regionali.*

11.276 The proceedings take place in two phases. Firstly, the instruction phase, where the applicant must prove that his claim is not manifestly unfounded. The administrative judges can order whatever measures are necessary in order to obtain evidence, in particular by requesting production of documents as well as any necessary verification and clarification. Secondly, the decision phase, where the *Tribunali* formally adopts a decision and either sets aside the act of a contracting authority under which a public contract was awarded or dismisses the application. The decision before the *Tribunali Amministrativi Regionali* for annulment of an administrative act, could take up to nine years at first instance and up to three years on appeal.

11.277 A decision of the *Tribunali Amministrativi Regionali* may be appealed to the Council of State at second instance within sixty days of the notification of the judgment to the claimant. The case is fully heard by the Council of State, which can issue a new decision on the merits replacing the ruling of the *Tribunali*. The case may be referred to the *Tribunali Amministrativi Regionali* where the appeal is allowed on the ground of procedural defects, or the judgment contained formal defects, or the *Tribunali* incorrectly declared itself incompetent. The judgment of the Council of State can be appealed before the Court of Cassation only on legal grounds. The enforcement of judgments of the *Tribunali Amministrativi Regionali* is not automatically suspended by an appeal, but only by a decision of the Council of State where immediate enforcement could give rise to serious and irreparable damage.

11.278 Where public authorities fail to observe a judgment of the *Tribunali Amministrativi Regionali*, the interested party may bring enforcement proceedings in the administrative courts (*giudizio di ottemperanza*). The *Tribunali* will then determine a period within which the public authority is bound to comply with the judgment, after which the court will adopt any necessary act to enforce the judgment or, alternatively, appoint an *ad hoc* officer to adopt any necessary act to enforce the judgment.

(11) Set aside and annulment orders in Luxembourg

11.279 An action for annulment is brought before possible the Administrative Tribunal, pursuant to an application for annulment (*recours en annulation*). *Locus standi* requirements before the Administrative Tribunals must satisfy that the applicant has an interest which is personal, direct, and current. In public procurement cases, this included tenderers who participated in an award procedure. However, those who did not participate directly in the award procedure do not have *locus standi*. The President of the Administrative Tribunal may grant an order setting aside decisions or parts of decisions, such the removal of discriminatory specifications taken unlawfully during the course of a contract award procedure. However, the President does not have any power to cancel the award of a contract by a public authority. The time limit for lodging an application with the Administrative Tribunal is three months after the notification of the decision in question. If the applicant is not a resident of Luxembourg, the time limit is extended to four months. These time limits may, however, be interrupted by an application to the Minister or the Tender Commission to reconsider the negative decision which has been taken. The deadlines run from the date of the formal notification of the decision, even if the recipient of the notification had knowledge of the irregularity before the decision has been notified.

The procedure before the Administrative Tribunal is mainly a written one, involv- **11.280** ing the exchange of written pleadings. The procedure is introduced by the complainant filing a petition (*requéte*) in writing with the Tribunal. The parties then exchange their written pleadings, known as *mémoires*, with each party being entitled to submit a maximum of two *mémoires*. After these have been exchanged, an oral hearing is fixed by the Tribunal, where the parties generally only give a few supplementary oral explanations regarding factual details. An oral hearing will always be held, although the most important part of the procedure remains the written pleadings.

The Tribunal does not have the power to substitute the quashed award decision of **11.281** a contracting authority but it refers the matter back to the administrative body requesting the adoption of a lawful decision. In the meantime, if the contract between the contracting authority and an undertaking has been concluded, the annulment of the award decision has no legal effects on the validity and legality of that contract. The judgments of the Administrative Tribunal can be appealed to the newly-created Administrative Court at second instance and the *Conseil d'Etat* for review of last instance.

The annulment of an administrative act by the Administrative Tribunal and any **11.282** interim suspension order granted by the Tribunal's President is binding. The Luxembourg administrative law system has conferred limited powers on complainants to enforce the judgment of the Administrative Tribunal after the challenged administrative decision has been set aside. If the public authority does not comply with the judgment, the applicant may apply to the Administrative Tribunal after three months have expired from the delivery of the judgment, for the nomination of a special commissioner who will then take a new decision in lieu of the administrative body in question. However, the enforcement of a judgment which annuls an act awarding a public contract has limited practical implications, as the concluded contract is not affected by an unlawful award decision.

For utilities operating in the public sector, the President of the Administrative **11.283** Tribunal has competence to set aside decisions awarding contracts taken by such utilities. For utilities which are private entities, the competent forum to set aside or annul a decision of the utility awarding a contract is vested with the President of the District Tribunal, sitting as a judge of summary proceedings. This civil judge is given the power to award interim orders and set aside orders, suspending the award procedure, or modifying or deleting technical specifications.[134] The President of the District Tribunal is also empowered to order dissuasive payments upon the private utility if a wrongful or illegal clause, which would cause damage, is not modified or deleted.[135] The President of the District Tribunal may also initiate the conciliation procedure provided by the Remedies Directive for utilities.[136]

(12) Set aside and annulment orders in The Netherlands

11.284 The District Court and the *Raad van Arbitrage* have the power to set aside unlawful decisions taken in the course of a procurement procedure. They may also order the annulment of a concluded contract awarded pursuant to such a procedure, provided the contract has not been performed.

11.285 An action before the *Raad van Arbitrage* must be brought within a period of three months after the written confirmation of the award of a public contract by a contracting authority.[137] Exceptionally, an action is only allowed after the three month period if the applicant proves that he was not aware of the contract award within the three months.

11.286 *Locus standi* before the *Raad van Arbitrage* requires that the complainant must have an interest and that the dispute in question falls under the jurisdictional remit (compulsorily or voluntarily) of the *Raad* by virtue of the *Uniform Aanbestedingsreglement* (Uniform Regulation of Procurement). An aggrieved tenderer must have participated in the award procedure. In cases where the contracting authority failed to observe either the open or restricted procedures, the *Uniform Aanbestedingsreglement* (Uniform Regulation of Procurement) does not apply, by default, and the dispute is declared inadmissible, as the *Raad* does not have competence. In such cases, the application should be addressed to the District Court. Trade organizations representing construction undertakings which may be registered in the Netherlands or in another European member state, do have *locus standi*. Complaints by other organizations would not normally be admissible.

11.287 Actions are commenced before the *Raad van Arbitrage* by way of a written request. The complainant has to pay a deposit for the costs of the proceedings. The President of the *Raad van Arbitrage* invites the parties to agree on the appointment

---

134 *See* Art.s 2.1(a) and 2.1(b) of Utilities Remedies Directive 92/13.
135 *See* Art. 2.1(c) of Directive 92/13.   136 *See* Art.s 9 to 11 of Directive 92/13.
137 *See* Art. 67.3 of the *Uniform Aanbestedingsreglement EG* 1991.

of arbitrators and, in case they fail to reach agreement, he appoints either one or three arbitrators from the list of members of the *Raad*. After delivering written memoranda, the parties appear in a hearing where each side presents its arguments. Intervention by third parties is permissible. In addition to the normal proceedings before the *Raad*, acceleration proceedings and interlocutory proceedings are allowed. The decision of the *Raad* is made in the form of an arbitration award which is legally binding and can be enforced by an enforcement order of a civil court. The decisions of the *Raad* are almost always given following accelerated proceedings, which lead to a decision on the substance of the case within four weeks. It is not considered necessary to apply for interlocutory proceedings before the *Raad*.

The Dutch Civil Code stipulates that a civil court can annul decisions of **11.288** arbitrators if, amongst other things, the decision its proceedings are contrary to the public order. Since compliance with public procurement rules is regarded as a matter of public order by both the *Raad* and the District Courts, a decision of the *Raad* can be appealed to a District Court on the ground that a Directive has been breached. The decisions of the *Raad* can be enforced with an enforcement order (*exequatur*) of the District Court.[138] The court may refuse to grant such an order if it considers the decision of the *Raad* to be manifestly contrary to public order. The *Raad* will usually impose a conditional penalty, which becomes payable in the event that its decision is not observed.

The District Court would grant set aside orders solely on the basis that there has **11.289** been an infringement of the procurement rules and without carrying out a detailed analysis of the balance of interests. The *Raad van Arbitrage* would annul a concluded contract only in cases that the award was made in breach of the procurement rules and the complainant would have been awarded the contract had the contracting authority observed the procurement rules.

Before the District Courts, there are no particular requirements for *locus standi*, **11.290** other than that the complainant must have a clear interest. Rejected tenderers or candidates have admissible claims. If the contract is awarded without publicity, every party which could have been a candidate if the procedure had been properly advertised may lodge a claim. However, undertakings which have not participated in the award procedure, and cannot substantiate that they would have been qualified had the infringement of the advertising rules not occurred, would not have *locus standi*. Trade organizations, such as trade associations which may be registered in the Netherlands or in another European member state, can bring an action before the District Court if the organization has a legal personality and its articles of association affirm that one of its objectives is to protect the interest of its members.

---

[138] *See* Art. 1062 of the Code on Civil Procedure.

11.291 An action before the District Courts is commenced by a writ of summons which must be served by a bailiff or a process server. For accelerated proceedings, an authorization of the President of the District Court is compulsory. In interlocutory proceedings, once the writ of summons has been served, a hearing is held. In other proceedings, the parties are requested to submit written memoranda and a hearing is held only if the parties request it.

11.292 In interlocutory proceedings, the President of the relevant District Court delivers his decision in an enforceable preliminary judgment which may contain an order to take interlocutory measures. In other proceedings on the substance of the case, an enforceable judgment is given by the relevant District Court. Before the District Courts, interlocutory proceedings are often followed. These proceedings last for two months but, if the matter is sufficiently urgent, the period may be shortened. Accelerated proceedings in the District Courts tend to last at least six months. Normal proceedings before the civil courts tend to last for at least a year.

11.293 All judgments of the District Court can be appealed before the Court of Appeal.[139] A judgment of the District Court is enforceable, since it is considered an executory title within the meaning of the Code on Civil Procedure. The District Court may impose a conditional penalty on a contracting authority when it suspects a possible breach of the judgment. If a decision of the District Court has not been observed, it is possible to demand the imposition of a penalty in interlocutory proceedings.

(13) Set aside and annulment orders in Portugal

11.294 A complainant may lodge an action for the annulment of the final award decision taken by a contracting authority before administrative courts. All directly-interested parties may bring an action to challenge an administrative act. In procurement cases, such parties would clearly include all those who participated in the award procedure and submitted bids for the contract in question. Other potentially-interested parties who did not take part in the procurement process will have *locus standi*. Any action for annulment in the administrative courts must be brought within two months if the complainant is domiciled in Portugal or within four months if the complainant is domiciled abroad.[140] These periods normally start to run from the date of notification or publication of the relevant administrative decision. However, in cases where an authority fails to take or communicate a particular decision, the time period is one year and begins to run from the date on which it is tacitly understood that an application has been

---

[139] *See* Art. 1065 of the Code on Civil Procedure.
[140] *See* the Law on Administrative Procedure (LPTA).

refused. In the context of procurement, the time limit starts to run from the date on which the necessary hierarchical appeal is expressly or tacitly rejected.

An action to annul an administrative decision begins with the filing of a written **11.295** claim (*recurso contencioso*) in the competent administrative court, which could be the *Supremo Tribunal Administrativo* (Administrative Supreme Court), or the *Tribunais Administrativos de Círculo* (Administrative Circle Courts). The entire procedure is conducted in writing and there are generally no oral hearings before the court.[141] In that claim, the complainant must *inter alia* set out the grounds for the complaint, referring to the rules and legal principles that have allegedly been infringed by the contracting authority adopting the challenged administrative decision. The claim must provide details of the parties and name any interested third parties who would be harmed if the administrative decision in question were annulled, such as the successful bidder to whom the contract in question has been awarded.

The contracting authority must submit its defence within one month after the **11.296** claim has been served upon it and, within the same time limit, deliver to the court the original or a certified copy of its administrative file for the award procedure in question. Then, any interested third parties are requested to submit their defences within twenty days. After all defences have been submitted, and before the court's decision is taken, the parties are requested to present their written point of law. Except in particular cases such as those involving administrative decisions of local or regional authorities, the only admissible evidence is documentary evidence and, when the court allows, expert witnesses. During the proceedings, the administrative judges are assisted by the Public Prosecution Service.

The administrative courts may annul other decisions or acts taken during the **11.297** course of the procurement procedure, to the extent that these decisions or acts bear a direct influence on the final award decision. The administrative courts may annul the final award decision even if the contract in question has been concluded. When the award of a contract is annulled, the contracting authority must launch fresh procurement procedures. However, where the contract has been concluded and been partially performed the contracting authority could successfully put forward grounds for non-execution of the annulment decision, namely impossibility or serious damage to the public interest.

The *Tribunais Administrativos de Círculo* (Administrative Circle Courts) are **11.298** courts of first instance and their rulings may be appealed to the *Supremo Tribunal Administrativo* (Administrative Supreme Court). The *Supremo Tribunal*

---

[141] *See* Arts. 24 to 58 of the Law on Administrative Procedure (LPTA) which stipulates all procedural requirements for bringing an action of annulling of an administrative decision, and actions for interim suspension orders.

Administrativo (Administrative Supreme Court) is both a court of first instance and a court of appeal. When exercising appellate jurisdiction, the Administrative Supreme Court is a court of last resort. When a proceeding is initiated at first instance to that court, its ruling may generally be appealed to the *Pleno da Secção di Contencioso Administrativo do Supremo Tribunal Administrativo* (Full Bench of the Administrative Division of the Supreme Administrative Court). An appeal may be submitted by the losing party, by a person directly harmed by the court's ruling, or by the Public Prosecution Service, within ten days following the notification of the court ruling.

11.299 Under the Portuguese constitution, administrative authorities are under a general duty to execute any decision by an administrative court which annuls an administrative decision. A duty to enforce the decision of an administrative court requires the replacement of the decision in question by a valid one and the correction of the effects of the annulled act. If the court's annulment order is not executed within thirty days, the complainant may request the execution of that decision. The authority is then obliged to execute the court's decision within sixty days of that request. If it fails to do so, the complainant may revert to the administrative court in order to seek further remedies, including the possible payment of an indemnity. Contracting authorities may claim that there are good grounds for not executing a court decision, such as the risk of serious damage to the public interest. In the absence of such grounds, continued non-execution of court decisions may ultimately result in civil, disciplinary, or criminal sanctions against the persons representing the contracting authority.

(14) Set aside and annulment orders in Spain

11.300 A complainant may apply to the court for the annulment of any administrative act taken during an award procedure which breaches public procurement rules. Any party who has had a direct interest in the effects of an administrative decision may seek to challenge that decision in the administrative courts, provided the preliminary administrative phase has first been exhausted. In relation to public procurement, any party which has taken part in the award procedure will be regarded as having the necessary direct interest in its outcome. Those tenderers who have not participated in the award procedure are not to be regarded as directly interested. The time limit for commencing an action before the administrative courts depends on the way in which the preliminary administrative phase is concluded. If the complaint to the administrative authority is expressly rejected, the deadline to bring an action before the competent administrative court is two months from the date on which that rejection is notified to the complainant. If the complaint is presumed to have been rejected by the administrative authority, an action before administrative courts may be brought within one year from the date on which the implicit rejection of the complaint is deemed to have taken place. In those cases where the contested decision is not subject to an administrative complaints phase, for example, where the contracting authority is not supervised by any superior authority, the time limit is two months from the date on which the contested administrative decision is notified or published.

An action before the administrative courts begins with the filing of a short writ **11.301** referring to the subject matter of the case, the writ, a power of attorney of the court *procurador* or attorney representing the complainant, a copy of the act being appealed, and a copy of the complainant's prior communication to the contracting authority of the complainant's intention to file the appeal. The court will then give notice of it in the relevant official bulletin. It will also demand a copy of the administrative file from the contracting authority, which the latter must then submit within twenty days.

Once the court has received the administrative file, it will deliver it to the com- **11.302** plainant. The complainant then files its claim within twenty days, following which the contracting authority and any other joined parties are given twenty days to file their reply. The claim and the reply must state the facts, the legal grounds relied on, and the demands of the parties, attaching or referring to any relevant documentary evidence. A hearing will take place if it is requested by both parties or if the court deems necessary. The court must issue its ruling within ten days after the hearing or after the date set for a ruling on the basis of written conclusions. A decision in an action for annulment will take approximately one year.

Under the theory of detachable acts (*actos separables*), administrative acts which **11.303** lead to the award of a public contract are separate from the contract itself, and can be reviewed exclusively by administrative courts, even if the contract to be awarded would be one subject to private law. The court may annul the act which awards the public contract in question, on grounds of invalidity or on grounds of absolute nullity. In the first instance, the contracting authority may validate the act by rectifying the breach that caused the invalidity, for example by inviting a previously-excluded tenderer to submit a bid. When, on the other hand, the administrative act that awards a public contract has been annulled on grounds of absolute nullity, the public authority has little opportunity to rectify it. In such cases, a fresh award procedure must be enacted.

Where the contract has not been concluded, the annulment of any of the **11.304** detachable acts leading to its award would mean that the contract may not be awarded until the infringement has been corrected. The declared invalidity of an administrative act in a public procurement procedure means, in theory, that any contract entered into pursuant to that act will also be void. However, if a contract has been concluded pending litigation for an action to annul its award decision, the contracting authority may declare to the court that the contract should be observed and performed, as its annulment would cause a serious harm to public interest.

11.305   The rulings of the *Sala de lo Contencioso-Administrativo de la Audiencia Nacional* (Chamber of Contentious Administrative Matters of the National Audience) and the *Salas de lo Contencioso-Administrativo de los Tribunales Superiores de Justicia* (Chambers of Contentious Administrative Matters of the Superior Courts of Justice) issued at first instance can be appealed to the *Sala del Tribunal Supremo* (the Supreme Court). Such appeals are only possible on certain legal grounds, such as abuse of jurisdiction, violation of essential procedural requirements or violation of the legal provisions or jurisprudence applied in resolving the case. The appeal must be filed within ten days before the court which issued the contested ruling, briefly setting out the reasons. Only parties which took part in the proceedings at first instance can file an appeal. Once the Supreme Court receives the file, it will call upon the parties to file full pleadings within thirty days.

11.306   Public authorities are under a general duty to take all measures necessary in order to comply with judgments without delay. They may fail to execute or delay in doing so only in certain highly exceptional circumstances. Any such action must be approved by the Council of Ministers. If the judgment entails the payment of a monetary amount such as damages, the authority will be allowed one month as from notification of the court decision within which to take any necessary budgetary steps. In cases where the public administration does not enforce a judgment, employees of the relevant authority at fault can be rendered personally and directly liable for the non-compliance. The court will generally begin by issuing orders designed to encourage compliance, but more stringent measures may be laid down if the judgment is still not respected after six months. The most common sanction is an order obliging the authority to compensate the complainant in respect of the non-compliance with the judgment. The court is not, however, empowered to place any charge over publicly-owned property.

(15) Set aside and annulment orders in Sweden

11.307   A set aside or an annulment order of the act of a contracting authority which awards a public contract may be requested before the *Länsrätt* when the contracting authority has violated a fundamental requirement to carry out its award procedures in an objective, transparent and non-discriminatory manner or has breached any procedural rule on public procurement.[142] *Locus standi* is afforded to any supplier, service provider, or works contractor who is, or would have been, interested in the award of the contract in question and who has been harmed, or risks being harmed, by an alleged infringement of public procurement rules

---

[142] *See* Art. 1:4 Lag 1997:1068.

governing an award procedure for a public contract. The complainant need not have taken part in the award procedure itself, although, in this case, it would be difficult to prove that he has been harmed, or risks being harmed, as a result of the alleged infringement. Actions for review before the *Länsrätt* (County Administrative Court) could only be brought during the contract award procedure and not after the decision to award the contract had been taken. The conclusion of the contract is the critical time before which any action for review must be brought.

There is no express requirement to give prior notice to the contracting authority **11.308** of the alleged infringement or of the complainant's intention to bring an action before the courts. Actions for review, including requests for interim measures, brought before the *Länsrätt* must be lodged by way of a written complaint specifying the type of the redress sought and the grounds for the action. The initial complaint should include detailed information concerning the parties and be accompanied by any supporting evidence, especially in the cases where interim measures are requested. The *Länsrätt* has responsibility for communicating written submissions between the parties and the procedure would be held in writing but court hearings may, rarely, be requested.

Provided the contract in question has not been concluded, the *Länsrätt* may annul **11.309** or set aside an unlawful act and order the contracting authority to start fresh award procedures. In addition, the set aside order may provide an obligation on the part of the contracting authority to suspend the award procedure until the infringement has been corrected. If the set aside or annulment order concerns an act of a utility awarding a contract, the *Länsrät* may only impose a conditional fine, which should be set below one per cent of the contract value, and prohibit the utility from continuing with the award procedure without correcting the infringement. In deciding a set aside or an annulment order, the *Länsrät* should only assess the legality of the act itself and the conduct of the contracting authority or the utility, without having recourse to any test regarding balance of interest between the contracting authority and the aggrieved tenderer. A concluded contract cannot be set aside or annulled. An action for annulment or set aside of a decision will be decided within a year. The relative promptness of the *Länsrätt* reflects the public interest considerations in public procurement litigation, especially the need to conclude and perform a public contract as quickly as possible.

The decisions of the *Länsrätt* (County Administrative Court) may be appealed to **11.310** the competent *Kammarrätt* (Administrative Court of Appeal) within three weeks from the date when the decision was delivered. The decisions of the *Kammarrätt* may in turn be appealed to the *Regeringsrätt* (Supreme Administrative Court).

Rulings by the administrative and civil courts in procurement cases may be **11.311** enforced by the *Kronofogdemyndigheten* (Swedish Enforcement Authority), only upon becoming *res judicata*, which means that no further appeal is allowed or any time limit for such appeals has expired. The *Kronofogdemyndigheten* may order the contracting entity to act in accordance with the judgment and may combine such an order with a conditional fine order. In addition, the Swedish Competition Authority has powers under a specific legal regime[143] to seek an order form a civil court in order to prohibit a contracting authority or a utility from having recourse to unfair procurement practices which discriminate against particular undertakings or which in other ways appreciably distort competition. Such a prohibition will be applicable immediately but extends only to the future conduct of the contracting authority or utility.

(16) Set aside and annulment orders in the United Kingdom

11.312 The High Court has competence to set aside or annul any decision or act taken unlawfully during a procurement procedure. This could be the decision to award the contract to a particular supplier or any earlier decision during the selection and qualification stages of the procedure. The set aside order would take the form of an injunction in that is decided before full trial and which is intended to have permanent effects. The High Court may also order the contracting authority to amend any act or documents which have been found in breach of either procedural or substantive procurement rules, such as documentation relating to technical specifications. Set aside and annulment orders may only be granted prior to the conclusion of the contract in question.

11.313 A necessary procedural requirement for admissibility of actions before the High Court in public procurement cases is the prior notification of the contracting authority.[144]

11.314 Proceedings before the High Court commence by Claim Form. This must be endorsed with either a full statement of the plaintiff's claim or a concise statement of the nature of the claim and the relief or remedy being sought. When the court has issued the writ, it must be served on the defendant within four months. A series of formal documents (pleadings) are communicated between the parties setting out their respective arguments. The pleadings should contain only material facts. The plaintiff's first pleading is his statement of claim, which may be part of the writ. The defendant subsequently answers with a defence, and other pleadings may follow. Pleadings are deemed to close fourteen days after service of the last pleading in the action. After the close of pleadings, the rules of the High Court provide that *discovery* will take place between the parties to the action. Discovery comprises two stages. Firstly, it includes the disclosure by way of a list of

---

[143] *See* Lag (1994:615) om Ingripande mot Otillbörligt beteende Avseende Offentlig Upphandling.
[144] *See* Case *The Queen v Portsmouth City Council, ex parte Bonaco Builders and others*, 6 June 1995.

documents by one party to the others of all relevant documents. Secondly, it embraces any inspection by the other party of such of those documents as are not legally privileged. The scope of discovery is very wide and extends to all documents that are or have been in a party's possession, or custody, provided such documents are not legally privileged.

Within one month of close of pleadings, the plaintiff must take out a summons for **11.315** directions, which normally the court would order without the claimant's request. This provides an opportunity for the court to consider the preparations for trial of the action. Among other things, the directions will deal with witness statements and expert evidence. Witness statements are prepared in order to support a case and are the equivalent of the factual oral evidence that is to be given if the witness is called at trial. They should therefore be comprehensive, as evidence of matters not covered in the statement will only be permitted at trial with the leave of the court. Experts will be able to give opinion evidence on any relevant matter on which they are qualified to speak. Witness statements and the reports of expert witnesses must normally be disclosed to the other parties in advance of the trial. The case will normally be decided by a single judge of the High Court, in public and without a jury.

An alternative, and completely distinct, approach is to proceed by way of judicial **11.316** review. This is the traditional procedure by which third parties have been able to challenge the actions and decisions of public authorities in the UK. The existence of the Regulations means it is no longer obligatory to challenge public procurement decisions by way of judicial review, but this option is still open to aggrieved tenderers and candidates in award procedures for public contracts. The aggrieved person wishing to bring judicial review proceedings must initially apply to a judge of the High Court for leave to do so. This is perhaps the main drawback of using judicial review rather than bringing an ordinary action under the Regulations. Indeed, the existence of the latter avenue could be one reason why a judge refuses to grant leave for judicial review. Any application for leave must be made promptly and, in any event, within three months from the date when the grounds for the application arose unless there is good reason for extending the period. If leave is granted, which may involve consideration of papers only or a hearing open to the public, the substantive application proceeds and the matter is heard by a judge or judges of the High Court.

Judicial review proceedings are usually determined by reference to affidavit **11.317** evidence without some of the other formal procedures which apply in ordinary civil cases. There is often little or no discovery. The following remedies are available in judicial review proceedings: an order restraining the decision-making body from acting outside its jurisdiction (prohibition) or quashing and requiring it to re-consider the matter (*certiorari*); an order requiring the body to carry out its judicial or other public duty (*mandamus*); the granting of a declaration as to the rights of the parties; the granting of an injunction; and, depending on the type of claim, in limited circumstances, an award of damages against the decision-making body. The remedies available under judicial review are similar to the remedies available under the Regulations, although the right to bring an action for damages is limited under judicial review.

E. Actions for Damages

11.318 Article 2(1)(c) in both Directives provides for award of damages to persons harmed by an infringement of public procurement law. The purpose behind this provision is to mobilize the interested contractors in order to supervise the application of Public Procurement Directives. The Public Procurement Directives do not require the provision of a remedy for the award of damages when there is a breach of a directly-effective rule. The reasons for that absence vary: in some cases the national court has held that the authority in breach of Community law did not owe any obligation directly to the plaintiff or that the plaintiff's losses were the results of foreseeable economic risk; in others, the award of damages has been seen as an unacceptable fetter on the freedom of authorities to enact legislative measures or administrative rules in good faith, pursuant to their general duty to safeguard public interest, such as human health. Damages may be available as a consequence of provisions of national law which make a national authority liable to compensate for breach of its obligations. Procuring authorities are subject to a duty to observe European rules and are liable for damages in breach of those rules. In the context of the Compliance Directives, a question arises as to whether an aspiring contractor seeking damages should prove that he would have been accepted as a tenderer or he would have won the contract, if not for the infringement.

11.319 The Directives provide that member states should establish judicial or administrative bodies responsible for their enforcement. Member states, therefore, have a choice as to the forum and procedures provided for hearing disputes or otherwise achieving the required result. In addition, they require that all decisions taken by bodies responsible for review procedures must be effectively enforced.

11.320 Damages largely remain to be determined by national law and practice. However, a pattern has emerged where a complainant seeking damages must prove that the contracting authority has committed an infringement of the procurement rules and, as a direct result and consequence of that infringement, he has suffered harm or loss. In some legal orders, the complainant does not have to prove a breach of procurement rules on the part of the contracting authority, if a previous set aside or annulment judgment of administrative court or tribunal has declared the awarding decision unlawful.

11.321 An aggrieved tenderer should, in principle, be entitled to recover the costs he has incurred in preparing his tender and participating in the award procedure (bid costs), as well as any loss of profit he would have achieved had he been awarded the contract. In most member states, the burden of proof concerning the headings of damages is set at relatively high level. The mere presence of a breach of procurement procedures, which could be proved by the applicant or through a previous set aside or annulment order of the awarding decision of a contracting authority, would be sufficient ground to trigger the award of damages relating to bid costs and costs necessary for the preparation and submission of a tender.

However, the most important issue emerging from actions for damages in the **11.322** legal systems of member states relates to the burden of proof on the part of the aggrieved tenderer seeking damages. In most legal orders, the recovery of damages relating to losses of profit is subject to the complainant proving that, in the absence of the alleged breach, he would have been awarded the contract. The Public Sector Remedies Directive 89/665 is silent on this issue, whereas Directive 92/13 provides some clarification as regards the recovery of bid costs as against utilities. Directive 92/13 provides that, where an aggrieved tenderer establishes that an infringement deprived him of a real chance of winning the contract, he is entitled (at least) to damages covering his bid costs. General principles and relevant case law in a number of member states suggest that this real chance test would apply more generally to any claim for damages under either Remedies Directive.

(1) Damages from the Court's jurisprudence

(a) *Ex proprio motu* investigation and causality

The Court covered review procedures concerning the award of public contracts **11.323** under the Remedies Directive 89/665/EEC and, in particular, the power of the body responsible for review procedures to consider infringements of its own motion.[145] The national court asked the European Court of Justice whether Directive 89/665 precludes the national court responsible for hearing review procedures, in an action brought by a tenderer with the ultimate aim of obtaining damages, for a declaration that the decision to award a public contract is unlawful, from raising of its own motion the unlawfulness of a decision of the contracting authority other than the one contested by the tenderer. On the other hand, the Directive does preclude the court from dismissing an application by a tenderer on the ground that, owing to the unlawfulness raised of its own motion, the award procedure was, in any event, unlawful, and that the harm the tenderer may have suffered would, therefore, have been caused even in the absence of the unlawfulness alleged by the tenderer.

---

[145] *See* Case C-315/01, *Gesellschaft für Abfallentsorgungs-Technik GmbH (GAT) and Österreichische Autobahnen und Schnellstraßen AG (ÖSAG)*, ECR [2003] I-6351;

11.324　In that regard, it is appropriate to recall that, as is apparent from the first and second recitals in the preamble, Directive 89/665 is intended to strengthen the existing mechanisms, both at national and Community levels, to ensure the effective application of Community Directives relating to public procurement, in particular at a stage when infringements can still be remedied. To that effect, Article 1(1) of that Directive requires member states to guarantee that unlawful decisions of contracting authorities can be subjected to effective review which is as swift as possible.[146] However, Directive 89/665 lays down only the minimum conditions to be satisfied by the review procedures established in domestic law to ensure compliance with the requirements of Community law concerning public contracts.[147]

11.325　If there is no specific provision governing the matter, it is therefore for the domestic law of each member state to determine whether, and in what circumstances, a court responsible for review procedures may raise *ex proprio motu* unlawfulness which has not been raised by the parties to the case brought before it. Neither the aims of Directive 89/665 nor the requirement it lays down that both parties be heard in review procedures preclude the introduction of that possibility in the domestic law of a member state.

11.326　The Court declared that, firstly, it cannot be inconsistent with the objective of that Directive, which is to ensure compliance with the requirements of Community law on public procurement by means of effective and swift review procedures, for the court responsible for the review procedures to raise *ex proprio motu* unlawfulness affecting an award procedure, without waiting for one of the parties to do so. Secondly, the requirement that both parties be heard in review procedures does not preclude the court responsible for those procedures from being able to raise *ex proprio motu* unlawfulness which it is the first to find, but simply means that before giving its ruling the court must observe the right of the parties to be heard on the unlawfulness raised *ex proprio motu*.

11.327　From the Court's stance, it follows that Directive 89/665 does not preclude the court responsible for hearing review procedures, in an action brought by a tenderer, with the ultimate aim of obtaining damages, for a declaration that the decision to award a public contract is unlawful, from raising of its own motion the unlawfulness of a decision of the contracting authority other than the one contested by the tenderer. However, it does not necessarily follow that the court may dismiss an application by a tenderer on the ground that, by reason of the unlawfulness raised of its own motion, the award procedure was in any event unlawful and that the harm the tenderer may have suffered would therefore have been caused even in the absence of the unlawfulness alleged by the tenderer.

---

[146]　*See* Case C-81/98 *Alcatel Austria and Others* [1999] ECR I-7671, paragraphs 33 and 34, and Case C-470/99 *Universale-Bau and Others* [2002] ECR I-11617, paragraph 74.
[147]　*See* Case C-327/00 *Santex* [2003] ECR I-1877, paragraph 47.

On the one hand, as is apparent from the case law of the Court, Article 1(1) of **11.328**
Directive 89/665 applies to all decisions taken by contracting authorities which are
subject to the rules of Community law on public procurement[148] and makes no
provision for any limitation as regards the nature and content of those decisions.[149]
On the other hand, among the review procedures which Directive 89/665 requires
the member states to introduce for the purposes of ensuring that the unlawful decisions of contracting authorities may be the subject of review procedures which are
effective and as swift as possible, is the procedure enabling damages to be granted
to the person harmed by an infringement, which is expressly stated in Article
2(1)(c). Therefore, a tenderer harmed by a decision to award a public contract, the
lawfulness of which he is contesting, cannot be denied the right to claim damages
for the harm caused by that decision on the ground that the award procedure was
in any event defective owing to the unlawfulness, raised *ex proprio motu*, of another
(possibly previous) decision of the contracting authority.

That conclusion is all the more obvious if a member state has exercised the power **11.329**
conferred on member states by the second subparagraph of Article 2(6) of
Directive 89/665 to limit, after the conclusion of the contract following the
award, the powers of the court responsible for the review procedures to award
damages. In such cases, the unlawfulness alleged by the tenderer cannot be subject
to any of the penalties provided for under Directive 89/665. The Court concluded that Directive 89/665 does not preclude the court responsible for hearing
review procedures, in an action brought by a tenderer, with the ultimate aim of
obtaining damages, for a declaration that the decision to award a public contract
is unlawful, from raising of its own motion the unlawfulness of a decision of the
contracting authority other than the one contested by the tenderer. However, the
Directive does preclude the court from dismissing an application by a tenderer on
the ground that, owing to the unlawfulness raised of its own motion, the award
procedure was in any event unlawful and that the harm which the tenderer may
have suffered would therefore have been caused even in the absence of the unlawfulness alleged by the tenderer.

(2) Action for damages in the Republic of Austria

A candidate or tenderer in a procurement award procedure may claim damages in **11.330**
the civil courts[150] if the contracting authority breached the provisions of the
Federal Procurement Act.

---

[148] *See* Case C-92/00 *HI* [2002] ECR I-5553, paragraph 37, and Case C-57/01 *Makedoniko
Metro and Michaniki* [2003] ECR I-1091, paragraph 68.
[149] *See* Case C-81/98 *Alcatel Austria and Others* [1999] ECR I-767, paragraph 35, and Case
C-92/00 *Hospital Ingenieure* [2002] ECR I-5553, paragraph 49.
[150] *See* § 122 of the *Bundesgesetz, mit dem das Bundesvergabegesetz geändert wird* Act, Federal Law
Gazette 1996/776.

11.331 For the admissibility of the action for damages before civil courts, a complainant seeking damages has to file a motion for a review procedure with the Public Procurement Agency. An action for damages is only admissible if the Agency has established that the contracting authority has violated public procurement rules. If such a violation has occurred, the Agency has to determine its impact upon the chances of the aggrieved tenderer of winning the contract. A claim for damages is dismissed if the Public Procurement Agency decides that the tenderer would have had no real chance of winning the contract.[151]

11.332 If the Public Procurement Agency ascertains that there was a breach and that the complainant had some chance of being awarded the contract in the event that the contracting authority had complied with the law, that complainant may take legal action against the contracting authority with little risk of failure, as the essential issue has already been decided. The procedure before the court will then concern only the extent of damages and the issue whether the contracting authority negligently breached the law.

11.333 When the Public Procurement Agency determines that there was a breach, and that the complainant had some chance of being awarded the contract in the event that the contracting authority had complied with the law, the burden of proof is no longer on the complainant. Instead, the contracting authority must prove that it did not breach the law in negligence. The shift of the burden of proof in such cases indicates a non-fault liability of contracting authorities, as they are legally obliged to comply with procurement rules.

11.334 Both Austrian civil law and the 1997 Act allow damages for loss of profit,[152] as well as preparation costs for submissions and bids, before the civil courts. The applicant must prove that he would have been awarded the contract had the procurement rules been complied with. In particular, the applicant will be able to recover damages for loss of profit in the civil courts only if the Public Procurement Agency concludes that it submitted the most economically advantageous tender and therefore, it should have been awarded the contract in the absence of the infringement.

11.335 For actions for damages for contracts awarded and which exceed the relevant thresholds stipulated in the Public Procurement Directives, the competent court is the *Landesgericht* where the contracting authority has its seat, regardless of the amount of damages sought.[153] The application has to indicate the competent

---

[151] *See* § 122(2) of the *Bundesgesetz, mit dem das Bundesvergabegesetz geändert wird* Act, Federal Law Gazette 1996/776.

[152] Under the general civil law, the Austrian Supreme Court of Civil Matters (*Oberster Gerichtshof*) may grant damages in respect of a violation of a legal provision of the public procurement regime based on the general principle of *cupla in contrahendo*.

[153] The amount of damages sought determines the courts' jurisdiction only in public contracts below the thresholds or ones which are governed by the Carinthian Procurement Act.

court, the parties to the civil suit, the matter in dispute, the requested amount of damages, the facts of the case, the facts in respect of jurisdiction of the civil court, a statement of reasons, the specific claim, and the name of the complainant. Civil procedures are led partly by the judge and partly by the parties. The judge controls the overall procedure which is principally based on adversarial oral hearings and is governed by formal procedural rules. The civil courts are under no stringent time constraints when dealing with an action for damages. On average, it takes one to two years to deliver a judgment for an action for damages.

(3) *Action for damages in Belgium*

An action for damages is admissible only before ordinary courts. In order to obtain damages, the complainant must prove that the contracting authority committed an unlawful act or fault and that this act was the direct cause of loss or damage suffered by the plaintiff. **11.336**

In cases where judgment for annulment has been given by the *Conseil d'Etat*, the ordinary civil court is bound to follow the decision of the *Conseil d'Etat* regarding the illegality of the award decision. Hence, the complainant will only be left to prove the existence of his damage and that this was caused by the unlawful decision. Where the complainant has not filed a request for annulment before the *Conseil d'Etat*, the ordinary court will itself review the legality of the contracting authority's conduct. **11.337**

In the case of a procedure (*adjudication*) where the award criterion is lowest price only, a rejected tenderer who can prove that he put forward the lowest regular tender will be automatically entitled to a compensation award of ten per cent of his tender price. Any additional request for damages will be refused, although the lowest regular tenderer is entitled to claim interest (at eight per cent per annum) on his indemnity for the period between the unlawful award decision and the payment. **11.338**

In a procedure (*appel d'offres*) where the award criterion is the most economically advantageous tender, a complainant is required to demonstrate the extent of his loss. The court will estimate the damages in order to compensate the prejudiced party as fully as possible, by putting him in the position he would have been in if there had been no illegality. The main criterion which helps the ordinary courts to establish the amount of the damages is the economic value of the contract. This value depends mainly on the expected economic profit. The case law shows that damages will principally and almost exclusively compensate the loss of profit, but not the bid costs linked to the tender, such as preparatory work, overheads, and administrative expenses. **11.339**

The courts have chosen a simple solution by estimating a fair profit to be ten per cent of the net amount of the tender. This percentage is deemed to correspond to **11.340** the usual net profit under public works contracts. The courts may increase this percentage in order to compensate monetary devaluation or if the plaintiff can demonstrate that both his expenses and his usual net profits are higher. However, the court may appoint experts to determine the loss of profit of the aggrieved contractor. In such cases, the expert bases his assessment on the profit obtained by the plaintiff when performing other works over the same period. Other elements can be taken into account in the estimation of damages such as the loss of references for future contracts and the under-utilization of equipment and staff, depending on whether they would have been used during the same period on other contracts, but as these elements are difficult to quantify, they are considered as damages covering loss of profit.

11.341 To bring an action before the ordinary courts, the complainant must have an interest which is concrete, personal and direct.[154] Group actions by associations of individuals are not possible. Actions before the ordinary courts are not subject to any special time limit for their commencement but solely to the thirty years' statute of limitation. Tort actions must be filed within thirty years from the date of the wrongful act for which damages are claimed. As for interim measures before ordinary courts, undue delay in bringing the action may cast doubt on the urgency of the proceedings.

11.342 The procedure is initiated by the notification of a summons by the process server. In some cases, the applicant may make a unilateral request, but he usually has to serve a copy on the other side beforehand so that both sides can be heard. The case is registered in the general list of the Court. There is then an exchange of conclusions. From the date of communication of the applicant's file, the defendant has one month to submit his conclusions. Similarly, the applicant benefits from another month from the date of communication of the defendant's conclusions to file his own conclusions.

11.343 Each party is allowed to file additional conclusions within fifteen days. Non-compliance with these time limits does not result in the action being declared void. Consequently, the written part of the procedure can take months or even several years. The fixing of a date for the hearing may be requested only when the case is 'en état', which means that the parties have exchanged all their arguments and documents through their conclusions and that the case is ready to be pleaded. Some special means are at the disposal of the petitioner in order to accelerate the procedure. For example, he may request an order to determine a timetable, which lays down the date on which each party must have filed their first and additional conclusions, as well as the date for a hearing. This timetable is compulsory, with the sanction that any conclusions submitted out of time will be disregarded.

---

[154] *See* Art. 17 of the Belgian Procedural Code.

Alternatively, the applicant can ask the court to determine a date by which the other party must have filed his conclusions. A failure to do so would lead to the issue of a judgment by default which could only be challenged before the Court of Appeal. The final decision of ordinary courts can be appealed to the Court of Appeal. In this case, the filing of an appeal will generally suspend the execution of the first ruling, except where that ruling specifies that it is enforceable notwithstanding any appeal. The supreme authority, to which points of law may be appealed, is the *Cour de Cassation*. Interim orders as well as definitive judgments (such as an award of damages) benefit from *res judicata* authority. However, the judgments operate only as between the parties. When the judgment is referred to the Court of Appeal, its *res judicata* authority remains and will only cease when the judgment is reviewed by the Court of Appeal. When an authority fails to comply with a ruling, enforcement can be ensured through charges on property (*attachments*) and the imposition of heavy daily fines.

(4) Action for damages in Denmark

An action for damages may be brought before ordinary courts against contracting **11.344** awarding authorities and utilities in breach procurement rules. Although the Complaints Board is not competent to award damages, a successful claim for annulment before the Complaints Board will be followed by subsequent court proceedings for damages. However, the courts may award damages even in the absence of a prior annulment decision by the Complaints Board.

The general principles of Danish law cover the availability and quantum of **11.345** damages in public procurement cases. Accordingly, a complainant is entitled to damages where he can prove that there has been an infringement of the procurement rules and that, as a direct and foreseeable consequence of that infringement, he has suffered an economic loss. A complainant will be also able to recover bid costs if it establishes that it had a reasonable chance of winning the contract and that this chance was adversely affected by the utility's breach of the procurement rules.[155] Hence, the complainant is not required to prove that he would in fact have been awarded the contract in the absence of the breach. In principle, the complainant should be placed in the same financial position as if the injury had not occurred. The Danish courts have traditionally been concerned not to over-compensate the complainant, who has a general duty to mitigate his loss.

The complainant in practice has a choice between compensation for bid costs and **11.346** loss of profits. For the recovery of bid costs, the complainant will only have to prove that he had a reasonable chance or a genuine possibility of being awarded

---

[155] *See* Art. 13(a) of the Remedies Act which implements Article 2.7 of Remedies Directive 92/13 as regards damages against utilities.

the contract and that this chance has been adversely affected.[156] Recovery for loss of profits will only be upheld if the complainant is able to prove that he would have been awarded the contract had the procurement rules not been infringed. It may be possible to establish such proof where the award criterion is the lowest price or where there were only a small number of bidders and the successful bid was obviously inferior. In the great majority of cases, however, it will be extremely difficult for the complainant to prove that he would have been awarded the contract in the absence of the infringement. Proceedings before the ordinary courts involve the exchange of written pleadings, beginning with the complainant's claim (writ of summons) and the defendant's reply. The case will then proceed to an oral hearing, where both sides present their evidence orally and are able to cross-examine each other. Finally, after the hearing, the judge pronounces the judgment. Decisions of ordinary courts, on an application to award damages, take at least two years. Decisions of the ordinary Bailiff's Court and City Courts may be appealed to the High Court. Any further appeal to the Supreme Court will only be allowed in exceptional circumstances. When the High Court is acting in its capacity as the court of first instance, its decisions, on the other hand, can be appealed to the Supreme Court. With regard to enforcement of decisions of the ordinary courts, it is a general rule of Danish law that court rulings may be enforced through the Bailiff's Court upon an application from the successful plaintiff.

(5) Action for damages in Finland

11.347 An action for damages may be brought by an aggrieved tenderer before ordinary courts.[157] Where a claim is made for damages representing the costs of bid preparation or the costs of participation in an award procedure, the applicant must prove an infringement of the relevant procurement rules and that he would have had a real chance of winning the contract. In addition to the above proof requirement, a causal link between the infringement and the damage suffered must be established.[158] An action for damages is independent from actions for an interim or set aside order before the Competition Council. However, a finding of an

---

[156] *See* the ruling of the Eastern High Court on 30th May 1996, which followed up the ruling of the European Court of Justice in the *Storebaelt Bridge* case of C-243/89 *Commission v Denmark*. In that case, the Danish court awarded damages around DKK23 million (ECU 3.1 million) to several firms who had tendered unsuccessfully for the Storebaelt Bridge contract. These damages covered bid costs only and were awarded even though the court did not find evidence that any of the complainants would have been awarded the contract.

[157] *See* Art. 8 of the Act on Public Procurement, which stipulates that a contracting authority is liable to pay damages where it causes damage by way of an infringement of the Procurement Act, of regulations passed under the Act or of the Treaty of Rome.

[158] *See* Art. 8(2) of the Act on Public Procurement. This rule in the Act corresponds with Article 2(7) of Remedies Directive 92/13, and covers not only utilities but also extents the real chance test to contracting authorities from the public sector.

infringement by the Competition Council is likely to have a positive impact in support of the complainant's claim for damages.

For actions for damages before the ordinary courts, no prior notification is **11.348** required. A complainant seeking damages must submit an application for a summons to a court of first instance. The application should set out the claim and the grounds on which it is based, together with details of the relevant course of events and of the evidence to be presented to the court. The contracting authority has to submit a written answer to the court. The court then invites both parties to a preparatory hearing in which the scope of the dispute is defined and the case is prepared for the main hearing. All written evidence has to be presented at the latest in the preparatory hearing. A main hearing takes place either immediately after the preparatory hearing or at a subsequent date. At the main hearing, oral submissions may be made by representatives of the parties as well as witnesses and experts.

There are no specific guidelines as to the quantum of damages. In practice, dam- **11.349** ages may be limited to the bid costs incurred by the complainant in participating in the award procedure. General principles of Finnish contract law only provide for compensation for loss of profits where there has been a breach of contract; therefore, such compensation is not available for a complainant who did not become a party to a contract.

For damages covering loss of profit, general principles of Finnish law suggest that **11.350** the complainant will have to satisfy a higher level of proof, exceeding the real chance test specified in the Compliance Directives, by demonstrating that there was a high probability that he would have won the contract had the contracting authority observed the procurement rules. The Competition Council has the power to order sanctions against defaulting contracting authorities in breach with public procurement law. If an aggrieved tenderer establishes that he would have had a real chance of winning the contract, the Competition Council may order the contracting entity to pay compensation to the applicant. This compensatory payment may be ordered if the application has been made after the conclusion of the contract or if the balance of interest test demonstrates that the application of other remedies would have harmful effects for the contracting authority in relation to the execution of the contract. The compensatory payment should take into account the value of the contract, the nature of the infringement, and the damages suffered by the aggrieved tenderer. An action before a County Administrative Court follows special time limits and procedures laid down in Finnish administrative legislation. A formal request for rectification should be made to the contracting authority itself within fourteen days after service of a decision. The authority is required to deal with the request without delay. If necessary, a further complaint can be filed with the County Administrative Court within thirty days after service of the decision. An action for damages before the ordinary courts is subject to the normal limitation period of ten years.

11.351 Rulings on damages by a court of first instance may be appealed to the Court of Appeal within thirty days. Before submitting such an appeal, the appellant party must have given notice to the court of first instance of his intent to appeal within seven days. A further appeal to the Supreme Court requires leave to appeal.

(6) Action for damages in France

11.352 A complainant may bring a claim for damages before the ordinary civil courts regardless of whether or not the contract has been concluded. French law suggests that a complainant may bring an action for damages where he has been deprived of a right as a result of fault or negligence by the defendant. An action for damages in the civil courts is commenced by a written summons (*assignation*), which is filed in the court and notified by a public server (*huissier*). Written pleadings are then exchanged before a judge. Finally, the parties and their representatives attend the final hearing at the court, where oral submissions are made. The judge usually delivers judgment within one month following the hearing. An action for damages before civil courts is completed on average within a year. Any appeal to the original judgment is resolved within approximately eighteen months.

11.353 The complainant has the burden of proof of the existence of the fault, the damage suffered and the causal link between the fault and the damage. A fault may consist in the violation of a legal obligation, constituting an unlawful act. Such fault is deemed to have occurred if the defendant, whether voluntarily or otherwise, with intention or by negligence, fails to comply with a duty expressly laid down by law. In cases where the fault results in a party losing the chance of concluding a contract, that party may recover damages. The complainant is, however, required to prove that its chance of being awarded the contract in question was significant.[159] Damages may cover loss of profits. In addition, the complainant may obtain compensation for its expenses related to the preparation of its submission and its bid. For actions for damages before civil courts, the general rule is that any action lapses after ten years from the infringement in question. A ruling of the civil courts upon an action for damages may be subject to an appeal, within one month, to the *Cour d'Appel* and ultimately to the *Cour de Cassation* (the supreme court for civil and commercial cases).

(7) Action for damages in Germany

11.354 An action for damages should be directed to the civil courts. Damages are the only remedy available once the contract in question has been concluded and

---

[159] There is no express provision implementing Article 2(7) of Directive 92/13 which provides that a complainant seeking to recover bid costs has to prove that a utility has committed an infringement of the procurement rules, that he had a real chance of being awarded the contract (in the absence of the breach) and that this chance was adversely affected as a result of the infringement.

cannot be annulled as void. The recovery of costs for preparing tenders and of cost related to the participation in the award procedure is expressly allowed, as these costs constitute direct losses.[160] A complainant is able to recover the bid costs, provided that the contracting authority has infringed a provision intended to protect the interests of the tenderers and that, in the absence of the breach, the applicant would have had a real chance of winning the contract. However, reimbursement of costs incurred for employees involved in the preparation of the bid can be claimed only if it can be shown that their working capacity could have been profitably used elsewhere and whether the costs for the preparation of the offer have been incurred solely for participation in a particular award procedure. The award of damages under the *Gesetzgegen Wettbewerbsbeschränkungen* exceeds the restrictive application of the traditional concept of *culpa in contrahendo*, under which damages may be claimed if a loss has been sustained as a result of detrimental collapse of legitimate expectation during contractual negotiations or pre-contractual arrangements, provided that the other party is in fault.

The award of damages that include indirect or potential loss may be granted in exceptional circumstances.[161] In such cases, the bidder has to be compensated as if he had obtained the contract.[162] Consequently, damages as a result of loss of profits may be allowed. The applicant has the burden of proof that, had the award procedures had been followed in accordance with the public procurement rules, the contract would have been awarded to him. **11.355**

In order to calculate the amount of lost profit, expenditure relating to materials, salaries, taxes, and fixed costs should be deducted from the contract remuneration. In addition, a causal link has to be established between the breach of a legal obligation on the part of the contracting authority and the injury sustained by the applicant. In the event of a breach of the procurement rules, all unsuccessful bidders might claim damages. To reduce the potential economic burden on contracting authorities, the courts have applied the causality of the link between the breach of procurement rules and the injury suffered by tenderers in a restrictive manner. The result is a very high standard of proof on the part of the applicant claiming damages, in the sense that he must provide undisputable evidence that he should have, beyond reasonable doubt and almost certainly, been awarded the contract in question. **11.356**

---

[160] *See* Art. § 126 of *Gesetzgegen Wettbewerbsbeschränkungen*.
[161] *See* Art. § 33 of *Gesetzgegen Wettbewerbsbeschränkungen*.
[162] *See* Art. § 823 II BGB Bürgerliches Gesetzbuch (German Civil Code) which generally provides a possibility to claim damages for the infringement of a statute intended for the protection of others. Article § 97 VII of *Gesetzgegen Wettbewerbsbeschränkungen* on the rules on public procurement constitute such a statute.

11.357 Another category of damages, those caused by the misuse of the right to apply or to appeal, are allowed.[163] An applicant or appellant has to pay for damages caused to his competitors and the contracting authority as a result of incorrect information in order to achieve the initial or further suspension of the award procedure, to harm competitors, to delay the award procedure, or to withdraw the complaint at a later stage in exchange for compensation.

11.358 It is not a pre-requisite for an action for damages before civil courts to exhaust the procedures before a Procurement Chamber or a Procurement Division at the Court of Appeal, although any damages awarded might be reduced on the grounds of contributory negligence or failure to mitigate damages. Any decisions before the Procurement Chamber or Division at the Court of Appeal which confirm that a contracting authority has breached public procurement rules are binding for the civil courts when subsequently they deal with action for damages.

11.359 The procedure before civil courts is governed by the Code on Civil Procedure (*Zivilprozeßordnung*, ZPO). Civil actions commence with the issue of a claim by the complainant, three copies of which must be registered with the court. The claim contains the names of the parties, the grounds, legal rules in support of the claim, and the amount in dispute. In the opening phase of the civil procedure, the court considers the admissibility of the claim and decides whether it opts for a written preliminary procedure or a procedure which involves an early oral hearing. A written preliminary procedure is mostly chosen if the matter seems to be complicated and may result in a longer process. As the case proceeds, the court determines what is necessary to decide the issue. When it has enough evidence it will declare this in court and the main hearing will take place, which usually lasts no more than a day. At this oral hearing there is a general duty imposed on the court to discuss the details of the case fully and to ensure that the parties are aware of all relevant legal aspects. The court summarizes the factual and legal issues and the arguments for the parties by reference to the written admissions and any legal points not raised by the parties. Means of proof of the facts include the use of expert witnesses and evidence, inspection by the court, documents, and questioning of the parties. The hearings are concluded by the opportunity provided to the parties to sum up orally by submitting a reference to all the pleadings and defence arguments previously considered, and a final plea on behalf of the client. A final judgment may be made at this stage, or a later date will be set for the reading of the judgment. Judgment is given orally after all evidence has been heard and the oral hearing closed. The judges retire to decide on the basis of a simple majority and the court will be recalled for the oral judgment to be read out. A detailed and reasoned written decision is given and forms the basis of any appeal to the next instance. Actions for damages in the civil courts usually last at least one year.

---

[163] *See* § 125 of *Gesetzgegen Wettbewerbsbeschränkungen*.

Actions for damages in the civil courts are subject to certain limitation periods. As a general rule the limitation period for non-contractual damages under German civil law is three years.[164] Damages under the concept of *culpa in contrahendo* may in principle be claimed within a period of thirty years.

(8) Action for damages in Greece

Actions for damages are available to aggrieved tenderers as a result of unlawful **11.360** decisions of contracting authorities. A complainant, under the general liability principles of the Greek Civil Code, has a right to recover damages from a contracting authority if its decision awarding a contract has been found to be unlawful by either administrative or civil courts. The claim for damages must be well founded in that the applicant must prove that he has suffered damage as a direct result of the unlawful act or omission by the contracting authority. The required causality link between the breach and the loss will be established if the applicant demonstrates that the breach, in all likelihoods, has resulted in the damage.

The quantum of damages covers both direct and indirect costs. The amount of **11.361** damages awarded should fully compensate the complainant for the entire financial loss which the applicant suffered as a result of the unlawful act. Damages are quantified by the decrease in the existing assets of the creditor (positive damage) as well as any loss of profit (negative damage). Loss of profit can be determined by estimating what can be reasonably anticipated as profit or gain in the ordinary course of events or by reference to the special circumstances and in particular the preparatory steps taken.[165] In a public procurement case, the damages should cover the positive loss of the tender and other costs incurred in participating in the award procedure, as well as the negative loss of the profit which the complainant could reasonably have expected to gain from the performance of the contract.

For actions for damages before civil courts, a first hearing usually takes place after **11.362** the filing of the suit. The court issues a preliminary decision containing the issues to be proved by witnesses and examines any witnesses proposed by the parties during the first hearing. A second hearing may take place after the completion of the examination of the witnesses in complex cases. If no further hearings or other procedural steps regarding the evidence are required by the court, a final decision will be issued within eight to fourteen months.

Decisions of the civil courts of first instance can be appealed to the Civil Court of **11.363** Appeal (branch for litigation and public works contracts), within thirty days from the delivery of the Court's decision. The final decision of the Civil Court of

---

[164] *See* Art.s § 823 II BGB and § 852 BGB *Bürgerliches Gesetzbuch* (German Civil Code).
[165] *See* Art. 298 of the Greek Civil Code.

Appeal can be appealed to the Supreme Court (*Areios Pagos*). The time limit for such appeals is thirty days.

11.364 Judgments of the civil courts awarding damages may not be enforced against the Greek state. The same applies to certain state-owned entities operating in the utilities sectors which, although subject to private law, enjoy special immunity under specific laws.

(9) Action for damages in Ireland

11.365 The High Court may, where a contract has been concluded subsequent to its award, award damages to any person harmed by an infringement of the procurement rules. The general principles and Irish case law regarding damages govern the availability and the quantum of damages in public procurement cases. Actions brought before the High Court commence proceedings by means of Special Summons. Once the Summons has been issued in the Central Office of the High Court, an initial hearing date within a number of weeks is allocated in the Master's List. A sworn statement (affidavit) by the complainant, verifying the claim in the Special Summons, is filed in the Central Office and a copy is given to the defendant. Unless the Court directs otherwise, proceedings commenced by Special Summons are heard on affidavit.

11.366 Public procurement cases are likely to be placed in the High Court list for hearing after initially appearing in the Master's List. Additional time may be allowed for the filing of further affidavits. However, it may be appropriate to request the Court that the matter is dealt with by way of plenary hearing, with the exchange of pleadings and examination and cross examination of witnesses. Even if the case is dealt with on affidavit, any party desiring to cross-examine anyone who has sworn an affidavit in the proceedings may serve a Notice of Cross Examination.

11.367 The Rules of the Superior Courts allow the parties to apply to the High Court for discovery of documents. An application must be preceded by a letter to the other party requesting voluntary discovery. If, within twenty-one days of such notification, agreement to give voluntary discovery is not forthcoming, the applicant may then seek an Order for Discovery from the High Court. Discovery comprises two stages: disclosure by way of a list of documents appended to an affidavit by one party to the other of all relevant documents, and an inspection by the other party of such of those documents that are not legally privileged. The scope of discovery is very wide and extends to all documents that are or have been in a party's possession, custody, or power relating to any matter in question in the case, save for those which are legally privileged (for example, communications between a party and a solicitor). Where they are privileged, the existence of the documents must be disclosed, but they are not required to be made available for inspection.

Expert evidence may be appropriate in some procurement proceedings. Experts will   **11.368**
be able to give opinion evidence on any relevant matter on which they are qualified to speak. Any witness statements are usually furnished to the other side in advance of the trial, although this is not compulsory. The case will normally be tried in public by a single judge of the High Court without a jury. The parties are normally represented by barristers who make submissions on their behalf and cross-examine witnesses based on their affidavits. In some cases, where parallel judicial review proceedings have been brought, and the judge has directed that the matter proceed by way of plenary hearing, it is likely that both sets of proceedings will be heard together.

Under general principles, the complainant will have to prove that a breach of the   **11.369**
procurement rules has in fact been committed and that he has suffered, or will suffer, loss as a result. A breach of the Directives and the Statutory Instruments is a breach of statutory duty and thus a tort. Under general principles, tort damages operate to put the plaintiff in the position he would have enjoyed had the tort not been committed. This could mean that, in order to recover damages in a procurement case, a complainant must prove that he would have been the successful tenderer, had the infringement of the procurement rules not occurred. However, as this test is very difficult to meet and its application would have the result of impeding the effectiveness of the Remedies Directives, Irish courts would normally allow recovery of damages even where the complainant is only able to prove that he had a reasonable chance of winning the contract.

The damages would be awarded to compensate the complainant for the loss of   **11.370**
that chance. A plaintiff should be able to recover all or part of his costs in participating in the tendering procedure if he can prove that he had a real chance of winning the contract and that, as a consequence of the infringement, that chance was adversely affected. Recovery of damages for loss of the potential profit is also possible. The complainant must prove the amount of profit which it would have made had it been awarded the contract. It is possible that a court would reduce that amount by a particular percentage in order to reflect the possibility that the complainant might not have been awarded the contract even if the procurement rules had not been infringed.

Where an award of damages is made, and a contracting authority has failed to   **11.371**
observe the judgment, the complainant could seek to register the judgment as a charge over the assets of the contracting authority or commence proceedings seeking to wind up the authority for failure to pay a debt following a demand to discharge the debt within twenty-one days of that demand. Finally, the complainant may apply to the court sheriff to seize goods or assets of the authority in order to discharge the amount of the debt.

(10) Action for damages in Italy

11.372 Traditionally, under Italian law, an aggrieved tenderer had only a legitimately protected interest (*interesse legittimo*) and not an individual right (*diritto soggettivo*) vis-à-vis the public administration and therefore was excluded from an action for damages against a contracting authority which violated procurement rules. Compensation for infringement of the relevant rules was classified as part of *interessi legittimi* and not as *diritti soggettivi*, with the disappointing consequence that the aggrieved tenderer was in fact deprived of any damages, which were recoverable only in the event of injuries to individual rights and not for injury to protected interests.

11.373 However for breaches in the field of public procurement, any person harmed by an act in breach of the Community rules concerning public supply and public works contracts, or in breach of the national implementing rules, may claim damages from the authority which has awarded the contract. Damages may be claimed before the ordinary courts only after the decision taken unlawfully has been set aside by a judgment of the administrative court.[166] Thus, a damages claim is only possible where the contracting authority has taken an unlawful administrative decision in breach of the procurement rules and that decision has been set aside by the *Tribunali Amministrativi Regionali*.

11.374 Proceedings in civil courts are commenced by serving a *citazione* (a writ with a full statement of claim endorsed) upon the defendant. The *citazione* must comply with specific procedural requirements[167] and methods of service of judicial documents and, in particular, it must contain a statement of the relief sought; the facts and rules of law giving rise to the claim; a specific indication of the evidence on which the complainant is going to rely; the power of attorney whereby the complainant appoints his lawyer to represent him in the proceedings; and the date of the first hearing, together with the invitation to the defendant to enter a Defence. Failure to comply with the above requirements and the proper methods of service may result in the nullity of the *citazione* and subsequent inadmissibility of the proceedings. The Defence must contain any counterclaims and an indication of the evidence on which the defendant is going to rely to rebut the allegations of the complainant. At the first hearing the judge may verify the proper notification of the *citazione* and the proper appearance of the defendant. A subsequent hearing will be fixed where he will informally question the parties, seek a possible settlement, clarify any issues and allow amendments to the pleadings. Following the closure of the written pleadings, the judge decides on the admissibility of the

---

[166] *See* Art. 13 of Law 142/92 which provides for damages for breaches of Community rules on public procurement.   [167] *See* Arts. 163–7 of the Civil Procedure Code.

evidence[168] proposed by the parties in the pleadings and of any new evidence requested by the parties at the hearing.[169] After this stage, new evidence can be admitted in the proceedings only in exceptional circumstances. Finally, the parties submit a brief summary of their conclusions. An oral hearing takes place only if requested by the parties and the case is decided by a single judge.

A claim for damages before ordinary courts may include the actual loss suffered **11.375** by an aggrieved tenderer, such as tender and bid costs, as well as loss of profits, including loss of opportunity. Bid and participating costs in the award procedure are recoverable if the claimant shows that he had a real chance of winning the contract. On the other hand, the standard of proof to recover damages for loss of profits is much higher, in the sense that such a claim would be successful only when the aggrieved tenderer is able to prove that the contract would have been awarded to him in the absence of the infringement of the procurement rules. The courts will have recourse to the principles governing non-contractual liability in the Italian legal system[170] which provide that loss of earnings must be assessed on a proportionate and equitable basis.

Claims for damages before the ordinary courts are subject to different limitation **11.376** periods of either ten or five years, depending on whether the liability of the public administration is regarded as contractual or non-contractual. In public procurement cases the right to compensation for damages for breach of the relevant rules is subject to the rules governing non-contractual liability and therefore the limitation period will be of five years, running from the date of the judgment of the administrative court setting aside the contested decision.

An action for damages before civil courts can only be brought once the **11.377** complainant has obtained an annulment order from the administrative court. The proceedings before the civil court at first instance would last between three to five years. Further periods of delay, averaging between two and five years, may be added if the judgment of either the administrative court or the ordinary court is appealed or if a question is referred to the European Court of Justice for a preliminary ruling. The judgments of civil courts may be appealed to the Court of Appeal at second instance within thirty days of the notification of the judgment to the claimant, or within one year of the deposit of the judgment in the Registry, if the judgment has not been notified). The ruling of the Court of Appeal may be appealed, on points of law only, to the Court of Cassation, which is the final court of review. The enforcement of judgments of the ordinary civil courts at first

---

[168] *See* Arts. 191–266 of the Code of Civil Procedure and in Arts. 2697–2739 of the Civil Code, dealing with rules of evidence such as the burden of proof, expert evidence, documents, inspection, admissions, oaths and witnesses.

[169] *See* Art. 184 of the Code of Civil Procedure.

[170] *See* Arts. 1226 and 2056 of the Civil Code.

instance may only be suspended by the Court of Appeal for serious reasons. For judgments of the ordinary courts awarding damages, enforcement proceedings are available under the Code of Civil Procedure which allow for liquidation of assets of the party responsible to recover any damage caused.

(11) Action for damages in Luxembourg

11.378 The laws implementing the Public Procurement Directives in Luxembourg do not lay down specific provisions on the availability of damages. Under general principles of Luxembourg law, damages are available for loss or damage that has been caused by an administrative decision which has been taken unlawfully. For an action for damages before the civil courts, the complainant must first have obtained the annulment of the challenged decision by an Administrative Tribunal. The annulment or *réformation* of an individual administrative decision implies *ipso facto* that the public administrative body is liable in a tort action. The procedure before the District Tribunal is a written one. The complainant introduces his action by a writ of summons (*assignation*). This is delivered by way of a bailiff (*huissier de Justice*) to the defendant. The parties then set out their arguments and counter-arguments by way of written pleadings, known as *conclusions*. Before the District Tribunal, there is no limit to the number of *conclusions* that may be put forward. Oral explanations are given in a court hearing only if this is necessary for the understanding of technical details.

11.379 In order to recover damages, it is sufficient for the complainant to prove loss of an opportunity (*perde d'une chance*) and it is not therefore essential to prove that the complainant would necessarily have been awarded the contract if there had been no breach.[171] Damages awarded may cover both bid costs and loss of profit. An action for damages against utilities must be directed to civil courts. As a general rule, actions for damages before the civil courts last between one and two years and their statute of limitation, under general Luxembourg civil law is thirty years. Judgments of the civil courts (the District Tribunals) can always be appealed to the Court of Appeal in Luxembourg.

(12) Action for damages in The Netherlands

11.380 A complainant who has suffered loss as a result of a breach of the procurement rules may apply to District Court or the *Raad van Arbitrage* for an award of damages. The contracting authority is in principle liable to compensate the

---

[171] The courts have relied on Art. 36 of the Act of 27 July 1936 concerning State Accountancy, rather than EU procurement rules, in order to award compensation for lost profit. Such reliance to the State Accountancy Act tends to favour the applicant as the burden of proof is relatively relaxed under the 1936 Act.

complainant for any damage he has suffered as a result of the unlawful act. Under the general principles of the Dutch Civil Code, damages can cover losses and expenses incurred, as well as loss of profit. However, recovery of loss of profit is possible provided that the complainant can establish that, in the absence of the breach, he would have been awarded the contract. The quantum of such damages includes a reasonable expectation of profitability arising from the performance of the contract in question or a similar contract and would normally not exceed ten per cent of the contract value. For reimbursement of tender costs, it is necessary to establish that, as a result of the unlawful breach of the procurement rules, these costs were actually incurred.

(13) Action for damages in Portugal

A complainant can bring an action for damages against a contracting authority **11.381** before the *Tribunais Administrativos de Circulo* (Administrative Circle Courts). The procedure for an action for damages before in the administrative courts involves three main stages.[172] Firstly, an exchange of written pleadings takes place. Secondly, the court organizes an interim hearing and the presentation of evidence. The administrative court will admit any witnesses put forward by the parties but will only hear oral presentations from either party if there is a request. Finally, the court orders the final hearing and legal submissions by the parties. There are no specific rules governing the availability and quantum of damages in public procurement cases and the applicable rules are those laid down in the Civil Code. Consequently, an award for damages could cover direct damages (*danos emergentes*) comprising of all the bid costs directly related to the tender, as well as loss of profit (*lucros cessantes*), being the net profit which the tenderer would have made, had he been awarded the contract in question. Direct damages and loss of profit will only be available to the extent that there is a sufficient causality link between the infringement of the procurement rules and the damages incurred by the applicant.

Any action for damages in the administrative courts is subject to the usual princi- **11.382** ple under civil law that the action must be brought within three years of the claimant being aware of the damage. The *Tribunais Administrativos de Circulo* (Administrative Circle Courts) are courts of first instance and their rulings may be appealed to the *Supremo Tribunal Administrativo* (Administrative Supreme Court).

The *Supremo Tribunal Administrativo* (Administrative Supreme Court) is both a **11.383** court of first instance and a court of appeal. When exercising appellate jurisdiction, the Administrative Supreme Court is a court of last resort. When a proceeding is

---

[172] *See* Arts. 71 and 72 of the Law on Administrative Procedure (LPTA). Art. 72 specifies that the general provisions of civil procedure shall apply in action for damages before administrative courts.

initiated at first instance that court, its ruling may generally be appealed to the *Pleno da Secção di Contencioso Administrativo do Supremo Tribunal Administrativo* (Full Bench of the Administrative Division of the Supreme Administrative Court). An appeal may be submitted by the losing party, by a person directly harmed by the court's ruling, or by the Public Prosecution Service, within ten days following the notification of the court ruling.

(14) Action for damages in Spain

11.384 An aggrieved tenderer may seek an award of damages from the contracting authority. The complainant must claim damages in the first instance from the authority itself, as part of a preliminary administrative phase. If the administrative claim to the contracting authority is unsuccessful, the complainant may bring an action before the administrative courts.

11.385 The court, in deciding a case for award of damages against a contracting authority, would first consider whether the complainant's legal position could be restored, if, for example, the contract in question has not yet been concluded. Such restoration by readmitting the complainant to the award procedure would reduce substantially any chance of damages being awarded, as the tenderer has not suffered any real and direct loss. However, in most cases, an action for an award of damages will follow the conclusion of the contract in question and, therefore, such restoration will not be possible, because any annulment of the contract itself might prejudice the general interest. In such cases, damages would have to be awarded as the only alternative means of redress. The complainant will need to show that he has suffered real damage or loss which was caused by the conduct of the contracting authority. The claim for damages may cover both direct losses, such as bid costs, as well as loss of profit, which include any profits which the complainant would have achieved in the normal course of events, had he been awarded the contract in question. Spanish law would normally allow compensation for loss of profits only in situations where the bidder demonstrates beyond reasonable doubt that he should have been awarded the contract, had the award procedure been lawfully conducted, because only then he would have suffered real and direct loss. When the contracting authority has failed to advertised a public contract and has subsequently awarded it to an undertaking of its choice, redress based on damages suffers by tenderers having a potential interest in taking part in the non-publicized award will be limited, as it would be difficult to establish the incurrence of any direct or indirect loss as a consequence of the infringement.

(15) Action for damages in Sweden

11.386 Actions for damages have to be brought before the competent *Tingsrätt* (District Court) within one year of the date of the conclusion of the contract. Failure to bring the damages action within the one-year time limit eliminates the right to bring such a claim. A complainant may bring an action for damages against a contracting authority which has infringed public procurement rules. The set aside or annulment of unlawful decisions is not a pre-condition for the admissibility of an action for damages before the *Tingsrätt*.

11.387 Actions for damages before the *Tingsrätt* must be made in writing by way of an application for a summons which includes a statement of the claim, detailed information concerning the parties, the grounds on which it is based, and any supporting evidence. The application should specify the evidence proposed for assessing the claim. The procedure is organized in writing and also by way of court hearings. Hearings are generally held both at the preparatory stage of the proceedings and at the final stage. Since an action for damages may not be brought before the contract is concluded, and as a signed contract cannot be set aside or annulled, interim measures before the *Tingsrätt* are not admissible.

11.388 The complainant must prove that he has incurred damages as a result of the infringement. The burden of proof is higher for damages sought from public authorities than for damages sought from utilities. In particular, the aggrieved tender seeking damages from a contracting authority which operates in the public sector must prove the existence of the claimed damages, the alleged infringement, and the causal link between the damages incurred and the infringement on the part of the contracting authority. The complainant must prove that he should have been awarded the contract, had the contracting authority observed the public procurement rules during the award procedures.

11.389 For damages claims against utilities, a more relaxed proof regime applies.[173] The complainant need not prove that he would have been awarded the contract in the absence of the infringement, but, instead, that that his chances of winning the contract were adversely affected as a result of the infringement on the party of the utility's defaulting procedures.

11.390 Damages against contracting authorities and utilities include, not only bid and preparatory costs, but also compensation for direct losses incurred and loss of profit.[174] The complainant should, in principle, be put in the financial position he would have been in, had he won the contract. The Swedish Procurement Act does not provide any guidance on how the quantum of damages should be assessed, but jurisprudence suggests that the calculation of loss of profit should take into account the anticipated margin from the turnover of the contract, excluding direct and indirect costs necessary for its performance. An action for damages may last for three years. Decisions of the *Tingsrätt* (District Court) may be appealed to

---

[173] *See* Art. 7:7 Lag 1997:1068.
[174] *See* Art. 7:6 Lag 1997:1068.

the competent *Hovrätt* (Court of Appeal) and ultimately to the *Högsta domstolen* (Supreme Court). Appeals to the Supreme Courts, in general cases, require a leave of appeal which, in principle, is granted only in cases turning on points of law. For decisions concerning an action for damages, appeals to the *Hovrätten* may be subject to a leave of appeal if the amount of the requested damages is less than €10,000. All appeals must be lodged within three weeks from the date of the delivery of the decision.

(16) Action for damages in the United Kingdom

11.391 The High Court is the competent forum to award damages to an aggrieved tenderer who has suffered loss or damage as a consequence of a breach of the procurement rules by a contracting authority, prior or after the conclusion of the contract in question. The British courts, in general, will apply existing principles of domestic law when considering claims for damages in public procurement cases. Thus, complainants are required to prove that the contracting authority has committed a breach of public procurement rules and, as a result of such breach, they have suffered harm or damage. A claim for damages may cover bid and preparation costs or the loss of profit that the aggrieved tenderer would have achieved, had been awarded the contract.

11.392 The Regulations do not provide detailed guidance on the availability and amount of damages. The only exception covers disputes in the utilities sectors, where the complainant must establish that an infringement deprived him of a real chance of winning a contract. For disputes in the utilities sectors, a complainant is not required to prove that, in the absence of the breach, he would necessarily have won the contract in question. A reasonable chance of winning the contract appears to be sufficient.

F. Dissuasive Penalty Payments

11.393 Under Article 2(1) of Remedies Directive 92/13, applicable to utilities, member states were given the option of introducing an alternative remedy to the usual combination of interim measures and set aside orders which must be made available, at least prior to the conclusion of the contract. Instead of those two remedies, member states could legislate for the availability of dissuasive penalty payments where an infringement is not corrected or prevented. The option of dissuasive penalty payments has only been taken up by three member states, Denmark (as regards offshore oil and gas utilities only), France, and Luxembourg.

(1) Imposition of fines in Denmark

Infringements of public procurement rules may result in the imposition of fines[175] **11.394**
by ordinary courts. Such fines do not affect possible claims for damages. Although
the Remedies Act does not specify the magnitude of the fines, these fines must be
sufficiently large to effectively discourage contracting authorities from infringing
the rules.[176] The imposition of fines on contracting authorities other than offshore
awarding authorities must be reserved for particularly serious infringements.
Conversely, for offshore awarding authorities, fines are intended to be the primary
sanction available to the Maritime and Commercial Court, due to the fact that
actions for interim measures and annulments of award decisions will have a
detrimental effect upon these entities.

Infringements committed by offshore awarding authorities may in exceptional **11.395**
circumstances[177] be dealt under the normal remedies[178] available to contracting
authorities. However, such exceptional circumstances are met when the alleged
infringement is of such a nature that it may result in imprisonment and that the
case has been initiated by the Public Prosecutor.

(2) Imposition of fines in France

For disputes covering contracts in the utilities sectors, the French system does not **11.396**
provide remedies aimed at interim relief. Instead, it has opted for the imposition
of dissuasive payments (penalty fines) as an alternative form of remedies in accordance with Article 2(1)(c) of Directive 92/13. An order for such penalties can be
brought in either the administrative courts[179] or the civil courts,[180] depending
upon whether or not the contract is administrative in nature.

A complainant alleging an infringement by a utility may, before the contract **11.397**
in question is concluded, apply to the president of the *Tribunal Administratif*
or the president of the civil court. The president may then order the utility to
comply with its obligations within a particular time limit. In deciding whether
to impose such an order, the president should apply a balance of interests test
by taking into account the probable effects of the measure as regards all the
interests potentially at stake, including the public interest, and should refrain

---

[175] *See* Art. 6(1) of the Remedies Act.   [176] *See* Art. 2(5) of Directive 92/13.
[177] *See* Art. 6(3) of the Remedies Act.   [178] *See* Art. 5(1) of the Remedies Act.
[179] *See* Law No. 93-1416 as amended by Art. 23 to the TA/CAA Code, for penalties sought
before the administrative courts.
[180] *See* Law No. 93-1416 as amended by Art. 7.1 to the law which implemented Utilities
Directive 90/531 (Law No. 92-1282), for penalties sought before the actions in the civil courts.

from granting the order where the negative consequences would exceed the benefits.[181]

11.398 At the same time, the president may also impose a provisional daily fine (*une astreinte provisoire*) as from the expiry of the specified time limit. If the infringement in question has not been corrected in accordance with the judge's directions, the judge may impose a final penalty (*une astreinte définitive*). A provisional or final penalty fine may be partially or fully annulled if it is proven that the utility's non-compliance, or delay in complying, with the president's order was due to any extraneous circumstances. The imposition of a penalty fine, whether provisional or final, is entirely independent of any action for damages. Thus, the imposition of such a fine will not hinder a complainant from also seeking an award of damages as against the utility.

(3) Imposition of fines in Luxembourg

11.399 The President of the District Tribunal is empowered to order dissuasive payments upon the private utility if a wrongful or illegal clause, which would cause damage, is not modified or deleted.[182]

G. Complaints to the European Commission

11.400 Under the Remedies Directives, the Commission may invoke a corrective procedure when, prior to a contract being concluded, it considers that a clear and manifest infringement of EU procurement rules has been committed. In such a case, the Commission will notify the awarding authority and the relevant member state government of the circumstances of the alleged infringement. The Commission will set a time limit of at least twenty-one days for public sector contracting authorities or thirty days for entities operating in the utility sectors, within which the national government has to respond. In practice the awarding authority is called upon to justify its conduct, rectify the infringement or suspend the award procedure.

11.401 In cases where the Commission is not satisfied with the explanations or actions of the awarding authority or the government of the respective member state, it may commence formal proceedings against the latter under Article 234 EC, seeking a declaration by the European Court of Justice for failure on the part of the

---

[181] *See Société Biwater Europe Ltd v Sivom de la région d'Aigues Mortes*, where the president of the administrative tribunal of Montpellier granted an order on 14 September 1994. Courrier des maires 11 November 1994, p. 57, Rep. Dalloz, *Droit communautaire, v marchés publics*, No 617.

[182] *See* Art. 2.1(c) of Directive 92/13.

member state to observe and comply with Community law. In particularly serious cases, the Commission might also ask the European Court of Justice to grant interim measures.

H. Conciliation Procedure for Utilities

Where a dispute arises in relation to procurement award procedures in the utilities **11.402** sectors, an aggrieved tenderer may initiate the conciliation procedure specified in the Remedies Directive 92/13 for the utilities sectors. Recourse to the conciliation procedure involves the following steps: the aggrieved tenderer forwards a request for use of the conciliation procedure to the European Commission; and the Commission asks the utility in question to state whether it is willing to take part in the conciliation procedure. The procedure can only continue if the utility gives its consent; then the Commission proposes a conciliator drawn from a list of independent persons. Both sides must state whether they accept the conciliator and each side designates an additional conciliator; then the aggrieved tenderer, the utility and any other relevant candidate or tenderer have the opportunity to make representations to the conciliators; and, finally, the conciliator endeavours to reach agreement between the parties which is in accordance with Community law.

The conciliation procedure must be distinguished from any pre-judicial adminis- **11.403** trative procedures at national level. Interestingly, there is no provision concerning the relationship between the two proceedings, and in a case where the same person were to initiate conciliation and judicial review proceedings under the Directive simultaneously, the relation between them is unclear. The utility or the aggrieved tenderer may withdraw from the procedure at any time.

CONCLUSIONS

Public procurement in the European Union has been an integral part of the concept of the common market. Its regulation provides for economic and policy justifications for eliminating existing non-tariff barriers in inter-state trade. The identification of public procurement as a major non-tariff barrier has revealed the economic importance of its regulation. Savings and price convergence appear as the main arguments for liberalizing the trade patterns of public procurement. The economic approach to the regulation of public procurement aims at the integration of public markets across the European Union. Through the principles of transparency, non-discrimination, and objectivity in the award of public contracts, it is envisaged that the regulatory system will bring about competitiveness in the relevant product and geographical markets, will increase import penetration of products and services destined for the public sector, will enhance the tradability of public contracts across the common market, will result in significant price convergence, and, finally, will be the catalyst for the necessary rationalisation and industrial restructuring of the European industrial base. Public procurement liberalization reflects the wish of European institutions to eliminate preferential and discriminatory purchasing patterns by the public sector and create seamless intra-community trade patterns between the public and private sectors. Public procurement by member states and their contracting authorities is often susceptible to a rationale and policy that favour indigenous undertakings at the expense of more efficient competitors. As the relevant markets have been sheltered from competition, distorted patterns emerge in the trade of goods, works, and services destined for the pubic sector. These trade patterns represent a serious impediment in the functioning of the common market and inhibit the fulfilment of the principles enshrined in the Treaties. Alongside the economic arguments, legal arguments have emerged supporting the regulation of public procurement, as a necessary ingredient of the fundamental principles of the Treaties such as the free movement of goods and services, the right of establishment, and the prohibition of discrimination of nationality grounds. The legal significance of the regulation of public procurement in the common market has been well documented through the jurisprudence of the European Court of Justice.

The influence of neo-classical economic theories on public procurement regulation has taken the relevant regime through the paces of the liberalization of public markets within the European Union and with reference to the World Trade

Organisation. Anti-trust and its remedies have played a seemingly important role in determining the necessary competitive conditions for the supply side to service the public sector. However, we have seen the emergence of a *sui generis* marketplace where the mere existence and functioning of anti-trust is not sufficient to achieve the envisaged objectives. Public markets require a positive regulatory approach in order to enhance market access. Whereas anti-trust and the neo-classical approach to economic integration depend heavily on price competition, public procurement regulation requires a system which primarily safeguards market access. Such a regulatory system could be described as public competition law and represents the first departure from the *stricto sensu* neo-classical perspective of public procurement. A policy orientation has emerged mainly through the jurisprudential approach of the regime and the willingness of the Court to expand on the element of flexibility that is inherent in the Public Procurement Directives.

The neo-classical versus the ordo-liberal approach reflects the frequently rehearsed debate about the origins of anti-trust law and policy *per se*. The European integration has benefited from a system where the neo-classical approach has contributed to the functioning of an environment of workable competition. However, consistently the rigidity of the neo-classical influence has been diluted with policy considerations, often attributed to national policy requirements. The reflection of the above picture is presented in public procurement regulation, although there are certain differences: the Court has allowed for a flexible policy-oriented application of public procurement, where in anti-trust the Commission has eroded the strict neo-classical approach of Article 81(1) EC with the plethora of policy considerations under 81(3) EC. Nevertheless, the similarity of balancing an economic exercise with policy choice is remarkable.

Public procurement regulation is an essential instrument of the common market. With the European Union in an expansion mode, European institutions need to provide a hint as to what public procurement stands for. The new generation of legal instruments intends to simplify and modernize the regime. In addition, there is strong evidence that the existence of competitive conditions within public markets would disengage the applicability of the relevant Directives. This development indicates the referral of public markets to anti-trust, perhaps as the ultimate regulatory regime. Public procurement remains one of the most influential instruments of policy choice in the hands of member states and also the European Commission. Its complementarity and compatibility with common policies is recognized and accepted by European institutions and member states.

In its jurisprudence, the European Court of Justice has reflected on the relative importance of public procurement to the fundamental freedoms of the common market, namely the right of establishment and the freedom to provide services. The approach taken by the Court revealed a positive yet restrictive interpretation of the Directives. By conferring direct effect upon their provisions, where appropriate, and inviting national courts to play prominent role in future public procurement litigation, the Court has hinted towards its preference for a decentralized enforcement of the Directives.

The Court's case law has also played an important function in delineating key concepts within the public procurement legal framework, such as *contracting authorities* and *award criteria*. This has exposed a significant characteristic of the Directives: *flexibility*. The Court developed a *ratione*, which recognises discretion in the hands of contracting authorities, discretion which is integral to the legal framework, compatible to the attainment of the fundamental freedoms of the common market, and complementary with other policies. The Court abandoned the *formality test* in determining the relationship between an entity and the state and instead adopted *the functionality* and *dependency tests* to define contracting authorities. In addition, *dualism* and the dual capacity of contracting authorities are irrelevant to the applicability of Public Procurement Directives. The Court also suggested that *commerciality* and *competitiveness* might lift the veil of compulsory tendering, thus rendering the public procurement rules inapplicable. Finally, the Court accepted, in principle, the complementarity of relevant policies of the European integration process, such as social policy and the protection of the environment, by conferring discretion to contracting authorities to award public contracts by reference to employee protection as well as socio-economic and environmental considerations. The Court's approach does not contradict its positive and restrictive interpretation of Public Procurement Directives and does not conflict with the *stricto sensu* and *de lege lata* approach of the Court. It rather recognises the fact that the relevant legal framework has to move on with the times, requirements and priorities of the common market. The fourth generation of the Public Procurement Directives has benefited immensely from the Court's jurisprudence, and the legislature has incorporated many of the themes that have emerged from the Court's jurisprudence in order to provide for a comprehensive regime that takes into account the needs of the public sector and the utilities as well as the needs of the private sector. The new regime of public procurement makes also clear its complementary relations with relevant policies of the common market.

Public procurement has been re-affirmed as a key parameter for the common market and at the same time as an important policy tool at domestic level. The new generation of legal instruments intends to simplify and modernize a regulatory regime which aims at gradually establishing a public market in the European Union. This regime seeks to accomplish unobstructed access to public markets through transparency of public expenditure relating to procurement, improved market information, elimination of technical standards capable of discriminating against potential contractors, and uniform application of objective criteria of participation in tendering and award procedures. The new regime has three principal objectives: simplification, modernization, and flexibility.

The objective of simplification has been met to a large extent. The new Public Sector Directive represents a notable example of codification of supranational administrative law. The objective of modernization is partly met, mainly as a result of the enormity of the newly introduced concepts. The ability of bodies governed by public law to tender for public contracts along private undertakings is a significant development. The use of framework procurement could assist in bringing the public sector closer to a seamless supply chain management. The introduction of electronic procurement and the use of information technology in public purchasing could process the logistics of public sector purchasing faster and more efficiently. However, the introduction of the competitive dialogue to facilitate the award of complex projects such as public–private partnerships and trans-European networks leaves many practical questions over its nature and conduct unanswered. This represents the biggest problem for the new regime. The exceptional nature of the competitive dialogue and its hierarchy with other award procedures (the wording of the Public Sector Directive puts the procedure on a par with the negotiated procedures with prior advertisement), the discretion of contracting authorities to initiate the procedure (who is to determine the nature of a particularly complex contract and the inability of the contracting authorities to draw precise specifications and the contact's financial and legal make-up), the internal structure and conduct of the procedure (the confusion surrounding the different stages pre-tender and post-tender), the response of the private sector (the predictably very high costs in participating), the degree of competition achieved (there is great potential for post tender negotiations), and, finally, the overall value for money results (in many instances the completive dialogue is less flexible than the negotiated procedures), are pertinent questions that have not been addressed by the new public procurement regime.

The objective of flexibility is the surprise element of the new regulatory package. The relaxation of the competitive tendering regime and the disengagement of the public procurement rules in industries that operate under competitive conditions in the utilities sectors indicate the links between procurement regulation and anti-trust. The non-applicability of the regime to telecommunications entities is an important development indicative of the future legal and regulatory blueprints. A rather disappointing feature of the new regime is the lack of clarity over the potential use of socio-economic and environmental considerations as part of the award criteria. Contrary to the Court's jurisprudential inferences, the new Directives do not confer the much-needed flexibility in this matter to contracting authorities, thus inviting the Court to continue its *rule of reason* approach into the legitimacy of policies, other than economic ones, through public procurement regulation.

The regulation of public procurement reflects on two opposite dynamics: one of a community-wide orientation and one of national priorities. Litigation and jurisprudential inferences will be extremely important in understanding the thrust of the new regime. The role of the Court has been instrumental in shaping many of the newly introduced concepts and in the future it will be invaluable in interpreting the new public procurement regime and pronouncing on the compatibility of implementing national provisions with the *acquis communautaire*.

Appendices

APPENDIX 1

Directive 2004/17/EC of the European Parliament and of the Council of 31 March 2004 coordinating the procurement procedures of entities operating in the water, energy, transport and postal services sectors

THE EUROPEAN PARLIAMENT AND THE COUNCIL OF THE EUROPEAN UNION,

Having regard to the Treaty establishing the European Community, and in particular Article 47(2) and Article 55 and Article 95 thereof,

Having regard to the proposal from the Commission,[1]

Having regard to the Opinion of the Economic and Social Committee,[2]

Having regard to the Opinion of the Committee of the Regions,[3]

Acting in accordance with the procedure laid down in Article 251 of the Treaty,[4] in the light of the joint text approved by the Conciliation Committee on 9 December 2003,

Whereas:

(1) On the occasion of new amendments being made to Council Directive 93/38/EEC of 14 June 1993 coordinating the procurement procedures of entities operating in the water, energy, transport and telecommunications sectors,[5] which

---

[1] OJ C 29 E, 30.1.2001, p. 112 and OJ C 203 E, 27.8.2002, p. 183.

[2] OJ C 193, 10.7.2001, p. 1.

[3] OJ C 144, 16.5.2001, p. 23.

[4] Opinion of the European Parliament of 17 January 2002 (OJ C 271 E, 7.11.2002, p. 293), Council Common Position of 20 Mars 2003 (OJ C 147 E, 24.6.2003, p. 137) and Position of the European Parliament of 2 July 2003 (not yet published in the Official Journal). Legislative Resolution of the European Parliament of 29 January 2004 and Decision of the Council of 2 February 2004.

[5] OJ L 199, 9.8.1993, p. 84. Directive as last amended by Commission Directive 2001/78/EC (OJ L 285, 29.10.2001, p. 1).

are necessary to meet requests for simplification and modernisation made by contracting entities and economic operators alike in their responses to the Green Paper adopted by the Commission on 27 November 1996, the Directive should, in the interests of clarity, be recast. This Directive is based on Court of Justice case-law, in particular case-law on award criteria, which clarifies the possibilities for the contracting entities to meet the needs of the public concerned, including in the environmental and/or social area, provided that such criteria are linked to the subject-matter of the contract, do not confer an unrestricted freedom of choice on the contracting entity, are expressly mentioned and comply with the fundamental principles mentioned in recital 9.

(2) One major reason for the introduction of rules coordinating procedures for the award of contracts in these sectors is the variety of ways in which national authorities can influence the behaviour of these entities, including participation in their capital and representation in the entities' administrative, managerial or supervisory bodies.

(3) Another main reason why it is necessary to coordinate procurement procedures applied by the entities operating in these sectors is the closed nature of the markets in which they operate, due to the existence of special or exclusive rights granted by the Member States concerning the supply to, provision or operation of networks for providing the service concerned.

(4) Community legislation, and in particular Council Regulation (EEC) No 3975/87 of 14 December 1987 laying down the procedure for the application of the rules on competition to undertakings in the air transport sector[1] and Regulation (EEC) No 3976/87 of 14 December 1987 on the application of Article 85(3) of the Treaty to certain categories of agreements and concerted practices in the air transport sector,[2] is designed to introduce more competition between carriers providing air transport services to the public. It is therefore not appropriate to include such entities in the scope of this Directive. In view of the competitive position of Community shipping, it would also be inappropriate to make the contracts awarded in this sector subject to the rules of this Directive.

(5) The scope of Directive 98/38/EEC covers, at present, certain contracts awarded by contracting entities operating in the telecommunications sector. A legislative framework, as mentioned in the Fourth report on the implementation of the telecommunications regulations of 25 November 1998, has been adopted to open this sector. One of its consequences has been the introduction of effective competition, both de jure and de facto, in this sector. For information purposes, and in the light of this situation, the Commission has published a list of telecommunications services[3] which may already be excluded from the scope of that Directive by virtue of Article 8 thereof. Further progress has been confirmed in the Seventh report on the implementation of telecommunications regulations of 26 November 2001. It is therefore no longer necessary to regulate purchases by entities operating in this sector.

(6) It is therefore no longer appropriate to maintain the Advisory Committee on Telecommunications Procurement set up by Council Directive 90/531/EEC of 17 September 1990 on the procurement procedures of entities operating in the water, energy transport and telecommunications sectors.[4]

(7) Nevertheless, it is appropriate to continue to monitor developments in the telecommunications sector and to reconsider the situation if it is established that there is no longer effective competition in that sector.

(8) Directive 93/38/EEC excludes from its scope purchases of voice telephony, telex, mobile telephone, paging and satellite services. Those exclusions were introduced to take account of the fact that the services in question could frequently be provided only by one service provider in a given geographical area because of the absence of effective competition and the existence of special or exclusive rights. The introduction of effective competition in the telecommunications sector removes the justification for these exclusions. It is therefore necessary to include the procurement of such telecommunications services in the scope of this Directive.

(9) In order to guarantee the opening up to competition of public procurement contracts awarded by entities operating in the water, energy, transport and postal services sectors, it is advisable to draw up provisions for Community coordination of contracts above a certain value. Such coordination is based on the requirements inferable from Articles 14, 28 and 49 of the EC Treaty and from Article 97 of the Euratom Treaty, namely the principle of equal treatment, of which the principle of non-discrimination is no more than a specific expression, the principle of mutual recognition, the principle of proportionality, as well as the principle of transparency. In view of the nature of the sectors affected by such coordination, the latter should, while safeguarding the application of those principles, establish a framework for sound commercial practice and should allow maximum flexibility.

---

[1] OJ L 374, 31.12.1987, p. 1. Regulation as last amended by Regulation (EC) No 1/2003 (OJ L 1, 4.1.2003, p. 1).

[2] OJ L 374, 31.12.1987, p. 9. Regulation as last amended by the 1994 Act of Accession.

[3] OJ C 156, 3.6.1999, p. 3.

[4] OJ L 297, 29.10.1990, p. 1. Directive as last amended by Directive 94/22/EC of the European Parliament and of the Council (OJ L 164, 30.6.1994, p. 3).

For public contracts the value of which is lower than that triggering the application of provisions of Community coordination, it is advisable to recall the case-law developed by the Court of Justice according to which the rules and principles of the Treaties referred to above apply.

(10) To ensure a real opening up of the market and a fair balance in the application of procurement rules in the water, energy, transport and postal services sectors it is necessary for the entities covered to be identified on a basis other than their legal status. It should be ensured, therefore, that the equal treatment of contracting entities operating in the public sector and those operating in the private sector is not prejudiced. It is also necessary to ensure, in keeping with Article 295 of the Treaty, that the rules governing the system of property ownership in Member States are not prejudiced.

(11) Member States should ensure that the participation of a body governed by public law as a tenderer in a procedure for the award of a contract does not cause any distortion of competition in relation to private tenderers.

(12) Under Article 6 of the Treaty, environmental protection requirements are to be integrated into the definition and implementation of the Community policies and activities referred to in Article 3 of the Treaty, in particular with a view to promoting sustainable development. This Directive therefore clarifies how the contracting entities may contribute to the protection of the environment and the promotion of sustainable development, whilst ensuring the possibility of obtaining the best value for money for their contracts.

(13) Nothing in this Directive should prevent the imposition or enforcement of measures necessary to protect public morality, public policy, public security, health, human and animal life or the preservation of plant life, in particular with a view to sustainable development, provided that these measures are in conformity with the Treaty.

(14) Council Decision 94/800/EC of 22 December 1994 concerning the conclusion on behalf of the European Community, as regards matters within its competence, of the Agreements reached in the Uruguay Round multilateral negotiations (1986 to 1994),[1] approved in particular the WTO Agreement on Government Procurement (hereinafter referred to as the 'Agreement'), the aim of which is to establish a multilateral framework of balanced rights and obligations relating to public contracts with the aim of achieving the liberalisation and expansion of world trade. In view of the international rights and commitments devolving on the Community as a result of the acceptance of the Agreement, the arrangements to be applied to tenderers and products from signatory third countries are those defined by the Agreement. The Agreement does not have direct effect. The contracting entities covered by the Agreement which comply with this Directive and which apply the latter to economic operators of third countries which are signatories to the Agreement should therefore be in conformity with the Agreement. It is also appropriate that this Directive should guarantee for Community economic operators conditions for participation in public procurement which are just as favourable as those reserved for economic operators of third countries which are signatories to the Agreement.

(15) Before launching a procurement procedure, contracting entities may, using a technical dialogue, seek or accept advice which may be used in the preparation of the specifications, provided, however, that such advice does not have the effect of precluding competition.

(16) In view of the diversity of works contracts, contracting entities should be able to make provision for contracts for the design and execution of work to be awarded either separately or jointly. It is not the intention of this Directive

---

[1] OJ L 336, 23.12.1994, p. 1.

to prescribe either joint or separate contract awards. The decision to award contracts separately or jointly should be determined by qualitative and economic criteria, which may be defined by national law.

A contract may be considered to be a works contract only if its subject-matter specifically covers the execution of activities listed in Annex XII, even if the contract covers the provision of other services necessary for the execution of such activities. Service contracts, in particular in the sphere of property management services, may in certain circumstances include works. However, insofar as such works are incidental to the principal subject-matter of the contract, and are a possible consequence thereof or a complement thereto, the fact that such works are included in the contract does not justify the qualification of the contract as a works contract.

For the purpose of calculating the estimated value of a works contract it is appropriate to take as a basis the value of the works themselves as well as the estimated value of supplies and services, if any, that the contracting entities place at the disposal of contractors, insofar as these services or supplies are necessary for the execution of the works in question. It should be understood that, for the purposes of this paragraph, the services concerned are those rendered by the contracting entities through their own personnel. On the other hand, calculation of the value of services contracts, whether or not to be placed at the disposal of a contractor for the subsequent execution of works, follows the rules applicable to service contracts.

(17) The field of services is best delineated, for the purpose of applying the procedural rules of this Directive and for monitoring purposes, by subdividing it into categories corresponding to particular headings of a common classification and by bringing them together in two Annexes, XVII A and XVII B, according to the regime to which they are subject. As regards services in Annex XVII B, the relevant provisions of this Directive should be without prejudice to the application of Community rules specific to the services in question.

(18) As regards service contracts, full application of this Directive should be limited, for a transitional period, to contracts where its provisions will permit the full potential for increased cross-frontier trade to be realised. Contracts for other services need to be monitored during this transitional period before a decision is taken on the full application of this Directive. In this respect, the mechanism for such monitoring needs to be defined. This mechanism should, at the same time, enable interested parties to have access to the relevant information.

(19) Obstacles to the free provision of services should be avoided. Therefore, service providers may be either natural or legal persons. This Directive should not, however, prejudice the application, at national level, of rules concerning the conditions for the pursuit of an activity or a profession, provided that they are compatible with Community law.

(20) Certain new electronic purchasing techniques are continually being developed. Such techniques help to increase competition and streamline public purchasing, particularly in terms of the savings in time and money which their use will allow. Contracting entities may make use of electronic purchasing techniques, provided that such use complies with the rules of this Directive and the principles of equal treatment, non-discrimination and transparency. To that extent, a tender submitted by a tenderer, in particular under a framework agreement or where a dynamic purchasing system is being used, may take the form of that tenderer's electronic catalogue if the latter uses the means of communication chosen by the contracting entity in accordance with Article 48.

(21) In view of the rapid expansion of electronic purchasing systems, appropriate rules should now be introduced to enable contracting entities to take full

advantage of the possibilities afforded by these systems. Against this background, it is necessary to define a completely electronic dynamic purchasing system for commonly used purchases and to lay down specific rules for setting up and operating such a system in order to ensure the fair treatment of any economic operator who wishes to join. Any economic operator which submits an indicative tender in accordance with the specification and meets the selection criteria should be allowed to join such a system. This purchasing technique allows the contracting entity, through the establishment of a list of tenderers already selected and the opportunity given to new tenderers to join, to have a particularly broad range of tenders, as a result of the electronic facilities available, and hence to ensure optimum use of funds through broad competition.

(22) Since use of the technique of electronic auctions is likely to increase, such auctions should be given a Community definition and be governed by specific rules in order to ensure that they operate fully in accordance with the principles of equal treatment, non-discrimination and transparency. To that end, provision should be made for such electronic auctions to deal only with contracts for works, supplies or services for which the specifications can be determined with precision. Such may in particular be the case for recurring supplies, works and service contracts. With the same objective, it should also be possible to establish the respective ranking of the tenderers at any stage of the electronic auction. Recourse to electronic auctions enables contracting entities to ask tenderers to submit new prices, revised downwards, and, when the contract is awarded to the most economically advantageous tender, also to improve elements of the tenders other than prices. In order to guarantee compliance with the principle of transparency, only the elements suitable for automatic evaluation by electronic means, without any intervention and/or

appreciation by the contracting entity, may be the object of electronic auctions, that is, only the elements which are quantifiable so that they can be expressed in figures or percentages. On the other hand, those aspects of tenders which imply an appreciation of non-quantifiable elements should not be the object of electronic auctions. Consequently, certain works contracts and certain service contracts having as their subject-matter intellectual performances, such as the design of works, should not be the object of electronic auctions.

(23) Certain centralised purchasing techniques have been developed in Member States. Several contracting authorities are responsible for making acquisitions or awarding contracts/framework agreements for contracting entities. In view of the large volumes purchased, those techniques help increase competition and streamline public purchasing. Provision should therefore be made for a Community definition of central purchasing bodies used by contracting entities. A definition should also be given of the conditions under which, in accordance with the principles of non-discrimination and equal treatment, contracting entities purchasing works, supplies and/or services through a central purchasing body may be deemed to have complied with this Directive.

(24) In order to take account of the different circumstances obtaining in Member States, Member States should be allowed to choose whether contracting entities may use central purchasing bodies, dynamic purchasing systems or electronic auctions, as defined and regulated by this Directive.

(25) There has to be an appropriate definition of the concept of special or exclusive rights. The consequence of the definition is that the fact that, for the purpose of constructing networks or port or airport facilities, an entity may take advantage of a procedure for the expropriation or use of property or may place network equipment on, under or over the public

highway will not in itself constitute exclusive or special rights within the meaning of this Directive. Nor does the fact that an entity supplies drinking water, electricity, gas or heat to a network which is itself operated by an entity enjoying special or exclusive rights granted by a competent authority of the Member State concerned in itself constitute an exclusive or special right within the meaning of this Directive. Nor may rights granted by a Member State in any form, including by way of acts of concession, to a limited number of undertakings on the basis of objective, proportionate and non-discriminatory criteria that allow any interested party fulfilling those criteria to enjoy those rights be considered special or exclusive rights.

(26) It is appropriate for the contracting entities to apply common procurement procedures in respect of their activities relating to water and for such rules also to apply where contracting authorities within the meaning of this Directive award contracts in respect of their projects in the field of hydraulic engineering, irrigation, land drainage or the disposal and treatment of sewage. However, procurement rules of the type proposed for supplies of goods are inappropriate for purchases of water, given the need to procure water from sources near the area in which it will be used.

(27) Certain entities providing bus transport services to the public were already excluded from the scope of Directive 93/38/EEC. Such entities should also be excluded from the scope of this Directive. In order to forestall the existence of a multitude of specific arrangements applying to certain sectors only, the general procedure that permits the effects of opening up to competition to be taken into account should also apply to all entities providing bus transport services that are not excluded from the scope of Directive 93/38/EEC pursuant to Article 2(4) thereof.

(28) Taking into account the further opening up of Community postal services to competition and the fact that such services are provided through a network by contracting authorities, public undertakings and other undertakings, contracts awarded by contracting entities providing postal services should be subject to the rules of this Directive, including those in Article 30, which, safeguarding the application of the principles referred to in recital 9, create a framework for sound commercial practice and allow greater flexibility than is offered by Directive 2004/18/EC of the European Parliament and of the Council of 31 March 2004 on the coordination of procedures for the award of public works contracts, public supply contracts and public service contracts.[1] For a definition of the activities in question, it is necessary to take into account the definitions of Directive 97/67/EC of the European Parliament and of the Council of 15 December 1997 on common rules for the development of the internal market of Community postal services and the improvement of quality of service.[2]

Whatever their legal status, entities providing postal services are not currently subject to the rules set out in Directive 93/38/EEC. The adjustment of contract award procedures to this Directive could therefore take longer to implement for such entities than for entities already subject to those rules which will merely have to adapt their procedures to the amendments made by this Directive. It should therefore be permissible to defer application of this Directive to accommodate the additional time required for this adjustment. Given the varying situations of such entities, Member States should have the option of providing for a transitional period for the application of this Directive to contracting entities operating in the postal services sector.

---

[1] See page 114 of this Official Journal.
[2] OJ L 15, 21.1.1998, p. 14. Directive as last amended by Regulation (EC) No 1882/2003 (OJ L 284, 31.10.2003, p. 1).

(29) Contracts may be awarded for the purpose of meeting the requirements of several activities, possibly subject to different legal regimes. It should be clarified that the legal regime applicable to a single contract intended to cover several activities should be subject to the rules applicable to the activity for which it is principally intended. Determination of the activity for which the contract is principally intended may be based on an analysis of the requirements which the specific contract must meet, carried out by the contracting entity for the purposes of estimating the contract value and drawing up the tender documents. In certain cases, such as the purchase of a single piece of equipment for the pursuit of activities for which information allowing an estimation of the respective rates of use would be unavailable, it might be objectively impossible to determine for which activity the contract is principally intended. The rules applicable to such cases should be indicated.

(30) Without prejudice to the international commitments of the Community, it is necessary to simplify the implementation of this Directive, particularly by simplifying the thresholds and by rendering applicable to all contracting entities, regardless of the sector in which they operate, the provisions regarding the information to be given to participants concerning decisions taken in relation to contract award procedures and the results thereof. Furthermore, in the context of Monetary Union, such thresholds should be established in euro in such a way as to simplify the application of these provisions while at the same time ensuring compliance with the thresholds laid down in the Agreement, which are expressed in Special Drawing Rights (SDR). In this context, provision should also be made for periodic reviews of the thresholds expressed in euro so as to adjust them, where necessary, in line with possible variations in the value of the euro in relation to the SDR. In addition, the thresholds applicable to design

contests should be identical to those applicable to service contracts.

(31) Provision should be made for cases in which it is possible to refrain from applying the measures for coordinating procedures on grounds relating to State security or secrecy, or because specific rules on the awarding of contracts which derive from international agreements, relating to the stationing of troops, or which are specific to international organisations are applicable.

(32) It is appropriate to exclude certain service, supply and works contracts awarded to an affiliated undertaking having as its principal activity the provision of such services, supply or works to the group of which it is part, rather than offering them on the market. It is also appropriate to exclude certain service, supply and works contracts awarded by a contracting entity to a joint venture which is formed by a number of contracting entities for the purpose of carrying out activities covered by this Directive and of which that entity is part. However, it is appropriate to ensure that this exclusion does not give rise to distortions of competition to the benefit of the undertakings or joint ventures that are affiliated with the contracting entities; it is appropriate to provide a suitable set of rules, in particular as regards the maximum limits within which the undertakings may obtain a part of their turnover from the market and above which they would lose the possibility of being awarded contracts without calls for competition, the composition of joint ventures and the stability of links between these joint ventures and the contracting entities of which they are composed.

(33) In the context of services, contracts for the acquisition or rental of immovable property or rights to such property have particular characteristics which make the application of procurement rules inappropriate.

(34) Arbitration and conciliation services are usually provided by bodies or individuals designated or selected in a manner which cannot be governed by procurement rules.

(35) In accordance with the Agreement, the financial services covered by this Directive do not include contracts relating to the issue, purchase, sale or transfer of securities or other financial instruments; in particular, transactions by the contracting entities to raise money or capital are not covered.

(36) This Directive should cover the provision of services only where based on contracts.

(37) Pursuant to Article 163 of the Treaty, the encouragement of research and technological development is a means of strengthening the scientific and technological basis of Community industry, and the opening up of service contracts contributes to this end. This Directive should not cover the cofinancing of research and development programmes: research and development contracts other than those where the benefits accrue exclusively to the contracting entity for its use in the conduct of its own affairs, on condition that the service provided is wholly remunerated by the contracting entity, are therefore not covered by this Directive.

(38) To forestall the proliferation of specific arrangements applicable to certain sectors only, the current special arrangements created by Article 3 of Directive 93/38/EEC and Article 12 of Directive 94/22/EC of the European Parliament and of the Council of 30 May 1994 on the conditions for granting and using authorisations for the prospection, exploration and production of hydrocarbons[1] governing entities exploiting a geographical area for the purpose of exploring for or extracting oil, gas, coal or other solid fuels should be replaced by the general procedure allowing for exemption of sectors directly exposed to competition. It has to be ensured, however, that this will be without prejudice to Commission Decision 93/676/EEC of 10 December 1993 establishing that the exploitation of geographical areas for the purpose of exploring for or extracting oil or gas does not constitute in the Netherlands an activity defined by Article 2(2)(b)(i) of Council Directive 90/531/EEC and that entities carrying on such an activity are not to be considered in the Netherlands as operating under special or exclusive rights within the meaning of Article 2(3)(b) of the Directive,[2] Commission Decision 97/367/EC of 30 May 1997 establishing that the exploitation of geographical areas for the purpose of exploring for or extracting oil or gas does not constitute in the United Kingdom an activity defined by Article 2(2)(b)(i) of Council Directive 93/38/EEC and that entities carrying on such an activity are not to be considered in the United Kingdom as operating under special or exclusive rights within the meaning of Article 2(3)(b) of the Directive,[3] Commission Decision 2002/205/EC of 4 March 2002 following a request by Austria applying for the special regime provided for in Article 3 of Directive 93/38/EEC[4] and Commission Decision 2004/73/EC on a request from Germany to apply the special procedure laid down in Article 3 of Directive 93/38/EEC.[5]

(39) Employment and occupation are key elements in guaranteeing equal opportunities for all and contribute to integration in society. In this context, sheltered workshops and sheltered employment programmes contribute efficiently towards the integration or reintegration of people with disabilities in the labour market. However, such workshops might not be able to obtain contracts under normal conditions of competition. Consequently, it is appropriate to provide that Member States may reserve the right to participate in award procedures for contracts to such workshops or reserve performance of contracts to the context of sheltered employment programmes.

---

[1] OJ L 164, 30.6.1994, p. 3.

[2] OJ L 316, 17.12.1993, p. 41.
[3] OJ L 156, 13.6.1997, p. 55.
[4] OJ L 68, 12.3.2002, p. 31.
[5] OJ L 16, 23.1.2004, p. 57.

(40) This Directive should apply neither to contracts intended to permit the performance of an activity referred to in Articles 3 to 7 nor to design contests organised for the pursuit of such an activity if, in the Member State in which this activity is carried out, it is directly exposed to competition on markets to which access is not limited. It is therefore appropriate to introduce a procedure, applicable to all sectors covered by this Directive, that will enable the effects of current or future opening up to competition to be taken into account. Such a procedure should provide legal certainty for the entities concerned, as well as an appropriate decisionmaking process, ensuring, within short time limits, uniform application of Community law in this area.

(41) Direct exposure to competition should be assessed on the basis of objective criteria, taking account of the specific characteristics of the sector concerned. The implementation and application of appropriate Community legislation opening a given sector, or a part of it, will be considered to provide sufficient grounds for assuming there is free access to the market in question. Such appropriate legislation should be identified in an annex which can be updated by the Commission. When updating, the Commission takes in particular into account the possible adoption of measures entailing a genuine opening up to competition of sectors other than those for which a legislation is already mentioned in Annex XI, such as that of railway transports. Where free access to a given market does not result from the implementation of appropriate Community legislation, it should be demonstrated that, de jure and de facto, such access is free. For this purpose, application by a Member State of a Directive, such as Directive 94/22/EC opening up a given sector to competition, to another sector, such as the coal sector, is a circumstance to be taken into account for the purposes of Article 30.

(42) The technical specifications drawn up by purchasers should allow public procurement to be opened up to competition. To this end, it should be possible to submit tenders which reflect the diversity of technical solutions. Accordingly, it should be possible to draw up the technical specifications in terms of functional performance and requirements and, where reference is made to the European standard or, in the absence thereof, to the national standard, tenders based on other equivalent arrangements which meet the requirements of the contracting entities and are equivalent in terms of safety should be considered by the contracting entities. To demonstrate equivalence, tenderers should be permitted to use any form of evidence. Contracting entities should be able to provide a reason for any decision that equivalence does not exist in a given case. Contracting entities that wish to define environmental requirements for the technical specifications of a given contract may lay down the environmental characteristics, such as a given production method, and/or specific environmental effects of product groups or services. They may use, but are not obliged to use appropriate specifications that are defined in eco-labels, such as the European Eco-label, (multi-) national eco-labels or any other eco-label provided that the requirements for the label are drawn up and adopted on the basis of scientific information using a procedure in which stakeholders, such as government bodies, consumers, manufacturers, distributors and environmental organisations can participate, and provided that the label is accessible and available to all interested parties. Contracting entities should, whenever possible, lay down technical specifications so as to take into account accessibility criteria for people with disabilities or design for all users. The technical specifications should be clearly indicated, so that all tenderers know what the requirements established by the contracting entity cover.

(43) In order to encourage the involvement of small and medium-sized undertakings in the public contracts procurement

market, it is advisable to include provisions on subcontracting.

(44) Contract performance conditions are compatible with the Directive provided that they are not directly or indirectly discriminatory and are indicated in the notice used to make the call for competition, or in the specifications. They may in particular be intended to encourage on-site vocational training, the employment of people experiencing particular difficulty in integration, the fight against unemployment or the protection of the environment. For example, mention may be made of the requirements—applicable during the performance of the contract—to recruit long-term jobseekers or to implement training measures for the unemployed or for young persons, to comply in substance with the provisions of the basic International Labour Organisation (ILO) Conventions, assuming that such provisions have not been implemented in national law, and to recruit more handicapped persons than are required under national legislation.

(45) The laws, regulations and collective agreements, at both national and Community level, which are in force in the areas of employment conditions and safety at work apply during the performance of a contract, provided that such rules, and their application, comply with Community law. In cross-border situations where workers from one Member State provide services in another Member State for the purpose of performing a contract, Directive 96/71/EC of the European Parliament and of the Council of 16 December 1996 concerning the posting of workers in the framework of the provision of services[1] lays down the minimum conditions which must be observed by the host country in respect of such posted workers. If national law contains provisions to this effect, non-compliance with those obligations may be considered to be grave misconduct or an offence concerning the professional conduct of the economic operator concerned, liable to lead to the exclusion of that economic operator from the procedure for the award of a contract.

(46) In view of new developments in information and telecommunications technology, and the simplifications these can bring in terms of publicising contracts and the efficiency and transparency of procurement procedures, electronic means should be put on a par with traditional means of communication and information exchange. As far as possible, the means and technology chosen should be compatible with the technologies used in the other Member States.

(47) The use of electronic means leads to savings in time. As a result, provision should be made for reducing the minimum periods where electronic means are used, subject, however, to the condition that they are compatible with the specific mode of transmission envisaged at Community level. However, it is necessary to ensure that the cumulative effect of reductions of time limits does not lead to excessively short time limits.

(48) Directive 1999/93/EC of the European Parliament and of the Council of 13 December 1999 on a Community framework for electronic signatures[2] and Directive 2000/31/EC of the European Parliament and of the Council of 8 June 2000 on certain legal aspects of information society services, in particular electronic commerce, in the internal market ('Directive on electronic commerce')[3] should, in the context of this Directive, apply to the transmission of information by electronic means. The public procurement procedures and the rules applicable to service contests require a level of security and confidentiality higher than that required by these Directives. Accordingly, the devices for the electronic receipt of offers, requests to participate and plans and projects should comply with specific additional requirements. To this end, use

---

[1] OJ L 18, 21.1.1997, p. 1.

[2] OJ L 13, 19.1.2000, p. 12.
[3] OJ L 178, 17.7.2000, p. 1.

of electronic signatures, in particular advanced electronic signatures, should, as far as possible, be encouraged. Moreover, the existence of voluntary accreditation schemes could constitute a favourable framework for enhancing the level of certification service provision for these devices.

(49) It is appropriate that the participants in an award procedure are informed of decisions to conclude a framework agreement or to award a contract or to abandon the procedure within time limits that are sufficiently short so as not to render the lodging of requests for review impossible; this information should therefore be given as soon as possible and in general within 15 days following the decision.

(50) It should be clarified that contracting entities which establish selection criteria in an open procedure should do so in accordance with objective rules and criteria, just as the selection criteria in restricted and negotiated procedures should be objective. These objective rules and criteria, just as the selection criteria, do not necessarily imply weightings.

(51) It is important to take into account Court of Justice case-law in cases where an economic operator claims the economic, financial or technical capabilities of other entities, whatever the legal nature of the link between itself and those entities, in order to meet the selection criteria or, in the context of qualification systems, in support of its application for qualification. In the latter case, it is for the economic operator to prove that those resources will actually be available to it throughout the period of validity of the qualification. For the purposes of that qualification, a contracting entity may therefore determine the level of requirements to be met and in particular, for example where the operator lays claim to the financial standing of another entity, it may require that that entity be held liable, if necessary jointly and severally.

Qualification systems should be operated in accordance with objective rules and criteria, which, at the contracting entities' choice, may concern the capacities of the economic operators and/or the characteristics of the works, supplies or services covered by the system. For the purposes of qualification, contracting entities may conduct their own tests in order to evaluate the characteristics of the works, supplies or services concerned, in particular in terms of compatibility and safety.

(52) The relevant Community rules on mutual recognition of diplomas, certificates or other evidence of formal qualifications apply when evidence of a particular qualification is required for participation in a procurement procedure or a design contest.

(53) In appropriate cases, in which the nature of the works and/or services justifies applying environmental management measures or schemes during the performance of a contract, the application of such measures or schemes may be required. Environmental management schemes, whether or not they are registered under Community instruments such as Regulation (EC) No 761/2001 (EMAS),[1] can demonstrate that the economic operator has the technical capability to perform the contract. Moreover, a description of the measures implemented by the economic operator to ensure the same level of environmental protection should be accepted as an alternative to environmental management registration schemes as a form of evidence.

(54) The award of public contracts to economic operators who have participated in a criminal organisation or who have been found guilty of corruption or of fraud to the detriment of the financial interests of the European Communities or of money laundering should be avoided. Given that contracting entities, which are not contracting authorities, might not have access to indisputable proof on the matter, it is appropriate to leave the choice of whether or not to apply the exclusion criteria listed

---

[1] Regulation (EC) No 761/2001 of the European Parliament and of the Council of 19 March 2001 allowing a voluntary participation by organisations in a Community eco-management and audit scheme (EMAS) (OJ L 114, 24.4.2001, p. 1).

in Article 45(1) of Directive 2004/18/EC to these contracting entities. The obligation to apply Article 45(1) should therefore be limited only to contracting entities that are contracting authorities. Where appropriate, the contracting entities should ask applicants for qualification, candidates or tenderers to supply relevant documents and, where they have doubts concerning the personal situation of these economic operators, they may seek the cooperation of the competent authorities of the Member State concerned. The exclusion of such economic operators should take place as soon as the contracting authority has knowledge of a judgment concerning such offences rendered in accordance with national law that has the force of res judicata.

If national law contains provisions to this effect, noncompliance with environmental legislation or legislation on unlawful agreements in contracts which has been the subject of a final judgment or a decision having equivalent effect may be considered an offence concerning the professional conduct of the economic operator concerned or grave misconduct.

Non-observance of national provisions implementing the Council Directives 2000/78/EC[1] and 76/207/EEC[2] concerning equal treatment of workers, which has been the subject of a final judgment or a decision having equivalent effect may be considered an offence concerning the professional conduct of the economic operator concerned or grave misconduct.

(55) Contracts must be awarded on the basis of objective criteria which ensure compliance with the principles of transparency, non-discrimination and equal treatment and which guarantee that tenders are assessed in conditions of effective competition. As a result, it is appropriate to allow the application of two award criteria only: 'the lowest price' and 'the most economically advantageous tender'.

To ensure compliance with the principle of equal treatment in the award of contracts, it is appropriate to lay down an obligation—established by case-law—to ensure the necessary transparency to enable all tenderers to be reasonably informed of the criteria and arrangements which will be applied to identify the most economically advantageous tender. It is therefore the responsibility of contracting entities to indicate the criteria for the award of the contract and the relative weighting given to each of those criteria in sufficient time for tenderers to be aware of them when preparing their tenders. Contracting entities may derogate from indicating the weighting of the criteria for the award of the contract in duly justified cases for which they must be able to give reasons, where the weighting cannot be established in advance, in particular on account of the complexity of the contract. In such cases, they must indicate the descending order of importance of the criteria.

Where contracting entities choose to award a contract to the most economically advantageous tender, they should assess the tenders in order to determine which one offers the best value for money. In order to do this, they should determine the economic and quality criteria which, taken as a whole, must make it possible to determine the most economically advantageous tender for the contracting entity. The determination of these criteria depends on the object of the contract since they must allow the level of performance offered by each tender to be assessed in the light of the object of the contract, as defined in the technical specifications, and the value for money of each tender to be measured. In order to guarantee equal treatment, the

---

[1] Council Directive 2000/78/EC of 27 November 2000 establishing a general framework for equal treatment in employment and occupation (OJ L 303, 2.12.2000, p. 16).
[2] Council Directive 76/207/EEC of 9 February 1976 on the implementation of the principle of equal treatment for men and women as regards access to employment, vocational training and promotion, and working conditions, (OJ L 39 of 14.2.1976, p. 40). Directive as amended by Directive 2002/73/EC of the European Parliament and of the Council (OJ L 269, 5.10.2002, p. 15).

criteria for the award of the contract must enable tenders to be compared and assessed objectively. If these conditions are fulfilled, economic and qualitative criteria for the award of the contract, such as meeting environmental requirements, may enable the contracting entity to meet the needs of the public concerned, as expressed in the specifications of the contract. Under the same conditions, a contracting entity may use criteria aiming to meet social requirements, in particular in response to the needs—defined in the specifications of the contract—of particularly disadvantaged groups of people to which those receiving/using the works, supplies or services which are the object of the contract belong.

(56) The award criteria must not affect the application of national provisions on the remuneration of certain services, such as the services provided by architects, engineers or lawyers.

(57) Council Regulation (EEC, Euratom) No 1182/71 of 3 June 1971 determining the rules applicable to periods, dates and time limits[1] should apply to the calculation of the time limits contained in this Directive.

(58) This Directive should be without prejudice to the existing international obligations of the Community or of the Member States and should not prejudice the application of the provisions of the Treaty, in particular Articles 81 and 86 thereof.

(59) This Directive should not prejudice the time-limits set out in Annex XXV, within which Member States are required to transpose and apply Directive 93/38/EEC.

(60) The measures necessary for the implementation of this Directive should be adopted in accordance with Council Decision 1999/468/EC of 28 June 1999 laying down the procedures for the exercise of implementing powers conferred on the Commission.[2]

HAVE ADOPTED THIS DIRECTIVE:

CONTENTS

---

[1] OJ L 124, 8.6.1971, p. 1.   [2] OJ L 184, 17.7.1999, p. 23.

TITLE III RULES GOVERNING SERVICE DESIGN CONTESTS

TITLE IV STATISTICAL OBLIGATIONS, EXECUTORY POWERS AND FINAL PROVISIONS

Title I

General Provisions Applicable to Contracts and Design Contests

Chapter I Basic Terms

Article 1
Definitions

1. For the purposes of this Directive, the definitions set out in this Article shall apply.

2. (a) 'Supply, works and service contracts' are contracts for pecuniary interest concluded in writing between one or more of the contracting entities referred to in Article 2(2), and one or more contractors, suppliers, or service providers.

(b) 'Works contracts' are contracts having as their object either the execution, or both the design and execution, of works related to one of the activities within the meaning of Annex XII or a work, or the realisation by whatever means of a work corresponding to the requirements specified by the contracting entity. A 'work' means the outcome of building or civil engineering works taken as a whole which is sufficient of itself to fulfil an economic or technical function.

(c) 'Supply contracts' are contracts other than those referred to in (b) having as their object the purchase, lease, rental or hire-purchase, with or without the option to buy, of products.

A contract having as its object the supply of products, which also covers, as an incidental matter, siting and installation operations shall be considered to be a 'supply contract';

(d) 'Service contracts' are contracts other than works or supply contracts having as their object the provision of services referred to in Annex XVII.

A contract having as its object both products and services within the meaning of Annex XVII shall be considered to be a 'service contract' if the value of the services in question exceeds that of the products covered by the contract.

A contract having as its object services within the meaning of Annex XVII and including activities within the meaning of Annex XII that are only incidental to the principal object of the contract shall be considered to be a service contract.

3. (a) A 'works concession' is a contract of the same type as a works contract except for the fact that the consideration for the works to be carried out consists either solely in the right to exploit the work or in that right together with payment;

(b) A 'service concession' is a contract of the same type as a service contract except for the fact that the consideration for the provision of services consists either solely in the right to exploit the service or in that right together with payment.

4. A 'framework agreement' is an agreement between one or more contracting entities referred to in Article 2(2) and one or more economic operators, the purpose of which is to establish the terms governing contracts to be awarded during a given period, in particular with regard to price and, where appropriate, the quantities envisaged.

5. A 'dynamic purchasing system' is a completely electronic process for making commonly used purchases, the characteristics of which, as generally available on the market, meet the requirements of the contracting entity, which is limited in duration and open throughout its validity to any economic operator which satisfies the selection criteria and has submitted an indicative tender that complies with the specification.

6. An 'electronic auction' is a repetitive process involving an electronic device for the presentation of new prices, revised downwards, and/or new values concerning certain elements of tenders, which occurs after an initial full evaluation of the tenders, enabling them to be ranked using automatic evaluation methods. Consequently, certain service contracts and certain works contracts having as their subject-matter intellectual performances, such as the design of works, may not be the object of electronic auctions.

7. The terms 'contractor', 'supplier' or 'service provider' mean either a natural or a legal person, or a contracting entity within the meaning of Article 2(2)(a) or (b), or a group of such persons and/or entities which offers on the market, respectively, the execution of works and/or a work, products or services.

The terms 'economic operator' shall cover equally the concepts of contractor, supplier and service provider. It is used merely in the interests of simplification.

A 'tenderer' is an economic operator who submits a tender, and 'candidate' means one who has sought an invitation to take part in a restricted or negotiated procedure.

8. A 'central purchasing body' is a contracting authority within the meaning of Article 2(1)(a) or a contracting authority within the meaning of Article 1(9) of Directive 2004/18/EC which:
—acquires supplies and/or services intended for contracting entities or
—awards public contracts or concludes framework agreements for works, supplies or services intended for contracting entities.

9. 'Open, restricted and negotiated procedures' are the procurement procedures applied by contracting entities, whereby:
(a) in the case of open procedures, any interested economic operator may submit a tender;
(b) in the case of restricted procedures, any economic operator may request to participate and only candidates invited by the contracting entity may submit a tender;
(c) in the case of negotiated procedures, the contracting entity consults the economic operators of its choice and negotiates the terms of the contract with one or more of these.

10. 'Design contests' are those procedures which enable the contracting entity to acquire, mainly in the fields of town and country planning, architecture, engineering or data processing, a plan or design selected by a jury after having been put out to competition with or without the award of prizes.

11. 'Written' or 'in writing' means any expression consisting of words or figures that can be read, reproduced and subsequently communicated. It may include information transmitted and stored by electronic means.

12. 'Electronic means' means using electronic equipment for the processing (including digital compression) and storage of data which is transmitted, conveyed and received by wire, by radio, by optical means or by other electromagnetic means.

13. 'Common Procurement Vocabulary (CPV)' means the reference nomenclature applicable to public contracts as adopted by Regulation (EC) No 2195/2002 of 5 November 2002 of the European Parliament and of the Council on the Common Procurement Vocabulary (CVP)[1] while ensuring equivalence with the other existing nomenclatures.

In the event of varying interpretations of the scope of this Directive, owing to possible differences between the CPV and NACE nomenclatures listed in Annex XII or between the CPV and CPC (provisional version) nomenclatures listed in Annex XVII, the NACE or the CPC nomenclature respectively shall take precedence.

CHAPTER II DEFINITION OF THE ACTIVITIES AND ENTITIES COVERED

Section 1 Entities

Article 2

Contracting entities

1. For the purposes of this Directive,
(a) 'Contracting authorities' are State, regional or local authorities, bodies governed by public law, associations formed by one or several such authorities or one or several of such bodies governed by public law.
'A body governed by public law' means any body:
— established for the specific purpose of meeting needs in the general interest, not having an industrial or commercial character,
— having legal personality and

---

[1] OJ L 340, 16.12.2002, p. 1.

— financed, for the most part, by the State, regional or local authorities, or other bodies governed by public law; or subject to management supervision by those bodies; or having an administrative, managerial or supervisory board, more than half of whose members are appointed by the State, regional or local authorities, or by other bodies governed by public law;

(b) a 'public undertaking' is any undertaking over which the contracting authorities may exercise directly or indirectly a dominant influence by virtue of their ownership of it, their financial participation therein, or the rules which govern it.

A dominant influence on the part of the contracting authorities shall be presumed when these authorities, directly or indirectly, in relation to an undertaking:

— hold the majority of the undertaking's subscribed capital, or

— control the majority of the votes attaching to shares issued by the undertaking, or

— can appoint more than half of the undertaking's administrative, management or supervisory body.

2. This Directive shall apply to contracting entities:

(a) which are contracting authorities or public undertakings and which pursue one of the activities referred to in Articles 3 to 7;

(b) which, when they are not contracting authorities or public undertakings, have as one of their activities any of the activities referred to in Articles 3 to 7, or any combination thereof and operate on the basis of special or exclusive rights granted by a competent authority of a Member State.

3. For the purposes of this Directive, 'special or exclusive rights' mean rights granted by a competent authority of a Member State by way of any legislative, regulatory or administrative provision the effect of which is to limit the exercise of activities defined in Articles 3 to 7 to one or more entities, and which substantially affects the ability of other entities to carry out such activity.

Section 2 Activities

Article 3

Gas, heat and electricity

1. As far as gas and heat are concerned, this Directive shall apply to the following activities:

(a) the provision or operation of fixed networks intended to provide a service to the public in connection with the production, transport or distribution of gas or heat; or

(b) the supply of gas or heat to such networks.

2. The supply of gas or heat to networks which provide a service to the public by a contracting entity other than a contracting authority shall not be considered a relevant activity within the meaning of paragraph 1 where:

(a) the production of gas or heat by the entity concerned is the unavoidable consequence of carrying out an activity other than those referred to in paragraphs 1 or 3 of this Article or in Articles 4 to 7; and

(b) supply to the public network is aimed only at the economic exploitation of such production and amounts to not more than 20 % of the entity's turnover having regard to the average for the preceding three years, including the current year.

3. As far as electricity is concerned, this Directive shall apply to the following activities:

(a) the provision or operation of fixed networks intended to provide a service to the public in connection with the production, transport or distribution of electricity; or

(b) the supply of electricity to such networks.

4. The supply of electricity to networks which provide a service to the public by a contracting entity other than a contracting authority shall not be considered a relevant activity within the meaning of paragraph 3 where:

(a) the production of electricity by the entity concerned takes place because its consumption is necessary for carrying out an activity other than those referred to in paragraphs 1 or 3 of this Article or in Articles 4 to 7; and

(b) supply to the public network depends only on the entity's own consumption and has not exceeded 30% of the entity's total production of energy, having regard to the average for the preceding three years, including the current year.

Article 4
Water

1. This Directive shall apply to the following activities:
(a) the provision or operation of fixed networks intended to provide a service to the public in connection with the production, transport or distribution of drinking water; or
(b) the supply of drinking water to such networks.

2. This Directive shall also apply to contracts or design contests awarded or organised by entities which pursue an activity referred to in paragraph 1 and which:
(a) are connected with hydraulic engineering projects, irrigation or land drainage, provided that the volume of water to be used for the supply of drinking water represents more than 20 % of the total volume of water made available by such projects or irrigation or drainage installations, or
(b) are connected with the disposal or treatment of sewage.

3. The supply of drinking water to networks which provide a service to the public by a contracting entity other than a contracting authority shall not be considered a relevant activity within the meaning of paragraph 1 where:
(a) the production of drinking water by the entity concerned takes place because its consumption is necessary for carrying out an activity other than those referred to in Articles 3 to 7; and
(b) supply to the public network depends only on the entity's own consumption and has not exceeded 30 % of the entity's total production of drinking water, having regard to the average for the preceding three years, including the current year.

Article 5
Transport services

1. This Directive shall apply to activities relating to the provision or operation of networks providing a service to the public in the field of transport by railway, automated systems, tramway, trolley bus, bus or cable.

As regards transport services, a network shall be considered to exist where the service is provided under operating conditions laid down by a competent authority of a Member State, such as conditions on the routes to be served, the capacity to be made available or the frequency of the service.

2. This Directive shall not apply to entities providing bus transport services to the public which were excluded from the scope of Directive 93/38/EEC pursuant to Article 2(4) thereof.

Article 6
Postal services

1. This Directive shall apply to activities relating to the provision of postal services or, on the conditions set out in paragraph 2(c), other services than postal services.

2. For the purpose of this Directive and without prejudice to Directive 97/67/EC:
(a) 'postal item': means an item addressed in the final form in which it is to be carried, irrespective of weight. In addition to items of correspondence, such items also include for instance books, catalogues, newspapers, periodicals and postal packages containing merchandise with or without commercial value, irrespective of weight;
(b) 'postal services': means services consisting of the clearance, sorting, routing and delivery of postal items. These services comprise:
— 'reserved postal services': postal services which are or may be reserved on the basis of Article 7 of Directive 97/67/EC,
— 'other postal services': postal services which may not be reserved on the basis of Article 7 of Directive 97/67/EC; and

(c) 'other services than postal services': means services provided in the following areas:

— mail service management services (services both preceding and subsequent to despatch, such as 'mailroom management services'),

— added-value services linked to and provided entirely by electronic means (including the secure transmission of coded documents by electronic means, address management services and transmission of registered electronic mail),

— services concerning postal items not included in point (a), such as direct mail bearing no address,

— financial services, as defined in category 6 of Annex XVII A and in Article 24(c) and including in particular postal money orders and postal giro transfers,

— philatelic services, and

— logistics services (services combining physical delivery and/or warehousing with other non-postal functions),

on condition that such services are provided by an entity which also provides postal services within the meaning of point (b), first or second indent, and provided that the conditions set out in Article 30(1) are not satisfied in respect of the services falling within those indents.

Article 7
Exploration for, or extraction of, oil, gas, coal or other solid fuels, as well as ports and airports

This Directive shall apply to activities relating to the exploitation of a geographical area for the purpose of:

(a) exploring for or extracting oil, gas, coal or other solid fuels, or

(b) the provision of airports and maritime or inland ports or other terminal facilities to carriers by air, sea or inland waterway.

Article 8
Lists of contracting entities

The non-exhaustive lists of contracting entities within the meaning of this Directive are contained in Annexes I to X. Member States shall notify the Commission periodically of any changes to their lists.

Article 9
Contracts covering several activities

1. A contract which is intended to cover several activities shall be subject to the rules applicable to the activity for which it is principally intended.

However, the choice between awarding a single contract and awarding a number of separate contracts may not be made with the objective of excluding it from the scope of this Directive or, where applicable, Directive 2004/18/EC.

2. If one of the activities for which the contract is intended is subject to this Directive and the other to the abovementioned Directive 2004/18/EC and if it is objectively impossible to determine for which activity the contract is principally intended, the contract shall be awarded in accordance with the abovementioned Directive 2004/18/EC.

3. If one of the activities for which the contract is intended is subject to this Directive and the other is not subject to either this Directive or the abovementioned Directive 2004/18/EC, and if it is objectively impossible to determine for which activity the contract is principally intended, the contract shall be awarded in accordance with this Directive.

Chapter III General Principles

Article 10
Principles of awarding contracts

Contracting entities shall treat economic operators equally and non-discriminatorily and shall act in a transparent way.

Title II
Rules Applicable to Contracts

Chapter I General Provisions

Article 11
Economic operators

1. Candidates or tenderers who, under the law of the Member State in which they are established, are entitled to provide the relevant service, shall not be rejected solely on the ground that, under the law of the Member State in which the contract is awarded, they would be required to be either natural or legal persons.

However, in the case of service and works contracts as well as supply contracts covering in addition services and/or siting and installation operations, legal persons may be required to indicate, in the tender or the request to participate, the names and relevant professional qualifications of the staff to be responsible for the performance of the contract in question.

2. Groups of economic operators may submit tenders or put themselves forward as candidates. In order to submit a tender or a request to participate, these groups may not be required by the contracting entities to assume a specific legal form; however, the group selected may be required to do so when it has been awarded the contract, to the extent to which this change is necessary for the satisfactory performance of the contract.

Article 12
Conditions relating to agreements concluded within the World Trade Organisation

For the purposes of the award of contracts by contracting entities, Member States shall apply in their relations conditions as favourable as those which they grant to economic operators of third countries in implementation of the Agreement. Member States shall, to this end, consult one another within the Advisory Committee for Public Contracts on the measures to be taken pursuant to the Agreement.

Article 13
Confidentiality

1. In the context of provision of technical specifications to interested economic operators, of qualification and selection of economic operators and of award of contracts, contracting entities may impose requirements with a view to protecting the confidential nature of information which they make available.

2. Without prejudice to the provisions of this Directive, in particular those concerning the obligations relating to the advertising of awarded contracts and to the information to candidates and tenderers set out in Articles 43 and 49, and in accordance with the national law to which the contracting entity is subject, the contracting authority shall not disclose information forwarded to it by economic operators which they have designated as confidential; such information includes, in particular, technical or trade secrets and the confidential aspects of tenders.

Article 14
Framework agreements

1. Contracting entities may regard a framework agreement as a contract within the meaning of Article 1(2) and award it in accordance with this Directive.

2. Where contracting entities have awarded a framework agreement in accordance with this Directive, they may avail themselves of Article 40(3)(i) when awarding contracts based on that framework agreement.

3. Where a framework agreement has not been awarded in accordance with this Directive, contracting entities may not avail themselves of Article 40(3)(i).

4. Contracting entities may not misuse framework agreements in order to hinder, limit or distort competition.

Article 15
Dynamic purchasing systems

1. Member States may provide that contracting entities may use dynamic purchasing systems.

2. In order to set up a dynamic purchasing system, contracting entities shall follow the rules of the open procedure in all its phases up to the award of the contracts to be concluded under this system. All tenderers who satisfy the selection criteria and have submitted an indicative tender which complies with the specification and any possible additional documents shall be admitted to the system; indicative tenders may be improved at any time provided that they continue to comply with the specification. With a view to setting up the system and to the award of contracts under that system, contracting entities shall use solely electronic means in accordance with Article 48(2) to (5).

3. For the purposes of setting up the dynamic purchasing system, contracting entities shall:

(a) publish a contract notice making it clear that a dynamic purchasing system is involved;

(b) indicate in the specification, amongst other matters, the nature of the purchases envisaged under that system, as well as all the necessary information concerning the purchasing system, the electronic equipment used and the technical connection arrangements and specifications;

(c) offer by electronic means, on publication of the notice and until the system expires, unrestricted, direct and full access to the specification and to any additional documents and shall indicate in the notice the internet address at which such documents may be consulted.

4. Contracting entities shall give any economic operator, throughout the entire period of the dynamic purchasing system, the possibility of submitting an indicative tender and of being admitted to the system under the conditions referred to in paragraph 2. They shall complete evaluation within a maximum of 15 days from the date of submission of the indicative tender. However, they may extend the evaluation period provided that no invitation to tender is issued in the meantime.

Contracting entities shall inform the tenderer referred to in the first subparagraph at the earliest possible opportunity of its admittance to the dynamic purchasing system or of the rejection of its indicative tender.

5. Each specific contract shall be the subject of an invitation to tender. Before issuing the invitation to tender, contracting entities shall publish a simplified contract notice inviting all interested economic operators to submit an indicative tender, in accordance with paragraph 4, within a time limit that may not be less than 15 days from the date on which the simplified notice was sent. Contracting entities may not proceed with tendering until they have completed evaluation of all the indicative tenders received within that time limit.

6. Contracting entities shall invite all tenderers admitted to the system to submit a tender for each specific contract to be awarded under the system. To that end, they shall set a time limit for the submission of tenders.

They shall award the contract to the tenderer which submitted the best tender on the basis of the award criteria set out in the contract notice for the establishment of the dynamic purchasing system. Those criteria may, if appropriate, be formulated more precisely in the invitation referred to in the first subparagraph.

7. A dynamic purchasing system may not last for more than four years, except in duly justified exceptional cases.

Contracting entities may not resort to this system to prevent, restrict or distort competition.

No charges may be billed to the interested economic operators or to parties to the system.

Chapter II Thresholds and Exclusion Provisions

Section 1 Thresholds

Article 16
Contract thresholds

Save where they are ruled out by the exclusions in Articles 19 to 26 or pursuant to Article 30, concerning the pursuit of the activity in question, this Directive shall apply to contracts which have a value excluding value-added tax (VAT) estimated to be no less than the following thresholds:

(a) EUR 499 000 in the case of supply and service contracts;

(b) EUR 6 242 000 in the case of works contracts.

Article 17
Methods of calculating the estimated value of contracts, framework agreements and dynamic purchasing systems

1. The calculation of the estimated value of a contract shall be based on the total amount payable, net of VAT, as estimated by the contracting entity. This calculation shall take account of the estimated total amount, including any form of option and any renewals of the contract.

Where the contracting entity provides for prizes or payments to candidates or tenderers it shall take them into account when calculating the estimated value of the contract.

2. Contracting entities may not circumvent this Directive by splitting works projects or proposed purchases of a certain quantity of supplies and/or services or by using special methods for calculating the estimated value of contracts.

3. With regard to framework agreements and dynamic purchasing systems, the estimated value to be taken into consideration shall be the maximum estimated value net of VAT of all the contracts envisaged for the total term of the agreement or system.

4. For the purposes of Article 16, contracting entities shall include in the estimated value of a works contract both the cost of the works and the value of any supplies or services necessary for the execution of the works, which they make available to the contractor.

5. The value of supplies or services which are not necessary for the performance of a particular works contract may not be added to the value of the works contract when to do so would result in removing the procurement of those supplies or services from the scope of this Directive.

6. (a) Where a proposed work or purchase of services may result in contracts being awarded at the same time in the form of separate lots, account shall be taken of the total estimated value of all such lots.

Where the aggregate value of the lots is equal to or exceeds the threshold laid down in Article 16, this Directive shall apply to the awarding of each lot.

However, the contracting entities may waive such application in respect of lots the estimated value of which, net of VAT, is less than EUR 80 000 for services or EUR 1 million for works, provided that the aggregate value of those lots does not exceed 20% of the aggregate value of the lots as a whole.

(b) Where a proposal for the acquisition of similar supplies may result in contracts being awarded at the same time in the form of separate lots, account shall be taken of the total estimated value of all such lots when applying Article 16.

Where the aggregate value of the lots is equal to or exceeds the threshold laid down in Article 16, this Directive shall apply to the awarding of each lot.

However, the contracting entities may waive such application in respect of lots, the estimated value of which, net of VAT, is less than EUR 80 000, provided that the aggregate cost of those lots does not exceed 20 % of the aggregate value of the lots as a whole.

7. In the case of supply or service contracts which are regular in nature or which are intended to be renewed within a given period, the calculation of the estimated contract value shall be based on the following:

(a) either the total actual value of the successive contracts of the same type awarded during the preceding twelve months or financial year adjusted, if possible, to take account of the changes in quantity or value which would occur in the course of the 12 months following the initial contract;

(b) or the total estimated value of the successive contracts awarded during the 12 months following the first delivery, or during the financial year if that is longer than 12 months.

8. The basis for calculating the estimated value of a contract including both supplies and services shall be the total value of the supplies and services, regardless of their respective

shares. The calculation shall include the value of the siting and installation operations.

9. With regard to supply contracts relating to the leasing, hire, rental or hire purchase of products, the value to be taken as a basis for calculating the estimated contract value shall be as follows:

(a) in the case of fixed-term contracts, if that term is less than or equal to 12 months, the total estimated value for the term of the contract or, if the term of the contract is greater than 12 months, the total value including the estimated residual value;

(b) in the case of contracts without a fixed term or the term of which cannot be defined, the monthly value multiplied by 48.

10. For the purposes of calculating the estimated contract value of service contracts, the following amounts shall, where appropriate, be taken into account:

(a) the premium payable, and other forms of remuneration, in the case of insurance services;

(b) fees, commissions, interest and other modes of remuneration, in the case of banking and other financial services;

(c) fees, commissions payable and other forms of remuneration, in the case of contracts involving design tasks.

11. In the case of service contracts which do not indicate a total price, the value to be used as the basis for calculating the estimated contract value shall be:

(a) in the case of fixed-term contracts, if that term is less than or equal to 48 months: the total value for their full term;

(b) in the case of contracts without a fixed term or with a term greater than 48 months: the monthly value multiplied by 48.

Section 2 Contracts and concessions and contracts subject to special arrangements

Subsection 1

Article 18

Works and service concessions

This Directive shall not apply to works and service concessions which are awarded by contracting entities carrying out one or more of the activities referred to in Articles 3 to 7, where those concessions are awarded for carrying out those activities.

Subsection 2 Exclusions applicable to all contracting entities and to all types of contract

Article 19

Contracts awarded for purposes of resale or lease to third parties

1. This Directive shall not apply to contracts awarded for purposes of resale or lease to third parties, provided that the contracting entity enjoys no special or exclusive right to sell or lease the subject of such contracts, and other entities are free to sell or lease it under the same conditions as the contracting entity.

2. The contracting entities shall notify the Commission at its request of all the categories of products or activities which they regard as excluded under paragraph 1. The Commission may periodically publish in the *Official Journal of the European Union*, for information purposes, lists of the categories of products and activities which it considers to be covered by this exclusion. In so doing, the Commission shall respect any sensitive commercial aspects that the contracting entities may point out when forwarding information.

Article 20

Contracts awarded for purposes other than the pursuit of an activity covered or for the pursuit of such an activity in a third country

1. This Directive shall not apply to contracts which the contracting entities award for purposes other than the pursuit of their activities as described in Articles 3 to 7 or for the pursuit of such activities in a third country, in conditions not involving the physical use of a network or geographical area within the Community.

2. The contracting entities shall notify the Commission at its request of any activities which they regard as excluded under paragraph 1. The Commission may periodically publish in the *Official Journal of the European Union* for information purposes, lists of the categories of activities which it considers to be covered by this exclusion. In so doing, the Commission shall respect any sensitive commercial aspects that the contracting entities may point out when forwarding this information.

Article 21
Contracts which are secret or require special security measures

This Directive shall not apply to contracts when they are declared to be secret by a Member State, when their performance must be accompanied by special security measures in accordance with the laws, regulations or administrative provisions in force in the Member State concerned, or when the protection of the basic security interests of that Member State so requires.

Article 22
Contracts awarded pursuant to international rules

This Directive shall not apply to contracts governed by different procedural rules and awarded:

(a) pursuant to an international agreement concluded in accordance with the Treaty between a Member State and one or more third countries and covering supplies, works, services or design contests intended for the joint implementation or exploitation of a project by the signatory States; all agreements shall be communicated to the Commission, which may consult the Advisory Committee for Public Contracts referred to in Article 68;

(b) pursuant to a concluded international agreement relating to the stationing of troops and concerning the undertakings of a Member State or a third country;

(c) pursuant to the particular procedure of an international organisation.

Article 23
Contracts awarded to an affiliated undertaking, to a joint venture or to a contracting entity forming part of a joint venture

1. For the purposes of this Article, 'affiliated undertaking' means any undertaking the annual accounts of which are consolidated with those of the contracting entity in accordance with the requirements of the Seventh Council Directive 83/349/EEC of 13 June 1983 based on the Article 44(2)(g) of the Treaty on consolidated accounts,[1,2] or, in the case of entities not subject to that Directive, any undertaking over which the contracting entity may exercise, directly or indirectly, a dominant influence within the meaning of Article 2(1)(b) hereof or which may exercise a dominant influence over the contracting entity or which, in common with the contracting entity, is subject to the dominant influence of another undertaking by virtue of ownership, financial participation, or the rules which govern it.

2. Provided that the conditions in paragraph 3 are met, this Directive shall not apply to contracts awarded:

(a) by a contracting entity to an affiliated undertaking, or

(b) by a joint venture, formed exclusively by a number of contracting entities for the purpose of carrying out activities within the meaning of Articles 3 to 7, to an undertaking which is affiliated with one of these contracting entities.

3. Paragraph 2 shall apply:

(a) to service contracts provided that at least 80 % of the average turnover of the affiliated undertaking with respect to services for the preceding three years derives from the provision of such services to undertakings with which it is affiliated;

(b) to supplies contracts provided that at least 80 % of the average turnover of the affiliated undertaking with respect to supplies for the preceding three years derives from the provision of such supplies to undertakings with which it is affiliated;

(c) to works contracts provided that at least 80 % of the average turnover of the affiliated undertaking with respect to works for the preceding three years derives from the provision of such works to undertakings with which it is affiliated.

When, because of the date on which an affiliated undertaking was created or commenced activities, the turnover is not available for the

---

[1] OJ L 193, 18.7.1983, p. 1. Directive as last amended by Directive 2001/65/EC of the European Parliament and of the Council (OJ L 283, 27.10.2001, p. 28).

[2] Editorial Note: The title of the Directive has been adjusted to take account of the renumbering of the Articles of the Treaty in accordance with Article 12 of the Treaty of Amsterdam; the original reference was to Article 54(3)(g) of the Treaty.

preceding three years, it will be sufficient for that undertaking to show that the turnover referred to in points (a), (b) or (c) is credible, particularly by means of business projections.

Where more than one undertaking affiliated with the contracting entity provides the same or similar services, supplies or works, the above percentages shall be calculated taking into account the total turnover deriving respectively from the provision of services, supplies or works by those affiliated undertakings.

4. This Directive shall not apply to contracts awarded:

(a) by a joint venture, formed exclusively by a number of contracting entities for the purpose of carrying out activities within the meaning of Articles 3 to 7, to one of these contracting entities, or

(b) by a contracting entity to such a joint venture of which it forms part, provided that the joint venture has been set up in order to carry out the activity concerned over a period of at least three years and that the instrument setting up the joint venture stipulates that the contracting entities, which form it, will be part thereof for at least the same period.

5. Contracting entities shall notify to the Commission, at its request, the following information regarding the application of paragraphs 2, 3 and 4:

(a) the names of the undertakings or joint ventures concerned,

(b) the nature and value of the contracts involved,

(c) such proof as may be deemed necessary by the Commission that the relationship between the undertaking or joint venture to which the contracts are awarded and the contracting entity complies with the requirements of this Article.

Subsection 3 Exclusions applicable to all contracting entities, but to service contracts only

Article 24
Contracts relating to certain services excluded from the scope of this Directive

This Directive shall not apply to service contracts for:

(a) the acquisition or rental, by whatever financial means, of land, existing buildings or other immovable property or concerning rights thereon; nevertheless, financial service contracts concluded at the same time as, before or after the contract of acquisition or rental, in whatever form, shall be subject to this Directive;

(b) arbitration and conciliation services;

(c) financial services in connection with the issue, sale, purchase or transfer of securities or other financial instruments, in particular transactions by the contracting entities to raise money or capital;

(d) employment contracts;

(e) research and development services other than those where the benefits accrue exclusively to the contracting entity for its use in the conduct of its own affairs, on condition that the service provided is wholly remunerated by the contracting entity.

Article 25
Service contracts awarded on the basis of an exclusive right

This Directive shall not apply to service contracts awarded to an entity which is itself a contracting authority within the meaning of Article 2(1)(a) or to an association of contracting authorities on the basis of an exclusive right which they enjoy pursuant to a published law, regulation or administrative provision which is compatible with the Treaty.

Subsection 4 Exclusions applicable to certain contracting entities only

Article 26
Contracts awarded by certain contracting entities for the purchase of water and for the supply of energy or of fuels for the production of energy

This Directive shall not apply:

(a) to contracts for the purchase of water if awarded by contracting entities engaged in one or both of the activities referred to in Article 4(1).

(b) to contracts for the supply of energy or of fuels for the production of energy, if awarded by contracting entities engaged in an activity referred to in Article 3(1), Article 3(3) or Article 7(a).

Subsection 5 Contracts subject to special arrangements, provisions concerning central purchasing bodies and the general procedure in case of direct exposure to competition

Article 27
Contracts subject to special arrangements

Without prejudice to Article 30 the Kingdom of the Netherlands, the United Kingdom, the Republic of Austria and the Federal Republic of Germany shall ensure, by way of the conditions of authorisation or other appropriate measures, that any entity operating in the sectors mentioned in Decisions 93/676/EEC, 97/367/EEC, 2002/205/EC and 2004/73/EC:

(a) observes the principles of non-discrimination and competitive procurement in respect of the award of supplies, works and service contracts, in particular as regards the information which the entity makes available to economic operators concerning its procurement intentions;

(b) communicates to the Commission, under the conditions defined in Commission Decision 93/327/EEC defining the conditions under which contracting entities exploiting geographical areas for the purpose of exploring for or extracting oil, gas, coal or other solid fuels must communicate to the Commission information relating to the contracts they award.[1]

Article 28
Reserved contracts

Member States may reserve the right to participate in contract award procedures to sheltered workshops or provide for such contracts to be performed in the context of sheltered employment programmes where most of the employees concerned are handicapped persons who, by reason of the nature or the seriousness of their disabilities, cannot carry on occupations under normal conditions.

The notice used to make the call for competition shall make reference to this Article.

---

[1] OJ L 129, 27.5.1993, p. 25.

Article 29
Contracts and framework agreements awarded by central purchasing bodies

1. Member States may prescribe that contracting entities may purchase works, supplies and/or services from or through a central purchasing body.

2. Contracting entities which purchase works, supplies and/ or services from or through a central purchasing body in the cases set out in Article 1(8) shall be deemed to have complied with this Directive insofar as the central purchasing body has complied with it or, where appropriate, with Directive 2004/ 18/EC.

Article 30
Procedure for establishing whether a given activity is directly exposed to competition

1. Contracts intended to enable an activity mentioned in Articles 3 to 7 to be carried out shall not be subject to this Directive if, in the Member State in which it is performed, the activity is directly exposed to competition on markets to which access is not restricted.

2. For the purposes of paragraph 1, the question of whether an activity is directly exposed to competition shall be decided on the basis of criteria that are in conformity with the Treaty provisions on competition, such as the characteristics of the goods or services concerned, the existence of alternative goods or services, the prices and the actual or potential presence of more than one supplier of the goods or services in question.

3. For the purposes of paragraph 1, access to a market shall be deemed not to be restricted if the Member State has implemented and applied the provisions of Community legislation mentioned in Annex XI.

If free access to a given market cannot be presumed on the basis of the first subparagraph, it must be demonstrated that access to the market in question is free de facto and de jure.

4. When a Member State considers that, in compliance with paragraphs 2 and 3, paragraph 1 is applicable to a given activity, it shall notify the Commission and inform it of all relevant facts,

and in particular of any law, regulation, administrative provision or agreement concerning compliance with the conditions set out in paragraph 1, where appropriate together with the position adopted by an independent national authority that is competent in relation to the activity concerned.

Contracts intended to enable the activity concerned to be carried out shall no longer be subject to this Directive if the Commission:

—has adopted a Decision establishing the applicability of paragraph 1 in accordance with paragraph 6 and within the period it provides for, or

—has not adopted a Decision concerning such applicability within that period.

However, where free access to a given market is presumed on the basis of the first subparagraph of paragraph 3, and where an independent national authority that is competent in the activity concerned has established the applicability of paragraph 1, contracts intended to enable the activity concerned to be carried out shall no longer be subject to this Directive if the Commission has not established the inapplicability of paragraph 1 by a Decision adopted in conformity with paragraph 6 and within the period it provides for.

5. When the legislation of the Member State concerned provides for it, the contracting entities may ask the Commission to establish the applicability of paragraph 1 to a given activity by a Decision in conformity with paragraph 6. In such a case, the Commission shall immediately inform the Member State concerned.

That Member State shall, taking account of paragraphs 2 and 3, inform the Commission of all relevant facts, and in particular of any law, regulation, administrative provision or agreement concerning compliance with the conditions set out in paragraph 1, where appropriate together with the position adopted by an independent national authority that is competent in the activity concerned.

The Commission may also begin the procedure for adoption of a Decision establishing the applicability of paragraph 1 to a given activity on its own initiative. In such a case, the Commission shall immediately inform the Member State concerned.

If, at the end of the period laid down in paragraph 6, the Commission has not adopted a Decision concerning the applicability of paragraph 1 to a given activity, paragraph 1 shall be deemed to be applicable.

6. For the adoption of a Decision under this Article, in accordance with the procedure under Article 68(2), the Commission shall be allowed a period of three months commencing on the first working day following the date on which it receives the notification or the request. However, this period may be extended once by a maximum of three months in duly justified cases, in particular if the information contained in the notification or the request or in the documents annexed thereto is incomplete or inexact or if the facts as reported undergo any substantive changes. This extension shall be limited to one month where an independent national authority that is competent in the activity concerned has established the applicability of paragraph 1 in the cases provided for under the third subparagraph of paragraph 4.

When an activity in a given Member State is already the subject of a procedure under this Article, further requests concerning the same activity in the same Member State before the expiry of the period opened in respect of the first request shall not be considered as new procedures and shall be treated in the context of the first request.

The Commission shall adopt detailed rules for applying paragraphs 4, 5 and 6 in accordance with the procedure under Article 68(2).

These rules shall include at least:

(a) the publication in the Official Journal, for information, of the date on which the three-month period referred to in the first subparagraph begins, and, in case this period is prolonged, the date of prolongation and the period by which it is prolonged;

(b) publication of the possible applicability of paragraph 1 in accordance with the second or third subparagraph of paragraph 4 or in accordance with the fourth subparagraph of paragraph 5; and

(c) the arrangements for forwarding positions adopted by an independent authority that is competent in the activity concerned, regarding questions relevant to paragraphs 1 and 2.

CHAPTER III RULES APPLICABLE TO SERVICE CONTRACTS

Article 31
Service contracts listed in Annex XVII A

Contracts which have as their object services listed in Annex XVII A shall be awarded in accordance with Articles 34 to 59.

Article 32
Service contracts listed in Annex XVII B

Contracts which have as their object services listed in Annex XVII B shall be governed solely by Articles 34 and 43.

Article 33
Mixed service contracts including services listed in Annex XVII A and services listed in Annex XVII B

Contracts which have as their subject-matter services listed both in Annex XVII A and in Annex XVII B shall be awarded in accordance with Articles 34 to 59 where the value of the services listed in Annex XVII A is greater than the value of the services listed in Annex XVII B. In other cases, contracts shall be awarded in accordance with Articles 34 and 43.

CHAPTER IV SPECIFIC RULES GOVERNING SPECIFICATIONS AND CONTRACT DOCUMENTS

Article 34
Technical specifications

1. Technical specifications as defined in point 1 of Annex XXI shall be set out in the contract documentation, such as contract notices, contract documents or additional documents. Whenever possible these technical specifications should be defined so as to take into account accessibility criteria for people with disabilities or design for all users.

2. Technical specifications shall afford equal access for tenderers and not have the effect of creating unjustified obstacles to the opening up of public procurement to competition.

3. Without prejudice to legally binding national technical rules, to the extent that they are compatible with Community law, the technical specifications shall be formulated:

(a) either by reference to technical specifications defined in Annex XXI and, in order of preference, to national standards transposing European standards, European technical approvals, common technical specifications, international standards, other technical reference systems established by the European standardisation bodies or—when these do not exist—national standards, national technical approvals or national technical specifications relating to the design, calculation and execution of the works and use of the products. Each reference shall be accompanied by the words 'or equivalent';

(b) or in terms of performance or functional requirements; the latter may include environmental characteristics. However, such parameters must be sufficiently precise to allow tenderers to determine the subject-matter of the contract and to allow contracting entities to award the contract;

(c) or in terms of performance or functional requirements as mentioned in subparagraph (b), with reference to the specifications mentioned in subparagraph (a) as a means of presuming conformity with such performance or functional requirements;

(d) or by referring to the specifications mentioned in subparagraph (a) for certain characteristics, and by referring to the performance or functional requirements mentioned in subparagraph (b) for other characteristics.

4. Where a contracting entity makes use of the option of referring to the specifications mentioned in paragraph 3(a), it cannot reject a tender on the ground that the products and services tendered for do not comply with the specifications to which it has referred, once the tenderer proves in his tender to the satisfaction of the contracting entity, by whatever appropriate means, that the solutions which he proposes satisfy in an equivalent manner the requirements defined by the technical specifications.

An appropriate means might be constituted by a technical dossier from the manufacturer or a test report from a recognised body.

5. Where a contracting entity uses the option provided for in paragraph 3 of laying down performance or functional requirements, it may not reject a tender for products, services or works which comply with a national standard transposing a European standard, with a European technical approval, a common technical specification, an international standard, or a technical reference system established by a European standardisation body, if these specifications address the performance or functional requirements which it has laid down.

In his tender, the tenderer shall prove to the satisfaction of the contracting entity and by any appropriate means that the product, service or work in compliance with the standard meets the performance or functional requirements of the contracting entity.

An appropriate means might be constituted by a technical dossier from the manufacturer or a test report from a recognised body.

6. Where contracting entities lay down environmental characteristics in terms of performance or functional requirements as referred to in paragraph 3(b) they may use the detailed specifications, or, if necessary, parts thereof, as defined by European or (multi-) national eco-labels, or by any other ecolabel, provided that:

— those specifications are appropriate to define the characteristics of the supplies or services that are the object of the contract,
— the requirements for the label are drawn up on the basis of scientific information,
— the eco-labels are adopted using a procedure in which all stakeholders, such as government bodies, consumers, manufacturers, distributors and environmental organisations can participate, and
— they are accessible to all interested parties.

Contracting entities may indicate that the products and services bearing the eco-label are presumed to comply with the technical specifications laid down in the contract documents; they must accept any other appropriate means of proof, such as a technical dossier from the manufacturer or a test report from a recognized body.

7. 'Recognised bodies', within the meaning of this Article, are test and calibration laboratories, and certification and inspection bodies which comply with applicable European standards.

Contracting entities shall accept certificates from recognised bodies established in other Member States.

8. Unless justified by the subject-matter of the contract, technical specifications shall not refer to a specific make or source, or to a particular process, or to trade marks, patents, types or a specific origin or production with the effect of favouring or eliminating certain undertakings or certain products. Such reference shall be permitted, on an exceptional basis, where a sufficiently precise and intelligible description of the subject-matter of the contract pursuant to paragraphs 3 and 4 is not possible; such reference shall be accompanied by the words 'or equivalent'.

Article 35
Communication of technical specifications

1. Contracting entities shall make available on request to economic operators interested in obtaining a contract the technical specifications regularly referred to in their supply, works or service contracts, or the technical specifications which they intend to apply to contracts covered by periodic indicative notices within the meaning of Article 41(1).

2. Where the technical specifications are based on documents available to interested economic operators, the inclusion of a reference to those documents shall be sufficient.

Article 36
Variants

1. Where the criterion for the award of the contract is that of the most economically advantageous tender, contracting entities may take account of variants which are submitted by a tenderer and meet the minimum requirements specified by the contracting entities.

Contracting entities shall indicate in the specifications whether or not they authorise variants and, if so, the minimum requirements to be met by the variants and any specific requirements for their presentation.

2. In procedures for awarding supply or service contracts, contracting entities which have authorised variants pursuant to paragraph 1 may not reject a variant on the sole ground that it would, if successful, lead either to a service contract rather than a supply contract or to a supply contract rather than a service contract.

Article 37
Subcontracting

In the contract documents, the contracting entity may ask, or may be required by a Member State to ask, the tenderer to indicate in his tender any share of the contract he intends to subcontract to third parties and any proposed subcontractors. This indication shall be without prejudice to the question of the principal economic operator's liability.

Article 38
Conditions for performance of contracts

Contracting entities may lay down special conditions relating to the performance of a contract, provided that these are compatible with Community law and are indicated in the notice used as a means of calling for competition or in the specifications. The conditions governing the performance of a contract may, in particular, concern social and environmental considerations.

Article 39
Obligations relating to taxes, environmental protection, employment protection provisions and working conditions

1. A contracting entity may state in the contract documents, or be required by a Member State so to state, the body or bodies from which a candidate or tenderer may obtain the appropriate information on the obligations relating to taxes, to environmental protection, to protection provisions and to the working conditions which are in force in the Member State, region or locality in which the services are to be provided and which shall be applicable to the works carried out on site or to the services provided during the performance of the contract.

2. A contracting entity which supplies the information referred to in paragraph 1 shall request the tenderers or candidates in the contract award procedure to indicate that they have taken account, when drawing up their tender, of the obligations relating to employment protection provisions and the working conditions which are in force in the place where the service is to be provided.

The first subparagraph shall be without prejudice to the application of Article 57.

Chapter V Procedures

Article 40
Use of open, restricted and negotiated procedures

1. When awarding supply, works or service contracts, contracting entities shall apply the procedures adjusted for the purposes of this Directive.

2. Contracting entities may choose any of the procedures described in Article 1(9)(a), (b) or (c), provided that, subject to paragraph 3, a call for competition has been made in accordance with Article 42.

3. Contracting entities may use a procedure without prior call for competition in the following cases:

(a) when no tenders or no suitable tenders or no applications have been submitted in response to a procedure with a prior call for competition, provided that the initial conditions of contract are not substantially altered;

(b) where a contract is purely for the purpose of research, experiment, study or development, and not for the purpose of securing a profit or of recovering research and development costs, and insofar as the award of such contract does not prejudice the competitive award of subsequent contracts which do seek, in particular, those ends;

(c) when, for technical or artistic reasons, or for reasons connected with the protection of exclusive rights, the contract may be executed only by a particular economic operator;

(d) insofar as is strictly necessary when, for reasons of extreme urgency brought about by events unforeseeable by the contracting entities, the time limits laid down for open procedures, restricted procedures and negotiated procedures with a prior call for competition cannot be adhered to;

(e) in the case of supply contracts for additional deliveries by the original supplier which are intended either as a partial replacement of normal supplies or installations or as the extension of existing supplies or installations, where a change of supplier would oblige the contracting entity to acquire material having different technical characteristics which would result in incompatibility or disproportionate technical difficulties in operation and maintenance;

(f) for additional works or services which were not included in the project initially awarded or in the contract first concluded but have, through unforeseen circumstances, become necessary to the performance of the contract, on condition that the award is made to the contractor or service provider executing the original contract:

— when such additional works or services cannot be technically or economically separated from the main contract without great inconvenience to the contracting entities, or

— when such additional works or services, although separable from the performance of the original contract, are strictly necessary to its later stages;

(g) in the case of works contracts, for new works consisting in the repetition of similar works assigned to the contractor to which the same contracting entities awarded an earlier contract, provided that such works conform to a basic project for which a first contract was awarded after a call for competition; as soon as the first project is put up for tender, notice shall be given that this procedure might be adopted and the total estimated cost of subsequent works shall be taken into consideration by the contracting entities when they apply the provisions of Articles 16 and 17;

(h) for supplies quoted and purchased on a commodity market;

(i) for contracts to be awarded on the basis of a framework agreement, provided that the condition referred to in Article 14(2) is fulfilled;

(j) for bargain purchases, where it is possible to procure supplies by taking advantage of a particularly advantageous opportunity available for a very short time at a price considerably lower than normal market prices;

(k) for purchases of supplies under particularly advantageous conditions from either a supplier definitively winding up his business activities or the receivers or liquidators of a bankruptcy, an arrangement with creditors or a similar procedure under national laws or regulations;

(l) when the service contract concerned is part of the followup to a design contest organised in accordance with the provisions of this Directive and shall, in accordance with the relevant rules, be awarded to the winner or to one of the winners of that contest; in the latter case, all the winners shall be invited to participate in the negotiations.

Chapter VI Rules on Publication and Transparency

Section 1 Publication of notices

Article 41
Periodic indicative notices and notices on the existence of a system of qualification

1. Contracting entities shall make known, at least once a year, by means of a periodic indicative notice as referred to in Annex XV A, published by the Commission or by themselves on their 'buyer profile', as described in point 2(b) of Annex XX:

(a) where supplies are concerned, the estimated total value of the contracts or the framework agreements by product area which they intend to award over the following 12 months, where the total estimated value, taking into account the provisions of Articles 16 and 17, is equal to or greater than EUR 750 000.

The product area shall be established by the contracting entities by reference to the CPV nomenclature:

(b) where services are concerned, the estimated total value of the contracts or the

638

framework agreements in each of the categories of services listed in Annex XVII A which they intend to award over the following 12 months, where such estimated total value, taking into account the provisions of Articles 16 and 17, is equal to or greater than EUR 750 000;

(c) where works are concerned, the essential characteristics of the works contracts or the framework agreements which they intend to award over the following 12 months, whose estimated value is equal to or greater than the threshold specified in Article 16, taking into account the provisions of Article 17.

The notices referred to in subparagraphs (a) and (b) shall be sent to the Commission or published on the buyer profile as soon as possible after the beginning of the budgetary year.

The notice referred to in subparagraph (c) shall be sent to the Commission or published on the buyer profile as soon as possible after the decision approving the planning of the works contracts or the framework agreements that the contracting entities intend to award.

Contracting entities which publish a periodic indicative notice on their buyer profiles shall transmit to the Commission, electronically, a notice of the publication of the periodic indicative notice on a buyer profile, in accordance with the format and procedures for the electronic transmission of notices indicated in point 3 of Annex XX.

The publication of the notices referred to in subparagraphs (a), (b) and (c) shall be compulsory only where the contracting entities take the option of reducing the time limits for the receipt of tenders as laid down in Article 45(4).

This paragraph shall not apply to procedures without prior call for competition.

2. Contracting entities may, in particular, publish or arrange for the Commission to publish periodic indicative notices relating to major projects without repeating information previously included in a periodic indicative notice, provided that it is clearly pointed out that these notices are additional ones.

3. Where contracting entities choose to set up a qualification system in accordance with Article 53, the system shall be the subject of a notice as referred to in Annex XIV, indicating the purpose of the qualification system and how to have access to the rules concerning its operation. Where the system is of a duration greater than three years, the notice shall be published annually. Where the system is of a shorter duration, an initial notice shall suffice.

Article 42
Notices used as a means of calling for competition

1. In the case of supply, works or service contracts, the call for competition may be made:
(a) by means of a periodic indicative notice as referred to in Annex XV A; or
(b) by means of a notice on the existence of a qualification system as referred to in Annex XIV; or
(c) by means of a contract notice as referred to in Annex XIII A, B or C.

2. In the case of dynamic purchasing systems, the system's call for competition shall be by contract notice as referred to in paragraph 1(c), whereas calls for competition for contracts based on such systems shall be by simplified contract notice as referred to in Annex XIII D.

3. When a call for competition is made by means of a periodic indicative notice, the notice shall:
(a) refer specifically to the supplies, works or services which will be the subject of the contract to be awarded;
(b) indicate that the contract will be awarded by restricted or negotiated procedure without further publication of a notice of a call for competition and invite interested economic operators to express their interest in writing; and
(c) have been published in accordance with Annex XX not more than 12 months prior to the date on which the invitation referred to in Article 47(5) is sent. Moreover, the contracting entity shall meet the time limits laid down in Article 45.

Article 43
Contract award notices

1. Contracting entities which have awarded a contract or a framework agreement shall,

within two months of the award of the contract or framework agreement, send a contract award notice as referred to in Annex XVI under conditions to be laid down by the Commission in accordance with the procedure referred to in Article 68(2).

In the case of contracts awarded under a framework agreement within the meaning of Article 14(2), the contracting entities shall not be bound to send a notice of the results of the award procedure for each contract based on that agreement.

Contracting entities shall send a contract award notice based on a dynamic purchasing system within two months after the award of each contract. They may, however, group such notices on a quarterly basis. In that case, they shall send the grouped notices within two months of the end of each quarter.

2. The information provided in accordance with Annex XVI and intended for publication shall be published in accordance with Annex XX. In this connection, the Commission shall respect any sensitive commercial aspects which the contracting entities may point out when forwarding this information, concerning the number of tenders received, the identity of economic operators, or prices.

3. Where contracting entities award a research-and-development service contract ('R&D contract') by way of a procedure without a call for competition in accordance with Article 40(3)(b), they may limit to the reference 'research and development services' the information to be provided in accordance with Annex XVI concerning the nature and quantity of the services provided.

Where contracting entities award an R&D contract which cannot be awarded by way of a procedure without a call for competition in accordance with Article 40(3)(b), they may, on grounds of commercial confidentiality, limit the information to be provided in accordance with Annex XVI concerning the nature and quantity of the services supplied.

In such cases, contracting entities shall ensure that any information published under this paragraph is no less detailed than that contained in the notice of the call for competition published in accordance with Article 42(1).

If they use a qualification system, contracting entities shall ensure in such cases that such information is no less detailed than the category referred to in the list of qualified service providers drawn up in accordance with Article 53(7).

4. In the case of contracts awarded for services listed in Annex XVII B, the contracting entities shall indicate in the notice whether they agree to publication.

5. Information provided in accordance with Annex XVI and marked as not being intended for publication shall be published only in simplified form and in accordance with Annex XX for statistical purposes.

Article 44
Form and manner of publication of notices

1. Notices shall include the information mentioned in Annexes XIII, XIV, XV A, XV B and XVI and, where appropriate, any other information deemed useful by the contracting entity in the format of standard forms adopted by the Commission in accordance with the procedure referred to in Article 68(2).

2. Notices sent by contracting entities to the Commission shall be sent either by electronic means in accordance with the format and procedures for transmission indicated in point 3 of Annex XX, or by other means.

The notices referred to in Articles 41, 42 and 43 shall be published in accordance with the technical characteristics for publication set out in point 1(a) and (b) of Annex XX.

3. Notices drawn up and transmitted by electronic means in accordance with the format and procedures for transmission indicated in point 3 of Annex XX, shall be published no later than five days after they are sent. Notices which are not transmitted by electronic means in accordance with the format and procedures for transmission indicated in point 3 of Annex XX shall be published not later than 12 days after they are transmitted. However, in exceptional cases, the contract notices referred to in Article 42(1)(c) shall be published within five days in response to a request by the contracting entity, provided that the notice has been sent by fax.

4. Contract notices shall be published in full in an official language of the Community as chosen by the contracting entity, this original

language version constituting the sole authentic text. A summary of the important elements of each notice shall be published in the other official languages.

The costs of publication of notices by the Commission shall be borne by the Community.

5. Notices and their contents may not be published at national level before the date on which they are sent to the Commission.

Notices published at national level shall not contain information other than that contained in the notices dispatched to the Commission or published on a buyer profile in accordance with the first subparagraph of Article 41(1), but shall mention the date of dispatch of the notice to the Commission or its publication on the buyer profile.

Periodic indicative notices may not be published on a buyer profile before the dispatch to the Commission of the notice of their publication in that form; they shall mention the date of that dispatch.

6. Contracting entities shall ensure that they are able to supply proof of the dates on which notices are dispatched.

7. The Commission shall give the contracting entity confirmation of the publication of the information sent, mentioning the date of that publication. Such confirmation shall constitute proof of publication.

8. Contracting entities may publish in accordance with paragraphs 1 to 7 contract notices which are not subject to the publication requirements laid down in this Directive.

Section 2 Time limits

Article 45
Time limits for the receipt of requests to participate and for the receipt of tenders

1. When fixing the time limits for requests to participate and the receipt of tenders, contracting entities shall take particular account of the complexity of the contract and the time required for drawing up tenders, without prejudice to the minimum time limits set by this Article.

2. In the case of open procedures, the minimum time limit for the receipt of tenders shall be 52 days from the date on which the contract notice was sent.

3. In restricted procedures and in negotiated procedures with a prior call for competition, the following arrangements shall apply:
(a) the time limit for the receipt of requests to participate, in response to a notice published under Article 42(1)(c), or in response to an invitation by the contracting entities under Article 47(5), shall, as a general rule, be fixed at no less than 37 days from the date on which the notice or invitation was sent and may in no case be less than 22 days if the notice is sent for publication by means other than electronic means or fax, and at no less than 15 days if the notice is transmitted by such means;
(b) the time limit for the receipt of tenders may be set by mutual agreement between the contracting entity and the selected candidates, provided that all candidates have the same time to prepare and submit their tenders;
(c) where it is not possible to reach agreement on the time limit for the receipt of tenders, the contracting entity shall fix a time limit which shall, as a general rule, be at least 24 days and shall in no case be less than 10 days from the date of the invitation to tender.

4. If the contracting entities have published a periodic indicative notice as referred to in Article 41(1) in accordance with Annex XX, the minimum time limit for the receipt of tenders in open procedures shall, as a general rule, not be less than 36 days, but shall in no case be less than 22 days from the date on which the notice was sent.

These reduced time limits are permitted, provided that the periodic indicative notice has included, in addition to the information required by Annex XV A, part I, all the information required by Annex XV A, part II, insofar as the latter information is available at the time the notice is published, and that the notice has been sent for publication between 52 days and 12 months before the date on which the contract notice referred to in Article 42(1)(c) is sent.

5. Where notices are drawn up and transmitted by electronic means in accordance with the format and procedures for transmission indicated in point 3 of Annex XX the time-limits for

the receipt of requests to participate in restricted and negotiated procedures, and for receipt of tenders in open procedures, may be reduced by seven days.

6. Except in the case of a time limit set by mutual agreement in accordance with paragraph 3(b), time limits for the receipt of tenders in open, restricted and negotiated procedures may be further reduced by five days where the contracting entity offers unrestricted and full direct access to the contract documents and any supplementary documents by electronic means from the date on which the notice used as a means of calling for competition is published, in accordance with Annex XX. The notice should specify the internet address at which this documentation is accessible.

7. In open procedures, the cumulative effect of the reductions provided for in paragraphs 4, 5 and 6 may in no case result in a time limit for the receipt of tenders of less than 15 days from the date on which the contract notice is sent.

However, if the contract notice is not transmitted by fax or electronic means, the cumulative effect of the reductions provided for in paragraphs 4, 5 and 6 may in no case result in a time limit for receipt of tenders in an open procedure of less than 22 days from the date on which the contract notice is transmitted.

8. The cumulative effect of the reductions provided for in paragraphs 4, 5 and 6 may in no case result in a time limit for receipt of requests to participate, in response to a notice published under Article 42(1)(c), or in response to an invitation by the contracting entities under Article 47(5), of less than 15 days from the date on which the contract notice or invitation is sent.

In restricted and negotiated procedures, the cumulative effect of the reductions provided for in paragraphs 4, 5 and 6 may in no case, except that of a time limit set by mutual agreement in accordance with paragraph 3(b), result in a time limit for the receipt of tenders of less than 10 days from the date of the invitation to tender.

9. If, for whatever reason, the contract documents and the supporting documents or additional information, although requested in good time, have not been supplied within the time limits set in Articles 46 and 47, or where tenders can be made only after a visit to the site or after on-the-spot inspection of the documents supporting the contract documents, the time limits for the receipt of tenders shall be extended accordingly, except in the case of a time-limit set by mutual agreement in accordance with paragraph 3(b), so that all economic operators concerned may be aware of all the information needed for the preparation of a tender.

10. A summary table of the time limits laid down in this Article is given in Annex XXII.

Article 46
Open procedures: specifications, additional documents and information

1. In open procedures, where contracting entities do not offer unrestricted and full direct access by electronic means in accor-dance with Article 45(6) to the specifications and any supporting documents, the specifications and supporting documents shall be sent to economic operators within six days of receipt of the request, provided that the request was made in good time before the time limit for the submission of tenders.

2. Provided that it has been requested in good time, additional information relating to the specifications shall be supplied by the contracting entities or competent departments not later than six days before the time limit fixed for the receipt of tenders.

Article 47
Invitations to submit a tender or to negotiate

1. In restricted procedures and negotiated procedures, contracting entities shall simultaneously and in writing invite the selected candidates to submit their tenders or to negotiate. The invitation to the candidates shall include either:

—a copy of the specifications and any supporting documents, or

—a reference to accessing the specifications and the supporting documents indicated in the first indent, when they are made directly available by electronic means in accordance with Article 45(6).

2. Where the specifications and/or any supporting documents are held by an entity other than the contracting entity responsible for the award procedure, the invitation shall

state the address from which those specifications and documents may be requested and, if appropriate, the closing date for requesting such documents, the sum payable for obtaining them and any payment procedures. The competent department shall send that documentation to the economic operator immediately upon receipt of the request.

3. The additional information on the specifications or the supporting documents shall be sent by the contracting entity or the competent department not less than six days before the final date fixed for the receipt of tenders, provided that it is requested in good time.

4. In addition, the invitation shall include at least the following:

(a) where appropriate, the time limit for requesting additional documents, as well as the amount and terms of payment of any sum to be paid for such documents;

(b) the final date for receipt of tenders, the address to which they are to be sent, and the language or languages in which they are to be drawn up;

(c) a reference to any published contract notice;

(d) an indication of any documents to be attached;

(e) the criteria for the award of the contract, where they are not indicated in the notice on the existence of a qualification system used as a means of calling for competition;

(f) the relative weighting of the contract award criteria or, where appropriate, the order of importance of such criteria, if this information is not given in the contract notice, the notice on the existence of a qualification system or the specifications.

5. When a call for competition is made by means of a periodic indicative notice, contracting entities shall subsequently invite all candidates to confirm their interest on the basis of detailed information on the contract concerned before beginning the selection of tenderers or participants in negotiations.

This invitation shall include at least the following information:

(a) nature and quantity, including all options concerning complementary contracts and,

if possible, the estimated time available for exercising these options for renewable contracts, the nature and quantity and, if possible, the estimated publication dates of future notices of competition for works, supplies or services to be put out to tender;

(b) type of procedure: restricted or negotiated;

(c) where appropriate, the date on which the delivery of supplies or the execution of works or services is to commence or terminate;

(d) the address and closing date for the submission of requests for tender documents and the language or languages in which they are to be drawn up;

(e) the address of the entity which is to award the contract and the information necessary for obtaining the specifications and other documents;

(f) economic and technical conditions, financial guarantees and information required from economic operators;

(g) the amount and payment procedures for any sum payable for obtaining tender documents;

(h) the form of the contract which is the subject of the invitation to tender: purchase, lease, hire or hire-purchase, or any combination of these; and

(i) the contract award criteria and their weighting or, where appropriate, the order of importance of such criteria, if this information is not given in the indicative notice or the specifications or in the invitation to tender or to negotiate.

Section 3 Communication and information

Article 48
Rules applicable to communication

1. All communication and information exchange referred to in this Title may be carried out by post, by fax, by electronic means in accordance with paragraphs 4 and 5, by telephone in the cases and circumstances referred to in paragraph 6, or by a combination of those means, according to the choice of the contracting entity.

2. The means of communication chosen shall be generally available and thus not restrict economic operators' access to the tendering procedure.

3. Communication and the exchange and storage of information shall be carried out in such a way as to ensure that the integrity of data and the confidentiality of tenders and requests to participate are preserved, and that the contracting entities examine the content of tenders and requests to participate only after the time limit set for submitting them has expired.

4. The tools to be used for communicating by electronic means, as well as their technical characteristics, shall be nondiscriminatory, generally available and interoperable with the information and communication technology products in general use.

5. The following rules are applicable to devices for the electronic transmission and receipt of tenders and to devices for the electronic receipt of requests to participate:

(a) information regarding the specifications necessary for the electronic submission of tenders and requests to participate, including encryption, shall be available to interested parties. Moreover, the devices for the electronic receipt of tenders and requests to participate shall conform to the requirements of Annex XXIV;

(b) Member States may, in compliance with Article 5 of Directive 1999/93/EC, require that electronic tenders be accompanied by an advanced electronic signature in conformity with paragraph 1 thereof;

(c) Member States may introduce or maintain voluntary accreditation schemes aiming at enhanced levels of certification service provision for these devices;

(d) tenderers or candidates shall undertake to submit, before expiry of the time limit laid down for the submission of tenders or requests to participate, the documents, certificates and declarations mentioned in Articles 52(2), 52(3), 53 and 54 if they do not exist in electronic format.

6. The following rules shall apply to the transmission of requests to participate:

(a) requests to participate in procedures for the award of contracts may be made in writing or by telephone;

(b) where requests to participate are made by telephone, a written confirmation must be sent before expiry of the time limit set for their receipt;

(c) contracting entities may require that requests for participation made by fax should be confirmed by post or by electronic means, where this is necessary for the purposes of legal proof. Any such requirement, together with the time limit for sending confirmation by post or electronic means, should be stated by the contracting entity in the notice used as a means of calling for competition or in the invitation referred to in Article 47(5).

Article 49
Information to applicants for qualification, candidates and tenderers

1. Contracting entities shall as soon as possible inform the economic operators involved of decisions reached concerning the conclusion of a framework agreement, the award of the contract, or admission to a dynamic purchasing system, including the grounds for any decision not to conclude a framework agreement or award a contract for which there has been a call for competition or to recommence the procedure, or not to implement a dynamic purchasing system; this information shall be provided in writing if the contracting entities are requested to do so.

2. On request from the party concerned, contracting entities shall, as soon as possible, inform:

—any unsuccessful candidate of the reasons for the rejection of his application,

— any unsuccessful tenderer of the reasons for the rejection of his tender, including, for the cases referred to in Article 34(4) and (5), the reasons for their decision of non-equivalence or their decision that the works, supplies or services do not meet the performance or functional requirements,

— any tenderer who has made an admissible tender of the characteristics and relative advantages of the tender selected, as well as the name of the successful tenderer or the parties to the framework agreement.

The time taken to do so may under no circumstances exceed 15 days from receipt of the written enquiry.

However, contracting entities may decide that certain information on the contract award or the conclusion of the framework agreement or on admission to a dynamic purchasing system, referred to in the paragraph 1, is to be withheld where release of such information would impede law enforcement or otherwise be contrary to the public interest or would prejudice the legitimate commercial interests of a particular economic operator, public or private, including the interests of the economic operator to whom the contract has been awarded, or might prejudice fair competition between economic operators.

3. Contracting entities which establish and operate a system of qualification shall inform applicants of their decision as to qualification within a period of six months.

If the decision will take longer than four months from the presentation of an application, the contracting entity shall inform the applicant, within two months of the application, of the reasons justifying the longer period and of the date by which his application will be accepted or refused.

4. Applicants whose qualification is refused shall be informed of this decision and the reasons for refusal as soon as possible and under no circumstances more than 15 days later than the date of the decision. The reasons shall be based on the criteria for qualification referred to in Article 53(2).

5. Contracting entities which establish and operate a system of qualification may bring the qualification of an economic operator to an end only for reasons based on the criteria for qualification referred to in Article 53(2). Any intention to bring qualification to an end shall be notified in writing to the economic operator beforehand, at least 15 days before the date on which qualification is due to end, together with the reason or reasons justifying the proposed action.

Article 50
Information to be stored concerning awards

1. Contracting entities shall keep appropriate information on each contract which shall be sufficient to permit them at a later date to justify decisions taken in connection with:
(a) the qualification and selection of economic operators and the award of contracts;

(b) the use of procedures without a prior call for competition by virtue of Article 40(3);
(c) the non-application of Chapters III to VI of this Title by virtue of the derogations provided for in Chapter II of Title I and in Chapter II of this Title.

Contracting entities shall take appropriate steps to document the progress of award procedures conducted by electronic means.

2. The information shall be kept for at least four years from the date of award of the contract so that the contracting entity will be able, during that period, to provide the necessary information to the Commission if the latter so requests.

CHAPTER VII CONDUCT OF THE PROCEDURE

Article 51
General provisions

1. For the purpose of selecting participants in their award procedures:
(a) contracting entities having provided rules and criteria for the exclusion of tenderers or candidates in accordance with Article 54(1), (2) or (4) shall exclude economic operators which comply with such rules and meet such criteria;
(b) they shall select tenderers and candidates in accordance with the objective rules and criteria laid down pursuant to Article 54;
(c) in restricted procedures and in negotiated procedures with a call for competition, they shall where appropriate reduce in accordance with Article 54 the number of candidates selected pursuant to subparagraphs (a) and (b).

2. When a call for competition is made by means of a notice on the existence of a qualification system and for the purpose of selecting participants in award procedures for the specific contracts which are the subject of the call for competition, contracting entities shall:
(a) qualify economic operators in accordance with the provisions of Article 53;
(b) apply to such qualified economic operators those provisions of paragraph 1 that are relevant to restricted or negotiated procedures.

3. Contracting entities shall verify that the tenders submitted by the selected tenderers comply with the rules and requirements applicable to tenders and award the contract on the basis of the criteria laid down in Articles 55 and 57.

Section 1 Qualification and qualitative selection

Article 52
Mutual recognition concerning administrative, technical or financial conditions, and certificates, tests and evidence

1. When selecting participants for a restricted or negotiated procedure, in reaching their decision as to qualification or when the criteria and rules are being updated, contracting entities shall not:

(a) impose administrative, technical or financial conditions on certain economic operators which would not be imposed on others;

(b) require tests or evidence which would duplicate objective evidence already available.

2. Where they request the production of certificates drawn up by independent bodies attesting the compliance of the economic operator with certain quality assurance standards, contracting entities shall refer to quality assurance systems based on the relevant European standards series certified by bodies conforming to the European standards series concerning certification.

Contracting entities shall recognise equivalent certificates from bodies established in other Member States. They shall also accept other evidence of equivalent quality assurance measures from economic operators.

3. For works and service contracts, and only in appropriate cases, the contracting entities may require, in order to verify the economic operator's technical abilities, an indication of the environmental management measures which the economic operator will be able to apply when carrying out the contract. In such cases, should the contracting entities require the production of certificates drawn up by

independent bodies attesting the compliance of the economic operator with certain environmental management standards, they shall refer to the EMAS or to environmental management standards based on the relevant European or international standards certified by bodies conforming to Community law or the relevant European or international standards concerning certification.

Contracting entities shall recognise equivalent certificates from bodies established in other Member States. They shall also accept other evidence of equivalent environmental management measures from economic operators.

Article 53
Qualification systems

1. Contracting entities which so wish may establish and operate a system of qualification of economic operators.

Contracting entities which establish or operate a system of qualification shall ensure that economic operators are at all times able to request qualification.

2. The system under paragraph 1 may involve different qualification stages.

It shall be operated on the basis of objective criteria and rules for qualification to be established by the contracting entity.

Where those criteria and rules include technical specifications, the provisions of Article 34 shall apply. The criteria and rules may be updated as required.

3. The criteria and rules for qualification referred to in paragraph 2 may include the exclusion criteria listed in Article 45 of Directive 2004/18/EC on the terms and conditions set out therein.

Where the contracting entity is a contracting authority within the meaning of Article 2(1)(a), those criteria and rules shall include the exclusion criteria listed in Article 45(1) of Directive 2004/18/EC.

4. Where the criteria and rules for qualification referred to in paragraph 2 include requirements relating to the economic and financial capacity of the economic operator, the latter may where necessary rely on the capacity of

other entities, whatever the legal nature of the link between itself and those entities. In this case the economic operator must prove to the contracting entity that these resources will be available to it throughout the period of the validity of the qualification system, for example by producing an undertaking by those entities to that effect.

Under the same conditions, a group of economic operators as referred to in Article 11 may rely on the capacity of participants in the group or of other entities.

5. Where the criteria and rules for qualification referred to in paragraph 2 include requirements relating to the technical and/or professional abilities of the economic operator, the latter may where necessary rely on the capacity of other entities, whatever the legal nature of the link between itself and those entities. In this case the economic operator must prove to the contracting entity that those resources will be available to it throughout the period of the validity of the qualification system, for example by producing an undertaking by those entities to make the necessary resources available to the economic operator.

Under the same conditions, a group of economic operators referred to in Article 11 may rely on the abilities of participants in the group or of other entities.

6. The criteria and rules for qualification referred to in paragraph 2 shall be made available to economic operators on request. The updating of these criteria and rules shall be communicated to interested economic operators.

Where a contracting entity considers that the qualification system of certain other entities or bodies meets its requirements, it shall communicate to interested economic operators the names of such other entities or bodies.

7. A written record of qualified economic operators shall be kept; it may be divided into categories according to the type of contract for which the qualification is valid.

8. When establishing or operating a qualification system, contracting entities shall in particular observe the provisions of Article 41(3) concerning notices on the existence of a system

of qualification, of Article 49(3), (4) and (5) concerning the information to be delivered to economic operators having applied for qualification, of Article 51(2) concerning the selection of participants when a call for competition is made by means of a notice on the existence of a qualification system as well as the provisions of Article 52 on mutual recognition concerning administrative, technical or financial conditions, certificates, tests and evidence.

9. When a call for competition is made by means of a notice on the existence of a qualification system, tenderers in a restricted procedure or participants in a negotiated procedure shall be selected from the qualified candidates in accordance with such a system.

Article 54
Criteria for qualitative selection

1. Contracting entities which establish selection criteria in an open procedure shall do so in accordance with objective rules and criteria which are available to interested economic operators.

2. Contracting entities which select candidates for restricted or negotiated procedures shall do so according to objective rules and criteria which they have established and which are available to interested economic operators.

3. In restricted or negotiated procedures, the criteria may be based on the objective need of the contracting entity to reduce the number of candidates to a level which is justified by the need to balance the particular characteristics of the procurement procedure with the resources required to conduct it. The number of candidates selected shall, however, take account of the need to ensure adequate competition.

4. The criteria set out in paragraphs 1 and 2 may include the exclusion criteria listed in Article 45 of Directive 2004/18/EC on the terms and conditions set out therein.

Where the contracting entity is a contracting authority within the meaning of Article 2(1)(a), the criteria and rules referred to in paragraphs 1 and 2 of this Article shall include the exclusion criteria listed in Article 45(1) of Directive 2004/18/EC.

5. Where the criteria referred to in paragraphs 1 and 2 include requirements relating to the

economic and financial capacity of the economic operator, the latter may where necessary and for a particular contract rely on the capacity of other entities, whatever the legal nature of the link between itself and those entities. In this case the economic operator shall prove to the contracting entity that the necessary resources will be available to it, for example by delivering an undertaking by those entities to that effect.

Under the same conditions, a group of economic operators as referred to in Article 11 may rely on the capacities of participants in the group or of other entities.

6. Where the criteria referred to in paragraphs 1 and 2 include requirements relating to the technical and/or professional abilities of the economic operator, the latter may where necessary and for a particular contract rely on the abilities of other entities, whatever the legal nature of the link between itself and those entities. In this case the economic operator must prove to the contracting entity that for the performance of the contract those resources will be available to it, for example by delivering an undertaking by those entities to make the necessary resources available to the economic operator.

Under the same conditions, a group of economic operators as referred to in Article 11 may rely on the abilities of participants in the group or of other entities.

Section 2 Award of the contract

Article 55
Contract award criteria

1. Without prejudice to national laws, regulations or administrative provisions on the remuneration of certain services, the criteria on which the contracting entities shall base the award of contracts shall:
(a) where the contract is awarded on the basis of the most economically advantageous tender from the point of view of the contracting entity, be various criteria linked to the subject-matter of the contract in question, such as delivery or completion date, running costs, cost-effectiveness, quality, aesthetic and functional characteristics, environmental

characteristics, technical merit, after-sales service and technical assistance, commitments with regard to parts, security of supply, and price or otherwise
(b) the lowest price only.

2. Without prejudice to the provisions of the third subparagraph, in the case referred to in paragraph 1(a), the contracting entity shall specify the relative weighting which it gives to each of the criteria chosen to determine the most economically advantageous tender.

Those weightings can be expressed by providing for a range with an appropriate maximum spread.

Where, in the opinion of the contracting entity, weighting is not possible for demonstrable reasons, the contracting entity shall indicate the criteria in descending order of importance.

The relative weighting or order of importance shall be specified, as appropriate, in the notice used as a means of calling for competition, in the invitation to confirm the interest referred to in Article 47(5), in the invitation to tender or to negotiate, or in the specifications.

Article 56
Use of electronic auctions

1. Member States may provide that contracting entities may use electronic auctions.

2. In open, restricted or negotiated procedures with a prior call for competition, the contracting entities may decide that the award of a contract shall be preceded by an electronic auction when the contract specifications can be established with precision.

In the same circumstances, an electronic auction may be held on the opening for competition of contracts to be awarded under the dynamic purchasing system referred to in Article 15.

The electronic auction shall be based:
(a) either solely on prices when the contract is awarded to the lowest price,
(b) or on prices and/or on the new values of the features of the tenders indicated in the specification, when the contract is

awarded to the most economically advantageous tender.

3. Contracting entities which decide to hold an electronic auction shall state that fact in the notice used as a means of calling for competition.

The specifications shall include, *inter alia*, the following details:

(a) the features whose values will be the subject of electronic auction, provided that such features are quantifiable and can be expressed in figures or percentages;

(b) any limits on the values which may be submitted, as they result from the specifications relating to the subject of the contract;

(c) the information which will be made available to tenderers in the course of the electronic auction and, where appropriate, when it will be made available to them;

(d) the relevant information concerning the electronic auction process;

(e) the conditions under which the tenderers will be able to bid and, in particular, the minimum differences which will, where appropriate, be required when bidding;

(f) the relevant information concerning the electronic equipment used and the arrangements and technical specifications for connection.

4. Before proceeding with the electronic auction, contracting entities shall make a full initial evaluation of the tenders in accordance with the award criterion/criteria set and with the weighting fixed for them.

All tenderers who have submitted admissible tenders shall be invited simultaneously by electronic means to submit new prices and/or new values; the invitation shall contain all relevant information concerning individual connection to the electronic equipment being used and shall state the date and time of the start of the electronic auction. The electronic auction may take place in a number of successive phases. The electronic auction may not start sooner than two working days after the date on which invitations are sent out.

5. When the contract is to be awarded on the basis of the most economically advantageous tender, the invitation shall be accompanied by the outcome of a full evaluation of the relevant tender carried out in accordance with the weighting provided for in the first subparagraph of Article 55(2).

The invitation shall also state the mathematical formula to be used in the electronic auction to determine automatic rerankings on the basis of the new prices and/or new values submitted. That formula shall incorporate the weighting of all the criteria established to determine the most economically advantageous tender, as indicated in the notice used as a means of calling for competition or in the specifications; for that purpose, any ranges shall, however, be reduced beforehand to a specified value.

Where variants are authorised, a separate formula shall be provided for each variant.

6. Throughout each phase of an electronic auction the contracting entities shall instantaneously communicate to all tenderers sufficient information to enable them to ascertain their relative rankings at any moment. They may also communicate other information concerning other prices or values submitted, provided that that is stated in the specifications. They may also at any time announce the number of participants in that phase of the auction. In no case, however, may they disclose the identities of the tenderers during any phase of an electronic auction.

7. Contracting entities shall close an electronic auction in one or more of the following manners:

(a) in the invitation to take part in the auction they shall indicate the date and time fixed in advance;

(b) when they receive no more new prices or new values which meet the requirements concerning minimum differences. In that event, the contracting entities shall state in the invitation to take part in the auction the time which they will allow to elapse after receiving the last submission before they close the electronic auction;

(c) when the number of phases in the auction, fixed in the invitation to take part in the auction, has been completed.

When the contracting entities have decided to close an electronic auction in accordance with subparagraph (c), possibly in combination with the arrangements laid down in subparagraph (b), the invitation to take part in the auction shall indicate the timetable for each phase of the auction.

8. After closing an electronic auction the contracting entities shall award the contract in accordance with Article 55 on the basis of the results of the electronic auction.

9. Contracting entities may not have improper recourse to electronic auctions nor may they use them in such a way as to prevent, restrict or distort competition or to change the subject-matter of the contract, as defined in the notice used as a means of calling for competition and in the specification.

Article 57
Abnormally low tenders

1. If, for a given contract, tenders appear to be abnormally low in relation to the goods, works or services, the contracting entity shall, before it may reject those tenders, request in writing details of the constituent elements of the tender which it considers relevant.

Those details may relate in particular to:

(a) the economics of the manufacturing process, of the services provided and of the construction method;

(b) the technical solutions chosen and/or any exceptionally favourable conditions available to the tenderer for the supply of the goods or services or for the execution of the work;

(c) the originality of the supplies, services or work proposed by the tenderer;

(d) compliance with the provisions relating to employment protection and working conditions in force at the place where the work, service or supply is to be performed;

(e) the possibility of the tenderer obtaining State aid.

2. The contracting entity shall verify those constituent elements by consulting the tenderer, taking account of the evidence supplied.

3. Where a contracting entity establishes that a tender is abnormally low because the tenderer

has obtained State aid, the tender can be rejected on that ground alone only after consultation with the tenderer where the latter is unable to prove, within a sufficient time limit fixed by the contracting entity, that the aid in question was granted legally. Where the contracting entity rejects a tender in these circumstances, it shall inform the Commission of that fact.

Section 3 Tenders comprising products originating in third countries and relations with those countries

Article 58
Tenders comprising products originating in third countries

1. This Article shall apply to tenders covering products originating in third countries with which the Community has not concluded, whether multilaterally or bilaterally, an agreement ensuring comparable and effective access for Community undertakings to the markets of those third countries. It shall be without prejudice to the obligations of the Community or its Member States in respect of third countries.

2. Any tender submitted for the award of a supply contract may be rejected where the proportion of the products originating in third countries, as determined in accordance with Council Regulation (EEC) No 2913/92 of 12 October 1992 establishing the Community Customs Code,[1] exceeds 50 % of the total value of the products constituting the tender. For the purposes of this Article, software used in telecommunications network equipment shall be regarded as products.

3. Subject to the second subparagraph, where two or more tenders are equivalent in the light of the contract award criteria defined in Article 55, preference shall be given to those tenders which may not be rejected pursuant to paragraph 2. The prices of those tenders shall be considered equivalent for the purposes of

---

[1] OJ L 302, 19.10.1992, p. 1. Regulation as last amended by Regulation (EC) No 2700/2000 of the European Parliament and of the Council (OJ L 311, 12.12.2000, p. 17).

this Article, if the price difference does not exceed 3%.

However, a tender shall not be preferred to another pursuant to the first subparagraph where its acceptance would oblige the contracting entity to acquire equipment having technical characteristics different from those of existing equipment, resulting in incompatibility, technical difficulties in operation and maintenance, or disproportionate costs.

4. For the purposes of this Article, those third countries to which the benefit of the provisions of this Directive has been extended by a Council Decision in accordance with paragraph 1 shall not be taken into account for determining the proportion, referred to in paragraph 2, of products originating in third countries.

5. The Commission shall submit an annual report to the Council, commencing in the second half of the first year following the entry into force of this Directive, on progress made in multilateral or bilateral negotiations regarding access for Community undertakings to the markets of third countries in the fields covered by this Directive, on any result which such negotiations may have achieved, and on the implementation in practice of all the agreements which have been concluded.

The Council, acting by a qualified majority on a proposal from the Commission, may amend the provisions of this Article in the light of such developments.

Article 59
Relations with third countries as regards works, supplies and service contracts

1. Member States shall inform the Commission of any general difficulties, in law or in fact, encountered and reported by their undertakings in securing the award of service contracts in third countries.

2. The Commission shall report to the Council before 31 December 2005, and periodically thereafter, on the opening up of service contracts in third countries and on progress in negotiations with these countries on this subject, particularly within the framework of the WTO.

3. The Commission shall endeavour, by approaching the third country concerned, to remedy any situation whereby it finds, on the basis either of the reports referred to in paragraph 2 or of other information, that, in the context of the award of service contracts, a third country:

(a) does not grant Community undertakings effective access comparable to that granted by the Community to undertakings from that country; or

(b) does not grant Community undertakings national treatment or the same competitive opportunities as are available to national undertakings; or

(c) grants undertakings from other third countries more favourable treatment than Community undertakings.

4. Member States shall inform the Commission of any difficulties, in law or in fact, encountered and reported by their undertakings and which are due to the non-observance of the international labour law provisions listed in Annex XXIII when these undertakings have tried to secure the award of contracts in third countries.

5. In the circumstances referred to in paragraphs 3 and 4, the Commission may at any time propose that the Council decide to suspend or restrict, over a period to be laid down in the decision, the award of service contracts to:

(a) undertakings governed by the law of the third country in question;

(b) undertakings affiliated to the undertakings specified in point (a) and having their registered office in the Community but having no direct and effective link with the economy of a Member State;

(c) undertakings submitting tenders which have as their subject-matter services originating in the third country in question.

The Council shall act, by qualified majority, as soon as possible.

The Commission may propose these measures on its own initiative or at the request of a Member State.

6. This Article shall be without prejudice to the commitments of the Community in relation to third countries ensuing from international agreements on public procurement, particularly within the framework of the WTO.

Title III
Rules Governing Service Design Contests

Article 60
General provision

1. The rules for the organisation of a design contest shall be in conformity with paragraph 2 of this Article and with Articles 61 and 63 to 66 and shall be made available to those interested in participating in the contest.

2. The admission of participants to design contests shall not be limited:

(a) by reference to the territory or part of the territory of a Member State;

(b) on the ground that, under the law of the Member State in which the contest is organised, they would have been required to be either natural or legal persons.

Article 61
Thresholds

1. This Title shall apply to design contests organised as part of a procurement procedure for services whose estimated value, net of VAT, is equal to or greater than EUR 499 000. For the purposes of this paragraph, 'threshold' means the estimated value net of VAT of the service contract, including any possible prizes and/or payments to participants.

2. This Title shall apply to all design contests where the total amount of contest prizes and payments to participants is equal to or greater than EUR 499 000.

For the purposes of this paragraph, 'threshold' means the total amount of the prizes and payments, including the estimated value net of VAT of the service contract which might subsequently be concluded under Article 40(3) if the contracting entity does not exclude such an award in the contest notice.

Article 62
Design contests excluded

This Title shall not apply to:

(1) contests which are organised in the same cases as referred to in Articles 20, 21 and 22 for service contracts;

(2) design contests organised for the pursuit, in the Member State concerned, of an activity to which the applicability of paragraph 1 of

Article 30 has been established by a Commission decision or has been deemed applicable pursuant to paragraph 4, second or third subparagraph, or to paragraph 5, fourth subparagraph, of that Article.

Article 63
Rules on advertising and transparency

1. Contracting entities which wish to organise a design contest shall call for competition by means of a contest notice. Contracting entities which have held a design contest shall make the results known by means of a notice. The call for competition shall contain the information referred to in Annex XVIII and the notice of the results of a design contest shall contain the information referred to in Annex XIX in accordance with the format of standard forms adopted by the Commission in accordance with the procedure in Article 68(2).

The notice of the results of a design contest shall be forwarded to the Commission within two months of the closure of the design contest and under conditions to be laid down by the Commission in accordance with the procedure referred to in Article 68(2). In this connection, the Commission shall respect any sensitive commercial aspects which the contracting entities may point out when forwarding this information, concerning the number of projects or plans received, the identity of the economic operators and the prices tendered.

2. Article 44(2) to (8) shall also apply to notices relating to design contests.

Article 64
Means of communication

1. Article 48(1), (2) and (4) shall apply to all communications relating to contests.

2. Communications, exchanges and the storage of information shall be such as to ensure that the integrity and the confidentiality of all information communicated by the participants in a contest are preserved and that the jury ascertains the contents of plans and projects only after the expiry of the time-limit for their submission.

3. The following rules shall apply to the devices for the electronic receipt of plans and projects:

(a) the information relating to the specifications which is necessary for the presentation of plans and projects by electronic means, including encryption, shall be available to the parties concerned. In addition, the devices for the electronic receipt of plans and projects shall comply with the requirements of Annex XXIV;

(b) Member States may introduce or maintain voluntary accreditation schemes aiming at enhanced levels of certification service provision for such devices.

Article 65
Rules on the organisation of design contests, the selection of participants and the jury

1. When organising design contests, contracting entities shall apply procedures which are adapted to the provisions of this Directive.

2. Where design contests are restricted to a limited number of participants, contracting entities shall establish clear and non-discriminatory selection criteria. In any event, the number of candidates invited to participate shall be sufficient to ensure genuine competition.

3. The jury shall be composed exclusively of natural persons who are independent of participants in the contest. Where a particular professional qualification is required of participants in a contest, at least a third of the jury members shall have the same qualification or an equivalent qualification.

Article 66
Decisions of the jury

1. The jury shall be autonomous in its decisions or opinions.

2. It shall examine the plans and projects submitted by the candidates anonymously and solely on the basis of the criteria indicated in the contest notice.

3. It shall record its ranking of projects in a report, signed by its members, made according to the merits of each project, together with its remarks and any points which may need clarification.

4. Anonymity must be observed until the jury has reached its opinion or decision.

5. Candidates may be invited, if need be, to answer questions which the jury has recorded in the minutes to clarify any aspects of the projects.

6. Complete minutes shall be drawn up of the dialogue between jury members and candidates.

Title IV
Statistical Obligations, Executory Powers and Final Provisions

Article 67
Statistical obligations

1. Member States shall ensure, in accordance with the arrangements to be laid down under the procedure provided for in Article 68(2), that the Commission receives every year a statistical report concerning the total value, broken down by Member State and by category of activity to which Annexes I to X refer, of the contracts awarded below the thresholds set out in Article 16 but which would be covered by this Directive were it not for those thresholds.

2. As regards the categories of activity to which Annexes II, III, V, IX and X refer, Member States shall ensure that the Commission receives a statistical report on contracts awarded no later than 31 October 2004 for the previous year, and before 31 October of each year thereafter, in accordance with arrangements to be laid down under the procedure provided for in Article 68(2). The statistical report shall contain the information required to verify the proper application of the Agreement.

The information required under the first subparagraph shall not include information concerning contracts for the R & D services listed in category 8 of Annex XVII A, for telecommunications services listed in category 5 of Annex XVII A whose CPV positions are equivalent to the CPC reference numbers 7524, 7525 and 7526, or for the services listed in Annex XVII B.

3. The arrangements under paragraphs 1 and 2 shall be laid down in such a way as to ensure that:

(a) in the interests of administrative simplification, contracts of lesser value may be excluded, provided that the usefulness of the statistics is not jeopardised;

(b) the confidential nature of the information provided is respected.

Article 68
Committee procedure

1. The Commission shall be assisted by the Advisory Committee for Public Contracts instituted by Article 1 of Council Decision 71/306/EEC[1] (hereinafter referred to as 'the Committee').

2. Where reference is made to this paragraph, Articles 3 and 7 of Decision 1999/468/EC shall apply, having regard to the provisions of Article 8 thereof.

3. The Committee shall adopt its rules of procedure.

Article 69
Revision of the thresholds

1. The Commission shall verify the thresholds established in Article 16 every two years from 30 April 2004, and shall, if necessary with regard to the second subparagraph, revise them in accordance with the procedure provided for in Article 68(2).

The calculation of the value of these thresholds shall be based on the average daily value of the euro, expressed in SDR, over the 24 months terminating on the last day of August preceding the revision with effect from 1 January. The value of the thresholds thus revised shall, where necessary, be rounded down to the nearest thousand euro so as to ensure that the thresholds in force provided for by the Agreement, expressed in SDR, are observed.

---

[1] OJ L 185, 16.8.1971, p. 15. Decision as amended by Decision 77/63/EEC (OJ L 13, 15.1.1977, p. 15).

2. At the same time as performing the revision under paragraph 1, the Commission shall, in accordance with the procedure provided for in Article 68(2), align the thresholds laid down in Article 61 (design contests) with the revised threshold applicable to service contracts.

The values of the thresholds laid down in accordance with paragraph 1 in the national currencies of Member States not participating in Monetary Union shall, in principle, be revised every two years from 1 January 2004. The calculation of such values shall be based on the average daily values of those currencies, expressed in euro, over the 24 months terminating on the last day of August preceding the revision with effect from 1 January.

3. The revised thresholds referred to in paragraph 1, their values in national currencies and the aligned thresholds referred to in paragraph 2 shall be published by the Commission in the *Official Journal of the European Union* at the beginning of the month of November following their revision.

Article 70
Amendments

The Commission may amend, in accordance with the procedure provided for in Article 68(2):

(a) the list of contracting entities in Annexes I to X so that they fulfil the criteria set out in Articles 2 to 7;

(b) the procedures for the drawing-up, transmission, receipt, translation, collection and distribution of the notices referred to in Articles 41, 42, 43 and 63;

(c) the procedures for specific references to particular positions in the CPV nomenclature in the notices;

(d) the reference numbers in the nomenclature set out in Annex XVII, in so far as this does not change the material scope of the Directive, and the procedures for reference in the notices to particular positions in this nomenclature within the categories of services listed in the Annex;

(e) the reference numbers in the nomenclature set out in Annex XII, insofar as this does not change the material scope of the Directive, and the procedures for reference to particular positions of this nomenclature in the notices;

(f) Annex XI;

(g) the procedure for sending and publishing data referred to in Annex XX, on grounds of technical progress or for administrative reasons;

(h) the technical details and characteristics of the devices for electronic receipt referred to in points (a), (f) and (g) of Annex XXIV;

(i) in the interests of administrative simplification as provided for in Article 67(3), the procedures for the use, drawing-up, transmission, receipt, translation, collection and distribution of the statistical reports referred to in Article 67(1) and (2);

(j) the technical procedures for the calculation methods set out in Article 69(1) and (2), second subparagraph.

Article 71
Implementation of the Directive

1. Member States shall bring into force the laws, regulations and administrative provisions necessary to comply with this Directive by 31 January 2006 at the latest. They shall forthwith inform the Commission thereof.

Member States may avail themselves of an additional period of up to 35 months after expiry of the time limit provided for in the first subparagraph for the application of the provisions necessary to comply with Article 6 of this Directive.

When Member States adopt those measures, they shall contain a reference to this Directive or be accompanied by such a reference on the occasion of their official publication. The methods of making such references shall be laid down by Member States.

The provisions of Article 30 are applicable from 30 April 2004.

2. Member States shall communicate to the Commission the text of the main provisions of national law which they adopt in the field covered by this Directive.

Article 72
Monitoring mechanisms

In conformity with Council Directive 92/13/EEC of 25 February 1992 coordinating the laws, regulations and administrative provisions relating to the application of Community rules on the procurement procedures of entities operating in the water, energy, transport and telecommunications sectors[1], Member States shall ensure implementation of this Directive by effective, available and transparent mechanisms.

For this purpose they may, among other things, appoint or establish an independent body.

Article 73
Repeal

Directive 93/38/EEC is hereby repealed, without prejudice to the obligations of the Member States concerning the time limits for transposition into national law set out in Annex XXV.

References to the repealed Directive shall be construed as being made to this Directive and shall be read in accordance with the correlation table in Annex XXVI.

Article 74
Entry into force

This Directive shall enter into force on the day of its publication in the *Official Journal of the European Union*.

Article 75
Addressees

This Directive is addressed to the Member States.

Done at Strasbourg, 31 March 2004.

For the European Parliament	*For the Council*
The President	*The President*
P. COX	D. ROCHE

The annexes to this Directive may found in the Official Journal

[2004] OJ LI 34, 30 March 2004

http://europa.eu.int/eur-lex/JOHtml.do?uri=OJ:L:2004:134:SOM:EN:HTML

---

[1] OJ L 76, 23.03.1992, p. 14. Directive amended by the 1994 Act of Accession (OJ 241, 29.8.1994, p. 228).

APPENDIX 2

Directive 2004/18/EC of the European Parliament and of the Council of 31 March 2004 on the coordination of procedures for the award of public works contracts, public supply contracts and public service contracts

THE EUROPEAN PARLIAMENT AND THE COUNCIL OF THE EUROPEAN UNION,

Having regard to the Treaty establishing the European Community, and in particular Article 47(2) and Article 55 and Article 95 thereof,

Having regard to the proposal from the Commission,[1]

Having regard to the opinion of the Economic and Social Committee,[2]

Having regard to the opinion of the Committee of the Regions,[3]

Acting in accordance with the procedure laid down in Article 251 of the Treaty,[4] in the light of the joint text approved by the Conciliation Committee on 9 December 2003,

Whereas:

(1) On the occasion of new amendments being made to Council Directives 92/50/EEC of 18 June 1992 relating to the coordination of procedures for the award of public service contracts,[5]

93/36/EEC of 14 June 1993 coordinating procedures for the award of public supply contracts[6] and 93/37/EEC of 14 June 1993 concerning the coordination of procedures for the award of public works contracts,[7] which are necessary to meet requests for simplification and modernisation made by contracting authorities and economic operators alike in their responses to the Green Paper adopted by the Commission on 27 November 1996, the Directives should, in the interests of clarity, be recast. This Directive is based on Court of Justice case-law, in particular case-law on award criteria, which clarifies the possibilities for the contracting authorities to meet the needs of the public concerned, including in the environmental and/or social area, provided that such criteria are linked to the subject-matter of the contract, do not confer an unrestricted freedom of choice on the contracting authority, are expressly mentioned and comply with the fundamental principles mentioned in recital 2.

(2) The award of contracts concluded in the Member States on behalf of the State, regional or local authorities and other bodies governed by public law entities, is subject to the respect of the principles of the Treaty and in particular to the principle of freedom of movement of goods,

---

[1] OJ C 29 E, 30.1.2001, p. 11 and OJ C 203 E, 27.8.2002, p. 210.

[2] OJ C 193, 10.7.2001, p. 7.

[3] OJ C 144, 16.5.2001, p. 23.

[4] Opinion of the European Parliament of 17 January 2002 (OJ C 271 E, 7.11.2002, p. 176), Council Common Position of 20 Mars 2003 (OJ C 147 E, 24.6.2003, p. 1) and Position of the European Parliament of 2 July 2003 (not yet published in the Official Journal). Legislative Resolution of the European Parliament of 29 January 2004 and Decision of the Council of 2 February 2004.

[5] OJ L 209, 24.7.1992, p. 1. Directive as last amended by Commission Directive 2001/78/EC (OJ L 285, 29.10.2001, p. 1).

[6] OJ L 199, 9.8.1993, p. 1. Directive as last amended by Commission Directive 2001/78/EC.

[7] OJ L 199, 9.8.1993, p. 54. Directive as last amended by Commission Directive 2001/78/EC.

the principle of freedom of establishment and the principle of freedom to provide services and to the principles deriving therefrom, such as the principle of equal treatment, the principle of non-discrimination, the principle of mutual recognition, the principle of proportionality and the principle of transparency. However, for public contracts above a certain value, it is advisable to draw up provisions of Community coordination of national procedures for the award of such contracts which are based on these principles so as to ensure the effects of them and to guarantee the opening-up of public procurement to competition. These coordinating provisions should therefore be interpreted in accordance with both the aforementioned rules and principles and other rules of the Treaty.

(3) Such coordinating provisions should comply as far as possible with current procedures and practices in each of the Member States.

(4) Member States should ensure that the participation of a body governed by public law as a tenderer in a procedure for the award of a public contract does not cause any distortion of competition in relation to private tenderers.

(5) Under Article 6 of the Treaty, environmental protection requirements are to be integrated into the definition and implementation of the Community policies and activities referred to in Article 3 of that Treaty, in particular with a view to promoting sustainable development. This Directive therefore clarifies how the contracting authorities may contribute to the protection of the environment and the promotion of sustainable development, whilst ensuring the possibility of obtaining the best value for money for their contracts.

(6) Nothing in this Directive should prevent the imposition or enforcement of measures necessary to protect public policy, public morality, public security, health, human and animal life or the preservation of plant life, in particular with a view to sustainable development, provided that these measures are in conformity with the Treaty.

(7) Council Decision 94/800/EC of 22 December 1994 concerning the conclusion on behalf of the European Community, as regards matters within its competence, of the Agreements reached in the Uruguay Round multilateral negotiations (1986 to 1994),[1] approved in particular the WTO Agreement on Government Procurement, hereinafter referred to as the 'Agreement', the aim of which is to establish a multilateral framework of balanced rights and obligations relating to public contracts with a view to achieving the liberalisation and expansion of world trade.

In view of the international rights and commitments devolving on the Community as a result of the acceptance of the Agreement, the arrangements to be applied to tenderers and products from signatory third countries are those defined by the Agreement. This Agreement does not have direct effect. The contracting authorities covered by the Agreement which comply with this Directive and which apply the latter to economic operators of third countries which are signatories to the Agreement should therefore be in conformity with the Agreement. It is also appropriate that those coordinating provisions should guarantee for Community economic operators conditions for participation in public procurement which are just as favourable as those reserved for economic operators of third countries which are signatories to the Agreement.

(8) Before launching a procedure for the award of a contract, contracting authorities may, using a technical dialogue, seek or accept advice which may be used in the preparation of the specifications provided, however, that such advice does not have the effect of precluding competition.

(9) In view of the diversity of public works contracts, contracting authorities should

---

[1] OJ L 336, 23.12.1994, p. 1.

be able to make provision for contracts for the design and execution of work to be awarded either separately or jointly. It is not the intention of this Directive to prescribe either joint or separate contract awards. The decision to award contracts separately or jointly must be determined by qualitative and economic criteria, which may be defined by national law.

(10) A contract shall be deemed to be a public works contract only if its subject matter specifically covers the execution of activities listed in Annex I, even if the contract covers the provision of other services necessary for the execution of such activities. Public service contracts, in particular in the sphere of property management services, may, in certain circumstances, include works. However, insofar as such works are incidental to the principal subject-matter of the contract, and are a possible consequence thereof or a complement thereto, the fact that such works are included in the contract does not justify the qualification of the contract as a public works contract.

(11) A Community definition of framework agreements, together with specific rules on framework agreements concluded for contracts falling within the scope of this Directive, should be provided. Under these rules, when a contracting authority enters into a framework agreement in accordance with the provisions of this Directive relating, in particular, to advertising, time limits and conditions for the submission of tenders, it may enter into contracts based on such a framework agreement during its term of validity either by applying the terms set forth in the framework agreement or, if all terms have not been fixed in advance in the framework agreement, by reopening competition between the parties to the framework agreement in relation to those terms. The reopening of competition should comply with certain rules the aim of which is to guarantee the required flexibility and to guarantee respect for the general principles, in particular the principle of equal treatment. For the same

reasons, the term of the framework agreements should not exceed four years, except in cases duly justified by the contracting authorities.

(12) Certain new electronic purchasing techniques are continually being developed. Such techniques help to increase competition and streamline public purchasing, particularly in terms of the savings in time and money which their use will allow. Contracting authorities may make use of electronic purchasing techniques, providing such use complies with the rules drawn up under this Directive and the principles of equal treatment, nondiscrimination and transparency. To that extent, a tender submitted by a tenderer, in particular where competition has been reopened under a framework agreement or where a dynamic purchasing system is being used, may take the form of that tenderer's electronic catalogue if the latter uses the means of communication chosen by the contracting authority in accordance with Article 42.

(13) In view of the rapid expansion of electronic purchasing systems, appropriate rules should now be introduced to enable contracting authorities to take full advantage of the possibilities afforded by these systems. Against this background, it is necessary to define a completely electronic dynamic purchasing system for commonly used purchases, and lay down specific rules for setting up and operating such a system in order to ensure the fair treatment of any economic operator who wishes to take part therein. Any economic operator which submits an indicative tender in accordance with the specification and meets the selection criteria should be allowed to join such a system. This purchasing technique allows the contracting authority, through the establishment of a list of tenderers already selected and the opportunity given to new tenderers to take part, to have a particularly broad range of tenders as a result of the electronic facilities available, and hence to ensure optimum use of public funds through broad competition.

(14) Since use of the technique of electronic auctions is likely to increase, such auctions should be given a Community definition and governed by specific rules in order to ensure that they operate in full accordance with the principles of equal treatment, non-discrimination and transparency. To that end, provision should be made for such electronic auctions to deal only with contracts for works, supplies or services for which the specifications can be determined with precision. Such may in particular be the case for recurring supplies, works and service contracts. With the same objective, it must also to be possible to establish the respective ranking of the tenderers at any stage of the electronic auction. Recourse to electronic auctions enables contracting authorities to ask tenderers to submit new prices, revised downwards, and when the contract is awarded to the most economically advantageous tender, also to improve elements of the tenders other than prices. In order to guarantee compliance with the principle of transparency, only the elements suitable for automatic evaluation by electronic means, without any intervention and/or appreciation by the contracting authority, may be the object of electronic auctions, that is, only the elements which are quantifiable so that they can be expressed in figures or percentages. On the other hand, those aspects of the tenders which imply an appreciation of nonquantifiable elements should not be the object of electronic auctions. Consequently, certain works contracts and certain service contracts having as their subjectmatter intellectual performances, such as the design of works, should not be the object of electronic auctions.

(15) Certain centralised purchasing techniques have been developed in Member States. Several contracting authorities are responsible for making acquisitions or awarding public contracts/framework agreements for other contracting authorities. In view of the large volumes purchased, those techniques help increase competition and streamline public purchasing. Provision should therefore be made for a Community definition of central purchasing bodies dedicated to contracting authorities. A definition should also be given of the conditions under which, in accordance with the principles of non-discrimination and equal treatment, contracting authorities purchasing works, supplies and/or services through a central purchasing body may be deemed to have complied with this Directive.

(16) In order to take account of the different circumstances obtaining in Member States, Member States should be allowed to choose whether contracting authorities may use framework agreements, central purchasing bodies, dynamic purchasing systems, electronic auctions or the competitive dialogue procedure, as defined and regulated by this Directive.

(17) Multiplying the number of thresholds for applying the coordinating provisions complicates matters for contracting authorities. Furthermore, in the context of monetary union such thresholds should be established in euro. Accordingly, thresholds should be set, in euro, in such a way as to simplify the application of such provisions, while at the same time ensuring compliance with the thresholds provided for by the Agreement which are expressed in special drawing rights. In this context, provision should also be made for periodic reviews of the thresholds expressed in euro so as to adjust them, where necessary, in line with possible variations in the value of the euro in relation to the special drawing right.

(18) The field of services is best delineated, for the purpose of applying the procedural rules of this Directive and for monitoring purposes, by subdividing it into categories corresponding to particular headings of a common classification and by bringing them together in two Annexes, II A and II B, according to the regime to which they are subject. As regards services in Annex II B, the relevant provisions of this Directive should be without prejudice to the application of Community rules specific to the services in question.

(19) As regards public service contracts, full application of this Directive should be limited, for a transitional period, to contracts where its provisions will permit the full potential for increased cross-frontier trade to be realised. Contracts for other services need to be monitored during this transitional period before a decision is taken on the full application of this Directive. In this respect, the mechanism for such monitoring needs to be defined. This mechanism should, at the same time, enable interested parties to have access to the relevant information.

(20) Public contracts which are awarded by the contracting authorities operating in the water, energy, transport and postal services sectors and which fall within the scope of those activities are covered by Directive 2004/17/EC of the European Parliament and of the Council of 31 March 2004 coordinating the procurement procedures of entities operating in the water, energy, transport and postal services sectors.[1] However, contracts awarded by the contracting authorities in the context of their service activities for maritime, coastal or river transport must fall within the scope of this Directive.

(21) In view of the situation of effective market competition in the telecommunications sector following the implementation of the Community rules aimed at liberalising that sector, public contracts in that area should be excluded from the scope of this Directive insofar as they are intended primarily to allow the contracting authorities to exercise certain activities in the telecommunications sector. Those activities are defined in accordance with the definitions used in Articles 1, 2 and 8 of Council Directive 93/38/EEC of 14 June 1993 coordinating the procurement procedures of entities operating in the water, energy, transport and telecommunications sector,[2] such that this Directive does not apply to contracts which have been excluded from the scope of Directive 93/38/EEC pursuant to Article 8 thereof.

(22) Provision should be made for cases in which it is possible to refrain from applying the measures for coordinating procedures on grounds relating to State security or secrecy, or because specific rules on the awarding of contracts which derive from international agreements, relating to the stationing of troops, or which are specific to international organisations are applicable.

(23) Pursuant to Article 163 of the Treaty, the encouragement of research and technological development is a means of strengthening the scientific and technological basis of Community industry, and the opening-up of public service contracts contributes to this end. This Directive should not cover the cofinancing of research and development programmes: research and development contracts other than those where the benefits accrue exclusively to the contracting authority for its use in the conduct of its own affairs, on condition that the service provided is wholly remunerated by the contracting authority, are not therefore covered by this Directive.

(24) In the context of services, contracts for the acquisition or rental of immovable property or rights to such property have particular characteristics which make the application of public procurement rules inappropriate.

(25) The awarding of public contracts for certain audiovisual services in the field of broadcasting should allow aspects of cultural or social significance to be taken into account which render application of procurement rules inappropriate. For these reasons, an exception must therefore be made for public service contracts for the purchase, development, production or co-production of off-the-shelf programmes and other preparatory services, such as those relating to scripts or artistic performances necessary for the production of the programme and

---

[1] See p. 1 of this Official Journal.
[2] OJ L 199, 9.8.1993, p. 84. Directive as last amended by Commission Directive 2001/78/EC (OJ L 285, 29.10.2001, p. 1).

contracts concerning broadcasting times. However, this exclusion should not apply to the supply of technical equipment necessary for the production, co-production and broadcasting of such programmes. A broadcast should be defined as transmission and distribution using any form of electronic network.

(26) Arbitration and conciliation services are usually provided by bodies or individuals designated or selected in a manner which cannot be governed by procurement rules.

(27) In accordance with the Agreement, the financial services covered by this Directive do not include instruments of monetary policy, exchange rates, public debt, reserve management or other policies involving transactions in securities or other financial instruments, in particular transactions by the contracting authorities to raise money or capital. Accordingly, contracts relating to the issue, purchase, sale or transfer of securities or other financial instruments are not covered. Central bank services are also excluded.

(28) Employment and occupation are key elements in guaranteeing equal opportunities for all and contribute to integration in society. In this context, sheltered workshops and sheltered employment programmes contribute efficiently towards the integration or reintegration of people with disabilities in the labour market. However, such workshops might not be able to obtain contracts under normal conditions of competition. Consequently, it is appropriate to provide that Member States may reserve the right to participate in award procedures for public contracts to such workshops or reserve performance of contracts to the context of sheltered employment programmes.

(29) The technical specifications drawn up by public purchasers need to allow public procurement to be opened up to competition. To this end, it must be possible to submit tenders which reflect the diversity of technical solutions. Accordingly, it must be possible to draw up the technical specifications in terms of functional performance and requirements, and, where reference is made to the European standard or, in the absence thereof, to the national standard, tenders based on equivalent arrangements must be considered by contracting authorities. To demonstrate equivalence, tenderers should be permitted to use any form of evidence. Contracting authorities must be able to provide a reason for any decision that equivalence does not exist in a given case. Contracting authorities that wish to define environmental requirements for the technical specifications of a given contract may lay down the environmental characteristics, such as a given production method, and/or specific environmental effects of product groups or services. They can use, but are not obliged to use appropriate specifications that are defined in ecolabels, such as the European Eco-label, (multi-)national eco-labels or any other eco-label providing the requirements for the label are drawn up and adopted on the basis of scientific information using a procedure in which stakeholders, such as government bodies, consumers, manufacturers, distributors and environmental organisations can participate, and providing the label is accessible and available to all interested parties. Contracting authorities should, whenever possible, lay down technical specifications so as to take into account accessibility criteria for people with disabilities or design for all users. The technical specifications should be clearly indicated, so that all tenderers know what the requirements established by the contracting authority cover.

(30) Additional information concerning contracts must, as is customary in Member States, be given in the contract documents for each contract or else in an equivalent document.

(31) Contracting authorities which carry out particularly complex projects may, without this being due to any fault on their part, find it objectively impossible to define the means of satisfying their needs

or of assessing what the market can offer in the way of technical solutions and/or financial/legal solutions. This situation may arise in particular with the implementation of important integrated transport infrastructure projects, large computer networks or projects involving complex and structured financing the financial and legal make-up of which cannot be defined in advance. To the extent that use of open or restricted procedures does not allow the award of such contracts, a flexible procedure should be provided which preserves not only competition between economic operators but also the need for the contracting authorities to discuss all aspects of the contract with each candidate. However, this procedure must not be used in such a way as to restrict or distort competition, particularly by altering any fundamental aspects of the offers, or by imposing substantial new requirements on the successful tenderer, or by involving any tenderer other than the one selected as the most economically advantageous.

(32) In order to encourage the involvement of small and medium-sized undertakings in the public contracts procurement market, it is advisable to include provisions on subcontracting.

(33) Contract performance conditions are compatible with this Directive provided that they are not directly or indirectly discriminatory and are indicated in the contract notice or in the contract documents. They may, in particular, be intended to favour on-site vocational training, the employment of people experiencing particular difficulty in achieving integration, the fight against unemployment or the protection of the environment. For instance, mention may be made, amongst other things, of the requirements—applicable during performance of the contract—to recruit long-term job-seekers or to implement training measures for the unemployed or young persons, to comply in substance with the provisions of the basic International Labour Organisation (ILO) Conventions,

assuming that such provisions have not been implemented in national law, and to recruit more handicapped persons than are required under national legislation.

(34) The laws, regulations and collective agreements, at both national and Community level, which are in force in the areas of employment conditions and safety at work apply during performance of a public contract, providing that such rules, and their application, comply with Community law. In cross-border situations, where workers from one Member State provide services in another Member State for the purpose of performing a public contract, Directive 96/71/EC of the European Parliament and of the Council of 16 December 1996 concerning the posting of workers in the framework of the provision of services[1] lays down the minimum conditions which must be observed by the host country in respect of such posted workers. If national law contains provisions to this effect, non-compliance with those obligations may be considered to be grave misconduct or an offence concerning the professional conduct of the economic operator concerned, liable to lead to the exclusion of that economic operator from the procedure for the award of a public contract.

(35) In view of new developments in information and communications technology, and the simplifications these can bring in terms of publicising contracts and the efficiency and transparency of procurement processes, electronic means should be put on a par with traditional means of communication and information exchange. As far as possible, the means and technology chosen should be compatible with the technologies used in other Member States.

(36) To ensure development of effective competition in the field of public contracts, it is necessary that contract notices drawn up by the contracting authorities of Member States be advertised

---

[1] OJ L 18, 21.1.1997, p. 1.

throughout the Community. The information contained in these notices must enable economic operators in the Community to determine whether the proposed contracts are of interest to them. For this purpose, it is appropriate to give them adequate information on the object of the contract and the conditions attached thereto. Improved visibility should therefore be ensured for public notices by means of appropriate instruments, such as standard contract notice forms and the Common Procurement Vocabulary (CPV) provided for in Regulation (EC) No 2195/2002 of the European Parliament and of the Council[1] as the reference nomenclature for public contracts. In restricted procedures, advertisement is, more particularly, intended to enable contractors of Member States to express their interest in contracts by seeking from the contracting authorities invitations to tender under the required conditions.

(37) Directive 1999/93/EC of the European Parliament and of the Council of 13 December 1999 on a Community framework for electronic signatures[2] and Directive 2000/31/EC of the European Parliament and of the Council of 8 June 2000 on certain legal aspects of information society services, in particular electronic commerce, in the internal market ('Directive on electronic commerce')[3] should, in the context of this Directive, apply to the transmission of information by electronic means. The public procurement procedures and the rules applicable to service contests require a level of security and confidentiality higher than that required by these Directives. Accordingly, the devices for the electronic receipt of offers, requests to participate and plans and projects should comply with specific additional requirements. To this end, use of electronic signatures, in particular advanced electronic signatures, should, as far as possible, be encouraged. Moreover, the existence of voluntary accreditation schemes could constitute a favourable framework for enhancing the level of certification service provision for these devices.

(38) The use of electronic means leads to savings in time. As a result, provision should be made for reducing the minimum periods where electronic means are used, subject, however, to the condition that they are compatible with the specific mode of transmission envisaged at Community level.

(39) Verification of the suitability of tenderers, in open procedures, and of candidates, in restricted and negotiated procedures with publication of a contract notice and in the competitive dialogue, and the selection thereof, should be carried out in transparent conditions. For this purpose, non-discriminatory criteria should be indicated which the contracting authorities may use when selecting competitors and the means which economic operators may use to prove they have satisfied those criteria. In the same spirit of transparency, the contracting authority should be required, as soon as a contract is put out to competition, to indicate the selection criteria it will use and the level of specific competence it may or may not demand of the economic operators before admitting them to the procurement procedure.

(40) A contracting authority may limit the number of candidates in the restricted and negotiated procedures with publication of a contract notice, and in the competitive dialogue. Such a reduction of candidates should be performed on the basis of objective criteria indicated in the contract notice. These objective criteria do not necessarily imply weightings. For criteria relating to the personal situation of economic operators, a general reference in the contract notice to the situations set out in Article 45 may suffice.

(41) In the competitive dialogue and negotiated procedures with publication of a contract notice, in view of the flexibility

[1] OJ L 340, 16.12.2002, p. 1.
[2] OJ L 13, 19.1.2000, p. 12.
[3] OJ L 178, 17.7.2000, p. 1.

which may be required and the high level of costs associated with such methods of procurement, contracting authorities should be entitled to make provision for the procedure to be conducted in successive stages in order gradually to reduce, on the basis of previously indicated contract award criteria, the number of tenders which they will go on to discuss or negotiate. This reduction should, insofar as the number of appropriate solutions or candidates allows, ensure that there is genuine competition.

(42) The relevant Community rules on mutual recognition of diplomas, certificates or other evidence of formal qualifications apply when evidence of a particular qualification is required for participation in a procurement procedure or a design contest.

(43) The award of public contracts to economic operators who have participated in a criminal organisation or who have been found guilty of corruption or of fraud to the detriment of the financial interests of the European Communities or of money laundering should be avoided. Where appropriate, the contracting authorities should ask candidates or tenderers to supply relevant documents and, where they have doubts concerning the personal situation of a candidate or tenderer, they may seek the cooperation of the competent authorities of the Member State concerned. The exclusion of such economic operators should take place as soon as the contracting authority has knowledge of a judgment concerning such offences rendered in accordance with national law that has the force of res judicata. If national law contains provisions to this effect, noncompliance with environmental legislation or legislation on unlawful agreements in public contracts which has been the subject of a final judgment or a decision having equivalent effect may be considered an offence concerning the professional conduct of the economic operator concerned or grave misconduct. Non-observance of national provisions implementing the Council Directives

2000/78/EC[1] and 76/207/EEC[2] concerning equal treatment of workers, which has been the subject of a final judgment or a decision having equivalent effect may be considered an offence concerning the professional conduct of the economic operator concerned or grave misconduct.

(44) In appropriate cases, in which the nature of the works and/or services justifies applying environmental management measures or schemes during the performance of a public contract, the application of such measures or schemes may be required. Environmental management schemes, whether or not they are registered under Community instruments such as Regulation (EC) No 761/2001[3] (EMAS), can demonstrate that the economic operator has the technical capability to perform the contract. Moreover, a description of the measures implemented by the economic operator to ensure the same level of environmental protection should be accepted as an alternative to environmental management registration schemes as a form of evidence.

(45) This Directive allows Member States to establish official lists of contractors, suppliers or service providers or a system of certification by public or private bodies, and makes provision for the effects of such registration or such certification in a contract award procedure in another Member State. As regards official lists of

---

[1] Council Directive 2000/78/EC of 27 November 2000 establishing a general framework for equal treatment in employment and occupation (OJ L 303, 2.12.2000, p. 16).

[2] Council Directive 76/207/EEC of 9 February 1976 on the implementation of the principle of equal treatment for men and women as regards access to employment, vocational training and promotion, and working conditions (OJ L 39, 14.2.1976, p. 40). Directive amended by Directive 2002/73/EC of the European Parliament and of the Council (OJ L 269, 5.10.2002, p. 15).

[3] Regulation (EC) No 761/2001 of the European Parliament and of the Council of 19 March 2001 allowing a voluntary participation by organisations in a Community eco-management and audit scheme (EMAS) (OJ L 114, 24.4.2001, p. 1).

approved economic operators, it is important to take into account Court of Justice case-law in cases where an economic operator belonging to a group claims the economic, financial or technical capabilities of other companies in the group in support of its application for registration. In this case, it is for the economic operator to prove that those resources will actually be available to it throughout the period of validity of the registration. For the purposes of that registration, a Member State may therefore determine the level of requirements to be met and in particular, for example where the operator lays claim to the financial standing of another company in the group, it may require that that company be held liable, if necessary jointly and severally.

(46) Contracts should be awarded on the basis of objective criteria which ensure compliance with the principles of transparency, non-discrimination and equal treatment and which guarantee that tenders are assessed in conditions of effective competition. As a result, it is appropriate to allow the application of two award criteria only: 'the lowest price' and 'the most economically advantageous tender'.

To ensure compliance with the principle of equal treatment in the award of contracts, it is appropriate to lay down an obligation—established by case-law—to ensure the necessary transparency to enable all tenderers to be reasonably informed of the criteria and arrangements which will be applied to identify the most economically advantageous tender. It is therefore the responsibility of contracting authorities to indicate the criteria for the award of the contract and the relative weighting given to each of those criteria in sufficient time for tenderers to be aware of them when preparing their tenders. Contracting authorities may derogate from indicating the weighting of the criteria for the award in duly justified cases for which they must be able to give reasons, where the weighting cannot be established in advance, in particular on account of the complexity of the contract. In such cases, they must indicate the descending order of importance of the criteria.

Where the contracting authorities choose to award a contract to the most economically advantageous tender, they shall assess the tenders in order to determine which one offers the best value for money. In order to do this, they shall determine the economic and quality criteria which, taken as a whole, must make it possible to determine the most economically advantageous tender for the contracting authority. The determination of these criteria depends on the object of the contract since they must allow the level of performance offered by each tender to be assessed in the light of the object of the contract, as defined in the technical specifications, and the value for money of each tender to be measured.

In order to guarantee equal treatment, the criteria for the award of the contract should enable tenders to be compared and assessed objectively. If these conditions are fulfilled, economic and qualitative criteria for the award of the contract, such as meeting environmental requirements, may enable the contracting authority to meet the needs of the public concerned, as expressed in the specifications of the contract. Under the same conditions, a contracting authority may use criteria aiming to meet social requirements, in response in particular to the needs—defined in the specifications of the contract—of particularly disadvantaged groups of people to which those receiving/using the works, supplies or services which are the object of the contract belong.

(47) In the case of public service contracts, the award criteria must not affect the application of national provisions on the remuneration of certain services, such as, for example, the services performed by architects, engineers or lawyers and, where public supply contracts are concerned, the application of national provisions setting out fixed prices for school books.

(48) Certain technical conditions, and in particular those concerning notices and statistical reports, as well as the

nomenclature used and the conditions of reference to that nomenclature, will need to be adopted and amended in the light of changing technical requirements. The lists of contracting authorities in the Annexes will also need to be updated. It is therefore appropriate to put in place a flexible and rapid adoption procedure for this purpose.

(49) The measures necessary for the implementation of this Directive should be adopted in accordance with Council Decision 1999/468/EC of 28 June 1999 laying down the procedures for the exercise of implementing powers conferred on the Commission.[1]

(50) It is appropriate that Council Regulation (EEC, Euratom) No 1182/71 of 3 June 1971 determining the rules applicable to periods, dates and time limits[2] should apply to the calculation of the time limits contained in this Directive.

(51) This Directive should not prejudice the time limits set out in Annex XI, within which Member States are required to transpose and apply Directives 92/50/EEC, 93/36/EEC and 93/37/EEC,

HAVE ADOPTED THIS DIRECTIVE:

TABLE OF CONTENTS

---

[1] OJ L 184, 17.7.1999, p. 23.   [2] OJ L 124, 8.6.1971, p. 1.

669

Title I
Definitions and General Principles

Article 1
Definitions

1. For the purposes of this Directive, the definitions set out in paragraphs 2 to 15 shall apply.

2. (a) 'Public contracts' are contracts for pecuniary interest concluded in writing between one or more economic operators and one or more contracting authorities and having as their object the execution of works, the supply of products or the provision of services within the meaning of this Directive.

   (b) 'Public works contracts' are public contracts having as their object either the execution, or both the design and execution, of works related to one of the activities within the meaning of Annex I or a work, or the realization, by whatever means, of a work corresponding to the requirements specified by the contracting authority. A 'work' means the outcome of building or civil engineering works taken as a whole which is sufficient of itself to fulfil an economic or technical function.

   (c) 'Public supply contracts' are public contracts other than those referred to in (b) having as their object the purchase, lease, rental or hire purchase, with or without option to buy, of products.

   A public contract having as its object the supply of products and which also covers, as an incidental matter, siting and installation operations shall be considered to be a 'public supply contract'.

   (d) 'Public service contracts' are public contracts other than public works or supply contracts having as their object the provision of services referred to in Annex II.

   A public contract having as its object both products and services within the meaning of Annex II shall be considered to be a 'public service contract' if the value of the services in question exceeds that of the products covered by the contract.

A public contract having as its object services within the meaning of Annex II and including activities within the meaning of Annex I that are only incidental to the principal object of the contract shall be considered to be a public service contract.

3. 'Public works concession' is a contract of the same type as a public works contract except for the fact that the consideration for the works to be carried out consists either solely in the right to exploit the work or in this right together with payment.

4. 'Service concession' is a contract of the same type as a public service contract except for the fact that the consideration for the provision of services consists either solely in the right to exploit the service or in this right together with payment.

5. A 'framework agreement' is an agreement between one or more contracting authorities and one or more economic operators, the purpose of which is to establish the terms governing contracts to be awarded during a given period, in particular with regard to price and, where appropriate, the quantity envisaged.

6. A 'dynamic purchasing system' is a completely electronic process for making commonly used purchases, the characteristics of which, as generally available on the market, meet the requirements of the contracting authority, which is limited in duration and open throughout its validity to any economic operator which satisfies the selection criteria and has submitted an indicative tender that complies with the specification.

7. An 'electronic auction' is a repetitive process involving an electronic device for the presentation of new prices, revised downwards, and/or new values concerning certain elements of tenders, which occurs after an initial full evaluation of the tenders, enabling them to be ranked using automatic evaluation methods.

Consequently, certain service contracts and certain works contracts having as their subject-matter intellectual performances, such as the design of works, may not be the object of electronic auctions.

8. The terms 'contractor', 'supplier' and 'service provider' mean any natural or legal person or legal entity or group of such persons and/or bodies which offers on the market, respectively, the execution of works and/or a work, products or services.

The term 'economic operator' shall cover equally the concepts of contractor, supplier and service provider. It is used merely in the interest of simplification.

An economic operator who has submitted a tender shall be designated a 'tenderer'. One which has sought an invitation to take part in a restricted or negotiated procedure or a competitive dialogue shall be designated a 'candidate'.

9. 'Contracting authorities' means the State, regional or local authorities, bodies governed by public law, associations formed by one or several of such authorities or one or several of such bodies governed by public law.

A 'body governed by public law' means any body:
(a) established for the specific purpose of meeting needs in the general interest, not having an industrial or commercial character;
(b) having legal personality; and
(c) financed, for the most part, by the State, regional or local authorities, or other bodies governed by public law; or subject to management supervision by those bodies; or having an administrative, managerial or supervisory board, more than half of whose members are appointed by the State, regional or local authorities, or by other bodies governed by public law.

Non-exhaustive lists of bodies and categories of bodies governed by public law which fulfil the criteria referred to in (a), (b) and (c) of the second subparagraph are set out in Annex III. Member States shall periodically notify the Commission of any changes to their lists of bodies and categories of bodies.

10. A 'central purchasing body' is a contracting authority which:
— acquires supplies and/or services intended for contracting authorities, or

— awards public contracts or concludes framework agreements for works, supplies or services intended for contracting authorities.

11. (a) 'Open procedures' means those procedures whereby any interested economic operator may submit a tender.
  (b) 'Restricted procedures' means those procedures in which any economic operator may request to participate and whereby only those economic operators invited by the contracting authority may submit a tender.
  (c) 'Competitive dialogue' is a procedure in which any economic operator may request to participate and whereby the contracting authority conducts a dialogue with the candidates admitted to that procedure, with the aim of developing one or more suitable alternatives capable of meeting its requirements, and on the basis of which the candidates chosen are invited to tender.

  For the purpose of recourse to the procedure mentioned in the first subparagraph, a public contract is considered to be 'particularly complex' where the contracting authorities:
  — are not objectively able to define the technical means in accordance with Article 23(3)(b), (c) or (d), capable of satisfying their needs or objectives, and/or
  — are not objectively able to specify the legal and/or financial make-up of a project.

  (d) 'Negotiated procedures' means those procedures whereby the contracting authorities consult the economic operators of their choice and negotiate the terms of contract with one or more of these.
  (e) 'Design contests' means those procedures which enable the contracting authority to acquire, mainly in the fields of town and country planning, architecture and engineering or data processing, a plan or design selected by a jury after being put out to competition with or without the award of prizes.

12. 'Written' or 'in writing' means any expression consisting of words or figures which can be read, reproduced and subsequently communicated. It may include information which is transmitted and stored by electronic means.

13. 'Electronic means' means using electronic equipment for the processing (including digital compression) and storage of data which is transmitted, conveyed and received by wire, by radio, by optical means or by other electromagnetic means.

14. The 'Common Procurement Vocabulary (CPV)' shall designate the reference nomenclature applicable to public contracts as adopted by Regulation (EC) No 2195/2002, while ensuring equivalence with the other existing nomenclatures.

In the event of varying interpretations of the scope of this Directive, owing to possible differences between the CPV and NACE nomenclatures listed in Annex I, or between the CPV and CPC (provisional version) nomenclatures listed in Annex II, the NACE or the CPC nomenclature respectively shall take precedence.

15. For the purposes of Article 13, Article 57(a) and Article 68(b), the following phrases shall have the following meanings:

(a) 'public telecommunications network' means the public telecommunications infrastructure which enables signals to be conveyed between defined network termination points by wire, by microwave, by optical means or by other electromagnetic means;

(b) a 'network termination point' means all physical connections and their technical access specifications which form part of the public telecommunications network and are necessary for access to, and efficient communication through, that public network;

(c) 'public telecommunications services' means telecommunications services the provision of which the Member States have specifically assigned, in particular, to one or more telecommunications entities;

(d) 'telecommunications services' means services the provision of which consists wholly or partly in the transmission and routing of signals on the public telecommunications network by means of telecommunications processes, with the exception of broadcasting and television.

Article 2
Principles of awarding contracts

Contracting authorities shall treat economic operators equally and non-discriminatorily and shall act in a transparent way.

Article 3
Granting of special or exclusive rights: non-discrimination clause

Where a contracting authority grants special or exclusive rights to carry out a public service activity to an entity other than such a contracting authority, the act by which that right is granted shall provide that, in respect of the supply contracts which it awards to third parties as part of its activities, the entity concerned must comply with the principle of non-discrimination on the basis of nationality.

TITLE II
RULES ON PUBLIC CONTRACTS

CHAPTER I GENERAL PROVISIONS

Article 4
Economic operators

1. Candidates or tenderers who, under the law of the Member State in which they are established, are entitled to provide the relevant service, shall not be rejected solely on the ground that, under the law of the Member State in which the contract is awarded, they would be required to be either natural or legal persons.

However, in the case of public service and public works contracts as well as public supply contracts covering in addition services and/or siting and installation operations, legal persons may be required to indicate in the tender or the request to participate, the names and relevant professional qualifications of the staff to be responsible for the performance of the contract in question.

2. Groups of economic operators may submit tenders or put themselves forward as candidates. In order to submit a tender or a request to participate, these groups may not be required by the contracting authorities to assume a specific legal form; however, the group selected may be required to do so when it has been awarded the contract, to the extent that this change is necessary for the satisfactory performance of the contract.

Article 5
Conditions relating to agreements concluded within the World Trade Organisation

For the purposes of the award of contracts by contracting authorities, Member States shall apply in their relations conditions as favourable as those which they grant to economic operators of third countries in implementation of the Agreement on Government Procurement (hereinafter referred to as 'the Agreement'), concluded in the framework of the Uruguay Round multilateral negotiations. Member States shall, to this end, consult one another within the Advisory Committee for Public Contracts referred to in Article 77 on the measures to be taken pursuant to the Agreement.

Article 6
Confidentiality

Without prejudice to the provisions of this Directive, in particular those concerning the obligations relating to the advertising of awarded contracts and to the information to candidates and tenderers set out in Articles 35(4) and 41, and in accordance with the national law to which the contracting authority is subject, the contracting authority shall not disclose information forwarded to it by economic operators which they have designated as confidential; such information includes, in particular, technical or trade secrets and the confidential aspects of tenders.

CHAPTER II SCOPE

Section 1 Thresholds
Article 7
Threshold amounts for public contracts

This Directive shall apply to public contracts which are not excluded in accordance with the exceptions provided for in Articles 10 and 11

and Articles 12 to 18 and which have a value exclusive of value-added tax (VAT) estimated to be equal to or greater than the following thresholds:

(a) EUR 162 000 for public supply and service contracts others than those covered by point (b), third indent, awarded by contracting authorities which are listed as central government authorities in Annex IV; in the case of public supply contracts awarded by contracting authorities operating in the field of defence, this shall apply only to contracts involving products covered by Annex V;

(b) EUR 249 000
  — for public supply and service contracts awarded by contracting authorities other than those listed in Annex IV,
  — for public supply contracts awarded by contracting authorities which are listed in Annex IV and operate in the field of defence, where these contracts involve products not covered by Annex V,
  — for public service contracts awarded by any contracting authority in respect of the services listed in Category 8 of Annex IIA, Category 5 telecommunications services the positions of which in the CPV are equivalent to CPC reference Nos 7524, 7525 and 7526 and/or the services listed in Annex II B;

(c) EUR 6 242 000 for public works contracts.

Article 8
Contracts subsidised by more than 50% by contracting authorities

This Directive shall apply to the awarding of:
(a) contracts which are subsidised directly by contracting authorities by more than 50 % and the estimated value of which, net of VAT, is equal to or greater than EUR 6 242 000,
  — where those contracts involve civil engineering activities within the meaning of Annex I,
  — where those contracts involve building work for hospitals, facilities intended for sports, recreation and leisure, school and university buildings and buildings used for administrative purposes;
(b) service contracts which are subsidised directly by contracting authorities by more

than 50% and the estimated value of which, net of VAT, is equal to or greater than EUR 249 000 and which are connected with a works contract within the meaning of point (a).

Member States shall take the necessary measures to ensure that the contracting authorities awarding such subsidies ensure compliance with this Directive where that contract is awarded by one or more entities other than themselves or comply with this Directive where they themselves award that contract for and on behalf of those other entities.

Article 9
Methods for calculating the estimated value of public contracts, framework agreements and dynamic purchasing systems

1. The calculation of the estimated value of a public contract shall be based on the total amount payable, net of VAT, as estimated by the contracting authority. This calculation shall take account of the estimated total amount, including any form of option and any renewals of the contract.

Where the contracting authority provides for prizes or payments to candidates or tenderers it shall take them into account when calculating the estimated value of the contract.

2. This estimate must be valid at the moment at which the contract notice is sent, as provided for in Article 35(2), or, in cases where such notice is not required, at the moment at which the contracting authority commences the contract awarding procedure.

3. No works project or proposed purchase of a certain quantity of supplies and/or services may be subdivided to prevent its coming within the scope of this Directive.

4. With regard to public works contracts, calculation of the estimated value shall take account of both the cost of the works and the total estimated value of the supplies necessary for executing the works and placed at the contractor's disposal by the contracting authorities.

5. (a) Where a proposed work or purchase of services may result in contracts being awarded at the same time in the form of separate lots, account shall be taken of the total estimated value of all such lots.

Where the aggregate value of the lots is equal to or exceeds the threshold laid down in Article 7, this Directive shall apply to the awarding of each lot.

However, the contracting authorities may waive such application in respect of lots the estimated value of which net of VAT is less than EUR 80 000 for services or EUR 1 million for works, provided that the aggregate value of those lots does not exceed 20 % of the aggregate value of the lots as a whole.

(b) Where a proposal for the acquisition of similar supplies may result in contracts being awarded at the same time in the form of separate lots, account shall be taken of the total estimated value of all such lots when applying Article 7(a) and (b).

Where the aggregate value of the lots is equal to or exceeds the threshold laid down in Article 7, this Directive shall apply to the awarding of each lot.

However, the contracting authorities may waive such application in respect of lots, the estimated value of which, net of VAT, is less than EUR 80 000, provided that the aggregate cost of those lots does not exceed 20 % of the aggregate value of the lots as a whole.

6. With regard to public supply contracts relating to the leasing, hire, rental or hire purchase of products, the value to be taken as a basis for calculating the estimated contract value shall be as follows:

(a) in the case of fixed-term public contracts, if that term is less than or equal to 12 months, the total estimated value for the term of the contract or, if the term of the contract is greater than 12 months, the total value including the estimated residual value;

(b) in the case of public contracts without a fixed term or the term of which cannot be defined, the monthly value multiplied by 48.

7. In the case of public supply or service contracts which are regular in nature or which are intended to be renewed within a given

period, the calculation of the estimated contract value shall be based on the following:

(a) either the total actual value of the successive contracts of the same type awarded during the preceding 12 months or financial year adjusted, if possible, to take account of the changes in quantity or value which would occur in the course of the 12 months following the initial contract;

(b) or the total estimated value of the successive contracts awarded during the 12 months following the first delivery, or during the financial year if that is longer than 12 months.

The choice of method used to calculate the estimated value of a public contract may not be made with the intention of excluding it from the scope of this Directive.

8. With regard to public service contracts, the value to be taken as a basis for calculating the estimated contract value shall, where appropriate, be the following:

(a) for the following types of services:

(i) insurance services: the premium payable and other forms of remuneration;

(ii) banking and other financial services: the fees, commissions, interest and other forms of remuneration;

(iii) design contracts: fees, commission payable and other forms of remuneration;

(b) for service contracts which do not indicate a total price:

(i) in the case of fixed-term contracts, if that term is less than or equal to 48 months: the total value for their full term;

(ii) in the case of contracts without a fixed term or with a term greater than 48 months: the monthly value multiplied by 48.

9. With regard to framework agreements and dynamic purchasing systems, the value to be taken into consideration shall be the maximum estimated value net of VAT of all the contracts envisaged for the total term of the framework agreement or the dynamic purchasing system.

Section 2 Specific situations

Article 10
Defence procurement

This Directive shall apply to public contracts awarded by contracting authorities in the field of defence, subject to Article 296 of the Treaty.

Article 11
Public contracts and framework agreements awarded by central purchasing bodies

1. Member States may stipulate that contracting authorities may purchase works, supplies and/or services from or through a central purchasing body.

2. Contracting authorities which purchase works, supplies and/or services from or through a central purchasing body in the cases set out in Article 1(10) shall be deemed to have complied with this Directive insofar as the central purchasing body has complied with it.

Section 3 Excluded contracts

Article 12
Contracts in the water, energy, transport and postal services sectors

This Directive shall not apply to public contracts which, under Directive 2004/17/EC, are awarded by contracting authorities exercising one or more of the activities referred to in Articles 3 to 7 of that Directive and are awarded for the pursuit of those activities, or to public contracts excluded from the scope of that Directive under Article 5(2) and Articles 19, 26 and 30 thereof. However, this Directive shall continue to apply to public contracts awarded by contracting authorities carrying out one or more of the activities referred to in Article 6 of Directive 2004/17/EC and awarded for those activities, insofar as the Member State concerned takes advantage of the option referred to in the second subparagraph of Article 71 thereof to defer its application.

Article 13
Specific exclusions in the field of telecommunications

This Directive shall not apply to public contracts for the principal purpose of permitting the contracting authorities to provide or exploit public telecommunications networks or to provide to the public one or more telecommunications services.

Article 14
Secret contracts and contracts requiring special security measures

This Directive shall not apply to public contracts when they are declared to be secret, when their performance must be accompanied by special security measures in accordance with the laws, regulations or administrative provisions in force in the Member State concerned, or when the protection of the essential interests of that Member State so requires.

Article 15
Contracts awarded pursuant to international rules

This Directive shall not apply to public contracts governed by different procedural rules and awarded:

(a) pursuant to an international agreement concluded in conformity with the Treaty between a Member State and one or more third countries and covering supplies or works intended for the joint implementation or exploitation of a work by the signatory States or services intended for the joint implementation or exploitation of a project by the signatory States; all agreements shall be communicated to the Commission, which may consult the Advisory Committee for Public Contracts referred to in Article 77;

(b) pursuant to a concluded international agreement relating to the stationing of troops and concerning the undertakings of a Member State or a third country;

(c) pursuant to the particular procedure of an international organisation.

Article 16
Specific exclusions

This Directive shall not apply to public service contracts for:

(a) the acquisition or rental, by whatever financial means, of land, existing buildings or other immovable property or concerning rights thereon; nevertheless, financial service contracts concluded at the same time as, before or after the contract of acquisition or rental, in whatever form, shall be subject to this Directive;

(b) the acquisition, development, production or co-production of programme material intended for broadcasting by broadcasters and contracts for broadcasting time;

(c) arbitration and conciliation services;

(d) financial services in connection with the issue, sale, purchase or transfer of securities or other financial instruments, in particular transactions by the contracting authorities to raise money or capital, and central bank services;

(e) employment contracts;

(f) research and development services other than those where the benefits accrue exclusively to the contracting authority for its use in the conduct of its own affairs, on condition that the service provided is wholly remunerated by the contracting authority.

Article 17
Service concessions

Without prejudice to the application of Article 3, this Directive shall not apply to service concessions as defined in Article 1(4).

Article 18
Service contracts awarded on the basis of an exclusive right

This Directive shall not apply to public service contracts awarded by a contracting authority to another contracting authority or to an association of contracting authorities on the basis of an exclusive right which they enjoy pursuant to a published law, regulation or administrative provision which is compatible with the Treaty.

Section 4 Special arrangement
Article 19
Reserved contracts

Member States may reserve the right to participate in public contract award procedures to sheltered workshops or provide for such contracts to be performed in the context of sheltered employment programmes where most of the employees concerned are handicapped persons who, by reason of the nature or the seriousness of their disabilities, cannot carry on occupations under normal conditions.

The contract notice shall make reference to this provision.

CHAPTER III ARRANGEMENTS FOR PUBLIC SERVICE CONTRACTS

Article 20
Service contracts listed in Annex II A

Contracts which have as their object services listed in Annex II A shall be awarded in accordance with Articles 23 to 55.

Article 21
Service contracts listed in Annex II B

Contracts which have as their object services listed in Annex II B shall be subject solely to Article 23 and Article 35(4).

Article 22
Mixed contracts including services listed in Annex II A and services listed in Annex II B

Contracts which have as their object services listed both in Annex II A and in Annex II B shall be awarded in accordance with Articles 23 to 55 where the value of the services listed in Annex II A is greater than the value of the services listed in Annex II B. In other cases, contracts shall be awarded in accordance with Article 23 and Article 35(4).

CHAPTER IV SPECIFIC RULES GOVERNING SPECIFICATIONS AND CONTRACT DOCUMENTS

Article 23
Technical specifications

1. The technical specifications as defined in point 1 of Annex VI shall be set out in the contract documentation, such as contract notices, contract documents or additional documents. Whenever possible these technical specifications should be defined so as to take into account accessibility criteria for people with disabilities or design for all users.

2. Technical specifications shall afford equal access for tenderers and not have the effect of creating unjustified obstacles to the opening up of public procurement to competition.

3. Without prejudice to mandatory national technical rules, to the extent that they are compatible with Community law, the technical specifications shall be formulated:

(a) either by reference to technical specifications defined in Annex VI and, in order of preference, to national standards transposing European standards, European technical approvals, common technical specifications, international standards, other technical reference systems established by the European standardisation bodies or—when these do not exist—to national standards, national technical approvals or national technical specifications relating to the design, calculation and execution of the works and use of the products. Each reference shall be accompanied by the words 'or equivalent';

(b) or in terms of performance or functional requirements; the latter may include environmental characteristics. However, such parameters must be sufficiently precise to allow tenderers to determine the subject-matter of the contract and to allow contracting authorities to award the contract;

(c) or in terms of performance or functional requirements as mentioned in subparagraph (b), with reference to the specifications mentioned in subparagraph (a) as a means of presuming conformity with such performance or functional requirements;

(d) or by referring to the specifications mentioned in subparagraph (a) for certain characteristics, and by referring to the performance or functional requirements mentioned in subparagraph (b) for other characteristics.

4. Where a contracting authority makes use of the option of referring to the specifications mentioned in paragraph 3(a), it cannot reject a tender on the grounds that the products and services tendered for do not comply with the specifications to which it has referred, once the tenderer proves in his tender to the satisfaction of the contracting authority, by whatever appropriate means, that the solutions which he proposes satisfy in an equivalent manner the requirements defined by the technical specifications.

An appropriate means might be constituted by a technical dossier of the manufacturer or a test report from a recognised body.

5. Where a contracting authority uses the option laid down in paragraph 3 to prescribe in

677

terms of performance or functional requirements, it may not reject a tender for works, products or services which comply with a national standard transposing a European standard, with a European technical approval, a common technical specification, an international standard or a technical reference system established by a European standardisation body, if these specifications address the performance or functional requirements which it has laid down.

In his tender, the tenderer must prove to the satisfaction of the contracting authority and by any appropriate means that the work, product or service in compliance with the standard meets the performance or functional requirements of the contracting authority.

An appropriate means might be constituted by a technical dossier of the manufacturer or a test report from a recognised body.

6. Where contracting authorities lay down environmental characteristics in terms of performance or functional requirements as referred to in paragraph 3(b) they may use the detailed specifications, or, if necessary, parts thereof, as defined by European or (multi-) national eco-labels, or by and any other eco-label, provided that:
— those specifications are appropriate to define the characteristics of the supplies or services that are the object of the contract,
— the requirements for the label are drawn up on the basis of scientific information,
— the eco-labels are adopted using a procedure in which all stakeholders, such as government bodies, consumers, manufacturers, distributors and environmental organisations can participate, and
— they are accessible to all interested parties.

Contracting authorities may indicate that the products and services bearing the eco-label are presumed to comply with the technical specifications laid down in the contract documents; they must accept any other appropriate means of proof, such as a technical dossier of the manufacturer or a test report from a recognised body.

7. 'Recognised bodies', within the meaning of this Article, are test and calibration laboratories and certification and inspection bodies which comply with applicable European standards.

Contracting authorities shall accept certificates from recognised bodies established in other Member States.

8. Unless justified by the subject-matter of the contract, technical specifications shall not refer to a specific make or source, or a particular process, or to trade marks, patents, types or a specific origin or production with the effect of favouring or eliminating certain undertakings or certain products. Such reference shall be permitted on an exceptional basis, where a sufficiently precise and intelligible description of the subject-matter of the contract pursuant to paragraphs 3 and 4 is not possible; such reference shall be accompanied by the words 'or equivalent'.

Article 24
Variants

1. Where the criterion for award is that of the most economically advantageous tender, contracting authorities may authorise tenderers to submit variants.

2. Contracting authorities shall indicate in the contract notice whether or not they authorise variants: variants shall not be authorised without this indication.

3. Contracting authorities authorising variants shall state in the contract documents the minimum requirements to be met by the variants and any specific requirements for their presentation.

4. Only variants meeting the minimum requirements laid down by these contracting authorities shall be taken into consideration.

In procedures for awarding public supply or service contracts, contracting authorities which have authorised variants may not reject a variant on the sole ground that it would, if successful, lead to either a service contract rather than a public supply contract or a supply contract rather than a public service contract.

Article 25
Subcontracting

In the contract documents, the contracting authority may ask or may be required by a Member State to ask the tenderer to indicate in his tender any share of the contract he may intend to subcontract to third parties and any proposed subcontractors.

This indication shall be without prejudice to the question of the principal economic operator's liability.

Article 26
Conditions for performance of contracts

Contracting authorities may lay down special conditions relating to the performance of a contract, provided that these are compatible with Community law and are indicated in the contract notice or in the specifications. The conditions governing the performance of a contract may, in particular, concern social and environmental considerations.

Article 27
Obligations relating to taxes, environmental protection, employment protection provisions and working conditions

1. A contracting authority may state in the contract documents, or be obliged by a Member State so to state, the body or bodies from which a candidate or tenderer may obtain the appropriate information on the obligations relating to taxes, to environmental protection, to the employment protection provisions and to the working conditions which are in force in the Member State, region or locality in which the works are to be carried out or services are to be provided and which shall be applicable to the works carried out on site or to the services provided during the performance of the contract.

2. A contracting authority which supplies the information referred to in paragraph 1 shall request the tenderers or candidates in the contract award procedure to indicate that they have taken account, when drawing up their tender, of the obligations relating to employment protection provisions and the working conditions which are in force in the place where the works are to be carried out or the service is to be provided.

The first subparagraph shall be without prejudice to the application of the provisions of Article 55 concerning the examination of abnormally low tenders.

CHAPTER V PROCEDURES

Article 28
Use of open, restricted and negotiated procedures and of competitive dialogue

In awarding their public contracts, contracting authorities shall apply the national procedures adjusted for the purposes of this Directive.

They shall award these public contracts by applying the open or restricted procedure. In the specific circumstances expressly provided for in Article 29, contracting authorities may award their public contracts by means of the competitive dialogue. In the specific cases and circumstances referred to expressly in Articles 30 and 31, they may apply a negotiated procedure, with or without publication of the contract notice.

Article 29
Competitive dialogue

1. In the case of particularly complex contracts, Member States may provide that where contracting authorities consider that the use of the open or restricted procedure will not allow the award of the contract, the latter may make use of the competitive dialogue in accordance with this Article.

A public contract shall be awarded on the sole basis of the award criterion for the most economically advantageous tender.

2. Contracting authorities shall publish a contract notice setting out their needs and requirements, which they shall define in that notice and/or in a descriptive document.

3. Contracting authorities shall open, with the candidates selected in accordance with the relevant provisions of Articles 44 to 52, a dialogue the aim of which shall be to identify and define the means best suited to satisfying their needs. They may discuss all aspects of the contract with the chosen candidates during this dialogue.

During the dialogue, contracting authorities shall ensure equality of treatment among all tenderers. In particular, they shall not provide information in a discriminatory manner which may give some tenderers an advantage over others.

Contracting authorities may not reveal to the other participants solutions proposed or other confidential information communicated by a candidate participating in the dialogue without his/her agreement.

4. Contracting authorities may provide for the procedure to take place in successive stages in order to reduce the number of solutions to be discussed during the dialogue stage by applying the award criteria in the contract notice or the descriptive document. The contract notice or the descriptive document shall indicate that recourse may be had to this option.

5. The contracting authority shall continue such dialogue until it can identify the solution or solutions, if necessary after comparing them, which are capable of meeting its needs.

6. Having declared that the dialogue is concluded and having so informed the participants, contracting authorities shall ask them to submit their final tenders on the basis of the solution or solutions presented and specified during the dialogue. These tenders shall contain all the elements required and necessary for the performance of the project.

These tenders may be clarified, specified and fine-tuned at the request of the contracting authority. However, such clarification, specification, fine-tuning or additional information may not involve changes to the basic features of the tender or the call for tender, variations in which are likely to distort competition or have a discriminatory effect.

7. Contracting authorities shall assess the tenders received on the basis of the award criteria laid down in the contract notice or the descriptive document and shall choose the most economically advantageous tender in accordance with Article 53.

At the request of the contracting authority, the tenderer identified as having submitted the most economically advantageous tender may be asked to clarify aspects of the tender or confirm commitments contained in the tender provided this does not have the effect of modifying substantial aspects of the tender or

of the call for tender and does not risk distorting competition or causing discrimination.

8. The contracting authorities may specify prices or payments to the participants in the dialogue.

Article 30
Cases justifying use of the negotiated procedure with prior publication of a contract notice

1. Contracting authorities may award their public contracts by negotiated procedure, after publication of a contract notice, in the following cases:

(a) in the event of irregular tenders or the submission of tenders which are unacceptable under national provisions compatible with Articles 4, 24, 25, 27 and Chapter VII, in response to an open or restricted procedure or a competitive dialogue insofar as the original terms of the contract are not substantially altered.

Contracting authorities need not publish a contract notice where they include in the negotiated procedure all of, and only, the tenderers which satisfy the criteria of Articles 45 to 52 and which, during the prior open or restricted procedure or competitive dialogue, have submitted tenders in accordance with the formal requirements of the tendering procedure;

(b) in exceptional cases, when the nature of the works, supplies, or services or the risks attaching thereto do not permit prior overall pricing;

(c) in the case of services, *inter alia* services within category 6 of Annex II A, and intellectual services such as services involving the design of works, insofar as the nature of the services to be provided is such that contract specifications cannot be established with sufficient precision to permit the award of the contract by selection of the best tender according to the rules governing open or restricted procedures;

(d) in respect of public works contracts, for works which are performed solely for purposes of research, testing or development and not with the aim of ensuring profitability or recovering research and development costs.

2. In the cases referred to in paragraph 1, contracting authorities shall negotiate with tenderers the tenders submitted by them in order to adapt them to the requirements which they have set in the contract notice, the specifications and additional documents, if any, and to seek out the best tender in accordance with Article 53(1).

3. During the negotiations, contracting authorities shall ensure the equal treatment of all tenderers. In particular, they shall not provide information in a discriminatory manner which may give some tenderers an advantage over others.

4. Contracting authorities may provide for the negotiated procedure to take place in successive stages in order to reduce the number of tenders to be negotiated by applying the award criteria in the contract notice or the specifications. The contract notice or the specifications shall indicate whether recourse has been had to this option.

Article 31
Cases justifying use of the negotiated procedure without publication of a contract notice

Contracting authorities may award public contracts by a negotiated procedure without prior publication of a contract notice in the following cases:

(1) for public works contracts, public supply contracts and public service contracts:

(a) when no tenders or no suitable tenders or no applications have been submitted in response to an open procedure or a restricted procedure, provided that the initial conditions of contract are not substantially altered and on condition that a report is sent to the Commission if it so requests;

(b) when, for technical or artistic reasons, or for reasons connected with the protection of exclusive rights, the contract may be awarded only to a particular economic operator;

(c) insofar as is strictly necessary when, for reasons of extreme urgency brought about by events unforeseeable by the contracting authorities in question, the time limit for the open, restricted or negotiated procedures with publication of a contract notice as referred to in Article 30 cannot be complied with. The circumstances invoked to justify extreme urgency must not in any event be attributable to the contracting authority;

(2) for public supply contracts:

(a) when the products involved are manufactured purely for the purpose of research, experimentation, study or development; this provision does not extend to quantity production to establish commercial viability or to recover research and development costs;

(b) for additional deliveries by the original supplier which are intended either as a partial replacement of normal supplies or installations or as the extension of existing supplies or installations where a change of supplier would oblige the contracting authority to acquire material having different technical characteristics which would result in incompatibility or disproportionate technical difficulties in operation and maintenance; the length of such contracts as well as that of recurrent contracts may not, as a general rule, exceed three years;

(c) for supplies quoted and purchased on a commodity market;

(d) for the purchase of supplies on particularly advantageous terms, from either a supplier which is definitively winding up its business activities, or the receivers or liquidators of a bankruptcy, an arrangement with creditors, or a similar procedure under national laws or regulations;

(3) for public service contracts, when the contract concerned follows a design contest and must, under the applicable rules, be awarded to the successful candidate or to one of the successful candidates, in the latter case, all successful candidates must be invited to participate in the negotiations;

(4) for public works contracts and public service contracts:

(a) for additional works or services not included in the project initially considered or in the original contract but which have, through unforeseen circumstances, become necessary for the performance of the works or services described therein, on condition that the award is made to the economic operator performing such works or services:

—when such additional works or services cannot be technically or economically separated from the original contract without major inconvenience to the contracting authorities,

or

—when such works or services, although separable from the performance of the original contract, are strictly necessary for its completion.

However, the aggregate value of contracts awarded for additional works or services may not exceed 50 % of the amount of the original contract;

(b) for new works or services consisting in the repetition of similar works or services entrusted to the economic operator to whom the same contracting authorities awarded an original contract, provided that such works or services are in conformity with a basic project for which the original contract was awarded according to the open or restricted procedure.

As soon as the first project is put up for tender, the possible use of this procedure shall be disclosed and the total estimated cost of subsequent works or services shall be taken into consideration by the contracting authorities when they apply the provisions of Article 7.

This procedure may be used only during the three years following the conclusion of the original contract.

Article 32
Framework agreements

1. Member States may provide that contracting authorities may conclude framework agreements.

2. For the purpose of concluding a framework agreement, contracting authorities shall follow the rules of procedure referred to in this Directive for all phases up to the award of contracts based on that framework agreement. The parties to the framework agreement shall be chosen by applying the award criteria set in accordance with Article 53.

Contracts based on a framework agreement shall be awarded in accordance with the procedures laid down in paragraphs 3 and 4. Those procedures may be applied only between the contracting authorities and the economic operators originally party to the framework agreement.

When awarding contracts based on a framework agreement, the parties may under no circumstances make substantial amendments to the terms laid down in that framework agreement, in particular in the case referred to in paragraph 3.

The term of a framework agreement may not exceed four years, save in exceptional cases duly justified, in particular by the subject of the framework agreement. Contracting authorities may not use framework agreements improperly or in such a way as to prevent, restrict or distort competition.

3. Where a framework agreement is concluded with a single economic operator, contracts based on that agreement shall be awarded within the limits of the terms laid down in the framework agreement.

For the award of those contracts, contracting authorities may consult the operator party to the framework agreement in writing, requesting it to supplement its tender as necessary.

4. Where a framework agreement is concluded with several economic operators, the latter must be at least three in number, insofar as there is a sufficient number of economic operators to satisfy the selection criteria and/or of admissible tenders which meet the award criteria.

Contracts based on framework agreements concluded with several economic operators may be awarded either:

— by application of the terms laid down in the framework agreement without reopening competition, or

— where not all the terms are laid down in the framework agreement, when the parties are again in competition on the basis of the same and, if necessary, more precisely formulated terms, and, where appropriate, other terms referred to in the specifications of the framework agreement, in accordance with the following procedure:

(a) for every contract to be awarded, contracting authorities shall consult in writing the economic operators capable of performing the contract;

(b) contracting authorities shall fix a time limit which is sufficiently long to allow tenders for each specific contract to be submitted, taking into account factors such as the complexity of the subject-matter of the contract and the time needed to send in tenders;

(c) tenders shall be submitted in writing, and their content shall remain confidential until the stipulated time limit for reply has expired;

(d) contracting authorities shall award each contract to the tenderer who has submitted the best tender on the basis of the award criteria set out in the specifications of the framework agreement.

Article 33
Dynamic purchasing systems

1. Member States may provide that contracting authorities may use dynamic purchasing systems.

2. In order to set up a dynamic purchasing system, contracting authorities shall follow the rules of the open procedure in all its phases up to the award of the contracts to be concluded under this system. All the tenderers satisfying the selection criteria and having submitted an indicative tender which complies with the specification and any possible additional documents shall be admitted to the system; indicative tenders may be improved at any time provided that they continue to comply with the specification. With a view to setting up the system and to the award of contracts under that system, contracting authorities shall use solely electronic means in accordance with Article 42(2) to (5).

3. For the purposes of setting up the dynamic purchasing system, contracting authorities shall:

(a) publish a contract notice making it clear that a dynamic purchasing system is involved;

(b) indicate in the specification, amongst other matters, the nature of the purchases envisaged under that system, as well as all the necessary information concerning the purchasing system, the electronic equipment used and the technical connection arrangements and specifications;

(c) offer by electronic means, on publication of the notice and up to the expiry of the system, unrestricted, direct and full access to the specification and to any additional documents and shall indicate in the notice the internet address at which such documents may be consulted.

4. Contracting authorities shall give any economic operator, throughout the entire period of the dynamic purchasing system, the possibility of submitting an indicative tender and of being admitted to the system under the conditions referred to in paragraph 2. They shall complete evaluation within a maximum of 15 days from the date of submission of the indicative tender. However, they may extend the evaluation period provided that no invitation to tender is issued in the meantime.

The contracting authority shall inform the tenderer referred to in the first subparagraph at the earliest possible opportunity of its admittance to the dynamic purchasing system or of the rejection of its indicative tender.

5. Each specific contract must be the subject of an invitation to tender. Before issuing the invitation to tender, contracting authorities shall publish a simplified contract notice inviting all interested economic operators to submit an indicative tender, in accordance with paragraph 4, within a time limit that may not be less than 15 days from the date on which the simplified notice was sent. Contracting authorities may not proceed with tendering until they have completed evaluation of all the indicative tenders received by that deadline.

6. Contracting authorities shall invite all tenderers admitted to the system to submit a tender for each specific contract to be awarded under the system. To that end they shall set a time limit for the submission of tenders

They shall award the contract to the tenderer which submitted the best tender on the basis of the award criteria set out in the contract notice for the establishment of the dynamic purchasing system. Those criteria may, if appropriate, be formulated more precisely in the invitation referred to in the first subparagraph.

7. A dynamic purchasing system may not last for more than four years, except in duly justified exceptional cases.

Contracting authorities may not resort to this system to prevent, restrict or distort competition.

No charges may be billed to the interested economic operators or to parties to the system.

Article 34
Public works contracts: particular rules on subsidised housing schemes

In the case of public contracts relating to the design and construction of a subsidised housing scheme the size and complexity of which, and the estimated duration of the work involved require that planning be based from the outset on close collaboration within a team comprising representatives of the contracting authorities, experts and the contractor to be responsible for carrying out the works, a special award procedure may be adopted for selecting the contractor most suitable for integration into the team.

In particular, contracting authorities shall include in the contract notice as accurate as possible a description of the works to be carried out so as to enable interested contractors to form a valid idea of the project. Furthermore, contracting authorities shall, in accordance with the qualitative selection criteria referred to in Articles 45 to 52, set out in such a contract notice the personal, technical, economic and financial conditions to be fulfilled by candidates.

Where such a procedure is adopted, contracting authorities shall apply Articles 2, 35, 36, 38, 39, 41, 42, 43 and 45 to 52.

Chapter VI Rules on Advertising and Transparency

Section 1 Publication of notices

Article 35
Notices

1. Contracting authorities shall make known, by means of a prior information notice published by the Commission or by themselves on their 'buyer profile', as described in point 2(b) of Annex VIII:

(a) where supplies are concerned, the estimated total value of the contracts or the framework agreements by product area which they intend to award over the following 12 months, where the total estimated value, taking into account Articles 7 and 9, is equal to or greater than €750 000.

The product area shall be established by the contracting authorities by reference to the CPV nomenclature;

(b) where services are concerned, the estimated total value of the contracts or the framework agreements in each of the categories of services listed in Annex II A which they intend to award over the following 12 months, where such estimated total value, taking into account the provisions of Articles 7 and 9, is equal to or greater than €750 000;

(c) where works are concerned, the essential characteristics of the contracts or the framework agreements which they intend to award, the estimated value of which is equal to or greater than the threshold specified in Article 7, taking into account Article 9.

The notices referred to in subparagraphs (a) and (b) shall be sent to the Commission or published on the buyer profile as soon as possible after the beginning of the budgetary year.

The notice referred to in subparagraph (c) shall be sent to the Commission or published on the buyer profile as soon as possible after the decision approving the planning of the works contracts or the framework agreements that the contracting authorities intend to award.

Contracting authorities who publish a prior information notice on their buyer profiles shall send the Commission, electronically, a notice of the publication of the prior information notice on a buyer profile, in accordance with the format and detailed procedures for sending notices indicated in point 3 of Annex VIII.

Publication of the notices referred to in subparagraphs (a), (b) and (c) shall be compulsory only where the contracting authorities take the option of shortening the time limits for the receipt of tenders as laid down in Article 38(4).

This paragraph shall not apply to negotiated procedures without the prior publication of a contract notice.

2. Contracting authorities which wish to award a public contract or a framework agreement by open, restricted or, under the conditions laid down in Article 30, negotiated procedure with the publication of a contract notice or, under the conditions laid down in Article 29, a competitive dialogue, shall make known their intention by means of a contract notice.

3. Contracting authorities which wish to set up a dynamic purchasing system shall make known their intention by means of a contract notice.

Contracting authorities which wish to award a contract based on a dynamic purchasing system shall make known their intention by means of a simplified contract notice.

4. Contracting authorities which have awarded a public contract or concluded a framework agreement shall send a notice of the results of the award procedure no later than 48 days after the award of the contract or the conclusion of the framework agreement.

In the case of framework agreements concluded in accordance with Article 32 the contracting authorities are not bound to send a notice of the results of the award procedure for each contract based on that agreement.

Contracting authorities shall send a notice of the result of the award of contracts based on a dynamic purchasing system within 48 days of the award of each contract. They may, however, group such notices on a quarterly basis. In that case, they shall send the grouped notices within 48 days of the end of each quarter.

In the case of public contracts for services listed in Annex II B, the contracting authorities shall indicate in the notice whether they agree to its publication. For such services contracts the Commission shall draw up the rules for establishing statistical reports on the basis of such notices and for the publication of such reports in accordance with the procedure laid down in Article 77(2).

Certain information on the contract award or the conclusion of the framework agreement may be withheld from publication where release of such information would impede law enforcement or otherwise be contrary to the public interest, would harm the legitimate commercial interests of economic operators, public or private, or might prejudice fair competition between them.

Article 36
Form and manner of publication of notices

1. Notices shall include the information mentioned in Annex VII A and, where appropriate, any other information deemed useful by the contracting authority in the format of standard forms adopted by the Commission in accordance with the procedure referred to in Article 77(2).

2. Notices sent by contracting authorities to the Commission shall be sent either by electronic means in accordance with the format and procedures for transmission indicated in Annex VIII, paragraph 3, or by other means. In the event of recourse to the accelerated procedure set out in Article 38(8), notices must be sent either by telefax or by electronic means, in accordance with the format and procedures for transmission indicated in point 3 of Annex VIII.

Notices shall be published in accordance with the technical characteristics for publication set out in point 1(a) and (b) of Annex VIII.

3. Notices drawn up and transmitted by electronic means in accordance with the format and procedures for transmission indicated in point 3 of Annex VIII, shall be published no later than five days after they are sent.

Notices which are not transmitted by electronic means in accordance with the format and procedures for transmission indicated in point 3 of Annex VIII, shall be published not later than 12 days after they are sent, or in the case of accelerated procedure referred to in Article 38(8), not later than five days after they are sent.

4. Contract notices shall be published in full in an official language of the Community as chosen by the contracting authority, this original language version constituting the sole authentic text. A summary of the important elements of each notice shall be published in the other official languages.

The costs of publication of such notices by the Commission shall be borne by the Community.

5. Notices and their contents may not be published at national level before the date on which they are sent to the Commission.

Notices published at national level shall not contain information other than that contained in the notices dispatched to the Commission or published on a buyer profile in accordance with the first subparagraph of Article 35(1), but shall mention the date of dispatch of the notice to the Commission or its publication on the buyer profile.

Prior information notices may not be published on a buyer profile before the dispatch to the Commission of the notice of their publication in that form; they shall mention the date of that dispatch.

6. The content of notices not sent by electronic means in accordance with the format and procedures for transmission indicated in point 3 of Annex VIII, shall be limited to approximately 650 words.

7. Contracting authorities must be able to supply proof of the dates on which notices are dispatched.

8. The Commission shall give the contracting authority confirmation of the publication of the information sent, mentioning the date of that publication. Such confirmation shall constitute proof of publication.

Article 37
Non-mandatory publication

Contracting authorities may publish in accordance with Article 36 notices of public contracts which are not subject to the publication requirement laid down in this Directive.

Section 2 Time limits

Article 38
Time limits for receipt of requests to participate and for receipt of tenders

1. When fixing the time limits for the receipt of tenders and requests to participate, contracting authorities shall take account in particular of the complexity of the contract and the time required for drawing up tenders, without prejudice to the minimum time limits set by this Article.

2. In the case of open procedures, the minimum time limit for the receipt of tenders shall be 52 days from the date on which the contract notice was sent.

3. In the case of restricted procedures, negotiated procedures with publication of a contract notice referred to in Article 30 and the competitive dialogue:
(a) the minimum time limit for receipt of requests to participate shall be 37 days from the date on which the contract notice is sent;
(b) in the case of restricted procedures, the minimum time limit for the receipt of tenders shall be 40 days from the date on which the invitation is sent.

4. When contracting authorities have published a prior information notice, the minimum time limit for the receipt of tenders under paragraphs 2 and 3(b) may, as a general rule, be shortened to 36 days, but under no circumstances to less than 22 days.

The time limit shall run from the date on which the contract notice was sent in open procedures, and from the date on which the invitation to tender was sent in restricted procedures.

The shortened time limits referred to in the first subparagraph shall be permitted, provided that the prior information notice has included all the information required for the contract notice in Annex VII A, insofar as that information is available at the time the notice is published and that the prior information notice was sent for publication between 52 days and 12 months before the date on which the contract notice was sent.

5. Where notices are drawn up and transmitted by electronic means in accordance with the format and procedures for transmission indicated in point 3 of Annex VIII, the time limits for the receipt of tenders referred to in paragraphs 2 and 4 in open procedures, and the time limit for the receipt of the requests to participate referred to in paragraph 3(a), in restricted and negotiated procedures and the competitive dialogue, may be shortened by seven days.

6. The time limits for receipt of tenders referred to in paragraphs 2 and 3(b) may be reduced by five days where the contracting authority offers unrestricted and full direct access by electronic means to the contract

documents and any supplementary documents from the date of publication of the notice in accordance with Annex VIII, specifying in the text of the notice the internet address at which this documentation is accessible.

This reduction may be added to that referred to in paragraph 5.

7. If, for whatever reason, the specifications and the supporting documents or additional information, although requested in good time, are not supplied within the time limits set in Articles 39 and 40, or where tenders can be made only after a visit to the site or after on-the-spot inspection of the documents supporting the contract documents, the time limits for the receipt of tenders shall be extended so that all economic operators concerned may be aware of all the information needed to produce tenders.

8. In the case of restricted procedures and negotiated procedures with publication of a contract notice referred to in Article 30, where urgency renders impracticable the time limits laid down in this Article, contracting authorities may fix:

(a) a time limit for the receipt of requests to participate which may not be less than 15 days from the date on which the contract notice was sent, or less than 10 days if the notice was sent by electronic means, in accordance with the format and procedure for sending notices indicated in point 3 of Annex VIII;

(b) and, in the case of restricted procedures, a time limit for the receipt of tenders which shall be not less than 10 days from the date of the invitation to tender.

Article 39
Open procedures: Specifications, additional documents and information

1. In open procedures, where contracting authorities do not offer unrestricted and full direct access by electronic means in accordance with Article 38(6) to the specifications and any supporting documents, the specifications and supplementary documents shall be sent to economic operators within six days of receipt of the request to participate, provided that the request was made in good time before the deadline for the submission of tenders.

2. Provided that it has been requested in good time, additional information relating to the specifications and any supporting documents shall be supplied by the contracting authorities or competent departments not later than six days before the deadline fixed for the receipt of tenders.

Section 3 Information content and means of transmission
Article 40
Invitations to submit a tender, participate in the dialogue or negotiate

1. In restricted procedures, competitive dialogue procedures and negotiated procedures with publication of a contract notice within the meaning of Article 30, contracting authorities shall simultaneously and in writing invite the selected candidates to submit their tenders or to negotiate or, in the case of a competitive dialogue, to take part in the dialogue.

2. The invitation to the candidates shall include either:
— a copy of the specifications or of the descriptive document and any supporting documents, or
— a reference to accessing the specifications and the other documents indicated in the first indent, when they are made directly available by electronic means in accordance with Article 38(6).

3. Where an entity other than the contracting authority responsible for the award procedure has the specifications, the descriptive document and/or any supporting documents, the invitation shall state the address from which those specifications, that descriptive document and those documents may be requested and, if appropriate, the deadline for requesting such documents, and the sum payable for obtaining them and any payment procedures. The competent department shall send that documentation to the economic operator without delay upon receipt of a request.

4. The additional information on the specifications, the descriptive document or the supporting documents shall be sent by the contracting authority or the competent department not less than six days before the deadline fixed for the receipt of tenders, provided that it is requested in good time. In the event of a restricted or an accelerated procedure, that period shall be four days.

5. In addition, the invitation to submit a tender, to participate in the dialogue or to negotiate must contain at least:

(a) a reference to the contract notice published;

(b) the deadline for the receipt of the tenders, the address to which the tenders must be sent and the language or languages in which the tenders must be drawn up;

(c) in the case of competitive dialogue the date and the address set for the start of consultation and the language or languages used;

(d) a reference to any possible adjoining documents to be submitted, either in support of verifiable declarations by the tenderer in accordance with Article 44, or to supplement the information referred to in that Article, and under the conditions laid down in Articles 47 and 48;

(e) the relative weighting of criteria for the award of the contract or, where appropriate, the descending order of importance for such criteria, if they are not given in the contract notice, the specifications or the descriptive document.

However, in the case of contracts awarded in accordance with the rules laid down in Article 29, the information referred to in (b) above shall not appear in the invitation to participate in the dialogue but it shall appear in the invitation to submit a tender.

Article 41
Informing candidates and tenderers

1. Contracting authorities shall as soon as possible inform candidates and tenderers of decisions reached concerning the conclusion of a framework agreement, the award of the contract or admittance to a dynamic purchasing system, including the grounds for any decision not to conclude a framework agreement or award a contract for which there has been a call for competition or to recommence the procedure or implement a dynamic purchasing system; that information shall be given in writing upon request to the contracting authorities.

2. On request from the party concerned, the contracting authority shall as quickly as possible inform:

— any unsuccessful candidate of the reasons for the rejection of his application,

— any unsuccessful tenderer of the reasons for the rejection of his tender, including, for the cases referred to in Article 23, paragraphs 4 and 5, the reasons for its decision of non-equivalence or its decision that the works, supplies or services do not meet the performance or functional requirements,

— any tenderer who has made an admissible tender of the characteristics and relative advantages of the tender selected as well as the name of the successful tenderer or the parties to the framework agreement.

The time taken may in no circumstances exceed 15 days from receipt of the written request.

3. However, contracting authorities may decide to withhold certain information referred to in paragraph 1, regarding the contract award, the conclusion of framework agreements or admittance to a dynamic purchasing system where the release of such information would impede law enforcement, would otherwise be contrary to the public interest, would prejudice the legitimate commercial interests of economic operators, whether public or private, or might prejudice fair competition between them.

Section 4 Communication
Article 42
Rules applicable to communication

1. All communication and information exchange referred to in this Title may be by post, by fax, by electronic means in accordance with paragraphs 4 and 5, by telephone in the cases and circumstances referred to in paragraph 6, or by a combination of those means, according to the choice of the contracting authority.

2. The means of communication chosen must be generally available and thus not restrict economic operators' access to the tendering procedure.

3. Communication and the exchange and storage of information shall be carried out in such a way as to ensure that the integrity of data and the confidentiality of tenders and requests to participate are preserved, and that the contracting authorities examine the content of tenders and requests to participate only after the time limit set for submitting them has expired.

4. The tools to be used for communicating by electronic means, as well as their technical

characteristics, must be nondiscriminatory, generally available and interoperable with the information and communication technology products in general use.

5. The following rules are applicable to devices for the electronic transmission and receipt of tenders and to devices for the electronic receipt of requests to participate:

(a) information regarding the specifications necessary for the electronic submission of tenders and requests to participate, including encryption, shall be available to interested parties. Moreover, the devices for the electronic receipt of tenders and requests to participate shall conform to the requirements of Annex X;

(b) Member States may, in compliance with Article 5 of Directive 1999/93/EC, require that electronic tenders be accompanied by an advanced electronic signature in conformity with paragraph 1 thereof;

(c) Member States may introduce or maintain voluntary accreditation schemes aiming at enhanced levels of certification service provision for these devices;

(d) tenderers or candidates shall undertake to submit, before expiry of the time limit laid down for submission of tenders or requests to participate, the documents, certificates and declarations referred to in Articles 45 to 50 and Article 52 if they do not exist in electronic format.

6. The following rules shall apply to the transmission of requests to participate:

(a) requests to participate in procedures for the award of public contracts may be made in writing or by telephone;

(b) where requests to participate are made by telephone, a written confirmation must be sent before expiry of the time limit set for their receipt;

(c) contracting authorities may require that requests for participation made by fax must be confirmed by post or by electronic means, where this is necessary for the purposes of legal proof. Any such requirement, together with the time limit for sending confirmation by post or electronic means, must be stated by the contracting authority in the contract notice.

Section 5 Reports

Article 43
Content of reports

For every contract, framework agreement, and every establishment of a dynamic purchasing system, the contracting authorities shall draw up a written report which shall include at least the following:

(a) the name and address of the contracting authority, the subject-matter and value of the contract, framework agreement or dynamic purchasing system;

(b) the names of the successful candidates or tenderers and the reasons for their selection;

(c) the names of the candidates or tenderers rejected and the reasons for their rejection;

(d) the reasons for the rejection of tenders found to be abnormally low;

(e) the name of the successful tenderer and the reasons why his tender was selected and, if known, the share of the contract or framework agreement which the successful tenderer intends to subcontract to third parties;

(f) for negotiated procedures, the circumstances referred to in Articles 30 and 31 which justify the use of these procedures;

(g) as far as the competitive dialogue is concerned, the circumstances as laid down in Article 29 justifying the use of this procedure;

(h) if necessary, the reasons why the contracting authority has decided not to award a contract or framework agreement or to establish a dynamic purchasing system.

The contracting authorities shall take appropriate steps to document the progress of award procedures conducted by electronic means.

The report, or the main features of it, shall be communicated to the Commission if it so requests.

CHAPTER VII CONDUCT OF THE PROCEDURE

Section 1 General provisions

Article 44
Verification of the suitability and choice of participants and award of contracts

1. Contracts shall be awarded on the basis of the criteria laid down in Articles 53 and 55,

taking into account Article 24, after the suitability of the economic operators not excluded under Articles 45 and 46 has been checked by contracting authorities in accordance with the criteria of economic and financial standing, of professional and technical knowledge or ability referred to in Articles 47 to 52, and, where appropriate, with the non-discriminatory rules and criteria referred to in paragraph 3.

2. The contracting authorities may require candidates and tenderers to meet minimum capacity levels in accordance with Articles 47 and 48.

The extent of the information referred to in Articles 47 and 48 and the minimum levels of ability required for a specific contract must be related and proportionate to the subject matter of the contract.

These minimum levels shall be indicated in the contract notice.

3. In restricted procedures, negotiated procedures with publication of a contract notice and in the competitive dialogue procedure, contracting authorities may limit the number of suitable candidates they will invite to tender, to negotiate or to conduct a dialogue with, provided a sufficient number of suitable candidates is available. The contracting authorities shall indicate in the contract notice the objective and non-discriminatory criteria or rules they intend to apply, the minimum number of candidates they intend to invite and, where appropriate, the maximum number.

In the restricted procedure the minimum shall be five. In the negotiated procedure with publication of a contract notice and the competitive dialogue procedure the minimum shall be three. In any event the number of candidates invited shall be sufficient to ensure genuine competition.

The contracting authorities shall invite a number of candidates at least equal to the minimum number set in advance. Where the number of candidates meeting the selection criteria and the minimum levels of ability is below the minimum number, the contracting authority may continue the procedure by inviting the candidate(s) with the required capabilities. In the context of this same procedure, the contracting authority may not include other economic operators who did not request to participate, or candidates who do not have the required capabilities.

4. Where the contracting authorities exercise the option of reducing the number of solutions to be discussed or of tenders to be negotiated, as provided for in Articles 29(4) and 30(4), they shall do so by applying the award criteria stated in the contract notice, in the specifications or in the descriptive document. In the final stage, the number arrived at shall make for genuine competition insofar as there are enough solutions or suitable candidates.

Section 2 Criteria for qualitative selection

Article 45
Personal situation of the candidate or tenderer

1. Any candidate or tenderer who has been the subject of a conviction by final judgment of which the contracting authority is aware for one or more of the reasons listed below shall be excluded from participation in a public contract:

(a) participation in a criminal organisation, as defined in Article 2(1) of Council Joint Action 98/733/JHA;[1]

(b) corruption, as defined in Article 3 of the Council Act of 26 May 1997[2] and Article 3(1) of Council Joint Action 98/742/JHA[3] respectively;

(c) fraud within the meaning of Article 1 of the Convention relating to the protection of the financial interests of the European Communities;[4]

(d) money laundering, as defined in Article 1 of Council Directive 91/308/EEC of 10 June 1991 on prevention of the use of the financial system for the purpose of money laundering.[5]

Member States shall specify, in accordance with their national law and having regard for Community law, the implementing conditions for this paragraph.

---

[1] OJ L 351, 29.12.1998, p. 1.
[2] OJ C 195, 25.6.1997, p. 1.
[3] OJ L 358, 31.12.1998, p. 2.
[4] OJ C 316, 27.11.1995, p. 48.
[5] OJ L 166, 28.6.1991, p. 77. Directive as amended by Directive 2001/97/EC (OJ L 344, 28.12.2001, p. 76).

They may provide for a derogation from the requirement referred to in the first subparagraph for overriding requirements in the general interest.

For the purposes of this paragraph, the contracting authorities shall, where appropriate, ask candidates or tenderers to supply the documents referred to in paragraph 3 and may, where they have doubts concerning the personal situation of such candidates or tenderers, also apply to the competent authorities to obtain any information they consider necessary on the personal situation of the candidates or tenderers concerned. Where the information concerns a candidate or tenderer established in a State other than that of the contracting authority, the contracting authority may seek the cooperation of the competent authorities. Having regard for the national laws of the Member State where the candidates or tenderers are established, such requests shall relate to legal and/or natural persons, including, if appropriate, company directors and any person having powers of representation, decision or control in respect of the candidate or tenderer.

2. Any economic operator may be excluded from participation in a contract where that economic operator:

(a) is bankrupt or is being wound up, where his affairs are being administered by the court, where he has entered into an arrangement with creditors, where he has suspended business activities or is in any analogous situation arising from a similar procedure under national laws and regulations;

(b) is the subject of proceedings for a declaration of bankruptcy, for an order for compulsory winding up or administration by the court or of an arrangement with creditors or of any other similar proceedings under national laws and regulations;

(c) has been convicted by a judgment which has the force of res judicata in accordance with the legal provisions of the country of any offence concerning his professional conduct;

(d) has been guilty of grave professional misconduct proven by any means which the contracting authorities can demonstrate;

(e) has not fulfilled obligations relating to the payment of social security contributions in accordance with the legal provisions of the country in which he is established or with those of the country of the contracting authority;

(f) has not fulfilled obligations relating to the payment of taxes in accordance with the legal provisions of the country in which he is established or with those of the country of the contracting authority;

(g) is guilty of serious misrepresentation in supplying the information required under this Section or has not supplied such information.

Member States shall specify, in accordance with their national law and having regard for Community law, the implementing conditions for this paragraph.

3. Contracting authorities shall accept the following as sufficient evidence that none of the cases specified in paragraphs 1 or 2(a), (b), (c), (e) or (f) applies to the economic operator:

(a) as regards paragraphs 1 and 2(a), (b) and (c), the production of an extract from the 'judicial record' or, failing that, of an equivalent document issued by a competent judicial or administrative authority in the country of origin or the country whence that person comes showing that these requirements have been met;

(b) as regards paragraph 2(e) and (f), a certificate issued by the competent authority in the Member State concerned.

Where the country in question does not issue such documents or certificates, or where these do not cover all the cases specified in paragraphs 1 and 2(a), (b) and (c), they may be replaced by a declaration on oath or, in Member States where there is no provision for declarations on oath, by a solemn declaration made by the person concerned before a competent judicial or administrative authority, a notary or a competent professional or trade body, in the country of origin or in the country whence that person comes.

4. Member States shall designate the authorities and bodies competent to issue the documents, certificates or declarations referred to in paragraph 3 and shall inform the Commission thereof. Such notification shall be without prejudice to data protection law.

Article 46
Suitability to pursue the professional activity

Any economic operator wishing to take part in a public contract may be requested to prove its enrolment, as prescribed in his Member State of establishment, on one of the professional or trade registers or to provide a declaration on oath or a certificate as described in Annex IX A for public works contracts, in Annex IX B for public supply contracts and in Annex IX C for public service contracts.

In procedures for the award of public service contracts, insofar as candidates or tenderers have to possess a particular authorisation or to be members of a particular organisation in order to be able to perform in their country of origin the service concerned, the contracting authority may require them to prove that they hold such authorisation or membership.

Article 47
Economic and financial standing

1. Proof of the economic operator's economic and financial standing may, as a general rule, be furnished by one or more of the following references:

(a) appropriate statements from banks or, where appropriate, evidence of relevant professional risk indemnity insurance;

(b) the presentation of balance-sheets or extracts from the balance-sheets, where publication of the balance-sheet is required under the law of the country in which the economic operator is established;

(c) a statement of the undertaking's overall turnover and, where appropriate, of turnover in the area covered by the contract for a maximum of the last three financial years available, depending on the date on which the undertaking was set up or the economic operator started trading, as far as the information on these turnovers is available.

2. An economic operator may, where appropriate and for a particular contract, rely on the capacities of other entities, regardless of the legal nature of the links which it has with them. It must in that case prove to the contracting authority that it will have at its disposal the resources necessary, for example, by producing an undertaking by those entities to that effect.

3. Under the same conditions, a group of economic operators as referred to in Article 4 may rely on the capacities of participants in the group or of other entities.

4. Contracting authorities shall specify, in the contract notice or in the invitation to tender, which reference or references mentioned in paragraph 1 they have chosen and which other references must be provided.

5. If, for any valid reason, the economic operator is unable to provide the references requested by the contracting authority, he may prove his economic and financial standing by any other document which the contracting authority considers appropriate.

Article 48
Technical and/or professional ability

1. The technical and/or professional abilities of the economic operators shall be assessed and examined in accordance with paragraphs 2 and 3.

2. Evidence of the economic operators' technical abilities may be furnished by one or more of the following means according to the nature, quantity or importance, and use of the works, supplies or services:

(a) (i) a list of the works carried out over the past five years, accompanied by certificates of satisfactory execution for the most important works. These certificates shall indicate the value, date and site of the works and shall specify whether they were carried out according to the rules of the trade and properly completed. Where appropriate, the competent authority shall submit these certificates to the contracting authority direct;

   (ii) a list of the principal deliveries effected or the main services provided in the past three years, with the sums, dates and recipients, whether public or private, involved. Evidence of delivery and services provided shall be given:
   — where the recipient was a contracting authority, in the form of certificates issued or countersigned by the competent authority,
   — where the recipient was a private purchaser, by the purchaser's certification or, failing this, simply by a declaration by the economic operator;

(b) an indication of the technicians or technical bodies involved, whether or not belonging directly to the economic operator's undertaking, especially those responsible for quality control and, in the case of public works contracts, those upon whom the contractor can call in order to carry out the work;

(c) a description of the technical facilities and measures used by the supplier or service provider for ensuring quality and the undertaking's study and research facilities;

(d) where the products or services to be supplied are complex or, exceptionally, are required for a special purpose, a check carried out by the contracting authorities or on their behalf by a competent official body of the country in which the supplier or service provider is established, subject to that body's agreement, on the production capacities of the supplier or the technical capacity of the service provider and, if necessary, on the means of study and research which are available to it and the quality control measures it will operate;

(e) the educational and professional qualifications of the service provider or contractor and/or those of the undertaking's managerial staff and, in particular, those of the person or persons responsible for providing the services or managing the work;

(f) for public works contracts and public services contracts, and only in appropriate cases, an indication of the environmental management measures that the economic operator will be able to apply when performing the contract;

(g) a statement of the average annual manpower of the service provider or contractor and the number of managerial staff for the last three years;

(h) a statement of the tools, plant or technical equipment available to the service provider or contractor for carrying out the contract;

(i) an indication of the proportion of the contract which the services provider intends possibly to subcontract;

(j) with regard to the products to be supplied:

(i) samples, descriptions and/or photographs, the authenticity of which must be certified if the contracting authority so requests;

(ii) certificates drawn up by official quality control institutes or agencies of recognised competence attesting the conformity of products clearly identified by references to specifications or standards.

3. An economic operator may, where appropriate and for a particular contract, rely on the capacities of other entities, regardless of the legal nature of the links which it has with them. It must in that case prove to the contracting authority that it will have at its disposal the resources necessary for the execution of the contract, for example, by producing an undertaking by those entities to place the necessary resources at the disposal of the economic operator.

4. Under the same conditions a group of economic operators as referred to Article 4 may rely on the abilities of participants in the group or in other entities.

5. In procedures for awarding public contracts having as their object supplies requiring siting or installation work, the provision of services and/or the execution of works, the ability of economic operators to provide the service or to execute the installation or the work may be evaluated in particular with regard to their skills, efficiency, experience and reliability.

6. The contracting authority shall specify, in the notice or in the invitation to tender, which references under paragraph 2 it wishes to receive.

Article 49
Quality assurance standards

Should they require the production of certificates drawn up by independent bodies attesting the compliance of the economic operator with certain quality assurance standards, contracting authorities shall refer to quality assurance systems based on the relevant European standards series certified by bodies conforming to the European standards series concerning certification. They shall recognise equivalent certificates from bodies established in other Member States. They shall also accept other evidence of equivalent quality assurance measures from economic operators.

Article 50
Environmental management standards

Should contracting authorities, in the cases referred to in Article 48(2)(f), require the production of certificates drawn up by independent bodies attesting the compliance of the economic operator with certain environmental management standards, they shall refer to the Community Eco-Management and Audit Scheme (EMAS) or to environmental management standards based on the relevant European or international standards certified by bodies conforming to Community law or the relevant European or international standards concerning certification. They shall recognise equivalent certificates from bodies established in other Member States. They shall also accept other evidence of equivalent environmental management measures from economic operators.

Article 51
Additional documentation and information

The contracting authority may invite economic operators to supplement or clarify the certificates and documents submitted pursuant to Articles 45 to 50.

Article 52
Official lists of approved economic operators and certification by bodies established under public or private law

1. Member States may introduce either official lists of approved contractors, suppliers or service providers or certification by certification bodies established in public or private law.

Member States shall adapt the conditions for registration on these lists and for the issue of certificates by certification bodies to the provisions of Article 45(1), Article 45(2)(a) to (d) and (g), Articles 46, Article 47(1), (4) and (5), Article 48(1), (2), (5) and (6), Article 49 and, where appropriate, Article 50. Member States shall also adapt them to Article 47(2) and Article 48(3) as regards applications for registration submitted by economic operators belonging to a group and claiming resources made available to them by the other companies in the group. In such case, these operators must prove to the authority establishing the official list that they will have these resources at their disposal throughout the period of validity of the certificate attesting to their being registered in the official list and that throughout the same period these companies continue to fulfil the qualitative selection requirements laid down in the Articles referred to in the second subparagraph on which operators rely for their registration.

2. Economic operators registered on the official lists or having a certificate may, for each contract, submit to the contracting authority a certificate of registration issued by the competent authority or the certificate issued by the competent certification body. The certificates shall state the references which enabled them to be registered in the list/to obtain certification and the classification given in that list.

3. Certified registration on official lists by the competent bodies or a certificate issued by the certification body shall not, for the purposes of the contracting authorities of other Member States, constitute a presumption of suitability except as regards Articles 45(1) and (2)(a) to (d) and (g), Article 46, Article 47(1)(b) and (c), and Article 48(2)(a)(i), (b), (e), (g) and (h) in the case of contractors, (2)(a)(ii), (b), (c), (d) and (j) in the case of suppliers and 2(a)(ii) and (c) to (i) in the case of service providers.

4. Information which can be deduced from registration on official lists or certification may not be questioned without justification. With regard to the payment of social security contributions and taxes, an additional certificate may be required of any registered economic operator whenever a contract is offered.

The contracting authorities of other Member States shall apply paragraph 3 and the first subparagraph of this paragraph only in favour of economic operators established in the Member State holding the official list.

5. For any registration of economic operators of other Member States in an official list or for their certification by the bodies referred to in paragraph 1, no further proof or statements can be required other than those requested of national economic operators and, in any event, only those provided for under Articles 45 to 49 and, where appropriate, Article 50.

However, economic operators from other Member States may not be obliged to undergo such registration or certification in order to participate in a public contract. The contracting authorities shall recognise equivalent certificates from bodies established in other Member States. They shall also accept other equivalent means of proof.

6. Economic operators may ask at any time to be registered in an official list or for a certificate to be issued. They must be informed within a reasonably short period of time of the decision of the authority drawing up the list or of the competent certification body.

7. The certification bodies referred to in paragraph 1 shall be bodies complying with European certification standards.

8. Member States which have official lists or certification bodies as referred to in paragraph 1 shall be obliged to inform the Commission and the other Member States of the address of the body to which applications should be sent.

Section 3 Award of the contract

Article 53

Contract award criteria

1. Without prejudice to national laws, regulations or administrative provisions concerning the remuneration of certain services, the criteria on which the contracting authorities shall base the award of public contracts shall be either:

(a) when the award is made to the tender most economically advantageous from the point of view of the contracting authority, various criteria linked to the subject-matter of the public contract in question, for example, quality, price, technical merit, aesthetic and functional characteristics, environmental characteristics, running costs, cost-effectiveness, after-sales service and technical assistance, delivery date and delivery period or period of completion, or

(b) the lowest price only.

2. Without prejudice to the provisions of the third subparagraph, in the case referred to in paragraph 1(a) the contracting authority shall specify in the contract notice or in the contract documents or, in the case of a competitive dialogue, in the descriptive document, the relative weighting which it gives to each of the criteria chosen to determine the most economically advantageous tender.

Those weightings can be expressed by providing for a range with an appropriate maximum spread.

Where, in the opinion of the contracting authority, weighting is not possible for demonstrable reasons, the contracting authority shall indicate in the contract notice or contract documents or, in the case of a competitive dialogue, in the descriptive document, the criteria in descending order of importance.

Article 54

Use of electronic auctions

1. Member States may provide that contracting authorities may use electronic auctions.

2. In open, restricted or negotiated procedures in the case referred to in Article 30(1)(a), the contracting authorities may decide that the award of a public contract shall be preceded by an electronic auction when the contract specifications can be established with precision.

In the same circumstances, an electronic auction may be held on the reopening of competition among the parties to a framework agreement as provided for in the second indent of the second subparagraph of Article 32(4) and on the opening for competition of contracts to be awarded under the dynamic purchasing system referred to in Article 33.

The electronic auction shall be based:

— either solely on prices when the contract is awarded to the lowest price,

— or on prices and/or on the new values of the features of the tenders indicated in the specification when the contract is awarded to the most economically advantageous tender.

3. Contracting authorities which decide to hold an electronic auction shall state that fact in the contract notice.

The specifications shall include, *inter alia*, the following details:

(a) the features, the values for which will be the subject of electronic auction, provided that such features are quantifiable and can be expressed in figures or percentages;

(b) any limits on the values which may be submitted, as they result from the specifications relating to the subject of the contract;

(c) the information which will be made available to tenderers in the course of the electronic auction and, where appropriate, when it will be made available to them;

(d) the relevant information concerning the electronic auction process;

(e) the conditions under which the tenderers will be able to bid and, in particular, the minimum differences which will, where appropriate, be required when bidding;

(f) the relevant information concerning the electronic equipment used and the arrangements and technical specifications for connection.

4. Before proceeding with an electronic auction, contracting authorities shall make a full initial evaluation of the tenders in accordance with the award criterion/criteria set and with the weighting fixed for them.

All tenderers who have submitted admissible tenders shall be invited simultaneously by electronic means to submit new prices and/or new values; the invitation shall contain all relevant information concerning individual connection to the electronic equipment being used and shall state the date and time of the start of the electronic auction. The electronic auction may take place in a number of successive phases. The electronic auction may not start sooner than two working days after the date on which invitations are sent out.

5. When the contract is to be awarded on the basis of the most economically advantageous tender, the invitation shall be accompanied by the outcome of a full evaluation of the relevant tenderer, carried out in accordance with the weighting provided for in the first subparagraph of Article 53(2).

The invitation shall also state the mathematical formula to be used in the electronic auction to determine automatic rerankings on the basis of the new prices and/or new values submitted. That formula shall incorporate the weighting of all the criteria fixed to determine the most economically advantageous tender, as indicated in the contract notice or in the specifications; for that purpose, any ranges shall, however, be reduced beforehand to a specified value.

Where variants are authorised, a separate formula shall be provided for each variant.

6. Throughout each phase of an electronic auction the contracting authorities shall instantaneously communicate to all tenderers at least sufficient information to enable them to ascertain their relative rankings at any moment. They may also communicate other information concerning other prices or values submitted, provided that that is stated in the specifications. They may also at any time

announce the number of participants in that phase of the auction. In no case, however, may they disclose the identities of the tenderers during any phase of an electronic auction.

7. Contracting authorities shall close an electronic auction in one or more of the following manners:

(a) in the invitation to take part in the auction they shall indicate the date and time fixed in advance;

(b) when they receive no more new prices or new values which meet the requirements concerning minimum differences. In that event, the contracting authorities shall state in the invitation to take part in the auction the time which they will allow to elapse after receiving the last submission before they close the electronic auction;

(c) when the number of phases in the auction, fixed in the invitation to take part in the auction, has been completed.

When the contracting authorities have decided to close an electronic auction in accordance with subparagraph (c), possibly in combination with the arrangements laid down in subparagraph (b), the invitation to take part in the auction shall indicate the timetable for each phase of the auction.

8. After closing an electronic auction contracting authorities shall award the contract in accordance with Article 53 on the basis of the results of the electronic auction.

Contracting authorities may not have improper recourse to electronic auctions nor may they use them in such a way as to prevent, restrict or distort competition or to change the subject-matter of the contract, as put up for tender in the published contract notice and defined in the specification.

Article 55
Abnormally low tenders

1. If, for a given contract, tenders appear to be abnormally low in relation to the goods, works or services, the contracting authority shall, before it may reject those tenders, request in writing details of the constituent elements of the tender which it considers relevant.

Those details may relate in particular to:

(a) the economics of the construction method, the manufacturing process or the services provided;

(b) the technical solutions chosen and/or any exceptionally favourable conditions available to the tenderer for the execution of the work, for the supply of the goods or services;

(c) the originality of the work, supplies or services proposed by the tenderer;

(d) compliance with the provisions relating to employment protection and working conditions in force at the place where the work, service or supply is to be performed;

(e) the possibility of the tenderer obtaining State aid.

2. The contracting authority shall verify those constituent elements by consulting the tenderer, taking account of the evidence supplied.

3. Where a contracting authority establishes that a tender is abnormally low because the tenderer has obtained State aid, the tender can be rejected on that ground alone only after consultation with the tenderer where the latter is unable to prove, within a sufficient time limit fixed by the contracting authority, that the aid in question was granted legally. Where the contracting authority rejects a tender in these circumstances, it shall inform the Commission of that fact.

TITLE III
RULES ON PUBLIC WORKS CONCESSIONS

CHAPTER I RULES GOVERNING PUBLIC WORKS CONCESSIONS

Article 56
Scope

This Chapter shall apply to all public works concession contracts concluded by the contracting authorities where the value of the contracts is equal to or greater than EUR 6 242 000.

The value shall be calculated in accordance with the rules applicable to public works contracts defined in Article 9.

Article 57
Exclusions from the scope

This Title shall not apply to public works concessions which are awarded:

(a) in the cases referred to in Articles 13, 14 and 15 of this Directive in respect of public works contracts;

(b) by contracting authorities exercising one or more of the activities referred to in Articles 3 to 7 of Directive 2004/17/EC where those concessions are awarded for carrying out those activities.

However, this Directive shall continue to apply to public works concessions awarded by contracting authorities carrying out one or more of the activities referred to in Article 6 of Directive 2004/17/EC and awarded for those activities, insofar as the Member State concerned takes advantage of the option referred to in the second subparagraph of Article 71 thereof to defer its application.

Article 58
Publication of the notice concerning public works concessions

1. Contracting authorities which wish to award a public works concession contract shall make known their intention by means of a notice.

2. Notices of public works concessions shall contain the information referred to in Annex VII C and, where appropriate, any other information deemed useful by the contracting authority, in accordance with the standard forms adopted by the Commission pursuant to the procedure in Article 77(2).

3. Notices shall be published in accordance with Article 36(2) to (8).

4. Article 37 on the publication of notices shall also apply to public works concessions.

Article 59
Time limit

When contracting authorities resort to a public works concession, the time limit for the presentation of applications for the concession shall be not less than 52 days from the date of dispatch of the notice, except where Article 38(5) applies.

Article 38(7) shall apply.

Article 60
Subcontracting

The contracting authority may either:

(a) require the concessionaire to award contracts representing a minimum of 30 %

of the total value of the work for which the concession contract is to be awarded, to third parties, at the same time providing the option for candidates to increase this percentage, this minimum percentage being specified in the concession contract, or

(b) request the candidates for concession contracts to specify in their tenders the percentage, if any, of the total value of the work for which the concession contract is to be awarded which they intend to assign to third parties.

Article 61
Awarding of additional works to the concessionaire

This Directive shall not apply to additional works not included in the concession project initially considered or in the initial contract but which have, through unforeseen circumstances, become necessary for the performance of the work described therein, which the contracting authority has awarded to the concessionaire, on condition that the award is made to the economic operator performing such work:

— when such additional works cannot be technically or economically separated from the initial contract without major inconvenience to the contracting authorities, or

— when such works, although separable from the performance of the initial contract, are strictly necessary for its completion.

However, the aggregate value of contracts awarded for additional works may not exceed 50 % of the amount of the original works concession contract.

Chapter II Rules on Contracts Awarded by Concessionaires Which are Contracting Authorities

Article 62
Applicable rules

Where the concessionaire is a contracting authority as referred to in Article 1(9), it shall comply with the provisions laid down by this Directive for public works contracts in the case of works to be carried out by third parties.

Chapter III Rules Applicable to Contracts Awarded by Concessionaires Which are Not Contracting Authorities

Article 63
Advertising rules: threshold and exceptions

1. The Member States shall take the necessary measures to ensure that public works concessionaires which are not contracting authorities apply the advertising rules defined in Article 64 when awarding works contracts to third parties where the value of such contracts is equal to or greater than EUR 6 242 000.

Advertising shall not, however, be required where a works contract satisfies the conditions listed in Article 31.

The values of contracts shall be calculated in accordance with the rules applicable to public works contracts laid down in Article 9.

2. Groups of undertakings which have been formed to obtain the concession or undertakings related to them shall not be considered third parties.

'Related undertaking' shall mean any undertaking over which the concessionaire can exert a dominant influence, whether directly or indirectly, or any undertaking which can exert a dominant influence on the concessionaire or which, as the concessionaire, is subject to the dominant influence of another undertaking as a result of ownership, financial participation or the rules which govern it. A dominant influence on the part of an undertaking is presumed when, directly or indirectly in relation to another undertaking, it:

(a) holds a majority of the undertaking's subscribed capital;

(b) controls a majority of the votes attached to the shares issued by the undertaking; or

(c) can appoint more than half of the undertaking's administrative, management or supervisory body.

The exhaustive list of such undertakings shall be included in the application for the concession. That list shall be brought up to date following any subsequent changes in the relationship between the undertakings.

Article 64
Publication of the notice

1. Works concessionaires which are not contracting authorities and which wish to award works contracts to a third party shall make known their intention by way of a notice.

2. Notices shall contain the information referred to in Annex VII C and, where appropriate, any other information deemed useful by the works concessionaire, in accordance with the standard form adopted by the Commission in accordance with the procedure in Article 77(2).

3. The notice shall be published in accordance with Article 36(2) to (8).

4. Article 37 on the voluntary publication of notices shall also apply.

Article 65
Time limit for the receipt of requests to participate and receipt of tenders

In works contracts awarded by a works concessionaire which is not a contracting authority, the time limit for the receipt of requests to participate, fixed by the concessionaire, shall be not less than 37 days from the date on which the contract notice was dispatched and the time limit for the receipt of tenders not less than 40 days from the date on which the contract notice or the invitation to tender was dispatched.

Article 38(5), (6) and (7) shall apply.

TITLE IV
RULES GOVERNING DESIGN CONTESTS

Article 66
General provisions

1. The rules for the organisation of design contests shall be in conformity with Articles 66 to 74 and shall be communicated to those interested in participating in the contest.

2. The admission of participants to design contests shall not be limited:
(a) by reference to the territory or part of the territory of a Member State;
(b) on the grounds that, under the law of the Member State in which the contest is organised, they would be required to be either natural or legal persons.

Article 67
Scope

1. In accordance with this Title, design contests shall be organised by:
(a) contracting authorities which are listed as central government authorities in Annex IV, starting from a threshold equal to or greater than EUR 162 000;
(b) contracting authorities not listed in Annex IV, starting from a threshold equal to or greater than EUR 249 000;
(c) by all the contracting authorities, starting from a threshold equal to or greater than EUR 249 000 where contests concern services in category 8 of Annex II A,

category 5 telecommunications services, the positions of which in the CPV are equivalent to reference Nos CPC 7524, 7525 and 7526 and/or services listed in Annex II B.

2. This Title shall apply to:
(a) design contests organised as part of a procedure leading to the award of a public service contract;
(b) design contests with prizes and/or payments to participants.

In the cases referred to in (a) the threshold refers to the estimated value net of VAT of the public services contract, including any possible prizes and/or payments to participants.

In the cases referred to in (b), the threshold refers to the total amount of the prizes and payments, including the estimated value net of VAT of the public services contract which might subsequently be concluded under Article 31(3) if the contracting authority does not exclude such an award in the contest notice.

Article 68
Exclusions from the scope

This Title shall not apply to:
(a) design contests within the meaning of Directive 2004/17/EC which are organised by contracting authorities exercising one or more of the activities referred to in

Articles 3 to 7 of that Directive and are organised for the pursuit of such activities; nor shall it apply to contests excluded from the scope of this Directive.

However, this Directive shall continue to apply to design contests awarded by contracting authorities carrying out one or more of the activities referred to in Article 6 of Directive 2004/17/EC and awarded for those activities, insofar as the Member State concerned takes advantage of the option referred to in the second subparagraph of Article 71 thereof to defer its application;

(b) contests which are organised in the same cases as those referred to in Articles 13, 14 and 15 of this Directive for public service contracts.

Article 69
Notices

1. Contracting authorities which wish to carry out a design contest shall make known their intention by means of a contest notice.

2. Contracting authorities which have held a design contest shall send a notice of the results of the contest in accordance with Article 36 and must be able to prove the date of dispatch.

Where the release of information on the outcome of the contest would impede law enforcement, be contrary to the public interest, prejudice the legitimate commercial interests of a particular enterprise, whether public or private, or might prejudice fair competition between service providers, such information need not be published.

3. Article 37 concerning publication of notices shall also apply to contests.

Article 70
Form and manner of publication of notices of contests

1. The notices referred to in Article 69 shall contain the information referred to in Annex VII D in accordance with the standard model notices adopted by the Commission in accordance with the procedure in Article 77(2).

2. The notices shall be published in accordance with Article 36(2) to (8).

Article 71
Means of communication

1. Article 42(1), (2) and (4) shall apply to all communications relating to contests.

2. Communications, exchanges and the storage of information shall be such as to ensure that the integrity and the confidentiality of all information communicated by the participants in a contest are preserved and that the jury ascertains the contents of plans and projects only after the expiry of the time limit for their submission.

3. The following rules shall apply to devices for the electronic receipt of plans and projects:

(a) the information relating to the specifications which is necessary for the presentation of plans and projects by electronic means, including encryption, shall be available to the parties concerned. In addition, the devices for the electronic receipt of plans and projects shall comply with the requirements of Annex X;

(b) the Member States may introduce or maintain voluntary arrangements for accreditation intended to improve the level of the certification service provided for such devices.

Article 72
Selection of competitors

Where design contests are restricted to a limited number of participants, the contracting authorities shall lay down clear and non-discriminatory selection criteria. In any event, the number of candidates invited to participate shall be sufficient to ensure genuine competition.

Article 73
Composition of the jury

The jury shall be composed exclusively of natural persons who are independent of participants in the contest. Where a particular professional qualification is required from participants in a contest, at least a third of the members of the jury shall have that qualification or an equivalent qualification.

Article 74
Decisions of the jury

1. The jury shall be autonomous in its decisions or opinions.

2. It shall examine the plans and projects submitted by the candidates anonymously and solely on the basis of the criteria indicated in the contest notice.

3. It shall record its ranking of projects in a report, signed by its members, made according to the merits of each project, together with its remarks and any points which may need clarification.

4. Anonymity must be observed until the jury has reached its opinion or decision.

5. Candidates may be invited, if need be, to answer questions which the jury has recorded in the minutes to clarify any aspects of the projects.

6. Complete minutes shall be drawn up of the dialogue between jury members and candidates.

TITLE V
STATISTICAL OBLIGATIONS, EXECUTORY POWERS AND FINAL PROVISIONS

Article 75
Statistical obligations

In order to permit assessment of the results of applying this Directive, Member States shall forward to the Commission a statistical report, prepared in accordance with Article 76, separately addressing public supply, services and works contracts awarded by contracting authorities during the preceding year, by no later than 31 October of each year.

Article 76
Content of statistical report

1. For each contracting authority listed in Annex IV, the statistical report shall detail at least:
(a) the number and value of awarded contracts covered by this Directive;
(b) the number and total value of contracts awarded pursuant to derogations to the Agreement.

As far as possible, the data referred to in point (a) of the first subparagraph shall be broken down by:
(a) the contract award procedures used; and
(b) for each of these procedures, works as given in Annex I and products and services as given in Annex II identified by category of the CPV nomenclature;
(c) the nationality of the economic operator to which the contract was awarded.

Where the contracts have been concluded according to the negotiated procedure, the data referred to in point (a) of the first subparagraph shall also be broken down according to the circumstances referred to in Articles 30 and 31 and shall specify the number and value of

contracts awarded, by Member State and third country of the successful contractor.

2. For each category of contracting authority which is not given in Annex IV, the statistical report shall detail at least:
(a) the number and value of the contracts awarded, broken down in accordance with the second subparagraph of paragraph 1;
(b) the total value of contracts awarded pursuant to derogations to the Agreement.

3. The statistical report shall set out any other statistical information which is required under the Agreement.

The information referred to in the first subparagraph shall be determined pursuant to the procedure under Article 77(2).

Article 77
Advisory Committee

1. The Commission shall be assisted by the Advisory Committee for Public Contracts set up by Article 1 of Decision 71/306/EEC[1] (hereinafter referred to as 'the Committee').

2. Where reference is made to this paragraph, Articles 3 and 7 of Decision 1999/468/EC shall apply, in compliance with Article 8 thereof.

3. The Committee shall adopt its rules of procedure.

Article 78
Revision of the thresholds

1. The Commission shall verify the thresholds established in Article 7 every two years

---

[1] OJ L 185, 16.8.1971, p. 15. Decision as amended by Decision 77/63/EEC (OJ L 13, 15.1.1977, p. 15).

from the entry into force of this Directive and shall, if necessary, revise them in accordance with the procedure laid down in Article 77(2).

The calculation of the value of these thresholds shall be based on the average daily value of the euro, expressed in SDRs, over the 24 months terminating on the last day of August preceding the revision with effect from 1 January. The value of the thresholds thus revised shall, where necessary, be rounded down to the nearest thousand euro so as to ensure that the thresholds in force provided for by the Agreement, expressed in SDRs, are observed.

2. At the same time as the revision under paragraph 1, the Commission, in accordance with the procedure under Article 77(2), shall align:

(a) the thresholds established in (a) of the first subparagraph of Article 8, in Article 56 and in the first subparagraph of Article 63(1) on the revised threshold applying to public works contracts;

(b) the thresholds established in (b) of the first subparagraph of Article 8, and in Article 67(1)(a) on the revised threshold applying to public service contracts concluded by the contracting authorities referred to in Annex IV;

(c) the threshold established in Article 67(1)(b) and (c) on the revised threshold applying to public service contracts awarded by the contracting authorities not included in Annex IV.

3. The value of the thresholds set pursuant to paragraph 1 in the national currencies of the Member States which are not participating in monetary union is normally to be adjusted every two years from 1 January 2004 onwards. The calculation of such value shall be based on the average daily values of those currencies expressed in euro over the 24 months terminating on the last day of August preceding the revision with effect from 1 January.

4. The revised thresholds referred to in paragraph 1 and their corresponding values in the national currencies referred to in paragraph 3 shall be published by the Commission in the *Official Journal of the European Union* at the beginning of the month of November following their revision.

Article 79
Amendments

1. In accordance with the procedure referred to in Article 77(2), the Commission may amend:

(a) the technical procedures for the calculation methods set out in the second subparagraph of Article 78(1) and in Article 78(3);

(b) the procedures for the drawing-up, transmission, receipt, translation, collection and distribution of the notices referred to in Articles 35, 58, 64 and 69 and the statistical reports provided for in the fourth subparagraph of Article 35(4), and in Articles 75 and 76;

(c) the procedures for specific reference to specific positions in the CPV nomenclature in the notices;

(d) the lists of bodies and categories of bodies governed by public law in Annex III, when, on the basis of the notifications from the Member States, these prove necessary;

(e) the lists of central government authorities in Annex IV, following the adaptations necessary to give effect to the Agreement;

(f) the reference numbers in the nomenclature set out in Annex I, insofar as this does not change the material scope of this Directive, and the procedures for reference to particular positions of this nomenclature in the notices;

(g) the reference numbers in the nomenclature set out in Annex II, insofar as this does not change the material scope of this Directive, and the procedures for reference in the notices to particular positions in this nomenclature within the categories of services listed in the Annex;

(h) the procedure for sending and publishing data referred to in Annex VIII, on grounds of technical progress or for administrative reasons;

(i) the technical details and characteristics of the devices for electronic receipt referred to in points (a), (f) and (g) of Annex X.

Article 80
Implementation

1. The Member States shall bring into force the laws, regulations and administrative provisions necessary to comply with this Directive no later than 31 January 2006. They

shall forthwith inform the Commission thereof.

When Member States adopt these measures, they shall contain a reference to this Directive or be accompanied by such reference on the occasion of their official publication. The methods of making such reference shall be laid down by Member States.

2. Member States shall communicate to the Commission the text of the main provisions of national law which they adopt in the field covered by this Directive.

Article 81
Monitoring mechanisms

In conformity with Council Directive 89/665/EEC of 21 December 1989 on the coordination of the laws, regulations and administrative provisions relating to the application of review procedures to the award of public supply and public works contracts,[1] Member States shall ensure implementation of this Directive by effective, available and transparent mechanisms.

For this purpose they may, among other things, appoint or establish an independent body.

Article 82
Repeals

Directive 92/50/EEC, except for Article 41 thereof, and Directives 93/36/EEC and 93/37/EEC shall be repealed with effect from the date shown in Article 80, without prejudice to the obligations of the Member States concerning the deadlines for transposition and application set out in Annex XI.

References to the repealed Directives shall be construed as references to this Directive and shall be read in accordance with the correlation table in Annex XII.

Article 83
Entry into force

This Directive shall enter into force on the day of its publication in the *Official Journal of the European Union*.

Article 84
Addressees

This Directive is addressed to the Member States.

Done at Strasbourg, 31 March 2004.

For the European Parliament   *For the Council*
The President   *The President*
P. COX   D. ROCHE

The annexes to this Directive may be found in the Official Journal
[2004] L 134, 30 March 2004
http://europa.eu.int/eur-lex/lex/JOHtml.do?uri=OJ:L:2004:134:SOM:EN:HTML

---

[1] OJ L 395, 30.12.1989, p. 33. Directive as amended by Directive 92/50/EEC.

INDEX

QM LIBRARY
(MILE END)

WITHDRAWN
FROM STOCK
QMUL LIBRARY